SAS® Language and Procedures: Usage

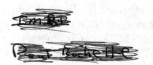

SAS Institute Inc.
SAS Campus Drive
Cary, NC 27513

The correct bibliographic citation for this manual is as follows: SAS Institute Inc., *SAS® Language and Procedures: Usage, Version 6, First Edition,* Cary, NC: SAS Institute Inc., 1989. 638 pp.

SAS® Language and Procedures: Usage, Version 6, First Edition*

SAS Institute Inc., SAS Campus Drive, Cary, North Carolina 27513.

1st printing, December 1989
2nd printing, November 1992
3rd printing, December 1993
4th printing, December 1995
5th printing, July 1997

The SAS® System is an integrated system of software providing complete control over data access, management, analysis, and presentation. Base SAS software is the foundation of the SAS System. Products within the SAS System include SAS/ACCESS®, SAS/AF®, SAS/ASSIST®, SAS/CALC®, SAS/CONNECT®, SAS/CPE®, SAS/DMI®, SAS/EIS®, SAS/ENGLISH®, SAS/ETS®, SAS/FSP®, SAS/GRAPH®, SAS/IMAGE®, SAS/IML®, SAS/IMS-DL/I®, SAS/INSIGHT®, SAS/IntrNet™, SAS/LAB®, SAS/MDDB™, SAS/NVISION®, SAS/OR®, SAS/PH-Clinical®, SAS/QC®, SAS/REPLAY-CICS®, SAS/SESSION®, SAS/SHARE®, SAS/SPECTRAVIEW®, SAS/STAT®, SAS/TOOLKIT®, SAS/TRADER®, SAS/TUTOR®, SAS/DB2™, SAS/GEO™, SAS/GIS™, SAS/PH-Kinetics™, SAS/SHARE*NET™, and SAS/SQL-DS™ software. Other SAS Institute products are SYSTEM 2000® Data Management Software, with basic SYSTEM 2000, CREATE™, Multi-User™, QueX™, Screen Writer™, and CICS interface software; InfoTap® software; JAZZ™ software; NeoVisuals® software; JMP®, JMP IN®, and JMP Serve® software; SAS/RTERM® software; and the SAS/C® Compiler and the SAS/CX® Compiler; Video Reality™ software; VisualSpace™ software; Budget Vision™, Campaign Vision™, CFO Vision™, Compensation Vision™, Enterprise Miner™, HR Vision™, and IT Service Vision™ software; Scalable Performance Data Server™ software; SAS OnlineTutor™ software; and Emulus® software. MultiVendor Architecture™, MVA™, MultiEngine Architecture™, and MEA™ are trademarks of SAS Institute Inc. SAS Institute also offers SAS Consulting® and SAS Video Productions® services. *Authorline®,* Books by Users™, The Encore Series®, ExecSolutions™, *JMPer Cable®, Observations®, SAS Communications®,* SAS OnlineDoc™, *SAS Professional Services™, SAS Views®,* the SASware Ballot®, SelecText™, and Solutions@Work™ documentation are published by SAS Institute Inc. The SAS Video Productions logo, the Books by Users SAS Institute's Author Service logo, the SAS Online Samples logo, and The Encore Series logo are registered service marks or registered trademarks of SAS Institute Inc. The Helplus logo, the SelecText logo, the Video Reality logo, the Quality Partner logo, the SAS Business Solutions logo, the SAS Rapid Warehousing Program logo, the SAS Publications logo, the Instructor-based Training logo, the Online Training logo, the Trainer's Kit logo, and the Video-based Training logo are service marks or trademarks of SAS Institute Inc. All trademarks above are registered trademarks or trademarks of SAS Institute Inc. in the USA and other countries. ® indicates USA registration.

The Institute is a private company devoted to the support and further development of its software and related services.

Other brand and product names are registered trademarks or trademarks of their respective companies.

*Version 7 compatible

Contents

Part 5 · Understanding Your SAS Session   279

Part 6 ▪ Producing Reports   331

Part 10 ▪ Understanding Your SAS Environment 513

Reference Aids

Displays

Figures

Tables

Special Topics

Credits

Documentation

Composition
Jim Byron, Gail C. Freeman, Cynthia Hopkins, Amanda G. Lemons, Pamela A. Troutman, Denise L. Truelove, David S. Tyree, June Zglinski

Graphics
Mary H. Cole, Ginny Matsey

Proofreading
Jennifer M. Ginn, Reid V. Harris III, Beth A. Heiney, Beryl C. Pittman, Josephine P. Pope, Toni P. Sherrill, Michael H. Smith, John M. West, Susan E. Willard

Technical Review
Johnny B. Andrews, Nancy L. Agnew, Stephen Beatrous, Patricia L. Berryman, Linda W. Binkley, John C. Boling, Bill Brideson, Eric C. Brinsfield, Lisa B. Brown, Dave Brumitt, Tracy C. Byrd, Joseph M. Carter, Oita C. Coleman, Anne Corrigan, Ottis R. Cowper, Ellen B. Daniels, Ginny Dineley, David A. Driggs, Ceci Edmiston, Cheryl A. Garner, Bary Allan Gold, Amerie Helton, Kevin Hobbs, Dale D. Ingold, Charles A. Jacobs, Christina A. Keene, Paul M. Kent, Bradley W. Klenz, Elizabeth C. Langston, Richard D. Langston, Sally B. Langthorn, Ann A. Lehman, Marty Light, Terrie Linker, Rusti Ludwick, A. Darrell Massengill, Jeffrey R. McDermott, James A. McKenzie, Paul W. Mortensen, Mason Nichols, Susan M. O'Connor, Diane D. Olson, Sally Painter, Lynn H. Patrick, Brian R. Perkinson, Denise M. Poll, Terry D. Poole, Paige Valentine-Query, Caroline Quinn, Joy Reel, Lisa M. Ripperton, Heman Robinson, David Ross, Alissa W. Schleich, Jeff Shaughnessy, W. David Shinn, Veronica L. Shores, David Shubert, Maura Stokes, Scott Sweetland, Annette Tharpe, Bruce Tindall, John S. Wallace, Charles Ray Walters, Jr., Becky Webb, Randolph S. Williams, Amanda W. Womble, Ann L. Yang, Thomas W. Zack

Writing and Editing
David D. Baggett, Deborah S. Blank, Catherine C. Carter, Rick Early, Christina N. Harvey, Stacy A. Hilliard, Brenda C. Kalt, Carol Austin Linden, N. Elizabeth Malcom, Gary R. Meek, Sonja R. Moore, Philip R. Shelton, Helen Weeks, Holly S. Whittle, John S. Williams, Helen F. Wolfson

Software

Complete software development, support, and quality assurance credits for base SAS Software are listed in the reference guides for this product. Refer to *SAS Language: Reference, Version 6, First Edition* and the *SAS Procedures Guide, Version 6, Third Edition.*

xx

Using This Book

Purpose

SAS Language and Procedures: Usage, Version 6, First Edition provides instructions and examples for accomplishing the primary tasks you need to complete in your daily use of the SAS System. This book is a tutorial for base SAS software beginning with Release 6.06. This guide does not attempt to cover all features of the system, all statements for a procedure, or all options for a statement. Instead, this guide focuses on common tasks and explains the simplest way of accomplishing them.

"Using This Book" contains important information to assist you as you use this book. This information includes how much experience of base SAS software is required before using this book, how to use this book, and what conventions are used in text and example code. In addition, an "Additional Documentation" section, found at the end of "Using This Book," provides references to other books that contain information on related topics.

Audience

SAS Language and Procedures: Usage, Version 6, First Edition is written for

- □ users who have not used the SAS System but have some computer programming experience and know the fundamentals of programming logic

- □ users who have an introductory-level knowledge of the SAS System

- □ experienced SAS users who want to learn new tasks.

Prerequisites

Before you use this book, you need to learn how to invoke the SAS System at your site. Contact the SAS Software Consultant at your site for instructions. In addition, you should have read the *SAS Introductory Guide, Third Edition* or have some knowledge of the SAS System or another programming language.

How to Use This Book

The following sections provide an overview of the information in this book, explain the organization, and describe how you can best use the book.

Organization

This book is divided into ten parts. Each part has one or more chapters to develop the topic for the part. The parts and chapters of the book are as follows:

Part 1: Introduction to the SAS System

Part 1 introduces you to the components of base SAS software, what it produces, and the primary methods of running the SAS System.

Chapter 1, "What Is the SAS System?"

Part 2: Getting Your Data into Shape

Part 2 explains the concept and use of the SAS data set. It tells how to create and store data using the SAS System.

Chapter 2, "Introduction to DATA Step Processing"

Chapter 3, "Starting with Raw Data"

Chapter 4, "Starting with SAS Data Sets"

Part 3: Basic Programming

Part 3 explains the basic techniques for handling data and programming with the SAS language.

Chapter 5, "Understanding DATA Step Processing"

Chapter 6, "Working with Numeric Variables"

Chapter 7, "Working with Character Variables"

Chapter 8, "Acting on Selected Observations"

Chapter 9, "Creating Subsets of Observations"

Chapter 10, "Working with Grouped or Sorted Observations"

Chapter 11, "Using More than One Observation in a Calculation"

Chapter 12, "Finding Shortcuts in Programming"

Chapter 13, "Working with Dates in the SAS System"

Part 4: Combining SAS Data Sets

Part 4 explains how to combine SAS data sets and compares the various methods.

Chapter 14, "Methods of Combining SAS Data Sets"

Chapter 15, "Concatenating SAS Data Sets"

Chapter 16, "Interleaving SAS Data Sets"

Chapter 17, "Merging SAS Data Sets"

Chapter 18, "Updating SAS Data Sets"

Chapter 19, "Manipulating SAS Data Sets"

Part 5: Understanding Your SAS Session

Part 5 explains the kinds of output produced by the SAS System and helps you avoid and diagnose errors.

Chapter 20, "Understanding and Enhancing Your Output"

Chapter 21, "Analyzing Your SAS Session with the SAS Log"

Chapter 22, "Directing the SAS Log and Output"

Chapter 23, "Diagnosing and Avoiding Errors"

Part 6: Producing Reports

Part 6 teaches you how to produce the most widely used reports: detailed reports, summary reports, and forms.

Chapter 24, "Printing Detail Reports"

Chapter 25, "Creating Summary Tables"

Chapter 26, "Producing Mailing Labels and Other Continuous-Feed Forms"

Part 7: Producing Plots and Charts

Part 7 teaches you how to produce a variety of plots and charts.

Chapter 27, "Plotting the Relationship between Variables"

Chapter 28, "Charting the Values of a Variable"

Part 8: Designing Your Own Output

Part 8 describes how to produce custom-designed reports.

Chapter 29, "Writing Output"

Chapter 30, "Customizing Output"

Part 9: Storing and Managing Data in SAS Files

Part 9 explains SAS data sets and SAS data libraries and tells how to manipulate the members of a SAS data library.

Chapter 31, "SAS Data Libraries"

Chapter 32, "Managing SAS Data Libraries"

Chapter 33, "Getting Information about Your Data Sets"

Chapter 34, "Modifying Data Set Names and Attributes"

Chapter 35, "Copying, Moving, and Deleting SAS Data Sets"

Part 10: Understanding Your SAS Environment

Part 10 shows you how to use the SAS Display Manager System to run jobs and use the SAS System.

Chapter 36, "Starting, Running, and Exiting the SAS System"

Chapter 37, "Using the SAS Display Manager System: the Basics"

Chapter 38, "Using Commands to Manipulate Your Full-Screen Environment"

Chapter 39, "Mastering Your Environment with Selected Windows"

What You Should Read

The following table explains what parts of the book you should read depending on your level of experience with base SAS software.

Level of Experience	Suggested Reading
no experience with the SAS System some experience with the SAS System completed the *SAS Introductory Guide*	Begin by reading Parts 1 and 2, which teach you the fundamental concepts of the SAS System. You should then read selected chapters in Part 3, which explains how to combine SAS data sets. After you have mastered the topics in the first three parts of the book, you can select topics as needed from the rest of the book.
experience with the fundamental concepts of the SAS System	Refer to the parts appropriate for the tasks you want to accomplish. Parts 3 through 10 explain how to use the SAS System to accomplish specific tasks that you need to do.

Reference Aids

SAS Language and Procedures: Usage provides a number of reference aids to help you find the information you need.

table of contents	lists page numbers for the major parts of the book.
table of reference aids	lists page numbers for all displays, figures, tables, and special topics boxes.
glossary	provides concise definitions of the terms used in the book.
index	provides page numbers where specific procedures, statements, and options are discussed. The index also lists many tasks that you need to accomplish and provides page numbers where you can find information on those tasks.
inside cover graphics	provide functional overviews of the SAS System. The inside front cover depicts the entire SAS System. The inside back cover illustrates how base SAS software is organized.

Each chapter provides special reference aids to help you find specific information.

chapter table of contents	lists the page numbers of sections within a single chapter.
Special Topics	highlights topics for which detailed information is given in one chapter for general reference throughout the book.
SAS Tools	appears at the end of most chapters. This section summarizes the elements of the SAS System discussed in the chapter by illustrating the syntax of each element. Note that the syntax summaries in this section do not necessarily include all possible arguments for a statement or procedure. This section shows all required syntax and any options that are explained in the text. For complete syntax, including all available options, refer to *SAS Language: Reference, Version 6, First Edition* and the *SAS Procedures Guide, Version 6, Third Edition*. For a detailed discussion of the syntax conventions used in this section, refer to "Syntax Conventions" later in "Using This Book."
Learning More	appears at the end of most chapters. This section lists other sources of information for topics discussed in the chapter. In addition, this section can contain brief summaries of related topics that may interest you. When a related topic is introduced, it also includes a reference to other documentation where you can learn more about the topic.

Conventions

This section explains the various conventions used in presenting text, SAS language syntax, examples, and printed output in this book.

Typographical Conventions

You will see several type styles used in this book. The following list explains the meaning of each style:

roman
: is the standard type style used for most text in this book.

UPPERCASE ROMAN
: is used for SAS statements, variable names, and other SAS language elements when they appear in the text. However, you can enter these elements in your own SAS code in lowercase, uppercase, or a mixture of the two.

italic
: is used for special terms defined in the text or in the glossary and to emphasize important information.

`monospace`
: is used to show examples of SAS statements. In most cases, this book uses lowercase type for SAS code, with the exception of some title characters. You can enter your own SAS code in lowercase, uppercase, or a mixture of the two. The SAS System ignores case except in character values. Therefore, enter any titles, footnotes, and character variable values exactly as you want them to appear on your output.

  Monospace is also used to show the values of character variables in text.

Syntax Conventions

Type styles have special meanings when used in the presentation of base SAS software syntax. The following list explains the style conventions for presenting syntax in this book:

UPPERCASE BOLD
: identifies SAS keywords such as the names of statements and procedures (for example, **PROC PRINT**).

UPPERCASE ROMAN
: identifies arguments and values that are literals (for example, DATA=).

italic
: identifies arguments or values that you supply. Items in italic can represent user-supplied values assigned to an argument (for example, *SAS-data-set* in DATA=*SAS-data-set*) or nonliteral arguments (for example, VAR *variable*;).

The following symbols are used to indicate other syntax conventions:

< > (angle brackets)   identify optional arguments. Any argument not enclosed in angle brackets is required.

| (vertical bar)   indicates that you can choose one value from a group. Values separated by bars are mutually exclusive.

. . . (ellipsis)   indicates that the argument or group of arguments following the ellipsis can be repeated any number of times. If the ellipsis and the following argument are enclosed in angle brackets, they are optional.

The following examples illustrate these syntax conventions:

□ **FILE** *your-output-file* <PRINT <HEADER=*your-label*>>;

□ **FORMAT** *variable-list-1 format-1* <. . . *variable-list-n format-n*>;

□ **PUT** <*variable-list* | _ALL_>;

FILE, FORMAT, and **PUT**
are all primary parts of the language so they appear in boldface type.

your-output-file
is required because it is not enclosed in angle brackets. The italic type indicates that you supply the value for this argument.

<HEADER=*your-label*>
is optional because it is enclosed in angle brackets. The uppercase roman type for HEADER= indicates that the argument must be spelled as shown. If you use HEADER=, you must supply the name of a statement label to replace *your-label*.

<PRINT <HEADER=*your-label*>>
are optional because they are enclosed in angle brackets, but if you use HEADER=, you must also use PRINT.

variable-list-1 format-1
is required and must have both a list of one or more variable names and a format.

<. . . *variable-list-n format-n*>
indicates that you can optionally specify multiple sets of variables and formats, but they must occur in pairs with each list of variables followed by a format.

<*variable-list* | _ALL_>
is separated by a vertical bar to indicate that you can use only one of these two arguments. The angle brackets indicate that both arguments are optional. Therefore, you can specify a list of variables with the PUT statement, or you can specify PUT _ALL_, or you can simply specify PUT with no arguments.

Conventions for Examples and Output

The examples in each chapter build on previous examples in the chapter to teach you how to combine statements and options to achieve the results you want. You can run any of the examples in this book as you read the chapters. The following conventions are used to simplify your use of examples:

☐ This book shows all of the code that creates all data sets.

☐ This book uses two methods to show input data used to create the data set: the CARDS statement and the INFILE statement. If the input data for the data set are lengthy, this book lists the data in the appendix, not in the main text of the chapter.

☐ This book uses the following form of the INFILE statement to simplify showing how to access an external file:

    INFILE 'your-input-file';

This form of the statement enables you to directly specify the name of the file as it is known on your operating system. This form of the INFILE statement is available in all environments except VSE. On VSE, you must use operating system control language to access external files. Refer to the SAS documentation for the VSE environment for more information. Other methods of accessing external data are briefly discussed in Chapter 2, but they are not generally used in this book.

☐ Most examples use permanent data sets because many examples in a chapter or part use the same data set. When a data set is reused, it is created once and used throughout the rest of the chapter or part. To help you find the data set more easily, a reference to the page where the data set is created is included in the index.

☐ The first time a data set is created or used, the example shows the LIBNAME statement that defines the libref for the data set. Subsequent examples use the same libref but do not repeat the LIBNAME statement. This use of the LIBNAME statement is available in all environments except VSE. On VSE, you must use operating system control language to define librefs. Refer to the SAS documentation for the VSE environment for more information.

Each page of output produced by a procedure is enclosed in a box. In each chapter, the procedure output is numbered consecutively starting with 1, and each output is given a title. Most of the output in this book is produced using the following SAS system options:

☐ LINESIZE=76

☐ PAGESIZE=60

☐ NODATE.

In examples where other options are used, the options appear in the SAS code that produces the output.

In examples that illustrate log output, the line numbers shown in the log will probably not match the line numbers of your log, regardless of the method you use to run the system. The difference in line numbers in the log is not important.

Additional Documentation

SAS Institute provides many publications about products of the SAS System and how to use it on specific hosts. For a complete list of SAS publications, you should refer to the current *Publications Catalog*. The catalog is produced twice a year. You can order a free copy of the catalog by writing to the following address:

> SAS Institute Inc.
> Book Sales Department
> SAS Campus Drive
> Cary, NC 27513

Base SAS Software Documentation

In addition to *SAS Language and Procedures: Usage*, you will find these other documents helpful when using base SAS software:

☐ *SAS Language and Procedures: Introduction, Version 6, First Edition* (order #A56074) helps you get started if you are unfamiliar with the SAS System or any other programming language.

☐ *SAS Language: Reference, Version 6, First Edition* (order #A56076) provides detailed reference information on SAS language statements, functions, formats, informats, display manager, or any other part of the base system except procedures.

☐ *SAS Procedures Guide, Version 6, Third Edition* (order #A56080) provides detailed reference information on SAS procedures.

☐ *SAS Guide to TABULATE Processing, Second Edition* (order #A56095) provides more information about the TABULATE procedure.

☐ *SAS Guide to the REPORT Procedure: Usage and Reference, Version 6, First Edition* (order #A56088) explains how to use the REPORT procedure to customize reports.

☐ SAS Technical Report P-258, *Using the Report Procedure in a Nonwindowing Environment, Release 6.07* (order #A59175) explains how to use the REPORT procedure in a non-windowing environment.

☐ *SAS Guide to Macro Processing, Version 6, Second Edition* (order #A56041) provides more information about macro variables and statements.

☐ *SAS Language and Procedures: Syntax, Version 6, First Edition* (order #A56077) provides a concise but complete reference to the syntax for portable SAS software.

□ *SAS Programming Tips: A Guide to Efficient SAS Processing, Version 6, First Edition* (order #A56150) suggests more than 100 tips for improving the efficiency of your SAS programs.

□ *SAS Language and Procedures: Usage 2, Version 6, First Edition* (order #A56078) builds on the tasks presented in this *Usage* book, and provides examples and instructions for accomplishing tasks of moderate difficulty for special purposes.

□ SAS Technical Report P-222, *SAS Software: Changes and Enhancements to Base SAS Software, Release 6.07* (order #A59139) provides changes and enhancements to base SAS software for Release 6.07.

□ SAS Technical Report P-242, *SAS Software: Changes and Enhancements, Release 6.08* (order #A59159) provides changes and enhancements to base SAS software for Release 6.08.

□ SAS Technical Report P-252, *SAS Software: Changes and Enhancements, Release 6.09* (order #A59169) provides changes and enhancements to base SAS software for Release 6.09.

□ The SAS Companion for your host system provides details for your specific host or operating system.

Documentation for Other SAS Software

The SAS System includes many software products in addition to the base SAS System. Several books that may be of particular interest to you are listed here:

□ *SAS/ASSIST Software: Your Interface to the SAS System* (order #A56086) provides information on using the SAS System in a menu-driven windowing environment that requires no programming.

□ *SAS/FSP Software: Usage and Reference, Version 6, First Edition* (order #A56001) provides information on using interactive procedures for creating SAS data sets and entering and editing data or for creating, editing, and printing form letters and reports.

□ *SAS/AF Software: Usage and Reference, Version 6, First Edition* (order #A56011) provides information on building windows for your own applications.

□ *SAS/GRAPH Software: Reference, Version 6, First Edition, Volume 1* and *Volume 2* (order #A56020) provides information on creating presentation graphics to illustrate relationships of data.

□ *SAS/GRAPH Software: Usage, Version 6, First Edition* (order #A56021) shows you in step-by-step format how to perform common graphing tasks.

□ *SAS/GRAPH Software: Introduction, Version 6, First Edition* (#A56019) introduces new users of SAS/GRAPH software to producing charts, maps, plots, and text slides.

Part 1
Introduction to the SAS® System

Chapter 1   **What Is the SAS® System?**

Chapter **1** What Is the SAS® System?

Introduction

The SAS System is an integrated system of software products. The SAS System enables you to perform data entry, retrieval, and management; report writing and graphics design; statistical and mathematical analysis; business forecasting and decision support; operations research and project management; and applications development. Some people use many of the SAS System's capabilities; others use only a few. What the SAS System is to you depends on what you want to do with it.

At the core of the SAS System is base SAS software, the software product you learn to use in this book. This chapter introduces the capabilities of base SAS software, addresses methods of running the SAS System, and outlines various types of output. This basic discussion will give you an overview of the SAS System.

Components of Base SAS Software

Base SAS software contains a data management facility, a programming language, and data analysis and reporting utilities. Learning to use base SAS software enables you to work with these features of the SAS System. It also prepares you to learn other software products in the SAS System, since all SAS software products follow the same basic rules.

Data Management Facility

The SAS System organizes data into a rectangular form called a *SAS data set*. In a SAS data set, each row represents information about an individual entity and is called an *observation*. Each column represents the same type of information and is called a *variable*. Each separate piece of information is a *data value*. In a SAS data set, an observation contains all the data values for an entity; a variable contains the same kind of data value for all entities. Figure 1.1 illustrates a SAS data set. The data describe participants in a 16-week weight program at a health and fitness club; the data for each participant are an identification number, name, team name, and weight at the beginning and end of the program.

Figure 1.1
Rectangular Form of a SAS Data Set

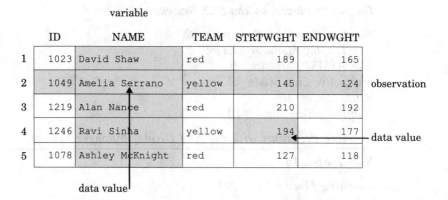

To build a SAS data set with base SAS software, you use statements in the SAS programming language. Here is a very simple SAS program that creates a SAS data set named WGHTCLUB from the health club data:

```
data wghtclub;
   input idno 1-4 name $ 6-24 team $ strtwght endwght;
   loss=strtwght-endwght;
   cards;
1023 David Shaw         red 189 165
1049 Amelia Serrano     yellow 145 124
1219 Alan Nance         red 210 192
1246 Ravi Sinha         yellow 194 177
1078 Ashley McKnight    red 127 118
;
run;
```

A SAS program or a portion of a program that begins with a DATA statement and ends with a RUN statement, another DATA statement, or a PROC statement (discussed later in this chapter) is called a *DATA step*. The DATA step that creates the data set WGHTCLUB comprises the following elements:

□ The DATA statement tells the SAS System to begin building a SAS data set named WGHTCLUB.

□ The INPUT statement identifies the fields to be read from the input data and names the SAS variables to be created from them (IDNO, NAME, TEAM, STRTWGHT, and ENDWGHT).

□ The third statement is an *assignment statement*; it calculates the weight each person lost and assigns the result to a new variable, LOSS.

□ The CARDS statement indicates that data lines follow.

□ The data lines follow the CARDS statement; this approach is useful when you have only a few data lines. (Later chapters show ways to access larger data files.) A single semi-colon on the following line signifies the end of the data lines.

□ The RUN statement tells the SAS System that the preceding statements are ready to be executed.

Note: By default, the data set WGHTCLUB is temporary; that is, it exists only for the current job or session. Chapter 2, "Introduction to DATA Step Processing," explains how to create a permanent SAS data set.

Programming Language

The statements that created the data set WGHTCLUB are part of the SAS programming language. The SAS language contains statements, expressions, functions, options, and formats—elements that many programming languages share. However, the way you use the elements of the SAS language depends on certain programming rules. The most important rules are listed in the next two sections.

Rules for SAS Statements

□ SAS statements end with a semicolon.

□ SAS statements can be entered in lowercase, uppercase, or a mixture of the two.

□ Any number of SAS statements can appear on a single line.

□ A SAS statement can be continued from one line to the next, as long as no word is split.

□ SAS statements can begin in any column. (The examples in this book show one set of conventions.)

□ Words in SAS statements are separated by blanks or by special characters (such as the equal sign and the minus sign in the calculation of the LOSS variable in the WGHTCLUB example).

Rules for SAS Names

□ SAS names are used for SAS data set names, variable names, and other items.

□ A SAS name can contain from one to eight characters.

□ The first character must be a letter or an underscore (_).

□ Subsequent characters must be letters, numbers, or underscores.

□ Blanks cannot appear in SAS names.

Data Analysis and Reporting Utilities

The SAS programming language is both powerful and flexible. You can program any number of analyses and reports with it. The SAS System can also simplify programming for you with its library of built-in programs known as *SAS procedures*. SAS procedures use data values from SAS data sets to produce preprogrammed reports, requiring minimal effort from you.

For example, suppose you want to display the values of the variables in the SAS data set WGHTCLUB. The following SAS program produces the report:

```
proc print data=wghtclub;
    title 'Health Club Data';
run;
```

This procedure, known as the PRINT procedure, displays the variables in a simple, organized form. Output 1.1 shows the result.

Output 1.1
Displaying the
Values in a
SAS Data Set

```
                              Health Club Data                               1

   OBS     IDNO     NAME             TEAM     STRTWGHT     ENDWGHT     LOSS

    1      1023     David Shaw       red         189         165        24
    2      1049     Amelia Serrano   yellow      145         124        21
    3      1219     Alan Nance       red         210         192        18
    4      1246     Ravi Sinha       yellow      194         177        17
    5      1078     Ashley McKnight  red         127         118         9
```

To produce a table showing mean starting weight, ending weight, and weight loss for each team, use the TABULATE procedure.

```
proc tabulate data=wghtclub;
    class team;
    var strtwght endwght loss;
    table team, mean*(strtwght endwght loss);
    title 'Mean Starting Weight, Ending Weight, and Weight Loss';
run;
```

Output 1.2 shows the result.

Output 1.2
Table of Mean
Values for Each
Team

```
            Mean Starting Weight, Ending Weight, and Weight Loss        1

         --------------------------------------------------------
         |                   |              MEAN                 |
         |                   |-----------------------------------|
         |                   | STRTWGHT |  ENDWGHT  |   LOSS     |
         |-------------------+----------+-----------+------------|
         |TEAM               |          |           |            |
         |-------------------|          |           |            |
         |red                |   175.33 |   158.33  |    17.00   |
         |-------------------+----------+-----------+------------|
         |yellow             |   169.50 |   150.50  |    19.00   |
         --------------------------------------------------------
```

A portion of a SAS program that begins with a PROC statement (short for
PROCEDURE statement) and ends with a RUN statement, a DATA statement, or
another PROC statement is called a *PROC step.** Both PROC steps that create
Output 1.1 and 1.2 comprise the following elements:

□ a PROC statement, which includes the word PROC, the name of the
procedure you want to use, and the name of the SAS data set containing the
values. (If you omit the DATA= option and data set name, the procedure
uses the SAS data set most recently created or updated in the program.)

□ additional statements that give the SAS System more information about what
you want to do, for example, CLASS, VAR, TABLE, and TITLE statements.

□ a RUN statement, which indicates that the preceding group of statements is
ready to be executed.

Output Produced by the SAS System

A SAS program can produce some or all of the following kinds of output:

□ a SAS data set. A SAS data set contains data values stored as a table of
observations and variables. It also stores descriptive information about the
data set, such as the names and arrangement of variables, the number of
observations, and when the data set was created. The SAS data set can be
temporary or permanent and can be stored on disk or tape. The examples in
this chapter create the data set WGHTCLUB.

□ the SAS log. By default, the SAS System creates the SAS log as a record of
the SAS statements you entered and messages from the SAS System about
the execution of your program. It can appear as a file on disk, a display on
your monitor, or a hardcopy listing. The exact appearance of the SAS log
varies according to your site, but a typical SAS log for the program in this
chapter looks like Output 1.3.

---

* Some procedures in the SAS System are interactive; in that case, a RUN statement executes the
preceding group of statements but does not end the PROC step.

Output 1.3
A SAS Log

```
1                          The SAS System

NOTE: Copyright(c) 1985,1986,1987,1988 SAS Institute Inc., Cary, NC USA.
NOTE: SAS (r) Proprietary Software Release 6.xx
      Licensed to SAS Institute Inc., Site xxxxxxxx


1          data wghtclub;
2              input idno 1-4 name $ 6-24 team $ strtwght endwght;
3              loss=strtwght-endwght;
4              cards;

NOTE: The data set WORK.WGHTCLUB has 5 observations and 6 variables.

10         run;
11         proc print data=wghtclub;
12             title 'Health Club Data';
13         run;

NOTE: The PROCEDURE PRINT printed page 1.

14         proc tabulate data=wghtclub;
15             class team;
16             var strtwght endwght loss;
17             table team, mean*(strtwght endwght loss);
18             title 'Mean Starting Weight, Ending Weight, and Weight Loss';
19         run;

NOTE: The PROCEDURE TABULATE printed page 2.


NOTE: SAS Institute Inc., SAS Circle, PO Box 8000, Cary, NC 27512-8000
```

□ procedure output. SAS procedure output contains the result of the analysis or the report produced. It can take the form of a file on disk, a display on your monitor, or hardcopy. The appearance of procedure output varies according to your site and the options specified in the program, but Output 1.1 and 1.2, shown earlier in this chapter, illustrate typical procedure output.

□ other SAS files, such as catalogs. SAS catalogs contain information that cannot be represented as tables of data values. Examples of items that can be stored in SAS catalogs include function key settings, letters produced by SAS/FSP software, and displays produced by SAS/GRAPH software.

□ external files or entries in other databases. The SAS System can create and update external files and some databases created by other software products. The information is stored on disk or tape.

Ways to Run SAS Programs

There are several ways to run SAS programs. They differ in the speed with which they run, the amount of computer resources required, and the amount of interaction you have with the program (that is, the kinds of changes you can make while the program is running).

The examples in this book produce the same results, regardless of the way you run the programs. However, in a few cases, the way you run a program determines the appearance of output or the way you write the program. The following sections briefly introduce different ways to run SAS programs.

SAS Display Manager System

In a SAS Display Manager session, you interact with the SAS System directly. The SAS System gives you a full-screen editor, a place for SAS log and procedure output, and windows that display information about your current environment (such as the SAS data sets available, the variables in them, and options currently in effect). You can prepare a program, submit it, see results, modify the program, and resubmit all or part of it, all within the same SAS session. You can scroll back and forth within windows and move freely between different parts of the session. At any point you can save the current program, the SAS log, or the procedure output. You can issue operating system commands from within the session or suspend the SAS session, enter the operating system's command environment, and resume the SAS session later.

Display manager is a quick and convenient way to program in the SAS System. It's especially useful for learning the SAS System and developing programs on small test files. Although it uses more computer resources than other techniques, display manager saves a lot of program development time.

SAS/ASSIST Software

One important feature of the SAS System is SAS/ASSIST software. SAS/ASSIST software provides a series of menus that allow you to select the tasks you want to perform. The SAS System then submits the SAS statements to accomplish those tasks. You do not need to know how to program in the SAS System in order to use SAS/ASSIST software.

SAS/ASSIST software works by submitting SAS statements just like the ones shown earlier in this chapter. In that way it provides a number of features, but its menus do not represent everything you can do with SAS software. If you want to perform tasks other than those listed in the menus, or if you want to bypass the menus, you need to learn to program in the SAS System as described in this book.

Interactive Line Mode

In an interactive line-mode session, you enter one line of a SAS program at a time, and the SAS System executes each DATA or PROC step automatically as soon as it recognizes the end of the step. You generally see procedure output immediately at your terminal. Depending on your site's computer system and on your terminal, you may be able to scroll backward and forward to see different parts of your log and procedure output, or you may lose them when they scroll off the top of your screen. There are limited facilities for modifying programs and correcting errors.

Interactive line mode sessions use fewer computer resources than display manager sessions, but they require more of your time to manage. If you use line mode, you should familiarize yourself with the %INCLUDE, %LIST, and RUN statements in *SAS Language: Reference, Version 6, First Edition*.

Batch Mode

To run a program in batch mode, you prepare a file containing SAS statements (and any statements in the operating system's command language that you need) and submit the program to the computer system. You can then work on something else at your terminal; while you are working, the computer's operating system schedules your job for execution (along with jobs submitted by other people) and runs it. When execution is complete, you look at the log and procedure output.

The central feature of batch execution is that it's completely separate from other activities at your terminal. You do not see the program while it's running, and you cannot correct errors at the time they occur. The log and procedure output go to prespecified destinations; you look at them when the program has finished running. To modify the SAS program, you edit the program with your system's editor and submit a new batch job.

When sites charge for computer resources, batch processing is a relatively inexpensive way to execute programs. It's particularly useful for large programs or when you need to use your terminal for other things while the program is executing. However, for learning the SAS System or developing and testing new programs, batch execution requires a lot of programming time.

Noninteractive Mode

In noninteractive mode, you prepare a file of SAS statements (and sometimes statements in the operating system's command language) and submit the program to the computer system. The program runs immediately and occupies your current terminal session. You can't do any other work in that session while the program is running,* and you generally can't interact with the program.** The log and procedure output go to prespecified destinations, and you usually don't see them until the program has ended. To modify the program or correct errors, you must re-edit and resubmit the program.

Noninteractive execution may be faster than batch execution because the computer system runs the program immediately rather than waiting to schedule your program among other programs.

Running Programs with the SAS Display Manager System

Most programs in this book can be run using any of the methods described in the previous sections. When it is necessary to show a SAS session as you are programming in it, this book uses display manager. The following example gives a brief overview of a display manager session. Instructions on how to use display manager appear in Chapter 37, "Using the SAS Display Manager System: the Basics."

---

*   In a workstation environment, you can switch to another window and continue working.
** Limited ways of interaction are available if the program was prepared with them in advance. For example, you can use the asterisk (*) option in the %INCLUDE statement

When you begin a display manager session, you see a display similar to the one in Display 1.1.

Display 1.1
Display Manager at the Beginning of a SAS Session

```
┌LOG─────────────────────────────────────────────────────────────────────┐
│ Command ===>                                                            │
│                                                                         │
│ NOTE: Copyright(c) 1989 SAS Institute Inc., Cary, NC 27512-8000, U.S.A. │
│ NOTE: SAS (r) Proprietary Software Release 6.xx                         │
│       Licensed to SAS Institute Inc., Site xxxxxxxx.                    │
│                                                                         │
│                                                                         │
│                                                                         │
│                                                                         │
└─────────────────────────────────────────────────────────────────────────┘
┌PROGRAM EDITOR──────────────────────────────────────────────────────────┐
│ Command ===>                                                            │
│                                                                         │
│ 00001                                                                   │
│ 00002                                                                   │
│ 00003                                                                   │
│ 00004                                                                   │
│ 00005                                                                   │
│ 00006                                                                   │
└─────────────────────────────────────────────────────────────────────────┘
```

The colors in the display, the messages, and some other details vary according to your site and your terminal's monitor. The window at the top of the display is the LOG window; it contains the SAS log for the session. The window at the bottom is the PROGRAM EDITOR window. This window provides a full-screen editor in which you edit your SAS programs.

To create the program for the health and fitness club, type the statements in the PROGRAM EDITOR window. Display 1.2 shows the display after you have typed part of the DATA step.

Display 1.2
Starting to Edit a Program in the PROGRAM EDITOR Window

```
┌LOG─────────────────────────────────────────────────────────────────────┐
│ Command ===>                                                            │
│                                                                         │
│ NOTE: Copyright(c) 1989 SAS Institute Inc., Cary, NC 27512-8000, U.S.A. │
│ NOTE: SAS (r) Proprietary Software Release 6.xx                         │
│       Licensed to SAS Institute Inc., Site xxxxxxxx.                    │
│                                                                         │
│                                                                         │
│                                                                         │
│                                                                         │
└─────────────────────────────────────────────────────────────────────────┘
┌PROGRAM EDITOR──────────────────────────────────────────────────────────┐
│ Command ===>                                                            │
│                                                                         │
│ 00001 data wghtclub;                                                    │
│ 00002    input idno 1-4 name $ 6-24 team $ strtwght endwght;            │
│ 00003    loss=strtwght-endwght;                                         │
│ 00004    cards;                                                         │
│ 00005 1023 David Shaw          red 189 165                              │
│ 00006 1049 Amelia Serrano      yellow 145 124                           │
└─────────────────────────────────────────────────────────────────────────┘
```

When you fill the PROGRAM EDITOR window, you can scroll down to get more lines so you can continue typing the program, as Display 1.3 shows.

Display 1.3
Scrolling Down in the PROGRAM EDITOR Window

```
┌LOG─────────────────────────────────────────────────────────────────
 Command ===>

 NOTE: Copyright(c) 1989 SAS Institute Inc., Cary, NC 27512-8000, U.S.A.
 NOTE: SAS (r) Proprietary Software Release 6.xx
       Licensed to SAS Institute Inc., Site xxxxxxxx.




└──────────────────────────────────────────────────────────────────────
┌PROGRAM EDITOR──────────────────────────────────────────────────────
 Command ===>

 00007 1219 Alan Nance         red 219 192
 00008 1246 Ravi Sinha         yellow 194 177
 00009 1078 Ashley McKnight    red 127 118
 00010 run;
 00011 proc print data=wghtclub;
 00012    title 'Health Club Data';
└──────────────────────────────────────────────────────────────────────
```

When you finish editing the program, submit it to the SAS System and view the output. Displays 1.4 and 1.5 show the OUTPUT window.

Display 1.4
First Page of Output in the OUTPUT Window

```
┌OUTPUT──────────────────────────────────────────────────────────────
 Command ===>
 NOTE: Procedure PRINT created 1 page(s) of output.
                     Health Club Data                         1

  OBS   IDNO   NAME            TEAM     STRTWGHT   ENDWGHT   LOSS

   1    1023   David Shaw      red        189       165      24
   2    1049   Amelia Serrano  yellow     145       124      21
   3    1219   Alan Nance      red        219       192      27
   4    1246   Ravi Sinha      yellow     194       177      17
   5    1078   Ashley McKnight red        127       118       9







                                                              R
└──────────────────────────────────────────────────────────────────────
```

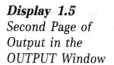

Display 1.5
Second Page of
Output in the
OUTPUT Window

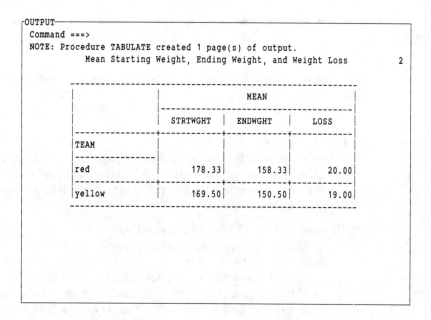

```
┌OUTPUT────────────────────────────────────────────────────────────────┐
│  Command ===>                                                          │
│  NOTE: Procedure TABULATE created 1 page(s) of output.                 │
│        Mean Starting Weight, Ending Weight, and Weight Loss          2 │
│                                                                        │
│         -----------------------------------------------------          │
│         |               |                   MEAN             |         │
│         |               |-----------------------------------|         │
│         |               | STRTWGHT | ENDWGHT |     LOSS      |         │
│         |---------------+----------+---------+---------------|         │
│         |TEAM           |          |         |               |         │
│         |---------------|          |         |               |         │
│         |red            |   178.33 |  158.33 |         20.00 |         │
│         |---------------+----------+---------+---------------|         │
│         |yellow         |   169.50 |  150.50 |         19.00 |         │
│         -----------------------------------------------------          │
│                                                                        │
│                                                                        │
└────────────────────────────────────────────────────────────────────────┘
```

After you finish viewing the output, you can return to the PROGRAM
EDITOR window, shown in Display 1.6, to begin editing a new program.

Display 1.6
The PROGRAM
EDITOR and LOG
Windows after a
Program Is
Executed

```
┌LOG─────────────────────────────────────────────────────────────────────┐
│  Command ===>                                                            │
│                                                                          │
│                                                                          │
│                                                                          │
│  14    proc tabulate data=wghtclub;                                      │
│  15       class team;                                                    │
│  16       var strtwght endwght loss;                                     │
│  17       table team, mean*(strtwght endwght loss);                      │
│  18       title 'Mean Starting Weight, Ending Weight, and Weight Loss';  │
│  19    run;                                                              │
│                                                                          │
│                                                                          │
└──────────────────────────────────────────────────────────────────────────┘
┌PROGRAM EDITOR────────────────────────────────────────────────────────────┐
│  Command ===>                                                            │
│  NOTE: 19 Lines submitted.                                               │
│  00001                                                                   │
│  00002                                                                   │
│  00003                                                                   │
│  00004                                                                   │
│  00005                                                                   │
│  00006                                                                   │
└──────────────────────────────────────────────────────────────────────────┘
```

By default, the output from all submissions remains in the OUTPUT window,
and all statements you submit remain in memory until the end of your session.
You can view the output at any time, and you can recall a previously submitted
program for editing and resubmitting. (You can also clear a window of its
contents if necessary.)

All the commands you use to move through display manager can be executed
as words or as function keys. You can also customize the display of windows and
the assignment of commands to function keys.

SAS Tools

This chapter introduces some basic SAS concepts, including both terminology and the rules for writing SAS statements. Most discussion of SAS syntax appears in later chapters, but you should remember the following points:

DATA *SAS-data-set*;
>   tells the SAS System to begin creating a SAS data set. A portion of a SAS program that begins with a DATA statement and ends with a RUN statement, another DATA statement, or a PROC statement is called a DATA step.

PROC *procedure* <DATA=*SAS-data-set*>;
>   tells the SAS System to invoke a particular SAS *procedure* to process the *SAS-data-set* specified in the DATA= option. If you omit the DATA= option, the procedure processes the most recently created SAS data set in the program. A portion of a SAS program that begins with a PROC statement and ends with a RUN statement, a DATA statement, or another PROC statement is called a PROC step.

RUN;
>   tells the SAS System to begin executing the preceding group of SAS statements.

Learning More

□   This book provides a mid-level introduction to the most commonly used parts of base SAS software. For an easier but more limited introduction, see the *SAS Introductory Guide*.* For complete reference information on the features shown here and related features, see *SAS Language: Reference, Version 6, First Edition*, and the *SAS Procedures Guide, Version 6, Third Edition*.

□   Part 2, "Getting Your Data into Shape," describes how to use DATA steps to create SAS data sets.

□   Part 3, "Basic Programming," expands on the concept of DATA step processing and shows a number of ways to manipulate data.

□   Part 9, "Storing and Managing Data in SAS Files," discusses temporary and permanent SAS data sets and how to store permanent SAS data sets.

□   Part 10, "Understanding Your SAS Environment," presents ways to execute SAS programs in general and display manager sessions in particular.

□   *SAS Language: Reference* documents the %INCLUDE statement's asterisk (*) option.

---

*   Also published in French, German, Japanese, and Spanish.

Part 2

Getting Your Data into Shape

Chapter 2 Introduction to DATA Step Processing

Introduction

This chapter introduces you to the basic structure, functioning, and components of the SAS DATA step. This information prepares you for the next chapters where you will learn to create your own SAS data sets. The purpose of this chapter is to help you understand

☐ what a SAS data set is and why it is needed

☐ how the DATA step works

☐ what information you have to supply to the SAS System so that it can construct a SAS data set for you.

The SAS Data Set: Your Key to the SAS System

You come to the SAS System with a problem to solve. You have data that you want to analyze or process in some way. The first task is to get the data into a form that the SAS System can recognize and handle. Once the data are in that form, you can analyze them and generate reports. Figure 2.1 shows the process in the simplest case.

You begin with *raw data*, that is, a collection of data that have not yet been processed by the SAS System. You use a set of statements known as a *SAS DATA step* to get your data into a SAS data set. Then you can further process your data with additional DATA step programming or with SAS procedures.

Figure 2.1
From Raw Data to Final Analysis

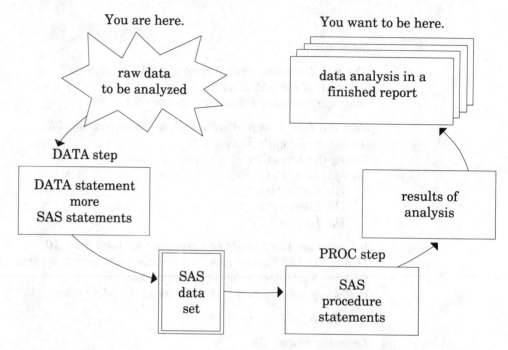

Part 2, "Getting Your Data into Shape," deals with only the first half of the process described in Figure 2.1, the DATA step. In its simplest form, the DATA step can be represented by the three components shown in Figure 2.2.

Figure 2.2
From Raw Data to a SAS Data Set

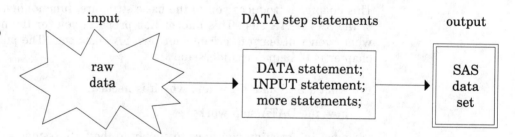

Once you have a SAS data set, you can use it as input to other SAS data steps, as shown in Figure 2.3.

Figure 2.3
Using One SAS Data Set to Create Another

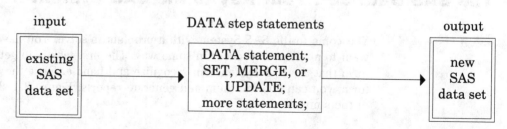

You use SAS statements in a DATA step to read your raw data and produce a SAS data set. In other parts of this book, you will learn about the programming power of the DATA step for performing such tasks as report writing and data management. Part 2 concentrates on only the basic steps necessary for reading data into a SAS data set.

Structure of the SAS Data Set

Think of a SAS data set as a rectangular structure that identifies and stores data. Once your data are in this structure, you use additional DATA steps for further processing or go on to perform many types of analysis with SAS procedures.

As introduced in Chapter 1, "What is the SAS System?," the structure of a SAS data set consists of rows and columns in which data values are stored. The rows in a SAS data set are called *observations*, while rows in a raw data file are called records. The columns, often called fields in a raw data file, become *variables* in a SAS data set. Variables are usually characteristics of whatever you are collecting data about.

As an example, look at the records of raw data shown in Figure 2.4. These data are taken from the health and fitness club example used in Chapter 1. Each record contains information about one participant.

Figure 2.4
Raw Data from the Health and Fitness Club

◄──────────────── data fields ────────────────►

Health and Fitness Club Data

Id	Name	Team	Starting Weight	Ending Weight
1023	David Shaw	red	189	165
1049	Amelia Serrano	yellow	145	124
1219	Alan Nance	red	210	192
1246	Ravi Sinha	yellow	194	177
1078	Ashley McKnight	red	127	118
1221	Jim Brown	yellow	220	—

raw data

Figure 2.5 shows how easily the health club records can be translated into parts of a SAS data set. The rows, or records, become observations. In this case, each observation represents a participant in the program. The columns, or fields, become variables. The variables are each participant's identification number, name, team name, and weight at the beginning and end of a 16-week program.

Figure 2.5
How Data Fit into
a SAS Data Set

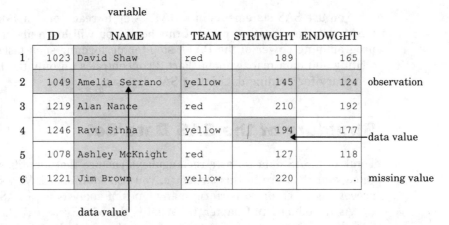

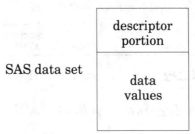

In a SAS data set, every variable exists for every observation. What if you don't have all the data for each observation? For example, suppose the data are incomplete because a value for ENDWGHT was not recorded for one observation. This *missing value* is represented by a period that serves as a placeholder, as shown in observation 6 in Figure 2.5. By coding a value as missing, you can add an observation to the data set for which the data are incomplete and still retain the rectangular shape necessary for a SAS data set.

There's one more important concept to remember about a SAS data set. As Figure 2.6 shows, every SAS data set contains a descriptor portion.

Figure 2.6
Parts of a SAS
Data Set

SAS data set

descriptor portion
data values

The descriptor portion consists of details the SAS System records about a data set, such as the names of all its variables, the attributes of all the variables, the number of observations in the data set, and the time the data set was created or updated. Depending on the operating system you use, additional information about SAS data sets may be stored.

Temporary versus Permanent SAS Data Sets

The data set WGHTCLUB, which was created in Chapter 1 from the raw data shown in Figures 2.4 and 2.5, is a *temporary SAS data set*. It exists until the end of the current SAS session. You can also create WGHTCLUB as a *permanent SAS data set*, one that exists after the end of the current session and can be used in future SAS sessions. The details of creating permanent SAS data sets vary according to your operating system. See "Special Topic: Using SAS Data Sets" for a synopsis of the differences between temporary and permanent SAS data sets.

Special Topic: Using SAS Data Sets

Creating and Using Temporary SAS Data Sets
When you use a DATA step to create a SAS data set with a *one-level name*, such as in

```
data wghtclub;
    input name $ strtwght endwght;
```

you normally create a *temporary* SAS data set, one that exists only for the duration of your current session. The SAS System places this data set in a *SAS data library* referred to as WORK. On most operating systems, everything stored there is deleted at the end of your session.*

The DATA statement above creates a SAS data set named WORK.WGHTCLUB. The SAS System always refers to this data set with its two-level name. For example, the SAS log may read

```
NOTE: The data set WORK.WGHTCLUB has 6 observations and
      5 variables.
```

However, because the SAS System assigns the first-level name WORK to all SAS data sets that are specified with only a one-level name, you can refer to it with the one-level name WGHTCLUB. When you specify a one-level name in a PROC PRINT statement, for example,

```
proc print data=wghtclub;
```

the SAS System automatically gives it the first-level name WORK and looks for the data set in the SAS data library WORK.

Creating and Using Permanent SAS Data Sets
To create a *permanent* SAS data set, you must indicate a SAS data library other than WORK to the SAS System. Use a LIBNAME statement, or an appropriate host system command, to assign a *libref* to a SAS data library on the host system.** (WORK is actually a reserved libref that the SAS System automatically assigns to a temporary SAS data

(continued on next page)

---

* For details, refer to the SAS documentation for your host system.

** Under the VSE operating system, you must use a host-level command, not a LIBNAME statement, to make this assignment. For more information, refer to the SAS documentation for using the SAS System under VSE.

(continued from previous page)

library.) The libref functions as a shorthand way of referring to a SAS data library. Here is the form of the LIBNAME statement.

LIBNAME *libref 'your-data-library';*

The *libref* must be a valid SAS name, that is, beginning with a letter or an underscore; containing letters, numbers, or the underscore; and having no more than eight characters.* Here is an example.

```
libname saveit 'your-data-library';

data saveit.wghtclub;
   input name $ strtwght endwght;
more program statements

proc print data=saveit.wghtclub;
run;
```

The LIBNAME statement associates the libref SAVEIT with *your-data-library*, where *your-data-library* is your operating system's name for a SAS data library. To create a new permanent SAS data set and store it in this SAS data library, you must use the two-level name in the DATA statement, for example,

```
data saveit.wghtclub;
```

To reference this SAS data set in a later DATA step or in a PROC statement, you must use the two-level name:

```
proc print data=saveit.wghtclub;
```

For more information, see Chapter 31, "SAS Data Libraries."

---

* Additional restrictions may apply under some operating systems. For more information, refer to the SAS documentation for your host system.

Conventions in This Manual
Throughout this manual, small data sets used for a single example are shown as temporary data sets specified with a one-level name, for example,

```
data fitness;
```

Data sets that are used throughout a chapter are created as permanent SAS data sets. These data sets are specified with a two-level name, and a LIBNAME statement precedes each DATA step in which a permanent SAS data set is created, for example,

```
libname saveit 'your-data-library';
data saveit.wghtclub;
```

How the DATA Step Works: a Basic Introduction

The DATA step consists of a group of SAS statements that begins with a DATA statement. The DATA statement begins the process of building a SAS data set and names the data set. The statements that make up the DATA step are first compiled, and the syntax is checked. If the syntax is correct, the statements are executed. Figure 2.7 illustrates the flow of action in a typical DATA step, showing that the DATA step, in its simplest form, is a loop with an automatic output and return action.

The next sections discuss the DATA step in terms of what happens during the compile phase and execution phase. These sections are followed by a sample program that demonstrates how the DATA step works.

Figure 2.7
Flow of Action in
a Typical DATA
Step

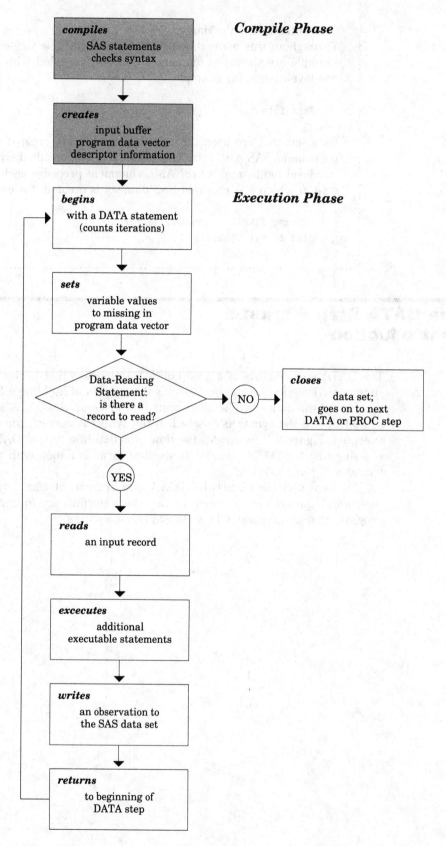

During the Compile Phase

When you submit a DATA step to the SAS System, the syntax of the SAS statements is checked, and the statements are compiled automatically; that is, your SAS statements are translated into machine code that can be further processed. Three items are defined at this time:

input buffer
    is the area of memory into which each record of data from the raw data file will be read when the program executes.

program data vector
    is the area of memory where the SAS System builds your data set, *one observation at a time*. When the program runs, data values are read from the input buffer and are assigned to the appropriate variable in the program data vector. Any variables created in the DATA step are also added to the program data vector. From here the variable values are written to disk as a single observation in a SAS data set.

descriptor portion
    contains information the SAS System creates and maintains about each SAS data set. Later, you will learn how to display this information.

During the Execution Phase

All executable statements in the DATA step are executed once for each iteration. A record is read into the input buffer. Values are read from the input buffer and are assigned to the appropriate variable in the program data vector. Values for variables created by program statements are calculated and are also written to the program data vector.

When the program reaches the end of the DATA step, three actions occur by default that make using the SAS language different from using most other programming languages:

1. The current observation is written to the data set from the program data vector.

2. The program loops back to the top of the DATA step.

3. Variables in the program data vector are reset to missing.*

If there is another record to read, the program executes again, building the second observation, and so on until there are no more records to read. The data set is then closed, and the SAS System goes on to the next DATA or PROC step.

---

* Exceptions to this rule include variables retained by default and variables specified in a RETAIN statement.

Example of a DATA Step

Here's a simple DATA step that produces a SAS data set from the data collected for the health and fitness club. As discussed earlier, the input data contain each participant's identification number, name, team name, and weight at the beginning and end of a 16-week weight program. This section shows a basic DATA step, explains each of the SAS statements used, and demonstrates the step-by-step execution of a DATA step.

The DATA Step

```
libname in 'your-data-library';

data in.wghtclub;
   input idno 1-4 name $ 6-24 team $ strtwght endwght;
   loss=strtwght-endwght;
   cards;
1023 David Shaw          red     189 165
1049 Amelia Serrano      yellow 145 124
1219 Alan Nance          red     210 192
1246 Ravi Sinha          yellow 194 177
1078 Ashley McKnight     red     127 118
1221 Jim Brown           yellow 220  .
1095 Susan Stewart       blue    135 127
1157 Rose Collins        green   155 141
1331 Jason Schock        blue    187 172
1067 Kanoko Nagasaka     green   135 122
1251 Richard Rose        blue    181 166
1333 Li-Hwa Lee          green   141 129
1192 Charlene Armstrong  yellow 152 139
1352 Bette Long          green   156 137
1262 Yao Chen            blue    196 180
1087 Kim Blackburn       red     148 135
1124 Adrienne Fink       green   156 142
1197 Lynne Overby        red     138 125
1133 John VanMeter       blue    180 167
1036 Becky Redding       green   135 123
1057 Margie Vanhoy       yellow 146 132
1328 Hisashi Ito         red     155 142
1243 Deanna Hicks        blue    134 122
1177 Holly Choate        red     141 130
1259 Raoul Sanchez       green   189 172
1017 Jennifer Brooks     blue    138 127
1099 Asha Garg           yellow 148 132
1329 Larry Goss          yellow 188 174
;
run;
```

The Statements

Note the following SAS statements in this DATA step:

□ The LIBNAME statement assigns a libref or shorthand name to the SAS data library in which your data set will be stored. (See "Special Topic: Using SAS Data Sets" earlier in this chapter for details.)

□ The DATA statement begins the DATA step and names the data set being created.

□ The INPUT statement creates five variables and indicates how values are to be read from the input buffer and assigned to variables in the program data vector.

□ The assignment statement, which follows the INPUT statement, creates an additional variable called LOSS, calculates the value of LOSS during each iteration of the DATA step, and writes it to the program data vector.

□ The CARDS statement marks the beginning of the input data. The single semicolon marks the end of the input data.

The Process

First, the DATA step is compiled.* At this time, the input buffer, program data vector, and descriptor portion are defined for the data set WGHTCLUB. As Figure 2.8 shows, the program data vector contains the variables named in the INPUT statement, as well as the variable LOSS. Also, note that all variable values are initially set to missing.**

Figure 2.8
*Variable Values
Set to Missing
Initially*

Input Buffer

```
----+----1----+----2----+----3----+----4----+----5----+----6----+----7----+----8
```

Program Data Vector

IDNO	NAME	TEAM	STRTWGHT	ENDWGHT	LOSS
.			.	.	.

The syntax is correct, so the DATA step executes. As Figure 2.9 illustrates, the INPUT statement causes the first record of raw data to be read into the input buffer. Then, according to the instructions in the INPUT statement, the data values in the input buffer are read and are assigned to variables in the program data vector.

---

* The SAS System automatically compiles the program when you submit the job for execution. It does not require an additional step.

** Missing numeric values are represented by a period. Missing character values are represented by a blank.

Figure 2.9
*Values Assigned
to Variables by
the INPUT
Statement*

Input Buffer

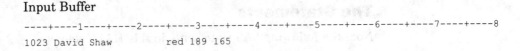

Program Data Vector

IDNO	NAME	TEAM	STRTWGHT	ENDWGHT	LOSS
1023	David Shaw	red	189	165	.

When values have been assigned for all variables listed in the INPUT
statement, the SAS System executes the next statement in the program, which in
this case is

```
loss=strtwght-endwght;
```

This assignment statement calculates the value for the variable LOSS and writes
that value to the program data vector, as Figure 2.10 shows.

Figure 2.10
*Value Computed
and Assigned to
LOSS*

Input Buffer

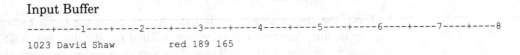

Program Data Vector

IDNO	NAME	TEAM	STRTWGHT	ENDWGHT	LOSS
1023	David Shaw	red	189	165	24

Now the end of the DATA step has been reached, so the program
automatically

1. writes the first observation to the data set

2. loops back to the top of the DATA step to begin the next iteration

3. sets all values in the program data vector to missing as Figure 2.11 shows.

Figure 2.11
Values Set to
Missing

Input Buffer

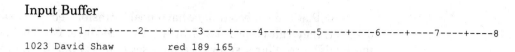

```
----+----1----+----2----+----3----+----4----+----5----+----6----+----7----+----8
1023 David Shaw        red 189 165
```

Program Data Vector

IDNO	NAME	TEAM	STRTWGHT	ENDWGHT	LOSS
.				.	.	.

Execution continues. The INPUT statement looks for another record to read. If there are no more records to read, the data set is closed and the system goes on to the next DATA or PROC step. In this example, there are more records, so the INPUT statement reads the second record into the input buffer, as Figure 2.12 shows.

Figure 2.12
Second Record Is
Read into Input
Buffer

Input Buffer

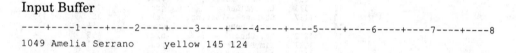

```
----+----1----+----2----+----3----+----4----+----5----+----6----+----7----+----8
1049 Amelia Serrano     yellow 145 124
```

Program Data Vector

IDNO	NAME	TEAM	STRTWGHT	ENDWGHT	LOSS
.				.	.	.

Figure 2.13 shows that values are assigned to variables in the program data vector, and the value for the variable LOSS is calculated, building the second observation just as the first was built.

Figure 2.13
Results of Second
Iteration of the
DATA Step

Input Buffer

```
----+----1----+----2----+----3----+----4----+----5----+----6----+----7----+----8
1049 Amelia Serrano     yellow 145 124
```

Program Data Vector

IDNO	NAME	TEAM	STRTWGHT	ENDWGHT	LOSS
1049	Amelia Serrano	yellow	145	124	21

This entire process continues until the SAS System detects the end of the file. The DATA step iterates as many times as there are records to read. Then the data set WGHTCLUB is closed, and the SAS System looks for the beginning of the next DATA or PROC step.

Now that the collected data have been transformed from raw data into a SAS data set, they can be processed by a SAS procedure. Output 2.1, produced with the PRINT procedure, shows the data set that has just been created.

```
proc print data=in.wghtclub;
    title 'Fitness Center Weight Club';
run;
```

Output 2.1
PROC PRINT
Output

```
                     Fitness Center Weight Club                          1

     OBS    IDNO    NAME                   TEAM      STRTWGHT   ENDWGHT   LOSS

       1    1023    David Shaw             red         189       165      24
       2    1049    Amelia Serrano         yellow      145       124      21
       3    1219    Alan Nance             red         210       192      18
       4    1246    Ravi Sinha             yellow      194       177      17
       5    1078    Ashley McKnight        red         127       118       9
       6    1221    Jim Brown              yellow      220        .        .
       7    1095    Susan Stewart          blue        135       127       8
       8    1157    Rose Collins           green       155       141      14
       9    1331    Jason Schock           blue        187       172      15
      10    1067    Kanoko Nagasaka        green       135       122      13
      11    1251    Richard Rose           blue        181       166      15
      12    1333    Li-Hwa Lee             green       141       129      12
      13    1192    Charlene Armstrong     yellow      152       139      13
      14    1352    Bette Long             green       156       137      19
      15    1262    Yao Chen               blue        196       180      16
      16    1087    Kim Blackburn          red         148       135      13
      17    1124    Adrienne Fink          green       156       142      14
      18    1197    Lynne Overby           red         138       125      13
      19    1133    John VanMeter          blue        180       167      13
      20    1036    Becky Redding          green       135       123      12
      21    1057    Margie Vanhoy          yellow      146       132      14
      22    1328    Hisashi Ito            red         155       142      13
      23    1243    Deanna Hicks           blue        134       122      12
      24    1177    Holly Choate           red         141       130      11
      25    1259    Raoul Sanchez          green       189       172      17
      26    1017    Jennifer Brooks        blue        138       127      11
      27    1099    Asha Garg              yellow      148       132      16
      28    1329    Larry Goss             yellow      188       174      14
```

Information You Supply to Create a SAS Data Set

This section briefly describes what the next chapter covers in detail: how to supply the SAS System with the necessary information for reading your data into a SAS data set. You must describe the raw data to the SAS System so that it can read them and create a SAS data set that you can use for further processing, data analysis, or report writing. You must

□ use an INPUT statement to tell the SAS System how to read the data

□ define the variables and indicate whether they are character or numeric

□ specify the location of the raw data.

Telling the SAS System How to Read the Data: Styles of Input

The SAS System provides many tools for reading raw data into a SAS data set. These tools include three basic input styles as well as various format modifiers and pointer controls.

List input is the easiest to use. Simply list the variable names in the INPUT statement and place at least one space between each value in the data lines. List input, however, places numerous restrictions on your data. These restrictions are discussed in detail in the next chapter. Here is an example of list input:

```
data scores;
   input name $ test1 test2 test3;
   cards;
Bill 187 97 103
John 156 76 74
Joe 99 102 129
;
run;
```

Note that there is at least one blank space between each data value.

Column input allows you to read the same data if they are entered in fixed columns:

```
data scores;
   input name $ 1-4 test1 6-8 test2 10-12 test3 14-16;
   cards;
Bill 187  97 103
John 156  76  74
Joe   99 102 129
;
run;
```

Formatted input allows you to supply special instructions in the INPUT statement for reading data. For example, to read numeric data containing special symbols, you need to supply the SAS System with special instructions so that it can read the data correctly. These instructions are called *informats*. In the INPUT statement, you can specify an informat to be used to read a data value, as in the following example:

```
data totsales;
   input date mmddyy8. +2 amount comma5.;
   cards;
9/5/88    1,382
10/19/88  1,235
11/30/88  2,391
;
run;
```

In this example, MMDDYY8. is the informat for the variable DATE, and COMMA5. is the informat for the variable AMOUNT.

The SAS System also allows you to mix these styles of input as required by the way values are arranged in the data records. The next chapter discusses in detail all these input styles, including their rules and restrictions, and additional data-reading tools.

Defining Variables to the SAS System

So far, you've seen the INPUT statement used to instruct the SAS System on how to read raw data lines. But at the same time that the INPUT statement provides instructions for reading data, it defines the variables for the data set. By assuming default values for variable attributes, the INPUT statement does a lot of work for you. Later in this book, you will learn other statements that allow you to define variables and assign attributes to variables, but this chapter and Chapter 3 concentrate on the use of the INPUT statement.

SAS variables can have the following attributes:

□ name

□ type

□ length

□ informat

□ format

□ label.

In an INPUT statement, you supply each variable name. The type is assumed to be numeric, and its length is assumed to be 8 bytes. Therefore, the INPUT statement

```
input idno test1 test2 test3;
```

creates four numeric variables, each with a length of 8 bytes, without requiring you to specify either type or length.

Name	Type	Length
idno	numeric	8 bytes
test1	numeric	8 bytes
test2	numeric	8 bytes
test3	numeric	8 bytes

Note that the values of numeric variables can contain only numbers. To store values that contain alphabetic or special characters, you must create a character variable. By following a variable name in an INPUT statement with a dollar sign ($), you create a character variable. The default length of a character variable is also 8 bytes. The statement

```
input idno name $ test1 test2 test3;
```

creates a data set containing one character variable and four numeric variables all with a default length of 8 bytes.

Name	Type	Length
idno	numeric	8 bytes
name	character	8 bytes
test1	numeric	8 bytes
test2	numeric	8 bytes
test3	numeric	8 bytes

In addition to specifying the types of variables in the INPUT statement, you can also specify the lengths of character variables. Character variables can be up to 200 characters in length. To specify the length of a character variable in an INPUT statement, you need to supply an informat or column numbers.* For example, by following a variable name in the INPUT statement with the informat $20., or with column specifications such as 1-20, you can create a character variable that is 20 bytes long.

Two other variable attributes, format and label, affect how variable values and names are represented when they are printed or displayed rather than how data are read or stored. They are assigned with different statements that you will learn about later.

Indicating the Location of Your Data to the SAS System

To create a SAS data set, you can read data from one of three locations:

□ raw data in the data stream, that is, following a CARDS statement

□ raw data in a file that you specify with an INFILE statement

□ data from an existing SAS data set.

In previous examples, data are placed directly in the data stream with the programming statements that make up the DATA step. The CARDS statement tells the SAS System that raw data follow. The single semicolon that follows the last line of data marks the end of the data. The CARDS statement and data lines must occur last in the DATA step statements.

If your raw data are already stored in a file, you don't have to bring that file into the data stream. Use an INFILE statement to specify the file containing the raw data. (See "Special Topic: Using External Files in Your SAS Job" for details on INFILE, FILE, and FILENAME statements.) The following statements

---

* The length of numeric variables is not affected by informats or column specifications in an INPUT statement.

demonstrate the same example, this time showing that the raw data are stored in an external file:

```
data wghtclub;
   infile 'your-input-file';
   input idno $ 1-4 name $ 6-23 strtwght 24-26 endwght 28-30;
   loss=strtwght-endwght;
run;
```

You can also use data already stored in a SAS data set as input to a new data set. To read data from an existing SAS data set, you must specify the existing data set's name in one of the following statements:

□ SET statement

□ MERGE statement

□ UPDATE statement.

For example, the following statements create a new SAS data set named RED that adds the variable LOSSPCT:

```
data red;
   set wghtclub;
   losspct=loss/strtwght*100;
run;
```

The SET statement indicates that the data being read are already in the structure of a SAS data set and gives the name of a SAS data set.

Special Topic: Using External Files in Your SAS Job

Your SAS programs often need to read raw data from a file or write data or reports to a file that is not a SAS data set. To use a file that is not a SAS data set in a SAS program, you need to tell the SAS System where to find it. You can

□ identify the file directly in the INFILE, FILE, or other SAS statement that uses the file

□ set up a *fileref* for the file by using the FILENAME statement and then use the fileref in the INFILE, FILE, or other SAS statement*

□ use operating system commands to set up a fileref and then use the fileref in the INFILE, FILE, or other SAS statement.

The first two methods are described here. The third method depends on the operating system you are using; this book does

---

* Under the VSE operating system, you must use a host-level command, not a FILENAME statement, to make this assignment. For more information, refer to the SAS documentation for using the SAS System under VSE.

not attempt to cover methods for various operating systems. Refer to the SAS documentation for your host system.

Identifying an External File Directly

The simplest method for referring to an external file is to use the name of the file in the INFILE, FILE, or other SAS statement that needs to reference the file. For example, if you have raw data stored in a file on your operating system and you want to read the data using a SAS DATA step, you can tell the SAS System where to find the raw data by putting the name of the file in the INFILE statement, for example,

```
data temp;
    infile 'your-input-file';
    input idno $ 1-4 name $ 6-23 strtwght 24-26 endwght 28-30;
run;
```

The INFILE statement for this example may appear as follows for MVS, VMS," and CMS environments:

```
    /* MVS example */
infile 'fitness.weight.rawdata(club1)';

    /* VMS example */
infile '[fitness.weight.rawdata]club1.dat';

    /* CMS example */
infile 'club1 weight a';
```

This method of referencing an external file is the one used throughout most of this book. For more information, refer to the SAS documentation for your host system.

Referencing an External File with a Fileref

An alternate method for referencing an external file is to use the FILENAME statement to set up a *fileref* for a file. The fileref functions as a shorthand way of referring to an external file. You then use the fileref in later SAS statements that reference the file, such as the FILE or INFILE statement.

Here is the form of the FILENAME statement:

FILENAME *fileref 'your-input-or-output-file'*;

The *fileref* must be a valid SAS name, that is, beginning with a letter or an underscore, containing letters, numbers, or the underscore; and having no more than eight characters.*

(continued)

VMS is a trademark of Digital Equipment Corporation.

* Additional restrictions may apply under some operating systems. For more information, refer to the SAS documentation for your host system.

(continued from previous page)

For example, you can reference the raw data stored in a file on your operating system by using the FILENAME statement to specify the name of the file and its fileref and the INFILE statement with the same fileref to reference the file.

```
filename fitclub 'your-input-file';

data temp;
   infile fitclub;
      input idno $ 1-4 name $ 6-23 strtwght 24-26 endwght 28-30;
run;
```

In this case, the INFILE statement stays the same for all operating systems; the FILENAME statement may appear as follows for MVS, VMS, and CMS environments:

```
    /* MVS example */
filename fitclub 'fitness.weight.rawdata(club1)';


    /* VMS example */
filename fitclub '[fitness.weight.rawdata]club1.dat';


    /* CMS example */
filename fitclub 'club1 weight a';
```

If you need to use several files or members from the same directory, PDS, or MACLIB, you can use the FILENAME statement to create a fileref that identifies the name of the directory, PDS, or MACLIB. Then you can use the fileref in the INFILE statement and enclose the name of the file, PDS member, or MACLIB member in parentheses immediately after the fileref, as in this example:

```
filename fitclub 'directory-or-PDS-or-MACLIB';

data temp;
   infile fitclub(club1);
      input idno $ 1-4 name $ 6-23 strtwght 24-26 endwght 28-30;
run;

data temp2;
   infile fitclub(club2);
      input idno $ 1-4 name $ 6-23 strtwght 24-26 endwght 28-30;
run;
```

In this case, the INFILE statements stay the same for all operating systems; the FILENAME statement may appear as follows for MVS, VMS, and CMS environments:

```
    /* MVS example */
filename fitclub 'fitness.weight.rawdata';

    /* VMS example */
filename fitclub 'fitness:[weight.rawdata]';

    /* CMS example */
filename fitclub 'fitness maclib a';
```

SAS Tools

This chapter introduces basic information on the DATA step. Specific DATA statement options are covered in detail in Chapters 3 and 4.

LIBNAME *libref 'your-SAS-data-library'*;
associates a *libref* with a SAS data library. Enclose the name of the library in quotes. The SAS System locates a permanent SAS data set by matching the libref in a two-level SAS data set name with the library associated with that libref in a LIBNAME statement. The rules for creating a SAS data library depend on your operating system.

DATA *<libref.>SAS-data-set*;
tells the SAS System to begin creating a SAS data set. If you give just a *SAS-data-set*, the SAS System creates a temporary SAS data set. (It attaches the libref WORK for its internal processing.) If you give a previously defined *libref* as the first level of the name, the SAS System stores the data set permanently in the library referenced by the libref. A SAS program or a portion of a program that begins with a DATA statement and ends with a RUN statement, another DATA statement, or a PROC statement is called a DATA step.

INPUT *variable<$>*;
reads raw data using list input. At least one blank must occur between any two data values. The $ denotes a character variable.

INPUT *variable<$>column-range*;
reads raw data that is aligned in columns. The $ denotes a character variable.

INPUT *variable informat*;
reads raw data using formatted input. An informat supplies special instructions for reading the data.

INFILE *fileref* | *'your-input-file'*;
identifies an external file to be read by an INPUT statement. Specify a *fileref* that has been assigned with a FILENAME statement or with an appropriate host system command, or specify the actual name of the external file.

FILENAME *fileref* *'your-input-or-output-file'*;
associates a *fileref* with an external file. Enclose the name of the external file in quotes.

Learning More

□ Chapter 4, "Starting with SAS Data Sets," discusses the SET statement in detail. In addition to the SET statement, you can also read a SAS data set with a MERGE or UPDATE statement. Chapter 17, "Merging SAS Data Sets," and Chapter 18, "Updating SAS Data Sets," discuss the MERGE and UPDATE statements.

□ Chapter 6, "Working with Numeric Variables," and Chapter 7, "Working with Character Variables," discuss in detail how the variable length affects what values you can store in a variable.

□ Chapter 13, "Working with Dates in the SAS System," discusses informats for dates.

□ *SAS Language: Reference, Version 6, First Edition* completely documents the ATTRIBUTE statement, which you can use to assign attributes to variables.

□ *SAS Language: Reference* provides complete documentation on using the LINESIZE= option in an INPUT statement to limit how much of the data lines is read by the INPUT statement.

□ This book deals with using the SAS System for reading files of raw data and SAS data sets and writing to SAS data sets; however, SAS documentation for SAS/ACCESS software provides complete information on using the SAS System to read and write information stored in several types of database files.

Chapter 3 Starting with Raw Data

Introduction

This chapter demonstrates how to use an INPUT statement, format modifiers, line-hold specifiers, and line-pointer controls to create a SAS data set from raw data. The SAS System provides you with three, basic input styles: list, column, and formatted. These styles may be used individually, in combination with each other, or in conjunction with various line-hold specifiers and line and column pointer controls.

You may be entering the data yourself or using an existing file of raw data. If your data are machine readable, you simply need to learn those tools that allow the SAS System to read them. If your data are not yet entered, you can choose the input style that allows you to enter the data most easily.

Choosing the Style of Input

The input style you use can depend on many factors:

□ how the data have been entered, for example, data fields aligned in columns or separated by blanks

□ how you would like to enter the data

□ whether character variables contain embedded blanks

□ whether numeric variables contain non-numeric characters such as commas

□ whether the data contain time or date values that require special instructions to be read

□ how data are placed for more than one observation in each input record

□ whether data for a single observation are spread over multiple input records.

The following sections give characteristics and examples of list, column, and formatted input. They also give guidelines for combining these styles of input in a single INPUT statement.

In the Simplest Case

Using List Input

List input uses the simplest form of the INPUT statement but places several restrictions on your data. The following program uses the health and fitness club data from Chapter 2 to illustrate a DATA step that contains an INPUT statement and uses list input. The CARDS statement marks the beginning of the data lines. The semicolon following the data lines marks the end of the data lines.

```
data club1;
   input idno name $ team $ strtwght endwght;
   cards;
1023 David red 189 165
1049 Amelia yellow 145 124
1219 Alan red 210 192
1246 Ravi yellow 194 177
1078 Ashley red 127 118
1221 Jim yellow 220
;
run;

proc print data=club1;
   title 'Weight Club Members';
run;
```

Output 3.1 shows the resulting data set. Note that this output is produced by the PROC PRINT statement that follows the DATA step.

Output 3.1
Data Set Created
with Simple List
Input

```
                          Weight Club Members                              1

      OBS    IDNO    NAME      TEAM       STRTWGHT    ENDWGHT

       1     1023    David     red          189         165
       2     1049    Amelia    yellow       145         124
       3     1219    Alan      red          210         192
       4     1246    Ravi      yellow       194         177
       5     1078    Ashley    red          127         118
       6     1221    Jim       yellow       220          .
```

In the records for this example, each data value is separated from the next by at least one blank space. Note also that the variable names are specified in the INPUT statement in *exactly* the same order as the fields in the raw data records. The last observation contains a missing value, represented by a period, for the value of ENDWGHT.

List input reads a data value until it reaches a blank space. It assumes the value has ended and assigns it to the appropriate variable in the program data vector. Then it scans the record in the input buffer until it reaches a nonblank space. There it begins reading the value to be assigned to the next variable.

List Input: Points to Remember

Keep in mind the following characteristics of list input:

□ Fields must be separated by at least one blank.

□ Each field must be specified in order.

□ Missing values must be represented by a place holder such as a period. (A blank field causes the matching of variable names and values to get out of sync.)

□ Character values can't contain embedded blanks.

□ The default length of character variables is 8 bytes. A longer value is truncated when it is written to the program data vector. (To read a character variable containing more than eight characters with list input, you can use a LENGTH statement. See Chapter 5, "Understanding DATA Step Processing.")

□ Data must be in standard character or numeric format.

List input requires the fewest specifications in the INPUT statement; however, the restrictions it places on the data may require that you learn other styles of input as well. For example, column input, which is discussed in the next section, is less restrictive. This section has introduced only *simple list input*. See also "Making List Input More Flexible" later in this chapter to learn about *modified list input*.

When Your Data Are in Columns

Using Column Input

With *column input*, data values occupy the same fields within each record. When using column input, you list in the INPUT statement the variable names and identify the location of the corresponding data fields in the data lines by specifying the column positions. You can use column input when your raw data are in fixed columns and in standard character or numeric format.

The following program also uses the health and fitness club data, but now two more data values are missing. The data are aligned in columns and are read with column input:

```
data club1;
   input idno 1-4 name $ 6-11 team $ 13-18 strtwght
      20-22 endwght 24-26;
   cards;
1023 David   red    189 165
1049 Amelia  yellow 145
1219 Alan    red    210 192
1246 Ravi    yellow     177
1078 Ashley  red    127 118
1221 Jim     yellow 220
;
run;

proc print data=club1;
   title 'Weight Club Members';
run;
```

Note that the specification following each variable name indicates the beginning and ending columns for the variable value. Also, when using column input you aren't required to indicate missing values with a placeholder such as a period. Note how the missing values appear in Output 3.2.

Output 3.2
Data Set Created
with Column Input

```
                         Weight Club Members                            1

          OBS    IDNO    NAME      TEAM      STRTWGHT    ENDWGHT

           1     1023    David     red         189        165
           2     1049    Amelia    yellow      145         .
           3     1219    Alan      red         210        192
           4     1246    Ravi      yellow       .         177
           5     1078    Ashley    red         127        118
           6     1221    Jim       yellow      220         .
```

Reading Embedded Blanks and Creating Longer Variables

One advantage to using column input over simple list input is that it allows character variables to contain embedded blanks. Look at the variable NAME in the data set CLUB1. It contains only the members' first names. Column input allows the variable to be longer than 8 bytes, and it can contain embedded blanks, allowing the first and last names to be read as a single value. These differences are possible for two reasons:

1. Column input uses the columns specified to determine the length of character variables.

2. Column input, unlike list input, reads data until it reaches the last specified column, *not* until it reaches a blank space.

For example, look at the following DATA step. It uses column input to create a new data set named CLUB2. The data are from the health and fitness club weight program used earlier, with one exception. They have been modified to include the members' first and last names. The value for the variable NAME now contains an embedded blank and is 18 bytes long.

```
data club2;
   input idno 1-4 name $ 6-23 team $ 25-30
         strtwght 32-34 endwght 36-38;
   cards;
1023 David Shaw         red    189 165
1049 Amelia Serrano     yellow 145 124
1219 Alan Nance         red    210 192
1246 Ravi Sinha         yellow 194 177
1078 Ashley McKnight    red    127 118
1221 Jim Brown          yellow 220
;
run;

proc print data=club2;
   title 'Weight Club Members';
run;
```

Output 3.3 shows the resulting data set.

Output 3.3
Data Set Created
with Column Input
(Embedded
Blanks)

```
                        Weight Club Members                        1

   OBS    IDNO    NAME             TEAM      STRTWGHT    ENDWGHT

    1     1023    David Shaw       red         189        165
    2     1049    Amelia Serrano   yellow      145        124
    3     1219    Alan Nance       red         210        192
    4     1246    Ravi Sinha       yellow      194        177
    5     1078    Ashley McKnight  red         127        118
    6     1221    Jim Brown        yellow      220          .
```

Using Column Input to Skip Fields When Reading Data Records

Column input also allows fields to be skipped altogether or to be read in any order. Using column input to read the same health and fitness club raw data, you can cause the value for the variable TEAM to be read first and the variable IDNO to be omitted altogether.

You can also cause only *part* of a value to be read or reread. For example, since the team names begin with different letters, you can save space by causing

only the first letter in the field containing the team name to be read. Consider
the INPUT statement in the following DATA step:

```
data club2;
    input team $ 25 name $ 6-23 strtwght 32-34 endwght 36-38;
    cards;
1023 David Shaw         red    189 165
1049 Amelia Serrano     yellow 145 124
1219 Alan Nance         red    210 192
1246 Ravi Sinha         yellow 194 177
1078 Ashley McKnight    red    127 118
1221 Jim Brown          yellow 220
;
run;

proc print data=club2;
    title 'Weight Club Members';
run;
```

Output 3.4 shows the PRINT procedure output. Note that the variable IDNO is
omitted altogether from this data set and that TEAM is the first variable in the
new data set; its values consist of only one character.

Output 3.4
Data Set Created
with Column Input
(Skipping Fields)

```
                        Weight Club Members                          1

      OBS    TEAM    NAME              STRTWGHT    ENDWGHT
      1      r       David Shaw          189         165
      2      y       Amelia Serrano      145         124
      3      r       Alan Nance          210         192
      4      y       Ravi Sinha          194         177
      5      r       Ashley McKnight     127         118
      6      y       Jim Brown           220           .
```

Column Input: Points to Remember

The advantages of column input can be summed up as follows:

□ Character variables can be up to 200 characters in length and are not
limited to the default length of 8 bytes.

□ Character variables can contain embedded blanks.

□ Fields can be read in any order.

□ No placeholder is required for missing data. A blank field is read as missing.
It does not cause other values to be read incorrectly.

□ Part of the data can be omitted from the input record.

□ Fields or parts of fields can be reread.

When Your Data Require Special Instructions

Using Formatted Input

Sometimes data may require special instructions to be read correctly. For example, numeric data may be stored in special formats such as binary or packed decimal or may contain special characters such as commas. In these situations use *formatted input*. Formatted input combines the features of column input with the ability to read nonstandard numeric or character values.

For example, the following data have numeric values that contain a comma, which is an invalid character for a numeric variable:

```
data jansales;
   input item $ 1-16 amount comma5.;
   cards;
trucks          1,382
jeeps           1,235
landrovers      2,391
;
run;

proc print data=jansales;
   title 'January Sales in Thousands';
run;
```

Note that the values for the variable AMOUNT cannot be read by the SAS System as valid numeric values without the additional instructions provided by an *informat*. Specify the informat COMMA5. to allow the SAS System to read and store these data as valid numeric values. Figure 3.1 shows that the informat COMMA5. instructs the program to read five characters of data (the comma counts as part of the length of the data), strip the comma from the data, and then write the resulting numeric value to the program data vector.

Figure 3.1
Reading a Value with an Informat

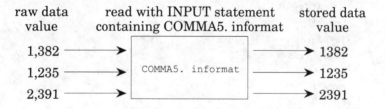

raw data value	read with INPUT statement containing COMMA5. informat	stored data value
1,382	COMMA5. informat	1382
1,235		1235
2,391		2391

Figure 3.2 shows that the data values are read into the input buffer *exactly* as they occur in the raw data records, but they are written to the program data vector (and then to the data set as an observation) as valid numeric values without any special characters.

Figure 3.2
Input Value
Compared to
Variable Value

Input Buffer

```
----+----1----+----2----+----3----+----4----+----5----+----6----+----7----+----8
trucks          1,382
```

Program Data Vector

ITEM	AMOUNT
trucks	1382

Output 3.5 shows the resulting data set. Note that the values for AMOUNT contain only numbers, no commas.*

Output 3.5
Data Set Created
with Column and
Formatted Input

```
                     January Sales in Thousands                        1

              OBS      ITEM          AMOUNT

               1       trucks         1382
               2       jeeps          1235
               3       landrovers     2391
```

Controlling the Position of the Pointer

As the INPUT statement reads data values, it uses an *input pointer* to keep track of its position in the input buffer.** *Column pointer controls* give you additional control over pointer movement and are especially useful with formatted input. Column pointer controls tell the SAS System how far to move the pointer before beginning to read the next value. For example, the data lines in the previous example could be read using formatted input with a column pointer control instead of a combination of column and formatted input.

Consider the following program:

```
data jansales;
   input item $10. @17 amount comma5.;
   cards;
trucks        1,382
jeeps         1,235
landrovers    2,391
;
run;
```

After reading the first value for the variable ITEM, the pointer is left in the next position, column 11. The *absolute column pointer control* @17 then directs the pointer to move to column 17 in the input buffer so that it is in the correct position to read a value for the variable AMOUNT.

---

*   In a report, you may want the comma to appear in numeric values to help readability. Just as the informat gives instructions for reading a value and stripping the comma out, a *format* provides instructions to a SAS procedure for adding characters to variable values in printed output.

** See "Effect of Input Style on Pointer Location" later in this chapter for a discussion of pointer movement.

In the next program, the *relative column pointer control* +6 instructs the pointer to move six columns to the right before reading the next data value.

```
data jansales;
   input item $10. +6 amount comma5.;
   cards;
trucks        1,382
jeeps         1,235
landrovers    2,391
;
run;
```

Note that the data in these two programs are aligned in columns. As with column input, you instruct the pointer to move from field to field. With column input you use column specifications; with formatted input you use the length specified in the informat together with pointer controls.

Formatted Input: Points to Remember

Keep in mind the following characteristics of formatted input:

□ Formatted input reads data until it has read the number of columns indicated by the informat. This is different from list input, which reads until it reaches a blank space.

□ You can position the pointer to read the next value by using pointer controls.

□ You can read data stored in nonstandard form such as packed decimal or data that contain commas.

□ You have the flexibility of using informats with all the features of column input, as described in "Column Input: Points to Remember" earlier in this chapter.

Making List Input More Flexible

Remember that list input places many restrictions on your data. Using format modifiers, you can take advantage of the simplicity of list input without the inconvenience of the usual restrictions. For example, you can used *modified list input* to give character variables a length longer than the default length of 8 bytes, to read numeric data with invalid characters, and to read character data that contain embedded blanks.

Reading Long Character Values and Numeric Data with Invalid Characters

With format modifiers, you can use list input rather than column or formatted input to read data, even when they contain values that require an informat to be read correctly. The *colon (:) format modifier* allows you to use list input for reading character data containing more than eight characters or data requiring informats (numeric data that contain invalid characters).

As an example, consider the following DATA step. The variable ITEM has a length of 10, and the variable AMOUNT requires an informat that strips commas from numbers so that they can be read as valid numeric values. To use the colon format modifier with list input, place the colon between the variable name and the informat. As in simple list input, at least one blank must separate each value from the next and character values can't contain embedded blanks.

```
data jansales;
    input item : $10. amount : comma5.;
    cards;
trucks 1,382
jeeps 1,235
landrovers 2,391
;
run;

proc print data=jansales;
    title 'January Sales in Thousands';
run;
```

Note that the data values are not aligned in columns as required in the preceding example, which uses formatted input to read the data. Output 3.6 shows the resulting data set.

Output 3.6
Data Set Created with Modified List Input (: comma5.)

```
                    January Sales in Thousands                    1

              OBS    ITEM        AMOUNT

               1     trucks        1382
               2     jeeps         1235
               3     landrovers    2391
```

Reading Character Data with Embedded Blanks

Because list input uses a blank space to determine where one value ends and the next one begins, values normally can't contain blanks. However, with the *ampersand* (&) *format modifier*, you can use list input to read data that contain *single* embedded blanks. The only restriction is that at least *two* blanks must divide each value from the *next* data value in the record.

For example, the following DATA step creates the data set CLUB2; the variable NAME contains members' first and last names. Using the ampersand format modifier, you can use list input rather than column input to read the data. (Column input was shown in an earlier example.) To use the ampersand format modifier with list input, place the ampersand between the variable name and the informat. Note that in the data lines there are *two* blank spaces between the values for the variable NAME and the variable TEAM.

```
data club2;
    input idno name & $18. team $ strtwght endwght;
    cards;
1023 David Shaw   red 189 165
1049 Amelia Serrano  yellow 145 124
1219 Alan Nance   red 210 192
1246 Ravi Sinha  yellow 194 177
1078 Ashley McKnight  red 127 118
1221 Jim Brown  yellow 220 .
;
run;

proc print data=club2;
    title 'Weight Club Members';
run;
```

Output 3.7 shows the resulting data set.

Output 3.7
Data Set Created with Modified List Input (& $18.)

```
                            Weight Club Members                              1

        OBS    IDNO    NAME             TEAM      STRTWGHT    ENDWGHT

         1     1023    David Shaw       red         189        165
         2     1049    Amelia Serrano   yellow      145        124
         3     1219    Alan Nance       red         210        192
         4     1246    Ravi Sinha       yellow      194        177
         5     1078    Ashley McKnight  red         127        118
         6     1221    Jim Brown        yellow      220          .
```

Mixing Styles of Input

An Example of Mixed Input

Once you begin an INPUT statement in a particular style (list, column, or formatted), you are not restricted to using that style alone. You can mix input styles in a single INPUT statement as long as you mix them in a way that appropriately describes the records of raw data. For example, look at the following DATA step, and note that all three input styles are used:

```
data club1;
    input idno name $18. team $ 25-30 strtwght endwght;
    cards;
1023 David Shaw          red    189 165
1049 Amelia Serrano      yellow 145 124
1219 Alan Nance          red    210 192
1246 Ravi Sinha          yellow 194 177
1078 Ashley McKnight     red    127 118
1221 Jim Brown           yellow 220  .
;
run;

proc print data=club1;
    title 'Weight Club Members';
run;
```

The variables IDNO, STRTWGHT, and ENDWGHT are read with list input. The variable NAME is read with formatted input, and the variable TEAM is read with column input. Output 3.8 demonstrates that mixing input styles in the example program causes the data to be read correctly.

Output 3.8
Data Set Created
with Mixed Styles
of Input

```
                         Weight Club Members                          1

    OBS    IDNO    NAME             TEAM      STRTWGHT    ENDWGHT

     1     1023    David Shaw       red         189         165
     2     1049    Amelia Serrano   yellow      145         124
     3     1219    Alan Nance       red         210         192
     4     1246    Ravi Sinha       yellow      194         177
     5     1078    Ashley McKnight  red         127         118
     6     1221    Jim Brown        yellow      220          .
```

Effect of Input Style on Pointer Location

As the INPUT statement reads data values from the record in the input buffer, it uses a *pointer* to keep track of its position. When you mix styles of input in a single INPUT statement, you can get unexpected results if you don't understand where the input pointer is left after a value in the input buffer has been read. This section explains the movement of the pointer when data records are read.

Pointer Location with Column and Formatted Input

With column and formatted input, you supply the instructions that determine the exact pointer location. With column input, the SAS System reads the columns you specify in the INPUT statement. With formatted input, the SAS System reads exactly the length you specify in the informat. In both cases, the pointer moves as far as you instruct it and stops. It is left in the column immediately following the last one read.

Here are two examples of input followed by an explanation of the pointer location. The first DATA step shows column input.

```
data tscores;
   input team $ 1-6 score 12-13;
   cards;
red        59
blue       95
yellow     63
green      76
;
run;
```

The second DATA step uses the same data to show formatted input.

```
data tscores;
   input team $6. +5 score 2.;
   cards;
red        59
blue       95
yellow     63
green      76
;
run;
```

Figure 3.3 shows that the pointer is located in column 7 after the first value is read with either of the two previous INPUT statements.

Figure 3.3
Pointer Position:
Column and
Formatted Input

```
----+----1----+----2
red          59
     ↑
```

Unlike list input, column and formatted input rely totally on your instructions to move the pointer so that the value for the second variable, SCORE, can be read. Column input uses column specifications to move the pointer to each data field; formatted input can use informats and pointer controls to control the position of the pointer.

In this INPUT statement using column input, the column specifications 12-13 move the pointer to column 12 to begin reading the value for the variable SCORE:

```
input team 1-6 score 12-13;
```

In this INPUT statement using formatted input, the +5 column pointer control moves the pointer to column 12 so that a value for the variable SCORE can then be read with the 2. numeric informat.

```
input team $6. +5 score 2.;
```

Without the use of a pointer control, which moves the pointer to the column where the value begins, this INPUT statement would attempt to read the value for SCORE in columns 7 and 8, which are blank.

Pointer Location with List Input

List input, on the other hand, uses a scanning method for determining the pointer location. With list input, the pointer reads until it reads a blank and then stops in the next column. To read the next variable value, the pointer then moves automatically to the first nonblank column, discarding any leading blanks it encounters. Here are the same data read with list input:

```
data tscores;
   input team $ score;
   cards;
red          59
blue         95
yellow       63
green        76
;
run;
```

Figure 3.4 shows that the pointer is located in column 5 after reading the value **red**. Because SCORE, the next variable, is read with list input, the pointer scans for the next nonblank space to begin reading a value for SCORE. Unlike with column and formatted input, you do not have to explicitly move the pointer to the beginning of the next field in list input.

Figure 3.4
Pointer Position:
List Input

```
----+----1----+----2
red          59
   ↑
```

Reading from the Same Record Twice

Sometimes you may need to tell the SAS System to hold a record and read from it again. This ability is useful when you need to test for a condition before creating an observation from a data record.

For example, to create a SAS data set that is a subset of a larger group of records, you may need to test for a condition before deciding if a particular record should be used to create an observation in the data set you want to create. Placing the *trailing at-sign* (@) before the semicolon at the end of an INPUT statement instructs the SAS System to hold the current data line in the input buffer so it is available for a subsequent INPUT statement.* You can set up this process, which requires that each record be read twice, by following these steps:

1. Use an INPUT statement to read a record.

2. Use a trailing @ at the end of the INPUT statement to hold the record in the input buffer for the execution of the next INPUT statement.

---

* Remember that an INPUT statement causes a new record to be read into the input buffer.

3. Use an IF statement to test for a condition.

4. If the condition is met, use another INPUT statement to read the record to create an observation.

To read from a record twice, you must prevent a new record from automatically being read into the input buffer when the second INPUT statement is executed. Use of a trailing @ in the first INPUT statement serves this purpose. The trailing @ is one of two *line-hold specifiers* that allow you to hold a record in the input buffer for further processing.

For example the health and fitness club data contain information about all members. The following DATA step creates a SAS data set that contains only members of the red team:

```
data redteam;
   input team $ 13-18 @;
   if team='red';
   input idno 1-4 strtwght 20-22 endwght 24-26;
   cards;
1023 David  red       189 165
1049 Amelia yellow 145 124
1219 Alan   red       210 192
1246 Ravi   yellow 194 177
1078 Ashley red       127 118
1221 Jim    yellow 220   .
;
run;

proc print data=redteam;
   title 'Red Team';
run;
```

In this DATA step, the following actions occur:

□ The first INPUT statement reads a record into the input buffer, reads a data value from columns 13 through 18, and assigns that value to the variable TEAM in the program data vector. Note that the single trailing @ affects the action of the second INPUT statement.

□ The IF statement allows the current iteration of the DATA step to continue only when the value for TEAM is **red**. When it is not, the current iteration stops and the SAS System returns to the top of the DATA step, resets values in the program data vector to missing, and releases the held record from the input buffer.

□ The second INPUT statement executes only when the value of TEAM is **red**. It does not cause a new record to be read into the input buffer; the single trailing @ at the end of the first INPUT statement instructs the system to hold the current record in the input buffer. It reads data values from the record in the input buffer and assigns values to the variables IDNO, STRTWGHT, and ENDWGHT.

□ The record is released from the input buffer when the program loops back to the top of the DATA step.

Output 3.9 shows the resulting data set.

Output 3.9
Subset Data Set
Created with
Trailing @

```
                              Red Team                              1

           OBS    TEAM    IDNO    STRTWGHT    ENDWGHT

            1     red     1023      189         165
            2     red     1219      210         192
            3     red     1078      127         118
```

Creating Multiple Observations from a Single Record

Sometimes you need to create multiple observations from a single record of raw data. One way to tell the SAS System how to read such a record is to use the other line-hold specifier, the *double trailing at-sign* (@@ or *double trailing @*). The double trailing @ not only prevents a new record from being read into the input buffer when a new INPUT statement is encountered, but it also prevents the record from being released when the program loops back to the top of the DATA step.* Note the double trailing @ in the following program:

```
data bodyfat;
   input sex $ fatpct @@;
   cards;
m 13.3 f 22
m 22   f 23.2
m 16   m 12
;
run;

proc print data=bodyfat;
   title 'Results of Bodyfat Testing';
run;
```

Output 3.10 shows the resulting data set.

Output 3.10
Data Set Created
with Double
Trailing @

```
                     Results of Bodyfat Testing                    1

                     OBS    SEX    FATPCT

                      1      m      13.3
                      2      f      22.0
                      3      m      22.0
                      4      f      23.2
                      5      m      16.0
                      6      m      12.0
```

---

* Remember that the trailing @ does not hold a record in the input buffer across iterations of the DATA step.

How the Double Trailing @ Affects Execution of the DATA Step

To understand how the data records in the previous example were read, look back at the lines of data in the DATA step. Each record contains the raw data for *two* observations instead of one. Consider this example in terms of the flow of the DATA step, as explained in Chapter 2.

When the SAS System reaches the end of the DATA step, it returns to the top of the program and begins the next iteration, executing until there are no more records to read. Each time it returns to the top of the DATA step and executes the INPUT statement, it *automatically* reads a new record into the input buffer. If that were the case in the previous example (and as shown below), the second set of data values in each record would never be read at all:

```
m 13.3 f 22
m 22   f 23.2
m 16   m 12
```

The double trailing @ tells the SAS System to hold the record in the input buffer. Each record is held in the input buffer until the end of the record is reached. The program does not automatically bring the next record into the input buffer each time it executes the INPUT statement, nor does it automatically release the record when it loops back to the top of the DATA step. As a result, the pointer location is maintained on the *current* record, allowing each value in that record to be read. Each time the DATA step completes an iteration, an observation is written to the data set.

Figures 3.5 through 3.9 demonstrate what happens in the input buffer when a double trailing @ appears in the INPUT statement, as in this example:

```
input sex $ fatpct @@;
```

Figure 3.5 shows that all values in the program data vector are set to missing. The INPUT statement reads the first record into the input buffer. The program begins reading values from the current pointer location, which is the beginning of the input buffer.

Figure 3.5
First Iteration:
First Record Is
Read

Input Buffer

```
----+----1----+----2----+----3----+----4----+----5----+----6----+----7----+----8
m 13.3 f 22
↑
```

Program Data Vector

SEX	FATPCT
	.

When the pointer reaches the blank space following 13.3, the complete value for the variable FATPCT has been read. The pointer stops in the next column, and the value 13.3 is written to the program data vector, as Figure 3.6 shows.

Figure 3.6
First Observation
Is Created

Input Buffer

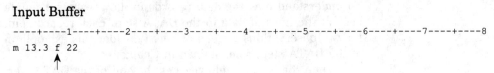

Program Data Vector

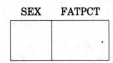

There are no other variables in the INPUT statement and no more statements in the DATA step, so three actions take place:

1. The first observation is written to the data set.

2. The DATA step begins its next iteration.

3. The values in the program data vector are set to missing.

Now note the position of the pointer in Figure 3.7. The SAS System is ready to read the next piece of data in the *same* record.

Figure 3.7
Second Iteration:
Still Reading from
First Record

Input Buffer

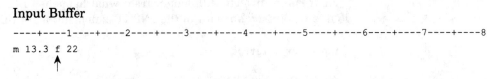

Program Data Vector

SEX	FATPCT
	.

Figure 3.8 shows that the INPUT statement reads the next two values from the input buffer and writes them to the program data vector.

Figure 3.8
Second
Observation Is
Created

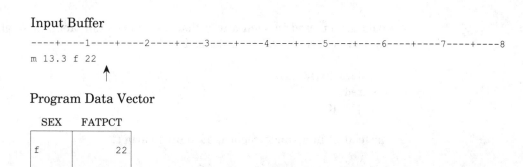

The DATA step has completed the second iteration, so the values in the program data vector are written to the data set as the second observation. Then the DATA step begins its third iteration. Values in the program data vector are set to missing, and the INPUT statement executes. The pointer, which is one column position after the last column read, continues reading. Because this is list input, the pointer scans for the next nonblank character to begin reading the next value. When it reaches the end of the input buffer, failing to find a nonblank character, a new record is read into the input buffer. Figure 3.9 shows that values for the third observation are read from the beginning of the second record.

Figure 3.9
Third Iteration:
Second Record Is
Read into the
Input Buffer

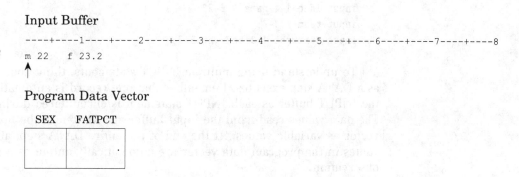

The process continues until all records have been read. The resulting SAS data set contains six observations instead of three.

  Note: Although this program successfully reads all of the data in the input records, it produces a message in the SAS log noting that it had to go to a new line.

Reading Multiple Records to Create a Single Observation

An example earlier in this chapter showed data for several observations appearing in a single record of raw data. Now consider the opposite situation: several records containing all the information to construct a single observation. This section looks at the health and fitness club data used earlier, but the raw data are entered in such a way that the information about a single member is spread across several records, as in

```
1023 David Shaw
red
189 165
```

instead of in a single record, as shown earlier.

```
1023 David Shaw       red 189 165
```

Using Multiple Input Statements

If you want to read all the data values arranged across the three records, you can use the following INPUT statement:

```
input idno 1-4 name $ 6-23 team $ strtwght endwght;
```

You can also use multiple INPUT statements, one for each record that needs to be read into the input buffer, as in the following:

```
input idno 1-4 name $ 6-23;
input team $ 1-6;
input strtwght 1-3 endwght 5-7;
```

To understand using multiple INPUT statements, think about what happens as a DATA step executes. Remember that one record is automatically read into the INPUT buffer as each INPUT statement is encountered during each iteration. The data values read from the input buffer are written to the program data vector as variable values. At the end of the entire DATA step, all the variable values in the program data vector are automatically output as a *single* observation.

In this example, you can use multiple INPUT statements in a DATA step to read only selected data fields and create a data set containing only the variables IDNO, STRTWGHT, and ENDWGHT.

```
data club2;
    input idno 1-4;
    input;
    input strtwght 1-3 endwght 5-7;
    cards;
1023 David Shaw
red
189 165
1049 Amelia Serrano
yellow
145 124
1219 Alan Nance
red
210 192
```

```
     1246 Ravi Sinha
     yellow
     194 177
     1078 Ashley McKnight
     red
     127 118
     1221 Jim Brown
     yellow
     220  .
     ;
     run;

     proc print data=club2;
        title 'Beginning and Ending Weights';
     run;
```

Note each of the three INPUT statements in this example.

□ The first INPUT statement reads only one data field in the first record and assigns a value to the variable IDNO.

□ The second INPUT statement has no arguments. This null INPUT statement reads the second record into the input buffer but doesn't assign a value to a variable.

□ The third INPUT statement causes the third record to be read into the input buffer and assigns values to the variables STRTWGHT and ENDWGHT.

Output 3.11. shows the resulting data set.

Output 3.11
Data Set Created with Multiple INPUT Statements

```
                    Beginning and Ending Weights              1

          OBS     IDNO    STRTWGHT     ENDWGHT

           1      1023      189          165
           2      1049      145          124
           3      1219      210          192
           4      1246      194          177
           5      1078      127          118
           6      1221      220           .
```

Using the / Line-Pointer Control

Writing a separate INPUT statement for each record that needs to be read is not the only way to create a single observation. You can write a single INPUT statement and use the */ line-pointer control*. This line-pointer control character forces a new record to be read into the input buffer and the pointer to return to the beginning of that record. Look at the INPUT statement in the following program:

```
data club2;
    input idno 1-4 / / strtwght 1-3 endwght 5-7;
    cards;
1023 David Shaw
red
189 165
1049 Amelia Serrano
yellow
145 124
1219 Alan Nance
red
210 192
1246 Ravi Sinha
yellow
194 177
1078 Ashley McKnight
red
127 118
1221 Jim Brown
yellow
220  .
;
run;

proc print data=club2;
    title 'Beginning and Ending Weights';
run;
```

Note that a / appears in this example exactly where a new INPUT statement begins in the previous example. What happens in the input buffer and program data vector as this DATA step executes is exactly the same as in the preceding example. The / is the signal to read a new record into the input buffer, which happens automatically when a new INPUT statement is encountered. Output 3.12 shows the resulting data set.

Output 3.12
Data Set Created with the
/ Line-Pointer Control

```
                    Beginning and Ending Weights                     1

          OBS    IDNO    STRTWGHT    ENDWGHT

           1     1023      189         165
           2     1049      145         124
           3     1219      210         192
           4     1246      194         177
           5     1078      127         118
           6     1221      220          .
```

Using the *#n* Line-Pointer Control

You can also read multiple records to create a single observation by pointing to a specific record in a set of input records with the *#n line-pointer control.* As you saw in the last section, the advantage of using the / line-pointer control over multiple INPUT statements is that it requires fewer statements. However, using the *#n* line-pointer control allows you to read the variables *in any order,* no matter which record contains the data values. It's also useful if you want to skip lines of raw data.

Note the order in which the data lines are read by the INPUT statement in the following program:

```
data club2;
    input #2 team $ 1-6 #1 name $ 6-23 idno 1-4
          #3 strtwght 1-3 endwght 5-7;
    cards;
1023 David Shaw
red
189 165
1049 Amelia Serrano
yellow
145 124
1219 Alan Nance
red
210 192
1246 Ravi Sinha
yellow
194 177
1078 Ashley McKnight
red
127 118
1221 Jim Brown
yellow
220   .
;
run;

proc print data=club2;
    title 'Fitness Center Weight Club';
run;
```

Output 3.13 shows the resulting data set. Compare it to Output 3.12. The order of the observations is the same, but the order of the variables in the INPUT statement differs in each data set. Note how the order in which the variables appear in the INPUT statements corresponds with their order in the resulting data sets.

Output 3.13
Data Set Created
with the #n
Line-Pointer
Control

```
                      Fitness Center Weight Club                      1

     OBS    TEAM      NAME              IDNO    STRTWGHT    ENDWGHT

      1     red       David Shaw        1023      189         165
      2     yellow    Amelia Serrano    1049      145         124
      3     red       Alan Nance        1219      210         192
      4     yellow    Ravi Sinha        1246      194         177
      5     red       Ashley McKnight   1078      127         118
      6     yellow    Jim Brown         1221      220          .
```

To understand the importance of the #n line-pointer control, remember the sequence of events in the DATA steps demonstrating the / line-pointer control and multiple INPUT statements. Each record is read into the input buffer one at a time. The data are read, and then a / or a new INPUT statement causes the next record to be read into the input buffer. It is impossible for a value from the first record to be read after one from the second record is read because the data in the first record are no longer available.

You can solve this problem by using the #n line-pointer control. The #n line-pointer control signals the program to create a multiple-line input buffer, making all data for a single observation available while the observation is being built in the program data vector. The #n line-pointer control also identifies the record in which data for each variable appear.

When the program compiles and builds the input buffer, it looks at the INPUT statement and creates an input buffer with as many lines as are necessary to contain the number of records for reading data for a single observation. In this example, the highest number of records specified was three, so the input buffer is built to contain three records at one time. Figures 3.10 through 3.14 demonstrate the flow of the DATA step in this example.

Figure 3.10 shows that values are set to missing in the program data vector and the INPUT statement reads the first three records into the input buffer.

Figure 3.10
Three Records Are
Read into the
Input Buffer

Input Buffer

```
----+----1----+----2----+----3----+----4----+----5----+----6----+----7----+----8
1023 David Shaw
red
189 165
```

Program Data Vector

TEAM	NAME	IDNO	STRTWGHT	ENDWGHT

In the INPUT statement, the first variable is preceded by #2, indicating that the value to be assigned to the variable TEAM is in the second record. Figure 3.11 shows that the pointer goes to the second line in the input buffer, reads the value, and writes it to the program data vector.

Figure 3.11
Reading from the
Second Record
First

Input Buffer

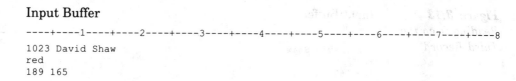

```
----+----1----+----2----+----3----+----4----+----5----+----6----+----7----+----8
1023 David Shaw
red
189 165
```

Program Data Vector

TEAM	NAME	IDNO	STRTWGHT	ENDWGHT
red		.	.	.

Figure 3.12 shows that the pointer then moves to the sixth column in the first record, reads a value, and assigns it to the variable NAME in the program data vector.

Figure 3.12
Reading from the
First Record

Input Buffer

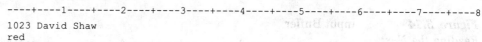

```
----+----1----+----2----+----3----+----4----+----5----+----6----+----7----+----8
1023 David Shaw
red
189 165
```

Program Data Vector

TEAM	NAME	IDNO	STRTWGHT	ENDWGHT
red	David Shaw	.	.	.

Figure 3.13 shows that the process continues with the pointer moving from record to record, as instructed by the INPUT statement, until a value is read and assigned to ENDWGHT, the last variable listed.

Figure 3.13
Reading from the
Third Record

Input Buffer

```
----+----1----+----2----+----3----+----4----+----5----+----6----+----7----+----8
1023 David Shaw
red
189 165
```

Program Data Vector

TEAM	NAME	IDNO	STRTWGHT	ENDWGHT
red	David Shaw	1023	189	165

The bottom of the DATA step is reached, and variable values in the program data vector are output as an observation to the data set. The DATA step loops back to the top, and values in the program data vector are set to missing. The INPUT statement executes, and Figure 3.14 shows that the next three records are read into the input buffer, ready to create the second observation.

Figure 3.14
Reading the Next
Three Records
into the Input
Buffer

Input Buffer

```
----+----1----+----2----+----3----+----4----+----5----+----6----+----7----+----8
1049 Amelia Serrano
yellow
145 124
```

Program Data Vector

TEAM	NAME	IDNO	STRTWGHT	ENDWGHT
		.	.	.

SAS Tools

This chapter discusses INPUT and CARDS statements. The syntax given here for the three styles of input shows only one *variable*. Subsequent variables in the INPUT statement may or may not be described in the same input style as the first one; any of the three styles of input (list, column, and formatted) may be used in a single INPUT statement.

CARDS;

indicates that data lines immediately follow. A semicolon must appear in the line immediately following the last data line.

INPUT *variable* <&> <$>;

reads raw data using list input. Using the & (ampersand format modifier) allows character values to contain embedded blanks. When you use the ampersand format modifier, two blanks are required to signal the end of a value. The $ indicates a character variable.

INPUT *variable start-column* <*-end-column*>;

reads raw data using column input. You can omit *end-column* if the data are only 1 byte long. This style of input allows you to skip columns of data that you do not want to read.

INPUT *variable* : *informat*;
INPUT *variable* & *informat*;

reads raw data using modified list input. The : (colon format modifier) indicates that the following informat is used to read the data value. The & (ampersand format modifier) used with an informat indicates that the following informat is used to read the data value and that two consecutive blanks are required to end the data value.

INPUT <*pointer-control*> *variable informat*;

reads raw data using formatted input. The *informat* supplies special instructions for reading the data. You can also use a *pointer-control* to direct the SAS System to start reading at a particular column.

This chapter discusses the following line-hold specifiers:

@

(trailing @) prevents a new record from automatically being read into the input buffer when a new INPUT statement is executed within the same iteration of the DATA step. When used, the trailing @ must be specified last in the INPUT statement.

@@

(double trailing @) prevents a new record from automatically being read into the input buffer when the next INPUT statement is executed, even if the DATA step loops back to the top for another iteration. When used, the double trailing @ must be specified last in the INPUT statement.

This chapter discusses the following column-pointer controls:

@*n*
>moves the pointer to the *n*th column in the input buffer.

+*n*
>moves the pointer forward *n* columns in the input buffer.

/
>moves the pointer to the next line in the input buffer.

#*n*
>moves the pointer to the *n*th line in the input buffer.

Learning More

☐ Chapter 8, "Acting on Selected Observations," and Chapter 9, "Creating Subsets of Observations," give information on the IF statement.

☐ Chapter 24, "Printing Detail Reports," provides information on using formats to control how values appear in reports.

☐ *SAS Language: Reference, Version 6, First Edition* provides a complete description of the INPUT statement. See also "INPUT, List"; "INPUT, Column"; "INPUT, Formatted"; and "INPUT, Named."

☐ *SAS Language: Reference* provides a complete listing and discussion of column-pointer controls, line-pointer controls, and line-hold specifiers.

☐ *SAS Language: Reference* gives information on using the DELIMITER= option in the INFILE statement. The DELIMITER= option is useful for reading data that are delimited by something other than blanks.

Chapter 4 Starting with SAS® Data Sets

Introduction

Chapter 3 demonstrated how to use an INPUT statement to create a SAS data set from records of raw data. This chapter introduces some simple techniques for creating a new SAS data set from an existing SAS data set rather than from records of raw data. Reading a SAS data set in a DATA step is simpler than reading raw data because the work of describing the data to the SAS System has already been done.

This chapter demonstrates using the SET statement and various data set options to control the structure and contents of a new SAS data set when the input is from a SAS data set. Topics include

☐ creating SAS data sets containing selected observations

☐ creating SAS data sets containing selected variables

☐ creating more than one SAS data set in a single DATA step.

Using a SAS Data Set as Input

If you want to work with data that have already been read into a SAS data set, but you need to work with only part of those data, you can use the existing SAS data set as input. In a DATA step, you create a new data set that is a subset of the original data set. For example, suppose you have a large data set of personnel data and you want to look at a subset of observations that meet certain conditions, such as observations for employees hired after a certain date. Or suppose you want to see all observations but only a few variables, such as the number of years of education or years of service to the company.

Working with subsets created from an existing SAS data set can make more efficient use of computer resources than working with the original, larger data set. Reading fewer variables means that a smaller program data vector is used, and reading fewer observations means that fewer iterations of the DATA step occur. Reading data directly from a SAS data set is more efficient than reading the raw data again because the work of describing and converting the data has already been done.

The next section introduces the SAS data set used as input in the examples in this chapter.

Checking the Structure of a SAS Data Set

Until now, the PRINT procedure has been used to show the SAS data set in each example. The CONTENTS procedure gives you another way to look at a SAS data set. Use it to display information that describes the structure of a SAS data set rather than the data values. If you need to work with a SAS data set that is unfamiliar to you, the CONTENTS procedure displays valuable information such as the name, type, and length of all the variables in the data set.

The examples in this chapter use a permanent SAS data set named IN.NASA, which contains information about National Aeronautics and Space Administration (NASA) expenditures.* It reports total NASA expenditures for the years 1966 through 1986 and divides the expenses into two major categories: Performance and Facilities.

```
libname in 'your-data-library';
proc contents data=in.nasa;
run;
```

Output 4.1 shows the results.

Output 4.1 The
Structure of
IN.NASA as
Shown by PROC
CONTENTS

```
                           The SAS System                              1
                         CONTENTS PROCEDURE

        Data Set Name: IN.NASA              Observations:          21
        Member Type:   DATA                 Variables:             10
        Engine:        V606                 Indexes:               0
        Created:       01AUG89:14:57:38     Observation Length:    80
        Last Modified: 01AUG89:14:57:38     Deleted Observations:  0
        Data Set Type:                      Compressed:            NO
        Label:

               -----Alphabetic List of Variables and Attributes-----

        #   Variable  Type  Len  Pos  Label
        --------------------------------------------------------------------
        10  FAIRTRAN  Num   8    72   Facilities: Air Transport and Other
        8   FFLIGHT   Num   8    56   Facilities: Space Flight
        9   FSCIENCE  Num   8    64   Facilities: Space Science Applications
        7   FTOTAL    Num   8    48   Facilities: Total
        6   PAIRTRAN  Num   8    40   Performance: Air Transport and Other
        4   PFLIGHT   Num   8    24   Performance: Space Flight
        5   PSCIENCE  Num   8    32   Performance: Space Science Applications
        3   PTOTAL    Num   8    16   Performance: Total
        2   TOTAL     Num   8    8    Total Outlays
        1   YEAR      Num   8    0
```

* The DATA step that created IN.NASA is shown in the Appendix.

Note what PROC CONTENTS tells you about the structure of a SAS data set. It reports

□ the number of variables and observations

□ the name, type, and length of each variable

□ the position of the variable in the observation

□ the format, informat, and label for each variable, if they exist

□ certain engine-specific and operating-system specific details (not shown here) that may vary from one operating system to another.* For more information, refer to the SAS documentation for your host system.

The rest of this chapter uses IN.NASA to demonstrate how you can use a DATA step and data set options to create a new SAS data set from an existing one.

Reading Selected Observations

If you are interested in only part of a large data set, you can use a DATA step to create a subset of a more manageable size. Using data set options, you can create a subset of a larger data set by specifying which observations you want the new data set to include. In Chapter 9, "Creating Subsets of Observations," you will learn how to use the subsetting IF statement to create a subset of a large SAS data set. For now, consider the FIRSTOBS= and OBS= data set options.

Suppose you don't want to read the observations at the beginning of the data set. You can use the FIRSTOBS= data set option to define which observation should be the first one processed. Consider the data set IN.NASA introduced earlier. If you are interested only in more recent expenditures, you can create a data set that excludes observations containing data prior to 1977 by specifying FIRSTOBS=12.

```
data in.NASA2;
   set in.NASA(firstobs=12);
run;

proc print;
   title 'NASA Expenditures';
   title2 '1977-1986';
run;
```

This program creates IN.NASA2, which contains the same number of variables but fewer observations than IN.NASA. Output 4.2 shows the resulting data set.

---

* An engine is the SAS System's mechanism for reading from and writing to files. At this point, you do not need to be concerned about engines.

Output 4.2
Subsetting a Data Set by Observations

```
                                 NASA Expenditures                          1
                                    1977-1986

                                           P      P
                                     P     S      A           F      F
                               T     F     C      I     F     F      S      A
                        Y      O     L     I      R     T     L      C      I
                        E      T     O     G      E     R     O      I      R
                 O      A       T    T     H      N     R     T      G      E    R
                 B      R       A    A      T     C     R     A      H      N    A
                 S             L    L             E     N     L             C    N

                 1    1977    3945  8402   2195   1002   643   105    56    4     45
                 2    1978    3984  8602   2204    964   692   124    56    8     60
                 3    1979    4187   542   2175   1144   735   133    41    9     83
                 4    1980    4850  7102   2556   1341   813   140    38    5     97
                 5    1981    5241  2743   3026   1380   868   147    26    4    117
                 6    1982    6035  9263   3526   1454   946   109    17    3     89
                 7    1983    6664  5564   4027   1486    43   108    26    .     82
                 8    1984    7048  8564   4037   1667   152   192    44   20    128
                 9    1985    7251    43   3852   1834   318   247    70   23    154
                10    1986    7404  1053   3787   2101   317   299   107   26    166
```

You can also specify the last observation you want included in a new data set with the OBS= data set option. For example, the following program creates a SAS data set containing only the observations for 1975-1980.

```
data in.nasa3;
    set in.nasa2(firstobs=10 obs=15);
run;
```

Reading Selected Variables

The SAS System allows you to create a subset of a larger data set not only by excluding observations but also by specifying which variables you want the new data set to contain. In a DATA step you can use the SET statement and the KEEP= or DROP= data set options (or the DROP and KEEP statements) to create a subset from a larger data set by specifying which variables you want the new data set to include.

Keeping Selected Variables

As an example, use the KEEP= data set option to create a new SAS data set that contains only the variables representing the performance-related expenditures of NASA.

```
data in.perform;
    set in.nasa(keep=year ptotal pflight pscience pairtran);
run;

proc print data=in.perform;
    title 'NASA Performance-Related Expenditures';
run;
```

Output 4.3 shows the resulting data set. Note that the data set IN.PERFORM contains only those variables specified in the KEEP= option. Note also that, like

IN.NASA, IN.PERFORM is a permanent SAS data set and therefore has a two-level name.

Output 4.3
Selecting Variables with the KEEP= Option

```
                    NASA Performance-Related Expenditures                     1

      OBS    YEAR    PTOTAL    PFLIGHT    PSCIENCE    PAIRTRAN

       1     1966     3613       3819       1120         422
       2     1967     1373       3477       1160         500
       3     1968     5993       3028       1061         510
       4     1969     1872       2754        893         540
       5     1970     6992       2195        963         541
       6     1971     3381       1877        926         535
       7     1972     3731       1727       1111         535
       8     1973     2711       1532       1220         519
       9     1974     1811       1448       1156         577
      10     1975     1811       1500       1076         606
      11     1976     5491       1934        969         646
      12     1977     8402       2195       1002         643
      13     1978     8602       2204        964         692
      14     1979      542       2175       1144         735
      15     1980     7102       2556       1341         813
      16     1981     2743       3026       1380         868
      17     1982     9263       3526       1454         946
      18     1983     5564       4027       1486          43
      19     1984     8564       4037       1667         152
      20     1985       43       3852       1834         318
      21     1986     1053       3787       2101         317
```

You can also use the KEEP statement to produce the same data set, as illustrated here.

```
data in.perform;
   set in.nasa;
   keep year ptotal pflight pscience pairtran;
run;
```

Dropping Selected Variables

Use the DROP= option to create a subset of a larger data set when you want to specify which variables are being *excluded* rather than the ones being included. The following DATA step reads the data set IN.NASA and uses the DROP= option to create a data set named IN.PERFORM2 that has the same contents as IN.PERFORM:

```
data in.perform2;
   set in.nasa (drop=total ftotal fflight fscience fairtran);
run;


proc print data=in.perform2;
   title 'NASA Performance-Related Expenditures';
run;
```

Output 4.4 shows the resulting data set.

Output 4.4
Excluding
Variables with the
DROP= Option

```
                    NASA Performance-Related Expenditures                    1

    OBS    YEAR    PTOTAL    PFLIGHT    PSCIENCE    PAIRTRAN

     1     1966     3613      3819        1120         422
     2     1967     1373      3477        1160         500
     3     1968     5993      3028        1061         510
     4     1969     1872      2754         893         540
     5     1970     6992      2195         963         541
     6     1971     3381      1877         926         535
     7     1972     3731      1727        1111         535
     8     1973     2711      1532        1220         519
     9     1974     1811      1448        1156         577
    10     1975     1811      1500        1076         606
    11     1976     5491      1934         969         646
    12     1977     8402      2195        1002         643
    13     1978     8602      2204         964         692
    14     1979      542      2175        1144         735
    15     1980     7102      2556        1341         813
    16     1981     2743      3026        1380         868
    17     1982     9263      3526        1454         946
    18     1983     5564      4027        1486          43
    19     1984     8564      4037        1667         152
    20     1985       43      3852        1834         318
    21     1986     1053      3787        2101         317
```

You can also use the DROP statement instead of the DROP= data set option, as follows:

```
data in.perform2;
   set in.nasa;
   drop total ftotal fflight fscience fairtrans;
run;
```

Choosing Data Set Options or Statements

As long as you're creating only one data set in the DATA step, the data set options to drop and keep variables have the same effect on the output data set as the statements to drop and keep variables. When your goal is to control which variables are read into the program data vector, using the data set options in the statement that reads the SAS data set, the SET statement in this case, is more efficient than using the statements. Later sections in this chapter show that the data set options can be used in some cases where the statements will not work.

Choosing DROP= or KEEP= Data Set Options

In a simple case, you may base your decision to use the DROP= or KEEP= options on which method allows you to specify fewer variables. If you are working with large production jobs that read data sets to which variables may be added between the times your batch jobs run, you may want to use the KEEP= option to be sure which variables are in the subset data set.

Figure 4.1 shows two data sets named SMALL. They have different contents because the new variable F was added to data set BIG before the DATA step was run on Tuesday. If this DATA step had used the KEEP= option to specify A, B, and C, then the data set named SMALL created on both days would have the same contents; the change to the original data set BIG would have had no effect on the new data set being created by this SAS job.

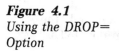

Figure 4.1
Using the DROP=
Option

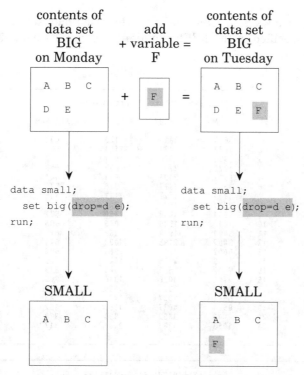

Creating More than One Data Set in a Single DATA Step

You can use a single DATA step to create more than one data set at a time. You can create data sets with different contents by using the KEEP= or DROP= data set options. For example, the following DATA step creates two SAS data sets: IN.PERFORM contains only variables that show performance-related expenditures; IN.FACIL contains variables that represent the facility-related expenditures. Using the KEEP= option after each data set name in the DATA statement determines which variables are written to each SAS data set being created.

```
data in.perform(keep=ptotal pflight pscience pairtran)
     in.facil(keep=ftotal fflight fscience fairtran);
   set in.nasa;
run;

proc print data=in.perform;
   title 'NASA Expenditures: Performance';
run;

proc print data=in.facil;
   title 'NASA Expenditures: Facilities';
run;
```

Output 4.5 shows both data sets. Note that each data set contains only the variables specified in the KEEP= option following its name in the DATA statement.

Output 4.5
Creating
IN.PERFORM and
IN.FACIL in One
DATA Step

```
                    NASA Expenditures: Performance                      1

       OBS    PTOTAL    PFLIGHT    PSCIENCE    PAIRTRAN

        1      3613      3819       1120         422
        2      1373      3477       1160         500
        3      5993      3028       1061         510
        4      1872      2754        893         540
        5      6992      2195        963         541
        6      3381      1877        926         535
        7      3731      1727       1111         535
        8      2711      1532       1220         519
        9      1811      1448       1156         577
       10      1811      1500       1076         606
       11      5491      1934        969         646
       12      8402      2195       1002         643
       13      8602      2204        964         692
       14       542      2175       1144         735
       15      7102      2556       1341         813
       16      2743      3026       1380         868
       17      9263      3526       1454         946
       18      5564      4027       1486          43
       19      8564      4037       1667         152
       20        43      3852       1834         318
       21      1053      3787       2101         317
```

```
                    NASA Expenditures: Facilities                       2

       OBS    FTOTAL    FFLIGHT    FSCIENCE    FAIRTRAN

        1       572       391        63          118
        2       289       172        47           70
        3       127        69        29           29
        4        65        27        21           17
        5        54        14        21           19
        6        44         8         6           30
        7        50        13         7           30
        8        45         5        11           29
        9        75        25        12           38
       10        85        35         9           42
       11       121        66        11           43
       12       105        56         4           45
       13       124        56         8           60
       14       133        41         9           83
       15       140        38         5           97
       16       147        26         4          117
       17       109        17         3           89
       18       108        26         .           82
       19       192        44        20          128
       20       247        70        23          154
       21       299       107        26          166
```

Note: In this case, you must use the KEEP= data set option. If you use the KEEP statement, all data sets created in the DATA step contain the same variables.

Where to Use Data Set Options

The DROP= and KEEP= data set options are valid in both the DATA statement and the SET statement. However, you can write a more efficient DATA step if you understand the consequences of using these options in the DATA statement as opposed to the SET statement.

In the SET statement, these options determine which variables are *read* from the SAS data set being used as input; therefore, they determine how the program data vector is built. In the DATA statement, these options affect which variables are *written* from the program data vector to the resulting SAS data set.

When you specify the DROP= or KEEP= option in the SET statement, the excluded variables are never read into the program data vector at all. If you are working with a large data set (perhaps one containing thousands or millions of observations), you can construct a more efficient DATA step by not reading unneeded variables from the input data set.

Note also that if you need to use a variable from the input data set (the one read with the SET statement) to perform a calculation, it must be read into the program data vector. If you do not want that variable to appear in the new data set, however, you can use the DROP= option in the DATA statement to exclude it.

The following DATA step creates the same two data sets as the DATA step in the previous example, but it does so without reading the variable TOTAL into the program data vector. Compare the SET statement here to the one in the preceding example.

```
data in.perform(keep=ptotal pflight pscience pairtran)
     in.facil  (keep=ftotal fflight fscience fairtran);
   set in.nasa(drop=total);
run;

proc print data=in.perform;
   title 'NASA Expenditures: Performance';
run;

proc print data=in.facil;
   title 'NASA Expenditures: Facilities';
run;
```

Note that here, unlike in previous examples, data set options appear in both the DATA and SET statements. In the SET statement, the DROP= option determines which variables are omitted from the program data vector. In the DATA statement, the KEEP= option controls which variables are written from the program data vector to each data set being created.

Note: Using a DROP or KEEP statement is comparable to using a DROP= or KEEP= option in the DATA statement. All variables are included in the program data vector; they are excluded when the observation is written from the program data vector to the new data set. When you are creating more than one data set in a single DATA step, using the data set options allows you to drop or keep different variables in each of the new data sets. A DROP or KEEP statement, on the other hand, affects all of the data sets being created.

SAS Tools

This chapter discusses the following data set options:

FIRSTOBS=*n*
> specifies the first observation to be read from the SAS data set you specify in the SET statement.

OBS=*n*
> specifies the last observation to be read from the SAS data set you specify in the SET statement.

KEEP=*variable(s)*
> specifies the variables to be included.
>
> Used in the SET statement, KEEP= specifies the variables to be read from the existing SAS data set into the program data vector. Used in the DATA statement, KEEP= specifies which variables in the program data vector are to be written to the data set being created.

DROP=*variable(s)*
> specifies the variables to be excluded.
>
> Used in the SET statement, DROP= specifies the variables not to be read from the existing SAS data set into the program data vector. Used in the DATA statement, DROP= specifies the variables to be excluded from the data set being created.

This chapter discusses the following statements:

DATA *SAS-data-set*<*(data-set-options)*>;
> begins a DATA step and names the SAS data set or data sets being created. You can specify the DROP= or KEEP= data set options in parentheses after each data set name to control which variables are written to the data set from the program data vector.

SET *SAS-data-set*<*(data-set-options)*>;
> reads observations from a SAS data set rather than records of raw data. You can specify the DROP= or KEEP= data set options in parentheses after a data set name to control which variables are written to the program data vector from the input data set.

KEEP *variable(s)*;
> specifies the variables to be written to the data set being created. See also the KEEP= data set option.

DROP *variable(s)*;
> specifies the variables to be excluded from the data set being created. See also the DROP= data set option.

This chapter discusses the CONTENTS procedure:

PROC CONTENTS <DATA=*SAS-data-set*>;
>   describes the structure of a SAS data set. The information provided includes the name, type, and length of all variables in the data set.

Learning More

This chapter discusses only the most basic ways to create one SAS data set from another.

□ Part 4, "Combining SAS Data Sets," covers the general topic of creating SAS data sets from other SAS data sets by merging, concatenating, interleaving, and updating.

□ Chapter 8, "Acting on Selected Observations," and Chapter 9, "Creating Subsets of Observations," discuss using the subsetting IF statement and IF-THEN logic in a DATA step that reads a SAS data set to create a new one.

□ *SAS Language: Reference, Version 6, First Edition* and the SAS documentation for your host system provide complete documentation on data set options.

□ *SAS Language: Reference* provides complete documentation on the DROP and KEEP statements.

□ *SAS Language: Reference* gives information on engines.

78

Part 3
Basic Programming

Chapter 5 Understanding DATA Step Processing

Introduction

In Part 1, "Introduction to the SAS System," you learned that the SAS System is a programming language, a data management facility, and a data analysis and reporting utility. You also learned that data for the SAS System are stored in SAS data sets. In Part 2, "Getting Your Data into Shape," you learned how to create a SAS data set using a DATA step. In Part 3, "Basic Programming," you learn

☐ more about how the DATA step works.

☐ how to manipulate data with basic SAS programming techniques as you create SAS data sets. Specifically, you learn how to

   ☐ work with numeric and character variables

   ☐ perform an action for some but not all observations

   ☐ select a subset of the original observations

   ☐ work with observations in groups or in sorted order

   ☐ work with data from more than one observation in a file at a time

   ☐ simplify some programming tasks by eliminating repetitive statements

   ☐ work with dates and times.

This chapter reviews how the SAS System processes a DATA step. Then it goes on to introduce the various kinds of program statements that can occur in the DATA step. **Note:** The examples in this chapter use some programming techniques that are described in detail in later chapters; for now, just notice the general form of the statements used and how the DATA step works when they are present.

Input File and SAS Data Set Example

The examples in Part 3 assume you are an employee of a travel agency, Tradewinds Travel Inc. You store information about tours in SAS data sets and manipulate the data to produce the information you need. The examples in this chapter assume information about some of your tours is available in an external file that looks like this:

```
France 8 793 575 Major
Spain 10 805 510 Hispania
India 10 . 489 Royal
Peru 7 722 590 Mundial
```

The first field contains the name of the country visited; the second field, the number of nights spent on the tour; third, the airfare; fourth, the cost of the land package; and finally, the name of the company that offers the tour.

You begin by creating a permanent SAS data set named SAVE.TRAVEL. The following program creates the data set, and Output 5.1 displays it:

```
libname save 'your-data-library';

data save.travel;
   infile 'your-input-file';
   input country $ nights aircost landcost vendor $;
run;

proc print data=save.travel;
   title 'Data Set SAVE.TRAVEL';
run;
```

Output 5.1
Data Set
SAVE.TRAVEL

```
                      Data Set SAVE.TRAVEL                              1

       OBS    COUNTRY    NIGHTS    AIRCOST    LANDCOST    VENDOR

        1     France       8         793        575      Major
        2     Spain       10         805        510      Hispania
        3     India       10          .         489      Royal
        4     Peru         7         722        590      Mundial
```

How the SAS System Processes a DATA Step

Some things that the SAS System does in processing a DATA step never vary. For example, the SAS System goes through the compilation and execution phases, described in Chapter 2, "Introduction to DATA Step Processing," in every DATA step:

□ During compilation, the SAS System reads the step through once from beginning to end. The SAS System

□ checks the syntax of each statement and the organization of the DATA step as a whole to be sure that all keywords are spelled correctly, that all statements are used in valid ways, and so on.

□ builds the program data vector for the step, the input buffer (if the DATA step reads data from an external file or following a CARDS statement), and the descriptive portion of the SAS data set.

□ During execution, the SAS System carries out the statements in the step, one by one, for the current observation in the input data and returns to the top of the DATA step for the next observation. Therefore, the execution phase of a DATA step consists of a loop. (Like other programming languages, the SAS System has statements that allow you to change the order in which statements in the step are carried out and to skip statements. However, the basic principle of processing in a loop still applies.) **Note:** The important point to remember is that by default the SAS System goes through the DATA step loop once for each observation it processes.

DATA steps vary in the number and kinds of program statements they contain. DATA step program statements do one of three main things:

□ Most statements tell the SAS System how to change or add to the input data, for example, to change the airfare or to add a note about a vendor's prices.

□ Some statements tell the SAS System more about the data set it is building or the data it is processing, for example, how much storage space to allow for a particular variable or how the observations are grouped.

□ Some statements delete observations that are not needed, output additional observations from a single input record, or change the order in which program statements are carried out.

The remainder of this chapter introduces each of these types of statements.

Adding Information to Observations with a DATA Step

One of the most common reasons for using program statements in the DATA step is to change the information read by the INPUT or SET/MERGE/UPDATE statement or to produce new information from the original information. How do you add information to observations with a DATA step?

The basic method of adding information to a SAS data set is to create a new variable in a DATA step with an assignment statement. An assignment statement has the following form:

variable = expression;

The *variable* receives the new information; the *expression* creates the new information. You figure out the calculation necessary to produce the information and write that as the expression; the SAS System evaluates the expression and stores the new information in the variable you name. It's important to remember that even if you need to add the information to only one or two observations out of many, the SAS System creates that variable for all observations. The SAS data set being created must have a rectangular structure.

The following sections show the three ways you can add information to or change information in a SAS data set with assignment statements.

Adding the Same Kind of Information to All Observations

At times, you want to make the same change in every observation. For example, at Tradewinds Travel you must increase the airfare for every tour by $10 because of a new tax. The following statement calculates the new airfare:

```
newacost=aircost+10;
```

The statement directs the SAS System to read the value of AIRCOST, add 10 to it, and assign the result to a new variable, NEWACOST. By default, the SAS System carries out each statement in the DATA step for each observation; therefore, the SAS System calculates NEWACOST in each iteration of the DATA step. It's easy to see that the SAS data set is rectangular in this case.

The following DATA step illustrates the use of the assignment statement above, and Output 5.2 shows the data set produced:

```
data newair;
   set save.travel;
   newacost=aircost+10;
run;

proc print data=newair;
   var country aircost newacost;
   title 'Increasing the Air Fare by $10 in All Observations';
run;
```

Output 5.2
Specifying Values for All Observations of a New Variable

```
        Increasing the Air Fare by $10 in All Observations            1

        OBS    COUNTRY    AIRCOST    NEWACOST

          1    France       793         803
          2    Spain        805         815
          3    India          .           .
          4    Peru         722         732
```

Note: In this example, the VAR statement in the PROC PRINT step determines the variables to be displayed in the output. The observation for India contains a missing value for AIRCOST; the SAS System therefore assigns a missing value to NEWACOST for that observation. The SAS data set remains rectangular.

Adding Information to Some Observations but Not Others

Often you need to add information to some observations but not others. For example, you know that some tour operators award bonus points to travel agencies for booking particular tours. Two companies, Hispania and Mundial, are offering bonus points this year. You want to add information about the bonus points to those observations, so you write the following statements:

```
if vendor='Hispania' then bonuspts='For 10+ people';
else if vendor='Mundial' then bonuspts='Yes';
```

The IF-THEN and ELSE statements cause the assignment statements to be carried out only when a condition is met. Remember that although the SAS System carries out the assignment statements only for two observations, the SAS System adds the variable BONUSPTS to *all* observations in order to maintain the rectangular structure of the data set. Placing the statements above in the following DATA step and printing the result produces Output 5.3:

```
data bonus;
   set save.travel;
   if vendor='Hispania' then bonuspts='For 10+ people';
   else if vendor='Mundial' then bonuspts='Yes';
run;

proc print data=bonus;
   var country vendor bonuspts;
   title 'The SAS System Creates a Variable for All Observations';
run;
```

Output 5.3
Specifying Values
for Only Certain
Observations of a
New Variable

```
         The SAS System Creates a Variable for All Observations          1

         OBS     COUNTRY     VENDOR      BONUSPTS

          1      France      Major
          2      Spain       Hispania    For 10+ people
          3      India       Royal
          4      Peru        Mundial     Yes
```

In the two observations not assigned a value for BONUSPTS, the SAS System assigns a missing value (represented by a blank in this case) to indicate the absence of a value. (The next two chapters discuss missing values in more detail.) In addition, because the value of BONUSPTS contains 14 characters in the first statement that uses it, the SAS System sets aside 14 bytes of storage in each observation for BONUSPTS, whether the actual value is a 14-character phrase or simply a blank.

Changing Information without Adding Variables

In the preceding examples, you changed information by adding a variable to the DATA step. You can also change the value of existing variables instead of adding new variables. For example, in one DATA step you created a new variable, NEWACOST, to contain the value of the airfare plus the new $10 tax:

```
newacost=aircost+10;
```

You can also decide to change the value of AIRCOST rather than create a new variable, as follows:

```
aircost=aircost+10;
```

The SAS System processes this statement just as it does other assignment statements: it evaluates the expression on the right side of the equal sign and assigns the result to the variable on the left side of the equal sign. The fact that the same variable appears on the right and left sides of the equal sign doesn't matter; the SAS System evaluates the expression on the right side of the equal sign before looking at the variable on the left side.

Writing the following program containing the assignment statement above and printing the result produces Output 5.4:

```
data newair2;
   set save.travel;
   aircost=aircost+10;
run;

proc print data=newair2;
   var country aircost;
   title 'Changing the Information in a Variable';
run;
```

Output 5.4
Changing the Information in a Variable

```
          Changing the Information in a Variable            1

              OBS    COUNTRY    AIRCOST

               1     France       803
               2     Spain        815
               3     India          .
               4     Peru         732
```

When you change the kind of information a variable contains, you change the meaning of that variable. In this case, you are changing the meaning of AIRCOST from airfare without tax to airfare with tax. If you keep track of the current meaning and if you know you don't need the original information, then changing a variable's values is useful. However, many people feel that keeping track of separate variables is easier than keeping track of one variable whose definition changes.

Using Variables Efficiently

The rectangular structure of SAS data sets gives a clue to good SAS programming. Creating variables to contain pieces of information that apply to only one or two observations uses a lot of storage space. When possible, create fewer variables that apply to more observations in the data set, and let the different values in different observations supply the information.

For example, suppose the Major company offers discounts (not bonus points) for groups of 30 or more people. An inefficient program creates separate variables for bonus points and discounts, as follows, with Output 5.5 showing the result:

```
/* inefficient use of variables */
data tourinfo;
   set save.travel;
   if vendor='Hispania' then bonuspts='For 10+ people';
   else if vendor='Mundial' then bonuspts='Yes';
   else if vendor='Major' then discount='For 30+ people';
run;

proc print data=tourinfo;
   var country vendor bonuspts discount;
   title 'Using Variables Inefficiently';
run;
```

Output 5.5
Scattering
Information
among Multiple
Variables

```
                    Using Variables Inefficiently                      1

    OBS    COUNTRY    VENDOR      BONUSPTS            DISCOUNT

     1     France     Major                       For 30+ people
     2     Spain      Hispania    For 10+ people
     3     India      Royal
     4     Peru       Mundial     Yes
```

Note: The first line in this program, the phrase marked with slashes and asterisks, is a comment. Comment statements allow you to document your program, but they have no effect on processing.

With a little planning, you can make the SAS data set much more efficient. In the following DATA step, you create one variable named REMARKS that contains information about bonus points, discounts, and any other special features of any tour, and Output 5.6 shows the result:

```
/* efficient use of variables */
data newinfo;
   set save.travel;
   if vendor='Hispania' then remarks='Bonus for 10+ people';
   else if vendor='Mundial' then remarks='Bonus points';
   else if vendor='Major' then remarks='Discount: 30+ people';
run;
```

```
proc print data=newinfo;
   var country vendor remarks;
   title 'Using Variables Efficiently';
run;
```

Output 5.6
Planning a
Variable to
Contain Maximum
Information

```
                    Using Variables Efficiently                         1

      OBS    COUNTRY    VENDOR      REMARKS

       1     France     Major       Discount: 30+ people
       2     Spain      Hispania    Bonus for 10+ people
       3     India      Royal
       4     Peru       Mundial     Bonus points
```

Describing the Data Set Being Created

The SAS System can determine many things about the data set you want to create by examining the DATA, INPUT (or SET/MERGE/UPDATE), and assignment statements in the DATA step, but at times you may need to give the SAS System additional information. For example, you may need to specify the amount of storage to allow for a particular variable. Suppose you are creating a variable named REMARKS to contain miscellaneous information about tours, as shown in the preceding section:

```
if vendor='Hispania' then remarks='Bonus for 10+ people';
```

By default, the SAS System allows as many bytes of storage space for REMARKS as there are characters in the first value assigned to it. If you don't want to think about putting the longest value first, you can simply specify a length for REMARKS before the first value is assigned to it, for example,

```
length remarks $ 30;
```

This statement, called a LENGTH statement, applies to the data set as a whole. It gives the number of bytes of storage used for variable REMARKS in every observation. The SAS System uses the LENGTH statement at compilation, not when it is processing statements on individual observations. (Such statements are called *declarative statements*.) The following DATA step shows the use of the LENGTH statement, and Output 5.7 shows the data set produced:

```
data newstmt;
   set save.travel;
   length remarks $ 30;
   if vendor='Hispania' then remarks='Bonus for 10+ people';
   else if vendor='Mundial' then remarks='Bonus points';
   else if vendor='Major' then remarks='Discount for 30+ people';
run;

proc print data=newstmt;
   var country vendor remarks;
   title 'Using a LENGTH Statement';
run;
```

Output 5.7
Setting the Length
of a Variable

```
                        Using a LENGTH Statement                         1

        OBS     COUNTRY     VENDOR      REMARKS

         1      France      Major       Discount for 30+ people
         2      Spain       Hispania    Bonus for 10+ people
         3      India       Royal
         4      Peru        Mundial     Bonus points
```

Output 5.7 is the same as Output 5.6 because the LENGTH statement affects variable storage, not the spacing of columns in printed output.*

Changing the Action of a DATA Step

A third type of statement in the DATA step changes the number of observations output to the data set being created, the number of statements processed for a given observation, the order in which they are processed, and so on. (The basic principle of operation in a loop still applies.) For example, suppose the tour to Peru has been discontinued and you don't want the observation for Peru to appear in the data set being created. The following example uses the DELETE statement to prevent the SAS System from writing that observation to the output data set:

```
if country='Peru' then delete;
```

(The DELETE statement is discussed in Chapter 9, "Creating Subsets of Observations.") Including the statement above in the following DATA step and printing the result produces Output 5.8:

```
data subset;
   set save.travel;
   if country='Peru' then delete;
run;

proc print data=subset;
   title 'Omitting a Discontinued Tour';
run;
```

Output 5.8
Deleting an
Observation

```
                        Omitting a Discontinued Tour                     1

     OBS   COUNTRY   NIGHTS   AIRCOST    LANDCOST   VENDOR

      1    France      8        793        575      Major
      2    Spain      10        805        510      Hispania
      3    India      10         .         489      Royal
```

---

* The DATASETS procedure shows the effect of the LENGTH statement on variable storage.

SAS Tools

This chapter discusses the following statements:

variable=expression;
>   is an assignment statement. It causes the SAS System to evaluate the *expression* on the right side of the equal sign and assign the result to the *variable* on the left. You must select the name of the variable and create the proper expression for calculating its value. The same variable name can appear on the left and right sides of the equal sign because the SAS System evaluates the right side before assigning the result to the variable on the left side.

IF *condition* **THEN** *action*;
<ELSE *action*;**>**
>   tests whether the *condition* is true. The *action* is one or more of a number of statements, including assignment statements. When the *condition* is false, the ELSE statement provides an alternative *action*.

/* comment */
>   describes portions of a program. The *comment*, enclosed by the delimiters /* and */, is ignored by the SAS System when it runs the program.

LENGTH *variable* **<$>** *length*;
>   assigns the number of bytes of storage (*length*) for a *variable*. Include a dollar sign ($) if the variable is character. The LENGTH statement must appear before the first use of the variable.

DELETE;
>   prevents the SAS System from writing a particular observation to the output data set. It usually appears as part of an IF-THEN/ELSE statement.

Learning More

□   Chapter 2, "Introduction to DATA Step Processing," gives background information on DATA step processing. See also *SAS Language: Reference, Version 6, First Edition*, for complete reference information on the DATA step.

□   Chapter 6, "Working with Numeric Variables," discusses expressions involving numbers and arithmetic calculations; Chapter 7, "Working with Character Variables," discusses expressions involving alphabetic and special characters as well as numbers. Both chapters also discuss the LENGTH statement.

□   Chapter 8, "Acting on Selected Observations," discusses IF-THEN and ELSE statements.

□ Chapter 33, "Getting Information about Your Data Sets," discusses using the DATASETS procedure to show the effect of the LENGTH statement on variable storage.

□ *SAS Language: Reference* gives complete reference information on the assignment, IF-THEN/ELSE, LENGTH, DELETE, and comment statements.

Chapter 6 Working with Numeric Variables

Introduction

Many tasks requiring computer processing involve numbers. You can use the SAS System to perform all kinds of mathematical operations. In this chapter you learn

☐ how to perform arithmetic calculations in the SAS System

☐ how to store numeric variables efficiently when disk space is limited.

A *numeric variable* is a variable whose values are numbers.* The SAS System accepts numbers in many forms, for example, scientific notation, hexadecimal, and so on. For simplicity, this book concentrates on numbers in standard representation, as shown here:

```
1254
 336.05
-243
```

Input File and SAS Data Set Example

Suppose you are using SAS software at Tradewinds Travel Inc. The external file shown here contains data about your most popular tours:

```
Japan        8  982 1020 Express
Greece      12    .  748 Express
New Zealand 16 1368 1539 Southsea
Ireland      7  787  628 Express
```

---
* To compare the SAS System with other programming languages, note that the SAS System uses double-precision floating point representation for calculations and, by default, for storing numeric variables in SAS data sets.

```
Venezuela     9  426   505 Mundial
Italy         8  852   598 Express
USSR         14 1106  1024 A-B-C
Switzerland   9  816   834 Tour2000
Australia    12 1299  1169 Southsea
Brazil        8  682   610 Almeida
```

The fields represent the country toured, the number of nights spent on the tour, the airfare, the cost of the land package, and the company offering the tour.

You begin by creating a permanent SAS data set named PERM.TOURS. The following program creates the data set, and Output 6.1 displays it:

```
libname perm 'your-data-library';

data perm.tours;
   infile 'your-input-file';
   input country $ 1-11 nights aircost landcost vendor $;
run;

proc print data=perm.tours;
   title 'Data Set PERM.TOURS';
run;
```

Output 6.1
Data Set
PERM.TOURS

```
                         Data Set PERM.TOURS                              1

     OBS    COUNTRY        NIGHTS    AIRCOST    LANDCOST    VENDOR

      1     Japan             8        982        1020      Express
      2     Greece           12         .          748      Express
      3     New Zealand      16       1368        1539      Southsea
      4     Ireland           7        787         628      Express
      5     Venezuela         9        426         505      Mundial
      6     Italy             8        852         598      Express
      7     USSR             14       1106        1024      A-B-C
      8     Switzerland       9        816         834      Tour2000
      9     Australia        12       1299        1169      Southsea
     10     Brazil            8        682         610      Almeida
```

In PERM.TOURS, variables NIGHTS, AIRCOST, and LANDCOST contain numbers; they are numeric variables. For comparison, variables COUNTRY and VENDOR contain alphabetic and special characters as well as numbers; they are character variables.

Calculating with Numeric Variables

To perform a calculation in a DATA step, write an assignment statement in which the expression contains arithmetic operators, SAS functions, or a combination of the two.

Using Arithmetic Operators

Arithmetic operators indicate addition, subtraction, multiplication, division, and exponentiation (raising to a power). Table 6.1 shows operators in arithmetic expressions.

Table 6.1
Operators in
Arithmetic
Expressions

Operation	Symbol	Example in Assignment Statement	Meaning of Operation
addition	+	x=y+z;	adds y and z
subtraction	−	x=y-z;	subtracts z from y
multiplication	*	x=y*z;	multiplies y by z
division	/	x=y/z;	divides y by z
exponentiation	**	x=y**z;	raises y to the z power

The following examples show some typical calculations using the Tradewinds Travel sample data.

□ Add the airfare and land cost to produce the total cost.

```
totcost=aircost+landcost;
```

□ Calculate the peak season airfares by increasing the basic fare by 10% and adding an $8 departure tax.

```
peakair=(aircost*1.10)+8;
```

□ Show the cost per night of each land package.

```
nitecost=landcost/nights;
```

In each case the variable on the left side of the equal sign receives the calculated value from the expression on the right side of the equal sign.* Including these statements in the following DATA step produces data set NEWTOUR, and Output 6.2 shows the new variables:

```
data newtour;
   set perm.tours;
   totcost=aircost+landcost;
   peakair=(aircost*1.10)+8;
   nitecost=landcost/nights;
run;
```

---

* The expressions can include spaces for easier reading, as in
```
totcost = aircost + landcost;
```

```
proc print data=newtour;
    var country nights aircost landcost totcost peakair nitecost;
    title 'New Variables Containing Calculated Values';
run;
```

Output 6.2
Creating New
Variables by Using
Arithmetic
Expressions

```
                    New Variables Containing Calculated Values              1

  OBS  COUNTRY      NIGHTS  AIRCOST  LANDCOST  TOTCOST  PEAKAIR  NITECOST

   1   Japan           8      982      1020      2002    1088.2   127.500
   2   Greece         12        .       748         .         .    62.333
   3   New Zealand    16     1368      1539      2907    1512.8    96.188
   4   Ireland         7      787       628      1415     873.7    89.714
   5   Venezuela       9      426       505       931     476.6    56.111
   6   Italy           8      852       598      1450     945.2    74.750
   7   USSR           14     1106      1024      2130    1224.6    73.143
   8   Switzerland     9      816       834      1650     905.6    92.667
   9   Australia      12     1299      1169      2468    1436.9    97.417
  10   Brazil          8      682       610      1292     758.2    76.250
```

The VAR statement in the PROC PRINT step causes only the variables listed in the statement to be displayed in the output.

Numeric expressions in the SAS System share some features with mathematical expressions:

□ When an expression contains more than one operator, the operations have the same order of precedence as in a mathematical expression: exponentiation is done first, then multiplication and division, and finally addition and subtraction.

□ When operators of equal precedence appear, the operations are performed from left to right (except exponentiation, which is performed right to left).

□ Parentheses are used to group parts of an expression; as in mathematical expressions, operations in parentheses are performed first.

It's important to remember that the equal sign in an assignment statement does not perform the same function as the equal sign in a mathematical equation. The sequence *variable=* in an assignment statement defines the statement, and the variable must appear on the left side of the equal sign. You cannot switch the positions of the result variable and the expression as in a mathematical equation.

Handling Missing Values

What if an observation lacks a value for a particular numeric variable? For example, in the data set PERM.TOURS the observation for Greece has no value for the variable AIRCOST. To maintain the rectangular structure of a SAS data set, the SAS System assigns a *missing value* to the variable in that observation. A missing value indicates that no information is present for the variable in that observation.

The following rules describe missing values in several situations:

□ In data lines, a missing numeric value is represented by a period, for example,

```
Greece      8 12   .   748 Express
```

By default, the SAS System interprets a single period in a numeric field as a missing value. (If the INPUT statement reads the value from particular columns, as in column input, a field containing only blanks also produces a missing value.)

□ In an expression, a missing numeric value is represented by a period, for example,

```
if aircost=. then status='Need air cost';
```

(The IF-THEN statement, which makes a comparison and takes an action based on the result, appears in Chapter 8, "Acting on Selected Observations.")

□ In a comparison and in sorting (discussed in Chapter 10, "Working with Grouped or Sorted Observations"), a missing numeric value is less than any other numeric value.

□ In procedure output, the SAS System by default represents a missing numeric value with a period (as in Output 6.1).

□ Some procedures eliminate missing values from their analyses; others don't. Documentation for individual procedures describes how each procedure handles missing values.

When you use a missing value in an arithmetic expression, the SAS System sets the result of the expression to missing. If you use that result in another expression, the next result is also missing. In the SAS System, this method of treating missing values is called *propagation of missing values*. For example, Output 6.2 shows that in data set NEWTOUR the values for TOTCOST and PEAKAIR are also missing in the observation for Greece.

Using SAS Functions

As you examine your data, you notice that vendors advertise many tours with odd prices: $748 instead of $750, $1299 instead of $1300, and so on. To make the prices easier to grasp, you decide to round the figures.

Programming a rounding calculation with just the arithmetic operators is a lengthy process. However, the SAS System contains over 90 built-in numeric expressions called *functions*. You can use them in expressions just as you do the arithmetic operators. For example, to round the value of AIRCOST to the nearest $50, write

```
roundair=round(aircost,50);
```

To calculate the total cost of each tour, rounded to the nearest $100, write

```
totcostr=round(aircost+landcost,100);
```

As another example, suppose you want to calculate a total cost for the tours based on all nonmissing costs. Therefore, when the airfare is missing (as it is for Greece) you want the total cost to represent the land cost, not a missing value.* The SUM function calculates the sum of its arguments, ignoring missing values. This example illustrates the SUM function:

```
sumcost=sum(aircost,landcost);
```

You can also combine functions. For example, to round the sum of all nonmissing airfares and land costs to the nearest $100, write

```
roundsum=round(sum(aircost,landcost),100);
```

Again, the SUM function ignores missing values.

Using the ROUND and SUM functions in the following DATA step creates the data set MORETOUR, and Output 6.3 shows it:

```
data moretour;
    set perm.tours;
    roundair=round(aircost,50);
    totcostr=round(aircost+landcost,100);
    sumcost=sum(aircost,landcost);
    roundsum=round(sum(aircost,landcost),100);
run;
proc print data=moretour;
    var country aircost landcost roundair totcostr sumcost roundsum;
    title 'Rounding and Summing Values';
run;
```

Output 6.3
Creating New Variables with ROUND and SUM Functions

```
                         Rounding and Summing Values                        1

OBS  COUNTRY      AIRCOST  LANDCOST  ROUNDAIR  TOTCOSTR  SUMCOST  ROUNDSUM

 1   Japan          982      1020      1000      2000      2002     2000
 2   Greece                   748        .         .        748      700
 3   New Zealand   1368      1539      1350      2900      2907     2900
 4   Ireland        787       628       800      1400      1415     1400
 5   Venezuela      426       505       450       900       931      900
 6   Italy          852       598       850      1500      1450     1500
 7   USSR          1106      1024      1100      2100      2130     2100
 8   Switzerland    816       834       800      1700      1650     1700
 9   Australia     1299      1169      1300      2500      2468     2500
10   Brazil         682       610       700      1300      1292     1300
```

In general, a SAS function performs the calculation indicated using the data values within parentheses (called *arguments*). Separate the arguments with commas. The ROUND function rounds the quantity given in the first argument to the nearest unit given in the second argument. The SUM function adds any number of arguments, ignoring missing values.

---

* Of course, you must decide whether skipping missing values in a particular calculation is a good idea.

Storing Numeric Variables Efficiently

The data sets shown in this chapter are very small, but in production jobs, data sets can be very large. At some point, you may need to think about the storage space your data set occupies. There are ways to save space when you store numeric variables in SAS data sets.

By default, the SAS System uses 8 bytes of storage in a data set for each numeric variable. Therefore, storing the variables for each observation in the earlier data set MORETOUR requires 75 bytes:

56 bytes for numeric variables
   (8 bytes per variable × 7 numeric variables)
11 bytes for COUNTRY
 8 bytes for VENDOR

-----

75 bytes for all variables

When numeric variables contain only integers (whole numbers), you can often shorten them in the data set being created. For example, a length of 4 bytes stores accurately all integers up to at least 2,000,000.* To change the number of bytes used for each variable, use a LENGTH statement.

A LENGTH statement contains the names of the variables followed by the number of bytes to be used for their storage. For numeric variables, the LENGTH statement affects only the data set being created; it does not affect the program data vector. The following program changes the storage space for all numeric variables in the data set SHORTER:

```
data shorter;
   set perm.tours;
   length nights aircost landcost roundair totcostr
         sumcost roundsum 4;
   roundair=round(aircost,50);
   totcostr=round(aircost+landcost,100);
   sumcost=sum(aircost,landcost);
   roundsum=round(sum(aircost,landcost),100);
run;
```

Calculating the storage space required for the variables in each observation of SHORTER shows the effect of the LENGTH statement:

28 bytes for numeric variables
   (4 bytes per variable in the LENGTH statement × 7 numeric variables)
11 bytes for COUNTRY
 8 bytes for VENDOR

-----

47 bytes for all variables

-----

* Under some operating systems, the number is much higher. For more information, refer to the documentation provided by the vendor for your host system.

Because most of the variables in SHORTER are numeric, using a LENGTH statement to change their lengths reduces the storage space for the variables in each observation by almost half.

▶ *Caution* . . . . ***Do not shorten fractions.***

You can safely shorten variables containing integers (whole numbers), but this book does not recommend shortening variables containing fractions. Using a LENGTH statement to shorten fractional values may alter the fraction significantly. You should use the default length of 8 bytes to store variables containing fractions. ▲

SAS Tools

This chapter discusses the following statements:

variable = expression;

is an assignment statement. It causes the SAS System to calculate the value of the *expression* on the right side of the equal sign and assign the result to the *variable* on the left. When *variable* is numeric, the expression can be an arithmetic calculation, a numeric constant, or a numeric function.

LENGTH *variable-list number-of-bytes*;

indicates that the variables in the *variable-list* are to be stored in the *number-of-bytes* you specify in the data set being created (numeric variables are not affected while they are in the program data vector). The default length for a numeric variable is 8 bytes; in general, the minimum you should use is 4 bytes for variables containing integers and 8 bytes for variables containing fractions. You can assign lengths to both numeric and character variables (discussed in the next chapter) in a single LENGTH statement.

This chapter discusses the following arithmetic operators:

+   addition
−   subtraction
*   multiplication
/   division
**   exponentiation

Parentheses are available for grouping terms in expressions.

This chapter discusses the following numeric functions:

ROUND(*expression, round-off-unit*)
> rounds the quantity in *expression* to the figure given in *round-off-unit*. The *expression* can be a numeric variable name, a numeric constant, or an arithmetic expression. Separate the *round-off-unit* from the *expression* with a comma.

SUM(*expression-1* <, . . . *expression-n*>)
> produces the sum of all *expressions* you specify in the parentheses. The SUM function ignores missing values as it calculates the sum of the *expressions*. Each *expression* can be a numeric variable, a numeric constant, another arithmetic expression, or another numeric function.

Learning More

□ Chapter 7, "Working with Character Variables," discusses character variables and how you can save space by treating some numeric values as character values.

□ Chapter 7 also discusses using base SAS software's character functions. *SAS Language: Reference, Version 6, First Edition* lists and describes base SAS software functions, including over 90 numeric functions in the following areas:

  □ arithmetic and algebraic expressions

  □ trigonometric and hyperbolic expressions

  □ probability distributions

  □ sample statistics

  □ random number generation.

  In addition, some other SAS software products provide additional functions. Those functions are described in the reference manual for each software product.

□ *SAS Language: Reference* lists the types of numbers the SAS System can read from data lines. Most types of numbers (other than those in standard representation) require an informat; they are listed in the same book. Types of numbers the SAS System accepts in expressions are also listed in *SAS Language: Reference*.

□ *SAS Language: Reference* describes arithmetic expressions in the SAS language and individual operators.

□ *SAS Language: Reference*, discusses how the SAS System allows you to distinguish between various kinds of numeric missing values. The SAS language contains 27 special missing values based on the letters A-Z and the underscore (_).

□ *SAS Language: Reference* documents using the DEFAULT= option in the LENGTH statement to assign a default storage length to all newly created numeric variables.

□ *SAS Language: Reference* lists ways to abbreviate lists of variables in function arguments. Many functions, including the SUM function, accept abbreviated lists of variables as arguments.

□ *SAS Language: Reference* presents a general discussion on numeric precision. The way a computer stores numbers, including the maximum and minimum representable values and the maximum number of decimal places stored accurately, is determined by the computer's hardware. The precision with which the SAS System can store numbers also depends on the hardware of the computer system on which it is installed. Specific limits for each hardware platform are discussed in the SAS documentation for each host system.

□ The SAS documentation for your host system provides information on storing numeric variables whose values are limited to 1 or 0 in the minimum number of bytes used by the SAS System (either 2 or 3 bytes, depending on your operating system).

Chapter **7** Working with Character Variables

Introduction

The SAS System can work with both variables that contain numbers and variables that can contain letters and special characters in addition to numeric digits. Variables whose values contain other kinds of characters as well as the digits 0 through 9 are called *character variables*.

In this chapter you learn to

- identify character variables

- set the length of character variables

- align character values within character variables

- handle missing values of character variables

- work with character variables, character constants, and character expressions in SAS program statements

- instruct the SAS System to read fields containing numbers as character variables in order to save space.

Input File and SAS Data Set Example

Suppose that at Tradewinds Travel, you are working with data on flight schedules for tours. Your data include the country to be visited, the number of cities in the tour, the city from which the tour leaves the U.S. (the gateway city), and the cities of arrival and departure in the other country.

The following DATA step reads the information and stores it in a data set named AIR.DEPART, and Output 7.1 displays the data set:

```
libname air 'your-data-library';

data air.depart;
   input country $ 1-9 cities 11-12 usgate $ 14-26 othrgate $ 28-48;
   cards;
Japan      5 San Francisco      Tokyo, Osaka
Italy      8 New York           Rome, Naples
Australia 12 Honolulu          Sydney, Brisbane
Venezuela  4 Miami             Caracas, Maracaibo
Brazil     4                 Rio de Janeiro, Belem
;
run;

proc print data=air.depart;
   title 'Data Set AIR.DEPART';
run;
```

Output 7.1
Data Set
AIR.DEPART

```
                        Data Set AIR.DEPART                        1

   OBS    COUNTRY     CITIES    USGATE         OTHRGATE

    1     Japan         5       San Francisco  Tokyo, Osaka
    2     Italy         8       New York       Rome, Naples
    3     Australia    12       Honolulu       Sydney, Brisbane
    4     Venezuela     4       Miami          Caracas, Maracaibo
    5     Brazil        4                      Rio de Janeiro, Belem
```

In AIR.DEPART, the variables COUNTRY, USGATE, and OTHRGATE contain information other than numbers. Variable CITIES contains only numbers.

Identifying Character Variables

To indicate a character variable in data lines, place a dollar sign after the variable name in the INPUT statement, as shown in the DATA step that created AIR.DEPART:

```
input country $ 1-9 cities 11-12 usgate $ 14-26 othrgate $ 28-48;
```

To indicate a character value in an assignment statement, enclose the value in quotes:

```
schedule='3-4 tours per season';
```

Either single quotes (apostrophes) or double quotes (quotation marks) are acceptable. If the value itself contains a single quote, surround the value with double quotes, as in

```
remarks="See last year's schedule";
```

Note: Matching quotes properly is important. Missing or extraneous quotes cause the SAS System to misread both the erroneous statement and the following statements.

When you refer to a character value in an expression, you must also enclose the value in quotes. For example, suppose you are recording the airport code for the U.S. departure cities. The following statement compares the value of USGATE to San Francisco and, when a match occurs, assigns the airport code SFO:

```
if usgate='San Francisco' then usairpt='SFO';
```

(You'll learn more about IF-THEN statements in Chapter 8, "Acting on Selected Observations.")

In character values, the SAS System distinguishes uppercase letters from lowercase ones. For example, in data set AIR.DEPART, the value of USGATE in the observation for New Zealand is `Honolulu`. The following IF condition is true, and the SAS System assigns USAIRPT the value HNL:

```
else if usgate='Honolulu' then usairpt='HNL';
```

However, the following condition is false:

```
if usgate='HONOLULU' then usairpt='HNL';
```

The SAS System doesn't select that observation because the characters Honolulu and HONOLULU are not equivalent. (Chapter 8 shows how to compare uppercase and lowercase characters.)

Placing these statements in the following DATA step and printing the data set produces Output 7.2:

```
data showchar;
   set air.depart;
   schedule='3-4 tours per season';
   remarks="See last year's schedule";
   if usgate='San Francisco' then usairpt='SFO';
   else if usgate='Honolulu' then usairpt='HNL';
run;

proc print data=showchar;
   var country schedule remarks usgate usairpt;
   title 'Examples of Some Character Variables';
run;
```

Output 7.2   *Character Variables in a DATA Step*

```
                         Examples of Some Character Variables                          1

       OBS    COUNTRY        SCHEDULE              REMARKS            USGATE        USAIRPT

        1     Japan       3-4 tours per season  See last year's schedule  San Francisco   SFO
        2     Italy       3-4 tours per season  See last year's schedule  New York
        3     Australia   3-4 tours per season  See last year's schedule  Honolulu        HNL
        4     Venezuela   3-4 tours per season  See last year's schedule  Miami
        5     Brazil      3-4 tours per season  See last year's schedule
```

Setting the Length of Character Variables

When you create character variables, the SAS System determines the length of the variable from its first occurrence in the DATA step. Therefore, you must allow for the longest possible value in the first statement that mentions the variable.

For example, as you enter the abbreviations for U.S. airports, you realize you don't know whether the flight listed as New York leaves from John F. Kennedy International Airport or Newark International Airport. You decide to list both, so you write the following DATA step; the results appear in Output 7.3:

```
    /* first attempt */
data aircode;
    set air.depart;
    if usgate='San Francisco' then usairpt='SFO';
    else if usgate='Honolulu' then usairpt='HNL';
    else if usgate='New York' then usairpt='JFK or EWR';
run;

proc print data=aircode;
    var country usgate usairpt;
    title 'Unexpected Truncation of Character Values';
run;
```

Output 7.3
Truncation of
Character Values

```
              Unexpected Truncation of Character Values          1

       OBS    COUNTRY    USGATE          USAIRPT

        1     Japan      San Francisco   SFO
        2     Italy      New York        JFK
        3     Australia  Honolulu        HNL
        4     Venezuela  Miami
        5     Brazil
```

Only the characters JFK appear in the observation for New York. The SAS System first encounters USAIRPT in the statement that assigns the value SFO. Therefore, the SAS System creates USAIRPT with a length of 3 bytes and uses only the first three characters in the New York observation.

To allow space to write JFK or EWR, use a LENGTH statement as the first reference to USAIRPT. The LENGTH statement has the form

LENGTH *variable-list$ number-of-bytes*;

where *variable-list* is the variable or variables to which you are assigning the length *number-of-bytes*. The dollar sign ($) indicates the variables are to be character. The LENGTH statement determines the length of a character variable both in the program data vector and in the data set being created. (In contrast, a LENGTH statement determines the length of a numeric variable only in the data set being created.) The maximum length of any character value in the SAS System is 200 bytes.

Here is a LENGTH statement for USAIRPT:

```
length usairpt $ 10;
```

The LENGTH statement must be the first reference to the character variables being assigned lengths. Therefore, the best position in the DATA step for a LENGTH statement is immediately after the DATA statement.

Output 7.4 shows the result of using the LENGTH statement in the following DATA step:*

```
    /* correct method */
data aircode2;
    length usairpt $ 10;
    set air.depart;
    if usgate='San Francisco' then usairpt='SFO';
    else if usgate='Honolulu' then usairpt='HNL';
    else if usgate='New York' then usairpt='JFK or EWR';
run;

proc print data=aircode2;
    var country usgate usairpt;
    title 'Using the Complete Character Value';
run;
```

Output 7.4
Setting the Length of a Character Variable with a LENGTH Statement

```
                     Using the Complete Character Value              1

          OBS    COUNTRY      USGATE          USAIRPT

           1     Japan        San Francisco   SFO
           2     Italy        New York        JFK or EWR
           3     Australia    Honolulu        HNL
           4     Venezuela    Miami
           5     Brazil
```

---

* You can use the DATASETS procedure to display the length of variables in a SAS data set.

Aligning Values in Character Variables

When an INPUT statement reads character fields in data lines, the SAS System reads the entire input field and removes any leading blanks before assigning the value to the variable. Therefore, character values read with an INPUT statement are left-aligned by default. If the value is shorter than the length of the variable, the SAS System adds blanks to the end of the value (known as *padding the value with blanks*) to make the value have the length specified. For example, notice the DATA step at the beginning of this chapter. The values for USGATE are left-aligned in the input field and the values of OTHRGATE are right-aligned, but the SAS System left-aligns both sets of values before assigning them to variables.

When you assign a character value in an assignment statement, the SAS System stores the value as it appears in the statement; the SAS System doesn't perform any alignment. In addition, if the length of the value in the assignment statement does not match a previously assigned length, the SAS System pads the value with blanks or truncates it to make it fit. The following DATA step centers the airport code for Miami, and Output 7.5 displays the results:

```
data aircode3;
   set air.depart;
   length usairpt $ 10;
   if usgate='San Francisco' then usairpt='SFO';
   else if usgate='Honolulu' then usairpt='HNL';
   else if usgate='New York' then usairpt='JFK or EWR';
   else if usgate='Miami' then usairpt='   MIA   ';
run;
proc print data=aircode3;
   var country usgate usairpt;
   title 'Alignment of Character Values';
run;
```

Output 7.5
How the SAS
System Aligns
Character Values

```
                     Alignment of Character Values                      1

         OBS    COUNTRY      USGATE         USAIRPT

          1     Japan        San Francisco  SFO
          2     Italy        New York       JFK or EWR
          3     Australia    Honolulu       HNL
          4     Venezuela    Miami             MIA
          5     Brazil
```

Handling Missing Values

Sometimes data for a character variable are missing. For example, the data line for Brazil lacks the departure city from the U.S.:

```
Brazil     4              Rio de Janeiro, Belem
```

The INPUT statement reads the value for USGATE from columns 14-26 (using column input), and all of those columns are blank. Therefore, the SAS System assigns a missing value to USGATE in the observation for Brazil.

One special case occurs when you are reading character data values with list input. In that case, you must use a period to represent a missing character value in data lines. (By default, blanks in list input indicate divisions between values; therefore, the SAS System interprets blanks as a signal to keep searching for the value, not as a missing value.)

The SAS System uses a blank to represent a missing character value in a data set. In the preceding examples, the observations for which you have not assigned values to USAIRPT contain missing values. You can also assign missing character values in assignment statements. In that case represent the missing value with a blank surrounded by quotes. For example, you don't know the departure city for the tour to Brazil. If you do not assign a value to USAIRPT for that observation, the value remains missing by default. However, you can also assign a missing value with an assignment statement as follows:

```
else if usgate=' ' then usairpt=' ';
```

The following DATA step assigns a missing value to USAIRPT when the departure city is missing, and Output 7.6 shows the resulting data set:

```
data aircode4;
   set air.depart;
   length usairpt $ 10;
   if usgate='San Francisco' then usairpt='SFO';
   else if usgate='Honolulu' then usairpt='HNL';
   else if usgate='New York' then usairpt='JFK or EWR';
   else if usgate='Miami' then usairpt='   MIA   ';
   else if usgate=' ' then usairpt=' ';
run;

proc print data=aircode4;
   var country usgate usairpt;
   title 'Assigning Missing Character Values';
run;
```

Output 7.6
Assigning Missing
Character Values

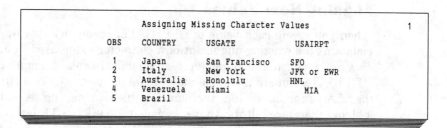

```
               Assigning Missing Character Values                    1

      OBS    COUNTRY      USGATE          USAIRPT

       1     Japan        San Francisco   SFO
       2     Italy        New York        JFK or EWR
       3     Australia    Honolulu        HNL
       4     Venezuela    Miami              MIA
       5     Brazil
```

Creating New Character Values

When values contain character data, you can work with them in several ways to create new character values. You can divide long values into pieces, combine existing values to make a longer value, and so on. This section shows you basic ways to create new character values.

Extracting a Portion of a Character Value

How do you isolate one piece of a character variable? For example, the value of OTHRGATE contains two cities: the city of arrival and the city of departure. How do you divide that value so that you can create separate variables for the two cities? The SCAN function gives you this capability.

The SCAN function selects a term from a character value; the term can be any character string and the divider for terms (the *delimiter*) can be any character or any of a list of characters:

SCAN(*source,n*<,*list-of-delimiters*>)

The *source* is the value you want to examine. It can be any kind of character expression, including character variables, character constants, and so on. The *n* is the number of the term to be selected from the source. The *list-of-delimiters* gives one or more delimiters. If you specify more than one delimiter, the SAS System uses any of them; if you omit the delimiter, the SAS System divides words according to a default list of delimiters (including the blank and some special characters). For example, to select the first term in the value of OTHRGATE and assign it to a new variable named ARVGATE, write

```
arvgate=scan(othrgate,1,',');
```

The SCAN function examines the value of OTHRGATE and selects the first term as identified by a comma. It's a good idea to specify the delimiter to be used; by default, in the observation for Brazil, the SAS System recognizes a blank space as the delimiter and selects `Rio` rather than `Rio de Janeiro` as the first term. Specifying the delimiter allows you to control the division.

To select the second term from OTHRGATE and assign it to a new variable term named DEPTGATE, write

```
deptgate=scan(othrgate,2,',');
```

Aligning New Values

When you create each value of DEPTGATE, remember that the SAS System maintains the existing alignment of a character value used in an expression; it does not perform any automatic realignment. In this example, the values of OTHRGATE contain a comma and a blank between the two city names. When the SCAN function divides the names at the comma, the second term begins with a blank; therefore, all the values assigned to DEPTGATE begin with a blank.

To left-align the values, use the LEFT function:

LEFT(*source*)

The LEFT function produces a value with all leading blanks in the *source* moved to the right side of the value; therefore, the result is left-aligned. The source can be any kind of character expression, including a character variable, a character constant enclosed in quotes, or another character function.

This example uses the LEFT function in a second assignment statement:

```
deptgate=scan(othrgate,2,',');
deptgate=left(deptgate);
```

You can also nest the two functions:

```
deptgate=left(scan(othrgate,2,','));
```

When you nest functions, the SAS System performs the action in the innermost function first. It uses the result of that function as the argument of the next function, and so on.

Creating ARVGATE and DEPTGATE with the following program and printing them produces Output 7.7:

```
data air.arvdept;
   set air.depart;
   arvgate=scan(othrgate,1,',');
   deptgate=left(scan(othrgate,2,','));
run;
proc print data=air.arvdept;
   var country othrgate arvgate deptgate;
   title 'Dividing Character Values into Terms';
run;
```

Output 7.7
Dividing Values into Separate Words with the SCAN Function

```
                    Dividing Character Values into Terms                      1

     OBS    COUNTRY      OTHRGATE               ARVGATE            DEPTGATE

      1     Japan        Tokyo, Osaka           Tokyo              Osaka
      2     Italy        Rome, Naples           Rome               Naples
      3     Australia    Sydney, Brisbane       Sydney             Brisbane
      4     Venezuela    Caracas, Maracaibo     Caracas            Maracaibo
      5     Brazil       Rio de Janeiro, Belem  Rio de Janeiro     Belem
```

Assigning Lengths to Variables Created by the SCAN Function

The SCAN function causes the SAS System to assign a length of 200 bytes to the result variable in an assignment statement. Most of the other character functions cause the target to have the same length as the original value. In the data set ARVDEPT, the variable ARVGATE has a length of 200 because the SCAN function creates it. The variable DEPTGATE also has a length of 200 because the argument of the LEFT function contains the SCAN function.

Setting the lengths of ARVGATE and DEPTGATE to the values you need rather than the default length saves a lot of storage space. Because the SAS System sets the length of a character variable the first time the SAS System encounters it, use a LENGTH statement before you use the variables ARVGATE and DEPTGATE in assignment statements:

```
data arvdept2;
   length arvgate $ 14 deptgate $ 9;
   set air.depart;
   arvgate=scan(othrgate,1,',');
   deptgate=left(scan(othrgate,2,','));
run;
```

Combining Character Values: Using Concatenation

The SAS System allows you to combine character values into longer ones using an operation known as *concatenation*. Concatenation combines character values by placing them one after the other. In SAS programming, the concatenation operator is the double vertical bar (||).* The length of the result is the sum of the lengths of the pieces, up to a maximum of 200 bytes. Figure 7.1 illustrates the concatenation operation.

Figure 7.1
Concatenating
Values

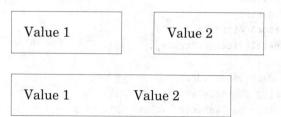

The following statement combines all the cities named as gateways into a single variable named ALLGATES:

```
allgates=usgate||othrgate;
```

The SAS System attaches the beginning of each value of OTHRGATE to the end of each value of USGATE. Including this statement in the following DATA step produces the data set shown in Output 7.8:

```
      /* first try */
data all;
   set air.depart;
   allgates=usgate||othrgate;
run;

proc print data=all;
   var country usgate othrgate allgates;
   title 'Simple Concatenation';
run;
```

---

* If your keyboard does not have a solid vertical bar, use a broken vertical bar (¦).

Output 7.8   *Simple Concatenation: Interior Blanks Not Removed*

```
                                 Simple Concatenation                                       1

    OBS   COUNTRY      USGATE        OTHRGATE                 ALLGATES

     1    Japan        San Francisco Tokyo, Osaka             San FranciscoTokyo, Osaka
     2    Italy        New York      Rome, Naples             New York    Rome, Naples
     3    Australia    Honolulu      Sydney, Brisbane         Honolulu    Sydney, Brisbane
     4    Venezuela    Miami         Caracas, Maracaibo       Miami       Caracas, Maracaibo
     5    Brazil                     Rio de Janeiro, Belem                Rio de Janeiro, Belem
```

Removing Interior Blanks

Why does the middle of ALLGATES contain blanks, or, in the Brazil observation, why is the first part of the value blank? When a character value is shorter than the length of the variable to which it belongs, the SAS System pads the value with trailing blanks. The length of USGATE is 13 bytes, but only San Francisco uses all of them. Therefore, the other values contain blanks at the end, and the value for Brazil is entirely blank. The SAS System concatenates USGATE and OTHRGATE without change; therefore, the middle of ALLGATES contains blanks for most observations. (Of course, most of the values of OTHRGATE also contain trailing blanks. If you concatenate another variable such as COUNTRY to OTHRGATE, you can see the trailing blanks in OTHRGATE.)

To eliminate trailing blanks, use the TRIM function:

TRIM(*source*)

The TRIM function produces a value without the trailing blanks in the *source*. (However, other rules about trailing blanks in the SAS System still apply. If the trimmed result is shorter than the length of the variable to which the result is assigned, the SAS System pads the result with new blanks as it makes the assignment.) To eliminate the trailing blanks in USGATE from ALLGATES, add the TRIM function to the expression:

```
allgate2=trim(usgate)||othrgate;
```

Using that statement in the following program produces Output 7.9:

```
    /* removing interior blanks */
data all2;
   set air.depart;
   allgate2=trim(usgate)||othrgate;
run;

proc print data=all2;
   var country usgate othrgate allgate2;
   title 'Trimming Blanks in a Concatenation';
run;
```

Output 7.9   *Removing Blanks with the TRIM Function*

```
                          Trimming Blanks in a Concatenation                              1

        OBS    COUNTRY      USGATE        OTHRGATE                ALLGATE2

         1     Japan        San Francisco Tokyo, Osaka            San FranciscoTokyo, Osaka
         2     Italy        New York      Rome, Naples            New YorkRome, Naples
         3     Australia    Honolulu      Sydney, Brisbane        HonoluluSydney, Brisbane
         4     Venezuela    Miami         Caracas, Maracaibo      MiamiCaracas, Maracaibo
         5     Brazil                     Rio de Janeiro, Belem   Rio de Janeiro, Belem
```

Adding Additional Characters

Data set ALL2 shows that removing the trailing blanks from USGATE causes all the values of OTHRGATE to come immediately after the corresponding values of USGATE. In the observation for Brazil, the value of OTHRGATE comes at the beginning of the value. To make the result easier to read, concatenate a comma and blank between the trimmed value of USGATE and the value of OTHRGATE. Use an IF-THEN statement to equate the value of ALLGATES with that of OTHRGATE in the observation for Brazil.

```
allgate3=trim(usgate)||', '||othrgate;
if country='Brazil' then allgate3=othrgate;
```

This DATA step produces the SAS data set shown in Output 7.10:

```
/* final version */
data all3;
   set air.depart;
   allgate3=trim(usgate)||', '||othrgate;
   if country='Brazil' then allgate3=othrgate;
run;

proc print data=all3;
   var country usgate othrgate allgate3;
   title 'Readable Concatenated Values';
run;
```

Output 7.10   *Concatenating Additional Characters for Readability*

```
                            Readable Concatenated Values                                  1

        OBS    COUNTRY      USGATE        OTHRGATE             ALLGATE3

         1     Japan        San Francisco Tokyo, Osaka         San Francisco, Tokyo, Osaka
         2     Italy        New York      Rome, Naples         New York, Rome, Naples
         3     Australia    Honolulu      Sydney, Brisbane     Honolulu, Sydney, Brisbane
         4     Venezuela    Miami         Caracas, Maracaibo   Miami, Caracas, Maracaibo
         5     Brazil                     Rio de Janeiro, Belem Rio de Janeiro, Belem
```

Troubleshooting: When New Variables Appear Truncated

This section discusses a common problem in using concatenation: the apparent loss of part of a concatenated value.

Earlier in this chapter you divided OTHRGATE into two new variables, ARVGATE and DEPTGATE, with default lengths of 200 bytes. For reference, this example recreates the DATA step:

```
data air.arvdept;
   set air.depart;
   arvgate=scan(othrgate,1,',');
   deptgate=left(scan(othrgate,2,','));
run;
```

Now that you have worked with the concatenation operator, suppose you decide to recombine ARVGATE and DEPTGATE into a new variable, OTHRGAT2, that is just like OTHRGATE. However, you forget to use the TRIM function on ARVGATE. The following DATA step shows the concatenation, and Output 7.11 shows the result:

```
   /* accidentally omitting the TRIM function */
data rebuild1;
   set air.arvdept;
   othrgat2=arvgate||', '||deptgate;
run;

proc print data=rebuild1;
   var country othrgate othrgat2;
   title 'Concatenation Seems to Use Only the First Piece';
run;
```

Output 7.11
Losing Part of a Concatenated Value

```
          Concatenation Seems to Use Only the First Piece          1

    OBS   COUNTRY     OTHRGATE              OTHRGAT2

     1    Japan       Tokyo, Osaka          Tokyo
     2    Italy       Rome, Naples          Rome
     3    Australia   Sydney, Brisbane      Sydney
     4    Venezuela   Caracas, Maracaibo    Caracas
     5    Brazil      Rio de Janeiro, Belem Rio de Janeiro
```

The value of OTHRGAT2 contains only the value of ARVGATE. The problem occurs because the sum of the lengths of ARVGATE, DEPTGATE, the comma, and the blank is 402 bytes; however, the maximum length that OTHRGAT2 can be is 200 bytes. The SAS System performs the complete concatenation, but it truncates the result on the right in order to make it fit the length of OTHRGAT2. Because the first piece, the value of ARVGATE, is 200 bytes, only that piece remains after the truncation.

There are two possible solutions to the problem. First, if you remember to trim the trailing blanks from ARVGATE with the TRIM function as shown in the preceding section, the significant characters from all three pieces fit within the first 200 bytes of the concatenation and are therefore assigned to OTHRGAT2.

Second, if you assign ARVGATE and DEPTGATE the lengths their values require (14 and 9 bytes, respectively), the sum of their lengths is 23 bytes. Then adding a comma and a blank for readability produces a concatenation with a total length of 25 bytes. Using the TRIM function as follows removes interior blanks from the concatenation, and Output 7.12 shows the result:

```
data rebuild2;
   length arvgate $ 14 deptgate $ 9;
   set air.arvdept;
   othrgat2=trim(arvgate)||', '||deptgate;
run;

proc print data=rebuild2;
   var country othrgate othrgat2;
   title 'All Concatenated Pieces Appear';
run;
```

Output 7.12
Showing All of a
Newly
Concatenated
Value

```
                       All Concatenated Pieces Appear                     1

        OBS    COUNTRY      OTHRGATE                 OTHRGAT2

         1     Japan        Tokyo, Osaka             Tokyo, Osaka
         2     Italy        Rome, Naples             Rome, Naples
         3     Australia    Sydney, Brisbane         Sydney, Brisbane
         4     Venezuela    Caracas, Maracaibo       Caracas, Maracaibo
         5     Brazil       Rio de Janeiro, Belem    Rio de Janeiro, Belem
```

Treating Numbers as Characters

Remember that the SAS System uses 8 bytes of storage for every numeric value in the DATA step; by default, the SAS System also uses 8 bytes of storage for numeric values in an output data set. However, a character value can contain a minimum of one character; in that case, the SAS System uses one byte for the character variable, both in the program data vector and in the output data set. In addition, the SAS System treats the digits 0 through 9 in a character value like any other character. Therefore, in some cases you can save space by treating a value containing digits as a character value.

For example, suppose some of your tours offer various prices, depending on the quality of the hotel room. The brochures rank the rooms as two stars, three stars, and so on. In this case the values 2, 3, and 4 are really the names of categories, and you don't expect to perform any arithmetic operations on them. Therefore, you can input the values into a character variable. The following DATA step reads HOTELRNK as a character variable, and Output 7.13 shows the result:

```
data hotels;
   input country $ 1-9 hotelrnk $ 11 landcost;
   cards;
Italy     2  498
Italy     4  698
Australia 2  915
```

```
Australia 3 1169
Australia 4 1399
;
proc print data=hotels;
   title 'Data Set HOTELS with Character Hotel Rankings';
run;
```

Output 7.13
Data Set HOTELS

```
           Data Set HOTELS with Character Hotel Rankings          1

           OBS     COUNTRY      HOTELRNK     LANDCOST

            1      Italy           2           498
            2      Italy           4           698
            3      Australia       2           915
            4      Australia       3          1169
            5      Australia       4          1399
```

In this DATA step the INPUT statement assigns HOTELRNK a length of 1 byte because the INPUT statement reads one column to find the value (shown by the use of column input). If you are using list input, place a LENGTH statement before the INPUT statement to set the length to 1 byte.

If you read a number as a character value and then discover that you need to use it in a numeric expression, you can do so without making changes in your program. The SAS System automatically produces a numeric value from the character value for use in the expression; it also issues a note that the conversion occurred. (Of course, the conversion causes the DATA step to use slightly more computer resources.) The original variable remains unchanged.

SAS Tools

This chapter discusses the following functions:

SCAN(*source,n*<*,list-of-delimiters*>)
   selects the *n*th term from the *source*. The source can be any kind of character expression, including a character variable, a character constant enclosed in quotes, or another character function. To choose the character that divides the terms, use a *delimiter*; if you omit the *delimiter*, the SAS System divides the terms using a default list of delimiters (the blank and some special characters).

LEFT(*source*)
   left-aligns the *source* by moving any leading blanks to the end of the value. The *source* can be any kind of character expression, including a character variable, a character constant enclosed in quotes, or another character function. Because any blanks removed from the left are added to the right, the length of the result matches the length of the source.

TRIM(*source*)

trims trailing blanks from the *source*. The *source* can be any kind of character expression, including a character variable, a character constant enclosed in quotes, or another character function. The TRIM function does not affect the way a variable is stored. If you use the TRIM function to remove trailing blanks and assign the trimmed value to a variable that is longer than that value, the SAS System pads the value with new trailing blanks to make the value match the length of the new variable.

This chapter discusses using the LENGTH statement for character variables:

LENGTH *variable-list* $ *number-of-bytes*;

assigns a length you specify in *number-of-bytes* to the character variable or variables in *variable-list*. You can assign any number of lengths in a single LENGTH statement, and you can assign lengths to both character and numeric variables in the same statement. Place a dollar sign ($) before the length of any character variable.

Learning More

□ This chapter illustrates the flexibility the SAS System allows you when manipulating character values. In addition to the functions described in this chapter, these character functions are frequently used:

COMPRESS	removes specified character(s) from the source.
INDEX	searches the source for a pattern of characters.
RIGHT	right-aligns the source.
SUBSTR	extracts a group of characters.
UPCASE	returns the source in uppercase.

The INDEX and UPCASE functions are discussed in Chapter 8, "Acting on Selected Observations." Complete descriptions of all character functions appear in *SAS Language: Reference, Version 6, First Edition*.

□ Chapter 8 describes using IF-THEN statements.

□ Chapter 33, "Getting Information about Your Data Sets," discusses using the DATASETS procedure to display the length of variables in a SAS data set.

□ *SAS Language: Reference* contains reference information on character variables.

□ *SAS Language: Reference* discusses the concatenation operator.

□ *SAS Language: Reference* provides complete information on the SAS System's numerous informats and formats for reading and writing character variables.

Chapter **8** Acting on Selected Observations

Introduction

One of the most useful features of the SAS System is its ability to perform an activity on only the observations you have selected. In this chapter you learn

☐ how the selection process works

☐ how to write statements that select observations based on a condition

☐ some special points about selecting numeric and character variables.

Input File and SAS Data Set Example

Suppose that at Tradewinds Travel you are putting together tours to art museums and galleries in various cities. You have the basic facts, but you need to make a lot of adjustments. For example, if the tour covers too many museums and galleries within a time period, you must either decrease the number of museums visited or change the number of days for the tour. If the guide you assigned to the tour is not available, you must assign another guide. Therefore, most of your work involves selecting observations that meet or don't meet various criteria and taking the required action.

The data you have collected about the tours are stored in an external file. The data look like this:

```
Rome        3  750 7 4 M, 3 G          D'Amico  Torres
Paris       8 1680 6 5 M, 1 other      Lucas    Lucas
London      6 1230 5 3 M, 2 G          Wilson   Lucas
New York 6    . 8 5 M, 1 G, 2 other Lucas    D'Amico
Madrid      3  370 5 3 M, 2 other      Torres   D'Amico
Amsterdam 4  580 6 3 M, 3 G                     Vandever
```

The first field contains the name of the city. Next come the number of nights in the city, the cost of the land package (not airfare), and the number of events the trip offers (such as visits to museums and galleries). The next field gives a brief description of the events (where M indicates a museum; G, a gallery; and other, another kind of event). The final two fields contain the name of the tour guide and a backup guide.

You have entered the data into a SAS data set named ARTS.ARTTOUR. The following DATA step creates ARTS.ARTTOUR, and Output 8.1 displays it:

```
libname arts 'your-data-library';

data arts.arttour;
    infile 'your-input-file';
    input city $ 1-9 nights 11 landcost 13-16 events 18
          describe $ 20-36 guide $ 38-45 backup $ 47-54;
run;

proc print data=arts.arttour;
    title 'Data Set ARTS.ARTTOUR';
run;
```

Output 8.1
ARTS.ARTTOUR

```
                           Data Set ARTS.ARTTOUR                          1

   OBS CITY       NIGHTS LANDCOST EVENTS DESCRIBE          GUIDE   BACKUP

     1  Rome         3      750      7   4 M, 3 G          D'Amico Torres
     2  Paris        8     1680      6   5 M, 1 other      Lucas   Lucas
     3  London       6     1230      5   3 M, 2 G          Wilson  Lucas
     4  New York     6        .      8   5 M, 1 G, 2 other Lucas   D'Amico
     5  Madrid       3      370      5   3 M, 2 other      Torres  D'Amico
     6  Amsterdam    4      580      6   3 M, 3 G                  Vandever
```

In ARTS.ARTTOUR, the variable EVENTS contains the number of attractions visited in the tour. DESCRIBE lists the number of museums (M), art galleries (G), and other attractions (other) visited. GUIDE gives the name of the guide assigned to the tour, and BACKUP is the alternate guide in case the original guide is unavailable.

How the Selection Process Works

The most common way the SAS System selects observations for action in a DATA step is through the IF-THEN statement:

    IF *condition* **THEN** *action*;

The *condition* is one or more comparisons, for example,

```
city='Rome'
events>nights
guide='Lucas' and nights>7
```

(The symbol $>$ stands for greater than. You'll see how to use symbols as comparison operators in "Writing Conditions" later in this chapter.)

For a given observation, a comparison is either true or false. In the first example, the value of CITY is either **Rome** or it is not. In the second example, the value of EVENTS in the current observation is either greater than the value of NIGHTS in the current observation or it is not. If the condition contains more than one comparison, as in the third example, the SAS System evaluates all of them according to its rules (discussed later) and declares the entire condition to be true or false.

When the condition is true, the SAS System takes the *action* in the THEN clause. The action must be expressed as a SAS statement that can be executed in an individual iteration of the DATA step. (Such statements are called *executable statements*.) The most common executable statements are assignment statements, for example,

```
landcost=landcost+30;
calendar='Check schedule';
guide='Torres';
```

This discussion concentrates on assignment statements in the THEN clause, but examples in other chapters show other statements used with the THEN clause.

Statements that provide information about a data set are not executable. For example, the LENGTH statement affects a variable as a whole, not how the variable is treated in a particular observation. (Such statements are called *declarative statements*.) Therefore, you can't use a LENGTH statement in a THEN clause.

When the condition is not true, the SAS System ignores the THEN clause and proceeds to the next statement in the DATA step.

The following DATA step uses these conditions and actions in IF-THEN statements, and Output 8.2 shows the result:

```
data revise;
   set arts.arttour;
   if city='Rome' then landcost=landcost+30;
   if events>nights then calendar='Check schedule';
   if guide='Lucas' and nights>7 then guide='Torres';
run;

proc print data=revise;
   var city nights landcost events guide calendar;
   title 'Examples of IF-THEN Statements';
run;
```

Output 8.2
Selecting
Observations with
IF-THEN
Statements

```
                         Examples of IF-THEN Statements                     1

   OBS    CITY        NIGHTS   LANDCOST   EVENTS    GUIDE      CALENDAR

    1    Rome           3        780        7     D'Amico   Check schedule
    2    Paris          8       1680        6     Torres
    3    London         6       1230        5     Wilson
    4    New York       6         .         8     Lucas     Check schedule
    5    Madrid         3        370        5     Torres    Check schedule
    6    Amsterdam      4        580        6               Check schedule
```

Providing an Alternative Action

Remember that the SAS System creates a variable in all observations, even if you don't assign it a value in all observations. In Output 8.2, the value of CALENDAR is blank in two observations. You can write a second IF-THEN statement to assign a different value, for example,

```
if events>nights then calendar='Check schedule';
if events<=nights then calendar='No problems';
```

(The symbol <= means less than or equal to.) In that case the SAS System compares the values of EVENTS and NIGHTS twice, once in each IF condition. A more efficient way to provide an alternative action is to use an ELSE statement:

ELSE *action*;

An ELSE statement names an alternative action to be taken when the IF condition is false. It must immediately follow the corresponding IF-THEN statement, as shown here:

```
if events>nights then calendar='Check schedule';
else calendar='No problems';
```

Adding the ELSE statement above to the previous DATA step produces Output 8.3:

```
data revise2;
   set arts.arttour;
   if city='Rome' then landcost=landcost+30;
   if events>nights then calendar='Check schedule';
   else calendar='No problems';
   if guide='Lucas' and nights>7 then guide='Torres';
run;

proc print data=revise2;
   var city nights landcost events guide calendar;
   title 'Alternative Value Assigned by ELSE';
run;
```

Output 8.3
Providing an
Alternative Action
with ELSE

```
                        Alternative Value Assigned by ELSE                    1

    OBS   CITY        NIGHTS   LANDCOST   EVENTS    GUIDE      CALENDAR

     1    Rome          3         780       7      D'Amico    Check schedule
     2    Paris         8        1680       6      Torres     No problems
     3    London        6        1230       5      Wilson     No problems
     4    New York      6           .       8      Lucas      Check schedule
     5    Madrid        3         370       5      Torres     Check schedule
     6    Amsterdam     4         580       6                 Check schedule
```

Writing a Series of Mutually Exclusive Conditions

Using an ELSE statement after an IF-THEN statement provides one alternative action when the IF condition is false. However, many cases involve a series of mutually exclusive conditions, each of which requires a separate action. For example, suppose you want to classify the tour prices as high, medium, or low, three alternatives.

In that case, write a series of IF-THEN and ELSE statements.

```
if landcost>=1500 then price='High  ';
else if landcost>=700 then price='Medium';
else price='Low';
```

(The symbol $>=$ is greater than or equal to.) To see how the SAS System executes this series of statements, consider two observations: Amsterdam, whose value of LANDCOST is 580, and Paris, whose value is 1680.

When the value of LANDCOST is 580:

1. The SAS System tests whether 580 is equal to or greater than 1500, determines that the comparison is false, ignores the THEN clause, and proceeds to the ELSE statement.

2. The action in the ELSE statement is to evaluate another condition. The SAS System tests whether 580 is equal to or greater than 700, determines that the comparison is false, ignores the THEN clause, and proceeds to the accompanying ELSE statement.

3. The SAS System executes the action in the ELSE statement and assigns PRICE the value **Low.**

When the value of LANDCOST is 1680:

1. The SAS System tests whether 1680 is greater than or equal to 1500, determines that the comparison is true, and executes the action in the THEN clause. The value of PRICE becomes **High.**

2. The SAS System ignores the ELSE statement. Because the entire remaining series is part of the first ELSE statement, the SAS System skips all remaining actions in the series.

A simple way to think of these actions is to remember that when an observation satisfies one condition in a series of mutually exclusive IF-THEN/ELSE statements, the SAS System processes that THEN action and skips the rest of the statements. (Therefore, you can increase the efficiency of a program by ordering the IF-THEN/ELSE statements so that the most common conditions appear first.)

Placing the series of statements above in the following DATA step and printing the result produces Output 8.4:

```
data prices;
   set arts.arttour;
   if landcost>=1500 then price='High  ';
   else if landcost>=700 then price='Medium';
   else price='Low';
run;

proc print data=prices;
   var city landcost price;
   title 'Mutually Exclusive Values';
run;
```

Output 8.4
Assigning
Mutually Exclusive
Values with
IF-THEN/ELSE
Statements

```
                         Mutually Exclusive Values                        1

        OBS    CITY         LANDCOST    PRICE

         1     Rome             750     Medium
         2     Paris           1680     High
         3     London          1230     Medium
         4     New York           .     Low
         5     Madrid           370     Low
         6     Amsterdam        580     Low
```

Writing Conditions

To write a condition in an IF-THEN statement, you make a comparison. You ask the SAS System to determine whether a value is equal to another value, greater than another value, and so on. The SAS System has six main comparison operators, which are shown in Table 8.1.

Table 8.1
Comparison
Operators

Symbol	Mnemonic Operator	Meaning
=	EQ	equal to
¬= ^= ~=	NE	not equal to (the ¬, ^, or ~ symbol depends on your keyboard)
>	GT	greater than
<	LT	less than
>=	GE	greater than or equal to
<=	LE	less than or equal to

The symbols in Table 8.1 are based on mathematical symbols; the letter abbreviations, known as *mnemonic operators*, have the same effect. Use the form that you prefer.* Both of the following statements compare the number of nights in the tour to six:

```
if nights>= 6 then stay='Week+';
if nights ge 6 then stay='Week+';
```

The terms on each side of the comparison operator can be variables, expressions, or constants. The side a particular term appears on does not matter, as long as you use the proper operator. All of the following comparisons are constructed correctly for use in SAS statements:

```
guide=' '

landcost ne .

landcost lt 600
600 ge landcost

events/nights>2
2<=events/nights
```

The following DATA step illustrates some of these conditions, and Output 8.5 shows the resulting SAS data set:

```
data changes;
   set arts.arttour;
   if nights>=6 then stay='Week+';
   else stay='days';
   if landcost ne . then remarks='OK  ';
   else remarks='Redo';
   if landcost lt 600 then budget='Low    ';
   else budget='Medium';
   if events/nights>2 then pace='Too fast';
   else pace='OK';
run;

proc print data=changes;
   var city nights landcost events stay remarks budget pace;
   title 'Using Various Conditions';
run;
```

---

* Use the mnemonic operators only in comparisons. For example, the equal sign in an assignment statement must be represented by the symbol =, not the mnemonic operator.

Output 8.5
Assigning Values
to Variables
According to
Specific
Conditions

```
                            Using Various Conditions                          1

   OBS   CITY       NIGHTS   LANDCOST   EVENTS   STAY    REMARKS   BUDGET   PACE

    1    Rome         3        750        7      days     OK       Medium   Too fast
    2    Paris        8       1680        6      Week+    OK       Medium   OK
    3    London       6       1230        5      Week+    OK       Medium   OK
    4    New York     6          .        8      Week+    Redo     Low      OK
    5    Madrid       3        370        5      days     OK       Low      OK
    6    Amsterdam    4        580        6      days     OK       Low      OK
```

Using More than One Comparison in a Condition

You can specify more than one comparison in a condition with these operators:

```
& or AND
| or OR
```

A condition can contain any number of ANDs, ORs, or both.

Using AND

When comparisons are connected by AND, all of the comparisons must be true for the condition to be true. Consider this example:

```
if city='Paris' and guide='Lucas' then remarks='Bilingual';
```

The comparison is true for observations in which the value of CITY is `Paris` and the value of GUIDE is `Lucas`.

A common comparison is to determine whether a value is between two quantities, greater than one quantity and less than another. For example, to select observations in which the value of LANDCOST is greater than or equal to 1000 and less than or equal to 1500, you can write a comparison with AND:

```
if landcost>=1000 and landcost<=1500 then price='1000-1500';
```

A simpler way to write this comparison is

```
if 1000<=landcost<=1500 then price='1000-1500';
```

This comparison has the same meaning as the previous one. You can use any of the operators $<$, $<=$, $>$, $>=$, or their mnemonic equivalents in this way.

Using the statements above in the following DATA step and printing the data set produces Output 8.6:

```
data showand;
   set arts.arttour;
   if city='Paris' and guide='Lucas' then remarks='Bilingual';
   if 1000<=landcost<=1500 then price='1000-1500';
run;
```

```
proc print data=showand;
   var city landcost guide remarks price;
   title 'Making Multiple Comparisons with AND';
run;
```

Output 8.6
Using AND When
Making Multiple
Comparisons

```
                  Making Multiple Comparisons with AND                      1

     OBS   CITY           LANDCOST     GUIDE      REMARKS        PRICE

      1    Rome              750       D'Amico
      2    Paris            1680       Lucas      Bilingual
      3    London           1230       Wilson                  1000-1500
      4    New York            .       Lucas
      5    Madrid            370       Torres
      6    Amsterdam        580
```

Using OR

When comparisons are connected by OR, only one of the comparisons needs to be true for the condition to be true. Consider the following example:

```
if landcost gt 1500 or landcost/nights gt 200 then level='Deluxe';
```

Any observation in which the land cost is over $1500, the cost per night is over $200, or both, satisfies the condition. The following DATA step shows this condition, and Output 8.7 shows the result:

```
data showor;
   set arts.arttour;
   if landcost gt 1500 or landcost/nights gt 200 then level='Deluxe';
run;

proc print data=showor;
   var city landcost nights level;
   title 'Making Multiple Comparisons with OR';
run;
```

Output 8.7
Using OR When
Making Multiple
Comparisons

```
                  Making Multiple Comparisons with OR                       1

     OBS   CITY           LANDCOST    NIGHTS    LEVEL

      1    Rome              750        3       Deluxe
      2    Paris            1680        8       Deluxe
      3    London           1230        6       Deluxe
      4    New York            .        6
      5    Madrid            370        3
      6    Amsterdam        580         4
```

Choosing AND or OR

Be careful when you combine negative operators with OR. Often, the operator you really need is AND. For example, suppose you have noticed some problems with the variable GUIDE. In the observation for Paris the guide and the backup are both Lucas; in the observation for Amsterdam, the name of the guide is missing. You want to label the observations that have no problems with GUIDE as OK. Should you write the IF condition with OR or with AND?

The following DATA step shows both conditions, and Output 8.8 shows the resulting data set:

```
data test;
   set arts.arttour;
   if guide ne backup or guide ne ' ' then use_or='OK';
   else use_or='No';
   if guide ne backup and guide ne ' ' then use_and='OK';
   else use_and='No';
run;

proc print data=test;
   var city guide backup use_or use_and;
   title 'Negative Operators with OR';
run;
```

Output 8.8
Using Negative
Operators When
Making
Comparisons

```
                    Negative Operators with OR                        1

        OBS    CITY        GUIDE      BACKUP      USE_OR    USE_AND

         1     Rome        D'Amico    Torres        OK        OK
         2     Paris       Lucas      Lucas         OK        No
         3     London      Wilson     Lucas         OK        OK
         4     New York    Lucas      D'Amico       OK        OK
         5     Madrid      Torres     D'Amico       OK        OK
         6     Amsterdam              Vandever      OK        No
```

In the IF-THEN/ELSE group that creates USE_OR, only one comparison needs to be true to make the condition true. In data set ARTS.ARTTOUR, the observation for Paris does not have a missing value for GUIDE; therefore, the comparison GUIDE NE ' ' is true. For Amsterdam, the comparison GUIDE NE BACKUP is true. Therefore, USE_OR has the value OK in all observations. The IF-THEN/ELSE group that creates USE_AND achieves the result you want, that is, selecting observations in which the value of GUIDE is not the same as BACKUP and is not missing.

Using AND and OR in the Same Condition

A condition can contain both ANDs and ORs. When it does, the SAS System evaluates the ANDs before the ORs. For example, suppose you want to specify a list of cities and a list of guides. Consider the following statement:

```
/* first attempt */
if city='Paris' or city='Rome' and guide='Lucas' or guide="D'Amico"
   then topic='Art history';
```

The SAS System first joins the items connected by AND:

```
city='Rome' and guide='Lucas'
```

The SAS System then makes the following OR comparisons:

```
city='Paris'
    or
city='Rome' and guide='Lucas'
    or
guide="D'Amico"
```

To group the CITY comparisons and the GUIDE comparisons, use parentheses:

```
/* correct method */
if (city='Paris' or city='Rome') and (guide='Lucas' or
    guide="D'Amico") then topic='Art history';
```

The SAS System evaluates the comparisons within parentheses first and uses the results as the terms of the larger comparison.

You can use parentheses in any condition to control the grouping of comparisons or to make the condition easier to read.

The following DATA step illustrates these conditions, and Output 8.9 shows the resulting data set:

```
data combine;
   set arts.arttour;
   if (city='Paris' or city='Rome') and (guide='Lucas' or
      guide="D'Amico") then topic='Art history';
run;

proc print data=combine;
   var city guide topic;
   title 'Grouping Comparisons with Parentheses';
run;
```

Output 8.9
Using Parentheses to Combine Comparisons with AND and OR

```
                  Grouping Comparisons with Parentheses              1

        OBS    CITY         GUIDE        TOPIC

         1     Rome         D'Amico      Art history
         2     Paris        Lucas        Art history
         3     London       Wilson
         4     New York     Lucas
         5     Madrid       Torres
         6     Amsterdam
```

Abbreviating Numeric Comparisons

Two points about numeric comparisons are helpful to know:

□ An abbreviated form of comparison is possible.

□ Abbreviated comparisons with OR require caution.

In computing terms, a value of TRUE is a 1 and a value of FALSE is a 0. In the SAS System, any numeric value other than 0 or missing is true; a value of 0 or missing is false. Therefore, a numeric variable or expression can stand alone in a condition. If its value is a number other than 0 or missing, the condition is true; if its value is 0 or missing, the condition is false.

For example, suppose you want to fill in variable REMARKS depending on whether the value of LANDCOST is present for a given observation. You can write the IF-THEN statement as

```
if landcost then remarks='Ready to budget';
```

This statement is equivalent to

```
if landcost ne . and landcost ne 0 then remarks='Ready to budget';
```

Be careful when you abbreviate comparisons with OR; it's easy to produce unexpected results. For example, suppose you want to select tours lasting six or eight nights. First you write this IF-THEN statement:

```
/* first try */
if nights=6 or 8 then stay='Medium';
```

The SAS System treats the condition as the following comparisons:

```
nights=6
    or
8
```

The second comparison does not use the values of NIGHTS; it is simply the number 8 standing alone. Because the number 8 is neither 0 nor a missing value, it always has the value TRUE. Because only one comparison in a series of OR comparisons needs to be true to make the condition true, *this condition is true for all observations*.

To select observations having six or eight nights, write the complete comparison each time:

```
/* correct way */
if nights=6 or nights=8 then stay='Medium';
```

Using these comparisons in the following DATA step produces the data set in Output 8.10:

```
data morecomp;
   set arts.arttour;
   if landcost then remarks='Ready to budget';
   else remarks='Need land cost';
   if nights=6 or nights=8 then stay='Medium';
   else stay='Short';
run;

proc print data=morecomp;
   var city nights landcost remarks stay;
   title 'More About Numeric Comparisons';
run;
```

Output 8.10
Abbreviating
Numeric
Comparisons

```
                        More About Numeric Comparisons                    1

        OBS    CITY         NIGHTS    LANDCOST      REMARKS         STAY

         1     Rome            3         750      Ready to budget   Short
         2     Paris           8        1680      Ready to budget   Medium
         3     London          6        1230      Ready to budget   Medium
         4     New York        6          .       Need land cost    Medium
         5     Madrid          3         370      Ready to budget   Short
         6     Amsterdam       4         580      Ready to budget   Short
```

Handling Character Comparisons

Some special situations arise when making character comparisons. You may
need to

□   compare uppercase and lowercase characters

□   select all values beginning with a particular group of characters

□   select all values beginning with a particular range of characters

□   find a particular value anywhere within another character value.

Each of these situations is discussed here.

Comparing Uppercase and Lowercase Characters

The SAS System distinguishes between uppercase and lowercase letters in
comparisons. For example, the values Madrid and MADRID are not equivalent.
To compare values that may occur in different cases, use the UPCASE function
to produce an uppercase value; then make the comparison between two
uppercase values, as shown here:

```
if upcase(city)='MADRID' then guide='Duncan';
```

Within the comparison, the SAS System produces an uppercase version of the
value of CITY and compares it to the uppercase constant MADRID. (The value of
CITY in the observation remains in its original case.) Using the statement above
in the following DATA step produces Output 8.11:

```
data newguide;
   set arts.arttour;
   if upcase(city)='MADRID' then guide='Duncan';
run;

proc print data=newguide;
   var city guide;
   title 'Using the UPCASE Function to Make a Comparison';
run;
```

Output 8.11
Data Set Produced
by an Uppercase
Comparison

```
               Using the UPCASE Function to Make a Comparison            1

                OBS    CITY           GUIDE

                 1     Rome           D'Amico
                 2     Paris          Lucas
                 3     London         Wilson
                 4     New York       Lucas
                 5     Madrid         Duncan
                 6     Amsterdam
```

Selecting All Values Beginning with the Same Group of Characters

In many situations you need to select a group of character values, such as all guides whose names begin with the letter D.

By default the SAS System compares values of different lengths by adding blanks to the end of the shorter value and testing the result against the longer value. Suppose you write this condition:

```
    /* first attempt */
if guide='D' then chosen='Yes';
else chosen='No';
```

The SAS System interprets the comparison as

```
guide='D        '
```

where **D** is followed by seven blanks (because GUIDE, a character variable created by list input, has a length of 8 bytes). Because the value of GUIDE never consists of the single letter D, the comparison is never true.

To compare a long value to a shorter standard, put a colon (:) after the operator, for example,

```
    /* correct method */
if guide=:'D' then chosen='Yes';
else chosen='No';
```

The colon causes the SAS System to compare the same number of characters in the shorter value and the longer value. In this case, the shorter string contains one character; therefore, the SAS System tests only the first character from the longer value. All names beginning with a D make the comparison true. (If you aren't sure that all the values of GUIDE begin with a capital letter, use the UPCASE function.) The following DATA step selects names beginning with D, and Output 8.12 shows the new data set:

```
data dguide;
   set arts.arttour;
   if guide=:'D' then chosen='Yes';
   else chosen='No';
run;

proc print data=dguide;
   var city guide chosen;
   title 'Guides Whose Names Begin with D';
run;
```

Output 8.12
Selecting All
Values Beginning
with a Particular
String

```
                      Guides Whose Names Begin with D                    1

          OBS    CITY         GUIDE       CHOSEN

           1     Rome         D'Amico     Yes
           2     Paris        Lucas       No
           3     London       Wilson      No
           4     New York     Lucas       No
           5     Madrid       Torres      No
           6     Amsterdam                No
```

Selecting a Range of Character Values

Suppose you want to select values beginning with a range of characters, such as all names beginning with A through L or M through Z. To select a range of character values, you need to understand the following points:

□ In computer processing, letters have magnitude. A is the smallest letter in the alphabet and Z is the largest. Therefore, the comparison A<B is true; so is the comparison D>C.*

□ A blank is smaller than any letter.

To divide the names of the guides into two groups beginning with A-L and M-Z, combine the comparison operator with the colon:

```
if guide<=:'L' then group='A-L';
else group='M-Z';
```

The following DATA step creates the groups, and Output 8.13 shows the result:

```
data guidegrp;
   set arts.arttour;
   if guide<=:'L' then group='A-L';
   else group='M-Z';

proc print data=guidegrp;
   var city guide group;
   title 'All Values Beginning with a Range of Characters';
run;
```

---

* The magnitude of letters in the alphabet is true for all host systems under which the SAS System runs. Other points, such as whether uppercase or lowercase letters are larger and how to treat numbers in character values, depend on your operating system. See Chapter 10, "Working with Grouped or Sorted Observations," for more information on how character values are sorted under various host operating systems.

Output 8.13
Selecting All
Values Beginning
with a Range of
Characters

```
                  All Values Beginning with a Range of Characters          1

              OBS      CITY          GUIDE        GROUP
               1       Rome          D'Amico      A-L
               2       Paris         Lucas        A-L
               3       London        Wilson       M-Z
               4       New York      Lucas        A-L
               5       Madrid        Torres       M-Z
               6       Amsterdam                  A-L
```

All names beginning with A through L, as well as the missing value, go into group A-L. The missing value goes into that group because a blank is smaller than any letter.

Finding a Value Anywhere within Another Character Value

Suppose you need to select tours that visit other attractions in addition to museums and galleries. In data set ARTS.ARTTOUR (illustrated in Output 8.1), the variable DESCRIBE refers to those events as `other`. However, the position of the word `other` varies in different observations. How can you find out whether `other` exists anywhere in the value of DESCRIBE for a given observation?

The INDEX function determines whether a specified character string (the excerpt) is present within a particular character value (the source):

INDEX(*source,excerpt*)

Both *source* and *excerpt* can be any kind of character expression, including character strings enclosed in quotes, character variables, and other character functions. If *excerpt* does occur within *source*, the function returns the position of the first character of *excerpt*, which is a positive number. If it doesn't, the function returns a 0. By testing for a value greater than 0, you can determine whether a particular character string is present in another character value.

The following statements select observations containing the string `other`:

```
if index(describe,'other')>0 then otherev='Yes';
else otherev='No';
```

You can also write the condition as

```
if index(describe,'other') then otherev='Yes';
else otherev='No';
```

The second example uses the fact that any value other than 0 or missing makes the condition true. Using these statements in a DATA step and printing the resulting data set produces Output 8.14:

```
data othrevnt;
   set arts.arttour;
   if index(describe,'other') then otherev='Yes';
   else otherev='No';
run;
```

```
proc print data=othrevnt;
   var city describe otherev;
   title 'Finding a Character String within Another Value';
run;
```

Output 8.14
Finding a
Character String
within Another
Value

```
             Finding a Character String within Another Value           1

     OBS    CITY        DESCRIBE             OTHEREV

      1     Rome        4 M, 3 G                No
      2     Paris       5 M, 1 other            Yes
      3     London      3 M, 2 G                No
      4     New York    5 M, 1 G, 2 other       Yes
      5     Madrid      3 M, 2 other            Yes
      6     Amsterdam   3 M, 3 G                No
```

In the observations for Paris and Madrid, the INDEX function returns the value 8; for New York, it returns 13. In the remaining observations, the function does not find the string `other` and returns a 0.

SAS Tools

This chapter discusses the following statements:

IF *condition* **THEN** *action*;
<ELSE *action*;>
> tests whether the *condition* is true; if so, the *action* in the THEN clause is carried out. If the *condition* is false and an ELSE statement is present, the ELSE *action* is carried out. If the *condition* is false and no ELSE statement is present, the next statement in the DATA step is processed. The *condition* is one or more numeric or character comparisons. The *action* must be an executable statement; that is, one that can be processed in an individual iteration of the DATA step. (Statements that affect the entire DATA step, such as LENGTH, are not executable.)
>
> In SAS processing, any numeric value other than 0 or missing is true; 0 and missing are false. Therefore, a numeric value can stand alone in a comparison. If its value is 0 or missing, the comparison is false; otherwise, the comparison is true.

This chapter discusses the following character functions:

UPCASE(*argument*)
> produces an uppercase value of *argument*, which can be any kind of character expression, such as character variables, character strings enclosed in quotes, other character functions, and so on.

INDEX(*source*,*excerpt*)
> searches the *source* for the string given in *excerpt*. Both the *source* and *excerpt* can be any kind of character expression, such as character variables, character strings enclosed in quotes, other character functions, and so on. When *excerpt* is present in *source*, the function returns the position of the first character of *excerpt* (a positive number). When *excerpt* is not present, the function returns a 0.

Learning More

□ *SAS Language: Reference, Version 6, First Edition* provides complete information on comparison and logical operators.

□ *SAS Language: Reference* documents the IF-THEN and ELSE statements.

□ *SAS Language: Reference* completely documents all SAS functions.

□ *SAS Language: Reference* documents the SELECT statement, which selects observations based on a condition; its action is equivalent to a series of IF-THEN/ELSE statements. If you have a long series of conditions and actions, the DATA step may be easier to read if you write them in a SELECT group.

□ *SAS Language: Reference* provides information on the IN operator. You can use the IN operator to shorten a comparison when you are comparing a value to a series of numeric or character constants (not variables or expressions).

Chapter 9 Creating Subsets of Observations

Introduction

This chapter explains how to create SAS data sets by selecting specific observations from existing SAS data sets. This information is useful if you want to

□ create a new SAS data set that includes only some of the observations from the input data source

□ create several new SAS data sets by writing observations from an input data source, using a single DATA step.

Input File and SAS Data Set Example

This chapter uses an example to illustrate how you can perform these tasks. At Tradewinds Travel, suppose you schedule tours to various art museums and galleries. You realize it would be convenient to keep different kinds of information in different SAS data sets. The following file contains data about your art tours:

```
Rome        3   750 Medium D'Amico
Paris       8  1680 High   Lucas
London      6  1230 High   Wilson
New York    6    .         Lucas
Madrid      3   370 Low    Torres
Amsterdam   4   580 Low
```

The fields represent the city, the number of nights spent on the tour, the cost of the land package, a rating of the budget, and the name of the guide.

You begin by creating a permanent SAS data set named PERM.ARTS. The following program creates the data set, and Output 9.1 displays it:

```
libname perm 'your-data-library';

data perm.arts;
    infile 'your-input-file';
    input city $ 1-9 nights 11 landcost 13-16 budget $ 18-23
        guide $ 25-32;
run;

proc print data=perm.arts;
    title 'Data Set PERM.ARTS';
run;
```

Output 9.1
Data Set
PERM.ARTS

```
                          Data Set PERM.ARTS                          1

        OBS    CITY        NIGHTS    LANDCOST    BUDGET    GUIDE

         1     Rome           3         750      Medium    D'Amico
         2     Paris          8        1680      High      Lucas
         3     London         6        1230      High      Wilson
         4     New York       6          .                 Lucas
         5     Madrid         3         370      Low       Torres
         6     Amsterdam      4         580      Low
```

Selecting Observations for a New SAS Data Set

There are two ways to select specific observations in a SAS data set when creating a new SAS data set:

1. Delete the observations that don't meet a condition, keeping only the ones that you want.

2. Accept only the observations that meet a condition.

Deleting Observations Based on a Condition

To delete an observation, first identify it with an IF condition; then use a DELETE statement in the THEN clause:

IF *condition* **THEN DELETE;**

Processing the DELETE statement for an observation causes the SAS System not to output that observation and to return immediately to the beginning of the DATA step for a new observation. For example, suppose that you want to delete observations containing a missing value for LANDCOST:

```
if landcost=. then delete;
```

Using the statement above in the following program produces Output 9.2:

```
data remove;
   set perm.arts;
   if landcost=. then delete;
run;

proc print data=remove;
   title 'Deleting Observations That Lack a Land Cost';
run;
```

Output 9.2
Deleting
Observations
Having a
Particular Value

```
               Deleting Observations That Lack a Land Cost                1

    OBS    CITY        NIGHTS    LANDCOST    BUDGET    GUIDE

     1     Rome           3        750       Medium    D'Amico
     2     Paris          8       1680       High      Lucas
     3     London         6       1230       High      Wilson
     4     Madrid         3        370       Low       Torres
     5     Amsterdam      4        580       Low
```

You can also delete observations as you input them from an external file. The following DATA step produces the same SAS data set as the one in Output 9.2, as Output 9.3 shows:

```
data remove2;
   infile 'your-input-file';
   input city $ 1-9 nights 11 landcost 13-16 budget $ 18-23
         guide $ 25-32;
   if landcost=. then delete;
run;

proc print data=remove2;
   title 'Deleting Observations While Inputting Them';
run;
```

Output 9.3
Deleting
Observations
While Reading
from an External
File

```
               Deleting Observations While Inputting Them                 1

    OBS    CITY        NIGHTS    LANDCOST    BUDGET    GUIDE

     1     Rome           3        750       Medium    D'Amico
     2     Paris          8       1680       High      Lucas
     3     London         6       1230       High      Wilson
     4     Madrid         3        370       Low       Torres
     5     Amsterdam      4        580       Low
```

Accepting Observations Based on a Condition

Suppose you decide to produce a data set that contains only tours lasting six nights. One way to make the selection is to delete observations in which the value of NIGHTS is not equal to 6:

```
if nights ne 6 then delete;
```

A more straightforward way is to select only observations meeting the criterion. The *subsetting IF statement* selects the observations you specify. It contains only a condition:

IF *condition*;

The implicit action in a subsetting IF statement is always the same: if the condition is true, continue processing the observation; if it is false, stop processing the observation and return to the top of the DATA step for a new observation. The statement is called subsetting because the result is a subset of the original observations. For example, if you want to select only observations in which the value of NIGHTS is equal to 6, you specify the following statement:

```
if nights=6;
```

Using the statement above in the following DATA step produces the data set shown in Output 9.4:

```
data subset6;
   set perm.arts;
   if nights=6;
run;

proc print data=subset6;
   title 'Producing a Subset with the Subsetting IF Statement';
run;
```

Output 9.4
Selecting Observations with a Subsetting IF Statement

```
          Producing a Subset with the Subsetting IF Statement          1

     OBS      CITY      NIGHTS    LANDCOST    BUDGET    GUIDE

      1      London        6        1230       High     Wilson
      2      New York      6          .                 Lucas
```

Comparing the DELETE and Subsetting IF Statements

The main reasons for choosing between a DELETE statement and a subsetting IF statement involve convenience:

□ It is usually easier to choose the statement that requires the fewest comparisons to identify the condition.

□ It is usually easier to think in positive terms than negative ones (this favors the subsetting IF).

One additional situation favors the subsetting IF: it is the safer method if your data have missing or misspelled values. Consider the following situation.

Suppose your manager asks you to produce a SAS data set of low- to medium-priced tours. Knowing that the values of BUDGET are `Low`, `Medium`, and `High`, you originally believe it is simplest to delete observations with a value of `High`. You write the following program, and Output 9.5 shows the result:

```
    /* first attempt */
data lowmed;
   set perm.arts;
   if upcase(budget)='HIGH' then delete;
run;

proc print data=lowmed;
   title 'Deleting High-Priced Tours';
run;
```

Output 9.5
Producing a
Subset by Deletion

```
                        Deleting High-Priced Tours                          1

     OBS   CITY         NIGHTS   LANDCOST   BUDGET    GUIDE

      1    Rome            3       750      Medium    D'Amico
      2    New York        6        .                 Lucas
      3    Madrid          3       370      Low       Torres
      4    Amsterdam       4       580      Low
```

Data set LOWMED contains both the tours you want and the tour to New York, which is erroneous because the value of BUDGET for the New York observation is missing. Using a subsetting IF statement ensures that the data set contains exactly the observations you want. This DATA step creates the subset with a subsetting IF statement, and Output 9.6 displays it:

```
    /* a safer method */
data lowmed2;
   set perm.arts;
   if upcase(budget)='MEDIUM' or upcase(budget)='LOW';
run;
```

```
proc print data=lowmed2;
   title 'Using Subsetting IF for an Exact Selection';
run;
```

Output 9.6
Producing an
Exact Subset with
Subsetting IF

```
                Using Subsetting IF for an Exact Selection            1

   OBS    CITY        NIGHTS   LANDCOST   BUDGET    GUIDE

    1     Rome          3        750      Medium    D'Amico
    2     Madrid        3        370      Low       Torres
    3     Amsterdam     4        580      Low
```

Selecting Observations for Multiple New SAS Data Sets

The SAS System allows you to create multiple SAS data sets in a single DATA step. This section shows you how to direct observations to the proper SAS data set when you are creating more than one data set in a DATA step.

Writing Observations to Multiple SAS Data Sets

Using an OUTPUT statement is an easy way to write observations to multiple SAS data sets:

OUTPUT *<SAS-data-set>* ;

When you use an OUTPUT statement without specifying a data set name, the SAS System writes the current observation to all data sets named in the DATA statement. If you want to write observations to a selected data set, specify that data set name directly in the OUTPUT statement. Any data set name appearing in the OUTPUT statement must also appear in the DATA statement. In the next example, the SAS System writes observations to two different data sets because both of the data sets are specified in OUTPUT statements.

Suppose you want to create two SAS data sets: one for tours guided by Ms. Lucas and one for tours led by other guides. Name both data sets in the DATA statement and select the observations with IF conditions. Use an OUTPUT statement in the THEN and ELSE clauses to output the observations to the data set you specify. Output 9.7 shows the results.

```
data ltour othrtour;
   set perm.arts;
   if guide='Lucas' then output ltour;
   else output othrtour;
run;

proc print data=ltour;
   title "Data Set with Guide='Lucas'";
run;
```

```
proc print data=othrtour;
   title "Data Set with Other Guides";
run;
```

Output 9.7
Creating Two Data Sets at Once

```
                    Data Set with Guide='Lucas'                    1

        OBS    CITY        NIGHTS    LANDCOST    BUDGET    GUIDE

         1     Paris          8        1680       High     Lucas
         2     New York       6          .                 Lucas
```

```
                    Data Set with Other Guides                     2

        OBS    CITY        NIGHTS    LANDCOST    BUDGET    GUIDE

         1     Rome           3         750      Medium    D'Amico
         2     London         6        1230      High      Wilson
         3     Madrid         3         370      Low       Torres
         4     Amsterdam      4         580      Low
```

Note that when you name more than one data set in a single DATA statement, the last name on the DATA statement (OTHRTOUR in the previous example) is the most recently created data set and the one that procedures use by default. To use another data set, such as LTOUR, specify it in the DATA= option in the PROC statement. In the previous example, both PROC PRINT statements use the DATA= option. The DATA= option is required in order to print LTOUR, and using it to print OTHRTOUR makes the program easier to read.

Using an OUTPUT statement suppresses the automatic output of observations at the end of the DATA step. Therefore, if you plan to use any OUTPUT statements in a DATA step, you must program all output for that step with OUTPUT statements. For example, in the previous DATA step you sent output to both LTOUR and OTHRTOUR. For comparison, suppose you omit the ELSE statement from the following DATA step. Output 9.8 shows the SAS log that results.

```
data ltour2 othrtou2;
   set perm.arts;
   if guide='Lucas' then output ltour2;
run;

proc print data=ltour2;
   title "Data Set with Guide='Lucas'";
run;

proc print data=othrtou2;
   title "Data Set with Other Guides";
run;
```

Output 9.8
Failing to Direct
Output to a
Second Data Set

```
7               data ltour2 othrtou2;
8                  set perm.arts;
9                  if guide='Lucas' then output ltour2;
10              run;

NOTE: The data set WORK.LTOUR2 has 2 observations and 5 variables.
NOTE: The data set WORK.OTHRTOU2 has 0 observations and 5 variables.

11
12              proc print data=ltour2;
13                 title "Data Set with Guide='Lucas'";
14              run;

NOTE: The PROCEDURE PRINT printed page 1.

15
16              proc print data=othrtou2;
17                 title "Data Set with Other Guides";
18              run;

NOTE: No observations in data set WORK.OTHRTOU2.
```

No observations are written to OTHRTOU2 because you didn't direct the output to it.

Understanding the OUTPUT Statement

An OUTPUT statement tells the SAS System to output the observation when the OUTPUT statement is processed, not at the end of the DATA step. For example, suppose you want to indicate the number of days in Ms. Lucas' and other guides' tours. At first you write the following DATA step, placing the assignment statement after the IF-THEN/ELSE group. Output 9.9 shows the result:

```
/* first attempt to combine assignment and OUTPUT statements */
data lday othrday;
   set perm.arts;
   if guide='Lucas' then output lday;
   else output othrday;
   days=nights+1;
run;

proc print data=lday;
   title "Number of Days in Lucas's Tours";
run;

proc print data=othrday;
   title "Number of Days in Other Guides' Tours";
run;
```

Output 9.9
Outputting
Observations
before Assigning
Values

```
                         Number of Days in Lucas's Tours                      1

          OBS    CITY        NIGHTS    LANDCOST    BUDGET    GUIDE    DAYS

           1     Paris          8        1680       High     Lucas     .
           2     New York       6          .                 Lucas     .
```

```
                      Number of Days in Other Guides' Tours                   2

          OBS    CITY        NIGHTS    LANDCOST    BUDGET    GUIDE     DAYS

           1     Rome           3         750      Medium    D'Amico    .
           2     London         6        1230      High      Wilson     .
           3     Madrid         3         370      Low       Torres     .
           4     Amsterdam      4         580      Low                  .
```

The value of DAYS is missing in all observations because the OUTPUT statement writes the observation to the SAS data sets before the assignment statement is processed. To have the value appear in the data sets, use the assignment statement before you use the OUTPUT statement. The following program shows the correct position, and the results appear in Output 9.10:

```
    /* correct position of assignment statement */
data lday2 othrday2;
   set perm.arts;
   days=nights+1;
   if guide='Lucas' then output lday2;
   else output othrday2;
run;

proc print data=lday2;
   title "Number of Days in Lucas's Tours";
run;

proc print data=othrday2;
   title "Number of Days in Other Guides' Tours";
run;
```

Output 9.10
Assigning Values
before Outputting
Observations

```
                         Number of Days in Lucas's Tours                      1

          OBS    CITY        NIGHTS    LANDCOST    BUDGET    GUIDE     DAYS

           1     Paris          8        1680       High     Lucas      9
           2     New York       6          .                 Lucas      7
```

```
                      Number of Days in Other Guides' Tours                   2

          OBS    CITY        NIGHTS    LANDCOST    BUDGET    GUIDE     DAYS

           1     Rome           3         750      Medium    D'Amico     4
           2     London         6        1230      High      Wilson      7
           3     Madrid         3         370      Low       Torres      4
           4     Amsterdam      4         580      Low                   5
```

After the SAS System processes an OUTPUT statement, the observation remains in the program data vector and you can continue programming with it. You can even output it again to the same SAS data set or to a different one. The following example creates two pairs of data sets, one pair based on the name of the tour guide and one pair based on the number of nights. Output 9.11 shows the results.

```
data ltour othrtour weektour daytour;
   set perm.arts;
   if guide='Lucas' then output ltour;
   else output othrtour;
   if nights>=6 then output weektour;
   else output daytour;
run;

proc print data=ltour;
   title "Lucas's Tours";
run;

proc print data=othrtour;
   title "Other Guides' Tours";
run;

proc print data=weektour;
   title 'Tours Lasting a Week or More';
run;

proc print data=daytour;
   title 'Tours Lasting Less Than a Week';
run;
```

Output 9.11
Assigning
Observations to
More than One
Data Set

```
                            Lucas's Tours                                1

        OBS    CITY      NIGHTS    LANDCOST    BUDGET    GUIDE

         1     Paris        8        1680       High     Lucas
         2     New York     6          .                 Lucas
```

```
                          Other Guides' Tours                            2

        OBS    CITY       NIGHTS    LANDCOST    BUDGET    GUIDE

         1     Rome         3         750       Medium    D'Amico
         2     London       6        1230       High      Wilson
         3     Madrid       3         370       Low       Torres
         4     Amsterdam    4         580       Low
```

```
                    Tours Lasting a Week or More                   3
          OBS    CITY       NIGHTS    LANDCOST    BUDGET    GUIDE

           1     Paris         8        1680      High      Lucas
           2     London        6        1230      High      Wilson
           3     New York      6          .                 Lucas
```

```
                    Tours Lasting Less Than a Week                 4
          OBS    CITY       NIGHTS    LANDCOST    BUDGET    GUIDE

           1     Rome          3         750      Medium    D'Amico
           2     Madrid        3         370      Low       Torres
           3     Amsterdam     4         580      Low
```

The first IF-THEN/ELSE group outputs all observations to either data set LTOUR or OTHRTOUR. The second IF-THEN/ELSE group outputs the same observations to a different pair of data sets, WEEKTOUR and DAYTOUR. This repetition is possible because each observation remains in the program data vector after the first OUTPUT statement is processed and can be output again.

SAS Tools

This chapter discusses the following statements:

DATA <*libref.-1*>*SAS-data-set-1*< . . . <*libref-n.*>*SAS-data-set-n*>;
    names the *SAS-data-set(s)* to be created in the DATA step.

DELETE;
    deletes the current observation. The DELETE statement is usually used as part of an IF-THEN/ELSE group.

IF *condition*;
    tests whether the *condition* is true. If it is true, the SAS System continues processing the current observation; if it isn't true, the SAS System stops processing the observation, doesn't add it to the SAS data set, and returns to the top of the DATA step. The *conditions* used are the same as in the IF-THEN/ELSE statements. This type of IF statement is called a subsetting IF statement because it produces a subset of the original observations.

OUTPUT <*SAS-data-set*>;
    immediately writes the current observation to the *SAS-data-set*. The observation remains in the program data vector, and you can continue programming with it, including outputting it again if you desire. When an OUTPUT statement appears in a DATA step, the SAS System doesn't automatically output observations to the SAS data set; you must specify the destination for all output in the DATA step with OUTPUT statements. Any SAS data set you specify in an OUTPUT statement must also appear in the DATA statement.

Learning More

□ Chapter 4, "Starting with SAS Data Sets," discusses using the FIRSTOBS= and OBS= data set options to select observations from the beginning, middle, or end of a SAS data set. They are documented completely in *SAS Language: Reference, Version 6, First Edition.*

□ Chapter 4 also discusses using the DROP= and KEEP= data set options to output a subset of variables to a SAS data set.

□ Chapter 8 "Acting on Selected Observations," discusses comparison and logical operators. They are also described in *SAS Language: Reference.*

□ Chapter 24, "Printing Detail Reports," discusses using the WHERE statement in PROC steps. The WHERE statement selects observations based on a condition. Its action is similar to that of a subsetting IF statement. The WHERE statement is extremely useful in PROC steps, and it can also be useful in DATA steps. The WHERE statement selects observations before they enter the program data vector (in contrast to the subsetting IF statement, which selects observations already in the program data vector).

   Note: In some cases, the same condition in a WHERE statement in the DATA step and in a subsetting IF statement produces different subsets. The difference is described in the discussion of the WHERE statement in *SAS Language: Reference.* Be sure you understand the difference before you use the WHERE statement in the DATA step. With that caution in mind, a WHERE statement can increase the efficiency of the DATA step considerably.

□ *SAS Language: Reference* completely documents the IF-THEN/ELSE, DELETE, and OUTPUT statements.

Chapter **10** Working with Grouped or Sorted Observations

Introduction

Some tasks depend on your being able to group observations according to the values of a particular variable. At times you may also need to sort observations by a variable, such as alphabetically. In this chapter you learn how to work with

☐ observations in groups and how to put the observations into groups if they are not already in them

☐ sorted observations and how to sort the observations if necessary.

Input File and SAS Data Set Example

At Tradewinds Travel, you're working with tours that emphasize either architecture or scenery. If you group the observations for those tours, the SAS System can produce reports on each group separately. In addition, if you need to put the observations in alphabetical order by country, the SAS System can reorganize them. The external file contains the following records:

```
Spain        architecture  10   510 World
Japan        architecture   8   720 Express
Switzerland  scenery        9   734 World
France       architecture   8   575 World
Ireland      scenery        7   558 Express
New Zealand  scenery       16  1489 Southsea
Italy        architecture   8   468 Express
Greece       scenery       12   698 Express
```

The first field is the name of the country. Next comes the tour's area of emphasis, followed by the number of nights on the tour, the cost of the land package, and the name of the tour vendor.

You begin by creating a permanent SAS data set named SAVE.TYPE. The following program creates the data set, and Output 10.1 displays it:

```
libname save 'your-data-library';

data save.type;
   infile 'your-input-file';
   input country $ 1-11 tourtype $ 13-24 nights
         landcost vendor $;
run;

proc print data=save.type;
   title 'Data Set SAVE.TYPE';
run;
```

Output 10.1
Data Set
SAVE.TYPE

```
                         Data Set SAVE.TYPE                          1

   OBS    COUNTRY        TOURTYPE       NIGHTS    LANDCOST    VENDOR

    1     Spain          architecture     10        510      World
    2     Japan          architecture      8        720      Express
    3     Switzerland    scenery           9        734      World
    4     France         architecture      8        575      World
    5     Ireland        scenery           7        558      Express
    6     New Zealand    scenery          16       1489      Southsea
    7     Italy          architecture      8        468      Express
    8     Greece         scenery          12        698      Express
```

Working with Grouped Data

The basic method for working with grouped data is to use a BY statement:

BY *list-of-variables*;

To use a BY statement, the data must meet these conditions:

1. The observations must be in a SAS data set, not an external file.

2. The variables that define the groups must appear in the BY statement.

3. All observations in a group must appear together in the data set.

You can create the groups in several ways. For example, you may decide to input all the tours that feature architecture and then all those that feature scenery. If the data are in a SAS data set but aren't arranged in the groups you want, you can use the SORT procedure (discussed in the next section) to make the groups. This chapter concentrates on using the BY statement in the DATA step and in the SORT procedure; other chapters in this book show using the BY statement with other SAS procedures.

Grouping Observations with the SORT Procedure

Suppose you want to group the observations by the values of TOURTYPE, `architecture` and `scenery`, so you write the following PROC SORT step:

```
proc sort data=save.type out=type2;
    by tourtype;
run;
```

The SORT procedure sorts data set SAVE.TYPE alphabetically according to the values of TOURTYPE; the sorted observations go into a new data set named TYPE2. (If you omit the OUT= option, the sorted version of the data set is named SAVE.TYPE and becomes the current version.) The SORT procedure does not produce printed output; instead, a message in the SAS log tells you that the SORT procedure was executed, as Output 10.2 shows.

Output 10.2
Message That the
SORT Procedure
Has Executed
Successfully

```
7          proc sort data=save.type out=type2;
8              by tourtype;
9          run;
NOTE: SAS sort was used.
NOTE: The data set WORK.TYPE2 has 8 observations and 5 variables.
```

To see the sorted data set, add a PROC PRINT step to the program. Output 10.3 shows the result.

```
proc sort data=save.type out=type2;
    by tourtype;
run;

proc print data=type2;
    var tourtype country nights landcost vendor;
    title 'The Simplest Sort--One Variable, Default Order of Groups';
run;
```

Output 10.3
Performing a
Simple Sort

```
          The Simplest Sort--One Variable, Default Order of Groups           1

   OBS    TOURTYPE       COUNTRY        NIGHTS    LANDCOST    VENDOR

     1    architecture   Spain             10        510      World
     2    architecture   Japan              8        720      Express
     3    architecture   France             8        575      World
     4    architecture   Italy              8        468      Express
     5    scenery        Switzerland        9        734      World
     6    scenery        Ireland            7        558      Express
     7    scenery        New Zealand       16       1489      Southsea
     8    scenery        Greece            12        698      Express
```

By default, the SAS System arranges groups in ascending order of the BY values, smallest to largest. Sorting a data set doesn't change the order of the variables within it. However, most examples in this chapter use a VAR statement in the PRINT procedure to display the BY variable in the first column.

(The PRINT procedure and other procedures used in this book can also produce a separate report for each BY group.)

Grouping by More than One Variable

You can group observations by as many variables as you want. This example groups observations by TOURTYPE, VENDOR, and LANDCOST. Output 10.4 shows the result.

```
proc sort data=save.type out=type3;
   by tourtype vendor landcost;
run;

proc print data=type3;
   var tourtype vendor landcost country nights;
   title 'Observations Grouped by Type of Tour, Vendor, and Price';
run;
```

Output 10.4
Grouping by
Several Variables

```
         Observations Grouped by Type of Tour, Vendor, and Price          1

   OBS   TOURTYPE        VENDOR      LANDCOST   COUNTRY        NIGHTS

    1    architecture    Express        468    Italy             8
    2    architecture    Express        720    Japan             8
    3    architecture    World          510    Spain            10
    4    architecture    World          575    France            8
    5    scenery         Express        558    Ireland           7
    6    scenery         Express        698    Greece           12
    7    scenery         Southsea      1489    New Zealand      16
    8    scenery         World          734    Switzerland       9
```

As Output 10.4 shows, the SAS System groups the observations by the first variable named; within those groups, by the second variable named; and so on. The groups defined by all variables contain only one observation each. In this example, no two observations have the same values for all of these observations.

Arranging Groups in Descending Order

In the data sets grouped by TOURTYPE, the group for `architecture` comes before the group for `scenery` because `architecture` begins with an "a"; "a" is smaller than "s" in computer processing. (The order of characters, known as their *collating sequence*, is discussed in "Special Topic: Collating Sequences" later in this chapter.) To produce a descending order for a particular variable, place the DESCENDING option before the name of the variable affected in the BY statement of the SORT procedure. The next example groups observations in descending order of TOURTYPE but ascending order of VENDOR and LANDCOST. Output 10.5 shows the result.

```
proc sort data=save.type out=type4;
   by descending tourtype vendor landcost;
run;
```

```
proc print data=type4;
   var tourtype vendor landcost country nights;
   title 'Descending and Ascending Orders';
run;
```

Output 10.5
Combining
Descending and
Ascending Sorts

```
                    Descending and Ascending Orders                        1

     OBS    TOURTYPE       VENDOR       LANDCOST    COUNTRY       NIGHTS

      1     scenery        Express        558       Ireland          7
      2     scenery        Express        698       Greece          12
      3     scenery        Southsea      1489       New Zealand     16
      4     scenery        World          734       Switzerland      9
      5     architecture   Express        468       Italy            8
      6     architecture   Express        720       Japan            8
      7     architecture   World          510       Spain           10
      8     architecture   World          575       France           8
```

Finding the First or Last Observation in a Group

Suppose you want to create a data set containing only the least expensive tour that features architecture and the least expensive tour that features scenery. How can you do that without stopping to display the data set and seeing which observations to select?

First, sort the data set by TOURTYPE and LANDCOST. The resulting data set appears in Output 10.6.

```
proc sort data=save.type out=type5;
   by tourtype landcost;
run;
```

```
proc print data=type5;
   var tourtype landcost country nights vendor;
   title 'Tours Arranged by TOURTYPE and LANDCOST';
run;
```

Output 10.6
Examining Tours
to Find the Least
Expensive Ones

```
                 Tours Arranged by TOURTYPE and LANDCOST                   1

    OBS    TOURTYPE       LANDCOST    COUNTRY       NIGHTS    VENDOR

     1     architecture     468       Italy            8      Express
     2     architecture     510       Spain           10      World
     3     architecture     575       France           8      World
     4     architecture     720       Japan            8      Express
     5     scenery          558       Ireland          7      Express
     6     scenery          698       Greece          12      Express
     7     scenery          734       Switzerland      9      World
     8     scenery         1489       New Zealand     16      Southsea
```

Because you sorted LANDCOST in ascending order, the first observation in each value of TOURTYPE has the lowest value of LANDCOST. If you can locate the first observation in each BY group in a DATA step, you can use a subsetting IF statement to select that observation. But how can you locate the first observation with each value of TOURTYPE?

When you use a BY statement in a DATA step, the SAS System automatically creates two additional variables for each variable in the BY statement. One is named FIRST.*variable*, where *variable* is the name of the BY variable, and the other is named LAST.*variable*. Their values are either 1 or 0. They exist in the program data vector and are available for DATA step programming, but the SAS System does not add them to the SAS data set being created. For example, suppose you begin a DATA step with these statements:

```
data lowcost;
   set type5;
   by tourtype;
   more SAS statements
```

The BY statement causes the SAS System to create one variable called FIRST.TOURTYPE and another variable called LAST.TOURTYPE. When the SAS System processes the first observation with the value `architecture`, the value of FIRST.TOURTYPE is 1; in other observations with the value `architecture`, it is 0. Similarly, when the SAS System processes the last observation with the value `architecture`, the value of LAST.TOURTYPE is 1; in other `architecture` observations, it is a 0. The same thing happens to observations in the `scenery` group.

Because the SAS System doesn't write FIRST. and LAST. variables to the output data set, you can't display their values with the PRINT procedure. Therefore, the simplest method of displaying the values of FIRST. and LAST. variables is to assign their values to other variables. This example assigns the value of FIRST.TOURTYPE to a variable named FRSTTOUR and the value of LAST.TOURTYPE to a variable named LASTTOUR. Output 10.7 shows the result.

```
data temp;
   set type5;
   by tourtype;
   frsttour=first.tourtype;
   lasttour=last.tourtype;
run;

proc print data=temp;
   var country tourtype frsttour lasttour;
   title 'Representing FIRST.TOURTYPE and LAST.TOURTYPE';
run;
```

Output 10.7
Representing FIRST. and LAST. Values

```
     Representing FIRST.TOURTYPE and LAST.TOURTYPE              1

  OBS   COUNTRY        TOURTYPE        FRSTTOUR      LASTTOUR

   1    Italy          architecture        1             0
   2    Spain          architecture        0             0
   3    France         architecture        0             0
   4    Japan          architecture        0             1
   5    Ireland        scenery             1             0
   6    Greece         scenery             0             0
   7    Switzerland    scenery             0             0
   8    New Zealand    scenery             0             1
```

In this data set, Italy is the first observation with the value `architecture`; for that observation, the value of FIRST.TOURTYPE is 1. Italy isn't the last observation with the value `architecture`, so its value of LAST.TOURTYPE is 0. The observations for Spain and France are neither the first nor the last with the value `architecture`; both FIRST.TOURTYPE and LAST.TOURTYPE are 0 for them. Japan is the last with the value `architecture`; the value of LAST.TOURTYPE is 1. The same rules apply to observations in the `scenery` group.

Now you're ready to use FIRST.TOURTYPE in a subsetting IF statement. When the data are sorted by TOURTYPE and LANDCOST, selecting the first observation in each type of tour gives you the lowest price of any tour in that category. The following program produces Output 10.8:

```
proc sort data=save.type out=type5;
   by tourtype landcost;
run;

data lowcost;
   set type5;
   by tourtype;
   if first.tourtype;
run;

proc print data=lowcost;
   title 'Least Expensive Tour for Each Type of Tour';
run;
```

Output 10.8
Selecting One
Observation from
Each BY Group

```
                     Least Expensive Tour for Each Type of Tour                   1

        OBS    COUNTRY    TOURTYPE        NIGHTS      LANDCOST     VENDOR

         1     Italy      architecture       8          468       Express
         2     Ireland    scenery            7          558       Express
```

Working with Sorted Data

The preceding sections show how to group data according to values of BY variables. By default, groups appear in ascending order of the BY values.

In some cases you want to emphasize the order in which the observations are sorted, not the fact that they can be grouped. For example, you may want to alphabetize the tours by country.

To sort your data in a particular order, use the SORT procedure just as you do for grouped data.* When the sorted order is more important than the grouping, you usually want only one observation with a given BY value in the resulting data set. Therefore, you may need to remove duplicate observations.

---

* The SORT procedure accesses either a sorting utility supplied as part of the SAS System or a sorting utility supplied by the host operating system. All examples in this book use the SAS sorting utility. Some host utilities don't accept various options, including the NODUPLICATES option described later in this chapter. The default sorting utility is set by your site. For more information on the utilities available to you, refer to the documentation provided by the vendor for your host system.

Sorting Data with the SORT Procedure

The following example sorts data set TYPE by COUNTRY. Output 10.9 shows the result.

```
proc sort data=save.type out=type6;
   by country;
run;

proc print data=type6;
   title 'Alphabetical Order by Country';
run;
```

Output 10.9
Sorting Data

```
                      Alphabetical Order by Country                     1

    OBS    COUNTRY        TOURTYPE        NIGHTS    LANDCOST    VENDOR

     1     France         architecture      8         575      World
     2     Greece         scenery          12         698      Express
     3     Ireland        scenery           7         558      Express
     4     Italy          architecture      8         468      Express
     5     Japan          architecture      8         720      Express
     6     New Zealand    scenery          16        1489      Southsea
     7     Spain          architecture     10         510      World
     8     Switzerland    scenery           9         734      World
```

Deleting Duplicate Observations

Suppose the external file contains a duplicate observation for Switzerland, as shown here:

```
Spain         architecture  10   510 World
Japan         architecture   8   720 Express
Switzerland   scenery        9   734 World
France        architecture   8   575 World
Switzerland   scenery        9   734 World
Ireland       scenery        7   558 Express
New Zealand   scenery       16  1489 Southsea
Italy         architecture   8   468 Express
Greece        scenery       12   698 Express
```

The following DATA step creates a permanent SAS data set named SAVE.DUPOBS. Output 10.10 shows that this data set has nine observations, whereas data set SAVE.TYPE has eight:

```
libname save 'your-data-library';

data save.dupobs;
    infile 'your-input-file';
    input country $ 1-11 tourtype $ 13-24 nights
        landcost vendor $;
run;

proc print data=save.dupobs;
    title 'Data Set SAVE.DUPOBS';
run;
```

Output 10.10
Data Set
SAVE.DUPOBS

```
                            Data Set SAVE.DUPOBS                        1

    OBS    COUNTRY        TOURTYPE        NIGHTS    LANDCOST    VENDOR

     1     Spain          architecture      10        510      World
     2     Japan          architecture       8        720      Express
     3     Switzerland    scenery            9        734      World
     4     France         architecture       8        575      World
     5     Switzerland    scenery            9        734      World
     6     Ireland        scenery            7        558      Express
     7     New Zealand    scenery           16       1489      Southsea
     8     Italy          architecture       8        468      Express
     9     Greece         scenery           12        698      Express
```

The NODUPLICATES option in the SORT procedure deletes any observation that duplicates the values of all variables (both BY variables and other variables) of another observation in the data set. The following steps sort SAVE.DUPOBS, remove the duplicate observation, and create a new data set called FIXED. Output 10.11 shows the message that appears in the SAS log and the data set that results.

```
proc sort data=save.dupobs out=fixed noduplicates;
    by country;
run;

proc print data=fixed;
    title 'Removing a Duplicate Observation with PROC SORT';
run;
```

Output 10.11
Sorting with the
NODUPLICATES
Option

```
4           proc sort data=save.dupobs out=fixed noduplicates;
5               by country;
6           run;

NOTE: SAS sort was used.
NOTE: 1 duplicate observations were deleted.
NOTE: The data set WORK.FIXED has 8 observations and 5 variables.

7
8           proc print data=fixed;
9               title 'Removing a Duplicate Observation with PROC SORT';
10          run;

NOTE: The PROCEDURE PRINT printed page 1.
```

```
                 Removing a Duplicate Observation with PROC SORT             1

     OBS    COUNTRY      TOURTYPE       NIGHTS    LANDCOST   VENDOR

      1     France       architecture      8        575     World
      2     Greece       scenery          12        698     Express
      3     Ireland      scenery           7        558     Express
      4     Italy        architecture      8        468     Express
      5     Japan        architecture      8        720     Express
      6     New Zealand  scenery          16       1489     Southsea
      7     Spain        architecture     10        510     World
      8     Switzerland  scenery           9        734     World
```

Special Topic: Collating Sequences

Both numeric and character variables can be sorted into ascending or descending order. For numeric variables, ascending or descending order is easy to understand, but what about the order of characters? Character values include uppercase and lowercase letters, special characters, and the digits 0 through 9 when treated as characters rather than as numbers. How does the SAS System sort these characters?

The order in which characters sort is called a *collating sequence*. By default, the SAS System sorts characters in one of two sequences: EBCDIC or ASCII, depending on the host environment under which the SAS System is running. For reference, both sequences are displayed here.

As long as you work under a single host, you seldom need to think about the details of collating sequences. However, when you transfer files from a host using EBCDIC to one using ASCII or vice versa, character values sorted on one host aren't necessarily in the correct order for the other host. The simplest solution to the problem is to re-sort character data (not numeric data) on the destination host. Refer to the documentation provided by the vendor for the host system(s) you are using for detailed information on collating sequences for that system(s).

ASCII Collating Sequence
The following operating systems use the ASCII collating sequence:

AOS/VS   PRIMOS®
MS-DOS®   UNIX® and its derivatives
OS/2®   VMS
PC DOS

From the smallest to the largest displayable character, the English-language ASCII sequence is

blank!"#$%&'()*+,−./0123456789:;<=>?@
ABCDEFGHIJKLMNOPQRSTUVWXYZ [\]^_`
abcdefghijklmnopqrstuvwxyz {|}~

The main features of the ASCII sequence are that digits are smaller than uppercase letters and uppercase letters are smaller than lowercase ones. The blank is the smallest displayable character, as shown here:

blank < digits < uppercase letters < lowercase letters

EBCDIC Collating Sequence
The following operating systems use the EBCDIC collating sequence:

CMS
MVS
VSE

From the smallest to largest displayable character, the English-language EBCDIC sequence is

blank¢.<(+ | &!$*);¬−/¦,%_>?`:#@'="
abcdefghijklmnopqr~stuvwxyz
{ABCDEFGHI}JKLMNOPQR\STUVWXYZ
0123456789

The main features of the EBCDIC sequence are that lowercase letters are smaller than uppercase ones and digits are larger than uppercase letters. The blank is the smallest displayable character, as shown here:

blank < lowercase letters < uppercase letters < digits

PRIMOS is a registered trademark of Prime Computer, Inc.
MS-DOS is a registered trademark of Microsoft Corp.
UNIX is a registered trademark of AT&T.
OS/2 is a registered trademark of International Business Machines Corp.

SAS Tools

This chapter discusses the SORT procedure and its BY statement and the DATA step BY statement.

PROC SORT <DATA=*SAS-data-set*> <OUT=*SAS-data-set*>
        <NODUPLICATES>;
    BY <DESCENDING> *variable-1* < . . . <DESCENDING> *variable-n*>;

PROC SORT <DATA=*SAS-data-set*> <OUT=*SAS-data-set*>
        <NODUPLICATES>;
        sorts a SAS data set by the values of variables listed in the BY statement.
        If you specify the OUT= option, the sorted data are stored in a different
        SAS data set than the input data. The NODUPLICATES option tells
        PROC SORT to eliminate identical observations.

BY <DESCENDING> *variable-1* < . . . <DESCENDING> *variable-n*>;
        sorts a SAS data set by the values of the variables listed in the BY
        statement. The BY statement can contain any number of variables. When
        more than one BY variable is present, the SAS System arranges all the
        observations in order by the first variable listed; then, within each of
        those groups, by the second variable listed; within each of those groups,
        by the third variable listed, and so on. By default, the SAS System
        arranges the groups in ascending order (smallest value to largest). The
        DESCENDING option reverses the order of groups for the variable that
        follows it (that is, largest to smallest).

The syntax for the BY statement in the DATA step follows:

BY <DESCENDING> *variable-1* < . . . <DESCENDING> *variable-n*>;
        in a DATA step causes the SAS System to create FIRST. and LAST.
        variables for each variable named in the statement. The value of
        FIRST.*variable-1* is 1 for the first observation with a given BY value and
        0 for other observations. Similarly, the value of LAST.*variable-1* is 1 for
        the last observation for a given BY value and 0 for other observations.
        The BY statement can follow a SET, MERGE, or UPDATE statement in
        the DATA step; it can't be used with an INPUT statement. By default,
        the SAS System assumes that data being read with a BY statement are in
        ascending order of the BY values. The DESCENDING option indicates
        that values of the variable that follow are in the opposite order, that is,
        largest to smallest.

Learning More

□ Chapters 16, 17, and 18 discuss interleaving, merging, and updating SAS data sets. These operations depend on the BY statement in the DATA step. Interleaving combines data sets in sorted order (Chapter 16, "Interleaving SAS Data Sets"); match-merging joins observations identified by the value of a BY variable (Chapter 17, "Merging SAS Data Sets"); and updating uses a data set containing transactions to change values in a master file (Chapter 18, "Updating SAS Data Sets").

□ Chapter 29, "Writing Output," discusses the NOTSORTED option. The NOTSORTED option can be used in both DATA and PROC steps, except for the SORT procedure. The NOTSORTED option is useful when data are grouped according to the values of a variable, but the groups are not in ascending or descending order. Using the NOTSORTED option in the BY statement allows the SAS System to process them.

□ *SAS Language: Reference, Version 6, First Edition* documents the BY statement in the DATA step and BY-group processing in the DATA step.

□ *SAS Language: Reference* provides information on an alternative to sorting observations: creating an index that identifies the observations with particular values of a variable. For details, see the "SAS Files" chapter.

□ *SAS Procedures Guide, Version 6, Third Edition* documents the SORT procedure and the role of the BY statement in it. It also describes how to specify different sorting utilities.

  □ When you work with large data sets, plan your work so that you sort the data set as few times as possible. For example, if you need to sort a data set by STATE at the beginning of a program and by CITY within STATE later, sort the data set by STATE and CITY at the beginning of the program.

  □ To eliminate observations whose BY values duplicate BY values in other observations (but not necessarily values of other variables), use the NODUPKEY option in the SORT procedure.

  □ The SAS System can sort data in sequences other than English-language EBCDIC or ASCII. Examples include the Danish-Norwegian and Finnish/Swedish sequences.

□ The SAS documentation for your host system presents host-specific information on the SORT procedure. In general, many points about sorting data depend on the operating system and other local conditions at your site (such as whether various operating system utilities are available).

Chapter 11 Using More than One Observation in a Calculation

Introduction

This chapter deals with calculations that require more than one observation. Examples of those calculations include:

- accumulating a total across a data set or a BY group

- saving a value from one observation in order to compare it to a value in a later observation.

This chapter explains each of these situations and uses an example to illustrate them.

Input File and SAS Data Set Example

Suppose at Tradewinds Travel it's time to see how much business the company did with various tour vendors during the peak season. You need to create data sets containing the total number of people booked on tours with various vendors and the total value of the tours booked.

The following external file contains data about your Tradewinds Travel tours:

```
France       575 Express  10
Spain        510 World    12
Brazil       540 World     6
India        489 Express   .
Japan        720 Express  10
Greece       698 Express  20
New Zealand 1489 Southsea  6
Venezuela    425 World     8
Italy        468 Express   9
```

```
USSR          924 World     6
Switzerland   734 World    20
Australia    1079 Southsea 10
Ireland       558 Express   9
```

The fields represent the country toured, the cost of the land package, the name of the vendor, and the number of people booked on that tour.

You begin by creating a permanent SAS data set called OUT.TOURREV. The following program creates the data set, and Output 11.1 displays it:

```
libname out 'your-data-library';

data out.tourrev;
   infile 'your-input-file';
   input country $ 1-11 landcost vendor $ bookings;
run;

proc print data=out.tourrev;
   title 'SAS Data Set OUT.TOURREV';
run;
```

Output 11.1
Data Set
OUT.TOURREV

```
                      SAS Data Set OUT.TOURREV                        1

        OBS    COUNTRY        LANDCOST     VENDOR      BOOKINGS

         1     France           575       Express        10
         2     Spain            510       World          12
         3     Brazil           540       World           6
         4     India            489       Express         .
         5     Japan            720       Express        10
         6     Greece           698       Express        20
         7     New Zealand     1489       Southsea        6
         8     Venezuela        425       World           8
         9     Italy            468       Express         9
        10     USSR             924       World           6
        11     Switzerland      734       World          20
        12     Australia       1079       Southsea       10
        13     Ireland          558       Express         9
```

Each observation in data set OUT.TOURREV contains the cost of a tour and the number of people who booked that tour (variable BOOKINGS). Suppose you need information from more than one observation; you want to know how much money was spent with each vendor and with all vendors together. You want to store the totals in a SAS data set separate from the individual vendors' records. You also want to find the tour that produced the most revenue, land cost times the number of people who booked the tour, and store just that information in a different SAS data set.

Accumulating a Total for an Entire Data Set

In performing your calculations on the data set OUT.TOURREV, first you decide to find out the total number of people who booked tours with Tradewinds Travel. You want the result to be in data set form. Therefore, you need a variable whose value starts at 0 and increases by the number of bookings in each observation. The sum statement gives you that capability:

variable + expression;

In a sum statement, the variable on the left side of the plus sign has the value 0 before the statement is processed for the first time. Processing the statement adds the value of the *expression* on the right side of the plus sign to the initial value; the sum variable retains the new value until the next processing of the statement. The sum statement ignores a missing value for the expression; the previous total remains unchanged.

To create the total number of bookings, you write the following statement:

```
totbook+bookings;
```

Using the sum statement above in the following DATA step produces Output 11.2:

```
data total;
   set out.tourrev;
   totbook+bookings;
run;

proc print data=total;
   var country bookings totbook;
   title 'Total Tours Booked';
run;
```

Output 11.2
Accumulating a
Total for a Data
Set

```
                          Total Tours Booked                        1

          OBS    COUNTRY        BOOKINGS      TOTBOOK

           1     France            10           10
           2     Spain             12           22
           3     Brazil             6           28
           4     India              .           28
           5     Japan             10           38
           6     Greece            20           58
           7     New Zealand        6           64
           8     Venezuela          8           72
           9     Italy              9           81
          10     USSR               6           87
          11     Switzerland       20          107
          12     Australia         10          117
          13     Ireland            9          126
```

The TOTBOOK variable in the last observation of the TOTAL data set contains the total number of bookings for the year. If that is the only information you need from the data set, you can create a data set containing only one observation, the total. Use the END= option in the SET statement to create a variable whose value is 1 when the DATA step is processing the last observation and 0 for other observations:

SET *SAS-data-set* <END=*variable*>;

(The SAS System does not add the END= variable to the data set being created.) Then you can test the value of the END= variable to find the last observation.

Select the last observation with a subsetting IF statement and use a KEEP= data set option to keep only the variable TOTBOOK in the data set. The result appears in Output 11.3.

```
data total2(keep=totbook);
   set out.tourrev end=lastobs;
   totbook+bookings;
   if lastobs;
run;

proc print data=total2;
   title 'Last Observation Shows Total Tours Booked';
run;
```

Output 11.3
Selecting the Last Observation in a Data Set

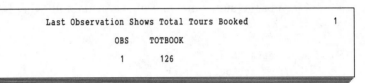

```
             Last Observation Shows Total Tours Booked              1

                          OBS     TOTBOOK

                           1        126
```

The condition in the subsetting IF statement is true when LASTOBS has the value 1. When the SAS System is processing the last observation from OUT.TOURREV, it assigns LASTOBS the value 1. Therefore, the subsetting IF statement accepts only the last observation from OUT.TOURREV, and the SAS System writes it to the data set TOTAL2.

Getting a Total for Each BY Group

You also need to find out the number of tours booked with each vendor, and you would like that information to be in data set form. Grouping by VENDOR means that you need a BY statement in the DATA step, plus a PROC SORT step if the data are not already grouped by VENDOR. To accumulate the bookings, you need a sum statement; the accumulation must begin with 0 for each vendor. You can use FIRST.VENDOR in an IF-THEN statement to set the sum variable to 0 in the first observation of each BY group. Using the following program produces Output 11.4:

```
proc sort data=out.tourrev out=out.sorttour;
   by vendor;
run;

data totalby;
   set out.sorttour;
   by vendor;
   if first.vendor then vendorbk=0;
   vendorbk+bookings;
run;

proc print data=totalby;
   title 'Setting the Sum Variable to 0 for BY Groups';
run;
```

Output 11.4
Creating Totals for
BY Groups

```
                    Setting the Sum Variable to 0 for BY Groups                   1

        OBS     COUNTRY        LANDCOST     VENDOR      BOOKINGS     VENDORBK

         1      France           575        Express        10          10
         2      India            489        Express         .          10
         3      Japan            720        Express        10          20
         4      Greece           698        Express        20          40
         5      Italy            468        Express         9          49
         6      Ireland          558        Express         9          58
         7      New Zealand     1489        Southsea        6           6
         8      Australia       1079        Southsea       10          16
         9      Spain            510        World          12          12
        10      Brazil           540        World           6          18
        11      Venezuela        425        World           8          26
        12      USSR             924        World           6          32
        13      Switzerland      734        World          20          52
```

To report the total bookings for each vendor group in data set form, you need only the variables VENDOR and VENDORBK from the last observation for each vendor; therefore, you can use the DROP= data set option to drop the variables COUNTRY, LANDCOST, and BOOKINGS. (You could have chosen to use the KEEP= data set option to keep VENDOR and VENDORBK.)

Using LAST.VENDOR in a subsetting IF statement writes only the last observation in each group to the data set TOTALBY. The following program creates data set TOTALBY and produces Output 11.5:

```
proc sort data=out.tourrev out=out.sorttour;
   by vendor;
run;

data totalby(drop=country landcost bookings);
   set out.sorttour;
   by vendor;
   if first.vendor then vendorbk=0;
   vendorbk+bookings;
   if last.vendor;
run;

proc print data=totalby;
   title 'Last Observation in BY Group Contains Group Total';
run;
```

Output 11.5
Putting Totals for
Each BY Group in
a New Data Set

```
             Last Observation in BY Group Contains Group Total           1

                OBS      VENDOR       VENDORBK

                 1       Express         58
                 2       Southsea        16
                 3       World           52
```

Writing Totals and Detail Records

Suppose you want overall information about the tours this year. In one SAS data set, you want to see information about each tour, including the total money spent on that tour. In another SAS data set, you want to see the total number of bookings with each vendor and the total money spent with that vendor. You can create these two data sets using the techniques you've learned so far.

Begin the program by creating two SAS data sets from the SAS data set OUT.SORTTOUR using the following DATA and SET statements:

```
data details vendgrps;
   set out.sorttour;
```

DETAILS is to contain the individual records, and VENDGRPS is to contain the information about vendors. The observations don't need to be grouped for DETAILS, but they need to be grouped by VENDOR for VENDGRPS.

If the data aren't already grouped by VENDOR, first use the SORT procedure. Add a BY statement to the DATA step for use with VENDGRPS.

```
proc sort data=out.tourrev out=out.sorttour;
   by vendor;
run;

data details vendgrps;
   set out.sorttour;
   by vendor;
```

The only calculation you need to make for the individual tours is the amount of money spent on each tour. Therefore, calculate the amount in an assignment statement and output the record to DETAILS.

```
money=landcost*bookings;
output details;
```

The portion of the DATA step that builds DETAILS is now complete. Because observations remain in the program data vector after an OUTPUT statement executes, you can continue using them in programming statements. The rest of the DATA step deals with information for the VENDGRPS data set.

Use the FIRST.VENDOR variable to tell when the SAS System is processing the first observation in each group. Then set the sum variables GRPBOOK and GRPMONEY to 0 in that observation. GRPBOOK totals the bookings for each vendor, and GRPMONEY totals the money. Add the following statements to the DATA step:*

```
if first.vendor then
   do;
      grpbook=0;
      grpmoney=0;
   end;
grpbook+bookings;
grpmoney+money;
```

The last observation in each BY group contains the totals for that vendor; therefore, use the following statement to output the last observation to data set VENDGRPS:

```
if last.vendor then output vendgrps;
```

As a final step, remove extraneous variables from the two data sets so that each data set has just the variables you want. The following program incorporates these statements, and Output 11.6 shows the two data sets:

```
proc sort data=out.tourrev out=out.sorttour;
   by vendor;
run;

data details(drop=grpbook grpmoney)
     vendgrps(keep=vendor grpbook grpmoney);
   set out.sorttour;
   by vendor;
   money=landcost*bookings;
   output details;
   if first.vendor then
      do;
         grpbook=0;
         grpmoney=0;
      end;
   grpbook+bookings;
   grpmoney+money;
   if last.vendor then output vendgrps;
run;

proc print data=details;
   title 'Detail Records: Dollars Spent on Individual Tours';
run;
```

---

* The program uses a DO group. Using DO groups allows you to evaluate a condition once and take more than one action as a result.

```
proc print data=vendgrps;
   title 'Group Totals: Dollars Spent and Bookings by Vendor';
run;
```

Output 11.6
*Detail Records in
One SAS Data Set
and Totals in
Another*

```
                  Detail Records: Dollars Spent on Individual Tours              1

        OBS    COUNTRY        LANDCOST     VENDOR      BOOKINGS     MONEY

         1     France           575       Express        10        5750
         2     India            489       Express         .           .
         3     Japan            720       Express        10        7200
         4     Greece           698       Express        20       13960
         5     Italy            468       Express         9        4212
         6     Ireland          558       Express         9        5022
         7     New Zealand     1489       Southsea        6        8934
         8     Australia       1079       Southsea       10       10790
         9     Spain            510       World          12        6120
        10     Brazil           540       World           6        3240
        11     Venezuela        425       World           8        3400
        12     USSR             924       World           6        5544
        13     Switzerland      734       World          20       14680
```

```
              Group Totals: Dollars Spent and Bookings by Vendor              2

           OBS     VENDOR     GRPBOOK     GRPMONEY

            1      Express       58        36144
            2      Southsea      16        19724
            3      World         52        32984
```

Using a Value in a Later Observation

As you examine the season's results, you decide to output the tour that
generated the most revenue to a separate SAS data set. (The revenue comes from
the price of the tour times the number of bookings.) One method takes three
steps: calculate the revenue in a DATA step, sort the data set in descending
order by the revenue, and use another DATA step with the OBS= data set
option to output that observation. A more efficient method compares the revenue
from all observations in a single DATA step. The SAS System can retain a value
from the current observation to use in future observations. When the processing
of the DATA step reaches the next observation, the held value represents
information from the previous observation.*

The RETAIN statement causes a variable created in the DATA step to retain
its value from the current observation into the next observation rather than
being set to missing at the beginning of each iteration of the DATA step. It is a
declarative statement, not an executable statement. This statement has the
following form:

RETAIN *variable-1* < ... *variable-n*>;

To compare the revenue in one observation to the revenue in the next
observation, create a retained variable named HOLDREV and assign the current
revenue to it. Therefore, in the next observation HOLDREV contains the
revenue from the previous observation, and you can compare its value to that of
REVENUE.

---

* A sum variable is an example of a variable that retains its value from one observation to the next.

To see how the RETAIN statement works, look at the next example. The following DATA step outputs observations to data set TEMP before the SAS System assigns the current revenue to HOLDREV, and Output 11.7 shows the data set TEMP:

```
data temp;
   set out.tourrev;
   retain holdrev;
   revenue=landcost*bookings;
   output;
   holdrev=revenue;
run;

proc print data=temp;
   var country landcost bookings revenue holdrev;
   title 'HOLDREV Shows REVENUE from Previous Observation';
run;
```

Output 11.7
Retaining a Value

```
                 HOLDREV Shows REVENUE from Previous Observation              1

     OBS    COUNTRY        LANDCOST    BOOKINGS    REVENUE    HOLDREV

      1     France           575          10        5750        .
      2     Spain            510          12        6120       5750
      3     Brazil           540           6        3240       6120
      4     India            489           .          .        3240
      5     Japan            720          10        7200        .
      6     Greece           698          20       13960       7200
      7     New Zealand     1489           6        8934      13960
      8     Venezuela        425           8        3400       8934
      9     Italy            468           9        4212       3400
     10     USSR             924           6        5544       4212
     11     Switzerland      734          20       14680       5544
     12     Australia       1079          10       10790      14680
     13     Ireland          558           9        5022      10790
```

The value of HOLDREV is missing at the beginning of the first observation; it is still missing when the OUTPUT statement writes the first observation to TEMP. After the OUTPUT statement, an assignment statement assigns the value of REVENUE to HOLDREV. Because HOLDREV is retained, that value is present at the beginning of the next iteration of the DATA step. When the OUTPUT statement executes again, the value of HOLDREV still contains that value.

To find the largest value of REVENUE, assign the value of REVENUE to HOLDREV only when REVENUE is larger than HOLDREV. The following program makes this specification, and Output 11.8 shows the data set MOSTREV:

```
data mostrev;
   set out.tourrev;
   retain holdrev;
   revenue=landcost*bookings;
   if revenue>holdrev then holdrev=revenue;
run;

proc print data=mostrev;
   var country landcost bookings revenue holdrev;
   title 'Collecting the Largest Value of REVENUE in HOLDREV';
run;
```

Output 11.8
Holding the
Largest Value in a
Retained Variable

```
          Collecting the Largest Value of REVENUE in HOLDREV              1

     OBS    COUNTRY        LANDCOST     BOOKINGS      REVENUE     HOLDREV
      1     France          575           10           5750        5750
      2     Spain           510           12           6120        6120
      3     Brazil          540            6           3240        6120
      4     India           489            .             .         6120
      5     Japan           720           10           7200        7200
      6     Greece          698           20          13960       13960
      7     New Zealand    1489            6           8934       13960
      8     Venezuela       425            8           3400       13960
      9     Italy           468            9           4212       13960
     10     USSR            924            6           5544       13960
     11     Switzerland     734           20          14680       14680
     12     Australia      1079           10          10790       14680
     13     Ireland         558            9           5022       14680
```

The value of HOLDREV in the last observation is the largest revenue generated by any tour. But how do you know which observation the value came from? Create a variable named HOLDCTRY to hold the name of the country from the observations with the largest revenue. Include HOLDCTRY in the RETAIN statement to retain its value until explicitly changed. Then use the END= data set option to select the last observation, and use the KEEP= data set option to keep only HOLDREV and HOLDCTRY in MOSTREV.* Output 11.9 displays the new data set:

```
data mostrev(keep=holdctry holdrev);
   set out.tourrev end=lastone;
   retain holdrev holdctry;
   revenue=landcost*bookings;
   if revenue>holdrev then
      do;
         holdrev=revenue;
         holdctry=country;
      end;
   if lastone;
run;
proc print data=mostrev;
   title 'Country with the Largest Value of REVENUE';
run;
```

Output 11.9
Selecting a New
Data Set Using
RETAIN and
Subsetting IF
Statements

```
          Country with the Largest Value of REVENUE                       1

              OBS      HOLDREV      HOLDCTRY

               1        14680       Switzerland
```

---

*   The program uses a DO group. DO groups allow you to perform two actions based on one IF condition.

SAS Tools

This chapter discusses the following statements:

variable + *expression*;

>   is called a sum statement; it adds the result of the *expression* on the
>   right side of the plus sign to the *variable* on the left side of the plus sign
>   and holds the new value of *variable* for use in subsequent observations.
>   The expression can be a numeric variable or expression. If the
>   expression is a missing value, the variable maintains its previous value.
>   Before the sum statement is executed for the first time, the default value
>   of the variable is 0.

SET *SAS-data-set* <END=*variable*>;

>   reads from the *SAS-data-set* you specify. The *variable* you specify in the
>   END= option has the value 0 until the SAS System is processing the last
>   observation in the data set. Then the variable has the value 1. The SAS
>   System doesn't add the END= variable to the data set being created.

RETAIN *variable-1* < . . . *variable-n*>;

>   retains the value of the *variable* for use in a subsequent observation. The
>   RETAIN statement prevents the value of the variable from being
>   reinitialized to missing when control returns to the top of the data set.
>
>   The RETAIN statement affects variables created in the current DATA
>   step (for example, variables created with an INPUT or assignment
>   statement). Variables read with a SET, MERGE, or UPDATE statement
>   are retained automatically; naming them in a RETAIN statement has no
>   effect.

Learning More

□   Chapter 4, "Starting with SAS Data Sets," discusses the KEEP= and
    DROP= data set options.

□   Chapter 12, "Finding Shortcuts in Programming," discusses DO groups.

□   Chapter 19, "Manipulating SAS Data Sets," presents another example of
    using the END= option in the SET statement.

□   Chapter 24, "Printing Detail Reports," discusses using the SUM and SUMBY
    statements in the PRINT procedure. You can use the SUM and SUMBY
    statements in the PRINT procedure if your only purpose in getting a total is
    to display it in a report.

□   Chapter 29, "Writing Output," discusses the automatic variable _N_, which
    provides a way to count the number of times the SAS System executes a
    DATA step. Using _N_ is more efficient than using a sum statement. The
    SAS System creates _N_ in each DATA step. The first time the SAS System
    begins to execute the DATA step, the value of _N_ is 1; the second time, 2;
    and so on. The SAS System does not add _N_ to the output data set.

□ *SAS Language: Reference, Version 6, First Edition* provides complete documentation on the RETAIN, sum, and SET statements. Keep in mind the following points about the RETAIN and sum statements.

□ The RETAIN statement can assign an initial value to a variable. If you need a variable to have the same value in all observations of a DATA step, it is more efficient to put the value in a RETAIN statement rather than in an assignment statement. The SAS System assigns the value in the RETAIN statement when it is compiling the DATA step, but it carries out the assignment statement during each execution of the DATA step.

□ The plus sign is required in the sum statement; to subtract successive values from a starting value, add negative values to the sum variable.

□ *SAS Language: Reference* documents the LAG family of functions. LAG functions provide another way to retain a value from one observation for use in a subsequent observation. LAG functions can retain a value for up to 100 observations.

□ The *SAS Procedures Guide, Version 6, Third Edition* provides complete documentation on the SUMMARY and MEANS procedures, which can also be used to compute totals.

Chapter 12 Finding Shortcuts in Programming

Introduction

The preceding chapters have shown you the basic points of DATA step programming, but you have probably realized that some of the programming is repetitive. This chapter shows you how to write DATA steps that are easier to code and read by

☐ performing more than one action after evaluating an IF condition

☐ performing the same action on more than one variable with a single group of statements.

Input File and SAS Data Set Example

The examples in this chapter assume that at Tradewinds Travel you are making adjustments to your data about tours to art museums and galleries. The data for the tours are as follows:

```
Rome       4 3 . D'Amico 2
Paris      5 . 1 Lucas   5
London     3 2 . Wilson  3
New York   5 1 2 Lucas   5
Madrid     . . 5 Torres  4
Amsterdam  3 3 .         .
```

The first field contains the name of the city; the second field, the number of museums to be visited; the third field, the number of art galleries; and the fourth field, the number of other attractions to be toured. The next field contains the last name of the tour guide, followed by the number of years of experience the guide has.

You begin by creating a permanent SAS data set called SAVE.ARTS. The following program creates the data set, and Output 12.1 displays it:

```
libname save 'your-data-library';

data save.arts;
    infile 'your-input-file';
    input city $ 1-9 museum 11 gallery 13
          other 15 guide $ 17-24 yrs_exp 26;
run;

proc print data=save.arts;
    title 'Data Set SAVE.ARTS';
run;
```

Output 12.1
Data Set
SAVE.ARTS

```
                          Data Set SAVE.ARTS                              1

   OBS    CITY        MUSEUM    GALLERY    OTHER    GUIDE     YRS_EXP

    1     Rome          4          3         .      D'Amico      2
    2     Paris         5          .         1      Lucas        5
    3     London        3          2         .      Wilson       3
    4     New York      5          1         2      Lucas        5
    5     Madrid        .          .         5      Torres       4
    6     Amsterdam     3          3         .                   .
```

Performing More than One Action in One IF-THEN Statement

Suppose you need to change several values in the observations for Madrid and Amsterdam. One way to select those observations is to evaluate an IF condition in a series of IF-THEN statements, as follows:

```
/* multiple actions based on the same condition */
data fixit;
    set save.arts;
    if city='Madrid' then museum=3;
    if city='Madrid' then other=2;
    if city='Amsterdam' then guide='Vandever';
    if city='Amsterdam' then yrs_exp=4;
run;
```

To avoid writing the IF condition twice for each city, use a DO group as the THEN clause, for example,

if *condition* then
  do;
    more SAS statements
  end;

The DO statement causes all statements following it to be treated as a unit until a matching END statement appears. A group of SAS statements beginning with DO and ending with END is called a *DO group*.

Placing DO groups into the following DATA step produces the data set shown in Output 12.2:

```
/* a more efficient method */
data fixit2;
   set save.arts;
   if city='Madrid' then
      do;
         museum=3;
         other=2;
      end;
   else if city='Amsterdam' then
      do;
         guide='Vandever';
         yrs_exp=4;
      end;
run;

proc print data=fixit2;
   title 'Using DO Groups';
run;
```

Output 12.2
Using DO Groups to Produce a Data Set

```
                              Using DO Groups                            1

    OBS   CITY       MUSEUM   GALLERY   OTHER   GUIDE      YRS_EXP

     1    Rome          4        3        .     D'Amico       2
     2    Paris         5        .        1     Lucas         5
     3    London        3        2        .     Wilson        3
     4    New York      5        1        2     Lucas         5
     5    Madrid        3        .        2     Torres        4
     6    Amsterdam     3        3        .     Vandever      4
```

Using the DO groups makes the program faster to write and easier to read. It also makes the program more efficient for the SAS System in two ways.

1. The IF condition is evaluated fewer times. (Although there are more statements in this DATA step than in the preceding one, the DO and END statements require very few computer resources.)

2. The conditions CITY='Madrid' and CITY='Amsterdam' are mutually exclusive, as condensing the multiple IF-THEN statements into two statements reveals. You can make the second IF-THEN statement part of an ELSE statement; therefore, the second IF condition is not evaluated when the first IF condition is true.

Performing the Same Action for a Series of Variables

In data set SAVE.ARTS, the variables MUSEUM, GALLERY, and OTHER contain missing values when the tour doesn't feature that kind of attraction. You decide to change the missing values to 0. One way to do that is to write a series of

IF-THEN statements with assignment statements, as the following program illustrates:

```
     /* same action for different variables */
data changes;
   set save.arts;
   if museum=. then museum=0;
   if gallery=. then gallery=0;
   if other=. then other=0;
run;
```

The pattern of action is the same in the three IF-THEN statements; only the variable name is different. You can make the program easier to read by telling the SAS System to perform the same action several times, changing only the variable affected. The technique is called *array processing*, and the following sections explain it in a three-step process:

1. grouping variables into arrays

2. repeating the action

3. selecting the current variable to be acted upon.

Grouping Variables into Arrays

In DATA step programming you can put variables into a temporary group called an *array*. To define an array, use an ARRAY statement. A simple ARRAY statement has the following form:

ARRAY *array-name{number-of-variables} variable-1* $<$ *. . . variable-n>*;

The *array-name* is a SAS name that you choose to identify the group of variables. The *number-of-variables*, enclosed in braces, tells the SAS System how many variables you are grouping, and *variable-1*$<$ *. . . variable-n* $>$ lists their names.*

The following ARRAY statement lists the three variables MUSEUM, GALLERY, and OTHER:

```
array chglist{3} museum gallery other;
```

This statement tells the SAS System to

□   make a group named CHGLIST for the duration of this DATA step

□   put three variable names in CHGLIST: MUSEUM, GALLERY, and OTHER.

In addition, listing a variable in an ARRAY statement assigns the variable an extra name with the form *array-name{position}*, where *position* is the position of

---

*   If you have worked with arrays in other programming languages, note that arrays in the SAS System are different from those in many other languages. In the SAS System, an array is simply a convenient way of temporarily identifying a group of variables. It is not a data structure, and it exists only for the duration of the DATA step. The *array-name* identifies the array and distinguishes it from any other arrays in the same DATA step; it is not a variable.

the variable in the list (1, 2, or 3 in this case). The position can be a number or the name of a variable whose value is the number. This additional name is called an *array reference*, and the *position* is often called the subscript. The previous ARRAY statement assigns MUSEUM the array reference CHGLIST{1}; GALLERY, CHGLIST{2}; and OTHER, CHGLIST{3}. From that point in the DATA step, you can refer to the variable by either its original name or by its array reference. For example, the names MUSEUM and CHGLIST{1} are equivalent.

Repeating the Action

To tell the SAS System to perform the same action several times, use an iterative DO loop of the following form:

> **DO** *index-variable*=1 TO *number-of-variables-in-array*;
>   *SAS statements*
> **END**;

An iterative DO loop begins with an iterative DO statement, contains other *SAS statements*, and ends with an END statement. The loop is processed repeatedly (iterates) according to the directions in the iterative DO statement. The iterative DO statement contains an *index-variable* whose name you choose and whose value changes in each iteration of the loop. In array processing, you usually want the loop to execute as many times as there are variables in the array; therefore, you specify that the values of *index-variable* are 1 TO *number-of-variables-in-array*. By default, the SAS System increases the value of *index-variable* by 1 before each new iteration of the loop. When the value becomes greater than *number-of-variables-in-array*, the SAS System stops processing the loop. By default the SAS System adds the index variable to the data set being created.

An iterative DO loop that processes three times and has an index variable named COUNT looks like this:

```
do count=1 to 3;
    SAS statements
end;
```

The first time the loop is processed, the value of COUNT is 1; the second time, 2; and the third time, 3. At the beginning of the fourth execution, the value of COUNT is 4, exceeding the specified range of 1 TO 3. The SAS System stops processing the loop.

Selecting the Current Variable

Now that you have grouped the variables and know how many times the loop will be processed, you must tell the SAS System which variable in the array to use in each iteration of the loop. Recall that variables in an array can be identified by their array references and that the subscript of the reference can be a variable name as well as a number. Therefore, you can write programming statements in which the index variable of the DO loop is the subscript of the array reference, in other words, *array-name*{*index-variable*}. When the value of the index variable changes, the subscript of the array reference (and, therefore, the variable referenced) also changes.

The following statement uses COUNT as the subscript of array references:

```
if chglist(count)=. then chglist(count)=0;
```

You can place this statement inside an iterative DO loop. When the value of COUNT is 1, the SAS System reads the array reference as CHGLIST{1} and processes the IF-THEN statement on CHGLIST{1}, that is, MUSEUM. The same thing happens when COUNT has the value 2 or 3; the SAS System processes the statement on CHGLIST{2}, that is, GALLERY, or CHGLIST{3}, OTHER. The complete iterative DO loop with array references looks like this:

```
do count=1 to 3;
   if chglist(count)=. then chglist(count)=0;
end;
```

These statements tell the SAS System to

□ perform the actions in the loop three times

□ replace the array subscript COUNT with the current value of COUNT for each iteration of the IF-THEN statement

□ locate the variable with that array reference and process the IF-THEN statement on it.

Using the ARRAY statement and iterative DO loop in the following DATA step produces the data set shown in Output 12.3:

```
data changes;
   set save.arts;
   array chglist{3} museum gallery other;
   do count=1 to 3;
      if chglist(count)=. then chglist(count)=0;
   end;
run;
```

```
proc print data=changes;
   title 'Data Set Produced with Array Processing';
run;
```

Output 12.3
Using an Array to Produce a Data Set

```
                    Data Set Produced with Array Processing                   1

  OBS   CITY        MUSEUM   GALLERY   OTHER    GUIDE     YRS_EXP   COUNT

   1    Rome          4         3        0      D'Amico      2        4
   2    Paris         5         0        1      Lucas        5        4
   3    London        3         2        0      Wilson       3        4
   4    New York      5         1        2      Lucas        5        4
   5    Madrid        0         0        5      Torres       4        4
   6    Amsterdam     3         3        0                   .        4
```

Data set CHANGES shows that the missing values for MUSEUM, GALLERY, and OTHER are now zero. In addition, the data set contains the variable COUNT with the value 4 (the value that caused processing of the loop to cease in each observation). To exclude COUNT from the data set, use a DROP= data set option in the following program to produce Output 12.4:

```
data chgdrop(drop=count);
   set save.arts;
   array chglist(3) museum gallery other;
   do count=1 to 3;
      if chglist(count)=. then chglist(count)=0;
   end;
run;

proc print data=chgdrop;
   title 'Data Set After Dropping Index Variable';
run;
```

Output 12.4
Dropping the
Index Variable
from a Data Set

```
                 Data Set After Dropping Index Variable              1

    OBS    CITY        MUSEUM    GALLERY    OTHER    GUIDE     YRS_EXP

     1     Rome          4          3         0     D'Amico      2
     2     Paris         5          0         1     Lucas        5
     3     London        3          2         0     Wilson       3
     4     New York      5          1         2     Lucas        5
     5     Madrid        0          0         5     Torres       4
     6     Amsterdam     3          3         0                  .
```

SAS Tools

This chapter discusses the following statements:

DO;
   SAS statements
END;
   treats the enclosed SAS statements as a unit. A group of statements beginning with DO and ending with END is called a DO group. DO groups usually appear in THEN clauses or ELSE statements.

ARRAY *array-name{number-of-variables} variable-1* < *. . . variable-n*>;
   creates a named, ordered list of variables that exists for processing of the current DATA step. The *array-name* must be a valid SAS name. Each *variable* is the name of a variable to be included in the array. *Number-of-variables* is the number of variables listed.
   When you place a variable in an array, the variable can also be accessed by *array-name{position}*, where *position* is the position of the variable in the list (from 1 to *number-of-variables*). This way of accessing the variable is called an array reference, and the *position* is known as the subscript of the array reference. After you list a variable in an ARRAY statement, programming statements in the same DATA step can use either the original name of the variable or the array reference.

(ARRAY continued)

This book uses curly braces around the subscript. Parentheses ( ) are also acceptable, and square brackets [ ] are acceptable on hosts that support those characters. Refer to the documentation provided by the vendor for your host system to determine the characters supported.

DO *index-variable*= 1 TO *number-of-variables-in-array*;
  SAS statements
END;

is known as an iterative DO loop. In each execution of the DATA step, an iterative DO loop is processed repeatedly (iterates) based on the value of *index-variable*. To create an index variable, simply use a SAS variable name in an iterative DO statement.

When you use iterative DO loops for array processing, the value of *index-variable* usually starts at 1 and increases by 1 before each iteration of the loop. When the value becomes greater than the *number-of-variables-in-array* (usually the number of variables in the array being processed), the SAS System stops processing the loop and proceeds to the next statement in the DATA step.

In array processing, the SAS statements in an iterative DO loop usually contain array references whose subscript is the name of the index variable (as in *array-name{index-variable}*). In each iteration of the loop, the SAS System replaces the subscript in the reference with the index variable's current value. Therefore, successive iterations of the loop cause the SAS System to process the statements on the first variable in the array, then the second variable, and so on.

Learning More

□ *SAS Language: Reference, Version 6, First Edition* completely documents DO groups, iterative DO loops, and the explicit ARRAY statement.

Iterative DO statements are flexible and powerful; they are useful in many situations other than array processing. The range of the index variable can start and stop with any number, and the increment can be any positive or negative number. The range of the index variable can be given as starting and stopping values; the values of the DIM, LBOUND, and HBOUND functions; a list of values separated by commas; or a combination of these. A range can also contain a WHILE or UNTIL clause. The index variable can also be a character variable (in that case, the range must be given as a list of character values). The DIM, LBOUND, and HBOUND functions are documented in *SAS Language: Reference*.

□ *SAS Language: Reference* provides information on both *explicit arrays* and *implicit arrays*. The arrays in this book are known as explicit arrays. They are more powerful and flexible than an older type of array in the SAS System (known as implicit arrays and often processed with DO OVER loops).

Explicit arrays can be multidimensional and can have bounds other than 1 and the number of variables. Explicit arrays can be made of existing SAS variables (as shown in this chapter), can create SAS variables, or can be made of temporary data elements that exist only for the duration of the DATA step (useful when the only purpose of an array is to perform a calculation). *SAS Language: Reference* discusses array processing.

□   *SAS Language: Reference* documents the SAS System's DO WHILE and DO UNTIL statements. A DO WHILE statement processes a loop as long as a condition is true; a DO UNTIL statement processes a loop until a condition is true. (A DO UNTIL loop always processes at least once; a DO WHILE loop is not processed at all if the condition is initially false.)

Chapter **13** Working with Dates in the SAS® System

Introduction

Date variables are generally recorded in some representation of a calendar date. None of these representations of dates can be sorted chronologically or used in mathematical calculations without using complicated programming techniques. The SAS System stores dates as single, unique numbers so you can use them in programs like any other numeric variable. How do you tell the SAS System to read a date in calendar form, such as 26JUL89, and convert that date to a single number? How do you tell the SAS System to display the number in a recognizable form? In this chapter you learn how to

☐ have the SAS System read dates in raw data files and store them as SAS date values

☐ indicate which calendar form the SAS System should use to display SAS date values

☐ calculate with dates, that is, determining the number of days between dates, finding the day of the week on which a date falls, and using today's date in calculations.

Understanding How the SAS System Processes Dates

Dates are written in many different ways. Some dates contain only numbers, while others contain various combinations of numbers, letters, and characters. For example, all the following forms represent the date July 26, 1989:

    072689 26JUL89   892607
    7/26/89 26JUL1989 July 26, 1989

Given the many different forms of dates, there must be some common ground, a way to store dates and use them in calculations, regardless of how dates are entered or displayed.

The common ground that the SAS System uses to represent dates is called a *SAS date value*. No matter how you write a date, the SAS System can convert and store that date as the number of days between January 1, 1960, and the date you enter. Figure 13.1 shows some dates written in calendar form and as SAS date values:

Figure 13.1
Comparing Calendar Dates to SAS Date Values

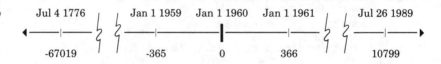

Calendar Date

SAS Date Value

In the SAS System, every date is a unique number on a number line. Dates before January 1, 1960, are negative numbers; those after January 1, 1960, are positive. Because SAS date values are numeric variables, you can sort them easily, determine time intervals, and use dates as constants, as arguments in SAS functions, or in calculations.

Note: SAS date values are valid for dates based on the Gregorian calendar from A.D. 1582 through A.D. 20,000.*

The first step for using dates is to tell the SAS System to convert them into SAS date values when the DATA step executes. The following section illustrates the method using a simple data set.

Input File and SAS Data Set Example

In the travel industry, many of the most important facts about a tour involve dates, when the tour leaves and returns, when payments are due, when refunds are allowed, and so on. At Tradewinds Travel you work with dates regularly,

---

*   Use caution when working with historical dates. Although the Gregorian calendar was used throughout most of Europe from 1582, Great Britain and the American colonies did not adopt the calendar until 1752.

and you decide to learn to program with them in the SAS System. Your list of popular tours includes the date that each tour leaves and the number of nights spent on the tour. The raw data are stored in an external file that looks like this:

```
Japan       13may89  8
Greece      17oct89  12
New Zealand 03feb90  16
Brazil      28feb90  8
Venezuela   10nov89  9
Italy       25apr89  8
USSR        03jun89  14
Switzerland 14jan90  9
Australia   24oct89  12
Ireland     27may89  7
```

The first field is the country toured followed by the departure date and the number of nights the tour lasts.

How does the SAS System know that the departure field contains SAS date values? The field contains letters, so the SAS System can't read it as an ordinary number. Because the SAS System needs to store the value as a number to do calculations, you can't instruct it to read the date as a character variable.

Entering Dates

To have the SAS System read the departure field as a SAS date value, you must give it a set of directions called an *informat*. By default, the SAS System reads numeric variables with a standard numeric informat that doesn't include letters or special characters. When a field contains data that don't match the standard patterns, you must specify the proper informat for reading it in an INPUT statement.

The SAS System provides a number of informats. Two commonly used date informats are MMDDYY8., which reads dates written as *mm/dd/yy*, and DATE7., which reads them in the form *ddMMMyy*. Note that each informat name ends with a period and contains a width specification that tells the SAS System how many columns to read.

To create a SAS data set for your Tradewinds Travel data, use the DATE7. informat in the INPUT statement to read the variable DEPART.

```
input country $ 1-11 @13 depart date7. nights;
```

Using an informat in the INPUT statement is called *formatted input*. The formatted input in this example contains the following items:

□ a pointer to indicate the column in which the value begins (@13)

□ the name of the variable to be read (DEPART)

□ the name of the informat to use (DATE7.).

Using the INPUT statement in the following program produces Output 13.1:

```
libname save 'your-data-library';

data save.dates;
   infile 'your-input-file';
   input country $ 1-11 a13 depart date7. nights;
run;

proc print data=save.dates;
   title 'Departure Dates as SAS Date Values';
run;
```

Output 13.1
Creating SAS Date Values from Calendar Dates

```
                Departure Dates as SAS Date Values                    1

         OBS     COUNTRY        DEPART     NIGHTS

          1      Japan           10725       8
          2      Greece          10882      12
          3      New Zealand     10991      16
          4      Brazil          11016       8
          5      Venezuela       10906       9
          6      Italy           10707       8
          7      USSR            10746      14
          8      Switzerland     10971       9
          9      Australia       10889      12
         10      Ireland         10739       7
```

Compare the values of the variable DEPART in Output 13.1 with the values of the raw data shown in the previous section. Data set SAVE.DATES shows that the SAS System read the departure dates and created SAS date values. Now you need a way to display the dates in a recognizable form.

Displaying Dates

To understand how to display the departure dates, you need to understand how the SAS System displays values in general. The SAS System displays all data values with a set of directions called a *format*. By default, the SAS System uses a standard numeric format with no commas, letters, or other special notation to display the values of numeric variables. As Output 13.1 shows, printing SAS date values with the standard numeric format produces numbers that are difficult to recognize. To display these numbers as calendar dates, you need to specify a SAS date format for the variable.

SAS date formats are available for the most common ways of writing calendar dates. The DATE7. format represents dates in the form *ddMMMyy*. You can ask for the month, day, and year spelled out by using the WORDDATE18. format. The WEEKDATE29. format includes the day of the week. There are also formats available for number representations such as the format MMDDYY8., which displays the calendar date in the form *mm/dd/yy*. Like informat names, each format name ends with a period and contains a width specification that tells the SAS System how many columns to use when displaying the date value.

You tell the SAS System which format to use by specifying the variable and the format name in a FORMAT statement. The following FORMAT statement assigns the MMDDYY8. format to the variable DEPART:

```
format depart mmddyy8.;
```

In this example, the FORMAT statement contains the following items:

□ the name of the variable (DEPART)

□ the name of the format to be used (MMDDYY8.).

Add the FORMAT statement to the following PROC PRINT step to produce Output 13.2:

```
proc print data=save.dates;
   title 'Departure Dates in Calendar Form';
   format depart mmddyy8.;
run;
```

Output 13.2
Displaying a
Formatted Date
Value

```
                  Departure Dates in Calendar Form               1

         OBS     COUNTRY          DEPART      NIGHTS

          1      Japan           05/13/89        8
          2      Greece          10/17/89       12
          3      New Zealand     02/03/90       16
          4      Brazil          02/28/90        8
          5      Venezuela       11/10/89        9
          6      Italy           04/25/89        8
          7      USSR            06/03/89       14
          8      Switzerland     01/14/90        9
          9      Australia       10/24/89       12
         10      Ireland         05/27/89        7
```

Placing a FORMAT statement in a PROC step associates the format with the variable only for that step. To associate a format with a variable permanently, use the FORMAT statement in a DATA step.

Assigning Permanent Date Formats to Variables

The next example creates a new permanent SAS data set and assigns the DATE7. format in the DATA step. From this point on, all procedures and DATA steps that use the variable DEPART use the DATE7. format by default. The PROC CONTENTS step displays the characteristics of the data set TOURDATE. Output

13.3 shows that the format DATE7. is listed as an attribute of the variable DEPART.

```
data save.tourdate;
   set save.dates;
   format depart date7.;
run;

proc contents data=save.tourdate;
run;
```

Output 13.3
Assigning a
Format in a DATA
Step

```
                              The SAS System                              1

                            CONTENTS PROCEDURE

       Data Set Name: SAVE.TOURDATE          Observations:           10
       Member Type:   DATA                   Variables:              3
       Engine:        V606                   Indexes:                0
       Created:       09AUG89:12:32:36       Observation Length:     27
       Last Modified: 09AUG89:12:32:36       Deleted Observations:   0
       Data Set Type:                        Compressed:             NO
       Label:

            -----Alphabetic List of Variables and Attributes-----

            #    Variable   Type   Len   Pos    Format
            --------------------------------------------------
            1    COUNTRY    Char    11     0
            2    DEPART     Num      8    11     DATE7.
            3    NIGHTS     Num      8    19
```

Changing Formats Temporarily

If you are preparing a report that requires the date in a different format, you can override the permanent format by using a FORMAT statement in a PROC step. For example, to display the full spelling for departure dates in the data set SAVE.TOURDATE, issue a FORMAT statement in a PROC PRINT step. In the following program specify the WORDDATE18. format for the variable DEPART to produce Output 13.4:

```
proc print data=save.tourdate;
   title 'Report with Departure Date Spelled Out';
   format depart worddate18.;
run;
```

Output 13.4
Overriding a
Previously
Specified Format

```
              Report with Departure Date Spelled Out              1

      OBS    COUNTRY                 DEPART      NIGHTS

        1    Japan            May 13, 1989          8
        2    Greece           October 17, 1989     12
        3    New Zealand      February 3, 1990     16
        4    Brazil           February 28, 1990     8
        5    Venezuela        November 10, 1989     9
        6    Italy            April 25, 1989        8
        7    USSR             June 3, 1989         14
        8    Switzerland      January 14, 1990      9
        9    Australia        October 24, 1989     12
       10    Ireland          May 27, 1989          7
```

The format DATE7. is still permanently assigned to DEPART, and calendar dates in the remaining examples are in the form *ddMMMyy* unless a FORMAT statement is included in the PROC PRINT step.

Using Dates in Calculations

Because SAS date values are numeric variables, you can sort them and use them in calculations. The following examples use the data set SAVE.TOURDATE to extract other information about your Tradewinds Travel data.

Sorting Dates

To help determine how frequently tours are scheduled, you can print a report with the tours listed in chronological order. The first step is to specify the following BY statement in a PROC SORT step to tell the SAS System to arrange the observations in ascending order of the date variable DEPART:

```
by depart;
```

By using a VAR statement in the following PROC PRINT step, you can list the departure date as the first column in the report. Output 13.5 shows the result.

```
proc sort data=save.tourdate out=sortdate;
   by depart;
run;

proc print data=sortdate;
   var depart country nights;
   title 'Departure Dates Listed in Chronological Order';
run;
```

Output 13.5
Sorting by SAS
Date Values

```
              Departure Dates Listed in Chronological Order                1

          OBS      DEPART     COUNTRY         NIGHTS

            1      25APR89    Italy              8
            2      13MAY89    Japan              8
            3      27MAY89    Ireland            7
            4      03JUN89    USSR              14
            5      17OCT89    Greece            12
            6      24OCT89    Australia         12
            7      10NOV89    Venezuela          9
            8      14JAN90    Switzerland        9
            9      03FEB90    New Zealand       16
           10      28FEB90    Brazil             8
```

The observations in the data set SORTDATE are now arranged in chronological order. Note that there are no FORMAT statements in this example, so the dates are displayed in the DATE7. format you assigned to DEPART when you created the data set SAVE.TOURDATE.

Creating New Date Variables

Because you know the departure date and the number of nights spent on each tour, you can calculate the return date for each tour. To start, create a new variable by adding the number of nights to the departure date, as follows:

```
return=depart+nights;
```

The result is a SAS date value for the return date that you can display by assigning it the DATE7. format, as follows. Output 13.6 shows the new data set.

```
data home;
   set save.tourdate;
   return=depart+nights;
   format return date7.;
run;

proc print data=home;
   title 'Dates of Departure and Return';
run;
```

Output 13.6
Adding Days to a
Date Value

```
                   Dates of Departure and Return                     1

     OBS    COUNTRY         DEPART      NIGHTS      RETURN

       1    Japan          13MAY89        8        21MAY89
       2    Greece         17OCT89       12        29OCT89
       3    New Zealand    03FEB90       16        19FEB90
       4    Brazil         28FEB90        8        08MAR90
       5    Venezuela      10NOV89        9        19NOV89
       6    Italy          25APR89        8        03MAY89
       7    USSR           03JUN89       14        17JUN89
       8    Switzerland    14JAN90        9        23JAN90
       9    Australia      24OCT89       12        05NOV89
      10    Ireland        27MAY89        7        03JUN89
```

Using Dates as Constants

Suppose you realize that the tour of Switzerland leaves on January 21, 1990, instead of January 14. You can use the following assignment statement to correct the error:

```
if country='Switzerland' then depart='21jan90'd;
```

The value '21jan90'D is a *SAS date constant*. To write a SAS date constant, enclose a date in quotes in the standard SAS form *ddMMMyy* and immediately follow the final quote with the letter D. The D suffix tells the SAS System to convert the calendar date to a SAS date value. Placing this statement in the following DATA step produces Output 13.7:

```
data corrdate;
   set save.tourdate;
   if country='Switzerland' then depart='21jan90'd;
run;

proc print data=corrdate;
   title 'Corrected Value for Switzerland';
run;
```

Output 13.7
Changing a Date
by Using a SAS
Date Constant

```
                    Corrected Value for Switzerland                    1

         OBS    COUNTRY        DEPART    NIGHTS

          1     Japan          13MAY89      8
          2     Greece         17OCT89     12
          3     New Zealand    03FEB90     16
          4     Brazil         28FEB90      8
          5     Venezuela      10NOV89      9
          6     Italy          25APR89      8
          7     USSR           03JUN89     14
          8     Switzerland    21JAN90      9
          9     Australia      24OCT89     12
         10     Ireland        27MAY89      7
```

Using SAS Date Functions

The SAS System has various functions that produce calendar dates from SAS date values. SAS date functions allow you to do such things as derive partial date information or use the current date in calculations.

Finding the Day of the Week

Suppose that customers must make the final payment for a tour 30 days before the tour leaves. You can find a date 30 days before departure by subtraction; however, Tradewinds Travel is closed on Sunday. If the payment is due on a Sunday, you must subtract an additional day to make the payment due on Saturday.

The WEEKDAY function returns the day of the week as a number from 1 through 7 (Sunday through Saturday). The following statements subtract 30 from the departure date, check the value returned by the WEEKDAY function, and subtract an additional day if necessary:

```
duedate=depart-30;
if weekday(duedate)=1 then duedate=duedate-1;
```

Constructing a data set with these statements produces a list of payment due dates. Adding the statements to the following program and assigning the format WEEKDATE29. to the new variable produces Output 13.8:

```
data pay;
   set save.tourdate;
   duedate=depart-30;
   if weekday(duedate)=1 then duedate=duedate-1;
   format duedate weekdate29.;
run;

proc print data=pay;
   var country duedate;
   title 'Date and Day of Week Payment Is Due';
run;
```

Output 13.8
Using the
WEEKDATE
Function

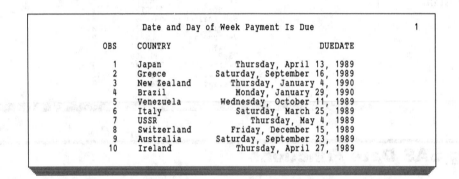

```
                  Date and Day of Week Payment Is Due                        1

        OBS    COUNTRY                        DUEDATE
         1     Japan              Thursday, April 13, 1989
         2     Greece           Saturday, September 16, 1989
         3     New Zealand        Thursday, January 4, 1990
         4     Brazil              Monday, January 29, 1990
         5     Venezuela        Wednesday, October 11, 1989
         6     Italy               Saturday, March 25, 1989
         7     USSR                  Thursday, May 4, 1989
         8     Switzerland       Friday, December 15, 1989
         9     Australia        Saturday, September 23, 1989
        10     Ireland             Thursday, April 27, 1989
```

Calculating a Date from Today

Suppose that Tradewinds Travel occasionally gets the opportunity to do special advertising promotions. In general, you like to advertise tours that depart more than 90 days from today but less than 120 days, as shown in Figure 13.2:

Figure 13.2
Optimum Interval
for Advertising
Tours Based on
Today's Date

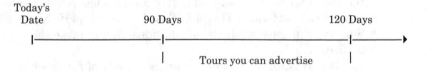

You need a program that determines which tours leave between 90 and 120 days from the date the program is run, regardless of when you run the program.

The TODAY function produces a SAS date value corresponding to the date the program is run: you can use the following statements to find which tours depart at least 90 days from today's date but not more than 120 days from now.

```
now=today();
if now+90<=depart<=now+120;
```

To print the value returned by the TODAY function, this example creates a variable equal to the value returned by the TODAY function. This step isn't necessary but is used here to clarify the program. You can use the function as part of the program statement just as well.

```
if today()+90<=depart<=today()+120;
```

Placing the statements in the following program and running it on August 9, 1989, produces Output 13.9:

```
data ads;
    set save.tourdate;
    now=today();
    if now+90<=depart<=now+120;
run;

proc print data=ads;
    title 'Tours Departing between 90 and 120 Days from Today';
    format now date7.;
run;
```

Note that the PROC PRINT step contains a FORMAT statement that temporarily assigns the format DATE7. to the variable NOW.

Output 13.9
Using the Current
Date as a SAS
Date Value

```
              Tours Departing between 90 and 120 Days from Today              1

         OBS      COUNTRY      DEPART     NIGHTS       NOW

          1       Venezuela    10NOV89       9       09AUG89
```

Comparing Durations and SAS Date Values

You can use SAS date values to find the units of time between dates. Suppose that Tradewinds Travel was founded on February 8, 1982. On September 28, 1989, you decide to find out how old Tradewinds Travel is, and you write the following program:

```
/* Calculating a duration in days */
data temp;
    start='08feb82'd;
    rightnow=today();
    age=rightnow-start;
    format start rightnow date7.;
run;

proc print data=temp;
    title 'Age of Tradewinds Travel';
run;
```

This DATA step produces a data set with one observation, and Output 13.10 shows the result.

Output 13.10
Calculating a
Duration in Days

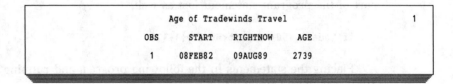

```
                          Age of Tradewinds Travel                            1

              OBS      START      RIGHTNOW      AGE

               1      08FEB82     09AUG89      2739
```

The value of AGE is 2789, a number that looks like an unformatted SAS date value. However, AGE is actually the difference between February 8, 1982, and September 28, 1989, and represents a duration in days, not a SAS date value. To make the value of AGE more understandable, divide the number of days by 365 (more precisely, 365.25) to produce a duration in years. The following DATA step calculates the age in years, and Output 13.11 shows the result:

```
    /* Calculating a duration in years */
data temp2;
    start='08feb82'd;
    rightnow=today();
    agedays=rightnow-start;
    ageyrs=agedays/365.25;
    format ageyrs 3.1 start rightnow date7.;
run;

proc print data=temp2;
    title 'Age in Years of Tradewinds Travel';
run;
```

Output 13.11
Calculating a
Duration in Years

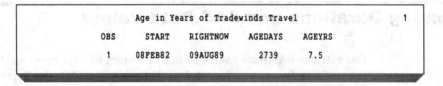

```
                       Age in Years of Tradewinds Travel                      1

          OBS      START      RIGHTNOW      AGEDAYS      AGEYRS

           1      08FEB82     09AUG89        2739         7.5
```

SAS Tools

This chapter discusses the conversion of calendar dates to date values so that you can treat them as numeric variables. As a part of this discussion, the chapter introduces a date informat, several date formats, and a SAS date constant for uses within the following SAS statements:

INPUT *date-variable date-informat;*
> tells the SAS System the form in which the values of the *date-variable* are entered. This chapter introduces the *date-informat* DATE7., which indicates that all values of the *date-variable* are of the form *ddMMMyy*, for example, 24AUG89.

FORMAT *date-variable date-format*;

> tells the SAS System how to display values of *date-variable*. The following *date-formats* produce dates in the forms indicated:

> DATE7.   05JUN89
> MMDDYY8.   06/05/89
> WORDDATE18. June 5, 1989
> WEEKDATE29. Monday, June 5, 1989

date-variable='*ddMMMyy*'D;

> is an assignment statement that tells the SAS System to convert the date in quotation marks to a numeric value (SAS date value) and assign it to *date-variable*. The SAS date constant '*ddMMMyy*'D specifies a particular date, for example, '21JAN90'D, and can be used in many SAS statements and expressions, not just assignment statements.

This chapter discusses the following date functions:

WEEKDAY(*SAS-date-value*)

> is a function that returns the day of the week on which the *SAS-date-value* falls as a number 1 through 7, with Sunday assigned the value 1.

TODAY()

> is a function that returns a SAS date value corresponding to the date on which the SAS program is run.

Learning More

□ Chapter 24, "Printing Detail Reports," discusses using the macro variable SYSDATE to include the current date in a title.

□ Chapter 32, "Managing SAS Data Libraries," discusses using the DATASETS procedure, which manages SAS data sets and data libraries, to assign or change a permanent format.

□ *SAS Language: Reference, Version 6, First Edition* completely documents the SAS System's informats, formats, and functions for working with SAS date values and *SAS time* and *datetime values*. *SAS Language: Reference* explains the following processes:

> □ The SAS System stores a time as the number of seconds since midnight of the current day. For example, 9:30 a.m. is 34200. A number of this type is known as a SAS time value. A SAS time value is independent of the date; the count begins at 0 each midnight.

> □ When a date and a time are both present, the SAS System stores the value as the number of seconds since midnight, January 1, 1960. For example, 9:30 a.m., June 5, 1989, is 928661400. This type of number is known as a SAS datetime value.

□ SAS date and time informats read fields of different widths. SAS date and time formats can display date variables in different ways according to the widths you specify in the format name. The number at the end of the format or informat name indicates the number of columns that the SAS System can use. For example, the DATE9. informat reads up to nine columns (as in 17OCT1990). The WEEKDATE9. format displays 9 columns, as in Wednesday, and WEEKDATE17. displays 17 columns, as in Wed, Oct 17, 1990.

□ *SAS Language: Reference* presents information on using the ATTRIB statement to assign or change a permanent format.

□ *SAS Language: Reference* documents using the PUT and INPUT functions for correcting two common errors in working with SAS dates: treating date values containing letters or symbols as character variables or storing dates written as numbers as ordinary numeric variables. Neither method enables you to use dates in calculations.

Part 4
Combining SAS® Data Sets

Chapter **14** Methods of Combining
SAS® Data Sets

Introduction

The SAS System provides several different methods for combining data sets.
Although you may know that you need to combine SAS data sets, you may not
know which method to use. In order to help you decide which method to use,
this chapter briefly introduces four methods of combining data sets:

□ concatenating

□ interleaving

□ merging

□ updating.

Subsequent chapters in this part teach you how to use these methods.

Concatenating

As Figure 14.1 illustrates, *concatenating* combines two or more data sets one
after the other into a single data set. You concatenate data sets using either the
SET statement in a DATA step or the APPEND procedure.

Figure 14.1
Concatenating SAS
Data Sets

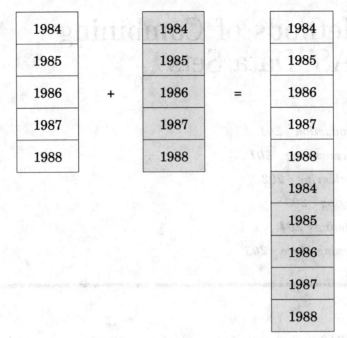

Interleaving

As Figure 14.2 illustrates, *interleaving* combines individual sorted data sets into one sorted data set. For each observation, the figure shows the value of the variable by which the data sets are sorted. You interleave data sets using a SET statement accompanied by a BY statement.

Figure 14.2
Interleaving SAS Data Sets

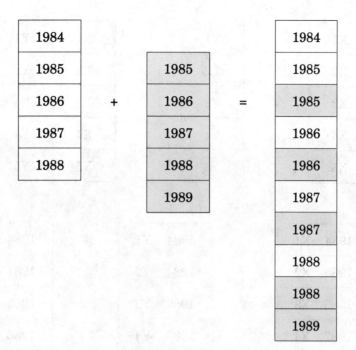

Merging

Merging combines observations from two or more data sets into a single observation in a new data set. A *one-to-one merge*, illustrated in Figure 14.3, combines observations based on their positions in the data sets. A *match-merge*, illustrated in Figure 14.4, combines observations based on the values of one or more common variables. You merge data sets using the MERGE statement and, if you are performing a match-merge, a BY statement.

Figure 14.3
A One-to-One
Merge

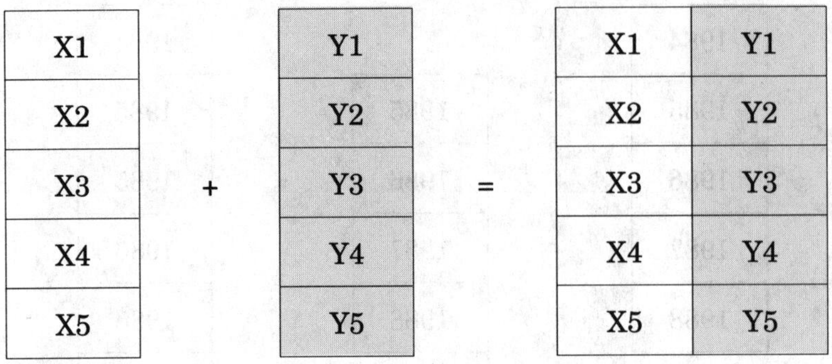

X1
X2
X3
X4
X5

+

Y1
Y2
Y3
Y4
Y5

=

X1	Y1
X2	Y2
X3	Y3
X4	Y4
X5	Y5

Figure 14.4
A Match-Merge

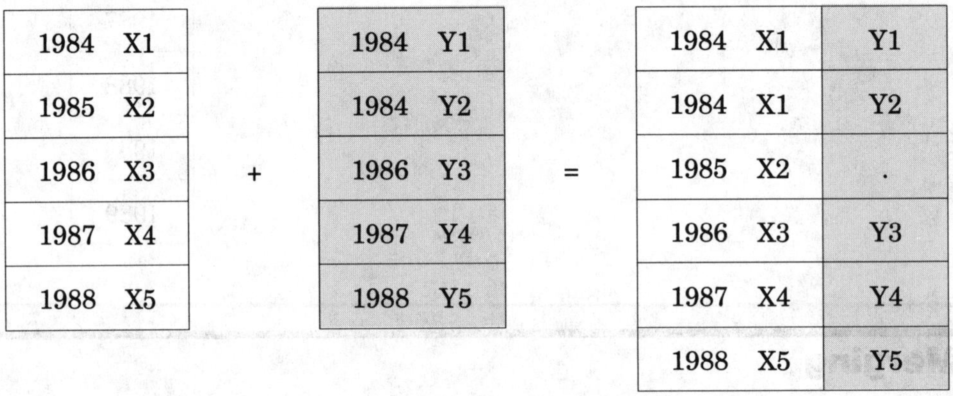

1984	X1
1985	X2
1986	X3
1987	X4
1988	X5

+

1984	Y1
1984	Y2
1986	Y3
1987	Y4
1988	Y5

=

1984	X1	Y1
1984	X1	Y2
1985	X2	.
1986	X3	Y3
1987	X4	Y4
1988	X5	Y5

Updating

As Figure 14.5 illustrates, *updating* replaces the values of variables in one data set (the master data set) with nonmissing values from another data set (the transaction data set). You update a data set using the UPDATE statement accompanied by a BY statement.

Figure 14.5
Updating a
SAS Data Set

1978	X1	Y1
1979	X1	Y1
1980	X1	Y1
1981	X1	Y1
1982	X1	Y1
1983	X1	Y1
1984	X1	Y1
1985	X1	Y1
1986	X1	Y1
1987	X1	Y1

+

1984	X2	.
1985	X2	Y2
1986	X2	.
1986	.	Y2
1988	X2	Y2

=

1978	X1	Y1
1979	X1	Y1
1980	X1	Y1
1981	X1	Y1
1982	X1	Y1
1983	X1	Y1
1984	X2	Y1
1985	X2	Y2
1986	X2	Y2
1987	X1	Y1
1988	X2	Y2

Learning More

□ Part 2, "Getting Your Data into Shape," explains how to create SAS data sets.

□ Chapter 15, "Concatenating SAS Data Sets," explains how to concatenate data sets.

□ Chapter 16, "Interleaving SAS Data Sets," explains how to interleave data sets.

□ Chapter 17, "Merging SAS Data Sets," explains how to merge data sets.

□ Chapter 18, "Updating SAS Data Sets," explains how to update data sets.

□ Chapter 19, "Manipulating SAS Data Sets," explains how to manipulate data sets as you combine them, for example, how to select certain observations from each data set and how to determine which data set an observation came from.

Chapter 15 Concatenating SAS® Data Sets

Introduction

Concatenating combines two or more SAS data sets one after the other into a single data set. The number of observations in the new data set is the sum of the numbers of observations in the original data sets.

    This chapter discusses two ways of concatenating SAS data sets: using the SET statement in a DATA step and using the APPEND procedure. If the data sets you concatenate contain the same variables and each variable has the same attributes in all data sets, the results of the SET statement and PROC APPEND are the same; in other cases, the results differ. This chapter explains both methods and contrasts them so that you can decide which one to use.

Using the SET Statement

The SET statement reads observations from one or more SAS data sets and uses them to build a new data set.

    The simplest form of the SET statement for concatenating data sets is

    SET *SAS-data-set-list*;

where

SAS-data-set-list	is a list of SAS data sets to concatenate. The observations from the first data set you name in the SET statement appear first in the new data set; the observations from the second data set follow those from the first data set, and so on. The list may contain any number of data sets.

The Simplest Case

In the simplest situation, the data sets you concatenate contain the same variables (variables with the same name). In addition, the type, length, informat, format, and label of each variable match across all data sets. In this case, the SAS System copies all observations from the first data set into the new data set, then copies all observations from the second data set into the new data set, and so on. Each observation is an exact copy of the original.

Suppose your company has six separate departments that use the SAS System to maintain personnel records. Management has decided to combine all personnel records. Two departments store their data in the same form. Each observation in both data sets contains values for the following variables:

SSN   is a character variable containing the employee's social security number.

NAME   is a character variable containing the employee's name in the form last name, comma, first name.

HIRED   is a numeric variable containing the date the employee was hired. This variable has a format of DATE7.

SALARY   is a numeric variable containing the employee's annual salary.

PHONE   is a character variable containing the employee's home phone number.

The following SAS program creates and prints the SAS data sets EMPLOYEE.DEPT1 and EMPLOYEE.DEPT2. Output 15.1 shows the data sets.

```
libname employee 'your-data-library';

data employee.dept1;
   input ssn $ 1-9 name $ 11-29 @30 hired date7. salary phone $;
   format hired date7.;
   cards;
429685482 Martin, Virginia    09aug80 34800 493-0824
244967839 Singleton, MaryAnn  24apr85 27900 929-2623
996740216 Leighton, Maurice   16dec83 32600 933-6908
675443925 Freuler, Carl       15feb88 29900 493-3993
845729308 Cage, Merce         19oct82 39800 286-0519
;
run;

proc print data=employee.dept1;
   title 'Data Set EMPLOYEE.DEPT1';
run;
```

```
data employee.dept2;
    input ssn $ 1-9 name $ 11-29 @30 hired date7. salary phone $;
    format hired date7.;
    cards;
324987451 Sayre, Jay        15nov84 44800 933-2998
596771321 Tolson, Andrew    18mar88 41200 929-4800
477562122 Jensen, Helga     01feb81 47400 286-2816
894724859 Kulenic, Marie    24jun83 41400 493-1472
988427431 Zweerink, Anna    07jul85 43700 929-3885
;
run;

proc print data=employee.dept2;
    title 'Data Set EMPLOYEE.DEPT2';
run;
```

Output 15.1
The Data Sets
EMPLOYEE.DEPT1
and
EMPLOYEE.DEPT2

```
                       Data Set EMPLOYEE.DEPT1                         1

    OBS      SSN       NAME              HIRED    SALARY    PHONE

     1    429685482   Martin, Virginia   09AUG80   34800    493-0824
     2    244967839   Singleton, MaryAnn 24APR85   27900    929-2623
     3    996740216   Leighton, Maurice  16DEC83   32600    933-6908
     4    675443925   Freuler, Carl      15FEB88   29900    493-3993
     5    845729308   Cage, Merce        19OCT82   39800    286-0519
```

```
                       Data Set EMPLOYEE.DEPT2                         2

    OBS      SSN         NAME            HIRED    SALARY    PHONE

     1    324987451   Sayre, Jay         15NOV84   44800    933-2998
     2    596771321   Tolson, Andrew     18MAR88   41200    929-4800
     3    477562122   Jensen, Helga      01FEB81   47400    286-2816
     4    894724859   Kulenic, Marie     24JUN83   41400    493-1472
     5    988427431   Zweerink, Anna     07JUL85   43700    929-3885
```

To concatenate the two data sets, simply list them in the SET statement. Use PROC PRINT to display the resulting data set. Output 15.2 shows the new data set. The data set contains all observations from EMPLOYEE.DEPT1 followed by all observations from EMPLOYEE.DEPT2.

```
data employee.dept1_2;
    set employee.dept1 employee.dept2;
run;

proc print data=employee.dept1_2;
    title 'Concatenating EMPLOYEE.DEPT1 and EMPLOYEE.DEPT2';
    title2 'to Create EMPLOYEE.DEPT1_2';
run;
```

Output 15.2
Concatenating
Data Sets with the
Same Variables
and the Same
Variable
Attributes

```
                   Concatenating EMPLOYEE.DEPT1 and EMPLOYEE.DEPT2                1
                           to Create EMPLOYEE.DEPT1_2

        OBS      SSN        NAME              HIRED     SALARY     PHONE

         1    429685482   Martin, Virginia    09AUG80    34800    493-0824
         2    244967839   Singleton, MaryAnn  24APR85    27900    929-2623
         3    996740216   Leighton, Maurice   16DEC83    32600    933-6908
         4    675443925   Freuler, Carl       15FEB88    29900    493-3993
         5    845729308   Cage, Merce         19OCT82    39800    286-0519
         6    324987451   Sayre, Jay          15NOV84    44800    933-2998
         7    596771321   Tolson, Andrew      18MAR88    41200    929-4800
         8    477562122   Jensen, Helga       01FEB81    47400    286-2816
         9    894724859   Kulenic, Marie      24JUN83    41400    493-1472
        10    988427431   Zweerink, Anna      07JUL85    43700    929-3885
```

When Data Sets Contain Different Variables

The data sets in the preceding example contain the same variables, and each variable is defined the same way in both data sets. However, you may want to concatenate data sets when not all variables are common to the data sets named in the SET statement. In this case, the new data set includes all variables from the SAS data sets named in the SET statement.

For example, the personnel records for the third department in your company don't include the variable PHONE. The records for the third department do contain a character variable, SEX, that isn't in the first two data sets. The SAS program for creating and displaying the third data set, EMPLOYEE.DEPT3, follows. Output 15.3 shows the data set.

```
data employee.dept3;
    input ssn $ 1-9 name $ 11-29 sex $ 30 @32 hired date7. salary;
    format hired date7.;
    cards;
744289612 Saparilas, Theresa  F 09may88 33400
824904032 Brosnihan, Dylan    M 04jan82 38200
242779184 Chao, Daeyong       M 28sep85 37500
544382887 Slifkin, Leah       F 24jul84 45000
933476520 Perry, Marguerite   F 19apr82 39900
;
run;

proc print data=employee.dept3;
    title 'Data Set EMPLOYEE.DEPT3';
run;
```

Output 15.3
The Data Set
EMPLOYEE.DEPT3

```
                        Data Set EMPLOYEE.DEPT3                           1

        OBS      SSN          NAME          SEX     HIRED     SALARY

         1    744289612   Saparilas, Theresa  F    09MAY88    33400
         2    824904032   Brosnihan, Dylan    M    04JAN82    38200
         3    242779184   Chao, Daeyong       M    28SEP85    37500
         4    544382887   Slifkin, Leah       F    24JUL84    45000
         5    933476520   Perry, Marguerite   F    19APR82    39900
```

The following program concatenates EMPLOYEE.DEPT1, EMPLOYEE.DEPT2, and EMPLOYEE.DEPT3 and displays the new data set, DEPT1_3. Output 15.4 shows the new data set.

```
data employee.dept1_3;
   set employee.dept1 employee.dept2 employee.dept3;
run;

proc print data=employee.dept1_3;
   title 'Combining Data Sets with Different Variables';
run;
```

Output 15.4
Combining Data
Sets with Different
Variables

```
            Combining Data Sets with Different Variables                1

OBS      SSN        NAME              HIRED    SALARY    PHONE       SEX

  1   429685482   Martin, Virginia   09AUG80   34800   493-0824
  2   244967839   Singleton, MaryAnn 24APR85   27900   929-2623
  3   996740216   Leighton, Maurice  16DEC83   32600   933-6908
  4   675443925   Freuler, Carl      15FEB88   29900   493-3993
  5   845729308   Cage, Merce        19OCT82   39800   286-0519
  6   324987451   Sayre, Jay         15NOV84   44800   933-2998
  7   596771321   Tolson, Andrew     18MAR88   41200   929-4800
  8   477562122   Jensen, Helga      01FEB81   47400   286-2816
  9   894724859   Kulenic, Marie     24JUN83   41400   493-1472
 10   988427431   Zweerink, Anna     07JUL85   43700   929-3885
 11   744289612   Saparilas, Theresa 09MAY88   33400               F
 12   824904032   Brosnihan, Dylan   04JAN82   38200               M
 13   242779184   Chao, Daeyong      28SEP85   37500               M
 14   544382887   Slifkin, Leah      24JUL84   45000               F
 15   933476520   Perry, Marguerite  19APR82   39900               F
```

All observations in the data set EMPLOYEE.DEPT1_3 have values for both the variable SEX and the variable PHONE. Observations from data sets EMPLOYEE.DEPT1 and EMPLOYEE.DEPT2, the data sets that don't contain the variable SEX, have missing values for SEX (indicated by blanks under the variable name); observations from EMPLOYEE.DEPT3, the data set that doesn't contain the variable PHONE, have missing values for PHONE (indicated by blanks under the variable name).

When Variables Have Different Attributes

Each variable in a SAS data set can have as many as six *attributes* associated with it. These attributes are

□ name

□ type

□ length

□ informat

□ format

□ label.

A variable's name is the attribute the SAS System uses to identify the variable. That is, when the SAS System looks at two or more data sets, it considers variables with the same name to be the same variable.

If the data sets you name in the SET statement contain variables with the same names and types, you can concatenate the data sets without modification. However, if variable types differ, you must modify one or more data sets before concatenating them. When lengths, formats, informats, or labels differ, you may want to modify one or more data sets before proceeding.

Different Types

If a variable is defined as character in one data set named in the SET statement and numeric in another, the SAS System issues an error message and doesn't concatenate the data sets.

Suppose the fourth department in your company treats social security number (SSN) as a numeric variable, whereas all other departments treat it as a character variable. The following program creates and displays EMPLOYEE.DEPT4. Output 15.5 shows the data set.

```
data employee.dept4;
    input ssn 1-9 name $ 11-29 sex $ 30 @32 hired date7. salary;
    format hired date7.;
    cards;
634875680 Gardinski, Barbara F 29may88 49800
824576630 Robertson, Hannah  F 14mar85 52700
744826703 Gresham, Jean       F 28apr82 54000
824447605 Kruize, Ronald      M 23may84 49200
988674342 Linzer, Fritz       M 23jul82 50400
;
run;

proc print data=employee.dept4;
    title 'Data Set EMPLOYEE.DEPT4';
run;
```

Output 15.5
The Data Set
EMPLOYEE.DEPT4

```
                         Data Set EMPLOYEE.DEPT4                          1

    OBS       SSN            NAME          SEX      HIRED      SALARY

     1     634875680   Gardinski, Barbara   F     29MAY88     49800
     2     824576630   Robertson, Hannah    F     14MAR85     52700
     3     744826703   Gresham, Jean        F     28APR82     54000
     4     824447605   Kruize, Ronald       M     23MAY84     49200
     5     988674342   Linzer, Fritz        M     23JUL82     50400
```

If you were to try concatenating the data sets for all four departments using the following program, the concatenation would fail.

```
data employee.dept1_4;
   set employee.dept1 employee.dept2
       employee.dept3 employee.dept4;
run;
```

You would receive the following error message in your SAS log:

```
ERROR: Variable SSN has been defined as both character and numeric.
```

Changing the Type of a Variable

One way to correct the previous error is to change the type of the variable SSN in EMPLOYEE.DEPT4 from numeric to character. Because you're unlikely to perform calculations on social security numbers, you can treat SSN as a character variable. You can't change the type of a variable once you have created a data set; you must re-create the data set to change the variable type. You can re-create the data set by changing the INPUT statement to make SSN a character variable, but, it's more efficient to use data set options with the existing SAS data set as the following program illustrates. Output 15.6 shows the new data set. The data set EMPLOYEE.NEWDEPT4 contains the same variables and values as EMPLOYEE.DEPT4. The only difference is that SSN is now a character variable.

```
data employee.newdept4 (drop=tempvar);
    length ssn $ 9;
    set employee.dept4(rename=(ssn=tempvar));
    ssn=tempvar;
run;

proc print data=employee.newdept4;
    title 'New Data Set with SSN as a Character Variable';
run;
```

Output 15.6
The Data Set
EMPLOYEE.NEWDEPT4

```
                New Data Set with SSN as a Character Variable                1

    OBS        SSN             NAME             SEX     HIRED      SALARY

     1      634875680    Gardinski, Barbara      F     29MAY88     49800
     2      824576630    Robertson, Hannah       F     14MAR85     52700
     3      744826703    Gresham, Jean           F     28APR82     54000
     4      824447605    Kruize, Ronald          M     23MAY84     49200
     5      988674342    Linzer, Fritz           M     23JUL82     50400
```

This program changes SSN from a numeric variable to a character variable in the following way:

□ The RENAME= data set option in the SET statement renames the numeric variable SSN to TEMPVAR.

□ A dollar sign in the LENGTH statement defines SSN as a character variable in the new data set.

□ The assignment statement

```
ssn=tempvar;
```

assigns the value of the numeric variable TEMPVAR to the character variable SSN. When it executes this assignment statement, the SAS System automatically converts the data in TEMPVAR from numeric to character because SSN is defined as a character variable.

□ The DROP= data set option in the DATA statement drops the numeric variable TEMPVAR, which has been replaced by the character variable SSN.

When you convert data from numeric to character in this way, the following note appears in your SAS log:

```
NOTE: Numeric values have been converted to character
      values at the places given by: (Number of times) at
      (Line):(Column).
```

Now that the types of all variables match, you can easily concatenate all four data sets using the following program. Output 15.7 shows the new data set.

```
data employee.dept1_4;
   set employee.dept1 employee.dept2
       employee.dept3 employee.newdept4;
run;

proc print data=employee.dept1_4;
   title 'Successful Concatenation After Changing the Type of SSN';
   title2 'from Numeric to Character';
run;
```

Output 15.7
The Data Set
EMPLOYEE.DEPT1_4

```
              Successful Concatenation After Changing the Type of SSN            1
                            from Numeric to Character

   OBS      SSN        NAME               HIRED     SALARY    PHONE       SEX

    1    429685482   Martin, Virginia    09AUG80    34800    493-0824
    2    244967839   Singleton, MaryAnn  24APR85    27900    929-2623
    3    996740216   Leighton, Maurice   16DEC83    32600    933-6908
    4    675443925   Freuler, Carl       15FEB88    29900    493-3993
    5    845729308   Cage, Merce         19OCT82    39800    286-0519
    6    324987451   Sayre, Jay          15NOV84    44800    933-2998
    7    596771321   Tolson, Andrew      18MAR88    41200    929-4800
    8    477562122   Jensen, Helga       01FEB81    47400    286-2816
    9    894724859   Kulenic, Marie      24JUN83    41400    493-1472
   10    988427431   Zweerink, Anna      07JUL85    43700    929-3885
   11    744289612   Saparilas, Theresa  09MAY88    33400                 F
   12    824904032   Brosnihan, Dylan    04JAN82    38200                 M
   13    242779184   Chao, Daeyong       28SEP85    37500                 M
   14    544382887   Slifkin, Leah       24JUL84    45000                 F
   15    933476520   Perry, Marguerite   19APR82    39900                 F
   16    634875680   Gardinski, Barbara  29MAY88    49800                 F
   17    824576630   Robertson, Hannah   14MAR85    52700                 F
   18    744826703   Gresham, Jean       28APR82    54000                 F
   19    824447605   Kruize, Ronald      23MAY84    49200                 M
   20    988674342   Linzer, Fritz       23JUL82    50400                 M
```

Different Formats, Informats, or Labels

When you concatenate data sets with the SET statement, the formats, informats, and labels associated with variables in the new data set are determined by the following rules:

□ An explicitly defined format, informat, or label overrides a default, regardless of the position of the data sets in the SET statement.

□ If two or more data sets explicitly define different formats, informats, or labels for the same variable, the variable in the new data set has the attribute of the first data set in the SET statement that explicitly defines the attribute.

Returning to the example, you may have noticed that all the data sets created so far used a FORMAT statement to explicitly assign a format of DATE7. to the variable HIRED. Therefore, although HIRED is a numeric variable, it appears in all displays as DDMMMYY (for example, 01FEB81). The data set from the fifth department, however, uses a format of DATE9. for HIRED (for example, 01FEB1981). In addition, the data sets from the first four departments use a default format for SALARY, whereas the data set for the fifth department uses an explicitly defined format, COMMA6., for the same variable. The COMMA6. format inserts a comma in the appropriate place when the SAS System displays the numeric variable SALARY.

The following program creates and displays the data set for the fifth department. Output 15.8 shows the data set.

```
data employee.dept5;
    input ssn $ 1-9 name $ 11-29 sex $ 30 ə32 hired date7.
        ə40 salary;
    format hired date9.
        salary comma6.;
    cards;
688774609 Carlton, Susan     F 28jan85 29200
922448328 Hoffmann, Gerald   M 12oct87 27600
544909752 DePuis, David      M 23aug84 32900
745609821 Hahn, Kenneth      M 23aug84 33300
634774295 Landau, Jennifer   F 30apr86 32900
;
run;

proc print data=employee.dept5;
    title 'Data Set EMPLOYEE.DEPT5';
    title2 'Has Different Formats for HIRED and SALARY';
run;
```

Output 15.8
The Data Set
EMPLOYEE.DEPT5

```
                          Data Set EMPLOYEE.DEPT5                          1
                    Has Different Formats for HIRED and SALARY

      OBS      SSN            NAME           SEX       HIRED      SALARY

       1    688774609    Carlton, Susan       F     28JAN1985    29,200
       2    922448328    Hoffmann, Gerald     M     12OCT1987    27,600
       3    544909752    DePuis, David        M     23AUG1984    32,900
       4    745609821    Hahn, Kenneth        M     23AUG1984    33,300
       5    634774295    Landau, Jennifer     F     30APR1986    32,900
```

Now consider what happens when you concatenate EMPLOYEE.DEPT5 with the previous four data sets. Output 15.9 shows the results.

```
data employee.dept1_5;
   set employee.dept1 employee.dept2
       employee.dept3 employee.newdept4
       employee.dept5;
run;

proc print data=employee.dept1_5;
   title 'Concatenating with Different Formats';
run;
```

This concatenation involves a variable (HIRED) with two different explicitly defined formats and a variable (SALARY) with a default and an explicit format. You can see from Output 15.9 that the SAS System creates the new data set according to the rules mentioned earlier:

□ In the case of HIRED, the format defined in the first data set named in the SET statement (DATE7. in EMPLOYEE.DEPT1) prevails.

□ In the case of SALARY, the explicit format (COMMA6.) prevails over the default format.

Output 15.9
Concatenating
Data Sets with
Different Formats

```
                        Concatenating with Different Formats              1

      OBS     SSN       NAME            HIRED    SALARY    PHONE     SEX

       1   429685482  Martin, Virginia  09AUG80   34,800   493-0824
       2   244967839  Singleton, MaryAnn 24APR85  27,900   929-2623
       3   996740216  Leighton, Maurice  16DEC83  32,600   933-6908
       4   675443925  Freuler, Carl      15FEB88  29,900   493-3993
       5   845729308  Cage, Merce        19OCT82  39,800   286-0519
       6   324987451  Sayre, Jay         15NOV84  44,800   933-2998
       7   596771321  Tolson, Andrew     18MAR88  41,200   929-4800
       8   477562122  Jensen, Helga      01FEB81  47,400   286-2816
       9   894724859  Kulenic, Marie     24JUN83  41,400   493-1472
      10   988427431  Zweerink, Anna     07JUL85  43,700   929-3885
      11   744289612  Saparilas, Theresa 09MAY88  33,400              F
      12   824904032  Brosnihan, Dylan   04JAN82  38,200              M
      13   242779184  Chao, Daeyong      28SEP85  37,500              M
      14   544382887  Slifkin, Leah      24JUL84  45,000              F
      15   933476520  Perry, Marguerite  19APR82  39,900              F
      16   634875680  Gardinski, Barbara 29MAY88  49,800              F
      17   824576630  Robertson, Hannah  14MAR85  52,700              F
      18   744826703  Gresham, Jean      28APR82  54,000              F
      19   824447605  Kruize, Ronald     23MAY84  49,200              M
      20   988674342  Linzer, Fritz      23JUL82  50,400              M
      21   688774609  Carlton, Susan     28JAN85  29,200              F
      22   922448328  Hoffmann, Gerald   12OCT87  27,600              M
      23   544909752  DePuis, David      23AUG84  32,900              M
      24   745609821  Hahn, Kenneth      23AUG84  33,300              M
      25   634774295  Landau, Jennifer   30APR86  32,900              F
```

Notice the difference if you perform a similar concatenation but reverse the order of the data sets in the SET statement. Output 15.10 shows the results.

```
data employee.dept5_1;
    set employee.dept5 employee.newdept4
        employee.dept3 employee.dept2
        employee.dept1;
run;

proc print data=employee.dept5_1;
    title 'Concatenating with Different Formats';
    title2 'and Reversing the Order of the Data Sets';
    title3 'in the SET Statement';
run;
```

Output 15.10
*Concatenating
Data Sets with
Different Formats
in a Different
Order*

```
                  Concatenating with Different Formats                    1
                 and Reversing the Order of the Data Sets
                           in the SET Statement

  OBS      SSN       NAME               SEX      HIRED     SALARY   PHONE

    1    688774609   Carlton, Susan      F    28JAN1985   29,200
    2    922448328   Hoffmann, Gerald    M    12OCT1987   27,600
    3    544909752   DePuis, David       M    23AUG1984   32,900
    4    745609821   Hahn, Kenneth       M    23AUG1984   33,300
    5    634774295   Landau, Jennifer    F    30APR1986   32,900
    6    634875680   Gardinski, Barbara  F    29MAY1988   49,800
    7    824576630   Robertson, Hannah   F    14MAR1985   52,700
    8    744826703   Gresham, Jean       F    28APR1982   54,000
    9    824447605   Kruize, Ronald      M    23MAY1984   49,200
   10    988674342   Linzer, Fritz       M    23JUL1982   50,400
   11    744289612   Saparilas, Theresa  F    09MAY1988   33,400
   12    824904032   Brosnihan, Dylan    M    04JAN1982   38,200
   13    242779184   Chao, Daeyong       M    28SEP1985   37,500
   14    544382887   Slifkin, Leah       F    24JUL1984   45,000
   15    933476520   Perry, Marguerite   F    19APR1982   39,900
   16    324987451   Sayre, Jay               15NOV1984   44,800   933-2998
   17    596771321   Tolson, Andrew           18MAR1988   41,200   929-4800
   18    477562122   Jensen, Helga            01FEB1981   47,400   286-2816
   19    894724859   Kulenic, Marie           24JUN1983   41,400   493-1472
   20    988427431   Zweerink, Anna           07JUL1985   43,700   929-3885
   21    429685482   Martin, Virginia         09AUG1980   34,800   493-0824
   22    244967839   Singleton, MaryAnn       24APR1985   27,900   929-2623
   23    996740216   Leighton, Maurice        16DEC1983   32,600   933-6908
   24    675443925   Freuler, Carl            15FEB1988   29,900   493-3993
   25    845729308   Cage, Merce              19OCT1982   39,800   286-0519
```

Output 15.10 shows that not only does the order of the observations change, but in the case of HIRED, the DATE9. format specified in EMPLOYEE.DEPT5 now prevails because that data set now appears first in the SET statement. The COMMA6. format prevails in any case because EMPLOYEE.DEPT5 is the only data set that explicitly specifies a format for the variable SALARY.

Different Lengths

If you use the SET statement to concatenate data sets in which the same variable is assigned different lengths, the outcome of the concatenation depends on whether the variable is numeric or character.

The SET statement determines the length of *numeric* variables by the same rules that govern formats, informats, and labels:

□ An explicitly defined length overrides a default, regardless of the position of the data sets in the SET statement.

□ If two or more data sets explicitly define different lengths for the same variable, the variable in the new data set has the length of the variable in the data set that appears first in the SET statement.

In contrast, if the length of a *character* variable differs among data sets, whether or not the differences are explicit, the length of the variable in the new data set is the length of the variable in the first data set you name in the SET statement that uses that variable.

The following program creates the data set EMPLOYEE.DEPT6. Notice that the INPUT statement for this data set creates NAME with a length of 27; in all other data sets, NAME has a length of 19. Output 15.11 shows the data set.

```
data employee.dept6;
    input ssn $ 1-9 name $ 11-37 sex $ 38 @40 hired date7. salary;
    format hired date7.;
    cards;
922854076 Schoenberg, Marguerite      F 19nov84 39800
770434994 Addison-Hardy, Jonathon     M 23feb82 41400
242784883 McNaughton, Elizabeth       F 24jul83 45000
377882806 Tharrington, Catherine      F 28sep84 38600
292450691 Frangipani, Christopher     M 12aug80 43900
;
run;

proc print data=employee.dept6;
    title 'Data Set EMPLOYEE.DEPT6';
run;
```

Output 15.11
The Data Set
EMPLOYEE.DEPT6

```
                        Data Set EMPLOYEE.DEPT6                           1

    OBS       SSN              NAME              SEX      HIRED    SALARY

     1      922854076    Schoenberg, Marguerite   F     19NOV84    39800
     2      770434994    Addison-Hardy, Jonathon  M     23FEB82    41400
     3      242784883    McNaughton, Elizabeth    F     24JUL83    45000
     4      377882806    Tharrington, Catherine   F     28SEP84    38600
     5      292450691    Frangipani, Christopher  M     12AUG80    43900
```

If you concatenate all six data sets, naming EMPLOYEE.DEPT6 in any position but the first in the SET statement, the SAS System defines NAME with a length of 19. Output 15.12 shows that the SAS System truncates the values for NAME from EMPLOYEE.DEPT6 (the last five observations in the new data set).

```
data employee.dept1_6;
    set employee.dept1 employee.dept2
        employee.dept3 employee.newdept4
        employee.dept5 employee.dept6;
run;
```

```
proc print data=employee.dept1_6;
   title 'Concatenating with Different Lengths';
run;
```

Output 15.12
Truncation of NAME

```
              Concatenating with Different Lengths                    1
 OBS    SSN        NAME              HIRED   SALARY   PHONE     SEX

   1  429685482  Martin, Virginia    09AUG80  34,800  493-0824
   2  244967839  Singleton, MaryAnn  24APR85  27,900  929-2623
   3  996740216  Leighton, Maurice   16DEC83  32,600  933-6908
   4  675443925  Freuler, Carl       15FEB88  29,900  493-3993
   5  845729308  Cage, Merce         19OCT82  39,800  286-0519
   6  324987451  Sayre, Jay          15NOV84  44,800  933-2998
   7  596771321  Tolson, Andrew      18MAR88  41,200  929-4800
   8  477562122  Jensen, Helga       01FEB81  47,400  286-2816
   9  894724859  Kulenic, Marie      24JUN83  41,400  493-1472
  10  988427431  Zweerink, Anna      07JUL85  43,700  929-3885
  11  744289612  Saparilas, Theresa  09MAY88  33,400            F
  12  824904032  Brosnihan, Dylan    04JAN82  38,200            M
  13  242779184  Chao, Daeyong       28SEP85  37,500            M
  14  544382887  Slifkin, Leah       24JUL84  45,000            F
  15  933476520  Perry, Marguerite   19APR82  39,900            F
  16  634875680  Gardinski, Barbara  29MAY88  49,800            F
  17  824576630  Robertson, Hannah   14MAR85  52,700            F
  18  744826703  Gresham, Jean       28APR82  54,000            F
  19  824447605  Kruize, Ronald      23MAY84  49,200            M
  20  988674342  Linzer, Fritz       23JUL82  50,400            M
  21  688774609  Carlton, Susan      28JAN85  29,200            F
  22  922448328  Hoffmann, Gerald    12OCT87  27,600            M
  23  544909752  DePuis, David       23AUG84  32,900            M
  24  745609821  Hahn, Kenneth       23AUG84  33,300            M
  25  634774295  Landau, Jennifer    30APR86  32,900            F
  26  922854076  Schoenberg, Marguer 19NOV84  39,800            F
  27  770434994  Addison-Hardy, Jona 23FEB82  41,400            M
  28  242784883  McNaughton, Elizabe 24JUL83  45,000            F
  29  377882806  Tharrington, Cather 28SEP84  38,600            F
  30  292450691  Frangipani, Christo 12AUG80  43,900            M
```

You can solve this problem two ways: by changing the order of data sets in the SET statement or by changing the length of NAME in the new data set. In the first case, simply list the data set that uses the longer length (EMPLOYEE.DEPT6) first:

```
data employee.dept6_1;
   set employee.dept6 employee.dept5
       employee.newdept4 employee.dept3
       employee.dept2 employee.dept1;
run;
```

If you don't want to change the order in which you concatenate the data sets, include a LENGTH statement in the DATA step that creates the new data set. If you're changing the length of a numeric variable, the LENGTH statement can appear anywhere in the DATA step. However, when you change the length of a character variable, the LENGTH statement must precede the SET statement. For example, the following program creates the data set EMPLOYEE.DEPT1_6A. The LENGTH statement gives the character variable NAME a length of 27, even though the first data set in the SET statement (EMPLOYEE.DEPT1) assigns it a length of 19. Output 15.13 shows that all values of NAME are complete. Note that the order of the variables in the new data set changes because NAME is the first variable encountered in the DATA step.

```
data employee.dept1_6a;
    length name $ 27;
    set employee.dept1 employee.dept2
        employee.dept3 employee.newdept4
        employee.dept5 employee.dept6;
run;

proc print data=employee.dept1_6a;
    title 'Changing the Length of a Character Variable';
    title2 'before Concatenating the Data Sets';
run;
```

Output 15.13
Fixing the
Problem of
Different Lengths
by Using a
LENGTH
Statement

```
               Changing the Length of a Character Variable            1
                      before Concatenating the Data Sets

    OBS  NAME                    SSN        HIRED   SALARY  PHONE     SEX

      1  Martin, Virginia        429685482  09AUG80  34,800  493-0824
      2  Singleton, MaryAnn      244967839  24APR85  27,900  929-2623
      3  Leighton, Maurice       996740216  16DEC83  32,600  933-6908
      4  Freuler, Carl           675443925  15FEB88  29,900  493-3993
      5  Cage, Merce             845729308  19OCT82  39,800  286-0519
      6  Sayre, Jay              324987451  15NOV84  44,800  933-2998
      7  Tolson, Andrew          596771321  18MAR88  41,200  929-4800
      8  Jensen, Helga           477562122  01FEB81  47,400  286-2816
      9  Kulenic, Marie          894724859  24JUN83  41,400  493-1472
     10  Zweerink, Anna          988427431  07JUL85  43,700  929-3885
     11  Saparilas, Theresa      744289612  09MAY88  33,400            F
     12  Brosnihan, Dylan        824904032  04JAN82  38,200            M
     13  Chao, Daeyong           242779184  28SEP85  37,500            M
     14  Slifkin, Leah           544382887  24JUL84  45,000            F
     15  Perry, Marguerite       933476520  19APR82  39,900            F
     16  Gardinski, Barbara      634875680  29MAY88  49,800            F
     17  Robertson, Hannah       824576630  14MAR85  52,700            F
     18  Gresham, Jean           744826703  28APR82  54,000            F
     19  Kruize, Ronald          824447605  23MAY84  49,200            M
     20  Linzer, Fritz           988674342  23JUL82  50,400            M
     21  Carlton, Susan          688774609  28JAN85  29,200            F
     22  Hoffmann, Gerald        922448328  12OCT87  27,600            M
     23  DePuis, David           544909752  23AUG84  32,900            M
     24  Hahn, Kenneth           745609821  23AUG84  33,300            M
     25  Landau, Jennifer        634774295  30APR86  32,900            F
     26  Schoenberg, Marguerite  922854076  19NOV84  39,800            F
     27  Addison-Hardy, Jonathon 770434994  23FEB82  41,400            M
     28  McNaughton, Elizabeth   242784883  24JUL83  45,000            F
     29  Tharrington, Catherine  377882806  28SEP84  38,600            F
     30  Frangipani, Christopher 292450691  12AUG80  43,900            M
```

Using the APPEND Procedure

The APPEND procedure adds the observations from one SAS data set to the end of another SAS data set. PROC APPEND doesn't process the observations in the first data set; it simply adds the observations in the second data set directly to the end of the original data set.

The form of the PROC APPEND statement is

PROC APPEND BASE=*base-SAS-data-set* <DATA=*SAS-data-set-to-append*>
<FORCE>;

where

base-SAS-data-set
> names the SAS data set to which you want to append the observations. If this data set doesn't exist, the SAS System creates it. At the completion of PROC APPEND, the *base-SAS-data-set* becomes the current (most recently created) SAS data set.

SAS-data-set-to-append
> names the SAS data set containing the observations to add to the end of the base data set. If you omit this option, PROC APPEND adds the observations in the current SAS data set to the end of the base data set.

FORCE
> forces PROC APPEND to concatenate the files in situations in which the procedure would normally fail. The following sections explain when to use the FORCE option.

The Simplest Case

Consider the following program, which appends the data set EMPLOYEE.DEPT2 to the data set EMPLOYEE.DEPT1 and displays the result. Recall that both data sets contain the same variables and that each variable has the same attributes in both data sets. Output 15.14 shows the output.

```
proc append base=employee.dept1 data=employee.dept2;
run;

proc print data=employee.dept1;
    title 'EMPLOYEE.DEPT1 After Appending EMPLOYEE.DEPT2';
run;
```

Output 15.14
Appending
EMPLOYEE.DEPT2
to
EMPLOYEE.DEPT1

```
                 EMPLOYEE.DEPT1 After Appending EMPLOYEE.DEPT2              1

   OBS      SSN       NAME                 HIRED    SALARY    PHONE

    1    429685482   Martin, Virginia     09AUG80   34800    493-0824
    2    244967839   Singleton, MaryAnn   24APR85   27900    929-2623
    3    996740216   Leighton, Maurice    16DEC83   32600    933-6908
    4    675443925   Freuler, Carl        15FEB88   29900    493-3993
    5    845729308   Cage, Merce          19OCT82   39800    286-0519
    6    324987451   Sayre, Jay           15NOV84   44800    933-2998
    7    596771321   Tolson, Andrew       18MAR88   41200    929-4800
    8    477562122   Jensen, Helga        01FEB81   47400    286-2816
    9    894724859   Kulenic, Marie       24JUN83   41400    493-1472
   10    988427431   Zweerink, Anna       07JUL85   43700    929-3885
```

The resulting data set is identical to the data set created by naming EMPLOYEE.DEPT1 and EMPLOYEE.DEPT2 in the SET statement (compare Output 15.14 to Output 15.2). However, it's important to realize that PROC APPEND permanently alters the base data set. EMPLOYEE.DEPT1 now contains observations from two departments.

When Data Sets Contain Different Variables

Recall that the third data set, EMPLOYEE.DEPT3, contains a variable, SEX, that isn't in either of the first two data sets, and it lacks the variable PHONE that is in the other two data sets. What happens if you try to use PROC APPEND to concatenate data sets that contain different variables?

If you were to try appending EMPLOYEE.DEPT3 to EMPLOYEE.DEPT1 using the following program, the concatenation would fail:

```
proc append base=employee.dept1 data=employee.dept3;
run;
```

You would receive the following warning messages:

```
WARNING:  Variable SEX was not found on BASE file.
WARNING:  Variable PHONE was not found on DATA file.
```

and the following error message:

```
ERROR:  No appending done because of anomalies listed above.
        Use FORCE option to append these files.
```

You must use the FORCE option with PROC APPEND when the DATA= data set contains a variable that isn't in the BASE= data set. If you modify the program to include the FORCE option, it successfully concatenates the files. Output 15.15 shows the results.

```
proc append base=employee.dept1 data=employee.dept3 force;
run;

proc print data=employee.dept1;
    title 'Using the FORCE Option to Append Data Sets that Contain';
    title2 'Different Variables';
run;
```

Output 15.15
Concatenating
Data Sets
Containing
Different Variables

```
                   Using the FORCE Option to Append Data Sets that Contain        1
                                      Different Variables
        OBS       SSN         NAME              HIRED     SALARY    PHONE

          1    429685482   Martin, Virginia    09AUG80    34800    493-0824
          2    244967839   Singleton, MaryAnn  24APR85    27900    929-2623
          3    996740216   Leighton, Maurice   16DEC83    32600    933-6908
          4    675443925   Freuler, Carl       15FEB88    29900    493-3993
          5    845729308   Cage, Merce         19OCT82    39800    286-0519
          6    324987451   Sayre, Jay          15NOV84    44800    933-2998
          7    596771321   Tolson, Andrew      18MAR88    41200    929-4800
          8    477562122   Jensen, Helga       01FEB81    47400    286-2816
          9    894724859   Kulenic, Marie      24JUN83    41400    493-1472
         10    988427431   Zweerink, Anna      07JUL85    43700    929-3885
         11    744289612   Saparilas, Theresa  09MAY88    33400
         12    824904032   Brosnihan, Dylan    04JAN82    38200
         13    242779184   Chao, Daeyong       28SEP85    37500
         14    544382887   Slifkin, Leah       24JUL84    45000
         15    933476520   Perry, Marguerite   19APR82    39900
```

Output 15.15 illustrates two important points about using PROC APPEND to concatenate data sets with different variables:

□ If the BASE= data set contains a variable that isn't in the DATA= data set (for example, PHONE), PROC APPEND concatenates the data sets and assigns a missing value to that variable in observations taken from the DATA= data set.

□ If the DATA= data set contains a variable that isn't in the BASE= data set (for example, SEX), the FORCE option in the PROC APPEND statement forces the procedure to concatenate the two data sets, but because that variable isn't in the descriptor portion of the base data set, the procedure can't include it in the concatenated data set.

Note: In this example both data sets contain a variable that isn't in the other. It is only the case of a variable in the DATA= data set that isn't in the BASE= data set that requires the use of the FORCE option. However, both cases display a warning in the log.

When Variables Have Different Attributes

If a variable has different attributes in the BASE= data set than it does in the DATA= data set, the attributes in the BASE= data set prevail. In the cases of differing formats, informats, and labels, the concatenation succeeds. If the length of a variable is longer in the BASE= data set than in the DATA= data set, the concatenation succeeds. However, if the length of a variable is longer in the DATA= data set than in the BASE= data set, or if the same variable is a character variable in one data set and a numeric variable in the other, PROC APPEND fails to concatenate the files unless you specify the FORCE option.

Using the FORCE option has the following consequences:

□ The length specified in the BASE= data set prevails. Therefore, the SAS System truncates values from the DATA= data set to fit them into the length specified in the BASE= data set.

□ The type specified in the BASE= data set prevails. The procedure replaces values of the wrong type (all values for the variable in the DATA= data set) with missing values.

Choosing between PROC APPEND and the SET Statement

If two data sets contain the same variables and the variables possess the same attributes, the file that results from concatenating them with PROC APPEND is the same as the file that results from concatenating them with the SET statement. PROC APPEND concatenates much faster than the SET statement, particularly when the BASE= data set is large, because PROC APPEND doesn't process the observations from the BASE= data set. However, the two methods of concatenating are sufficiently different that when the variables or their attributes differ between data sets, you must consider the differences in behavior before you decide which method to use. Table 15.1 summarizes the major differences between the SET statement and PROC APPEND.

Table 15.1
Differences between the SET Statement and PROC APPEND

Condition	SET Statement	PROC APPEND
Number of data sets you can concatenate	Any number	Two
Data sets contain different variables	Uses all variables. Assigns missing values where appropriate.	Uses all variables in the BASE= data set. Assigns missing values to observations from the DATA= data set where appropriate. Requires the FORCE option to concatenate if the DATA= data set contains variables that aren't in the BASE= data set. Can't include variables found only in the DATA= data set when concatenating the data sets.

(continued)

Table 15.1
(continued)

Condition	SET Statement	PROC APPEND
Different formats, informats, or labels	Uses explicitly defined formats, informats, and labels over defaults. If two or more data sets explicitly define the format, informat, or label, uses the definition from the data set you name first in the SET statement.	Uses formats, informats, and labels from the BASE= data set.
Different lengths	If the same variable has a different length in two or more data sets, uses the length from the data set you name first in the SET statement.	Requires the FORCE option if the length of a variable is longer in the DATA= data set. Truncates the values of the variable to match the length in the BASE= data set.
Different types	Doesn't concatenate.	Requires the FORCE option to concatenate. Uses type from the BASE= data set and assigns missing values to the variable in observations from the DATA= data set.

SAS Tools

This chapter discusses using the SET and DATA statements to concatenate SAS data sets:

DATA *SAS-data-set*;
SET *SAS-data-set-list*;
> read multiple SAS data sets and create a single SAS data set.
> *SAS-data-set* is the name of the SAS data set you want to create, and
> *SAS-data-set-list* is a list of SAS data sets to concatenate.

This chapter discusses using the APPEND procedure to concatenate SAS data sets:

PROC APPEND BASE=*base-SAS-data-set*<DATA=*SAS-data-set-to-append*>
       <FORCE>;
> appends the DATA= data set to the BASE= data set. *Base-SAS-data-set*
> names the SAS data set to which you want to append the observations. If
> this data set doesn't exist, the SAS System creates it. At the completion
> of PROC APPEND the base data set becomes the current (most recently
> created) SAS data set. *SAS-data-set-to-append* names the SAS data set
> containing the observations to add to the end of the base data set. If you

(PROC APPEND BASE= continued)

omit this option, PROC APPEND adds the observations in the current SAS data set to the end of the base data set. FORCE forces PROC APPEND to concatenate the files in situations in which the procedure would, by default, fail.

Learning More

□ Chapter 19, "Manipulating SAS Data Sets," discusses using the IN= data set option and the END= option in the SET statement. The IN= option allows you to process observations from each data set differently. The END= option allows you to determine when the SAS System is processing the last observation in the DATA step.

□ Chapter 32, "Managing SAS Data Libraries," describes how to use the CONTENTS statement in the DATASETS procedure to display information about a data set, including the names, positions, and types of all variables. This information reveals any problems you may have when you try to concatenate data sets and helps you decide whether to use the SET statement or PROC APPEND.

□ *SAS Language: Reference, Version 6, First Edition* provides information on variable attributes.

□ The *SAS Procedures Guide, Version 6, Third Edition* provides documentation on using the APPEND statement in the DATASETS procedure to concatenate SAS data sets.

Chapter 16 Interleaving SAS® Data Sets

Introduction

Interleaving combines individual sorted SAS data sets into one sorted data set. You interleave data sets using a SET statement and a BY statement in a DATA step. The number of observations in the new data set is the sum of the number of observations in the original data sets.

This chapter discusses how to use the BY statement, how to sort data sets to prepare for interleaving, and how to use the SET and BY statements together to interleave observations.

Using BY-Group Processing

The BY statement specifies the variable or variables by which you want to interleave the data sets. In order to understand interleaving, you must understand BY variables, BY values, and BY groups.

BY variable
> is a variable named in a BY statement.

BY value
> is the value of a BY variable.

BY group
> is all observations with the same values for all BY variables. In discussions of interleaving, BY groups commonly span more than one data set. If you use more than one variable in a BY statement, a BY group is a group of observations with a unique combination of values for those variables.

When interleaving, the SAS System creates a new data set as follows:

1. Before executing the SET statement, the SAS System reads the descriptor portion of each data set you name in the SET statement and creates a program data vector that, by default, contains all the variables from all data sets as well as any variables created by the DATA step. It sets the value of each variable to missing.

2. It looks at the first BY group in each data set you name in the SET statement in order to determine which BY group should appear first in the new data set.

3. It copies all observations in that BY group from each data set containing observations in the BY group to the new data set. It copies from the data sets in the same order as they appear in the SET statement.

4. It looks at the next BY group in each data set to determine which BY group should appear next in the new data set.

5. It sets the value of each variable in the program data vector to missing.

6. It repeats steps 3 through 5 until it has copied all observations to the new data set.

Preparing to Interleave Data Sets

Before you can interleave data sets, the data must be sorted by the same variable or variables you will use with the BY statement that accompanies your SET statement.

Suppose the Research and Development division and the Publications division of your company both maintain data sets containing information about each project currently under way. Each data set includes the following variables:

PROJECT	is a unique code that identifies the project.
DEPT	is the name of a department involved in the project.
MANAGER	is the last name of the manager from DEPT.
HEADCOUN	is the number of people working for MANAGER on this project.

You want to combine the data sets by PROJECT so that the new data set shows the resources that both divisions are devoting to each project. Both data sets must be sorted by PROJECT before you can interleave them.

The following program creates and displays INTLEAVE.RANDD. Output 16.1 shows the data set. Note that the data are already sorted by PROJECT.

```
libname intleave 'your-data-library';

data intleave.randd;
   length dept manager $ 10;
   input project $ dept $ manager $ headcoun;
   cards;
MP971 Designing Daugherty 10
MP971 Coding Newton 8
MP971 Testing Miller 7
SL827 Designing Robinson 8
SL827 Coding Moore 10
SL827 Testing Baker 7
WP057 Designing Cliver 11
WP057 Coding Constant 13
WP057 Testing Slivko 10
;
run;

proc print data=intleave.randd;
   title 'Data Set INTLEAVE.RANDD';
run;
```

Output 16.1
The Data Set
INTLEAVE.RAND

```
                        Data Set INTLEAVE.RANDD                         1

        OBS    DEPT         MANAGER       PROJECT    HEADCOUN

         1     Designing    Daugherty     MP971         10
         2     Coding       Newton        MP971          8
         3     Testing      Miller        MP971          7
         4     Designing    Robinson      SL827          8
         5     Coding       Moore         SL827         10
         6     Testing      Baker         SL827          7
         7     Designing    Cliver        WP057         11
         8     Coding       Constant      WP057         13
         9     Testing      Slivko        WP057         10
```

The following program creates, sorts, and displays the second data set, INTLEAVE.PUBS. Output 16.2 shows the data set sorted by PROJECT.

```
data intleave.pubs;
   length dept manager $ 10;
   input manager $ dept $ project $ headcoun;
   cards;
Cook Writing WP057 5
Deakins Writing SL827 7
Franscombe Editing MP971 4
Henry Editing WP057 3
King Production SL827 5
Krysonski Production WP057 3
Lassiter Graphics SL827 3
Miedema Editing SL827 5
Morard Writing MP971 6
Posey Production MP971 4
Spackle Graphics WP057 2
;
run;

proc sort data=intleave.pubs;
   by project;
run;

proc print data=intleave.pubs;
   title 'Data Set INTLEAVE.PUBS Sorted by Project';
run;
```

Output 16.2
The Sorted Data
Set
INTLEAVE.PUBS

```
              Data Set INTLEAVE.PUBS Sorted by Project            1

     OBS      DEPT        MANAGER       PROJECT      HEADCOUN

      1      Editing     Franscombe     MP971           4
      2      Writing     Morard         MP971           6
      3      Production  Posey          MP971           4
      4      Writing     Deakins        SL827           7
      5      Production  King           SL827           5
      6      Graphics    Lassiter       SL827           3
      7      Editing     Miedema        SL827           5
      8      Writing     Cook           WP057           5
      9      Editing     Henry          WP057           3
     10      Production  Krysonski      WP057           3
     11      Graphics    Spackle        WP057           2
```

Interleaving the Data Sets

To interleave the data set INTLEAVE.RANDD and the data set INTLEAVE.PUBS, use the SET statement and the BY statement. Output 16.3 shows the new data set.

```
data intleave.randdpub;
   set intleave.randd intleave.pubs;
   by project;
run;
```

```
proc print data=intleave.randdpub;
   title 'Interleaving INTLEAVE.RANDD and INTLEAVE.PUBS';
   title2 'by PROJECT';
run;
```

Output 16.3
Results of
Interleaving the
Data Sets

```
        Interleaving INTLEAVE.RANDD and INTLEAVE.PUBS          1
                          by PROJECT

   OBS     DEPT         MANAGER       PROJECT    HEADCOUN

     1    Designing    Daugherty      MP971         10
     2    Coding       Newton         MP971          8
     3    Testing      Miller         MP971          7
     4    Editing      Franscombe     MP971          4
     5    Writing      Morard         MP971          6
     6    Production   Posey          MP971          4
     7    Designing    Robinson       SL827          8
     8    Coding       Moore          SL827         10
     9    Testing      Baker          SL827          7
    10    Writing      Deakins        SL827          7
    11    Production   King           SL827          5
    12    Graphics     Lassiter       SL827          3
    13    Editing      Miedema        SL827          5
    14    Designing    Cliver         WP057         11
    15    Coding       Constant       WP057         13
    16    Testing      Slivko         WP057         10
    17    Writing      Cook           WP057          5
    18    Editing      Henry          WP057          3
    19    Production   Krysonski      WP057          3
    20    Graphics     Spackle        WP057          2
```

The new data set INTLEAVE.RANDDPUB includes all observations from both data sets. Each BY group in the new data set contains observations from INTLEAVE.RANDD followed by observations from INTLEAVE.PUBS.

SAS Tools

This chapter discusses using the SET statement with the BY statement to interleave SAS data sets:

SET *SAS-data-set-list*;
BY *variable-list*;

> read multiple sorted SAS data sets and create one sorted SAS data set. *SAS-data-set-list* is a list of the SAS data sets to interleave; *variable-list* is a list of the variables by which to interleave the data sets. The data sets must be sorted by the same list of variables before you can interleave them.

Learning More

- □ Chapter 10, "Working with Grouped or Sorted Observations," explains how to use the SORT procedure and the BY statement.

- □ Chapter 15, "Concatenating SAS Data Sets," presents information on concatenating data sets when they contain different variables or when the same variables have different attributes. The same rules apply to interleaving data sets as to concatenating them.

- □ *SAS Language: Reference, Version 6, First Edition* and the *SAS Procedures Guide, Version 6, Third Edition* provide more information on indexing. You don't need to sort unordered data sets before interleaving them if the data sets have an index on the variable or variables by which you want to interleave.

Chapter **17** Merging SAS® Data Sets

Introduction

Merging combines observations from two or more SAS data sets into a single observation in a new SAS data set. The new data set contains all variables from all the original data sets unless you specify otherwise.

This chapter discusses two types of merging: one-to-one merging and match merging. In *one-to-one merging*, you don't use a BY statement. Observations are combined based on their postions in the input data sets. In *match merging*, you use a BY statement to combine observations from the input data sets based on common BY groups.

Using the MERGE Statement

You merge data sets using the MERGE statement in a DATA step. The form of the MERGE statement used in this chapter is

> **MERGE** *SAS-data-set-list*;
> **BY** *variable-list*;

where

SAS-data-set-list   is a list of the SAS data sets to merge. The list may contain any number of data sets.

variable-list   is a list of variables by which to merge the data sets. If you use a BY statement, the data sets must be sorted by the same BY variables before you can merge them.

One-to-One Merging

When you use the MERGE statement without a BY statement, the SAS System combines the first observation in all data sets you name in the MERGE statement into the first observation in the new data set, the second observation in all data sets into the second observation in the new data set, and so on. In a one-to-one merge, the number of observations in the new data set is equal to the number of observations in the largest data set you name in the MERGE statement.

A Simple One-to-One Merge

Suppose you teach an improvisational acting class. At the beginning of the semester, you want to schedule a conference with each student. You have one data set, IMPROV.CLASS, that contains the following variables:

NAME   is the student's name.

YEAR   is the student's year: freshman, sophomore, junior, or senior.

MAJOR   is the student's area of specialization (missing for freshmen and sophomores, who haven't selected a major subject yet).

The following SAS program creates and displays the data set IMPROV.CLASS. Output 17.1 shows the data set.

```
libname improv 'your-data-library';

data improv.class;
   input name $ 1-25 year $ 26-34 major $ 36-50;
   cards;
Abbott, Jennifer          freshman
Carter, Tom               junior     Theater
Kirby, Elissa             senior     Mathematics
Tucker, Rachel            freshman
Uhl, Roland               sophomore
Wacenske, Maurice         junior     Theater
;
run;

proc print data=improv.class;
   title 'The Data Set IMPROV.CLASS';
run;
```

Output 17.1
The Data Set
IMPROV.CLASS

```
                    The Data Set IMPROV.CLASS                          1

        OBS    NAME                  YEAR        MAJOR

         1     Abbott, Jennifer      freshman
         2     Carter, Tom           junior      Theater
         3     Kirby, Elissa         senior      Mathematics
         4     Tucker, Rachel        freshman
         5     Uhl, Roland           sophomore
         6     Wacenske, Maurice     junior      Theater
```

Your second data set contains a list of the dates and times you have
scheduled conferences and the rooms in which the conferences are to take place.
The following program creates and displays the data set IMPROV.TIMESLOT.
Note the use of the date format and informat. Output 17.2 shows the data set.

```
data improv.timeslot;
   input date date7. @10 time $ @17 room $;
   format date date7.;
   cards;
12sep88  10:00  103
12sep88  10:30  103
12sep88  11:00  207
13sep88  10:00  105
13sep88  10:30  105
15sep88  11:00  207
;
run;

proc print data=improv.timeslot;
   title 'Dates, Times, and Locations of Conferences';
run;
```

Output 17.2
The Data Set
IMPROV.TIMESLOT

```
              Dates, Times, and Locations of Conferences              1

              OBS     DATE      TIME    ROOM

               1     12SEP88   10:00    103
               2     12SEP88   10:30    103
               3     12SEP88   11:00    207
               4     13SEP88   10:00    105
               5     13SEP88   10:30    105
               6     15SEP88   11:00    207
```

The following program performs a one-to-one merge of these data sets, assigning a time slot for a conference to each student in the class. Output 17.3 shows the conference schedule data set.

```
data improv.schedule;
   merge improv.class improv.timeslot;
run;

proc print data=improv.schedule;
   title 'Merging IMPROV.CLASS and IMPROV.TIMESLOT to Assign';
   title2 'Conference Times to Students';
run;
```

Output 17.3
Conference Schedule Created by One-to-One Merge of IMPROV.CLASS and IMPROV.TIMESLOT

```
         Merging IMPROV.CLASS and IMPROV.TIMESLOT to Assign             1
                     Conference Times to Students

OBS   NAME                  YEAR          MAJOR          DATE    TIME   ROOM

 1    Abbott, Jennifer      freshman                    12SEP88  10:00  103
 2    Carter, Tom           junior        Theater       12SEP88  10:30  103
 3    Kirby, Elissa         senior        Mathematics   12SEP88  11:00  207
 4    Tucker, Rachel        freshman                    13SEP88  10:00  105
 5    Uhl, Roland           sophomore                   13SEP88  10:30  105
 6    Wacenske, Maurice     junior        Theater       15SEP88  11:00  207
```

Output 17.3 shows that the new data set combines the first observation from IMPROV.CLASS with the first observation from IMPROV.TIMESLOT, the second from IMPROV.CLASS with the second from IMPROV.TIMESLOT, and so on.

Data Sets with the Same Variables

The previous example illustrates the simplest case of a one-to-one merge: the data sets contain the same number of observations, all variables have unique names, and you want to keep all variables from both data sets in the new data set. Now consider merging data sets that contain the same variables (variables with the same names).

Suppose you teach two improvisational acting classes. In addition to the data set IMPROV.CLASS, you also have the data set IMPROV.CLASS2, which contains the same variables as IMPROV.CLASS but one more observation. The following program creates and displays the data set IMPROV.CLASS2. Output 17.4 shows the data set.

```
data improv.class2;
   input name $ 1-25 year $ 26-34 major $ 36-50;
   cards;
Hitchcock-Tyler, Erin     sophomore
Keil, Deborah             junior    Theater
Nacewicz, Chester         junior    Theater
Norgaard, Rolf            sophomore
Prism, Lindsay            senior    Anthropology
Singh, Rajiv              sophomore
Wittich, Stefan           junior    Physics
;
run;
```

```
proc print data=improv.class2;
   title 'The Data Set IMPROV.CLASS2';
run;
```

Output 17.4
The Data Set
IMPROV.CLASS2

```
                     The Data Set IMPROV.CLASS2                      1

          OBS    NAME                    YEAR        MAJOR

           1     Hitchcock-Tyler, Erin   sophomore
           2     Keil, Deborah           junior      Theater
           3     Nacewicz, Chester       junior      Theater
           4     Norgaard, Rolf          sophomore
           5     Prism, Lindsay          senior      Anthropology
           6     Singh, Rajiv            sophomore
           7     Wittich, Stefan         junior      Physics
```

Instead of scheduling conferences for one class, you want to schedule improvisational exercises for pairs of students, one student from each class. You want to create a data set in which each observation contains the name of one student from each class and the date, time, and location of the exercise. You don't want the variables YEAR and MAJOR in the new data set.

You can create this new data set by merging the data sets IMPROV.CLASS, IMPROV.CLASS2, and IMPROV.TIMESLOT. Because you don't want YEAR and MAJOR in the new data set, use the DROP= data set option to drop them. Notice that the data sets IMPROV.CLASS and IMPROV.CLASS2 both contain the variable NAME, but the values for NAME are different in each data set. To preserve both sets of values, you must use the RENAME= data set option to rename the variable in one of the data sets.

The following program uses these data set options to merge the three data sets. Output 17.5 shows the new data set.

```
data improv.exercise;
   merge improv.class (drop=year major)
         improv.class2 (drop=year major rename=(name=name2))
         improv.timeslot;
run;


proc print data=improv.exercise;
   title 'Merging Three Data Sets While Dropping and Renaming';
   title2 'Some Variables';
run;
```

Output 17.5
Creating a
Schedule for Pairs
of Students by
Merging Three
Data Sets

```
        Merging Three Data Sets While Dropping and Renaming        1
                          Some Variables

  OBS   NAME                NAME2                  DATE     TIME   ROOM

   1    Abbott, Jennifer    Hitchcock-Tyler, Erin  12SEP88  10:00  103
   2    Carter, Tom         Keil, Deborah          12SEP88  10:30  103
   3    Kirby, Elissa       Nacewicz, Chester      12SEP88  11:00  207
   4    Tucker, Rachel      Norgaard, Rolf         13SEP88  10:00  105
   5    Uhl, Roland         Prism, Lindsay         13SEP88  10:30  105
   6    Wacenske, Maurice   Singh, Rajiv           15SEP88  11:00  207
   7                        Wittich, Stefan            .
```

Here's an explanation of how the SAS System merges the data sets.

1. Before executing the DATA step, the SAS System reads the descriptor portion of each data set you name in the MERGE statement and creates a program data vector for the new data set that, by default, contains all the variables from all data sets, as well as variables created by the DATA step. In this case, however, the DROP= data set option excludes the variables YEAR and MAJOR from the program data vector. The RENAME= data set option adds the variable NAME2 to the program data vector. Therefore, the program data vector contains the variables NAME, NAME2, DATE, TIME, and ROOM.

2. The SAS System sets the value of each variable in the program data vector to missing, as Figure 17.1 illustrates.

Figure 17.1
Program Data Vector before Reading from Data Sets

NAME	NAME2	DATE	TIME	ROOM
		.		

3. Next, the SAS System reads and copies the first observation from each data set into the program data vector (reading the data sets in the same order they appear in the MERGE statement), as Figure 17.2 illustrates.

Figure 17.2
Program Data Vector after Reading from Each Data Set

NAME	NAME2	DATE	TIME	ROOM
Abbott, Jennifer		.		

NAME	NAME2	DATE	TIME	ROOM
Abbott, Jennifer	Hitchcock-Tyler, Erin	.		

NAME	NAME2	DATE	TIME	ROOM
Abbott, Jennifer	Hitchcock-Tyler, Erin	12SEP88	10:00	103

4. After processing the first observation from the last data set and executing any other statements in the DATA step, the SAS System writes the contents of the program data vector to the new data set. If the DATA step attempts to read past the end of a data set, the values of all variables from that data set in the program data vector are set to missing.

This behavior has two important consequences:

□ If a variable exists in more than one data set, the value from the last data set the SAS System reads is the value that goes into the new data set (even if that value is missing). If you want to keep all the values for like-named variables from different data sets, you must rename one or more of the variables with the RENAME= data set option so that each variable has a unique name.

□ Once the SAS System has processed all observations in a data set, the program data vector and all subsequent observations in the *new* data set have missing values for the variables unique to that data set. So, as Figure 17.3 shows, the program data vector for the last observation in the new data set contains missing values for all variables except NAME2.

Figure 17.3
Program Data Vector for the Last Observation

NAME	NAME2	DATE	TIME	ROOM
	Wittich, Stefan	.		

5. The SAS System continues to merge observations until it has copied all observations from all data sets.

Match-Merging

Merging with a BY statement allows you to match observations according to the values of the BY variables you specify. Before you can perform a match-merge, all data sets must be sorted by the variables you want to use for the merge.

In order to understand match-merging, you must understand BY variables, BY values, and BY groups.

BY variable
is a variable named in a BY statement.

BY value
is the value of a BY variable.

BY group
is all observations with the same values for all BY variables. In discussions of match-merging, BY groups commonly span more than one data set. If you use more than one variable in a BY statement, a BY group is a group of observations with a unique combination of values for those variables.

Suppose you are the director of a small repertory theater company. You maintain company records in two SAS data sets. One data set, THEATER.COMPANY, contains the following variables:

NAME   is the name of the player.

AGE   is the player's age.

SEX   is the player's sex.

A second data set, THEATER.FINANCE, contains these variables:

NAME   is the player's name.

SSN   is the player's social security number.

SALARY   is the player's annual salary.

The following program creates, displays, and sorts THEATER.COMPANY and THEATER.FINANCE. Output 17.6 shows the data sets.

```
data theater.company;
    input name $ 1-25 age 27-28 sex $ 30;
    cards;
Vincent, Martina          34 F
Phillipon, Marie-Odile    28 F
Gunter, Thomas            27 M
Harbinger, Nicholas       36 M
Benito, Gisela            32 F
Rudelich, Herbert         39 M
Sirignano, Emily          12 F
Morrison, Michael         32 M
;
run;

proc sort data=theater.company;
   by name;
run;

proc print data=theater.company;
    title 'The Data Set THEATER.COMPANY Sorted by NAME';
run;

data theater.finance;
    input ssn $ 1-11 name $ 13-40 salary;
    cards;
074-53-9892 Vincent, Martina           35000
776-84-5391 Phillipon, Marie-Odile     29750
929-75-0218 Gunter, Thomas             27500
446-93-2122 Harbinger, Nicholas        33900
228-88-9649 Benito, Gisela             28000
029-46-9261 Rudelich, Herbert          35000
442-21-8075 Sirignano, Emily           5000
;
run;
```

```
proc sort data=theater.finance;
   by name;
run;

proc print data=theater.finance;
   title 'The Data Set THEATER.FINANCE Sorted by NAME';
run;
```

Output 17.6
The Data Sets
THEATER.COMPANY
and
THEATER.FINANCE

```
                    The Data Set THEATER.COMPANY Sorted by NAME                  1

           OBS      NAME                      AGE    SEX

            1       Benito, Gisela             32     F
            2       Gunter, Thomas             27     M
            3       Harbinger, Nicholas        36     M
            4       Morrison, Michael          32     M
            5       Phillipon, Marie-Odile     28     F
            6       Rudelich, Herbert          39     M
            7       Sirignano, Emily           12     F
            8       Vincent, Martina           34     F
```

```
                    The Data Set THEATER.FINANCE Sorted by NAME                  2

        OBS        SSN            NAME                    SALARY

         1      228-88-9649    Benito, Gisela             28000
         2      929-75-0218    Gunter, Thomas             27500
         3      446-93-2122    Harbinger, Nicholas        33900
         4      776-84-5391    Phillipon, Marie-Odile     29750
         5      029-46-9261    Rudelich, Herbert          35000
         6      442-21-8075    Sirignano, Emily            5000
         7      074-53-9892    Vincent, Martina           35000
```

You decide that you don't need to maintain two separate data sets, so you want to merge the records for each player from both data sets into a new data set that contains all the variables. The variable common to both data sets is NAME. Therefore, NAME is the appropriate BY variable.

Because the data sets are already sorted by NAME, you can use the following SAS program to merge them by NAME. Output 17.7 shows the new data set.

```
data theater.compfin;
   merge theater.company theater.finance;
   by name;
run;

proc print data=theater.compfin;
   title 'Merging THEATER.COMPANY and THEATER.FINANCE';
run;
```

Output 17.7
Result of Merging
THEATER.COMPANY
and
THEATER.FINANCE

```
                    Merging THEATER.COMPANY and THEATER.FINANCE               1

    OBS    NAME                    AGE    SEX        SSN        SALARY

     1     Benito, Gisela           32     F      228-88-9649    28000
     2     Gunter, Thomas           27     M      929-75-0218    27500
     3     Harbinger, Nicholas      36     M      446-93-2122    33900
     4     Morrison, Michael        32     M                         .
     5     Phillipon, Marie-Odile   28     F      776-84-5391    29750
     6     Rudelich, Herbert        39     M      029-46-9261    35000
     7     Sirignano, Emily         12     F      442-21-8075     5000
     8     Vincent, Martina         34     F      074-53-9892    35000
```

The new data set contains one observation for each player in the company. Each observation contains all the variables from both data sets. Notice in particular the fourth observation. The data set THEATER.FINANCE doesn't have an observation for Michael Morrison. In this case, the values of the variables unique to THEATER.FINANCE (SSN and SALARY) are missing.

Data Sets with Multiple Observations in a BY Group

When neither data set has more than one observation in a BY group, merging is simple. The following example illustrates what happens when a data set does have more than one observation in a BY group.

While trying to work out casting for the season, you created a third data set, THEATER.REPTORY, that contains the following variables:

PLAY   is the name of one of the plays in the repertory.

ROLE   is the name of a character in PLAY.

SSN   is the social security number of the player playing ROLE.

The following program creates and displays THEATER.REPTORY. Output 17.8 shows the data set.

```
data theater.reptory;
   input play $ 1-23 role $ 25-48 ssn $ 50-60;
   cards;
No Exit                 Estelle                 074-53-9892
No Exit                 Inez                    776-84-5391
No Exit                 Valet                   929-75-0218
No Exit                 Garcin                  446-93-2122
Happy Days              Winnie                  074-53-9892
Happy Days              Willie                  446-93-2122
The Glass Menagerie     Amanda Wingfield        228-88-9649
The Glass Menagerie     Laura Wingfield         776-84-5391
The Glass Menagerie     Tom Wingfield           929-75-0218
The Glass Menagerie     Jim O'Connor            029-46-9261
The Dear Departed       Mrs. Slater             228-88-9649
The Dear Departed       Mrs. Jordan             074-53-9892
The Dear Departed       Henry Slater            029-46-9261
The Dear Departed       Ben Jordan              446-93-2122
The Dear Departed       Victoria Slater         442-21-8075
The Dear Departed       Abel Merryweather       929-75-0218
;
run;

proc print data=theater.reptory;
   title 'The Data Set THEATER.REPTORY';
run;
```

Output 17.8
The Data Set
THEATER.REPTORY

```
                   The Data Set THEATER.REPTORY                           1

     OBS  PLAY                 ROLE                  SSN

       1  No Exit              Estelle               074-53-9892
       2  No Exit              Inez                  776-84-5391
       3  No Exit              Valet                 929-75-0218
       4  No Exit              Garcin                446-93-2122
       5  Happy Days           Winnie                074-53-9892
       6  Happy Days           Willie                446-93-2122
       7  The Glass Menagerie  Amanda Wingfield      228-88-9649
       8  The Glass Menagerie  Laura Wingfield       776-84-5391
       9  The Glass Menagerie  Tom Wingfield         929-75-0218
      10  The Glass Menagerie  Jim O'Connor          029-46-9261
      11  The Dear Departed    Mrs. Slater           228-88-9649
      12  The Dear Departed    Mrs. Jordan           074-53-9892
      13  The Dear Departed    Henry Slater          029-46-9261
      14  The Dear Departed    Ben Jordan            446-93-2122
      15  The Dear Departed    Victoria Slater       442-21-8075
      16  The Dear Departed    Abel Merryweather     929-75-0218
```

To maintain confidentiality during preliminary casting, this data set identifies players by social security number. However, casting decisions are now final, and you want to replace each social security number with the player's name. You can, of course, re-create the data set, entering each player's name instead of the social security number in the raw data. Or, you can make use of the data set THEATER.FINANCE, which already contains the name and social security number of all players (see Output 17.7). If you merge the data sets, the SAS System takes care of adding the players' names to the data set for you.

Of course, before you can merge the data sets, you must sort them by SSN. Output 17.9 shows the sorted data sets.

```
proc sort data=theater.finance;
   by ssn;
run;

proc sort data=theater.reptory;
   by ssn;
run;

proc print data=theater.finance;
   title 'The Data Set THEATER.FINANCE Sorted by SSN';
run;

proc print data=theater.reptory;
   title 'The Data Set THEATER.REPTORY Sorted by SSN';
run;
```

Output 17.9
Sorting
THEATER.FINANCE
and
THEATER.REPTORY
by SSN

```
                    The Data Set THEATER.FINANCE Sorted by SSN                   1

        OBS        SSN          NAME                    SALARY

         1     029-46-9261    Rudelich, Herbert          35000
         2     074-53-9892    Vincent, Martina           35000
         3     228-88-9649    Benito, Gisela             28000
         4     442-21-8075    Sirignano, Emily            5000
         5     446-93-2122    Harbinger, Nicholas        33900
         6     776-84-5391    Phillipon, Marie-Odile     29750
         7     929-75-0218    Gunter, Thomas             27500
```

```
                    The Data Set THEATER.REPTORY Sorted by SSN                   2

       OBS    PLAY                 ROLE                    SSN

         1    The Glass Menagerie  Jim O'Connor         029-46-9261
         2    The Dear Departed    Henry Slater         029-46-9261
         3    No Exit              Estelle              074-53-9892
         4    Happy Days           Winnie               074-53-9892
         5    The Dear Departed    Mrs. Jordan          074-53-9892
         6    The Glass Menagerie  Amanda Wingfield     228-88-9649
         7    The Dear Departed    Mrs. Slater          228-88-9649
         8    The Dear Departed    Victoria Slater      442-21-8075
         9    No Exit              Garcin               446-93-2122
        10    Happy Days           Willie               446-93-2122
        11    The Dear Departed    Ben Jordan           446-93-2122
        12    No Exit              Inez                 776-84-5391
        13    The Glass Menagerie  Laura Wingfield      776-84-5391
        14    No Exit              Valet                929-75-0218
        15    The Glass Menagerie  Tom Wingfield        929-75-0218
        16    The Dear Departed    Abel Merryweather    929-75-0218
```

These two data sets contain seven BY groups, that is, among the 23 observations are seven different values for the BY variable, SSN. The first BY group has a value of 029-46-9261 for SSN. THEATER.FINANCE has one observation in this BY group; THEATER.REPTORY has two. The last BY group has a value of 929-75-0218 for SSN. THEATER.FINANCE has one observation in this BY group; THEATER.REPTORY has three.

The following program merges the data sets THEATER.FINANCE and THEATER.REPTORY. The OPTIONS statement extends the line size to 120 so that PROC PRINT can display all variables on one line. Output 17.10 shows the new data set. It contains all variables from both data sets.

Note: Most output in this chapter is created with line size set to 76 in the OPTIONS statement. An OPTIONS statement appears only in examples using a different line size. Once you set the LINESIZE= option, it remains in effect until you reset it or end the SAS session.

```
options linesize=120;

data theater.finrep;
   merge theater.finance theater.reptory;
   by ssn;
run;

proc print data=theater.finrep;
   title 'Adding Players'' Names to THEATER.REPTORY';
   title2 'by';
   title3 'Merging It with THEATER.FINANCE';
run;
```

Output 17.10   *The Data Set THEATER.FINREP Contains All Variables from THEATER.REPTORY and THEATER.FINANCE*

```
                            Adding Players' Names to THEATER.REPTORY                                    1
                                              by
                              Merging It with THEATER.FINANCE

      OBS      SSN          NAME                    SALARY      PLAY                  ROLE

       1    029-46-9261   Rudelich, Herbert          35000    The Glass Menagerie   Jim O'Connor
       2    029-46-9261   Rudelich, Herbert          35000    The Dear Departed     Henry Slater
       3    074-53-9892   Vincent, Martina           35000    No Exit               Estelle
       4    074-53-9892   Vincent, Martina           35000    Happy Days            Winnie
       5    074-53-9892   Vincent, Martina           35000    The Dear Departed     Mrs. Jordan
       6    228-88-9649   Benito, Gisela             28000    The Glass Menagerie   Amanda Wingfield
       7    228-88-9649   Benito, Gisela             28000    The Dear Departed     Mrs. Slater
       8    442-21-8075   Sirignano, Emily            5000    The Dear Departed     Victoria Slater
       9    446-93-2122   Harbinger, Nicholas        33900    No Exit               Garcin
      10    446-93-2122   Harbinger, Nicholas        33900    Happy Days            Willie
      11    446-93-2122   Harbinger, Nicholas        33900    The Dear Departed     Ben Jordan
      12    776-84-5391   Phillipon, Marie-Odile     29750    No Exit               Inez
      13    776-84-5391   Phillipon, Marie-Odile     29750    The Glass Menagerie   Laura Wingfield
      14    929-75-0218   Gunter, Thomas             27500    No Exit               Valet
      15    929-75-0218   Gunter, Thomas             27500    The Glass Menagerie   Tom Wingfield
      16    929-75-0218   Gunter, Thomas             27500    The Dear Departed     Abel Merryweather
```

Carefully examine the first few observations in the new data set in Output 17.10 and consider how the SAS System creates them.

1. Before executing the DATA step, the SAS system reads the descriptor portion of the two data sets and creates a program data vector that contains all variables from both data sets: SSN, NAME, and SALARY from THEATER.FINANCE; PLAY and ROLE from THEATER.REPTORY (SSN is already in the program data vector because it's in THEATER.FINANCE). It sets the values of all variables to missing, as Figure 17.4 illustrates.

Figure 17.4
Program Data
Vector before
Reading from
Data Sets

SSN	NAME	SALARY	PLAY	ROLE
		.		

2. The SAS System looks at the first BY group in each data set to determine which BY group should appear first. In this case, the first BY group, observations with the value 029-46-9261 for SSN, is the same in both data sets.

3. The SAS System reads and copies the first observation from THEATER.FINANCE into the program data vector, as Figure 17.5 illustrates.

Figure 17.5
Program Data
Vector after
Reading
THEATER.FINANCE

SSN	NAME	SALARY	PLAY	ROLE
029-46-9261	Rudelich, Herbert	35000		

4. The SAS System reads and copies the first observation from THEATER.REPTORY into the program data vector, as Figure 17.6 illustrates. If a data set doesn't have any observations in a BY group, the program data vector contains missing values for the variables unique to that data set.

Figure 17.6
Program Data
Vector after
Reading
THEATER.REPTORY

SSN	NAME	SALARY	PLAY	ROLE
029-46-9261	Rudelich, Herbert	35000	The Glass Menagerie	Jim O'Connor

5. The SAS System writes the observation to the new data set and retains the values in the program data vector. (If the program data vector contained variables created by the DATA step, the SAS System would set them to missing after writing to the new data set.)

6. The SAS System looks for a second observation in the BY group in each data set. THEATER.REPTORY has one; THEATER.FINANCE doesn't. The MERGE statement reads the second observation in the BY group from THEATER.REPTORY. Because THEATER.FINANCE has only one observation in the BY group, the statement uses the values of NAME (`Rudelich, Herbert`) and SALARY (35000) retained in the program data vector for the second observation in the new data set, as Figure 17.7 illustrates.

Figure 17.7
Program Data Vector with Second Observation in the BY Group

SSN	NAME	SALARY	PLAY	ROLE
029-46-9261	Rudelich, Herbert	35000	The Dear Departed	Henry Slater

7. The SAS System writes the observation to the new data set. Neither data set contains any more observations in this BY group. Therefore, as Figure 17.8 illustrates, the SAS System sets all values in the program data vector to missing and begins processing the next BY group. It continues processing observations until it exhausts all observations in both data sets.

Figure 17.8
Program Data Vector before New BY Groups

SSN	NAME	SALARY	PLAY	ROLE
		.		

Now that casting decisions are final, you want to post the casting list. However, you don't want the variable SALARY in the data set. Nor do you need the variable SSN now that NAME is in the data set. As the following SAS program illustrates, you can easily eliminate SALARY and SSN by using the DROP= data set option when you create the new data set. Output 17.11 shows the new data set.

```
data theater.newrep (drop=ssn);
   merge theater.finance (drop=salary) theater.reptory;
   by ssn;
run;

proc print data=theater.newrep;
   title 'Replacing Players'' Social Security Numbers';
   title2 'with Their Names';
run;
```

Note: The difference in placement of the two DROP= data set options is crucial. Dropping SSN in the DATA statement means that the variable is available to the MERGE and BY statements (to which it is essential) but that it doesn't go into the new data set. Dropping SALARY in the MERGE statement means that the MERGE statement doesn't even read this variable, so SALARY is unavailable to the program statements.

Output 17.11
Dropping SALARY
and SSN while
Merging
THEATER.REPTORY
and
THEATER.FINANCE

```
                        Replacing Players' Social Security Numbers                1
                                   with Their Names

       OBS    NAME                    PLAY                    ROLE

        1     Rudelich, Herbert       The Glass Menagerie      Jim O'Connor
        2     Rudelich, Herbert       The Dear Departed        Henry Slater
        3     Vincent, Martina        No Exit                  Estelle
        4     Vincent, Martina        Happy Days               Winnie
        5     Vincent, Martina        The Dear Departed        Mrs. Jordan
        6     Benito, Gisela          The Glass Menagerie      Amanda Wingfield
        7     Benito, Gisela          The Dear Departed        Mrs. Slater
        8     Sirignano, Emily        The Dear Departed        Victoria Slater
        9     Harbinger, Nicholas     No Exit                  Garcin
       10     Harbinger, Nicholas     Happy Days               Willie
       11     Harbinger, Nicholas     The Dear Departed        Ben Jordan
       12     Phillipon, Marie-Odile  No Exit                  Inez
       13     Phillipon, Marie-Odile  The Glass Menagerie      Laura Wingfield
       14     Gunter, Thomas          No Exit                  Valet
       15     Gunter, Thomas          The Glass Menagerie      Tom Wingfield
       16     Gunter, Thomas          The Dear Departed        Abel Merryweather
```

Data Sets with the Same Variables

You can match-merge data sets that contain the same variables (variables with the same name) by using the RENAME= data set option, just as you would when performing a one-to-one merge (see the section "Data Sets with the Same Variables," under "One-to-One Merging," earlier in this chapter).

If you don't use the RENAME= option and a variable exists in more than one data set, the value of that variable in the last data set read is the value that goes into the new data set.

Data Sets That Lack a Common Variable

You can name any number of data sets in the MERGE statement. However, if you are match-merging the data sets, you must be sure they all have a common variable and are sorted by that variable. If the data sets don't have a common variable, you may be able to use another data set that has variables common to the original data sets to merge them.

For instance, consider the data sets used in the match-merge examples. Table 17.1 shows the names of the data sets and the names of the variables in each data set.

Table 17.1 *Data Sets and* *Variables Used in* *Match-Merge* *Examples*	Data Set	Variables
	THEATER.COMPANY	NAME AGE SEX
	THEATER.FINANCE	NAME SSN SALARY
	THEATER.REPTORY	PLAY ROLE SSN

These data sets don't share a common variable. However, THEATER.COMPANY and THEATER.FINANCE share the variable NAME. Similarly, THEATER.FINANCE and THEATER.REPTORY share the variable SSN. Therefore, as the following SAS program shows, you can merge the data sets into one with two separate DATA steps. As usual, you must sort the data sets by the appropriate BY variable. (THEATER.REPTORY is already sorted by SSN.) Output 17.12 shows the data set.

```
options linesize=120;

proc sort data=theater.finance;
   by name;
run;

proc sort data=theater.company;
   by name;
run;

   /* Merge THEATER.COMPANY and THEATER.FINANCE into a */
   /* temporary data set.                              */
data temp;
   merge theater.company theater.finance;
   by name;
run;

proc sort data=temp;
   by ssn;
run;

   /* Merge the temporary data set with THEATER.REPTORY */
data theater.all;
   merge temp theater.reptory;
   by ssn;
run;

proc print data=theater.all;
   title 'Merging Three Data Sets that Lack a Common Variable';
run;
```

In order to merge the three data sets, this program

□ sorts THEATER.FINANCE and THEATER.COMPANY by NAME

□ merges THEATER.COMPANY and THEATER.FINANCE into a temporary data set, TEMP

□ sorts TEMP by SSN

□ merges TEMP and THEATER.REPTORY by SSN.

Output 17.12   *Match-Merging Data Sets That Lack a Common Variable*

```
                    Merging Three Data Sets that Lack a Common Variable                    1

    OBS   NAME                     AGE   SEX      SSN       SALARY    PLAY                 ROLE

     1    Morrison, Michael         32    M                                               
     2    Rudelich, Herbert         39    M    029-46-9261   35000    The Glass Menagerie  Jim O'Connor
     3    Rudelich, Herbert         39    M    029-46-9261   35000    The Dear Departed    Henry Slater
     4    Vincent, Martina          34    F    074-53-9892   35000    No Exit              Estelle
     5    Vincent, Martina          34    F    074-53-9892   35000    Happy Days           Winnie
     6    Vincent, Martina          34    F    074-53-9892   35000    The Dear Departed    Mrs. Jordan
     7    Benito, Gisela            32    F    228-88-9649   28000    The Glass Menagerie  Amanda Wingfield
     8    Benito, Gisela            32    F    228-88-9649   28000    The Dear Departed    Mrs. Slater
     9    Sirignano, Emily          12    F    442-21-8075    5000    The Dear Departed    Victoria Slater
    10    Harbinger, Nicholas       36    M    446-93-2122   33900    No Exit              Garcin
    11    Harbinger, Nicholas       36    M    446-93-2122   33900    Happy Days           Willie
    12    Harbinger, Nicholas       36    M    446-93-2122   33900    The Dear Departed    Ben Jordan
    13    Phillipon, Marie-Odile    28    F    776-84-5391   29750    No Exit              Inez
    14    Phillipon, Marie-Odile    28    F    776-84-5391   29750    The Glass Menagerie  Laura Wingfield
    15    Gunter, Thomas            27    M    929-75-0218   27500    No Exit              Valet
    16    Gunter, Thomas            27    M    929-75-0218   27500    The Glass Menagerie  Tom Wingfield
    17    Gunter, Thomas            27    M    929-75-0218   27500    The Dear Departed    Abel Merryweather
```

One-to-One Merging versus Match-Merging

Use one-to-one merging when you want to combine one observation from each data set and it doesn't matter which observations merge with each other. The first example in this chapter merged an observation containing a student's name, year, and major with an observation containing a date, time, and location for a conference. It doesn't matter which student gets which time slot; therefore, a one-to-one merge is appropriate.

In cases where you must merge certain observations, use a match-merge. In the last example, it's crucial that you first merge observations with the same name, then observations with the same social security number. You must also merge one observation from TEMP with from one to three observations in THEATER.REPTORY. Therefore, you must use a match-merge.

Sometimes you may want to merge by a particular variable, but your data are arranged in such a way that you can see that a one-to-one merge will work. The following example illustrates a case when you could use a one-to-one merge for matching observations because you're certain your data are ordered correctly. However, as a subsequent example shows, it is risky to use a one-to-one merge in such situations. Consider the data set THEATER.COMPANY2. Each observation in this data set corresponds to an observation with the same value of NAME in THEATER.FINANCE. The following program creates and displays THEATER.COMPANY2; it also displays THEATER.FINANCE for comparison. Output 17.3 shows the data set.

```
data theater.company2;
    input name $ 1-25 age 27-28 sex $ 30;
    cards;
Benito, Gisela           32 F
Gunter, Thomas           27 M
Harbinger, Nicholas      36 M
Phillipon, Marie-Odile   28 F
Rudelich, Herbert        39 M
Sirignano, Emily         12 F
Vincent, Martina         34 F
;
run;

proc print data=theater.company2;
    title 'The Data Set THEATER.COMPANY2';
run;

proc print data=theater.finance;
    title 'The Data Set THEATER.FINANCE';
run;
```

Output 17.13
The Data Sets
THEATER.COMPANY2
and
THEATER.FINANCE

```
                 The Data Set THEATER.COMPANY2                    1

          OBS    NAME                     AGE    SEX

           1     Benito, Gisela            32     F
           2     Gunter, Thomas            27     M
           3     Harbinger, Nicholas       36     M
           4     Phillipon, Marie-Odile    28     F
           5     Rudelich, Herbert         39     M
           6     Sirignano, Emily          12     F
           7     Vincent, Martina          34     F
```

```
                   The Data Set THEATER.FINANCE                    2

        OBS       SSN           NAME                  SALARY

         1    228-88-9649    Benito, Gisela           28000
         2    929-75-0218    Gunter, Thomas           27500
         3    446-93-2122    Harbinger, Nicholas      33900
         4    776-84-5391    Phillipon, Marie-Odile   29750
         5    029-46-9261    Rudelich, Herbert        35000
         6    442-21-8075    Sirignano, Emily          5000
         7    074-53-9892    Vincent, Martina         35000
```

The following program shows that because both data sets are sorted by NAME and because each observation in one data set has a corresponding observation in the other data set, a one-to-one merge has the same result as merging by NAME. Output 17.14 shows the two new data sets. You can see that they are identical.

```
    /* One-to-one merge */
data theater.onetoone;
    merge theater.company2 theater.finance;
run;
```

```
proc print data=theater.onetoone;
   title 'Using a One-to-One Merge to Combine';
   title2 'THEATER.COMPANY2 and THEATER.FINANCE';
run;


   /* Match-merge */
data theater.match;
   merge theater.company2 theater.finance;
   by name;
run;

proc print data=theater.match;
   title 'Using a Match-Merge to Combine';
   title2 'THEATER.COMPANY2 and THEATER.FINANCE';
run;
```

Output 17.14
Comparing a
One-to-One Merge
with a
Match-Merge when
Observations
Correspond

```
                    Using a One-to-One Merge to Combine                  1
                   THEATER.COMPANY2 and THEATER.FINANCE

      OBS   NAME                 AGE   SEX      SSN       SALARY

       1    Benito, Gisela        32    F    228-88-9649   28000
       2    Gunter, Thomas        27    M    929-75-0218   27500
       3    Harbinger, Nicholas   36    M    446-93-2122   33900
       4    Phillipon, Marie-Odile 28   F    776-84-5391   29750
       5    Rudelich, Herbert     39    M    029-46-9261   35000
       6    Sirignano, Emily      12    F    442-21-8075    5000
       7    Vincent, Martina      34    F    074-53-9892   35000
```

```
                     Using a Match-Merge to Combine                      2
                   THEATER.COMPANY2 and THEATER.FINANCE

      OBS   NAME                 AGE   SEX      SSN       SALARY

       1    Benito, Gisela        32    F    228-88-9649   28000
       2    Gunter, Thomas        27    M    929-75-0218   27500
       3    Harbinger, Nicholas   36    M    446-93-2122   33900
       4    Phillipon, Marie-Odile 28   F    776-84-5391   29750
       5    Rudelich, Herbert     39    M    029-46-9261   35000
       6    Sirignano, Emily      12    F    442-21-8075    5000
       7    Vincent, Martina      34    F    074-53-9892   35000
```

Even though the resulting data sets are identical, it isn't wise to use a one-to-one merge when it's essential to merge a particular observation from one data set with a particular observation from another data set.

In the preceding example, you can easily determine that the data sets contain the same values for NAME and that the values appear in the same order. However, if the data sets contained hundreds of observations, it would be difficult to ascertain that all the values match. If the observations don't match, serious problems can occur. The following example illustrates why you shouldn't use a one-to-one merge for matching observations.

Consider the original data set, THEATER.COMPANY, which contains an observation for Michael Morrison (see Output 17.7). THEATER.FINANCE has no corresponding observation. Suppose you didn't realize this fact and tried to use the following program to perform a one-to-one merge with THEATER.FINANCE. Output 17.15 shows the new data set and reveals several problems.

```
data theater.badmerge;
    merge theater.company theater.finance;
run;

proc print data=theater.badmerge;
    title 'Using a One-to-One Merge Instead of a Match-Merge';
run;
```

Output 17.15
The Data Set
THEATER.BADMERGE
Pairs Some
Observations
Incorrectly

```
                 Using a One-to-One Merge Instead of a Match-Merge              1

  OBS    NAME                  AGE    SEX       SSN          SALARY

   1     Benito, Gisela         32     F     228-88-9649      28000
   2     Gunter, Thomas         27     M     929-75-0218      27500
   3     Harbinger, Nicholas    36     M     446-93-2122      33900
   4     Phillipon, Marie-Odile 32     M     776-84-5391      29750
   5     Rudelich, Herbert      28     F     029-46-9261      35000
   6     Sirignano, Emily       39     M     442-21-8075       5000
   7     Vincent, Martina       12     F     074-53-9892      35000
   8     Vincent, Martina       34     F                          .
```

The first three observations merge correctly. However, THEATER.FINANCE doesn't have an observation for Michael Morrison. A one-to-one merge makes no attempt to match parts of the observations from the different data sets. It simply combines observations based on their positions in the data sets you name in the MERGE statement. Therefore, the fourth observation in THEATER.BADMERGE combines the fourth observation in THEATER.COMPANY (Michael's name, age, and sex) with the fourth observation in THEATER.FINANCE (Marie-Odile's name, social security number, and salary). As the SAS System combines the observations, Marie-Odile's name overwrites Michael's. After writing this observation to the new data set, the SAS System processes the next observation in each data set. These observations are similarly mismatched.

This type of mismatch continues until the seventh observation when the MERGE statement exhausts the observations in the smaller data set, THEATER.FINANCE. After writing the seventh observation to the new data set, the SAS System begins the next iteration of the DATA step. Because the SAS System has read all observations in THEATER.FINANCE, it sets the values for variables from that data set to missing in the program data vector. Then it reads the values for NAME, AGE, and SEX from THEATER.COMPANY and writes the contents of the program data vector to the new data set. Therefore, the last observation has the same value for NAME as the previous observation and contains missing values for SSN and SALARY.

These missing values and the duplication of the value for NAME might make you suspect that the observations didn't merge as you intended them to. However, if instead of being an additional observation, the observation for Michael Morrison replaced another observation in THEATER.COMPANY2, no observations would have missing values, and the problem wouldn't be so easy to spot. Therefore, you're safer using a match-merge in situations that call for it even if you think the data are arranged so that a one-to-one merge will have the same results.

SAS Tools

This chapter discusses using the MERGE statement to combine observations from one or more SAS data sets:

MERGE *SAS-data-set-list*;
BY *variable-list*;

> read observations in multiple SAS data sets and combine them into one observation in one new SAS data set. *SAS-data-set-list* is a list of the SAS data sets to merge. The list may contain any number of data sets; *variable-list* is a list of variables by which to merge the data sets. If you use a BY statement, the data sets must be sorted by the same BY variables before you can merge them. If you don't use a BY statement, the SAS System merges observations based on their positions in the original data sets.

Learning More

□ *SAS Language: Reference, Version 6, First Edition* documents SAS date and time formats and informats. The examples in this chapter read TIME as a character variable, and they read DATE with a SAS date informat. You could read TIME using special SAS time informats.

□ *SAS Language: Reference* and the *SAS Procedures Guide, Version 6, Third Edition* present information on indexes. If a data set has an index on the variable or variables named in the BY statement that accompanies the MERGE statement, you don't need to sort that data set.

Chapter **18** Updating SAS® Data Sets

Introduction

Updating replaces the values of variables in one data set with nonmissing values from another data set. When you update, you work with two SAS data sets. The data set containing the original information is the *master data set*. The data set containing the new information is the *transaction data set*. Many applications, such as maintaining mailing lists and inventories, call for periodic updates of information.

Using the UPDATE Statement

The UPDATE statement, which you use in the DATA step, reads observations from the transaction data set to update corresponding observations (observations with the same value of all BY variables) from the master data set. All nonmissing values for variables in the transaction data set replace the corresponding values read from the master data set. The SAS System writes the modified observations to the data set you name in the DATA statement without modifying either the master or the transaction data set.

The general form of the UPDATE statement is

UPDATE *master-SAS-data-set transaction-SAS-data-set*;
BY *identifier-list*;

where

master-SAS-data-set	is the SAS data set containing information you want to update.
transaction-SAS-data-set	is the SAS data set containing information with which you want to update the master data set.
identifier-list	is the list of BY variables by which you identify corresponding observations.

The SAS System writes all observations from the master data set that don't correspond to any observation in the transaction data set to the new data set without modification. An observation from the transaction data set that doesn't correspond to any observation in the master data set becomes the basis for a new observation. The new observation may be modified by other observations from the transaction data set before it's written to the new data set.

Selecting the BY Variables

The master data set and the transaction data set must be sorted by the same variable or variables you specify in the BY statement accompanying the UPDATE statement. Select a variable that meets the following criteria:

□ The value of the variable is unique for each observation in the master data set. If you use more than one BY variable, no two observations in the master data set should have the same values for all BY variables.

□ The variable or variables never need to be updated.

Some variables that you can use in the BY statement include social security number, other forms of identification, and the names of objects in an inventory.

If you are updating a data set, you probably don't want duplicate values of BY variables in the master data set. For example, if you update by NAME, each observation in the master data set should have a unique value of NAME. If you update by NAME and AGE, two or more observations can have the same value for either NAME or AGE but shouldn't have the same values for both. The SAS System warns you if it finds duplicates but proceeds with the update. It applies all transactions only to the first observation in the BY group in the master data set.

Updating a Data Set

Suppose you work for a magazine whose mailing list contains tens of thousands of names. Your job is to maintain the mailing list. Each magazine contains a form for readers to fill out when they change their names or addresses. To simplify your job, the form requests that readers send only new information. New subscribers can start a subscription by completing the entire form. When you receive a form, you enter the information on the form into a raw data file. Once a month you update the mailing list.

The mailing list includes the following information for each subscriber:

ID

> is a unique number assigned to the subscriber at the time the subscription begins. A subscriber's ID never changes.

NAME

> is the subscriber's name. The last name appears first, followed by a comma and the first name.

STREET

> is the subscriber's street address.

CITY

> is the subscriber's city.

STATE

> is the subscriber's state.

ZIP

> is the subscriber's ZIP code.

The following program creates and displays a small version of this data set. The raw data are already sorted by ID. Output 18.1 shows the data set.

```
data mailing.master;
   input id 1-8 name $ 9-27 street $ 28-47 city $ 48-62
         state $ 63-64 zip $ 67-71;
   cards;
1001    Ericson, Jane      111 Clancey Court   Chapel Hill    NC  27514
1002    Dix, Martin        4 Shepherd St.      Norwich        VT  05055
1003    Gabrielli, Theresa 24 Ridgetop Rd.     Westboro       MA  01581
1004    Clayton, Aria      14 Bridge St.       San Francisco  CA  94124
1005    Archuleta, Ruby    Box 108             Milagro        NM  87429
1006    Misiewicz, Jeremy  43-C Lakeview Apts.  Madison        WI  53704
1007    Ahmadi, Hafez      5203 Marston Way    Boulder        CO  80302
1008    Jacobson, Becky    1 Lincoln St.       Tallahassee    FL  32312
1009    An, Ing            95 Willow Dr.       Charlotte      NC  28211
1010    Slater, Emily      1009 Cherry St.     York           PA  17407
;
run;

proc print data=mailing.master;
   title 'The Master Mailing List Is Sorted by ID';
run;
```

Output 18.1
The Data Set
MAILING.MASTER

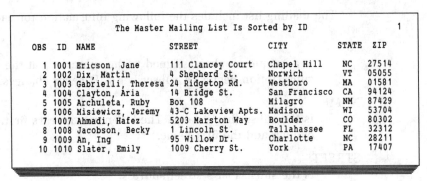

```
                        The Master Mailing List Is Sorted by ID                1

    OBS   ID  NAME               STREET               CITY          STATE  ZIP

     1  1001  Ericson, Jane      111 Clancey Court    Chapel Hill    NC   27514
     2  1002  Dix, Martin        4 Shepherd St.       Norwich        VT   05055
     3  1003  Gabrielli, Theresa 24 Ridgetop Rd.      Westboro       MA   01581
     4  1004  Clayton, Aria      14 Bridge St.        San Francisco  CA   94124
     5  1005  Archuleta, Ruby    Box 108              Milagro        NM   87429
     6  1006  Misiewicz, Jeremy  43-C Lakeview Apts.  Madison        WI   53704
     7  1007  Ahmadi, Hafez      5203 Marston Way     Boulder        CO   80302
     8  1008  Jacobson, Becky    1 Lincoln St.        Tallahassee    FL   32312
     9  1009  An, Ing            95 Willow Dr.        Charlotte      NC   28211
    10  1010  Slater, Emily      1009 Cherry St.      York           PA   17407
```

This month you receive the following information for updating the mailing list:

□ Martin Dix changed his name to Martin Dix-Rosen.

□ Jane Ericson's ZIP code changed.

□ Jeremy Misiewicz moved to a new street address. His city, state, and ZIP code remain the same.

□ Ing An moved from Charlotte, North Carolina, to Raleigh, North Carolina.

□ Martin Dix-Rosen, shortly after changing his name, moved from Norwich, Vermont, to Hanover, New Hampshire.

□ Two new subscribers joined the list. You assign them IDs 1011 and 1012.

You enter each change into your raw data file as soon as you receive it. In each case, you enter only the customer's ID and the new information. The raw data file looks like this:

```
1002    Dix-Rosen, Martin
1001                                                                      27516
1006                       932 Webster St.
1009                       2540 Pleasant St.   Raleigh                    27622
1011    Mitchell, Wayne    28 Morningside Dr.  New York       NY  10017
1002                       R.R. 2, Box 1850    Hanover        NH  03755
1012    Stavros, Gloria    212 Northampton Rd. South Hadley   MA  01075
```

The data are in fixed columns, matching the INPUT statement that created MAILING.MASTER.

First, you must transform the raw data into a SAS data set and sort that data set by ID so that you can use it to update the master list. Output 18.2 shows the sorted data set.

```
data mailing.trans;
   infile 'your-input-file';
   input id 1-8 name $ 9-27 street $ 28-47 city $ 48-62
         state $ 63-64 zip $ 67-71;
run;

proc sort data=mailing.trans;
   by id;
run;

proc print data=mailing.trans;
   title 'Transaction Data Set Sorted by ID';
run;
```

Output 18.2
The Data Set
MAILING.TRANS
Sorted by ID

```
                        Transaction Data Set Sorted by ID                    1

  OBS  ID    NAME              STREET           CITY        STATE  ZIP
   1  1001                                                         27516
   2  1002  Dix-Rosen, Martin
   3  1002                     R.R. 2, Box 1850  Hanover     NH    03755
   4  1006                     932 Webster St.
   5  1009                     2540 Pleasant St. Raleigh           27622
   6  1011  Mitchell, Wayne    28 Morningside Dr. New York   NY    10017
   7  1012  Stavros, Gloria    212 Northampton Rd. South Hadley MA  01075
```

Now that your new data are in a sorted SAS data set, the following program updates the mailing list. The new data set, MAILING.NEWLIST, appears in Output 18.3.

```
data mailing.newlist;
   update mailing.master mailing.trans;
   by id;
run;

proc print data=mailing.newlist;
   title 'Updated Mailing List';
run;
```

Output 18.3
The Updated
Mailing List in the
Data Set
MAILING.NEWLIST

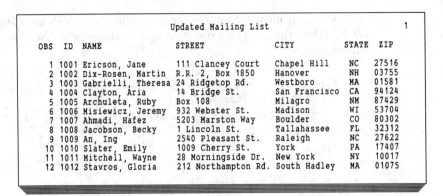

```
                          Updated Mailing List                              1

OBS  ID   NAME              STREET              CITY          STATE  ZIP

  1  1001 Ericson, Jane     111 Clancey Court   Chapel Hill    NC    27516
  2  1002 Dix-Rosen, Martin R.R. 2, Box 1850    Hanover        NH    03755
  3  1003 Gabrielli, Theresa 24 Ridgetop Rd.    Westboro       MA    01581
  4  1004 Clayton, Aria     14 Bridge St.       San Francisco  CA    94124
  5  1005 Archuleta, Ruby   Box 108             Milagro        NM    87429
  6  1006 Misiewicz, Jeremy 932 Webster St.     Madison        WI    53704
  7  1007 Ahmadi, Hafez     5203 Marston Way    Boulder        CO    80302
  8  1008 Jacobson, Becky   1 Lincoln St.       Tallahassee    FL    32312
  9  1009 An, Ing           2540 Pleasant St.   Raleigh        NC    27622
 10  1010 Slater, Emily     1009 Cherry St.     York           PA    17407
 11  1011 Mitchell, Wayne   28 Morningside Dr.  New York       NY    10017
 12  1012 Stavros, Gloria   212 Northampton Rd. South Hadley   MA    01075
```

The data for subscriber 1002, who has two update transactions, is used below to show what happens when you update an observation in the master data set with corresponding observations from the transaction data set.

1. Before executing the DATA step, the SAS System reads the descriptor portion of each data set named in the UPDATE statement and, by default, creates a program data vector that contains all the variables from all data sets. As Figure 18.1 illustrates, the SAS System sets the value of each variable to missing. (Use the DROP= or KEEP= data set option to exclude one or more variables.)

Figure 18.1
Program Data
Vector before
Execution of the
DATA Step

ID	NAME	STREET	CITY	STATE	ZIP
.					

2. Next, the SAS System reads the first observation from the master data set and copies it into the program data vector, as Figure 18.2 illustrates.

Figure 18.2
Program Data
Vector after
Reading the First
Observation from
the Master Data
Set

ID	NAME	STREET	CITY	STATE	ZIP
1002	Dix, Martin	4 Shepherd St.	Norwich	VT	05055

3. The SAS System applies the first transaction by copying all nonmissing values (the value of NAME) from the first observation in this BY group (ID=1002) into the program data vector, as Figure 18.3 illustrates.

Figure 18.3
Program Data Vector after Applying the First Transaction

ID	NAME	STREET	CITY	STATE	ZIP
1002	Dix-Rosen, Martin	4 Shepherd St.	Norwich	VT	05055

4. After completing this transaction, the SAS System looks for another observation in the same BY group in the transaction data set. When it finds another observation with the same value for ID, it applies that transaction too (new values for STREET, CITY, STATE, and ZIP). Now the observation contains the new values from both transactions, as Figure 18.4 illustrates.

Figure 18.4
Program Data Vector after Applying the Second Transaction

ID	NAME	STREET	CITY	STATE	ZIP
1002	Dix-Rosen, Martin	R.R. 2, Box 1850	Hanover	NH	03755

5. After completing the second transaction, the SAS System looks for a third observation in the same BY group. Because no such observation exists, it writes the observation in its current form to the new data set and sets the values in the program data vector to missing.

The UPDATE statement continues processing observations in this way until it reaches the end of the master and transaction data sets. The two observations in the transaction data set that describe new subscribers (and therefore have no corresponding observation in the master data set) become part of the new data set.

Updating with Incremental Values

Often you update variables in a data set by reading new values from the transaction data set. However, some applications require you to update a variable by mathematically manipulating its value based on the value of a variable in the transaction data set.

Suppose you manage a bookstore and use the SAS System to keep track of your weekly sales and your year-to-date sales. The following program creates, sorts by TITLE, and displays the data set INVNTRY.YRSALES, which contains the year-to-date information. Output 18.4 shows the data set.

```
data invntry.yrsales;
   input title $ 1-25 author $ 27-50 sales;
   cards;
The Milagro Beanfield War Nichols, John            303
The Golden Gate           Seth, Vikran             150
Always Coming Home        LeGuin, Ursula            79
Falling through Space     Gilchrist, Ellen         128
Ender's Game              Card, Orson Scott         87
The Handmaid's Tale       Atwood, Margaret          64
;
run;

proc sort data=invntry.yrsales;
   by title;
run;

proc print data=invntry.yrsales;
   title 'Sales to Date';
   title2;
   title3 'Sorted by TITLE';
run;
```

Output 18.4
The Data Set
INVNTRY.YRSALES

```
                         Sales to Date                        1
                        Sorted by TITLE

      OBS   TITLE                        AUTHOR          SALES

       1    Always Coming Home           LeGuin, Ursula    79
       2    Ender's Game                 Card, Orson Scott 87
       3    Falling through Space        Gilchrist, Ellen 128
       4    The Golden Gate              Seth, Vikran     150
       5    The Handmaid's Tale          Atwood, Margaret  64
       6    The Milagro Beanfield War    Nichols, John    303
```

Every Saturday you create a SAS data set containing information about all the books you sold during the past week. The following program creates, sorts by TITLE, and displays the data set INVNTRY.WEEKLIST, which contains this week's information. Output 18.5 shows the data set, which contains the same variables as the year-to-date data set, but the variable SALES represents sales for only one week.

```
data invntry.weeklist;
    input title $ 1-25 author $ 27-50 sales;
    cards;
The Milagro Beanfield War Nichols, John        32
The Golden Gate           Seth, Vikran         17
Always Coming Home        LeGuin, Ursula       10
Falling through Space     Gilchrist, Ellen     12
The Accidental Tourist    Tyler, Anne          15
The Handmaid's Tale       Atwood, Margaret      8
;
run;

proc sort data=invntry.weeklist;
    by title;
run;

proc print data=invntry.weeklist;
    title 'This Week''s Sales Sorted by TITLE';
run;
```

Output 18.5
The Data Set
INVNTRY.WEEKLIST

```
                This Week's Sales Sorted by TITLE                     1

     OBS    TITLE                        AUTHOR            SALES

      1     Always Coming Home           LeGuin, Ursula      10
      2     Falling through Space        Gilchrist, Ellen    12
      3     The Accidental Tourist       Tyler, Anne         15
      4     The Golden Gate              Seth, Vikran        17
      5     The Handmaid's Tale          Atwood, Margaret     8
      6     The Milagro Beanfield War    Nichols, John       32
```

Note: If you were updating only titles that are already in INVNTRY.YRSALES, you wouldn't need the variable AUTHOR in the transaction data set. However, by leaving this variable in the data set, you can use the transaction data set to add complete observations to the master data set.

The following program uses the weekly information to update the year-to-date data set and displays the new data set. Output 18.6 shows the updated data set.

```
data invntry.totsales;
    update invntry.yrsales invntry.weeklist (rename=(sales=newsales));
    by title;
    sales=sum(sales,newsales);
    drop newsales;
run;

proc print data=invntry.totsales;
    title 'Updated Year-to-Date Sales';
run;
```

The RENAME= data set option in this program's UPDATE statement changes the name of the variable SALES in the transaction data set (INVNTRY.WEEKLIST) to NEWSALES so that these values don't replace the value of SALES read from the master data set (INVNTRY.YRSALES). The value used for SALES in the updated data set (INVNTRY.TOTSALES) is the sum of the year-to-date sales and the weekly sales. The program drops the variable NEWSALES because it isn't needed in the new data set.

Output 18.6 shows that in addition to updating sales information for the titles already in the master data set, the UPDATE statement has added a new title, `The Accidental Tourist.`

Output 18.6
Updating
Year-to-Date Sales
with Weekly Sales

```
                        Updated Year-to-Date Sales                    1

        OBS    TITLE                      AUTHOR            SALES

         1     Always Coming Home         LeGuin, Ursula       89
         2     Ender's Game               Card, Orson Scott    87
         3     Falling through Space      Gilchrist, Ellen    140
         4     The Accidental Tourist     Tyler, Anne          15
         5     The Golden Gate            Seth, Vikran        167
         6     The Handmaid's Tale        Atwood, Margaret     72
         7     The Milagro Beanfield War  Nichols, John       335
```

Updating versus Merging

The MERGE statement, which is discussed in Chapter 17, "Merging SAS Data Sets," and the UPDATE statement both match observations from two SAS data sets; however, the two statements differ significantly. It's important to distinguish between the two processes and to choose the one that is appropriate for your application.

The most straightforward differences are

□ The UPDATE statement uses only two data sets. The number of data sets the MERGE statement can use is limited only by machine-dependent factors.

□ A BY statement must accompany an UPDATE statement. The MERGE statement performs a one-to-one merge if no BY statement follows it.

The two statements also process observations differently. To illustrate the differences, compare updating the SAS data set MAILING.MASTER with the data set MAILING.TRANS to merging the two data sets. You have already seen the results of updating in the example that created Output 18.3. That output appears again in Output 18.7 for easy comparison.

Output 18.7
Results of
Updating the
Master Data Set
with the
Transaction Data
Set

```
                        Updated Mailing List                         1

     OBS  ID   NAME                STREET             CITY          STATE  ZIP

      1  1001 Ericson, Jane       111 Clancey Court  Chapel Hill    NC   27516
      2  1002 Dix-Rosen, Martin   R.R. 2, Box 1850   Hanover        NH   03755
      3  1003 Gabrielli, Theresa  24 Ridgetop Rd.    Westboro       MA   01581
      4  1004 Clayton, Aria       14 Bridge St.      San Francisco  CA   94124
      5  1005 Archuleta, Ruby     Box 108            Milagro        NM   87429
      6  1006 Misiewicz, Jeremy   932 Webster St.    Madison        WI   53704
      7  1007 Ahmadi, Hafez       5203 Marston Way   Boulder        CO   80302
      8  1008 Jacobson, Becky     1 Lincoln St.      Tallahassee    FL   32312
      9  1009 An, Ing             2540 Pleasant St.  Raleigh        NC   27622
     10  1010 Slater, Emily       1009 Cherry St.    York           PA   17407
     11  1011 Mitchell, Wayne     28 Morningside Dr. New York       NY   10017
     12  1012 Stavros, Gloria     212 Northampton Rd. South Hadley  MA   01075
```

In contrast, the following program merges the two data sets. Output 18.8 shows the output from this program.

```
data mailing.merged;
   merge mailing.master mailing.trans;
      by id;
run;


proc print data=mailing.merged;
   title 'Merging the Master and Transaction Data Sets';
   title2 'instead of Updating Them';
run;
```

Output 18.8
Results of Merging
the Master and
Transaction Data
Sets

```
             Merging the Master and Transaction Data Sets           1
                      instead of Updating Them

     OBS  ID     NAME              STREET             CITY          STATE  ZIP

      1  1001                                                            27516
      2  1002 Dix-Rosen, Martin
      3  1002                     R.R. 2, Box 1850   Hanover        NH   03755
      4  1003 Gabrielli, Theresa  24 Ridgetop Rd.    Westboro       MA   01581
      5  1004 Clayton, Aria       14 Bridge St.      San Francisco  CA   94124
      6  1005 Archuleta, Ruby     Box 108            Milagro        NM   87429
      7  1006                     932 Webster St.
      8  1007 Ahmadi, Hafez       5203 Marston Way   Boulder        CO   80302
      9  1008 Jacobson, Becky     1 Lincoln St.      Tallahassee    FL   32312
     10  1009                     2540 Pleasant St.  Raleigh             27622
     11  1010 Slater, Emily       1009 Cherry St.    York           PA   17407
     12  1011 Mitchell, Wayne     28 Morningside Dr. New York       NY   10017
     13  1012 Stavros, Gloria     212 Northampton Rd. South Hadley  MA   01075
```

The MERGE statement produces a data set containing 13 observations, whereas UPDATE produces a data set containing 12 observations. In addition, merging the data sets results in several missing values, whereas updating doesn't.

The differences between the merged and updated data sets result from the ways the two statements handle missing values and multiple observations in a BY group. Using the wrong statement may result in incorrect data. The following sections describe the functional differences between the two statements.

Processing Missing Values

During an update, if a value for a variable is missing in the transaction data set, the SAS System uses the value from the master data set when it writes the observation to the new data set. When merging the same observations, the SAS System overwrites the value in the program data vector with the missing value. For instance, consider the following observation from the data set MAILING.MASTER:

```
1001   ERICSON, JANE      111 CLANCEY COURT   CHAPEL HILL    NC   27514
```

and the corresponding observation in MAILING.TRANS:

```
1001                                                               27516
```

Updating combines the two observations into this one:

```
1001   ERICSON, JANE      111 CLANCEY COURT   CHAPEL HILL    NC   27516
```

while merging creates this observation:

```
1001                                                               27516
```

Processing Multiple Observations in a BY Group

The SAS System doesn't write an updated observation to the new data set until it has applied all transactions in a BY group. When merging data sets, the SAS System writes one new observation for each observation in the data set with the largest number of observations in the BY group. For example, consider the following observation from MAILING.MASTER:

```
1002   DIX, MARTIN       4 SHEPHERD ST.       NORWICH        VT   05055
```

and the corresponding observations from MAILING.TRANS:

```
1002   DIX-ROSEN, MARTIN
1002                      R.R. 2, BOX 1850     HANOVER        NH   03755
```

Updating applies both transactions and combines these observations into a single one:

```
1002   DIX-ROSEN, MARTIN R.R. 2, BOX 1850      HANOVER        NH   03755
```

Merging, on the other hand, first merges the observation from MAILING.MASTER with the first observation in the corresponding BY group in MAILING.TRANS. All values of variables from the observation in MAILING.TRANS are used, regardless of whether they're missing. Then the SAS System writes the observation to the new data set:

```
1002   DIX-ROSEN, MARTIN
```

Next, the SAS System looks for other observations in the same BY group in each data set. Because more observations are in the BY group in MAILING.TRANS, all the values in the program data vector are retained. The SAS System merges them with the second observation in the BY group from MAILING.TRANS and writes the result to the new data set:

```
1002                    R.R. 2, BOX 1850    HANOVER       NH  03755
```

Therefore, merging creates two observations for the new data set, whereas updating creates only one.

SAS Tools

This chapter discusses using the UPDATE statement to update information in one SAS data set with information in another SAS data set:

UPDATE *master-SAS-data-set transaction-SAS-data-set*;
BY *identifier-list*;
> replace the values of variables in one SAS data set with nonmissing values from another SAS data set. *Master-SAS-data-set* is the SAS data set containing information you want to update; *transaction-SAS-data-set* is the SAS data set containing information with which you want to update the master data set; *identifier-list* is the list of BY variables by which you identify corresponding observations.

Learning More

□ Part 9, "Storing and Managing Data in SAS Files," explains using the DATASETS procedure. When you update a data set, you create a new data set containing the updated information. Typically, you want to use PROC DATASETS to delete the old master data set and rename the new one so you can use the same program the next time you update the information.

□ Chapter 17, "Merging SAS Data Sets," describes the MERGE statement in detail.

□ *SAS Language: Reference, Version 6, First Edition* and the *SAS Procedures Guide, Version 6, Third Edition* describe indexes. If a data set has an index on the variable or variables named in the BY statement that accompanies the UPDATE statement, you don't need to sort that data set.

Chapter 19 Manipulating SAS® Data Sets

Introduction

This chapter teaches you how to manipulate data while combining SAS data sets and describes how to

□ determine which data set the current observation is from

□ create a new data set that includes only selected observations from the data sets you combine

□ determine when the SAS System is processing the last observation in the DATA step.

You have seen some of these concepts in earlier chapters, but this chapter applies them to processing multiple data sets.

The examples in this chapter use the SET statement, but you can also use all the features discussed with both the MERGE and UPDATE statements.

Determining the Source of an Observation

Suppose you have two similar SAS data sets, one for each major political party in the United States. Each data set contains the following variables:

YEAR   is the year of a presidential election. Both data sets include data for all presidential elections from 1920 to 1984.

PRES   is the name of the party's presidential candidate.

VICEPRES   is the name of the party's vice-presidential candidate.

RESULT   is the outcome of the election. The value for winners is won; for losers, lost.

The data set POLITICS.DONKEY contains data for the Democratic party; POLITICS.ELEPHANT contains data for the Republican party. The following program creates and displays these data sets. Output 19.1 shows the data sets. The observations in both data sets are ordered by YEAR because the raw data are ordered by YEAR.

```
libname politics 'your-data-library';

data politics.donkey;
    input year 1-4 pres $ 6-29 vicepres $ 31-55 result $ 60-64;
    cards;
1920 James M. Cox            Franklin D. Roosevelt        lost
1924 John W. Davis           Charles W. Bryan             lost
1928 Alfred E. Smith         Joseph T. Robinson           lost
1932 Franklin D. Roosevelt   John N. Garner               won
1936 Franklin D. Roosevelt   John N. Garner               won
1940 Franklin D. Roosevelt   Henry A. Wallace             won
1944 Franklin D. Roosevelt   Harry S. Truman              won
1948 Harry S. Truman         Alben W. Barkley             won
1952 Adlai E. Stevenson      John J. Sparkman             lost
1956 Adlai E. Stevenson      Estes Kefauver               lost
1960 John F. Kennedy         Lyndon B. Johnson            won
1964 Lyndon B. Johnson       Hubert H. Humphrey           won
1968 Hubert H. Humphrey      Edmund S. Muskie             lost
1972 George S. McGovern      R. Sargent Shriver Jr.       lost
1976 Jimmy Carter            Walter F. Mondale            won
1980 Jimmy Carter            Walter F. Mondale            lost
1984 Walter F. Mondale       Geraldine Ferraro            lost
;
run;

proc print data=politics.donkey;
    title 'Democratic Presidential and Vice-Presidential Candidates';
    title2 'from 1920 to 1984';
run;
```

```
data politics.elephant;
    input year 1-4 pres $ 6-29 vicepres $ 31-55 result $ 60-64;
    cards;
1920 Warren G. Harding         Calvin Coolidge            won
1924 Calvin Coolidge           Charles G. Dawes           won
1928 Herbert Hoover            Charles Curtis             won
1932 Herbert Hoover            Charles Curtis             lost
1936 Alfred M. Landon          Frank Knox                 lost
1940 Wendell L. Willkie        Charles McNary             lost
1944 Thomas E. Dewey           John W. Bricker            lost
1948 Thomas E. Dewey           Earl Warren                lost
1952 Dwight D. Eisenhower      Richard M. Nixon           won
1956 Dwight D. Eisenhower      Richard M. Nixon           won
1960 Richard M. Nixon          Henry Cabot Lodge          lost
1964 Barry M. Goldwater        William E. Miller          lost
1968 Richard M. Nixon          Spiro T. Agnew             won
1972 Richard M. Nixon          Spiro T. Agnew             won
1976 Gerald R. Ford            Robert J. Dole             lost
1980 Ronald Reagan             George Bush                won
1984 Ronald Reagan             George Bush                won
;
run;

proc print data=politics.elephant;
    title 'Republican Presidential and Vice-Presidential Candidates';
    title2 'from 1920 to 1984';
run;
```

Output 19.1
The Data Sets
POLITICS.DONKEY
and
POLITICS.ELEPHANT

```
            Democratic Presidential and Vice-Presidential Candidates        1
                             from 1920 to 1984

    OBS   YEAR   PRES                   VICEPRES                 RESULT

     1    1920   James M. Cox           Franklin D. Roosevelt    lost
     2    1924   John W. Davis          Charles W. Bryan         lost
     3    1928   Alfred E. Smith        Joseph T. Robinson       lost
     4    1932   Franklin D. Roosevelt  John N. Garner           won
     5    1936   Franklin D. Roosevelt  John N. Garner           won
     6    1940   Franklin D. Roosevelt  Henry A. Wallace         won
     7    1944   Franklin D. Roosevelt  Harry S. Truman          won
     8    1948   Harry S. Truman        Alben W. Barkley         won
     9    1952   Adlai E. Stevenson     John J. Sparkman         lost
    10    1956   Adlai E. Stevenson     Estes Kefauver           lost
    11    1960   John F. Kennedy        Lyndon B. Johnson        won
    12    1964   Lyndon B. Johnson      Hubert H. Humphrey       won
    13    1968   Hubert H. Humphrey     Edmund S. Muskie         lost
    14    1972   George S. McGovern     R. Sargent Shriver Jr.   lost
    15    1976   Jimmy Carter           Walter F. Mondale        won
    16    1980   Jimmy Carter           Walter F. Mondale        lost
    17    1984   Walter F. Mondale      Geraldine Ferraro        lost
```

```
          Republican Presidential and Vice-Presidential Candidates        2
                            from 1920 to 1984

    OBS    YEAR    PRES                    VICEPRES             RESULT

      1    1920    Warren G. Harding       Calvin Coolidge      won
      2    1924    Calvin Coolidge         Charles G. Dawes     won
      3    1928    Herbert Hoover          Charles Curtis       won
      4    1932    Herbert Hoover          Charles Curtis       lost
      5    1936    Alfred M. Landon        Frank Knox           lost
      6    1940    Wendell L. Willkie      Charles McNary       lost
      7    1944    Thomas E. Dewey         John W. Bricker      lost
      8    1948    Thomas E. Dewey         Earl Warren          lost
      9    1952    Dwight D. Eisenhower    Richard M. Nixon     won
     10    1956    Dwight D. Eisenhower    Richard M. Nixon     won
     11    1960    Richard M. Nixon        Henry Cabot Lodge    lost
     12    1964    Barry M. Goldwater      William E. Miller    lost
     13    1968    Richard M. Nixon        Spiro T. Agnew       won
     14    1972    Richard M. Nixon        Spiro T. Agnew       won
     15    1976    Gerald R. Ford          Robert J. Dole       lost
     16    1980    Ronald Reagan           George Bush          won
     17    1984    Ronald Reagan           George Bush          won
```

Use the SET statement with a BY statement to combine the two data sets into one data set containing all the observations in chronological order (see Chapter 16, "Interleaving SAS Data Sets"). Output 19.2 shows the new data set.

```
data politics.intleave;
   set politics.donkey politics.elephant;
   by year;
run;


proc print data=politics.intleave;
   title 'Presidential and Vice-Presidential Candidates';
   title2 'from 1920 to 1984';
run;
```

Output 19.2
Interleaving
Democratic and
Republican
Candidates by
YEAR to Form
POLITICS.INTLEAVE

```
                Presidential and Vice-Presidential Candidates          1
                           from 1920 to 1984

     OBS    YEAR    PRES                    VICEPRES              RESULT

      1     1920    James M. Cox            Franklin D. Roosevelt  lost
      2     1920    Warren G. Harding       Calvin Coolidge        won
      3     1924    John W. Davis           Charles W. Bryan       lost
      4     1924    Calvin Coolidge         Charles G. Dawes       won
      5     1928    Alfred E. Smith         Joseph T. Robinson     lost
      6     1928    Herbert Hoover          Charles Curtis         won
      7     1932    Franklin D. Roosevelt   John N. Garner         won
      8     1932    Herbert Hoover          Charles Curtis         lost
      9     1936    Franklin D. Roosevelt   John N. Garner         won
     10     1936    Alfred M. Landon        Frank Knox             lost
     11     1940    Franklin D. Roosevelt   Henry A. Wallace       won
     12     1940    Wendell L. Willkie      Charles McNary         lost
     13     1944    Franklin D. Roosevelt   Harry S. Truman        won
     14     1944    Thomas E. Dewey         John W. Bricker        lost
     15     1948    Harry S. Truman         Alben W. Barkley       won
     16     1948    Thomas E. Dewey         Earl Warren            lost
     17     1952    Adlai E. Stevenson      John J. Sparkman       lost
     18     1952    Dwight D. Eisenhower    Richard M. Nixon       won
     19     1956    Adlai E. Stevenson      Estes Kefauver         lost
     20     1956    Dwight D. Eisenhower    Richard M. Nixon       won
     21     1960    John F. Kennedy         Lyndon B. Johnson      won
     22     1960    Richard M. Nixon        Henry Cabot Lodge      lost
     23     1964    Lyndon B. Johnson       Hubert H. Humphrey     won
     24     1964    Barry M. Goldwater      William E. Miller      lost
     25     1968    Hubert H. Humphrey      Edmund S. Muskie       lost
     26     1968    Richard M. Nixon        Spiro T. Agnew         won
     27     1972    George S. McGovern      R. Sargent Shriver Jr. lost
     28     1972    Richard M. Nixon        Spiro T. Agnew         won
     29     1976    Jimmy Carter            Walter F. Mondale      won
     30     1976    Gerald R. Ford          Robert J. Dole         lost
     31     1980    Jimmy Carter            Walter F. Mondale      lost
     32     1980    Ronald Reagan           George Bush            won
     33     1984    Walter F. Mondale       Geraldine Ferraro      lost
     34     1984    Ronald Reagan           George Bush            won
```

The original data sets, POLITICS.DONKEY and POLITICS.ELEPHANT, don't need a variable identifying the candidates' parties because all observations in POLITICS.DONKEY pertain to the Democratic party, and all observations in POLITICS.ELEPHANT pertain to the Republican party. However, when you combine the data sets, you lose this information. The following section explains how to avoid this loss.

Using the IN= Data Set Option

The IN= data set option allows you to determine which data sets have contributed to the observation currently in the program data vector. The syntax for this option is

SAS-data-set(IN=*variable*)

When you place the IN= option in parentheses next to the name of a data set in a SET, MERGE, or UPDATE statement, the SAS System creates a temporary *variable* associated with that data set. The value of *variable* is 1 if the data set has contributed to the observation currently in the program data vector; 0 if it hasn't. You can use the IN= option with any or all the data sets you name in a SET, MERGE, or UPDATE statement, but use a different variable name in each case. Although the DATA step can use IN= variables, the SAS System doesn't add them to the data set.

As the following SAS program shows, you can use the IN= option in conjunction with IF-THEN/ELSE statements to avoid losing information on a political party when you combine POLITICS.DONKEY and POLITICS.ELEPHANT. By testing which data set an observation comes from, you can assign the appropriate value to a new variable, PARTY, while you build the new data set. Output 19.3 shows the data set.

```
data politics.party;
    set politics.donkey (in=D) politics.elephant;
    by year;
    if D then party='Democratic';
    else party='Republican';
run;

proc print data=politics.party;
    title 'Presidential and Vice-Presidential Candidates';
    title2 'from 1920 to 1984';
    title3 'including Candidates'' Party';
run;
```

The IN= option in the SET statement tells the SAS System to create a variable named D. When the current observation comes from the data set POLITICS.DONKEY, the value of D is 1; otherwise, its value is 0. The IF-THEN/ELSE statements execute one of two assignment statements, depending on the value of D. If the observation comes from the data set POLITICS.DONKEY, the value assigned to PARTY is `Democratic`. If the observation comes from the data set POLITICS.ELEPHANT, the value assigned to PARTY is `Republican`.

Output 19.3
Using the IN=
Data Set Option to
Assign a Value to
PARTY

```
                  Presidential and Vice-Presidential Candidates          1
                              from 1920 to 1984
                           including Candidates' Party

    OBS   YEAR   PRES                   VICEPRES                RESULT   PARTY

     1    1920   James M. Cox           Franklin D. Roosevelt   lost     Democratic
     2    1920   Warren G. Harding      Calvin Coolidge         won      Republican
     3    1924   John W. Davis          Charles W. Bryan        lost     Democratic
     4    1924   Calvin Coolidge        Charles G. Dawes        won      Republican
     5    1928   Alfred E. Smith        Joseph T. Robinson      lost     Democratic
     6    1928   Herbert Hoover         Charles Curtis          won      Republican
     7    1932   Franklin D. Roosevelt  John N. Garner          won      Democratic
     8    1932   Herbert Hoover         Charles Curtis          lost     Republican
     9    1936   Franklin D. Roosevelt  John N. Garner          won      Democratic
    10    1936   Alfred M. Landon       Frank Knox              lost     Republican
    11    1940   Franklin D. Roosevelt  Henry A. Wallace        won      Democratic
    12    1940   Wendell L. Willkie     Charles McNary          lost     Republican
    13    1944   Franklin D. Roosevelt  Harry S. Truman         won      Democratic
    14    1944   Thomas E. Dewey        John W. Bricker         lost     Republican
    15    1948   Harry S. Truman        Alben W. Barkley        won      Democratic
    16    1948   Thomas E. Dewey        Earl Warren             lost     Republican
    17    1952   Adlai E. Stevenson     John J. Sparkman        lost     Democratic
    18    1952   Dwight D. Eisenhower   Richard M. Nixon        won      Republican
    19    1956   Adlai E. Stevenson     Estes Kefauver          lost     Democratic
    20    1956   Dwight D. Eisenhower   Richard M. Nixon        won      Republican
    21    1960   John F. Kennedy        Lyndon B. Johnson       won      Democratic
    22    1960   Richard M. Nixon       Henry Cabot Lodge       lost     Republican
    23    1964   Lyndon B. Johnson      Hubert H. Humphrey      won      Democratic
    24    1964   Barry M. Goldwater     William E. Miller       lost     Republican
    25    1968   Hubert H. Humphrey     Edmund S. Muskie        lost     Democratic
    26    1968   Richard M. Nixon       Spiro T. Agnew          won      Republican
    27    1972   George S. McGovern     R. Sargent Shriver Jr.  lost     Democratic
    28    1972   Richard M. Nixon       Spiro T. Agnew          won      Republican
    29    1976   Jimmy Carter           Walter F. Mondale       won      Democratic
    30    1976   Gerald R. Ford         Robert J. Dole          lost     Republican
    31    1980   Jimmy Carter           Walter F. Mondale       lost     Democratic
    32    1980   Ronald Reagan          George Bush             won      Republican
    33    1984   Walter F. Mondale      Geraldine Ferraro       lost     Democratic
    34    1984   Ronald Reagan          George Bush             won      Republican
```

Combining Portions of SAS Data Sets

Suppose that instead of simply interleaving the two data sets you want to create a data set that contains observations only for the winning candidates. You can easily select these observations with the subsetting IF statement while you combine the data sets.

The following program uses a subsetting IF statement to create a SAS data set, POLITICS.WINNERS, that contains only those observations for which the value of RESULT is `won`. The DROP= data set option drops the variable RESULT from the new data set because all values for this variable will be the same. Output 19.4 shows the data set.

```
data politics.winners(drop=result);
    set politics.donkey (in=D) politics.elephant;
    by year;
    if result='won';
    if D then party='Democratic';
    else party='Republican';
run;

proc print data=politics.winners;
    title 'Winning Ticket from 1920 to 1984';
    title2 'including Candidates'' Party';
run;
```

Output 19.4
Combining
Selected
Observations

```
                      Winning Ticket from 1920 to 1984                      1
                          including Candidates' Party

    OBS    YEAR    PRES                      VICEPRES              PARTY

     1     1920    Warren G. Harding         Calvin Coolidge       Republican
     2     1924    Calvin Coolidge           Charles G. Dawes      Republican
     3     1928    Herbert Hoover            Charles Curtis        Republican
     4     1932    Franklin D. Roosevelt     John N. Garner        Democratic
     5     1936    Franklin D. Roosevelt     John N. Garner        Democratic
     6     1940    Franklin D. Roosevelt     Henry A. Wallace      Democratic
     7     1944    Franklin D. Roosevelt     Harry S. Truman       Democratic
     8     1948    Harry S. Truman           Alben W. Barkley      Democratic
     9     1952    Dwight D. Eisenhower      Richard M. Nixon      Republican
    10     1956    Dwight D. Eisenhower      Richard M. Nixon      Republican
    11     1960    John F. Kennedy           Lyndon B. Johnson     Democratic
    12     1964    Lyndon B. Johnson         Hubert H. Humphrey    Democratic
    13     1968    Richard M. Nixon          Spiro T. Agnew        Republican
    14     1972    Richard M. Nixon          Spiro T. Agnew        Republican
    15     1976    Jimmy Carter              Walter F. Mondale     Democratic
    16     1980    Ronald Reagan             George Bush           Republican
    17     1984    Ronald Reagan             George Bush           Republican
```

Identifying the Last Observation

Many applications require you to determine when the SAS System is processing the last observation in the DATA step; for example, you may want to perform calculations only on the last observation in a data set. For this purpose, the SAS System provides the END= option for the SET, MERGE, and UPDATE statements. The syntax for this option is

SET *SAS-data-set-list* END=*variable*;

The END= option defines a temporary *variable* whose value is 1 when the DATA step is processing the last observation. At all other times, the value of *variable* is 0. Although the DATA step can use the END= *variable*, the SAS System doesn't add it to the data set.*

Suppose you want to use the data in POLITICS.DONKEY and POLITICS.ELEPHANT to calculate how many years each party was in the White House from 1921 to 1989. (The president and vice president take office in the year following their election.) Now you must know not only which party the winners were from but also how many times each party won the election. Therefore, you must keep separate tallies of Democratic and Republican victories in your DATA step. After processing all observations, multiply the final tally for each party by 4 (the length of the term of office) to determine the length of time each party has been in the White House. Because the final observation contains variables whose values are the total length of time each party spent in the White House, it's the only observation you want to send to the new data set. The following program shows how to do all this in the DATA step. Output 19.5 shows the data set.

```
data politics.timespan (keep=yrsdem yrsrep);
    set politics.donkey (in=D) politics.elephant end=lastyear;
    by year;
    if result='won' then
        do;
            if D then dwins+1;
            else rwins+1;
    end;
    if lastyear then
        do;
            yrsdem=dwins*4;
            yrsrep=rwins*4;
            output;
        end;
run;

proc print data=politics.timespan;
    title 'Total Years of Administration of Each Major Party';
    title2 'from 1921 to 1989';
run;
```

Output 19.5
Using the END=
Option to
Specially Process
the Last
Observation in the
Data Sets

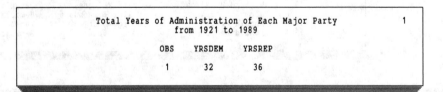

```
      Total Years of Administration of Each Major Party          1
                        from 1921 to 1989

                 OBS     YRSDEM     YRSREP

                  1        32         36
```

---

* Chapter 11, "Using More than One Observation in a Calculation," explains how to use the END= option in the SET statement with a single data set. The END= option works the same way with multiple data sets, but it's important to note that END= is set to 1 only when the last observation from all input data sets is being processed.

Here's an explanation of this program:

1. The END= option creates the temporary variable LASTYEAR. This option tells the SAS System to assign a value of 0 to LASTYEAR until the DATA step begins processing the last observation.

2. Two new variables, DWINS and RWINS, keep a running tally of the number of victories each party achieves. If an observation with a value of **won** for RESULT comes from the data set POLITICS.DONKEY, a sum statement (DWINS+1) adds 1 to the value of DWINS. If an observation with a value of **won** comes from POLITICS.ELEPHANT, a sum statement adds 1 to the value of RWINS.

3. When the DATA step begins processing the last observation, the value of LASTYEAR changes from 0 to 1. When this change occurs, the conditional statement IF LASTYEAR becomes true, and the statements following it are executed. The SAS System multiplies the total number of victories for each party by 4 and assigns the result to the appropriate variable, YRSDEM or YRSREP.

4. The OUTPUT statement sends the observation to the newly created data set. Remember that the OUTPUT statement overrides the automatic writing of data to the new data set by specifying exactly which observations to write. Therefore, the DATA step writes only the last observation to POLITICS.TIMESPAN. As the DATA step writes the observation, it keeps only two variables, YRSDEM and YRSREP, as directed by the KEEP= data set option in the DATA statement.

SAS Tools

This chapter discusses using the IN= data set option, the END= option, and the subsetting and conditional IF statements to manipulate data as you combine data sets:

SET *SAS-data-set* (IN=*variable*) *SAS-data-set-list*;
> creates a *variable* associated with a SAS data set. The value of *variable* is 1 if the data set has contributed to the observation currently in the program data vector; 0 if it hasn't. You can use the option with any data set you name in the SET, MERGE, or UPDATE statement, but use a different variable name for each one.
>
> Although the DATA step can use IN= variables, the SAS System doesn't add them to the data set being created.

SET *SAS-data-set-list* END=*variable*;
> creates a *variable* whose value is 0 until the the DATA step starts to process its last observation. When processing of the last observation begins, the value of *variable* changes to 1. You can also use the END= option with the MERGE and UPDATE statements.
>
> Although the DATA step can use the END= variable, the SAS System doesn't add it to the data set being created.

IF *condition*;

> tests whether the *condition* is true. If it's true, the SAS System continues processing the current observation; if it isn't, the SAS System stops processing the observation and returns to the beginning of the DATA step. This type of IF statement is called a *subsetting* IF statement because it produces a subset of the original observations.

IF *condition* **THEN** *action*;
<**ELSE** *action*;>

> tests whether the *condition* is true; if so, the *action* in the THEN clause is executed. If the *condition* is false and an ELSE statement is present, the ELSE *action* is executed. If the *condition* is false and no ELSE statement is present, execution proceeds to the next statement in the DATA step.

Learning More

□ Chapter 4, "Starting with SAS Data Sets," provides an introduction to data set options in general.

□ Chapter 8, "Acting on Selected Observations," discusses subsetting and conditional IF statements.

□ Chapter 9, "Creating Subsets of Observations," discusses the OUTPUT statement and the subsetting IF statement in greater detail.

□ Chapter 11, "Using More than One Observation in a Calculation," discusses the sum statement and the END= option.

□ Chapter 12, "Finding Shortcuts in Programming," discusses the DO statement.

Part 5

Understanding Your SAS® Session

Chapter 20 Understanding and Enhancing Your Output

Introduction

This chapter helps you to understand your output so you can make it more informative and enhance its appearance. It discusses

- □ DATA step and PROC step output

- □ output destinations.

This chapter tells you how to enhance the output's appearance by

- □ adding titles, footnotes, and labels

- □ numbering pages

- □ printing date and time values

- □ representing missing values.

Understanding Output

Output from Procedures

When you invoke a SAS procedure, you are telling the SAS System to analyze or in some other way process your data. You may be telling it to read a SAS data set, compute statistics, print results, or create a new data set. The possibilities are many. One of the results of executing a SAS procedure is *procedure output*. Its destination varies with the method of running the SAS System, the operating system, and the options used. Form and content vary with each procedure. Some procedures, such as the SORT procedure, don't produce printed output at all.

The SAS System has numerous procedures with which you can process your data. For example, you can use the PRINT procedure to print a simple list of the values of each variable. You can use the MEANS procedure to produce simple univariate descriptive statistics for numeric variables. For a graphic representation, you can use the CHART procedure. As you have already discovered from using this book, many other procedures are available through the SAS System.

Output from DATA Step Applications

Although output is usually generated by a procedure, it may also be generated by a DATA step application. For example, you can use the FILE and PUT statements together within the DATA step to generate output. First, use the FILE statement to identify your current output file. Then use the PUT statement to write lines that contain variable values or text strings to the output file. You can write the values in column, list, or formatted style. Note that if a FILE statement is not executed before a PUT statement in the current execution of a DATA step, the lines are written to the SAS log. The FILE and PUT statements can be used to target only a subset of data. If you have a large data set that includes unnecessary information, this kind of DATA step processing can save time and computer resources.

Suppose you are conducting a study of standardized test scores. You have a data set containing Scholastic Aptitude Test (SAT) information for college-bound high school seniors from 1967 through 1986. For selected years between 1967 and 1986, the data set shows estimated scores based on the total number of students nationwide taking the test. Scores are estimated for male and female students both for the verbal and math portions of the test. The following PROC PRINT step produces Output 20.1:*

```
libname out 'your-data-library';

proc print data=out.sats1;
run;
```

---

*   The DATA step that created this data set is shown in the Appendix. The data set is stored in a SAS data library that is referenced by the libref OUT throughout the rest of this chapter.

Output 20.1
Obtaining a List with the PRINT Procedure

```
                          Using the PRINT Procedure                      1

         OBS     TEST     SEX     YEAR     SCORE

          1     math       m      1967      514
          2     math       f      1967      467
          3     math       m      1970      509
          4     math       f      1970      465
          5     math       m      1975      495
          6     math       f      1975      449
          7     math       m      1977      497
          8     math       f      1977      445
          9     math       m      1980      491
         10     math       f      1980      443
         11     math       m      1981      492
         12     math       f      1981      443
         13     math       m      1982      493
         14     math       f      1982      443
         15     math       m      1983      493
         16     math       f      1983      445
         17     math       m      1984      495
         18     math       f      1984      449
         19     math       m      1985      499
         20     math       f      1985      452
         21     math       m      1986      501
         22     math       f      1986      451
         23     verbal     m      1967      463
         24     verbal     f      1967      468
         25     verbal     m      1970      459
         26     verbal     f      1970      461
         27     verbal     m      1975      437
         28     verbal     f      1975      431
         29     verbal     m      1977      431
         30     verbal     f      1977      427
         31     verbal     m      1980      428
         32     verbal     f      1980      420
         33     verbal     m      1981      430
         34     verbal     f      1981      418
         35     verbal     m      1982      431
         36     verbal     f      1982      421
         37     verbal     m      1983      430
         38     verbal     f      1983      420
         39     verbal     m      1984      433
         40     verbal     f      1984      420
         41     verbal     m      1985      437
         42     verbal     f      1985      425
         43     verbal     m      1986      437
         44     verbal     f      1986      426
```

Now suppose you need to create an external file from the SAS data set so you can process the records with a pre-existing FORTRAN program for analyzing test scores. You know the FORTRAN program expects the data to appear like this:

Variable	Column location
YEAR	10–13
TEST	15–25
SEX	30
SCORE	35–37

You can use the FILE and PUT statements, as shown in the following SAS program, to create the file that can be read by the FORTRAN program:

```
data _null_;
   set out.sats1;
    file 'your-output-file';
    put @10 year @15 test
        @30 sex @35 score;
run;
```

Locating Procedure Output

The destination of your procedure output depends on the method you're using to start, run, and exit the SAS System. It also depends on the operating system you're using and the setting of SAS system options. Table 20.1 shows the default destination for each method of operation.

Table 20.1
Default
Destinations for
Procedure Output

Method of Operation	Destination of Procedure Output
SAS Display Manager System (interactive full-screen)	OUTPUT window
interactive line mode	on the terminal display, as each step executes
noninteractive SAS programs	depends on the operating system
batch jobs	line printer or disk file

Making Output Informative

Any time you generate output, you can make it more informative by adding titles, footnotes, and labels.

Adding Titles

At the top of each page of output, the SAS System automatically prints the title

```
The SAS System
```

You can make your output more informative if you specify your own title. Suppose you have generated a plot with the PLOT procedure and you want to call it 'SAT Scores by Year, 1967-1976'. Simply specify

```
title 'SAT Scores by Year, 1967-1976';
```

Within a SAS session, the SAS System continues to use the most recently created title until you change or eliminate it, even if you generate different output later.

You can specify up to ten titles per page by numbering them in ascending order. If you want to add a subtitle to your previous title, for instance, the subtitle 'Separate Statistics by Test Type', number your titles by the order in which you want them to appear. To add a blank line between titles, simply skip a number as you number your TITLE statements. Your TITLE statements now become

```
title1 'SAT Scores by Year, 1967-1976';
title3 'Separate Statistics by Test Type';
```

You can change the text of one title of a series and then resubmit your job, including all the TITLE statements, for execution. But be aware that executing a numbered TITLE statement without a text string eliminates all higher-numbered titles.

For example, if you want to change TITLE1 to 'SAT Scores for College-Bound Seniors, 1967-1976', executing the following statement by itself makes the change you want but also eliminates the subtitle added earlier:

```
title1 'SAT Scores for College-Bound Seniors, 1967-1976';
```

To eliminate all titles including the default title, specify

```
title;
```

or

```
title1;
```

Although the TITLE statement can appear anywhere in your program, you can associate it with a particular PROC step by positioning it

- □ after the RUN statement for the previous step
- □ after the PROC statement but before the next DATA, PROC, or RUN statement.

Footnoting Results

The guidelines for the TITLE statement also apply to the FOOTNOTE statement.*
Suppose you want to add the footnote '1967 and 1970 SAT scores estimated based on total number of people taking the SAT'. Anywhere in your program, specify

```
footnote1 '1967 and 1970 SAT scores estimated based on total number';
footnote2 'of people taking the SAT';
```

As with the TITLE statement, the SAS System uses the most recently created footnote until you change or eliminate it.

---

* Note that when you are using display manager, you can also use the TITLES window to specify titles and the FOOTNOTES window to specify footnotes for output that you subsequently generate within a session.

You can specify up to ten lines of footnotes per page by numbering them in ascending order. When you alter the text of one footnote in a series and re-execute your whole program, only the text of the one footnote is changed. However, if you execute a numbered FOOTNOTE statement without a text string, all higher-numbered footnotes are eliminated. To eliminate all footnotes, specify

```
footnote;
```

or

```
footnote1;
```

Although the FOOTNOTE statement can appear anywhere in your program, you can associate it with a particular PROC step by positioning it

□ after the RUN statement for the previous step

□ after the PROC statement but before the next DATA, PROC, or RUN statement.

Note: Footnotes don't appear in reports generated in the DATA step with a FILE statement.

Labeling Variables

In procedure output, the SAS System automatically prints the variables with the names you specify. However, you can label some or all of your variables by specifying a LABEL statement either in the DATA step or, with some procedures, in the PROC step of your program. Your label can be up to 40 characters long, including blanks.

Suppose you want to describe the variable SCORE with the phrase 'SAT score'. Simply specify

```
label score ='SAT score';
```

If you specify the LABEL statement in the DATA step, the label is permanently stored in the data set. If you specify the LABEL statement in the PROC step, the label is associated with the variable for the duration of the PROC step only. In either case, when a label is assigned, it is printed with almost all SAS procedures. The exception is the PRINT procedure. Whether you put the LABEL statement in the DATA step or in the PROC step, with the PRINT procedure you must specify the LABEL option, as follows:

```
proc print data=sats label;
run;
```

Note that specifying a label in the PROC step overrides any labels stored in the data set.

Developing Descriptive Output

The following example incorporates the TITLE, LABEL, and FOOTNOTE statements and produces Output 20.2. Note the change of the line size from 76 to 120 to accommodate the plot.

```
options linesize=120 nonumber nodate;

proc sort data=out.sats1;
   by test;
run;

proc plot data=out.sats1;
   by test;
   label score='SAT score';
   plot score*year / haxis=1967 1970 1975 1977 1980
         1981 1982 1983 1984 1985 1986;
   title1 'SAT Scores by Year, 1967-1976';
   title3 'Separate Statistics by Test Type';
   footnote1 '1967 and 1970 SAT scores estimated based on total number';
   footnote2 'of people taking the SAT';
run;
```

Output 20.2   *Using TITLE, FOOTNOTE, and LABEL Statements*

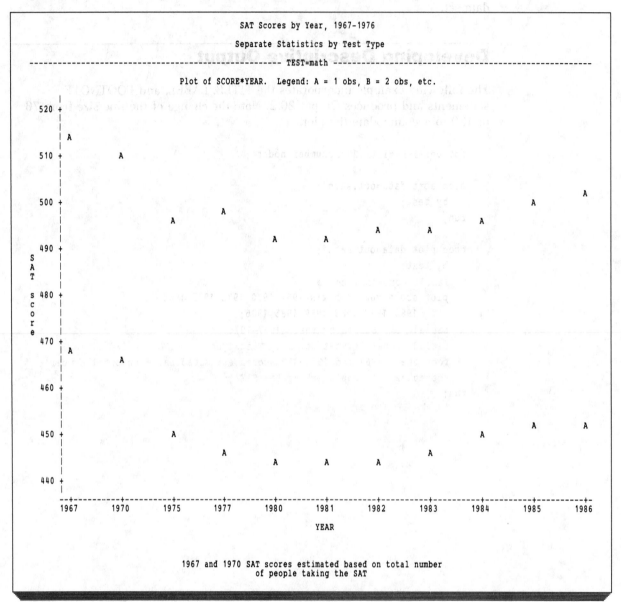

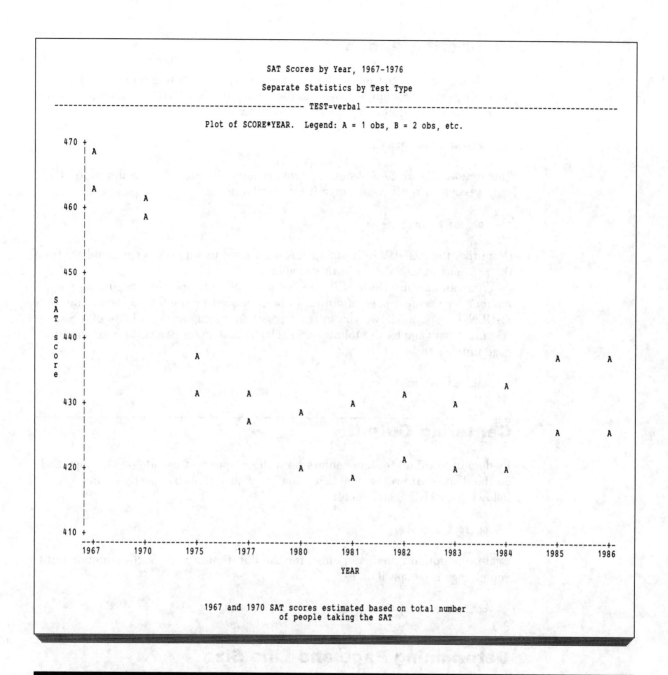

Controlling Output Appearance

You can enhance the appearance of your output by specifying SAS system options. You can specify some of these options when you invoke the SAS System or from the OPTIONS window of display manager. The options in this section are specified in OPTIONS statements.

Numbering Pages

By default, the SAS System numbers pages of output, starting with page 1. However, you can suppress page numbers with the NONUMBER system option.* Simply specify the following OPTIONS statement:

```
options nonumber;
```

This option, like all SAS system options, remains in effect for the duration of your session or until you change it by specifying

```
options number;
```

(Note that the NONUMBER option has been used to suppress page numbers for the previous output shown in this chapter.)

You can also use the PAGENO= system option to specify a beginning page number for the next page of output to be produced by the SAS System. The PAGENO= option allows you to reset page numbering in the middle of a SAS session. For example, the following OPTIONS statement resets the next output page number to 5:

```
options pageno=5
```

Centering Output

By default, the SAS System centers both the output and its title on the page and on the display. However, you can left-align your output by specifying the following OPTIONS statement:

```
options nocenter;
```

Again, the option remains in effect for the duration of your SAS session or until you change it by specifying

```
options center;
```

Determining Page and Line Size

Procedure output is scaled automatically to fit the size of the page and line. The number of lines per page and the number of characters per line of printed output are determined by the settings of the PAGESIZE= and LINESIZE= system options. The default settings vary from site to site and are further affected by the machine, operating system, and method of running the SAS System. For example, when the SAS System is running in an interactive environment, the PAGESIZE= option by default assumes the size of the default device specified. However, you can adjust both your page size and line size by resetting the PAGESIZE= and LINESIZE= options.

---

* Default option settings may vary among sites. To determine the defaults at your site, execute the OPTIONS procedure or browse the OPTIONS window in display manager.

For example, you can specify the following OPTIONS statement:

```
options pagesize=40 linesize=64;
```

The PAGESIZE= and LINESIZE= options remain in effect for the duration of your SAS session or until you change them.

Printing Date and Time Values

By default, the SAS System prints at the top of your output the beginning date and time of the SAS session during which your job was run. This automatic record is especially useful when you execute a program many times. However, if you prefer, you can use the NODATE system option to specify that these values not appear. In an OPTIONS statement, specify

```
options nodate;
```

The NODATE option remains in effect for the duration of your SAS session or until you change it. (Note that the NODATE option has been used to suppress dates for the previous output shown in this chapter.)

Choosing Options Selectively

So far, all the output in this chapter has been centered and unnumbered. It hasn't been dated. Except for the plot in Output 20.2, all the output has a line size of 76. But suppose you want to use a line size of 64 and you want to left-align and number the results. In addition, you want to keep a record of when the output was generated.

The following program, which uses the conditional IF-THEN statement to subset the data set, includes the options you have chosen for your output and produces Output 20.3 The OPTIONS statement specifies a line size of 64 and left-aligns the output. The DATE and NUMBER system options signal the SAS System to date and number the results.

```
options linesize=64 nocenter number date;

data hisats;
   set out.sats1;
   if score < 500 then delete;
run;

proc print;
   title 'Changing Option Settings to Customize Output';
run;
```

Output 20.3
Tailoring Results
with SAS System
Options

```
Changing Option Settings to Customize Output                    1
                                 15:39 Friday, August 18, 1989

OBS    TEST    SEX    YEAR    SCORE

 1     math     m     1967     514
 2     math     m     1970     509
 3     math     m     1986     501
```

Representing Missing Values

Recognizing the Default

Suppose the scores from the SAT data are missing for 1967 and 1970, as shown
in the following program. Output 20.4 shows the results. By default, the SAS
System prints a period to represent missing values if they are numeric.

```
data out.sats2;
    input test $ 1-8 sex $ 18 year 20-23
        score 25-27;
    cards;
verbal          m 1967
verbal          f 1967
verbal          m 1970
verbal          f 1970
math            m 1967
math            f 1967
math            m 1970
math            f 1970
;
run;

proc sort data=out.sats2;
   by test;
run;

proc print data=out.sats2;
   by test;
   title 'Processing Missing Values--the Default';
run;
```

Output 20.4
Using the Default
to Represent
Missing Values

```
                         Processing Missing Values--the Default                  1
        ------------------------------ TEST=math ------------------------------

                          OBS   SEX   YEAR   SCORE

                           1     m    1967     .
                           2     f    1967     .
                           3     m    1970     .
                           4     f    1970     .


        ------------------------------ TEST=verbal ----------------------------

                          OBS   SEX   YEAR   SCORE

                           5     m    1967     .
                           6     f    1967     .
                           7     m    1970     .
                           8     f    1970     .
```

Customizing Output of Missing Values

To customize results, you can use the MISSING= system option in the
OPTIONS statement to display missing values as a single character instead of as
a period, as the following program illustrates. Output 20.5 shows the results.

```
options missing='M';

proc print data=out.sats2;
    title 'Processing Missing Values--the MISSING= Option';
run;
```

Output 20.5
Customizing
Missing Values
with the
MISSING=
Option

```
              Processing Missing Values--the MISSING= Option              1
          OBS    TEST     SEX    YEAR    SCORE
           1     math      m     1967      M
           2     math      f     1967      M
           3     math      m     1970      M
           4     math      f     1970      M
           5     verbal    m     1967      M
           6     verbal    f     1967      M
           7     verbal    m     1970      M
           8     verbal    f     1970      M
```

The FORMAT procedure gives you another, perhaps more informative way
to represent the missing values. The following program shows that you can use
the FORMAT procedure to customize missing values by formatting them. First
use the FORMAT procedure to define a format, and then use a FORMAT
statement in the PROC or DATA step to associate the format with the variable
SCORE. Note that you don't follow the format name with a period in the VALUE

statement but a period always accompanies the format when used in a FORMAT statement. Output 20.6 shows the results.

```
proc format;
    value xscore .='scores unavailable';
run;

proc print data=out.sats2;
    format score xscore.;
    title 'Customizing Missing Values--the FORMAT Procedure';
run;
```

Output 20.6
Using the
FORMAT
Procedure to
Represent Missing
Values

```
        Customizing Missing Values--the FORMAT Procedure         1

    OBS    TEST     SEX    YEAR        SCORE

     1     math      m     1967     scores unavailable
     2     math      f     1967     scores unavailable
     3     math      m     1970     scores unavailable
     4     math      f     1970     scores unavailable
     5     verbal    m     1967     scores unavailable
     6     verbal    f     1967     scores unavailable
     7     verbal    m     1970     scores unavailable
     8     verbal    f     1970     scores unavailable
```

SAS Tools

The following statements are discussed in this chapter:

FILE *file-specification*;
specifies the current output file you indicate with *file-specification*.

PUT <*variable-list*>;
writes lines to the SAS log, the output file, or to any file you specify in a FILE statement. *Variable-list* names the variables whose values are to be written.

TITLE <*n*> <*'title'*>;
specifies up to ten title lines to be printed on each page of the SAS print file and other SAS output, where *n* specifies the number of the title line and *title* specifies the text of the title.

FOOTNOTE<*n*> <*'text'*>;
specifies up to ten footnote lines to be printed at the bottom of a page of output, where *n* specifies the relative line to be occupied by the footnote and *text* specifies the text of the footnote.

LABEL *variable*='*label*';
associates the variable you specify with the descriptive text you specify as the *label*. You can use the LABEL statement in either the DATA step or the PROC step.

OPTIONS *option-1* <. . . *option-n*>;
changes one or more SAS system options from the default value set at a site. *Option* specifies a SAS system option to be changed.

IF *condition* **THEN** *action*;
>for the observations from a file that meet the *condition* you specify in the IF clause, executes the *action* following the THEN clause. *Condition* is any valid SAS expression, and *action* is any executable SAS statement or DO group.

FORMAT *variable-list* <*format*>;
>associates a format with variables in a PROC or DATA step. *Variable-list* names the variables to be formatted, and *format* identifies the format.

The following SAS system options are discussed in this chapter; they are used to enhance SAS output. In this chapter they are specified in OPTIONS statements.

NUMBER | NONUMBER
>controls whether the page number prints on the first title line of each page of output.

PAGENO=*n*
>resets the page number for the next page of output.

CENTER | NOCENTER
>controls whether SAS procedure output is centered.

PAGESIZE=*n*
>specifies the number of lines that can be printed per page of output.

LINESIZE=*n*
>specifies the printer line width for the SAS log and the standard SAS print file used by the DATA step and procedures.

DATE | NODATE
>controls whether the date and time are printed at the top of each page of the SAS log, the standard print file, or any file with the PRINT attribute.

MISSING='*character*'
>specifies the *character* to be printed for missing numeric variable values.

The following SAS procedures are discussed in this chapter:

PROC PRINT <DATA=*SAS-data-set*> <LABEL>;
>prints the observations in a SAS data set using some or all of the variables. DATA=*SAS-data-set* specifies the data set, and LABEL tells the SAS System to use variable labels as column headings.

PROC FORMAT;
VALUE *name range*='*formatted-value*';

PROC FORMAT;
>defines a format for character or numeric variables.

VALUE *name range*='*formatted-value*';
>defines a format that writes a variable's value as a different value. *Name* specifies the format being created, *range* specifies one or more values, and *formatted-value* is the output value that is printed instead of the actual variable value.

Learning More

- The other chapters in Part 5 provide more information on your SAS session.

- Part 6, "Producing Reports," provides details on report writing procedures. Part 7, "Producing Plots and Charts," discusses plots and charts. For complete reference information about procedures, see the *SAS Procedures Guide, Version 6, Third Edition.*

- Chapter 3, "Starting with Raw Data," provides information on formatting variables. See also *SAS Language: Reference, Version 6, First Edition* and the *SAS Procedures Guide.*

- Chapter 21, "Analyzing Your SAS Session with the SAS Log," discusses the PUT statement and the SAS log.

- Chapter 29, "Writing Output," and Chapter 30, "Customizing Output," provide details on the FILE and PUT statements. See also *SAS Language: Reference.*

- Chapter 36, "Starting, Running, and Exiting the SAS System," discusses methods of running the SAS System. For a brief discussion, see also Chapter 1, "What Is the SAS System?," and *SAS Language: Reference.*

- Chapter 36 also discusses the SAS command. Chapter 39, "Mastering Your Environment with Selected Windows," discusses the OPTIONS window.

- Chapter 37, "Using the SAS Display Manager System: the Basics," discusses interactive full-screen processing in display manager.

- *SAS Language: Reference* provides complete information on SAS output.

- The SAS documentation for your host system describes host-dependent options, the default settings for system options, and the default destination for procedure output.

Chapter 21 Analyzing Your SAS® Session with the SAS® Log

Introduction

This chapter shows you how to analyze your SAS session with the SAS log. It discusses

□ the log in relation to output

□ the log's structure

□ the log's default destination, depending on your method of running the SAS System.

This chapter also tells you how to

□ write to the log

□ suppress information to the log.

Understanding the SAS Log

Gaining a Perspective

The SAS log is one result of executing a SAS program, and in that sense it is output. It acts as a record of everything you do in your SAS session or with your SAS program, from the names of the data sets you have created to the number of observations and variables you have created. This record can tell you what statements were executed, how much time the DATA and PROC steps required, and whether your program contains errors.

As with SAS output, the destination of the SAS log varies depending on your method of running the system and your operating system. Its content varies according to the DATA and PROC steps executed and the options used.

The sample log in Output 21.1 was generated by a SAS program that contains two PROC steps. Among other things, it tells you that the data set OUT.SATS1 has 44 observations and 4 variables.* Another typical log is described in detail later in the chapter.

Output 21.1

A Sample SAS Log

```
NOTE: Libref OUT was successfully assigned as follows:
      Engine:        V606
      Physical Name: YOUR-DATA-LIBRARY
4
5          libname out 'your-data-library';
6          options linesize=120;
7
8          proc sort data=out.sats1;
9             by test;
10         run;

NOTE: SAS sort was used.
NOTE: The data set OUT.SATS1 has 44 observations and 4 variables.

11
12         proc plot data=out.sats1;
13            by test;
14            label score='SAT score';
15            plot score*year / haxis=1967 1970 1975 1977 1980
16               1981 1982 1983 1984 1985 1986;
17            title1 'SAT Scores by Year, 1967-1976';
18            title3 'Separate Statistics by Test Type';
19            footnote1 '1967 and 1970 SAT scores estimated based on total n
20            footnote2 'of people taking the SAT';
21         run;

NOTE: The PROCEDURE PLOT printed pages 1-2.
```

Recognizing the Log as a Problem Solver

The SAS program that generated the log in Output 21.1 ran without errors. If the program had contained errors, those errors would have been reflected, as part of the session, in the log. The SAS System generates messages for data

---

* The DATA step that created this data set is shown in the Appendix in "Data Sets for Chapter 20." The data set is stored in a SAS data library referenced by the libref OUT throughout the rest of this chapter.

errors, syntax errors, and programming errors. You can browse those messages, make necessary changes to your program, and then rerun it successfully.

Locating the SAS Log

The destination of your log depends on the method you're using to start, run, and exit the SAS System. It also depends on the operating system you're using and the setting of SAS system options. Table 21.1 shows the default destination for each method of operation.

Table 21.1
Default
Destinations for
the SAS Log

Method of Operation	Destination of SAS Log
SAS Display Manager System (interactive full-screen)	LOG window
interactive line mode	on the terminal display, as statements are entered
noninteractive SAS programs	depends on the operating system
batch jobs	line printer or disk file

Understanding the Log's Structure

Detecting a Syntax Error

Suppose you execute the following program, which contains one DATA step and two PROC steps. However, having inadvertently omitted the semicolon from the DATA statement, you make a syntax error.

```
     /* omitted semicolon */
data out.sats4
    infile 'your-input-file';
    input test $ 1-8 sex $ 18 year 20-23
         score 25-27;
run;

proc sort data=out.sats4;
   by test;
run;

proc print data=out.sats4;
   by test;
run;
```

Output 21.2 shows the results. Although some variation occurs across operating systems and among methods of running the SAS System, the log in Output 21.2 is a representative sample.

Output 21.2

Analyzing a SAS Log with Error Messages

```
NOTE: Libref OUT was successfully assigned as follows:
      Engine:        V606
      Physical Name: YOUR-DATA-LIBRARY
4
5          libname out 'your-data-library';
6             /* omitted semicolon */
7          data out.sats4                                          1
8             infile 'your-input-file';                            2
                     74
9             input test $ 1-8 sex $ 18 year 20-23
10                  score 25-27;
11         run;

ERROR 74-322: The symbol is being ignored.                         3

ERROR: No CARDS or INFILE statement.
NOTE: The SAS System stopped processing this step because of errors.  4
NOTE: SAS set option OBS=0 and will continue to check statements.
      This may cause NOTE: No observations in data set.
WARNING: The data set OUT.SATS4 may be incomplete.  When this step was5
         stopped there were 0 observations and 4 variables.
WARNING: Data set OUT.SATS4 was not replaced because this step was stopped.
WARNING: The data set WORK.INFILE may be incomplete.  When this step was
         stopped there were 0 observations and 4 variables.

12
13         proc sort data=out.sats4;                               1
14            by test;
15         run;

16
17         proc print data=out.sats4;                              1
18            by test;
19         run;

NOTE: The SAS System stopped processing this step because of errors.  4

ERROR: Errors printed on page 1.                                   3

NOTE: SAS Institute Inc., SAS Circle, PO Box 8000, Cary, NC 27512-80006
```

Examining the Components of a Log

The following list describes the components of the log in Output 21.2. It provides valuable information, especially if you have questions and need to contact your SAS Software Consultant or the Technical Support Department at SAS Institute Inc.

The boldface numbers on the log correspond to the following items:

1. SAS statements for the DATA and PROC steps.

2. point at which the SAS System detects an error (signified by an underline).

3. error messages.

4. notes, which may include warning messages.

5. notes that contain the number of observations and variables for each data set created.

6. name and address of SAS Institute Inc. (this note appears when you end a session).

Writing to the SAS Log

In the previous sample logs, you have seen what information appears on the log by default. You can also write to the log with the PUT statement or the LIST statement.

Using the PUT Statement

The PUT statement allows you to write selected lines, including text strings and variable values, to the log. Values can be written in column, list, or formatted style. Used in this chapter as a screening device, the PUT statement can also be a useful debugging tool. For example, the following statement writes the values of all variables, including _ERROR_ and _N_, defined in the current DATA step using named output:

```
put _all_;
```

The following program reads the data set OUT.SATS1 (described in Chapter 20, "Understanding and Enhancing Your Output") and uses the PUT statement to write to the SAS log the records for which the score is 500 points or more. Ouput 21.3 shows that three records are written to the log immediately after the SAS statements.

```
libname out 'your-data-library';

data _null_;
   set out.sats1;
   if score >= 500 then put test sex year;
run;
```

Output 21.3
Writing to the SAS
Log with the PUT
Statement

```
NOTE: Libref OUT was successfully assigned as follows:
      Engine:        V606
      Physical Name: YOUR-DATA-LIBRARY
4
5           libname out 'your-data-library';
6           data _null_;
7              set out.sats1;
8              if score >= 500 then put test sex year;
9           run;

math m 1967
math m 1970
math m 1986
```

Using the LIST Statement

Use the LIST statement in the DATA step to list on the log the current input record. The following program shows that the LIST statement, like the PUT statement, can be very effective when combined with conditional processing to write selected information to the log:

```
        libname out 'your-data-library';

    data out.sats3;
         infile 'your-input-file';
         input test $ 1-8 sex $ 18 year 20-23 score 25-27;
         if score < 500 then delete;
         else list;
    run;
```

When the LIST statement is executed, the SAS System causes the current input buffer to be printed following the DATA step. Output 21.4 shows the results. Note the presence of the columns ruler before the first line. The ruler indicates that input data have been written to the log. It can be used to reference column position in the input buffer.

Output 21.4
Writing to the SAS Log with the LIST Statement

```
NOTE: Libref OUT was successfully assigned as follows:
      Engine:       V606
      Physical Name: YOUR-DATA-LIBRARY
4
5          libname out 'your-data-library';
6          data out.sats3;
7               infile 'your-input-file';
8               input test $ 1-8 sex $ 18 year 20-23 score 25-27;
9               if score < 500 then delete;
10              else list;
11         run;

NOTE: The infile 'your-input-file' is:
      Dsname=YOUR-INPUT-FILE

RULE:       ----+----1----+----2----+----3----+----4----+----5----+----6----+
23          math            m 1967 514
25          math            m 1970 509
43          math            m 1986 501
NOTE: 44 records were read from the infile 'your-input-file'.
NOTE: The data set OUT.SATS3 has 3 observations and 4 variables.
```

Suppressing Information to the SAS Log

There may be times when you want to suppress some information to the SAS log. You can suppress SAS statements, system messages, and error messages with SAS system options. You can specify these options when you invoke the SAS System, in the OPTIONS window, or in an OPTIONS statement. In this chapter, the options are specified in OPTIONS statements.

Note that all SAS system options remain in effect for the duration of your session or until you change them.

Suppressing SAS Statements

If you regularly execute large SAS programs without making changes, you can use the NOSOURCE system option as follows to suppress the listing of the SAS statements to the log:

```
options nosource;
```

The NOSOURCE option causes only source lines containing errors to be printed. You can return to the default by specifying the SOURCE system option as follows:

```
options source;
```

The SOURCE option causes all subsequent source lines to be printed.

You can also control whether secondary source statements from files included with a %INCLUDE statement are printed on the SAS log. Specify the following statement to suppress secondary statements:

```
options nosource2;
```

The following OPTIONS statement causes secondary source statements to print to the log:

```
options source2;
```

Suppressing System Notes

Much of the information supplied by the log appears as notes, including the following:

□ copyright information

□ licensing and site information

□ number of observations and variables in the data set.

The SAS System also issues a note to tell you that it has stopped processing a step because of errors.

If you do not want the notes to appear on the log, use the NONOTES system option to suppress their printing:

```
options nonotes;
```

All messages starting with NOTE: are suppressed. You can return to the default by specifying the NOTES system option:

```
options notes;
```

Limiting the Number of Error Messages

The SAS System prints messages for data input errors that appear in your SAS program; the default number is usually twenty.* Use the ERRORS= system option to specify the maximum number of observations for which error messages are printed.

Note that this option limits only the error messages that are produced for incorrect data. This kind of error is caused primarily by trying to read character values for a variable the INPUT statement defines as numeric.

If data errors are detected in more observations than the number you specify, processing continues but error messages don't print for the additional errors. For example, the following OPTIONS statement specifies printing for a maximum of five observations:

```
options errors=5;
```

However, as discussed later in this chapter, it may be dangerous to suppress error messages.

Note: No option is available to eliminate warning messages.

Suppressing SAS Statements, Notes, and Error Messages

Suppose you're reading the test scores data again, but this time you accidentally omit the character symbol for the variable SEX. You also forget to sort the data before using a BY statement with PROC PRINT. At the same time, for efficiency, you decide to suppress the SAS statements, notes, and error messages.

```
libname out 'your-data-library';
options nosource nonotes errors=0;

data out.sats5;
    infile 'your-input-file';
    input test $ 1-8 sex 18 year 20-23
        score 25-27;
run;

proc print;
    by test;
run;
```

This program doesn't generate output, but Output 21.5 shows the SAS log. Because you specified ERRORS=0, the log shows one line of data but doesn't include an error message about the data input errors that result from trying to read SEX as a numeric value. Also, specifying the NOSOURCE and NONOTES system options causes the log to contain no SAS statements that you can doublecheck and no notes to explain what happened. The log does contain an

---

* The default number of error messages may vary among sites.

error message telling you that OUT.SATS5 isn't sorted in ascending sequence. This error isn't caused by invalid input data, so the ERRORS=0 option has no effect on this error.

Output 21.5
Suppressing Information to the SAS Log

```
NOTE: Libref OUT was successfully assigned as follows:
      Engine:        V606
      Physical Name: YOUR-DATA-LIBRARY
4
5         libname out 'your-data-library';
6         options nosource nonotes errors=0;


RULE:      ----+----1----+----2----+----3----+----4----+----5----+----6----+
1          verbal       m 1967 463
TEST=verbal SEX=. YEAR=1967 SCORE=463 _ERROR_=1 _N_=1


ERROR: Data set OUT.SATS5 is not sorted in ascending sequence. The current
       by-group has TEST = verbal and the next by-group has TEST = math.
```

▶ *Caution* . . . . ***Knowing when not to suppress information.***

The NOSOURCE, NONOTES, and ERRORS= system options are space savers. They are most suitable when used with an already-tested program, perhaps one that you run regularly. However, as demonstrated in the previous section, they aren't always appropriate. If you're developing a new program, the error messages in the log may be essential for debugging, and you should not limit them. Similarly, notes shouldn't be suppressed because they may pinpoint problems with your program. They are especially important if you seek help in debugging your program from someone not already familiar with it. In fact, you're advised not to suppress any information in the log until you have already executed the program without errors. ▲

Suppose you re-execute the program that generated Output 21.5, but this time you specify the SOURCE, NOTES, and ERRORS= options. Output 21.6 shows the results.

Output 21.6
Debugging with the SAS Log

```
6          options source notes errors=5;
7          data out.sats5;
8              infile 'your-input-file';
9              input test $ 1-8 sex 18 year 20-23
10                   score 25-27;
11         run;

NOTE: The infile 'your-input-file' is:
      Dsname=YOUR-INPUT-FILE

NOTE: Invalid data for SEX in line 1 18-18.
RULE:      ----+----1----+----2----+----3----+----4----+----5----+----6----+
1          verbal    point   m 1967 463
TEST=verbal SEX=. YEAR=1967 SCORE=463 _ERROR_=1 _N_=1
NOTE: Invalid data for SEX in line 2 18-18.
2          verbal    point   f 1967 468
TEST=verbal SEX=. YEAR=1967 SCORE=468 _ERROR_=1 _N_=2
NOTE: Invalid data for SEX in line 3 18-18.
3          verbal    point   m 1970 459
TEST=verbal SEX=. YEAR=1970 SCORE=459 _ERROR_=1 _N_=3
NOTE: Invalid data for SEX in line 4 18-18.
```

(continued on next page)

```
(continued from previous page)
4          verbal    point   f 1970 461
TEST=verbal SEX=. YEAR=1970 SCORE=461 _ERROR_=1 _N_=4
NOTE: Invalid data for SEX in line 5 18-18.
ERROR: Limit set by ERRORS= option reached.  Further errors of this type
       will not be printed.
5          verbal    point   m 1975 437
TEST=verbal SEX=. YEAR=1975 SCORE=437 _ERROR_=1 _N_=5
NOTE: 44 records were read from the infile 'your-input-file'.
NOTE: The data set OUT.SATS5 has 44 observations and 4 variables.

12         proc print;
13            by test;
```

```
2
                              The SAS System
14       run;

ERROR: Data set OUT.SATS5 is not sorted in ascending sequence. The current
       by-group has TEST = verbal and the next by-group has TEST = math.
NOTE: The SAS System stopped processing this step because of errors.
```

Again, this program doesn't generate output, but this time the log is a more effective problem-solving tool. It includes all the SAS statements from your program, which you can doublecheck, as well as many informative notes. Specifically, it includes enough messages about the invalid data for the variable SEX that you can spot the problem. With this information, you can modify your program and rerun it successfully.

Changing the Log's Appearance

Chapter 20 showed you how you can customize your output. Except in an interactive session, you can also customize the log by using the PAGE and SKIP statements. Use the PAGE statement to move to a new page on the log; use the SKIP statement to skip lines on the log. With the SKIP statement, specify the number of lines you want to skip; if you don't specify a number, one line is skipped. If the number you specify exceeds the number of lines remaining on the page, the SAS System treats the SKIP statement like a PAGE statement and skips to the top of the next page. The PAGE and SKIP statements don't appear on the log.

Suppose you insert the PAGE statement before the PROC PRINT step in the previous example. Output 21.7 shows the results.

Output 21.7
Using the PAGE
Statement

```
6          options source notes errors=5;
7          data out.sats5;
8             infile 'your-input-file';
9             input test $ 1-8 sex 18 year 20-23
10                score 25-27;
11         run;

NOTE: The infile 'your-input-file' is:
      Dsname=YOUR-INPUT-FILE

NOTE: Invalid data for SEX in line 1 18-18.
RULE:      ----+----1----+----2----+----3----+----4----+----5----+----6----+
1          verbal   point   m 1967 463
TEST=verbal SEX=. YEAR=1967 SCORE=463 _ERROR_=1 _N_=1
NOTE: Invalid data for SEX in line 2 18-18.
2          verbal   point   f 1967 468
TEST=verbal SEX=. YEAR=1967 SCORE=468 _ERROR_=1 _N_=2
NOTE: Invalid data for SEX in line 3 18-18.
3          verbal   point   m 1970 459
TEST=verbal SEX=. YEAR=1970 SCORE=459 _ERROR_=1 _N_=3
NOTE: Invalid data for SEX in line 4 18-18.
4          verbal   point   f 1970 461
TEST=verbal SEX=. YEAR=1970 SCORE=461 _ERROR_=1 _N_=4
NOTE: Invalid data for SEX in line 5 18-18.
ERROR: Limit set by ERRORS= option reached.  Further errors of this type
       will not be printed.
5          verbal   point   m 1975 437
TEST=verbal SEX=. YEAR=1975 SCORE=437 _ERROR_=1 _N_=5
NOTE: 44 records were read from the infile 'your-input-file.
NOTE: The data set OUT.SATS5 has 44 observations and 4 variables.
```

```
2
                              The SAS System
13         proc print;
14            by test;
15         run;

ERROR: Data set OUT.SATS5 is not sorted in ascending sequence. The current
       by-group has TEST = verbal and the next by-group has TEST = math.
NOTE: The SAS System stopped processing this step because of errors.
```

SAS Tools

This chapter discusses the following statements, which are used to write to the log and to change the log's appearance:

PUT <variable-list> | <_ALL_>;

writes lines to the SAS log, the output file, or any file you specify in a FILE statement. If no FILE statement has been executed in this iteration of the DATA step, the PUT statement writes to the SAS log. *Variable-list* names the variables whose values are to be written, and _ALL_ signifies that the values of all variables, including _ERROR_ and _N_, are to be written to the log.

LIST;

lists on the SAS log the contents of the input buffer for the observation being processed.

PAGE;

skips to a new page on the log.

SKIP*n*;

on the SAS log, skips the number of lines you specify with the value *n*. If the number is greater than the number of lines remaining on the page, the SAS System treats the SKIP statement like a PAGE statement and skips to the top of the next page.

This chapter discusses the following SAS system options; they are used to suppress information to the log. In this chapter, they are specified in OPTIONS statements.

SOURCE | NOSOURCE

controls whether SAS statements are printed to the log.

SOURCE2 | NOSOURCE2

controls whether secondary SAS statements from files included by %INCLUDE statements are printed to the log.

NOTES | NONOTES

controls whether notes are printed to the log.

ERRORS=*n*

specifies the maximum number of observations for which error messages about data input errors are printed.

Learning More

□ The other chapters in Part 5 provide more information on your SAS session. See especially Chapter 23, "Diagnosing and Avoiding Errors," which contains more information about error messages.

□ Chapter 20, "Understanding and Enhancing Your Output," and Chapter 30, "Customizing Output," discuss the FILE and PUT statements.

□ Chapter 23, "Diagnosing and Avoiding Errors," discusses the automatic variables _N_ and _ERROR_.

□ Chapter 36, "Starting, Running, and Exiting the SAS System," provides information on methods of operation and on specifying SAS system options when you invoke the SAS System.

□ Chapter 36 also discusses executing SAS statements automatically.

□ Chapter 37, "Using the SAS Display Manager System: the Basics," discusses the LOG window.

□ *SAS Language: Reference, Version 6, First Edition* provides complete reference information about the SAS log.

□ *SAS Language: Reference* provides complete reference information on the SAS statements discussed in this chapter.

□ *SAS Language: Reference* provides complete reference information on the SAS system options that work across all operating systems. Refer to the SAS documentation for your host system for information concerning host-specific options.

□ The SAS documentation for your host system contains information concerning the appearance and destination of the SAS log, as well as for routing output.

Chapter 22 Directing the SAS® Log and Output

Introduction

This chapter builds on your basic understanding of SAS output and the SAS log. It shows you how to direct your log and procedure output to another destination. You can use the

- PRINTTO procedure from within a program or session to route the log and procedure output from their destinations to the destination you choose

- FILE command from within the SAS Display Manager System to store copies of the contents of the LOG and OUTPUT windows in files

- PRINT= and LOG= system options as you invoke the SAS System to redefine the default for an entire session or program by specifying a default destination.

Routing Procedure Output and the SAS Log in Any Method of Operation

In any method of operation, you can use the PRINTTO procedure to route procedure output or the SAS log to one of the following destinations:

- a printer

- a permanent file

- a dummy file, which serves to suppress the output.

Routing Output to an Alternate Location

The PRINTTO procedure reroutes SAS procedure output to an alternate location. All output produced after PROC PRINTTO is executed is sent to the alternate location until another PROC PRINTTO statement has been executed or until the program or session has ended.

The new output file is specified using the FILE= option (also called the PRINT= option) in the PROC PRINTTO statement. The value you specify for the FILE= option can be either the complete name of the file in quotes or a fileref for the file. (See "Special Topic: Using External Files in Your SAS Job" in Chapter 2, "Introduction to DATA Step Processing," for more information on filerefs and filenames.) If you specify the NEW option in the PROC PRINTTO statement, PROC PRINTTO writes over the previous contents of the output file. Otherwise, the output is appended to the output already in the file.

Suppose you want to route to an alternate file output for a program that reads the SAT data described in Chapter 20, "Understanding and Enhancing Your Output." Simply insert a PROC PRINTTO step in the following program before the PROC PRINT statement. Then submit the program.

```
data sats;
   infile 'your-input-file';
   input test $ 1-8 sex $ 18 year 20-23
         score 25-27;
run;

proc printto file='your-alternate-output-file' new;
run;

proc print;
   title 'Routing Output--the PRINTTO Procedure';
run;
```

A check of *your-alternate-output-file* should verify that your output has been routed.

The PRINTTO procedure itself doesn't produce printed output but instead tells the SAS System to route the results of all subsequent procedures until another PROC PRINTTO statement has been executed. Therefore, the PROC PRINTTO statement must precede the procedure whose output is to be routed.

You can execute the PRINTTO procedure as many times in a program as necessary. Therefore, it can be especially useful for routing output from different steps of a SAS job to different files.

Figure 22.1 illustrates how the SAS System uses the PRINTTO procedure to route output.

Figure 22.1
Using the PRINTTO Procedure to Route Output

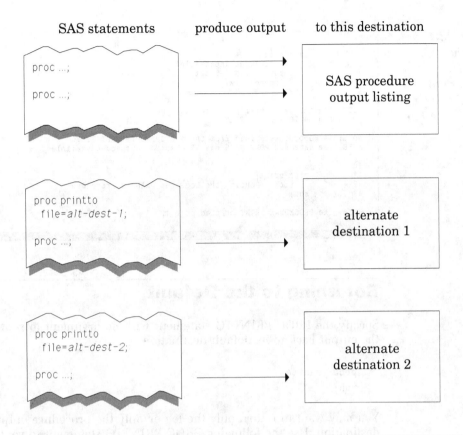

Routing the SAS Log to an Alternate Location

To route the SAS log to an alternate file, specify the LOG= option in the PROC PRINTTO statement, as in the following program. Output 22.1 shows the results.

```
proc printto log='your-alternate-log-file';
run;

data sats;
   infile 'your-input-file';
   input test $ 1-8 sex $ 18 year 20-23
         score 25-27;
run;

proc print;
   title 'Routing the Log--the PRINTTO Procedure';
run;
```

A check of *your-alternate-log-file* should verify that the log has been routed, starting with the messages following the PROC PRINTTO step.

Output 22.1
Using the
PRINTTO
Procedure to
Route the Log to
an Alternate File

```
5           data sats;
6             infile 'your-input-file';
7             input test $ 1-8 sex $ 18 year 20-23
8               score 25-27;
9           run;

NOTE: The infile 'your-input-file' is:
      Dsname=YOUR-INPUT-FILE

NOTE: 44 records were read from the infile YOUR-INPUT-FILE.
NOTE: The data set WORK.SATS has 44 observations and 4 variables.

10
11          proc print;
12            title 'Routing the Log--the PRINTTO Procedure';
13          run;

NOTE: The PROCEDURE PRINT printed page 1.
```

Returning to the Default

Specify the PROC PRINTTO statement with no argument to route the log and
the output back to its default destination:

```
proc printto;
run;
```

You may want to return only the log or only the procedure output to its default
destination. Use the following PROC PRINTTO statement to route the log back to
the default destination:

```
proc printto log=log;
run;
```

Use the following PROC PRINTTO statement to route the procedure output to
the default destination:

```
proc printto file=print;
run;
```

Storing Output and the SAS Log from the
SAS Display Manager System

Understanding the Default

Within the SAS Display Manager System, the default destination for most base
procedures' output is the OUTPUT window. Each time you execute a procedure
within a single session, the output is appended to the already-existing output. To
browse the results, you can

□ scroll the OUTPUT window, which contains the output by the order in
  which it was generated

□ execute the selection-field command B in the OUTPUT MANAGER window
  to display a browse window for one piece of output.

You can also browse a listing of all output in the OUTPUT MANAGER window. In the OUTPUT window, execute the PRINT command to print your output and the CLEAR command to clear the contents of the window. When you end your session, the output is automatically cleared from the window. You can also use the selection-field command P in the OUTPUT MANAGER window to print your output.

In display manager, the default destination for the SAS log messages is the LOG window. When you execute a procedure, the log messages are appended to the already-existing log messages in the LOG window. You can scroll the LOG window to browse the results. Execute the PRINT command to print your log messages and the CLEAR command to clear the contents of the window. When your session ends, the window is automatically cleared.

Within display manager, you can use the PRINTTO procedure to route log messages or output to a location other than the default, just as you can in other methods of operation. For details, see "Routing Procedure Output and the SAS Log in Any Method of Operation" earlier in this chapter.

Storing the Contents of the LOG or OUTPUT Windows

If you want to store a copy of the contents of the OUTPUT or LOG window in a file, use the display manager FILE command. On the command line of the OUTPUT or LOG window, specify the FILE command followed by the name of the file:

file '*file-to-store-contents-of-window*'

The SAS System has a built-in safeguard that prevents you from accidentally overwriting a file. Whether you inadvertently specify an existing file by omitting the FILE operand or by specifying an already-existing file as the operand, a *requestor window* appears. A requestor window is a window that the SAS System displays to prompt you to choose a course of action, to provide you with information, and sometimes to prevent you from doing something dangerous. It asks you whether you want

□ the contents of the file replaced

□ the contents of the file appended

□ the FILE command canceled.

Note that you can also use the selection-field command F in the OUTPUT MANAGER window to store a copy of your output in a file.

Redefining the Default Destination in a Batch Environment

Understanding the Default

Normally, in a batch environment, procedure output is routed to the list file and the SAS log is routed to a log file. These files are usually defined by your installation and are created automatically when you invoke the SAS System. Consult your SAS Software Representative if you have questions pertaining to your site.

Redefining the Default

If you want to redefine the default destination for procedure output, use the PRINT= system option. To redefine the default destination for the SAS log, use the LOG= system option. You can specify these options only at initialization. For more information on SAS system options that can be specified only at initialization, see "Special Topic: System Options for Initializing the SAS System" later in this chapter. For details on how the PRINT= and LOG= options work at your site, refer to the SAS documentation for your host system.

Special Topic: System Options for Initializing the SAS System

Some options must be specified at initialization. These options affect

- □ the initialization of the SAS System
- □ the SAS System's interface with the hardware
- □ the SAS System's interface with the operating system.

Such options are sometimes called *configuration options*. In contrast to other SAS system options, which affect appearance of output, file handling, use of system variables, and processing of observations, configuration options can't be changed in the middle of a program. They must be specified when you invoke the SAS System, either in the configuration file or in the SAS command.

The configuration file is a special file that contains configuration options as well as other SAS system options and their settings. Each time it is invoked, the SAS System checks the settings of this special file. Note that the options in this special file are specified in the same format as they are in the SAS command on a host system. For example, under MVS this file's contents may typically include the following:

```
WORK=WORK
SASUSER=SASUSER
DMS
SASMSG=SASMSG
```

The SAS System automatically puts into effect the settings of the options as they appear in the configuration file. If you specify options both in the configuration file and in the SAS command, the options are concatenated. If you specify the same option in the SAS command and in the configuration file, the setting in the SAS command overrides the setting in the file. For example, specifying the NODMS option in the SAS command overrides the DMS option in the configuration file and tells the SAS System to bring up a line-mode session.

SAS Tools

This chapter discusses the PRINTTO procedure:

PROC PRINTTO <LOG='*your-alternate-log-file*'>
　　　　　　　　<FILE='*your-alternate-output-file*'>
　　　　　　　　<NEW>;
　　　　routes the SAS log or procedure output to an alternate location. The
　　　　LOG= option identifies the location for the log and the FILE= option
　　　　identifies the location for the output. NEW signifies that the log or
　　　　output is to write over the previous contents.

The following display manager commands are discussed in this chapter:

B
　　　　is a selection-field command you can use to display a browse window.

PRINT
　　　　prints the contents of the window.

P
　　　　is a selection-field command you can use in the OUTPUT MANAGER
　　　　window to print your output.

CLEAR
　　　　clears a window as specified.

FILE<'*file-to-store-contents-of-window*'>
　　　　routes a copy of the contents of a window to the file you specify; the
　　　　original remains in place.

F
　　　　is a selection-field command you can use in the OUTPUT MANAGER
　　　　window to store a copy of your output in a file.

The following SAS system options are discussed in this chapter:

PRINT=*system-filename*
　　　　redefines the default destination for procedure output.

LOG=*system-filename*
　　　　redefines the default destination for the SAS log.

Learning More

□ The other chapters in Part 5 provide more information on SAS output.

□ Part 10, "Understanding Your SAS Environment," contains details about methods of operating the SAS System and about interactive processing in the SAS Display Manager System. For a brief discussion, see also Chapter 1, "What Is the SAS System?," and *SAS Language: Reference, Version 6, First Edition.*

□ Chapter 36, "Starting, Running, and Exiting the SAS System," gives details about SAS system options, including configuration options. See also *SAS Language: Reference.*

□ Chapter 37, "Using the SAS Display Manager System: the Basics," discusses the LOG and OUTPUT windows and the FILE command.

□ *SAS Language: Reference* provides complete reference information on the SAS log and procedure output.

□ The *SAS Procedures Guide, Version 6, Third Edition* completely documents the PRINTTO procedure, including the UNIT= option. Use the UNIT= option for rerouting output if your operating system uses FORTRAN unit numbers. Refer also to the SAS documentation for your host system.

□ The SAS documentation for your host system contains additional host-specific information about routing output.

□ The SAS documentation for your host system presents host-specific details about the PRINT= and LOG= options and about other SAS system options.

Chapter 23 Diagnosing and Avoiding Errors

Introduction

This chapter shows you how to diagnose errors in your programs, thereby helping you to avoid other errors. It also provides a quality control checklist that you should use as you develop programs.

Many factors are involved in diagnosing and avoiding errors. As this chapter explains, you should

☐ understand how the SAS System checks a job

☐ distinguish among the types of errors

☐ understand the notes, warning messages, and error messages that appear on the log.

Understanding How the SAS System Checks a Job

To better understand the errors you make so you can avoid others, it's important to understand how the SAS System checks a job. The SAS supervisor is the part of the SAS System that is responsible for executing SAS programs. To check the syntax of SAS programs, the SAS supervisor

☐ reads SAS statements and data

☐ translates program statements into executable machine code or intermediate code

☐ creates data sets

☐ calls SAS procedures, as requested

□ prints error messages

□ ends a job.

The SAS supervisor knows

□ the forms and types of statements that can be present in a DATA step

□ the types of statements and the options that can be present in a PROC step.

To process a program, the SAS supervisor scans all of the SAS statements and breaks each statement into words. Each word is processed separately; when all of the words in a step are processed, the step is executed. If the SAS supervisor detects an error, it flags the error at its location and prints an explanation. The SAS supervisor considers anything it doesn't recognize an error.

Understanding How the SAS System Processes Errors

When the SAS System detects an error, it usually underlines the error or underlines the point at which it detects the error, identifying it by a number. Each number is uniquely associated with a message. Then it enters *syntax check mode*. The SAS System reads the following statements, checks their syntax, and underlines additional errors if necessary.

In a batch or noninteractive program, an error in a DATA step statement causes the SAS System to remain in syntax check mode for the rest of the program. It doesn't execute any more DATA or PROC steps that create external files or SAS data sets. Procedures that read from SAS data sets execute with 0 observations, and procedures that don't read SAS data sets execute normally. A syntax error in a PROC step usually affects only that step. At the end of the step, the SAS System writes a message in the SAS log for each error detected.

Distinguishing Types of Errors

The SAS System recognizes three kinds of errors:

□ syntax errors

□ execution-time errors

□ data errors.

Recognizing Syntax Errors

Syntax errors are errors made in the SAS statements of a program. They include misspelled keywords and missing or invalid punctuation. The SAS System detects syntax errors as it compiles each DATA or PROC step.

Recognizing Execution-Time Errors

Execution-time errors cause a program to fail when it is submitted for execution. Most execution-time errors that aren't serious produce notes but allow the program to run to completion. For more serious errors, the SAS System issues error messages and stops all processing.

Recognizing Data Errors

Data errors are actually a type of execution-time error. They occur when the raw data you are analyzing with a SAS program contain invalid values. For example, a data error occurs if you specify numeric variables in the INPUT statement for character data. Data errors don't cause a program to stop but instead elicit notes.

Diagnosing Errors

Suppose you are continuing to analyze the data introduced in Chapter 20, "Understanding and Enhancing Your Output." The data consist of nationwide test results from the Scholastic Aptitude Test (SAT) for college-bound high school seniors from 1967 through 1986.* This section shows what happens when errors occur.

Diagnosing Syntax Errors

As already noted, the SAS supervisor detects syntax errors as it compiles each step. It

□ prints the word ERROR

□ identifies the error's location

□ prints an explanation of the error.

Suppose you want to use the CHART procedure to analyze your data. However, as the following program shows, you omit a semicolon in the DATA statement and you misspell the keyword INFILE. Output 23.1 shows the results of the two syntax errors.

```
  /* omitted semicolon and misspelled keyword */
  libname out 'your-data-library';

data out.error1
   infill 'your-input-file';
   input test $ 1-8 sex $ 18 year 20-23
         score 25-27;
run;
```

---

* Refer to the Appendix for a complete listing of the input data used to create the data sets in this chapter.

```
proc chart data=out.error1;
    hbar test / sumvar=score type=mean group=sex discrete;
run;
```

Output 23.1
Diagnosing Syntax
Errors

```
NOTE: Libref OUT was successfully assigned as follows:
      Engine:        V606
      Physical Name: YOUR-DATA-LIBRARY
4
5            /* omitted semicolon and misspelled keyword */
6            libname out 'your-data-library';
7
8            data out.error1
9                infill 'your-input-file';
                       74
10               input test $ 1-8 sex $ 18 year 20-23
11                   score 25-27;
12           run;
ERROR 74-322: The symbol is being ignored.

ERROR: No CARDS or INFILE statement.
NOTE: The SAS System stopped processing this step because of errors.
NOTE: SAS set option OBS=0 and will continue to check statements.
      This may cause NOTE: No observations in data set.
WARNING: The data set OUT.ERROR1 may be incomplete.  When this step was
         stopped there were 0 observations and 4 variables.
WARNING: Data set OUT.ERROR1 was not replaced because this step was stopped.
WARNING: The data set WORK.INFILL may be incomplete.  When this step was
         stopped there were 0 observations and 4 variables.


13
14           proc chart data=out.error1;
15               hbar test / sumvar=score type=mean group=sex discrete;
16           run;
NOTE: The SAS System stopped processing this step because of errors.

ERROR: Errors printed on page 1.

NOTE: SAS Institute Inc., SAS Circle, PO Box 8000, Cary, NC 27512-8000
```

As the log indicates, the SAS System recognizes the keyword DATA and attempts to process the DATA step. Because the DATA statement must end with a semicolon, the SAS System assumes that INFILL is a data set name and that two data sets are being created: OUT.ERROR1 and WORK.INFILL. Because it considers INFILL the name of a data set, it doesn't recognize it as part of another statement and, therefore, doesn't detect the spelling error. Because the quoted string is invalid in a DATA statement, the SAS System stops processing here and creates no observations for either data set.

The SAS System attempts to execute your program logically based on what you have told it, according to the steps outlined earlier in this chapter. The second syntax error, the misspelled keyword, is never recognized because the SAS System considers the DATA statement in effect until it finds a semicolon. The point to remember is that when multiple errors are made in the same program, not all of them may be detected the first time you execute the program or they may be flagged differently in a group than if they were made alone. You may find that one correction may uncover another error or at least change its explanation in the log.

As an illustration, suppose you re-execute the previous program with the semicolon added to the DATA statement. An attempt to correct the misspelled keyword simply introduces a different spelling error, as follows. Output 23.2 shows the results.

```
/* misspelled keyword */
libname out 'your-data-library';

data out.error2;
   unfile 'your-input-file';
   input test $ 1-8 sex $ 18 year 20-23
         score 25-27;
run;

proc chart data=out.error1;
   hbar test / sumvar=score type=mean group=sex discrete;
run;
```

Output 23.2
Correcting Syntax and Finding Different Error Messages

```
NOTE: Libref OUT was successfully assigned as follows:
      Engine:        V606
      Physical Name: YOUR-DATA-LIBRARY
5          libname out 'your-data-library';
6
7             /* misspelled keyword */
8
9          data out.error2;
10            unfile 'your-input-file';
              180
11            input test $ 1-8 sex $ 18 year 20-23
12                  score 25-27;
13         run;

ERROR 180-322: Statement is not valid or it is used out of proper order.

ERROR: No CARDS or INFILE statement.
NOTE: The SAS System stopped processing this step because of errors.
NOTE: SAS set option OBS=0 and will continue to check statements.
      This may cause NOTE: No observations in data set.
WARNING: The data set OUT.ERROR2 may be incomplete.  When this step was
         stopped there were 0 observations and 4 variables.
WARNING: Data set OUT.ERROR2 was not replaced because this step was stopped.


14
15         proc chart data=out.error1;
16            hbar test / sumvar=score type=mean group=sex discrete;
17         run;

NOTE: The SAS System stopped processing this step because of errors.

ERROR: Errors printed on page 1.

NOTE: SAS Institute Inc., SAS Circle, PO Box 8000, Cary, NC 27512-8000
```

With the semicolon added, the SAS System now attempts to create only one data set. From that point on, the SAS System reads the SAS statements as it did before and issues many of the same messages. However, this time the SAS System considers the UNFILE statement invalid and out of proper order, and it creates no observations for the data set.

Diagnosing Execution-Time Errors

Several types of errors are detected at execution time. Execution-time errors include the following:

□ illegal mathematical operations

□ observations out of order for BY-group processing

□ an incorrect reference in an INFILE statement (for example, misspelling or otherwise incorrectly stating the external file).

When the SAS supervisor encounters an execution-time error, it

□ prints a note, warning, or error message, depending on the seriousness of the error

□ in some cases, lists the values stored in the program data vector

□ continues or stops processing, depending on the seriousness of the error.

Suppose you re-execute the previous program, but instead of misspelling INFILE you misspell the file identified in the INFILE statement. This error doesn't allow the data to be read.

```
/* misspelled file in the INFILE statement */
libname out 'your-data-library';

data out.error3;
   infile 'an-incorrect-filename';
   input test $ 1-8 sex $ 18 year 20-23
         score 25-27;
run;

proc chart data=out.error3;
   hbar test / sumvar=score type=mean group=sex discrete;
run;
```

As the SAS log in Output 23.3 indicates, the SAS System can't find the file. The SAS system stops processing because of errors and creates no observations in the data set.

Output 23.3
Diagnosing an
Error in the
INFILE Statement

```
NOTE: Libref OUT was successfully assigned as follows:
      Engine:        V606
      Physical Name: YOUR-DATA-LIBRARY
4
5             /* misspelled file in the INFILE statement */
6             libname out 'your-data-library';
7
8             data out.error3;
9                infile 'an-incorrect-filename';
10               input test $ 1-8 sex $ 18 year 20-23
11                     score 25-27;
12            run;

ERROR: AN-INCORRECT-FILENAME        - OPEN failed. Specified member was not
       found.
NOTE: The SAS System stopped processing this step because of errors.
NOTE: SAS set option OBS=0 and will continue to check statements.
      This may cause NOTE: No observations in data set.
WARNING: The data set OUT.ERROR3 may be incomplete.  When this step was
         stopped there were 0 observations and 4 variables.
WARNING: Data set OUT.ERROR3 was not replaced because this step was stopped.


13
14            proc chart data=out.error3;
15               hbar test / sumvar=score type=mean group=sex discrete;
16            run;


NOTE: The SAS System stopped processing this step because of errors.


ERROR: Errors printed on page 1.

NOTE: SAS Institute Inc., SAS Circle, PO Box 8000, Cary, NC 27512-8000
```

Diagnosing Data Errors

The SAS System detects data errors during execution and continues processing. It

□   prints a note describing the error

□   lists the values stored in the input buffer

□   lists the values stored in the program data vector.

Note that the values listed in the program data vector include two variables created automatically by the SAS System:

_N_   counts the number of times the DATA step iterates after it first executes.

ERROR   indicates the occurrence of an error during an execution of the DATA step.

The value assigned to the variable _ERROR_ is 0 when no error is encountered and 1 when an error is encountered.

These automatic variables are assigned temporarily to each observation and aren't stored with the data set.

Suppose you submit a program that uses formats to assign values to variables. The raw data are shown below:

```
----+----1----+----2----+----3----+----4----+----5
verbal        m 1967 463
verbal        f 1967 468
verbal        m 1970 459
verbal        f 1970 461
math          m 1967 514
 math          f 1967 467
math          m 1970 509
math          f 1970 509
```

However, the data aren't correctly aligned in the columns described by the INPUT statement. The sixth data line is shifted two spaces to the right, and the rest of the data lines are shifted one space to the right, as evidenced by a comparison of the raw data with the following program. Output 23.4 shows the output, and Output 23.5 shows the SAS log.

```
   /* data in wrong columns */
libname out 'your-data-library';

proc format;
   value xscore .='accurate scores unavailable';
run;

data out.error4;
   infile 'your-input-file';
   input test $ 1-8 sex $ 18 year 20-23
        score 25-27;
   format score xscore.;
run;

proc print data=out.error4;
   title 'Viewing Incorrect Output';
run;
```

Output 23.4
Detecting Data Errors with Incorrect Output

```
                    Viewing Incorrect Output                        1

     OBS     TEST     SEX    YEAR              SCORE

       1    verbal           196                      46
       2    verbal           196                      46
       3    verbal           197                      45
       4    verbal           197                      46
       5    math             196                      51
       6    math              .     accurate scores unavailable
       7    math             197                      50
       8    math             197                      46
```

This program generates output, but it isn't the output you expected. The values for the variable SEX are missing altogether. Only the first three digits of the value for the variable YEAR are shown except in the sixth observation where a missing value is indicated. The third digit of the value for the variable SCORE is missing, again except in the sixth observation, which does show the assigned value for the missing value.

Now check the SAS log, in Output 23.5, for an explanation.

Output 23.5
Diagnosing Data
Errors

```
NOTE: Libref OUT was successfully assigned as follows:
      Engine:        V606
      Physical Name: YOUR-DATA-LIBRARY
4
5              /* data in wrong columns */
6              libname out 'your-data-library';
7
8              proc format;
9                  value xscore .='accurate scores unavailable';
NOTE: Format XSCORE has been output.
10             run;


11
12             data out.error4;
13                 infile 'your-input-file';
14                 input test $ 1-8 sex $ 18 year 20-23
15                       score 25-27;
16                 format score xscore.;
17             run;

NOTE: The infile 'your-input-file' is:
      Dsname=YOUR-INPUT-FILE

NOTE: Invalid data for YEAR in line 6 20-23.
NOTE: Invalid data for SCORE in line 6 25-27.
RULE:      ----+----1----+----2----+----3----+----4----+----5----+----6----+
6          math          f 1967 467
TEST=math SEX=  YEAR=. SCORE=accurate scores unavailable _ERROR_=1 _N_=6
NOTE: 8 records were read from the infile 'your-input-file'              .
NOTE: The data set OUT.ERROR4 has 8 observations and 4 variables.

18
19             proc print data=out.error4;
20                 title 'Viewing Incorrect Output';
21             run;

NOTE: The PROCEDURE PRINT printed page 1.
```

The errors are flagged, starting with the first message that line 6 contains invalid data for the variable YEAR. The rule indicates that input data have been written to the log. The SAS System lists on the log the values stored in the program data vector. The following line from the log indicates that the SAS System has encountered an error.

```
TEST=math SEX= YEAR=. SCORE=accurate scores unavailable_ERROR_=1 _N_=6
```

Missing values are shown for the variables SEX and YEAR. The automatic variables _ERROR_ and _N_ indicate that the sixth line of input contained the error.

To debug your program, either reposition the raw data or rewrite the INPUT statement, remembering that all the data lines were shifted at least one space to the right. The variable TEST was unaffected, but the variable SEX was completely removed from its designated field; therefore, the SAS System read it as a missing value. In the sixth observation, for which the data were shifted right an additional space, the character value for SEX occupied part of the field for the numeric variable YEAR. When the SAS System encounters invalid data, it treats the value as a missing value but also notes on the log that the data are invalid. The important point to remember is that the SAS System can use only the information you provide it, not what you *intend* to provide it.

Using a Quality Control Checklist

If you follow some basic guidelines as you develop a program, you can avoid common errors. Use the following checklist to flag and correct common mistakes before you submit your program.

1. *Check the syntax of your program.* In particular, check the following:

   □ All SAS statements end with a semicolon; be sure you haven't omitted any semicolons or accidentally typed the wrong character.

   □ Any starting and ending quotes must match; you can use either single or double quotes.

   □ Most SAS statements begin with a SAS keyword. (Exceptions are the assignment statement and sum statement.) Be sure you haven't misspelled or omitted any of the keywords.

   □ Every DO statement must be followed by an END statement.

2. *Check the order of your program.* The SAS System usually executes the statements in a DATA step one by one, in the order they appear. After executing the DATA step, the SAS System moves to the next step and continues in the same fashion. Be sure that all the SAS statements appear in order so the SAS System can execute them properly. For example, an INFILE statement, if used, must precede an INPUT statement.

   Also, be sure to end steps with the RUN statement. This is especially important at the end of your program since the RUN statement causes the previous step to be executed.

3. *Check your INPUT statement and your data.* The SAS System classifies all variables as either character or numeric. The assignment in the INPUT statement as either character or numeric must correspond to the actual values of variables in your data. Also, the SAS System allows for list, column, formatted, or named input. The method of input you specify in the INPUT statement must correspond with the actual arrangement of raw data.

Learning More

□ The other chapters in Part 5 provide more information on your SAS session. Chapter 22, "Directing the SAS Log and Output," discusses warnings, notes, and error messages and presents debugging guidelines.

□ Chapter 2, "Introduction to DATA Step Processing," and Chapter 3, "Starting with Raw Data," contain information on the program data vector and the input buffer.

□ *SAS Language: Reference, Version 6, First Edition* contains complete reference information about the SAS log.

□ *SAS Language: Reference* contains complete reference information about SAS output.

□ *SAS Language: Reference* contains information on using the MISSOVER and STOPOVER options in the INFILE statement as debugging tools. The

MISSOVER option prevents a SAS program from going past the end of a line to read values with list input if it doesn't find values in the current line for all INPUT statement variables. Then the SAS System assigns missing values to variables for which no values appear on the current input line. The STOPOVER option stops processing the DATA step when an INPUT statement using list input reaches the end of the current record without finding values for all variables in the statement. Then the SAS System sets _ERROR_ to 1, stops building the data set, and prints an incomplete data line.

Part 6
Producing Reports

Chapter 24 Printing Detail Reports

Introduction

This chapter shows you how to use the PRINT procedure to produce *detail reports*. Detail reports are computer output that list every item that is processed. For example, a detail report for a sales company may list all the information about every sale made during a particular quarter of the year.

In this chapter, you learn how to

□ produce simple reports using a few basic PROC PRINT statements

□ produce enhanced reports by adding more complex statements

□ improve the appearance of reports by adding titles, footnotes, and labels and by using other options

□ use macro variables to substitute text.

Input File and SAS Data Set Examples

This chapter uses one input file and five SAS data set examples to illustrate certain aspects of the PRINT procedure. The input file contains sales records for TruBlend Coffee Makers, Inc. and looks like this: *

```
01      1       Hollingsworth   Deluxe      260     29.50
01      1       Smith           Standard     41     19.95
01      1       Hollingsworth   Deluxe      330     29.50
01      1       Jones           Standard   1110     19.95
01      1       Smith           Standard    715     19.95
01      1       Jones           Deluxe      675     29.50
02      1       Jones           Standard     45     19.95
02      1       Smith           Deluxe       10     29.50

more data ...

12      4       Hollingsworth   Deluxe      125     29.50
12      4       Jones           Standard   1254     19.95
12      4       Hollingsworth   Deluxe      175     29.50
```

The input file contains the month and quarter of the year a sale was made; the name of the sales representative; type of coffee maker sold, either standard or deluxe; the number of units sold; and the price of each unit.

The first of the five SAS data sets is named SALES.ALLYEAR and contains all the sales records from the input file and a new variable named AMTSOLD, which is UNITS multiplied by PRICE. The other four SAS data sets, SALES.QTR01, SALES.QTR02, SALES.QTR03, and SALES.QTR04, contain sales records for the four quarters of the year.

---

* Refer to the Appendix for a complete listing of the input data.

The following program creates the five SAS data sets used in this chapter:

```
libname sales 'your-data-library';

data sales.allyear;
    infile 'your-input-file';
    input mth $ qtr $ salesrep $14. type $ units price;
    amtsold=units*price;
run;

data sales.qtr01 sales.qtr02 sales.qtr03 sales.qtr04;
    set sales.allyear;
    if qtr='1' then output sales.qtr01;
    if qtr='2' then output sales.qtr02;
    if qtr='3' then output sales.qtr03;
    if qtr='4' then output sales.qtr04;
run;
```

Printing Simple Reports

Suppose you work for TruBlend Coffee Makers, Inc. and you need to produce several reports showing sales information for the first three months of the year. As the examples in this section illustrate, you can use PROC PRINT to produce a series of simple reports that deal with first quarter sales information based on the SAS data set SALES.QTR01.

Printing All Variables

The simplest way to use the PRINT procedure is to list the values of all the variables and observations in the data set. For example, the following PROC PRINT step prints the SAS data set SALES.QTR01. Output 24.1 shows that all the values of all the variables in SALES.QTR01 are printed.

```
proc print data=sales.qtr01;
    title 'Printing All Variables';
run;
```

Output 24.1
Reports: Printing
All Variables

```
                        Printing All Variables                        1

 OBS    MTH    QTR    SALESREP        TYPE        UNITS    PRICE    AMTSOLD

   1     01     1     Hollingsworth   Deluxe        260    29.50    7670.00
   2     01     1     Smith           Standard       41    19.95     817.95
   3     01     1     Hollingsworth   Standard      330    19.95    6583.50
   4     01     1     Jones           Standard      110    19.95    2194.50
   5     01     1     Smith           Deluxe        715    29.50   21092.50
   6     01     1     Jones           Standard      675    19.95   13466.25
   7     02     1     Smith           Standard     2045    19.95   40797.75
   8     02     1     Smith           Deluxe         10    29.50     295.00
   9     02     1     Smith           Standard       40    19.95     798.00
  10     02     1     Hollingsworth   Standard     1030    19.95   20548.50
  11     02     1     Jones           Standard      153    19.95    3052.35
  12     02     1     Smith           Standard       98    19.95    1955.10
  13     03     1     Hollingsworth   Standard      125    19.95    2493.75
  14     03     1     Jones           Standard      154    19.95    3072.30
  15     03     1     Smith           Standard      118    19.95    2354.10
  16     03     1     Hollingsworth   Standard       25    19.95     498.75
  17     03     1     Jones           Standard      525    19.95   10473.75
  18     03     1     Smith           Standard      310    19.95    6184.50
```

Notice a few things about Output 24.1. First, look at the OBS column on the far left. It identifies the number of each observation in the data set. Second, notice that the top of the report has a title, which reads "Printing All Variables," and a page number, 1. The title is a result of the TITLE statement in the PROC PRINT step. The TITLE statement is discussed in more detail in the section "Improving the Appearance of Reports" later in this chapter. For now, just be aware that all the examples contain at least one TITLE statement that produces a descriptive title similar to the one in this example.

Although the report doesn't differ from the contents of the original data set SALES.QTR01, the report is easy to produce and improve.

Suppressing the Observation Column

The first improvement you decide to make to the report is to suppress the printing of the OBS column because you don't need to identify each observation by number. (In some cases, you may want to keep the observation numbers, but for this report they aren't necessary.) To suppress the OBS column, add the NOOBS option to the PROC PRINT statement as the following SAS program illustrates. Output 24.2 shows the report.

```
proc print data=sales.qtr01 noobs;
   title 'Suppressing the Observation Column';
run;
```

Output 24.2
Reports:
Suppressing the
Observation
Column

```
                        Suppressing the Observation Column                        1

      MTH   QTR   SALESREP         TYPE        UNITS   PRICE     AMTSOLD

      01     1    Hollingsworth    Deluxe        260   29.50     7670.00
      01     1    Smith            Standard       41   19.95      817.95
      01     1    Hollingsworth    Standard      330   19.95     6583.50
      01     1    Jones            Standard      110   19.95     2194.50
      01     1    Smith            Deluxe        715   29.50    21092.50
      01     1    Jones            Standard      675   19.95    13466.25
      02     1    Smith            Standard     2045   19.95    40797.75
      02     1    Smith            Deluxe         10   29.50      295.00
      02     1    Smith            Standard       40   19.95      798.00
      02     1    Hollingsworth    Standard     1030   19.95    20548.50
      02     1    Jones            Standard      153   19.95     3052.35
      02     1    Smith            Standard       98   19.95     1955.10
      03     1    Hollingsworth    Standard      125   19.95     2493.75
      03     1    Jones            Standard      154   19.95     3072.30
      03     1    Smith            Standard      118   19.95     2354.10
      03     1    Hollingsworth    Standard       25   19.95      498.75
      03     1    Jones            Standard      525   19.95    10473.75
      03     1    Smith            Standard      310   19.95     6184.50
```

Suppressing the observation numbers by specifying NOOBS is an easy way to simplify a report; however, there are numerous other SAS statements and options available that allow you to tailor reports to your specific needs, as the following examples illustrate.

Emphasizing a Key Variable

You can use the ID statement with the PRINT procedure to emphasize a key variable from your data set. The variable that you identify in the ID statement is emphasized in that its values are printed in the first column of the report. Highlighting a key variable in this way can help answer questions about your data. For example, suppose you want to produce a report that answers this question: "For each sales representative, what are the sales figures for the first quarter of the year?" The next two examples help answer this question.

Using the ID Statement with Unsorted Data

To produce a report that emphasizes the sales representative, add an ID statement to the PROC PRINT step. In the ID statement specify the variable SALESREP. When you add the ID statement, you can delete the NOOBS option from the PROC PRINT statement because the ID statement automatically suppresses the observation numbers.

The revised PROC PRINT step follows. Output 24.3 shows the report.

```
proc print data=sales.qtr01;
   id salesrep;
   title 'Using the ID Statement with Unsorted Data';
run;
```

Output 24.3
Reports: Using the
ID Statement with
Unsorted Data

```
                    Using the ID Statement with Unsorted Data                1

    SALESREP        MTH    QTR     TYPE       UNITS    PRICE     AMTSOLD

    Hollingsworth   01     1       Deluxe       260    29.50     7670.00
    Smith           01     1       Standard      41    19.95      817.95
    Hollingsworth   01     1       Standard     330    19.95     6583.50
    Jones           01     1       Standard     110    19.95     2194.50
    Smith           01     1       Deluxe       715    29.50    21092.50
    Jones           01     1       Standard     675    19.95    13466.25
    Smith           02     1       Standard    2045    19.95    40797.75
    Smith           02     1       Deluxe        10    29.50      295.00
    Smith           02     1       Standard      40    19.95      798.00
    Hollingsworth   02     1       Standard    1030    19.95    20548.50
    Jones           02     1       Standard     153    19.95     3052.35
    Smith           02     1       Standard      98    19.95     1955.10
    Hollingsworth   03     1       Standard     125    19.95     2493.75
    Jones           03     1       Standard     154    19.95     3072.30
    Smith           03     1       Standard     118    19.95     2354.10
    Hollingsworth   03     1       Standard      25    19.95      498.75
    Jones           03     1       Standard     525    19.95    10473.75
    Smith           03     1       Standard     310    19.95     6184.50
```

Notice that the names of the sales representatives are not in any particular order. The report would be easier to read if you could group the observations together in alphabetical order by sales representative. The next example illustrates how to group alphabetically by a variable.

Using the ID Statement with Sorted Data

The following program shows how to group the observations in alphabetical order by sales representative. You must precede the PROC PRINT step with a PROC SORT step that includes a BY statement. In the BY statement you specify the variable SALESREP. The PROC SORT step rearranges the observations in the data set before they are printed. Output 24.4 shows the report.

```
proc sort data=sales.qtr01;
   by salesrep;
run;

proc print data=sales.qtr01;
   id salesrep;
   title 'Using the ID Statement with Sorted Data';
run;
```

Output 24.4
Reports: Using the
ID Statement with
Sorted Data

```
                       Using the ID Statement with Sorted Data                   1

       SALESREP      MTH    QTR      TYPE       UNITS    PRICE     AMTSOLD

       Hollingsworth  01     1      Deluxe       260     29.50     7670.00
       Hollingsworth  01     1      Standard     330     19.95     6583.50
       Hollingsworth  02     1      Standard    1030     19.95    20548.50
       Hollingsworth  03     1      Standard     125     19.95     2493.75
       Hollingsworth  03     1      Standard      25     19.95      498.75
       Jones          01     1      Standard     110     19.95     2194.50
       Jones          01     1      Standard     675     19.95    13466.25
       Jones          02     1      Standard     153     19.95     3052.35
       Jones          03     1      Standard     154     19.95     3072.30
       Jones          03     1      Standard     525     19.95    10473.75
       Smith          01     1      Standard      41     19.95      817.95
       Smith          01     1      Deluxe       715     29.50    21092.50
       Smith          02     1      Standard    2045     19.95    40797.75
       Smith          02     1      Deluxe        10     29.50      295.00
       Smith          02     1      Standard      40     19.95      798.00
       Smith          02     1      Standard      98     19.95     1955.10
       Smith          03     1      Standard     118     19.95     2354.10
       Smith          03     1      Standard     310     19.95     6184.50
```

The report in Output 24.4 clearly shows what each sales representative sold during the first three months of the year.

Printing Selected Variables

By default, the PRINT procedure prints the values of all the variables in the data set. However, you can control which variables are printed and in what order by adding the VAR statement to the PROC PRINT step.

For example, assume you no longer need to show the variables QTR, TYPE, and PRICE. That is, you want to print only the following variables in this order:

```
SALESREP  MTH  UNITS  AMTSOLD
```

To print the four variables in this order, list them in the VAR statement as shown in the following program. Output 24.5 shows the report.

```
proc print data=sales.qtr01 noobs ;
   var salesrep mth units amtsold;
      title 'Printing Selected Variables';
run;
```

Notice two changes in this program. First, you don't need the ID statement any more because the variable SALESREP is listed as the first variable in the VAR statement. Second, the NOOBS option has been added to the PROC PRINT statement to suppress the observation numbers.

Output 24.5
Reports: Printing
Selected Variables

```
                         Printing Selected Variables                       1

          SALESREP         MTH     UNITS      AMTSOLD

          Hollingsworth    01       260       7670.00
          Hollingsworth    01       330       6583.50
          Hollingsworth    02      1030      20548.50
          Hollingsworth    03       125       2493.75
          Hollingsworth    03        25        498.75
          Jones            01       110       2194.50
          Jones            01       675      13466.25
          Jones            02       153       3052.35
          Jones            03       154       3072.30
          Jones            03       525      10473.75
          Smith            01        41        817.95
          Smith            01       715      21092.50
          Smith            02      2045      40797.75
          Smith            02        10        295.00
          Smith            02        40        798.00
          Smith            02        98       1955.10
          Smith            03       118       2354.10
          Smith            03       310       6184.50
```

Now you have a concise report that contains only those variables listed in the VAR statement. In the next example, you see how to tailor the report further to print only those observations that meet a particular condition.

Selecting Observations Conditionally

The WHERE statement allows you to select observations from a data set based on a particular condition. The condition you define with a WHERE statement is a sequence of operands and operators that specify one or more comparisons.* Note that when you compare character values, you must enclose them in single or double quotes, and the values must match exactly, including capitalization.

Making a Single Comparison

To see how you can select observations based on a single comparison, suppose you want to produce a report that shows the sales activity during the first quarter of the year for the sales representative named Smith. The following program produces the report, and Output 24.6 shows it.

```
proc print data=sales.qtr01 noobs;
   var salesrep mth units amtsold;
   where salesrep='Smith';
   title 'Making a Single Comparison';
run;
```

In this program's WHERE statement, the value Smith is enclosed in quotes because SALESREP is a character variable. (See the SAS program in the section "Input File and SAS Data Set Examples" earlier in this chapter.) In addition, the letter S in the value Smith is uppercase so that it matches exactly the way the value appears in the data set SALES.QTR01.

---

* The construction of WHERE statements is similar to the construction of IF and IF-THEN statements.

Output 24.6
Reports: Making a
Single Comparison

```
                        Making a Single Comparison                          1

                   SALESREP   MTH   UNITS    AMTSOLD

                    Smith      01      41      817.95
                    Smith      01     715    21092.50
                    Smith      02    2045    40797.75
                    Smith      02      10      295.00
                    Smith      02      40      798.00
                    Smith      02      98     1955.10
                    Smith      03     118     2354.10
                    Smith      03     310     6184.50
```

Making Multiple Comparisons

You can also select observations based on two or more comparisons. For
example, suppose you want to produce a report that shows how many coffee
makers Smith sold during the first month of the year.

The WHERE statement in the following program combines the two
comparisons by using a logical AND; therefore, both comparisons must be true
for an observation to be included in the report. Output 24.7 shows the report.

```
proc print data=sales.qtr01 noobs;
   var salesrep mth units amtsold;
   where salesrep='Smith' and mth='01';
   title 'Testing for Two Conditions';
run;
```

Output 24.7
Reports: Testing
for Two
Conditions

```
                         Testing for Two Conditions                         1

                   SALESREP   MTH   UNITS    AMTSOLD

                    Smith      01      41      817.95
                    Smith      01     715    21092.50
```

You may also want to select observations that must meet only one of several
conditions. For example, suppose you want to produce a report that shows every
sale during the first quarter of the year that was for more than 500 coffee
makers *or* for more than $20,000.

The WHERE statement in the following program combines the two
comparisons by using a logical OR; therefore, only one of the comparisons must
be true for an observation to be included in the report. Output 24.8 shows the
report.

```
proc print data=sales.qtr01 noobs;
   var salesrep mth units amtsold;
   where units>500 or amtsold>20000;
   title 'Testing for One Condition or Another';
run;
```

Output 24.8
Reports: Testing
for One Condition
or Another

```
                 Testing for One Condition or Another                  1

            SALESREP        MTH     UNITS     AMTSOLD

            Hollingsworth    02      1030     20548.50
            Jones            01       675     13466.25
            Jones            03       525     10473.75
            Smith            01       715     21092.50
            Smith            02      2045     40797.75
```

Printing Enhanced Reports

As the previous examples illustrate, you can use just a few PROC PRINT statements and options to produce a variety of detail reports. However, there are many more statements and options you can use with PROC PRINT to enhance your reports.

The examples in this section use the SAS data set SALES.QTR02, which was created in the section "Input File and SAS Data Set Examples" earlier in this chapter. The examples illustrate several ways to enhance output from the PROC PRINT step. In particular, the examples in this section show you how to

□ specify output formats of variables

□ sum numeric variables

□ group observations based on variable values

□ sum groups of variable values

□ group observations on separate pages.

Specifying Output Formats of Variables

By adding the FORMAT statement to your program, you can specify output formats for variables. The output format of a variable is the pattern the SAS System uses to write the values of the variables. For example, the SAS System contains output formats for including commas in numeric values, for adding dollar signs to figures, for printing values as Roman numerals, and many other formats.

Specifying output formats of variables is a simple yet effective way to enhance the readability of reports. For instance, suppose you want to print the values of the variables UNITS and AMTSOLD in a way that is easier to read than in the previous reports. Specifically, for the values of the variable UNITS, you want a total field width of 7, including commas, to separate every three digits. You don't need any decimal places.

For the values of the variable AMTSOLD, you want a total field width of 14, including commas, to separate every three digits; a decimal point; two decimal places; and a dollar sign.

As the following program illustrates, you can use the COMMA7. format for the values of the variable UNITS and the DOLLAR14.2 format for the values of the variable AMTSOLD. Output 24.9 shows the report.

```
proc print data=sales.qtr02 noobs;
    var salesrep mth units amtsold;
    where units>500 or amtsold>20000;
    format units comma7.
           amtsold dollar14.2;
    title 'Specifying Output Formats of Variables';
run;
```

Output 24.9
Reports:
Specifying Output
Formats of
Variables

```
                 Specifying Output Formats of Variables                    1

        SALESREP        MTH      UNITS         AMTSOLD

        Hollingsworth   04         530      $10,573.50
        Jones           04       1,110      $22,144.50
        Smith           04       1,715      $34,214.25
        Jones           04         675      $13,466.25
        Hollingsworth   05       1,120      $22,344.00
        Hollingsworth   05       1,030      $20,548.50
        Smith           06         512      $10,214.40
        Smith           06       1,000      $19,950.00
```

Take a closer look at the way the FORMAT statement works. In the DOLLAR14.2 format, the 14 specifies a maximum of 14 columns for the value of the variables. The 2 specifies that two of those columns are for the decimal part of the values. The remaining 12 places are for the decimal point, whole numbers, the dollar sign, commas, and minus sign if the value is negative. The same syntax applies to the COMMA7. format except there are no dollar signs or decimal points. Formats don't affect the actual data values as they are stored in the SAS data set. That is, output formats only affect the way values are printed.

Note: Be sure to specify enough columns in the format to contain the largest value. If the format you specify isn't wide enough to contain the largest value, including special characters such as commas and dollar signs, the SAS System prints the value using the most appropriate format.

Summing Numeric Variables

So far, the reports in this chapter have listed only the values of the variables that were processed. That is, no subtotals or totals of the numeric values have been printed. You can obtain subtotals and totals for numeric values by specifying one or more variables in the SUM statement. For instance, to produce a report that shows totals for the variables UNITS and AMTSOLD, add the SUM statement to the PROC PRINT step. Output 24.10 shows the report.

```
proc print data=sales.qtr02 noobs;
   var salesrep mth units amtsold;
   where units>500 or amtsold>20000;
   format units comma7.
          amtsold dollar14.2;
   sum units amtsold;
   title 'Summing Numeric Variables';
run;
```

Output 24.10
Reports: Summing
Numeric Variables

```
                    Summing Numeric Variables                            1

          SALESREP        MTH       UNITS         AMTSOLD

          Hollingsworth   04          530      $10,573.50
          Jones           04        1,110      $22,144.50
          Smith           04        1,715      $34,214.25
          Jones           04          675      $13,466.25
          Hollingsworth   05        1,120      $22,344.00
          Hollingsworth   05        1,030      $20,548.50
          Smith           06          512      $10,214.40
          Smith           06        1,000      $19,950.00
                                   =======  ===============
                                     7,692     $153,455.40
```

Notice that the totals for UNITS and AMTSOLD are for all three sales representatives as a group. As the next example illustrates, the PRINT procedure can also subtotal the variables UNITS and AMTSOLD for each of the sales representatives.

Grouping Observations by Variable Values

The BY statement allows you to obtain separate analyses on groups of observations. In the previous example, you used the SUM statement to print totals for the variables UNITS and AMTSOLD, but the totals were for all three sales representatives as one group. The next two examples show how you can use the BY and ID statements as a part of the PRINT procedure to separate the sales representatives into three groups with three separate subtotals and one grand total.

Grouping Observations with the BY Statement

To obtain separate subtotals of the variables UNITS and AMTSOLD for each sales representative, add a BY statement to the PROC PRINT step. In the BY statement specify the variable SALESREP. Also, remove the variable SALESREP from the VAR statement. (If you list SALESREP in the BY statement *and* in the VAR statement, the values of SALESREP are printed twice on the report, as a header across the page and in columns down the page.)

Also, be aware that when you add a BY statement to a PROC PRINT step, the PRINT procedure expects the input data to be sorted by the BY variables.

Therefore, if the data aren't already sorted in the proper order, you should add a PROC SORT step before the PROC PRINT step.

In addition, when you use the BY statement with the PRINT procedure, the values of the BY variables are printed in dashed lines, called BY lines, above the printed output for the BY group.

The program now includes a PROC SORT step and the BY statement and excludes SALESREP from the VAR statement. Output 24.11 shows the report. Notice that the report contains subtotals for three separate groups, one for each sales representative, and a grand total at the end.

```
proc sort data=sales.qtr02;
   by salesrep;
run;

proc print data=sales.qtr02 noobs;
   var mth units amtsold;
   where units>500 or amtsold>20000;
   format units comma7.
          amtsold dollar14.2;
   sum units amtsold;
   by salesrep;
   title 'Grouping Observations with the BY Statement';
run;
```

Output 24.11
Grouping
Observations with
the BY Statement

```
        Grouping Observations with the BY Statement              1
-------------------------- SALESREP=Hollingsworth --------------------------

        MTH        UNITS          AMTSOLD

        04           530      $10,573.50
        05         1,120      $22,344.00
        05         1,030      $20,548.50
                 -------   --------------
        SALESREP   2,680      $53,466.00

---------------------------- SALESREP=Jones ----------------------------

        MTH        UNITS          AMTSOLD

        04         1,110      $22,144.50
        04           675      $13,466.25
                 -------   --------------
        SALESREP   1,785      $35,610.75

---------------------------- SALESREP=Smith ----------------------------

        MTH        UNITS          AMTSOLD

        04         1,715      $34,214.25
        06           512      $10,214.40
        06         1,000      $19,950.00
                 -------   --------------
        SALESREP   3,227      $64,378.65
                 =======   ==============
                   7,692     $153,455.40
```

Grouping Observations with the BY and ID Statements

You can use both the BY and ID statements as part of the PRINT procedure to modify the appearance of your report. When you specify the same variables in both the BY and ID statements, the PRINT procedure uses the ID variable to identify the beginning of the BY group. For example, add the following ID statement to the PROC PRINT step. Output 24.12 shows the report.

```
proc print data=sales.qtr02;
   var mth units amtsold;
   where units>500 or amtsold>20000;
   format units comma7.
          amtsold dollar14.2;
   sum units amtsold;
   by salesrep;
   id salesrep;
   title 'Grouping Observations with the BY and ID Statements';
run;
```

Output 24.12
Grouping Observations with the BY and ID Statements

```
         Grouping Observations with the BY and ID Statements            1

         SALESREP         MTH      UNITS        AMTSOLD

         Hollingsworth    04         530      $10,573.50
                          05       1,120      $22,344.00
                          05       1,030      $20,548.50
         -------------             ------   --------------
         Hollingsworth            2,680      $53,466.00

         Jones            04       1,110      $22,144.50
                          04         675      $13,466.25
         -------------             ------   --------------
         Jones                    1,785      $35,610.75

         Smith            04       1,715      $34,214.25
                          06         512      $10,214.40
                          06       1,000      $19,950.00
         -------------             ------   --------------
         Smith                    3,227      $64,378.65
                                  =======   ==============
                                  7,692     $153,455.40
```

Notice two things about the report in Output 24.12. First, it is broken into groups, and repetitive values of the BY and ID variables are suppressed. Second, when you use the BY and ID statements together in a PROC PRINT step, the BY lines (the dashed lines that appear above the BY groups) don't print.

Keep in mind these general rules about the SUM, BY, and ID statements:

□ You can specify a variable in the SUM statement that is not listed in the VAR statement. PROC PRINT simply adds the variable to the VAR list.

□ Don't specify variables in the SUM statement that are also listed in the ID or BY statement.

Also,

□ when you use a BY statement and specify only one BY variable, the SUM variable is subtotaled for each BY group containing more than one observation.

□ when you use a BY statement and specify multiple BY variables, subtotals are printed for a BY variable only when it changes value and there is more than one observation with that value.

Grouping Observations with Multiple BY Variables

You can also use two or more variables in a BY statement to define groups, subgroups, and so on. For example, to produce a report that groups observations first by sales representative and then by month, add the variable MTH to the BY statement and remove the variable MTH from the VAR statement so its values are not printed twice on the report. Also, remove the ID statement and add the NOOBS option. The program now looks like this. Output 24.13 shows the report.

```
proc print data=sales.qtr02 noobs;
    var units amtsold;
    where units>500 or amtsold>20000;
    format units comma7.
            amtsold dollar14.2;
    sum units amtsold;
    by salesrep mth;
    title 'Grouping Observations with Multiple BY Variables';
run;
```

Output 24.13
Grouping
Observations with
Multiple BY
Variables

```
              Grouping Observations with Multiple BY Variables            1
---------------------- SALESREP=Hollingsworth MTH=04 ----------------------

                    UNITS          AMTSOLD

                     530         $10,573.50


---------------------- SALESREP=Hollingsworth MTH=05 ----------------------

                    UNITS          AMTSOLD

                   1,120        $22,344.00
                   1,030        $20,548.50
                   -------      --------------
                   2,150   M    $42,892.50
                   2,680   S    $53,466.00

------------------------- SALESREP=Jones MTH=04 -------------------------

                    UNITS          AMTSOLD

                   1,110        $22,144.50
                     675        $13,466.25
                   -------      --------------
                   1,785   M    $35,610.75
                   1,785   S    $35,610.75

------------------------- SALESREP=Smith MTH=04 -------------------------

                    UNITS          AMTSOLD

                   1,715        $34,214.25


------------------------- SALESREP=Smith MTH=06 -------------------------

                    UNITS          AMTSOLD

                     512        $10,214.40
                   1,000        $19,950.00
                   -------      --------------
                   1,512   M    $30,164.40
                   3,227   S    $64,378.65
                   =======      ==============
                   7,692       $153,455.40
```

When a BY group contains two or more observations, PROC PRINT includes totals for each of the BY variables listed in the BY statement. For example, in the report in Output 24.13, the totals for the variable MTH are indicated by the letter M, and the totals for the variable SALESREP are indicated by the letter S.

Summing in Groups

When you have multiple BY variables as in the previous example, you may not want to obtain subtotals every time one of the BY values changes. Use the SUMBY statement to control which BY variable causes subtotaling. The following program removes the monthly subtotals for each sales representative by designating SALESREP as the variable by which to sum. Output 24.14 shows the report.

```
proc print data=sales.qtr02;
   var units amtsold;
   where units>500 or amtsold>20000;
   format units comma7.
          amtsold dollar14.2;
   sum units amtsold;
   by salesrep mth;
   id salesrep mth;
   sumby salesrep;
   title 'Summing in Groups';
run;
```

Output 24.14
Summing in
Groups

```
                         Summing in Groups                        1

        SALESREP        MTH     UNITS        AMTSOLD

        Hollingsworth   04       530        $10,573.50

        Hollingsworth   05     1,120        $22,344.00
                               1,030        $20,548.50
        -------------   ---   -------     --------------
        Hollingsworth          2,680        $53,466.00

        Jones           04     1,110        $22,144.50
                                 675        $13,466.25
        -------------   ---   -------     --------------
        Jones                  1,785        $35,610.75

        Smith           04     1,715        $34,214.25

        Smith           06       512        $10,214.40
                               1,000        $19,950.00
        -------------   ---   -------     --------------
        Smith                  3,227        $64,378.65
                               =======     ==============
                               7,692       $153,455.40
```

You can specify only one SUMBY variable, and it must be one of the variables listed in the BY statement. Sums are produced each time the value of the SUMBY variable changes. Sums are also produced when the value changes for any variable that's listed in the BY statement before the SUMBY variable. For example, consider the following statements:

```
by qtr salesrep mth;
sumby salesrep;
```

SALESREP is the SUMBY variable. In the BY statement, QTR comes before SALESREP, and MTH comes after SALESREP. Therefore, these statements cause PROC PRINT to print totals when either QTR or SALESREP changes value, but not when MTH changes value.

Grouping Observations on Separate Pages

The PAGEBY statement causes the PRINT procedure to begin printing a new page when the BY variable you specify changes value or when any BY variable listed before it in the BY statement changes value. For example, the following PROC PRINT step includes a PAGEBY statement that causes page breaks to occur when the value of the SALESREP variable changes from `Hollingsworth` to `Jones` and from `Jones` to `Smith`. Output 24.15 shows the report.

```
proc print data=sales.qtr02 noobs;
   var units amtsold;
   where units>500 or amtsold>20000;
   format units comma7.
          amtsold dollar14.2;
   sum units amtsold;
   by salesrep mth;
   id salesrep mth;
   sumby salesrep;
   pageby salesrep;
   title 'Grouping Observations on Separate Pages';
run;
```

Output 24.15
Reports: Grouping
Observations on
Separate Pages

```
                Grouping Observations on Separate Pages              1
           SALESREP        MTH      UNITS        AMTSOLD

           Hollingsworth   04        530       $10,573.50

           Hollingsworth   05      1,120       $22,344.00
                                    1,030       $20,548.50
           -------------   ---    -------    --------------
           Hollingsworth           2,680       $53,466.00
```

```
                Grouping Observations on Separate Pages              2
           SALESREP        MTH      UNITS        AMTSOLD

           Jones           04      1,110       $22,144.50
                                     675       $13,466.25
           -------------   ---    -------    --------------
           Jones                   1,785       $35,610.75
```

```
            Grouping Observations on Separate Pages           3
      SALESREP      MTH       UNITS        AMTSOLD

      Smith         04        1,715      $34,214.25

      Smith         06          512      $10,214.40
                              1,000      $19,950.00
      --------------  ---    -------    ---------------
      Smith                   3,227      $64,378.65
                              =======    ===============
                              7,692     $153,455.40
```

Improving the Appearance of Reports

As you have seen from the previous examples, you can use the PRINT procedure to produce simple detail reports quickly and easily. You have also seen how you can use a few statements and options to enhance the readability of your reports. In this section, you learn how to improve the appearance of reports. Specifically, you learn how to

□ add descriptive titles and footnotes

□ define and split labels

□ add double spacing

□ print variables in uniform columns across pages.

Adding Titles and Footnotes

Adding descriptive titles and footnotes is one of the easiest and most effective ways to improve the appearance of a report. You can use the TITLE statement to print up to ten lines of text at the top of the output.

In the TITLE statement you can specify *n*, which is a number from 1 to 10 that immediately follows the word TITLE, with no intervening blank; *n* specifies the level of the TITLE statement. The text of each title can be up to 132 characters long and must be enclosed in single or double quotes. Skipping over some values of *n* indicates that those lines are to be blank. For example, if you specify TITLE1 and TITLE3 statements and skip TITLE2, a blank line appears between the first and third lines.

Once you specify a title for a line, that title is used for *all* subsequent output until you cancel it or define another title for that line. A TITLE statement for a given line cancels the previous TITLE statement for that line and for all lines below it, that is, those with larger *n* values.

To cancel all existing titles, specify a TITLE statement without the *n* value, for example,

```
title;
```

To suppress the *n*th title and all titles below it, use the following statement:

```
titlen;
```

Footnotes work the same way as titles. You can use the FOOTNOTE statement to print up to ten lines of text at the bottom of the output.

In the FOOTNOTE statement you can specify *n*, which is a number from 1 to 10 that immediately follows the word FOOTNOTE, with no intervening blank; *n* specifies the line number of the FOOTNOTE. The text of each footnote can be up to 132 characters long and must be enclosed in single or double quotes. As with the TITLE statement, you can print blank footnote lines by skipping over some values of *n*.

Keep in mind that footnotes are pushed up from the bottom of the output. In other words, the FOOTNOTE statement with the largest number appears on the bottom line.

Once you specify a footnote for a line, that footnote is used for *all* subsequent output until you cancel it or define another footnote for that line. You cancel and suppress footnotes the same way you cancel and suppress titles.

To illustrate using titles and footnotes, assume you want to produce a report for TruBlend Coffee Makers, Inc. that shows observations from SALES.QTR02 for the month of April. The report should have three title lines. On the first line, you want to print a description of the report. You want the second line blank, and on the third line, you want the company's name.

You also want two footnote lines. On the first line, you want the phrase "April Sales Totals," and on the second, the note "COMPANY CONFIDENTIAL INFORMATION."

In addition, you want to suppress the observation numbers by using the NOOBS option and show only the values of the variables SALESREP, MTH, UNITS, and AMTSOLD.

The following program produces the report in Output 24.16.

```
proc print data=sales.qtr02 noobs;
    var salesrep mth units amtsold;
    where mth='04';
    format units comma7.
           amtsold dollar14.2;
    sum units amtsold;
    title1 'Adding Titles and Footnotes';
    title3 'TruBlend Coffee Makers, Inc.';
    footnote1 'April Sales Totals';
    footnote2 'COMPANY CONFIDENTIAL INFORMATION';
run;
```

Output 24.16
Reports: Adding
Titles and
Footnotes

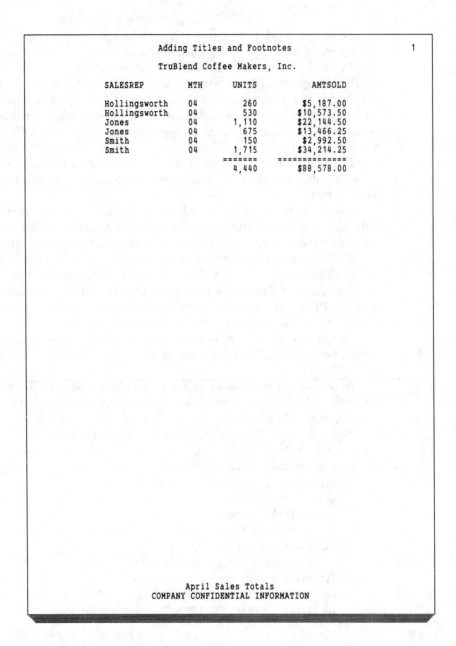

```
                    Adding Titles and Footnotes                      1

                    TruBlend Coffee Makers, Inc.

        SALESREP        MTH      UNITS          AMTSOLD

        Hollingsworth   04        260          $5,187.00
        Hollingsworth   04        530         $10,573.50
        Jones           04      1,110         $22,144.50
        Jones           04        675         $13,466.25
        Smith           04        150          $2,992.50
        Smith           04      1,715         $34,214.25
                                =======     ===============
                                  4,440        $88,578.00




                             April Sales Totals
                       COMPANY CONFIDENTIAL INFORMATION
```

Defining Labels

By default, the SAS System uses variable names for column headings. However, you may want to improve the appearance of a report by specifying your own column headings. For example, suppose you don't want to use the variable names SALESREP, MTH, UNITS, and AMTSOLD as the column headings. Instead you want SALESREP to be replaced with Sales Rep., MTH to be replaced with Month, UNITS to be replaced with Units Sold, and AMTSOLD to be replaced with Amt Sold.

To override the default headings, you need to do two things. First, add the LABEL option to the PROC PRINT statement. This option indicates to the PRINT procedure that you want to use labels for column headings in your report. Second, define the labels by adding the LABEL statement.* In the LABEL statement you specify the variable to be labeled and its label. The label can be up to 40 characters long, including blanks, and must be enclosed in single or double quotes.

The following program builds on the previous program; now it defines labels for the variables SALESREP, MTH, UNITS, and AMTSOLD. It also contains a TITLE statement that redefines the first title and cancels titles from the second level down and a FOOTNOTE statement that cancels all footnotes. Output 24.17 shows the report.

```
proc print data=sales.qtr02 noobs label;
     var salesrep mth units amtsold;
     where mth='04';
     format units comma7.
            amtsold dollar14.2;
     sum units amtsold;
     title 'Defining Labels';
     footnote;
     label salesrep = 'Sales Rep.'
           mth      = 'Month'
           units    = 'Units Sold'
           amtsold  = 'Amt Sold';
run;
```

Output 24.17
Reports: Defining
Labels

```
                          Defining Labels                        1

                                   Units
        Sales Rep.      Month       Sold        Amt Sold

        Hollingsworth    04          260       $5,187.00
        Hollingsworth    04          530      $10,573.50
        Jones            04        1,110      $22,144.50
        Jones            04          675      $13,466.25
        Smith            04          150       $2,992.50
        Smith            04        1,715      $34,214.25
                                  =======   ==============
                                    4,440      $88,578.00
```

Notice that the label Units Sold is split between two lines. The PRINT procedure splits labels if necessary to conserve space. The next section illustrates how you can control the splitting of labels.

---

* If you created and stored labels when you created the SAS data set, you don't need to use the LABEL statement. Simply specify the LABEL option in the PROC PRINT statement.

Splitting Labels onto Two or More Lines

When labels are too long to fit on one line or when you want to split a label onto two or more lines, use the SPLIT= option. The SPLIT= option replaces the LABEL option in the PROC PRINT statement. (You don't need to use both SPLIT= and LABEL because SPLIT= implies labels are to be used.) In the SPLIT= option you specify an alphanumeric character that indicates where to split labels.

To use the SPLIT= option, you must do two things. First, define the split character as a part of the PROC PRINT statement. Second, include the split character in the LABEL statements as a part of the labels that you want to split. For example, the following PROC PRINT step defines the slash (/) as the split character and includes slashes in the LABEL statements to split the labels Sales Representative, Units Sold, and Amount Sold onto two lines each. Output 24.18 shows the report.

```
proc print data=sales.qtr02 noobs split='/';
    var salesrep mth units amtsold;
    where mth='04';
    format units comma7.
           amtsold dollar14.2;
    sum units amtsold;
    title 'Splitting Labels Onto Two Lines';
    label salesrep = 'Sales/Representative'
          mth      = 'Month'
          units    = 'Units/Sold'
          amtsold  = 'Amount/Sold';
run;
```

Output 24.18
Reporting:
Splitting Labels
onto Two Lines

```
                     Splitting Labels Onto Two Lines                   1

        Sales                         Units           Amount
    Representative     Month          Sold             Sold

    Hollingsworth       04             260          $5,187.00
    Hollingsworth       04             530         $10,573.50
    Jones               04           1,110         $22,144.50
    Jones               04             675         $13,466.25
    Smith               04             150          $2,992.50
    Smith               04           1,715         $34,214.25
                                     =======      ===============
                                       4,440        $88,578.00
```

Adding Double Spacing

For some reports and other types of printouts, you may want to improve the appearance of the output by double spacing. The following program uses the DOUBLE option in the PROC PRINT statement to double space output. Output 24.19 shows the report.

```
proc print data=sales.qtr02 noobs split='/' double;
    var salesrep mth units amtsold;
    where mth='04';
    format units comma7.
           amtsold dollar14.2;
    sum units amtsold;
    title 'Adding Double Spacing';
    label salesrep = 'Sales/Representative'
          mth      = 'Month'
          units    = 'Units/Sold'
          amtsold  = 'Amount/Sold';
run;
```

Output 24.19
Reports: Adding
Double Spacing

```
                           Adding Double Spacing                      1
                Sales                 Units           Amount
                Representative  Month  Sold             Sold

                Hollingsworth    04      260         $5,187.00

                Hollingsworth    04      530        $10,573.50

                Jones            04    1,110        $22,144.50

                Jones            04      675        $13,466.25

                Smith            04      150         $2,992.50

                Smith            04    1,715        $34,214.25

                                      =======    ==============
                                        4,440        $88,578.00
```

Printing Variables in Uniform Columns

The example in this section uses the SAS data set SALES.QTR03 to illustrate the UNIFORM option in the PRINT procedure. SALES.QTR03 contains sales records for the third quarter of the year and was created in the section "Input File and SAS Data Set Examples" earlier in this chapter.

The UNIFORM option makes reports easier to read by ensuring the columns of data line up from one page to the next. Without the UNIFORM option, the PRINT procedure fits as many variables and observations on a page as possible. As a result, different numbers of variables can be printed on each page or in columns that can be shifted from one page to the next.

For example, suppose you sort the data set SALES.QTR03 by SALESREP, print all the values of all the variables, and don't use the UNIFORM option.

When you print your report, the columns of values on page one don't line up with those on page two. In other words, the columns shift from page to page.

The shift occurs because of the differences in the length of the names of the sales representatives. Without the UNIFORM option, the PRINT procedure lines up the columns on the first page of the report, allowing enough space for the longest name, `Hollingsworth.` On the second page the longest name is `Smith`, so the columns shift relative to the first page.

To prevent the shifting of columns, add the UNIFORM option to the PROC PRINT statement. Output 24.20 shows the report.

```
proc sort data=sales.qtr03;
   by salesrep;
run;

proc print data=sales.qtr03 split='/' uniform;
   var salesrep mth units amtsold;
   format units comma7.
          amtsold dollar14.2;
   sum units amtsold;
   title 'Printing Variables in Uniform Columns';
   label salesrep = 'Sales/Representative'
         mth      = 'Month'
         units    = 'Units/Sold'
         amtsold  = 'Amount/Sold';
run;
```

Output 24.20
Reporting:
Printing Variables
in Uniform
Columns

```
                     Printing Variables in Uniform Columns                    1

                 Sales                      Units          Amount
         OBS     Representative   Month      Sold            Sold

          1      Hollingsworth      07         60        $1,770.00
          2      Hollingsworth      07         30          $885.00
          3      Hollingsworth      07        130        $2,593.50
          4      Hollingsworth      07         60        $1,770.00
          5      Hollingsworth      07        330        $6,583.50
          6      Hollingsworth      08        120        $2,394.00
          7      Hollingsworth      08        230        $4,588.50
          8      Hollingsworth      08        230        $6,785.00
          9      Hollingsworth      08        290        $5,785.50
         10      Hollingsworth      08        330        $6,583.50
         11      Hollingsworth      08         50        $1,475.00
         12      Hollingsworth      09        125        $2,493.75
         13      Hollingsworth      09      1,000       $19,950.00
         14      Hollingsworth      09        125        $2,493.75
         15      Hollingsworth      09        175        $3,491.25
         16      Jones              07        110        $2,194.50
         17      Jones              07        110        $2,194.50
         18      Jones              07        275        $5,486.25
         19      Jones              07        110        $2,194.50
         20      Jones              07        110        $2,194.50
         21      Jones              07        675       $13,466.25
         22      Jones              08        145        $2,892.75
         23      Jones              08        453        $9,037.35
         24      Jones              08        453        $9,037.35
         25      Jones              08         45        $1,327.50
         26      Jones              08        145        $2,892.75
         27      Jones              08        453        $9,037.35
         28      Jones              08        225        $6,637.50
         29      Jones              09        254        $5,067.30
         30      Jones              09        284        $5,665.80
         31      Jones              09        275        $8,112.50
         32      Jones              09        876       $17,476.20
         33      Jones              09        254        $5,067.30
         34      Jones              09        284        $5,665.80
         35      Jones              09        275        $8,112.50
         36      Jones              09        876       $17,476.20
```

```
          37    Smith              07          250      $4,987.50
          38    Smith              07           90      $1,795.50
          39    Smith              07           90      $1,795.50
          40    Smith              07          265      $5,286.75
          41    Smith              07        1,250     $24,937.50
          42    Smith              07           90      $1,795.50
          43    Smith              07           90      $1,795.50
          44    Smith              07          465      $9,276.75
          45    Smith              08          110      $3,245.00
          46    Smith              08          240      $4,788.00
          47    Smith              08          198      $3,950.10
          48    Smith              08        1,198     $23,900.10
          49    Smith              08          110      $3,245.00
          50    Smith              08          240      $4,788.00
          51    Smith              08          198      $3,950.10
          52    Smith              09          118      $2,354.10
          53    Smith              09          412      $8,219.40
          54    Smith              09          100      $1,995.00
          55    Smith              09        1,118     $22,304.10
```

```
                Printing Variables in Uniform Columns                    2

                    Sales                      Units            Amount
          OBS    Representative    Month        Sold              Sold

          56    Smith              09          412      $8,219.40
          57    Smith              09          100      $1,995.00
                                             =======   ===============
                                              17,116      $355,502.70
```

Making Your Reports Easy to Change

The SAS System includes a macro facility that allows you to substitute text in SAS programs. One of the major advantages of using macro variables to substitute text is that it allows you to change the value of a variable in one place in your program and then have the change appear in multiple references throughout your program. You can substitute text by using automatic macro variables or by using your own macro variables, which you define and to which you assign values.

There are two sample reports in this section based on fourth quarter sales figures for TruBlend Coffee Makers, Inc. The two reports use the SAS data set SALES.QTR04, which was created earlier in the section "Input File and SAS Data Set Examples" earlier in this chapter. These reports illustrate how to use macro variables to substitute text. The first report illustrates how to use the automatic macro variable SYSDATE to print the date on a report. (The SYSDATE automatic macro variable gives the date on which the SAS job started execution.) The second report illustrates how to use your own macro variables by defining them with the %LET statement and by referring to them with the ampersand (&) prefix.

Using Automatic Macro Variables

The SAS macro facility includes many automatic macro variables. The values associated with the automatic macro variables are assigned by the SAS System depending on your operating system environment. Therefore, you don't have to define automatic macro variables.

There are automatic macro variables that give the time, day of the week, and date based on your computer system's clock/calendar as well as other processing information. For example, assume you want to include in your report a TITLE2 statement that contains the word "Printed" followed by the value for SYSDATE. To do so, add the following TITLE statement to your program:

```
title2 "Printed &SYSDATE";
```

Notice a few things about this statement. First, the ampersand that precedes SYSDATE indicates to the SAS macro facility that it should replace the reference with its assigned value. In this case, the assigned value is the date the SAS job starts and is expressed as *ddmmmyy* where *dd* is the day of the month, *mmm* is a three-letter abbreviation of the month name, and *yy* is the year. Second, the text of the TITLE statement is enclosed in double quotes because the SAS macro facility resolves macro variable references in TITLE and FOOTNOTE statements only if they are in double quotes.

The following program, which includes a PROC SORT step and the TITLE statement, illustrates using the SYSDATE. Output 24.21 shows the report.

```
proc sort data=sales.qtr04;
   by salesrep;
run;

proc print data=sales.qtr04 noobs split='/' uniform;
   var salesrep mth units amtsold;
   format units comma7.
          amtsold dollar14.2;
   sum units amtsold;
   title1 'Using Automatic Macro Variables';
   title2 "Printed &SYSDATE";
   label salesrep = 'Sales/Representative'
         mth      = 'Month'
         units    = 'Units/Sold'
         amtsold  = 'Amount/Sold';
run;
```

Output 24.21
Reports: Using
Automatic Macro
Variables

```
                       Using Automatic Macro Variables                   1
                            Printed 12JAN90

                Sales                     Units             Amount
           Representative     Month        Sold               Sold

           Hollingsworth        10          530          $10,573.50
           Hollingsworth        10          265           $5,286.75
           Hollingsworth        11        1,230          $24,538.50
           Hollingsworth        11          150           $4,425.00
           Hollingsworth        12          125           $3,687.50
           Hollingsworth        12          175           $3,491.25
           Jones                10          975          $19,451.25
           Jones                10           55           $1,097.25
           Jones                11          453           $9,037.35
           Jones                11           70           $1,396.50
           Jones                12          876          $17,476.20
           Jones                12        1,254          $25,017.30
           Smith                10          250           $4,987.50
           Smith                10          365           $7,281.75
           Smith                11          198           $3,950.10
           Smith                11          120           $2,394.00
           Smith                12        1,000          $19,950.00
                                       =======      ==============
                                         8,091         $164,041.70
```

Using Your Own Macro Variables

In addition to automatic macro variables, you can use your own macro variables by defining them with the %LET statement and referring to them with the ampersand prefix. Defining macro variables at the beginning of your program allows you to change parts of the program easily. The next example illustrates how to define two macro variables, QTR and YR, and how to refer to them in a TITLE statement.

Defining Macro Variables

Suppose you want to add to the previous report a TITLE3 statement that uses two macro variables. You want to name the first macro variable QTR and assign it the value Fourth. You want to name the second macro variable YR and assign it the value 1989.

The following %LET statements define these macro variables:

```
%let Qtr=Fourth;
%let Yr=1989;
```

Macro variable names such as these must follow the rules for SAS names. Specifically, macro variable names can be one to eight characters long; must begin with a letter or an underscore; and can have letters, numbers, and underscores following the first character.

In these simple situations, the values assigned to macro variables shouldn't contain unmatched quotes or semicolons. If the values contain leading or trailing blanks, the blanks are dropped.

So far, you have only defined the macro variables. The next section shows how to use the ampersand prefix to refer to the value of a macro variable.

Referring to Macro Variables

To refer to the value of a macro variable, place an ampersand prefix in front of the name of the variable. For example, the following TITLE statement contains references to the values of the macro variables QTR and YR, which were previously defined in %LET statements:

```
title3 "&Qtr Quarter &Yr Sales Totals";
```

The complete program, which includes the two %LET statements and the TITLE3 statement, follows. Output 24.22 shows the report.

```
%let Qtr=Fourth;
%let Yr=1989;

proc print data=sales.qtr04 noobs split='/' uniform;
   var salesrep mth units amtsold;
   format units comma7.
          amtsold dollar14.2;
   sum units amtsold;
   title1 'Using Your Own Macro Variables';
   title2 "Printed &SYSDATE";
   title3 "&Qtr Quarter &Yr Sales Totals";
   label salesrep = 'Sales/Representative'
         mth      = 'Month'
         units    = 'Units/Sold'
         amtsold  = 'Amount/Sold';
run;
```

Notice a few things about this program. First, the ampersands that precede QTR and YR indicate to the SAS macro facility to replace the references with their assigned values, Fourth and 1989, respectively. Second, as in the previous example, the texts of the TITLE2 and TITLE3 statements are enclosed in double quotes so the SAS macro facility can resolve them.

Output 24.22
Reports: Using
Your Own Macro
Variables

```
                  Using Your Own Macro Variables                    1
                         Printed 12JAN90
                    Fourth Quarter 1989 Sales Totals

        Sales                    Units           Amount
        Representative   Month   Sold            Sold

        Hollingsworth    10        530        $10,573.50
        Hollingsworth    10        265         $5,286.75
        Hollingsworth    11      1,230        $24,538.50
        Hollingsworth    11        150         $4,425.00
        Hollingsworth    12        125         $3,687.50
        Hollingsworth    12        175         $3,491.25
        Jones            10        975        $19,451.25
        Jones            10         55         $1,097.25
        Jones            11        453         $9,037.35
        Jones            11         70         $1,396.50
        Jones            12        876        $17,476.20
        Jones            12      1,254        $25,017.30
        Smith            10        250         $4,987.50
        Smith            10        365         $7,281.75
        Smith            11        198         $3,950.10
        Smith            11        120         $2,394.00
        Smith            12      1,000        $19,950.00
                               =======    ===============
                                 8,091       $164,041.70
```

Using macro variables can make your programs easy to modify. For example, if the previous program contained many references to QTR and YR, you could produce an entirely different report by making changes in only three places, the two values in the %LET statements and the data set name in the PROC PRINT statement.

SAS Tools

This chapter discusses the PRINT and SORT procedures:

PROC PRINT <DATA=*SAS-data-set*> <*print-options*>;
  ID *variables*;
  VAR *variables*;
  WHERE *where-expression*;
  FORMAT *variable format-name*;
  SUM *variables*;
  BY *variables*;
  SUMBY *variable*;
  PAGEBY *variable*;
  TITLE<*n*> <*'title'*>;
  FOOTNOTE<*n*> <*'footnote'*>;
  LABEL *variable='label'*;

PROC PRINT <DATA=*SAS-data-set*> <*print-options*>;
    starts the procedure and, when used alone, prints all variables for all observations in the *SAS-data-set*. Other statements allow you to control what to print.
    You can specify the following *print-options* in the PROC PRINT statement:

DATA=*SAS-data-set*
    names the SAS data set to be used by the PRINT procedure. If you omit DATA=, the most recently created data set is used.

NOOBS
    causes the observation numbers to be suppressed. It is most useful when you don't want to use an ID statement but you don't want the observation numbers to be printed.

LABEL
    causes the PRINT procedure to use variable labels instead of variable names as column headings for any variables that have labels defined. Variable labels appear only if you use the LABEL option or the SPLIT= option. You can specify labels in LABEL statements in the DATA step that creates the data set or in the PROC PRINT step. If you don't specify the LABEL option or if there is no label for a variable, the variable name is used.

SPLIT=*'split-character'*
    splits labels used as column headings wherever the designated split character appears. Variable labels are used only if you use the LABEL option or the SPLIT= option. When you define the value of the split character, you must enclose it in single quotes. It isn't necessary to use both the LABEL and SPLIT= options because SPLIT= implies that labels are to be used. The split character isn't printed. Blanks in the label are permitted.

(PROC PRINT continued)

DOUBLE | D
>   causes the printed output to be double-spaced.

UNIFORM | U
>   requests that the values of a variable be printed in the same
>   columns of each page in the output. Without the UNIFORM
>   option, the PRINT procedure fits as many variables and
>   observations on a page as possible. Therefore, different numbers
>   of variables may be printed on each page.

You can use the following statements in the PRINT procedure.

ID *variables;*
>   specifies that the values of the *variables* are to be used instead of
>   observation numbers to identify observations in the output. You can
>   specify more than one variable.

VAR *variables;*
>   names the *variables* to be printed. The variables are printed in the order
>   in which they appear in the VAR statement. If you don't use the VAR
>   statement, all variables in the data set are printed.

WHERE *where-expression;*
>   defines a condition on which observations are selected from a data set.
>   *Where-expression* defines the condition. The condition you define is a
>   sequence of operands and operators that specify one or more
>   comparisons.

FORMAT *variable format-name;*
>   allows you to print the value of a *variable* using a special pattern that
>   you specify as *format-name*.

SUM *variables;*
>   specifies *variables* whose values are to be totaled. You can specify a
>   variable in the SUM statement that is not listed in the VAR statement,
>   and the procedure adds the variable to the VAR list. PROC PRINT
>   ignores requests for totals on BY and ID variables. In general, when
>   used with the BY statement, the SUM statement produces subtotals each
>   time the value of a BY variable changes.

BY *variables;*
>   causes separate analyses to be performed on observations in groups
>   defined by the *variables* you specify. When a BY statement appears, the
>   procedure expects the input data set to be sorted in order of the
>   *variables*.

SUMBY *variable;*
>   prints totals when the *variable* you specify changes value or when any
>   variable listed before it in the BY statement changes value. You must use
>   a BY statement with the SUMBY statement.

PAGEBY *variable;*
> causes the PRINT procedure to begin printing a new page when the *variable* you specify changes value or when any variable listed before it in the BY statement changes value. You must use a BY statement with the PAGEBY statement.

TITLE<*n*> <*'title'*>;
> specifies titles. The argument *n* is a number from 1 to 10 that immediately follows the word TITLE, with no intervening blank, and specifies the level of the TITLE. The text of each *title* can be up to 132 characters long and must be enclosed in single or double quotes.

FOOTNOTE<*n*> <*'footnote'*>;
> specifies footnotes. The argument *n* is a number from 1 to 10 that immediately follows the word FOOTNOTE, with no intervening blank, and specifies the line number of the FOOTNOTE. The text of each *footnote* can be up to 132 characters long and must be enclosed in single or double quotes.

LABEL *variable='label';*
> specifies labels to be used for column headings. *Variable* names the variable to be labeled, and *label* specifies a string of up to 40 characters, including blanks. The *label* must be enclosed in single or double quotes.

PROC SORT <DATA=*SAS-data-set*>;
  BY *variable;*

PROC SORT<DATA=*SAS-data-set*>;
> sorts a SAS data set by the values of variables listed in the BY statement.

BY *variable;*
> sorts a SAS data set by the values of the variables listed in the BY statement. By default, the SAS System arranges the groups in ascending order (smallest value to largest).

The following macro statements and variables are discussed in this chapter:

SYSDATE
> is an automatic macro variable that allows you to include the date, in *mmdddyy* format, in your printed output. To refer to it in a program, you must use an ampersand (&) prefix before SYSDATE.

%LET *macro-variable=value;*
> is a macro statement that defines a *macro-variable* and assigns it a *value*. The *value* you define in the %LET statement is substituted for the *macro-variable* in printed output. To refer to the *macro-variable* in a program, you must use an ampersand (&) prefix before it.

Learning More

□ Chapter 8, "Acting on Selected Observations," describes the WHERE statement and the UPCASE function, which is useful for comparing values in WHERE statements. Chapter 8 also provides information on writing conditional statements in general. See also *SAS Language: Reference, Version 6, First Edition* for complete reference documentation on the WHERE statement.

□ Chapter 10, "Working with Grouped or Sorted Observations," discusses the SORT procedure. See also the *SAS Procedures Guide, Version 6, Third Edition* for complete reference documentation on the SORT procedure.

□ *SAS Language: Reference* provides information on indexing. You don't need to sort data sets before using a BY statement in the PRINT procedure if the data sets have an index on the variable or variables specified in the BY statement.

□ *SAS Language: Reference* completely documents SAS formats. There are many formats available with the SAS System, including ones for fractions, hexadecimal values, Roman numerals, social security numbers, date and time values, and numbers written as words.

□ The *SAS Procedures Guide* completely documents the PRINT procedure.

□ The *SAS Guide to Macro Processing, Version 6, Second Edition* describes macro processing in detail.

Chapter 25 Creating Summary Tables

Introduction

This chapter shows you how to use the TABULATE Procedure to create *summary tables*; it assumes you are familiar with the SAS DATA step. A summary table is a report that provides a concise overview of the relationships that exist among variables in a data set. PROC TABULATE allows you to create summary tables that use variables to form rows, columns, and pages.

The next section describes the input file and SAS data set used throughout this chapter. The subsequent section, "Understanding the Basics of the TABULATE Procedure," presents several key ideas you need to know before reading the remainder of the chapter. All the sample programs that follow use and build on the basic ideas in that section. The section "Using the TABULATE Procedure to Obtain Information about Your Data" uses sample SAS programs and output to show you how to use PROC TABULATE to create and modify summary tables.

Input File and SAS Data Set Example

This chapter uses an input file and a SAS data set example to illustrate certain aspects of PROC TABULATE. The input file contains sales records for TruBlend Coffee Makers, Inc. and looks like this:*

```
01    1    Hollingsworth Deluxe    260   29.50
01    1    Smith         Standard   41   19.95
01    1    Hollingsworth Standard  330   19.95
01    1    Jones         Standard  110   19.95
01    1    Smith         Deluxe    715   29.50
01    1    Jones         Standard  675   19.95
02    1    Jones         Standard 2045   19.95
02    1    Smith         Deluxe     10   29.50


          more data ...


12    4    Hollingsworth Deluxe    125   29.50
12    4    Jones         Standard 1254   19.95
12    4    Hollingsworth Standard  175   19.95
```

The input file contains the month and quarter of the year a sale was made; the name of the sales representative; type of coffee maker sold, either standard or deluxe; the number of units sold; and the price of each unit.

In addition to the input file, this chapter uses a SAS data set named SALES.YEAR; it contains all the sales records from the input file and a new variable named AMTSOLD. The variable AMTSOLD is UNITS multiplied by PRICE.

The following program creates SALES.YEAR:

```
libname sales 'your-data-library';

data sales.year;
    infile 'your-input-file';
    input mth $ qtr $ salesrep $14. type $ units price;
    amtsold=units*price;
run;
```

Understanding the Basics of the TABULATE Procedure

PROC TABULATE produces tables that give you summary statistics on categories of data. PROC TABULATE associates the statistics with the categories they describe in a visually effective way so you can extract information quickly.

---

* Refer to the Appendix for a complete listing of the input data.

Before you look at the sample programs and output in the other sections of this chapter, you need to be be familiar with the following PROC TABULATE statements and options:

□ PROC TABULATE statement

    □ DATA= option

    □ FORMAT= option

□ CLASS statement

□ VAR statement

□ TABLE statement.

The PROC TABULATE Statement

The TABULATE procedure begins with a PROC TABULATE statement. There are many options available with the PROC TABULATE statement. However, for the examples in this chapter, only two are needed: the DATA= option and the FORMAT= option.

Using the DATA= Option

The DATA= option specifies the SAS data set to be used by PROC TABULATE. If you omit the DATA= option, the TABULATE procedure uses the SAS data set created most recently in the current job or session. All the examples in this chapter use the SAS data set SALES.YEAR.

Using the FORMAT= Option

The FORMAT= option specifies a default format for formatting the value in each *cell* in the table. A cell is a single unit of the table where a row and a column intersect and where a single statistic value is printed. You can specify any valid SAS numeric format or user-defined format. COMMA10. is the default format used for all the examples in this chapter. The following PROC TABULATE statement is used for all the examples in this chapter:

```
proc tabulate data=sales.year format=comma10.;
```

The CLASS, VAR, and TABLE Statements

In addition to the PROC TABULATE statement, you must also use at least two other statements. First, you must use either a CLASS statement or a VAR statement (or both). Second, you must use at least one TABLE statement. Every variable that occurs in a TABLE statement must appear in either a CLASS statement or a VAR statement, but not both.

Using the CLASS Statement

The CLASS statement specifies which variables are to be used as *class variables*. A class variable organizes your data into distinct categories. You can obtain descriptive statistics about the categories formed by the class variables.

Variables you specify in the CLASS statement can be either character or numeric and should be categorical or discrete in nature. For example, the following CLASS statement specifies the character variable SALESREP as a class variable:

```
class salesrep;
```

Recall from the section "Input File and SAS Data Set Example" earlier in this chapter that the variable SALESREP has only three possible values: `Hollingsworth`, `Jones`, or `Smith`. When you specify SALESREP as a class variable, PROC TABULATE constructs a category for the value `Hollingsworth`, a second category for the value `Jones`, and a third category for the value `Smith`. You can use PROC TABULATE to obtain descriptive statistics about each category. For example, you might want to know how many sales each sales representative made.

Using the VAR Statement

The VAR statement identifies which variables are to be used as *analysis variables*. An analysis variable contains values for which you want to compute statistics. For example, the following VAR statement specifies the variable AMTSOLD as an analysis variable:

```
var amtsold;
```

Recall from the section "Input File and SAS Data Set Example" earlier in this chapter that the variable AMTSOLD is the result of multiplying the variables UNITS and PRICE. The variable AMTSOLD has many possible values. When you specify AMTSOLD as an analysis variable, you can use the values of AMTSOLD to request a wide variety of descriptive statistics.

For example, you might want to know the dollar amount that each sales representative sold during the year. In other words, suppose you ask, "For each sales representative, what is the sum of the values of the variable AMTSOLD?" (By default, PROC TABULATE sums the values of analysis variables.)

Guidelines for Class and Analysis Variables

Use the following guidelines to help determine whether you should specify a variable as a class variable in the CLASS statement or as an analysis variable in the VAR statement. Keep in mind that all variables you use in the TABLE statement you must also specify in either the CLASS statement or the VAR statement, but not both.

□ Class variables can be either character or numeric.

□ Class variable values form categories about which you want to obtain information.

□ Usually, a variable should be specified as a class variable to report on how frequently each value of the variable occurs or to print distinct values for the variable as row, column, or page headings.

□ The TABULATE procedure prints a separate heading for each value of each class variable; therefore, in most cases, you should specify as class variables only those variables that have a few distinct values.

□ Analysis variables must be numeric.

□ When used as a statement in the TABULATE procedure, the VAR statement specifies analysis variables. Unlike the VAR statement in many SAS procedures, the VAR statement in PROC TABULATE is used only for those variables that are to be treated as analysis variables.

□ A variable should be specified as an analysis variable if you want to obtain descriptive statistics using the values of the variable.

Using the TABLE Statement

PROC TABULATE allows you to create summary tables that have one, two, or three dimensions. One-dimensional summary tables only have columns; two-dimensional summary tables have rows and columns; and three-dimensional summary tables print the output on separate pages with rows and columns on each page. For example, the summary table in Output 25.3 (later in this chapter) has three dimensions. It has separate pages for the values of the variable SALESREP, rows for the values of the variable QTR, and columns for the values of the variable AMTSOLD.

You use the TABLE statement to define the table you want PROC TABULATE to produce. The TABLE statement defines the following aspects of the table:

□ the number of dimensions

□ which variables, statistics, and other elements go in which dimension

□ the relationship among variables, statistics, and other elements within a dimension.

You must specify at least one TABLE statement in a PROC TABULATE step. There are no default tables for the TABULATE procedure.

In the TABLE statement you specify page expressions, row expressions, and column expressions, all of which are constructed in the same way and are referred to collectively as *dimension expressions*. You use commas to separate dimension expressions from one another.

The number of dimension expressions you specify in the TABLE statement and their positions relative to one another tell PROC TABULATE how to construct the table. If you specify one dimension expression, it defines columns. If you specify two dimension expressions, the first expression in the TABLE statement defines rows, and the second one defines columns. If you specify three dimension expressions, the first expression defines pages, the second one defines rows, and the third one defines columns.

For example, the following TABLE statement defines a three-dimensional summary table that places the values of the variable SALESREP in the page dimension, the values of the variable TYPE in the row dimension, and the values of the variable AMTSOLD in the column dimension:

```
table salesrep,
      type,
      amtsold;
```

The examples in the next section show you how to create and modify one-, two-, and three-dimensional summary tables using the basics of PROC TABULATE.

Multiple TABLE Statements in a Single TABULATE Step

Note that you can use more than one TABLE statement in the same step, but you can't define variables in the CLASS or VAR statements more than once in a single PROC TABULATE step. In other words, you can't change how you use a variable in the middle of a PROC TABULATE step. For example, the following program produces three tables during one execution of the TABULATE procedure:

```
proc tabulate data=sales.year format=comma10.;
   class salesrep type;
   var amtsold;
   table type;
   table type,units;
   table salesrep,type,amtsold;
run;
```

Using the TABULATE Procedure to Obtain Information about Your Data

The examples in this chapter use the data set SALES.YEAR, introduced in the section "Input File and SAS Data Set Example" earlier in this chapter. The examples show how to use PROC TABULATE to obtain sales information about TruBlend Coffee Makers, Inc. Specifically, the examples that follow show you how to

□ count frequencies of occurrence

□ obtain totals for single variables

□ obtain totals for subgroups by crossing variables

□ obtain two sets of totals by concatenating variables

□ obtain averages

□ obtain totals for all class variables.

Counting Frequencies of Occurrence

The data set SALES.YEAR contains 110 observations. Each observation represents a sale made during the year. Some of the sales were made by the sales representative Hollingsworth, some by Jones, and some by Smith. Suppose you want to answer this question: "How many times did each sales representative make a sale?" In other words, you want to know how many times the values `Hollingsworth`, `Jones`, and `Smith` occur in the data set SALES.YEAR.

The following PROC TABULATE step answers this question by producing a one-dimensional summary table. Output 25.1 shows the table.

```
proc tabulate data=sales.year format=comma10.;
   title 'Counting Frequencies of Occurrence';
   class salesrep;
   table salesrep;
run;
```

Notice a few things about this program. First, the variable SALESREP is specified as a class variable in the CLASS statement. Second, the variable SALESREP is listed as the only variable in the TABLE statement. Third, there is no VAR statement because the table doesn't use analysis variables. Fourth, the CLASS statement comes before the TABLE statement. (This isn't necessary, but it is a convention used throughout this chapter.) Last, there is a TITLE statement followed by the title "Counting Frequencies of Occurrence." All the examples in this chapter include a TITLE statement with a similar descriptive title.

Output 25.1
Tables: Counting
Frequencies of
Occurrence

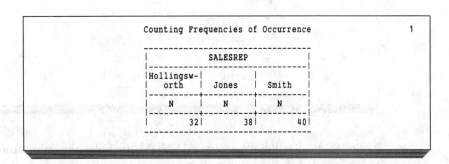

The default statistic for class variables is N, which is the number of observations in the data set for which there are nonmissing variable values. The values 32, 38, and 40 in Output 25.1 indicate the frequency (N) with which the values `Hollingsworth`, `Jones`, and `Smith` occur.

Obtaining Totals for Single Variables

Suppose you ask, "What was the amount sold by each sales representative?" The following PROC TABULATE step answers this question by producing a two-dimensional table with one variable in each dimension. Output 25.2 shows the table.

```
proc tabulate data=sales.year format=comma10.;
    title 'Obtaining Totals for Single Variables in Two Dimensions';
    class salesrep;
    var amtsold;
    table salesrep,
          amtsold;
run;
```

Notice that the variable SALESREP is specified as a class variable and is listed first in the TABLE statement. The values of SALESREP appear in the row dimension. The program includes a VAR statement, which specifies AMTSOLD as an analysis variable. AMTSOLD is also included in the TABLE statement after a comma; therefore, it appears in the column dimension. (The comma separates the row expression containing SALESREP from the column expression containing AMTSOLD.)

Output 25.2
Tables: Obtaining Totals for Single Variables in Two Dimensions

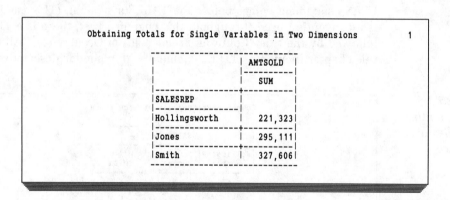

```
     Obtaining Totals for Single Variables in Two Dimensions          1

                          ----------------------------
                          |               | AMTSOLD |
                          |               |---------|
                          |               |   SUM   |
                          |---------------+---------|
                          |SALESREP       |         |
                          |---------------|         |
                          |Hollingsworth  |  221,323|
                          |---------------+---------|
                          |Jones          |  295,111|
                          |---------------+---------|
                          |Smith          |  327,606|
                          ----------------------------
```

Notice that the column heading AMTSOLD includes the subheading SUM. The values printed in the column dimension are sums of the amount sold by each sales representative because, by default, PROC TABULATE sums the values of analysis variables.

You can also produce three-dimensional summary tables that show totals for single variables. To illustrate, suppose you ask this question: "What was the amount sold during each quarter of the year by each sales representative?" The following PROC TABULATE step produces a three-dimensional table with the totals for one variable in each dimension. Output 25.3 shows the table.

```
proc tabulate data=sales.year format=comma10.;
    title 'Obtaining Totals for Single Variables in Three Dimensions';
    class salesrep qtr;
    var amtsold;
    table salesrep,
          qtr,
          amtsold;
run;
```

Notice changes in two of the statements in this program. First, the CLASS statement includes the variable QTR. Second, the TABLE statement contains three dimension expressions, which are separated by commas. The variable SALESREP is listed first in the TABLE statement; therefore, the values of SALESREP appear on the page dimension. The variable QTR is listed second, so its values appear in the row dimension. The variable AMTSOLD is listed third; it appears in the column dimension.

Output 25.3
Tables: Obtaining Totals for Single Variables in Three Dimensions

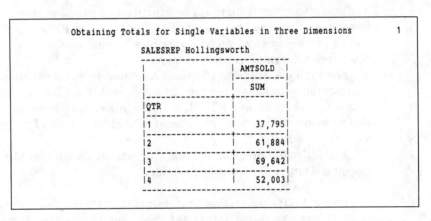

```
Obtaining Totals for Single Variables in Three Dimensions          1

  SALESREP Hollingsworth
  ---------------------------------------
  |                         | AMTSOLD   |
  |                         |-----------|
  |                         | SUM       |
  |-------------------------+-----------|
  |QTR                      |           |
  |-------------------------|           |
  |1                        |    37,795 |
  |-------------------------+-----------|
  |2                        |    61,884 |
  |-------------------------+-----------|
  |3                        |    69,642 |
  |-------------------------+-----------|
  |4                        |    52,003 |
  ---------------------------------------
```

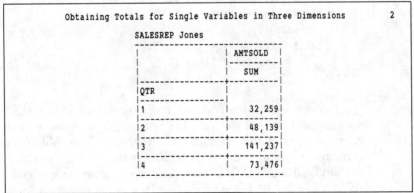

```
Obtaining Totals for Single Variables in Three Dimensions          2

  SALESREP Jones
  ---------------------------------------
  |                         | AMTSOLD   |
  |                         |-----------|
  |                         | SUM       |
  |-------------------------+-----------|
  |QTR                      |           |
  |-------------------------|           |
  |1                        |    32,259 |
  |-------------------------+-----------|
  |2                        |    48,139 |
  |-------------------------+-----------|
  |3                        |   141,237 |
  |-------------------------+-----------|
  |4                        |    73,476 |
  ---------------------------------------
```

```
                Obtaining Totals for Single Variables in Three Dimensions        3

                      SALESREP Smith
                      ----------------------------------------
                      |                        | AMTSOLD |
                      |                        |---------|
                      |                        |  SUM    |
                      |------------------------+---------|
                      |QTR                     |         |
                      |------------------------|         |
                      |1                       |   74,295|
                      |------------------------+---------|
                      |2                       |   70,124|
                      |------------------------+---------|
                      |3                       |  144,624|
                      |------------------------+---------|
                      |4                       |   38,563|
                      ----------------------------------------
```

Obtaining Totals for Subgroups by Crossing Variables

You can also create subgroups of your data by *crossing* elements within a dimension. Crossing is the operation that instructs PROC TABULATE to combine two or more elements, such as variables, format modifiers, or statistics. You use the asterisk operator to cross elements.

For example, suppose you want to obtain sales information about each sales representative based on the type of coffee maker sold. In other words, you're asking for information on TYPE *by* SALESREP. Specifically, you want to answer this question: "What was the amount sold of each type of coffee maker by each sales representative?"

The following program creates a two-dimensional table that answers this question. Output 25.4 shows the table.

```
proc tabulate data=sales.year format=comma10.;
   title 'Obtaining Totals for Subgroups by Crossing Variables';
   class salesrep type;
   var amtsold;
   table salesrep*type,
         amtsold*f=dollar16.2;
run;
```

The row dimension contains one expression, SALESREP*TYPE, which crosses the values of the variable SALESREP with those of the variable TYPE. Note the asterisk that combines the variables. The column dimension also contains one expression, AMTSOLD*F=DOLLAR16.2, which crosses the values of the variable AMTSOLD with the format modifier F= and the SAS format DOLLAR16.2. The format DOLLAR16.2 is better suited for dollar figures than the format COMMA10., which is specified as the default in the PROC TABULATE statement. (See the section "Using the FORMAT= Option" earlier in this chapter.)

Output 25.4
Tables: Obtaining
Totals for
Subgroups by
Crossing Variables

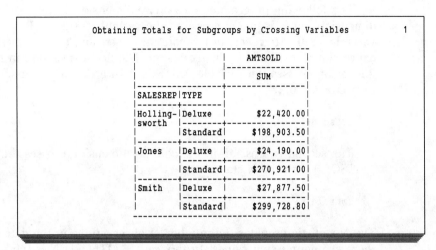

```
              Obtaining Totals for Subgroups by Crossing Variables              1
         --------------------------------------------
         |               |        |   AMTSOLD   |
         |               |        |-------------|
         |               |        |     SUM     |
         |---------------+--------+-------------|
         |SALESREP |TYPE  |             |
         |---------+------|-------------|
         |Holling- |Deluxe |    $22,420.00|
         |sworth   |-------+-------------|
         |         |Standard|   $198,903.50|
         |---------+------+-------------|
         |Jones    |Deluxe |    $24,190.00|
         |         |-------+-------------|
         |         |Standard|   $270,921.00|
         |---------+------+-------------|
         |Smith    |Deluxe |    $27,877.50|
         |         |-------+-------------|
         |         |Standard|   $299,728.80|
         --------------------------------------------
```

When you cross variables, the asterisk operator tells PROC TABULATE to place values for one variable within the values for the other variable in the same dimension. The order that you list the variables in the crossing determines the order of the headings in the table. In the column dimension, variables are stacked top to bottom; in the row dimension, left to right; and in the page dimension, front to back.

The result of crossing elements depends on what type of elements are crossed. Crossings fall into these general categories:

□ class variables crossed with other class variables

□ class variables crossed with an analysis variable

□ any variable crossed with a statistic

□ any variable crossed with a format modifier (to format values in the table cells).

Note that you *can't* cross two statistics or two analysis variables. Because there is an implied crossing between dimensions, all statistics must occur in one dimension, and all analysis variables must occur in one dimension. However, statistics and analysis variables don't have to be in the same dimension.

Obtaining Two Sets of Totals by Concatenating Variables

You can also create summary tables that report on two or more statistics by *concatenating* variables. Concatenating is the operation that joins the information of two or more elements, such as class variables, analysis variables, or statistics, by placing the output of the second and subsequent elements immediately after the output of the first element. To concatenate elements in a dimension expression, put a blank space between them.

For example, suppose you want to know the total number of sales *and* the total dollar amount sold. In other words, you're asking for totals on the frequency (N) of AMTSOLD *and* on the sum of AMTSOLD. That is, you want to answer this question: "How many sales were made, and what was the total sales figure of each type of coffee maker by each sales representative?"

The following program creates a two-dimensional table. In the row dimension, there is one expression: the variable SALESREP is crossed with the variable TYPE. However, in the column dimension, there are two concatenated expressions, separated by blank spaces. The first expression in the column dimension crosses the variable AMTSOLD with the format modifier F=DOLLAR16.2:

```
amtsold*f=dollar16.2
```

The second expression in the column dimension crosses the variable AMTSOLD with the N statistic:

```
amtsold*n
```

The N statistic provides the number of observations in the data set for which there are nonmissing values. In this case, AMTSOLD*N is the number of sales that were made during the year. Output 25.5 shows the table.

```
proc tabulate data=sales.year format=comma10.;
    title 'Obtaining Two Sets of Totals by Concatenating Variables';
    class salesrep type;
    var amtsold;
    table salesrep*type,
          amtsold*f=dollar16.2 amtsold*n;
run;
```

Output 25.5
Tables: Obtaining Two Sets of Totals by Concatenating Variables

```
        Obtaining Two Sets of Totals by Concatenating Variables          1
    ---------------------------------------------------------------
    |                   |         AMTSOLD    | AMTSOLD |
    |                   |--------------------+---------|
    |                   |         SUM        |    N    |
    |-------------------+--------------------+---------|
    |SALESREP |TYPE     |                    |         |
    |---------+---------|                    |         |
    |Holling- |Deluxe   |       $22,420.00   |       8 |
    |sworth   |---------+--------------------+---------|
    |         |Standard |      $198,903.50   |      24 |
    |---------+---------+--------------------+---------|
    |Jones    |Deluxe   |       $24,190.00   |       4 |
    |         |---------+--------------------+---------|
    |         |Standard |      $270,921.00   |      34 |
    |---------+---------+--------------------+---------|
    |Smith    |Deluxe   |       $27,877.50   |       4 |
    |         |---------+--------------------+---------|
    |         |Standard |      $299,728.80   |      36 |
    ---------------------------------------------------------------
```

You can request other descriptive statistics by crossing variables with the appropriate statistic keyword. When you cross either a class variable or an analysis variable with a statistic, you're telling PROC TABULATE what type of calculations to perform. If the crossing contains no analysis variables, you can cross the class variables with only the statistics N or PCTN. When you cross class variables and don't include an analysis variable or statistic, PROC TABULATE by default crosses the N statistic with the class variables. For example, this code:

```
class salesrep type;
table salesrep*type;
```

is treated the same as this code:

```
class salesrep type;
table salesrep*type*N;
```

Analysis variables can be crossed with any of the many descriptive statistics that are available with PROC TABULATE. If you don't specify a statistic when you include an analysis variable in the crossing, PROC TABULATE automatically crosses the analysis variable with SUM. For example, look back at the program used to produce Output 25.3. Although no statistic is explicitly stated for the analysis variable AMTSOLD, the TABULATE procedure supplies the default statistic SUM.

Obtaining Averages

You can cross the statistic MEAN with a variable to obtain averages. For example, suppose you ask this question: "How many sales were made, what was the average amount per sale, and what was the amount sold of each type of coffee maker by each sales representative?" The following program creates a two-dimensional table that answers this question. Output 25.6 shows the table.

```
proc tabulate data=sales.year format=comma10.;
   title 'Obtaining Averages';
   class salesrep type;
   var amtsold;
   table salesrep*type,
         amtsold*f=dollar16.2 amtsold*mean*f=dollar16.2 amtsold*n;
run;
```

Notice a few things about the TABLE statement in this program. As before, the row dimension contains one expression, SALESREP*TYPE. However, in the column dimension, three concatenated expressions are separated by blank spaces. The first expression in the column dimension, as before, crosses the variable AMTSOLD with the format modifier F=DOLLAR16.2:

```
amtsold*f=dollar16.2
```

The second expression in the column dimension crosses the variable AMTSOLD with the statistic MEAN and with the format modifier F=DOLLAR16.2:

```
amtsold*mean*f=dollar16.2
```

The MEAN statistic provides the arithmetic mean.

The third expression in the column dimension, as in the previous example, crosses the variable AMTSOLD with the N statistic:

```
amtsold*n
```

The output provides a great deal of summary information with one omission: there are no totals for the sales representatives as a group. The next example shows you how to use the universal class variable ALL to obtain totals for the sales representatives as a class.

Output 25.6
Tables: Obtaining
Averages

```
 Obtaining Averages                                                      1
 ---------------------------------------------------------------------------
 |              |        | AMTSOLD     |  AMTSOLD      | AMTSOLD  |
 |              |        |-------------+---------------+----------|
 |              |        |  SUM        |  MEAN         | N        |
 |--------------+--------+-------------+---------------+----------|
 |SALESREP|TYPE |        |             |               |          |
 |--------+------|        |             |               |          |
 |Holling-|Deluxe |   $22,420.00|    $2,802.50|        8|
 |sworth  |------+-------------+---------------+----------|
 |        |Standard|  $198,903.50|    $8,287.65|       24|
 |--------+------+-------------+---------------+----------|
 |Jones   |Deluxe |   $24,190.00|    $6,047.50|        4|
 |        |------+-------------+---------------+----------|
 |        |Standard|  $270,921.00|    $7,968.26|       34|
 |--------+------+-------------+---------------+----------|
 |Smith   |Deluxe |   $27,877.50|    $6,969.38|        4|
 |        |------+-------------+---------------+----------|
 |        |Standard|  $299,728.80|    $8,325.80|       36|
 ---------------------------------------------------------------------------
```

Obtaining Totals for All Class Variables

You can use the universal class variable ALL to obtain totals for all the class variables in a dimension. For example, suppose you want sales information about each sales representative separately and about all the sales representatives as a class. That is, suppose you ask, "For each sales representative and for all the sales representatives as a group, how many sales were made, what was the average amount per sale, and what was the amount sold?"

The following program produces a two-dimensional summary table that answers this question. Output 25.7 shows the table.

```
proc tabulate data=sales.year format=comma10.;
    title 'Obtaining Totals for All Class Variables';
    class salesrep type;
    var amtsold;
    table salesrep*type all,
          amtsold*f=dollar16.2 amtsold*mean*f=dollar16.2 amtsold*n;
run;
```

Notice that this program differs from the previous one in only one way: the TABLE statement now includes the universal class variable ALL in the row dimension.

Output 25.7
Tables: Obtaining
Totals for All
Class Variables

```
                 Obtaining Totals for All Class Variables                  1

           |        | AMTSOLD    | AMTSOLD    | AMTSOLD  |
           |        |------------+------------+----------|
           |        | SUM        | MEAN       | N        |
           |--------+------------+------------+----------|
|SALESREP|TYPE     |            |            |          |
|--------+---------|            |            |          |
|Holling-|Deluxe   |  $22,420.00|  $2,802.50 |        8 |
|sworth  |---------+------------+------------+----------|
|        |Standard | $198,903.50|  $8,287.65 |       24 |
|--------+---------+------------+------------+----------|
|Jones   |Deluxe   |  $24,190.00|  $6,047.50 |        4 |
|        |---------+------------+------------+----------|
|        |Standard | $270,921.00|  $7,968.26 |       34 |
|--------+---------+------------+------------+----------|
|Smith   |Deluxe   |  $27,877.50|  $6,969.38 |        4 |
|        |---------+------------+------------+----------|
|        |Standard | $299,728.80|  $8,325.80 |       36 |
|--------+---------+------------+------------+----------|
|ALL     |         | $844,040.80|  $7,673.10 |      110 |
```

SAS Tools

This chapter discusses the TABULATE procedure:

PROC TABULATE <DATA=*SAS-data-set*> <FORMAT=*format-name*>;
  CLASS *variables*;
  VAR *variables*;
  TABLE <<*page-expression*,> *row-expression*,> *column-expression*;

Each PROC TABULATE step requires at least one TABLE statement and either a CLASS statement, a VAR statement, or both.

PROC TABULATE <DATA=*SAS-data-set*> <FORMAT=*format-name*>;
  starts the TABULATE procedure. DATA= specifies the *SAS-data-set* to be used by PROC TABULATE. If you omit the DATA= option, the TABULATE procedure uses the SAS data set created most recently in the current job or session.
  FORMAT= specifies the default format for formatting the value in each cell in the table. You can specify any valid SAS numeric format or user-defined format.

CLASS *variables;*
  identifies variables in the input data set as class variables. Any class variable you use in a TABLE statement must have been previously listed in the CLASS statement. The variables may have either numeric or character values. Normally, each class variable has a small number of discrete values or unique levels.

VAR *variables;*
  identifies variables in the input data set as analysis variables. Any analysis variable you use in a TABLE statement must have been previously listed in the VAR statement. The variables must be numeric and may contain continuous values.

TABLE <<*page-expression,*> *row-expression,*> *column-expression;*
defines the table you want PROC TABULATE to produce. You must specify at least one TABLE statement. In the TABLE statement you specify *page-expressions*, *row-expressions*, and *column-expressions*, all of which are constructed in the same way and are referred to collectively as *dimension expressions*. Use commas to separate dimension expressions from one another. You define relationships among variables, statistics, and other elements within a dimension by combining them with one or more *operators*. Operators are symbols that tell PROC TABULATE what actions to perform on the variables, statistics, and other elements. Table 25.1 lists the common operators and the actions they symbolize:

Table 25.1
TABLE Statement
Operators

Operator	Action
, (comma)	separates dimensions of the table
* (asterisk)	crosses elements within a dimension
(blank space)	concatenates elements in a dimension
= (equal)	overrides default cell format or assigns label to an element

Learning More

□ The *SAS Guide to TABULATE Processing, 1987 Edition* presents information on the class variable ALL. You can use the universal class variable ALL to obtain many levels of subtotals as well as totals of an entire dimension.

□ The *SAS Guide to TABULATE Processing* provides information about using the LABEL, KEYLABEL, BY, FREQ, and WEIGHT statements with PROC TABULATE. Only the PROC TABULATE, CLASS, VAR, and TABLE statements are necessary to use the TABULATE procedure. All other statements available for use with PROC TABULATE are optional.

□ The *SAS Guide to TABULATE Processing* presents a complete discussion of the statistics available with PROC TABULATE.

□ The *SAS Guide to TABULATE Processing* presents information about TABLE statement options. Numerous options are available for use with the TABLE statement. For example, you can use the CONDENSE option in the TABLE statement to print multiple logical pages on single physical pages.

Chapter **26** Producing Mailing Labels and
Other Continuous-Feed Forms

Introduction

This chapter shows you how to use the FORMS procedure; it assumes you are familiar with the SAS DATA step. This procedure allows you to select variables and print their values onto continuous-feed forms such as mailing labels.

The next section, "Input File and SAS Data Set Example," describes the input file and SAS data set used throughout this chapter. The subsequent section, "Understanding the Basics of the FORMS Procedure," discusses three key ideas you need to know before reading the remainder of the material. All of the sample programs that follow use and build on the basic ideas presented in that section.

The other sections in this chapter use sample SAS programs and output to illustrate how to

- use the default options in PROC FORMS to display mailing labels
- route the output to an external file for printing
- improve the appearance of the mailing labels
- control the layout of the forms.

Input File and SAS Data Set Example

This chapter uses one input file and one SAS data set to illustrate certain aspects of PROC FORMS. The input file looks like this:

```
Johnson, Lee. R.      P. O. Box 243     Montgomery,   AL   36113
Abbott, Brenda K.     568 Trillion Ct.  Denver,       CO   80237
Rodriquez, Juan       619 Powell Dr.    Charleston,   SC   29412
Stevenson, Mary K.    22 Meredith Blvd. Austin,       TX   78702
Hawks, Patrick E.     Rt. 1, Box 523    Taylorsville, NC   28681
Lee, Chen             123 Maple St.     Raleigh,      NC   27606
Weinstein, Joseph M.  Rt. 4, Box 466    Dixon,        IL   61021
Baskowski, Bonnie G.  P. O. Box 42      Sacramento,   CA   95841
```

The input file contains the names and addresses of customers of TruBlend Coffee Makers, Inc.

In addition to the input file, this chapter uses a SAS data set named CUSTOMER.LABELS. The following program creates the SAS data set CUSTOMER.LABELS and sorts the observations by ZIP code:

```
libname customer 'your-data-library';
data customer.labels;
   infile 'your-input-file';
   input name   $ 1-20
         street $ 22-42
         city   $ 44-64
         state  $ 66-67
         zip    $ 69-73;
run;


proc sort data=customer.labels;
   by zip;
run;
```

Understanding the Basics of the FORMS Procedure

Before you look at the sample programs and output in this chapter, you need to be familiar with the following aspects of PROC FORMS:

□ form units

□ form pages

□ form layouts.

Form Units

For each observation in the input SAS data set, PROC FORMS prints data in a rectangular block called a *form unit*.* For example, a mailing label is a form unit. You specify what goes into each form unit with LINE statements and LINE statement options.

Each form unit contains print lines, which you define using one or more LINE statements. LINE statements come after the PROC FORMS statement and specify the line number and the variables to be printed on a particular line. At least one LINE statement is required with the FORMS procedure. For example, the following LINE statement specifies to print the values of the variable STREET on line 2:

```
line 2 street;
```

You can use options in the LINE statement to control the way lines are printed. However, no options are required. If you omit a LINE statement option from your program, PROC FORMS uses its default value for processing. Use of these options is explained in the section "Improving the Appearance of Mailing Labels" later in this chapter.

Form Pages

An individual form unit, such as a mailing label, is printed on a *form page*. A form page has a line size and page size associated with it. Figure 26.1 illustrates continuous-feed mailing labels that have one form unit across a form page and two form units down a form page.

Figure 26.1
Mailing Labels:
Sample Form Page

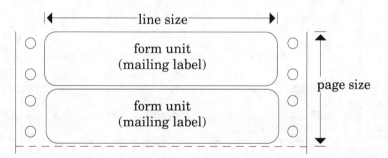

Form Layout

Form layout refers to the number and arrangement of form units on a form page. You control the form layout with *form placement options*, which you specify as a part of the PROC FORMS statement. Form placement options

---

* PROC FORMS writes blanks for missing values of character variables *and* numeric variables.

control how many form units are printed on a form page and where they're printed.

If you omit a form placement option from your program, PROC FORMS uses its default value. Form placement options include

□ DOWN=*number*

□ INDENT=*number*

□ LINES=*number*

□ WIDTH=*number*

□ ACROSS=*number*

□ BETWEEN=*number*

□ SKIP=*number*.

Figure 26.2 illustrates a sample form layout. The form placement options are shown in uppercase letters.

Figure 26.2
Mailing Labels:
Sample Form
Layout

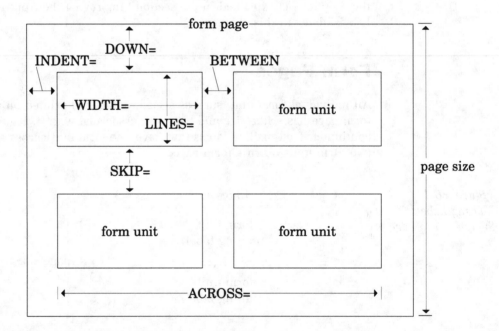

Using the FORMS Procedure's Default Options

The FORMS procedure has many statements and options that allow you to tailor forms to your needs. However, the easiest way to get started with PROC FORMS is to use the default values of the procedure.

In this section, you learn how to use the following values of PROC FORMS:

□ the default values of the form placement options

□ the default values of the LINE statement options

□ the default specification for the output file.

Using Default Form Placement and LINE Statement Options

To illustrate how to use the default values of PROC FORMS, suppose you want to mail questionnaires to several of the customers who have bought products from TruBlend Coffee Makers, Inc. You have mailing labels that line up with the default values of the form placement and LINE statement options. In other words, the mailing labels have the following format:

□ The first label begins at the top of the page; that is, it is *down* 0 lines from the top.

□ The labels are *indented* 0 spaces from the left margin.

□ Each label has room for three *lines*.

□ Each line can be up to 40 characters *wide*.

□ There is one label *across* the page.

□ There is one *skip* line between each label.

Figure 26.3 illustrates this format.

Figure 26.3
Mailing Labels:
Format of Labels
for Default Values

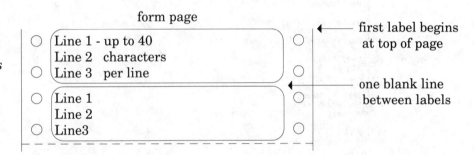

Previewing Your File before Printing

Before actually printing the mailing labels, you want to display the output so that you can see the results and make changes to the PROC FORMS step if necessary. The default destination for the output file depends on which method you're using to run the SAS System: batch, noninteractive, interactive line-mode, or the SAS Display Manager System.

□ For batch processing, the default output file is the SAS procedure output file.

□ For noninteractive processing, the default output file depends on the operating system.

□ For interactive line-mode processing, the default output file is the terminal.

□ For display manager, the default output file is the OUTPUT window.

The following PROC FORMS step uses the SAS data set
CUSTOMER.LABELS, created earlier in this chapter, and the default values of
PROC FORMS mentioned so far; that is, the program contains no form
placement or LINE statement options. Display 26.1, which assumes you're using
display manager, shows this program's output.

```
proc forms data=customer.labels;
   line 1 name;
   line 2 street;
   line 3 city state zip;
run;
```

Display 26.1
Mailing Labels:
Using the Default
Output File

```
┌OUTPUT─────────────────────────────────────────────────────────┐
│ Command ===>                                                    │
│                                                                 │
│                          The SAS System                       1 │
│                                    11:28 Wednesday, April 25, 1990│
│ Stevenson, Mary K.                                              │
│ 22 Meredith Blvd.                                               │
│ Austin,            TX 07611                                     │
│                                                                 │
│ Weinstein, Joseph M.                                            │
│ Rt. 4, Box 466                                                  │
│ Dixon,             IL 17191                                     │
│                                                                 │
│ Baxley, Allison T.                                              │
│ 752 Lee Ave.                                                    │
│ Wellington,        KS 17612                                     │
│                                                                 │
│ Baskowski, Bonnie G.                                            │
│ P. O. Box 42                                                    │
│ Sacramento,        CA 26701                                     │
│                                                                 │
│ Lee, Chen                                                       │
│ 123 Maple St.                                                   │
│ Raleigh            NC 27408                                     │
│                                                                 │
│ Abbott, Brenda K.                                               │
│ 568 Trillion Ct.                                                │
│ Denver,            CO 37201                                     │
│                                                                 │
│                                                               R │
└─────────────────────────────────────────────────────────────────┘
```

Notice the following about the output in Display 26.1:

□ The default title, "The SAS System," the page number, and the time and date appear at the top of the output.

□ The last name of each customer is displayed first and is followed by a comma. This same format was used in the input file.

□ There are several blanks between the CITY and STATE variables due to a field length of 21 for the variable CITY specified in the INPUT statement when the data set was created.

□ The CITY, STATE, and ZIP variables for each customer are displayed on line 3.

Routing Output to an External File for Printing

In the previous section, you saw how to preview the PROC FORMS output before printing it. However, to actually print the mailing labels, you must route the output to an *external file*. An external file isn't part of the SAS data library.

You store external files on disk or tape and use your operating system's print commands to print them.*

To route the PROC FORMS output to an external file, you must first define the file in your SAS program by adding the FILENAME statement and the FILE= option to your SAS program.

Using the FILENAME Statement

Use the FILENAME statement to associate a SAS *fileref* with the *filename* of your external file. Fileref is an abbreviation for *file reference*. You use filerefs in PROC FORMS and in other SAS procedures to identify external files to the SAS System. Filename refers to the entire definition of a file according to the naming convention of your computer's operating system.

The FILENAME statement must appear before PROC FORMS so that the procedure can make the association between the fileref and the filename of your external file before it begins processing. Also, the filename must appear in either single or double quotes. For more information about the FILENAME statement, see "Special Topic: Using External Files in Your SAS Job" in Chapter 2, *Introduction to DATA Step Processing*.

Using the FILE= Option

Use the FILE= option in the PROC FORMS statement to write to an external file that you define in the FILENAME statement. When you use the FILE= option in the PROC FORMS statement, the procedure automatically invokes another option, the ALIGN= option. The ALIGN= option causes PROC FORMS to write rows of *alignment form units* at the beginning of the print file followed by a page break. An alignment form unit is a group of Xs printed the same size as the form units (see Output 26.1). You can use alignment form units to test whether the output from PROC FORMS lines up correctly with the mailing labels.

The default value of the ALIGN= option is 8 rows of alignment form units if the FILE= option is used and 0 if the FILE= option isn't used. However, you can override the default values of the ALIGN= option by specifying it as a part of the PROC FORMS statement. For example, ALIGN=2 specifies 2 rows of alignment form units. Therefore, if you have 4 mailing labels per row, ALIGN=2 prints 8 individual alignment form units.

The following program includes the FILENAME statement and the FILE= option. The FILENAME statement comes before the PROC FORMS statement and associates a fileref called EXTERNAL with *'your-file-name'*, which is the name of a file that follows the naming convention of your computer's operating system. Using the FILE= option in the PROC FORMS statement causes the FORMS procedure to write to the file associated with the fileref EXTERNAL. In

---

*   Some external files, such as print files on IBM mainframe operating systems (for example, RECFM=VBA), require carriage-control characters. To add carriage-control characters to an external file, add the CC option to the PROC FORMS statement. For details, see the *SAS Procedures Guide, Version 6, Third Edition.*

addition, the following program uses the ALIGN= option, which overrides the default value by specifying ALIGN=1. Output 26.1 shows the results.

```
filename external 'your-file-name';

proc forms data=customer.labels file=external align=1;
   line 1 name;
   line 2 street;
   line 3 city state zip;
run;
```

Output 26.1
Mailing Labels:
Routing Output to
an External File

```
xxxxxxxxxxxxxxxxxxxxxxxxxxxxx
xxxxxxxxxxxxxxxxxxxxxxxxxxxxx
xxxxxxxxxxxxxxxxxxxxxxxxxxxxx
Stevenson, Mary K.
22 Meredith Blvd.
Austin,          TX 07611

Weinstein, Joseph M.
Rt. 4, Box 466
Dixon,           IL 17191

Baskowski, Bonnie G.
P. O. Box 42
Sacramento,      CA 26701

Lee, Chen
123 Maple St.
Raleigh,         NC 27408

Abbott, Brenda K.
568 Trillion Ct.
Denver,          CO 37201

Johnson, Lee. R.
P. O. Box 243
Montgomery,      AL 57806

Hawks, Patrick E.
Rt. 1, Box 523
Taylorsville,    WA 68681

Rodriquez, Juan
619 Powell Dr.
Charleston,      SC 71607
```

Improving the Appearance of Mailing Labels

The labels produced in the previous example are easy to produce, and they look acceptable. However, by adding a few simple LINE statement options to the program, you can improve the appearance of the mailing labels. The following sections show you how to reverse the order of last and first names and how to remove unwanted blanks from lines.

Reversing the Order of Last and First Names

So far, the name of each customer has been printed with the last name first as shown in Figure 26.4.

Figure 26.4
Mailing Labels:
Sample Label with
the Last Name
First

The last-name-first format is fine for alphabetical lists, but for mailing labels going to customers, such a format may seem too impersonal. Therefore, you want to use the LASTNAME option, which causes PROC FORMS to print labels in the following form:

FIRSTNAME INITIAL. LASTNAME

So on line one, add a slash (/) and the LASTNAME option after the variable NAME. The revised program follows. Output 26.2 shows the results.

```
proc forms data=customer.labels file=external align=1;
    line 1 name /lastname;
    line 2 street;
    line 3 city state zip;
run;
```

The LASTNAME option reverses the order in which the last names and first names are printed by looking for a comma in character variables. If a comma is found, the words that appear before the comma are switched with the words that appear after the comma, and the comma is dropped.

Output 26.2
Mailing Labels:
Reversing the
Order of First and
Last Names

```
XXXXXXXXXXXXXXXXXXXXXXXXXXXXXX
XXXXXXXXXXXXXXXXXXXXXXXXXXXXXX
XXXXXXXXXXXXXXXXXXXXXXXXXXXXXX

Mary K. Stevenson
22 Meredith Blvd.
Austin,            TX 07611

Joseph M. Weinstein
Rt. 4, Box 466
Dixon,             IL 17191

Bonnie G. Baskowski
P. O. Box 42
Sacramento,        CA 26701

Chen Lee
123 Maple St.
Raleigh,           NC 27408

Brenda K. Abbott
568 Trillion Ct.
Denver,            CO 37201

Lee. R. Johnson
P. O. Box 243
Montgomery,        AL 57806

Patrick E. Hawks
Rt. 1, Box 523
Taylorsville,      WA 68681

Juan Rodriquez
619 Powell Dr.
Charleston,        SC 71607
```

Removing Unwanted Blanks

Another easy way to improve the appearance of the labels is to use the PACK option in the LINE statement to remove extra blanks. For instance, the labels in the previous example contain unnecessary blanks between the variables CITY and STATE. (The blanks are there because the INPUT statement reserved 21 spaces for the variable CITY when the data set was created.) With the PACK option, you can remove the extra blanks so that all the values are separated by only one space.

For example, to remove the extra blanks from line 3, add a slash (/) and the PACK option as a part of the LINE 3 statement. The revised program follows. Output 26.3 shows the results.

```
proc forms data=customer.labels file=external align=1;
    line 1 name/lastname;
    line 2 street;
    line 3 city state zip/pack;
run;
```

Output 26.3
Mailing Labels:
Removing
Unwanted Blanks

```
xxxxxxxxxxxxxxxxxxxxxxxxxxxxxx
xxxxxxxxxxxxxxxxxxxxxxxxxxxxxx
xxxxxxxxxxxxxxxxxxxxxxxxxxxxxx
Mary K. Stevenson
22 Meredith Blvd.
Austin, TX 07611

Joseph M. Weinstein
Rt. 4, Box 466
Dixon, IL 17191

Bonnie G. Baskowski
P. O. Box 42
Sacramento, CA 26701

Chen Lee
123 Maple St.
Raleigh, NC 27408

Brenda K. Abbott
568 Trillion Ct.
Denver, CO 37201

Lee. R. Johnson
P. O. Box 243
Montgomery, AL 57806

Patrick E. Hawks
Rt. 1, Box 523
Taylorsville, WA 68681

Juan Rodriquez
619 Powell Dr.
Charleston, SC 71607
```

Printing Multiple Labels across a Form Page

Not all continuous forms come with one form unit across the form page. For example, mailing labels are often available commercially with two, three, and four labels across the page.

This section shows you how to use the form placement options to make PROC FORMS output match the layout of continuous-feed forms, such as mailing labels with four labels across a form page.

Suppose you have a second box of continuous-feed mailing labels with the following characteristics:

□ The labels begin 2 lines *down* from the top of the page.

□ The labels are *indented* 5 spaces (print positions) from the left margin.

□ Each label has room for up to 4 *lines*.

□ Each label is *wide* enough for up to 25 characters (print positions) per line.

□ There are 4 labels in each row *across* the form page.

□ There are 4 print positions *between* each label.

□ Two lines are *skipped* between each row of labels.

The form layout for these labels is shown in Figure 26.5.

Figure 26.5
*Mailing Labels:
Four across Each
Page*

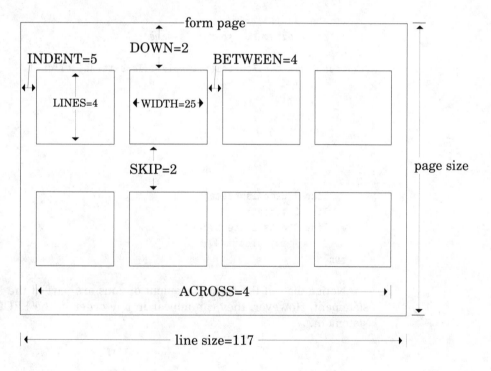

To make the PROC FORMS output print properly on the four-across mailing labels, you need to

□ add an OPTIONS LINESIZE= statement to increase the line size so that it's wide enough to contain all the characters to be printed on one line. You can use the following formula:

$$(INDENT + ((ACROSS-1) * BETWEEN) + (ACROSS * WIDTH)) = LINESIZE$$

In this example, the values are

$$(5 + (3 * 4) + (4 * 25)) = 117 \quad .$$

□ add the following form placement options to the PROC FORMS statement:

    □ DOWN=2

    □ INDENT=5

    □ LINES=4

    □ WIDTH=25

    □ ACROSS=4

    □ BETWEEN=4

    □ SKIP=2.

□ add a fourth LINE statement that contains the ZIP variable and the INDENT= line statement option.

□ remove the ZIP variable from line 3.

The revised program follows. Output 26.4 shows the results.

```
options linesize=117;
filename external 'your-file-name';

proc forms data=customer.labels file=external align=1
     down=2
     indent=5
     lines=4
     width=25
     across=4
     between=4
     skip=2;
   line 1 name/lastname;
   line 2 street;
   line 3 city state/pack;
   line 4 zip/indent=12;
run;
```

Notice that all the form placement options are part of the PROC FORMS statement. However, they can appear in any order in the PROC FORMS statement.

Output 26.4   *Mailing Labels: Using Form Layout Options*

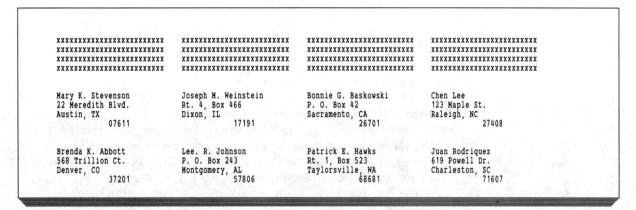

```
xxxxxxxxxxxxxxxxxxxxxxxxx    xxxxxxxxxxxxxxxxxxxxxxxxx    xxxxxxxxxxxxxxxxxxxxxxxxx    xxxxxxxxxxxxxxxxxxxxxxxxx
xxxxxxxxxxxxxxxxxxxxxxxxx    xxxxxxxxxxxxxxxxxxxxxxxxx    xxxxxxxxxxxxxxxxxxxxxxxxx    xxxxxxxxxxxxxxxxxxxxxxxxx
xxxxxxxxxxxxxxxxxxxxxxxxx    xxxxxxxxxxxxxxxxxxxxxxxxx    xxxxxxxxxxxxxxxxxxxxxxxxx    xxxxxxxxxxxxxxxxxxxxxxxxx
xxxxxxxxxxxxxxxxxxxxxxxxx    xxxxxxxxxxxxxxxxxxxxxxxxx    xxxxxxxxxxxxxxxxxxxxxxxxx    xxxxxxxxxxxxxxxxxxxxxxxxx


Mary K. Stevenson           Joseph M. Weinstein          Bonnie G. Baskowski          Chen Lee
22 Meredith Blvd.           Rt. 4, Box 466               P. O. Box 42                 123 Maple St.
Austin, TX                  Dixon, IL                    Sacramento, CA               Raleigh, NC
            07611                        17191                        26701                        27408


Brenda K. Abbott            Lee. R. Johnson              Patrick E. Hawks             Juan Rodriquez
568 Trillion Ct.            P. O. Box 243                Rt. 1, Box 523               619 Powell Dr.
Denver, CO                  Montgomery, AL               Taylorsville, WA             Charleston, SC
            37201                        57806                        68681                        71607
```

Printing Multiple Labels for Each Observation

You can use PROC FORMS to print multiple copies of form units, or mailing labels, with the SETS= option or with the COPIES= option. If you want the entire list repeated as a whole, use the SETS= option. If you want each observation repeated in adjacent form units, use the COPIES= option. You can use these options either separately or together. Figure 26.6 compares the results of using the SETS= option and the COPIES= option.

Figure 26.6
Comparison of SETS= Option and COPIES= Option

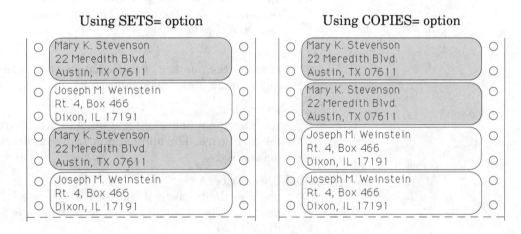

SAS Tools

This chapter discusses the FORMS procedure:

PROC FORMS <DATA=*SAS-data-set*> <*forms-options*>;
   LINE *line-number variables* </ *line-options*>;

PROC FORMS <DATA=*SAS-data-set*> <*forms-options*>;

    starts the FORMS procedure. Use the DATA= option to specify the *SAS-data-set* that contains the variables you specify in the LINE statements. If you omit the DATA= option, PROC FORMS uses the SAS data set created most recently in the SAS job or session.

    You can use the following *form-options* to control the number, placement, and destination of the form in the PROC FORMS statement:

WIDTH=*number*

    specifies the number of horizontal print positions of each form unit. The minimum is 1, the maximum is 255, and the default is 40.

LINES=*number*

    specifies the number of print lines on a form unit. The minimum is 1, the maximum is 200, and the default is the maximum number you specify in LINE statements.

DOWN=*number*

    specifies the number of lines to skip on a form page before printing the first form unit. The minimum is 0, the maximum is 200, and the default is 0.

SKIP=*number*

    specifies the number of lines that separate form units. The minimum is 0, the maximum is 200, and the default is 1.

ACROSS=*number*

    specifies the number of form units to print horizontally across the form page. The minimum is 1, the maximum is 200, and the default is 1.

BETWEEN=*number*

    specifies the number of spaces that separate form units across the page. The minimum is 0, the maximum is 200, and the default is 1.

INDENT=*number*

    specifies the left margin indention of form units. The minimum is 0, the maximum is 200, and the default is 0.

SETS=*number*

    specifies the *number* of copies of the entire list to be printed. This option is different from COPIES=, which prints the multiples in adjacent positions.

COPIES=*number*

    specifies the *number* of copies to be produced for each observation in the input data set. The copies are produced together rather than in separate sets (as in the SETS= option).

ALIGN=*number*
> controls the *number* of rows of alignment form units. The default is 8 if you specify the FILE= option; otherwise it is 0.

FILE=*fileref*
> specifies an external file where PROC FORMS writes the forms. If you don't specify the FILE= option, PROC FORMS uses the SAS print file.

LINE *line-number variables* </ *line-options*>;
> specifies the *line-number* on which the *variables* you designate are to be printed. You can use the following *line-options* in the LINE statement after a slash (/):

LASTNAME
> looks for commas in a character variable containing a name; if a comma is present, the words after the comma are switched with the words before the comma. By default, PROC FORMS doesn't switch names.

PACK
> removes extra blanks from the line so that all the values are separated by one space. By default, PROC FORMS doesn't remove extra blanks.

INDENT=*number*
> specifies that the line is to be indented a certain *number* of characters. This indent is done within the form unit (in contrast to the INDENT= option for the PROC FORMS statement). The default value is 0.

This chapter also discusses the FILENAME statement:

FILENAME *fileref* '*filename*';
> defines a *fileref* or abbreviated name for the file. The filename is the entire definition of the file according to your operating system's conventions.

Learning More

□ Chapter 2, "Introduction to DATA Step Processing," discusses the FILENAME statement.

□ Chapter 36, "Starting, Running, and Exiting the SAS System," and Chapter 37, "Using the SAS Display Manager System: the Basics," provide information on methods of running the SAS System.

□ *SAS Language: Reference, Version 6, First Edition* provides information on the BY statement and indexes. In page-mode operation, you can use a BY statement with PROC FORMS to force new pages to be started when the BY values change. When a BY statement appears, the procedure expects the input data set to be sorted in order of the BY variables. If your input data set isn't sorted in ascending order, use the SORT procedure with a similar

BY statement to sort the data, or, if appropriate, use the BY statement options NOTSORTED or DESCENDING. In addition, you don't need to sort data before using a BY statement if the data set has an index on the variables you specify in the BY statement.

□ The *SAS Procedures Guide, Version 6, Third Edition* describes PROC FORMS in detail.

□ The *SAS Procedures Guide* describes how to run PROC FORMS in page-mode operation.

□ Your computer center staff should be able to provide you with specific details (such as suitable control statements) for handling special forms you may want to use.

At many installations, the operating system automatically skips to a new page after printing a given number of lines. Check with your computer center staff to disable this skip for continuous forms.

Part 7
Producing Plots and Charts

Chapter 27 Plotting the Relationship between Variables

Introduction

Often the clearest way to describe the relationship between variables is to plot their values. The PLOT procedure produces a picture that shows the relationship between variables. This chapter teaches you how to use the PLOT procedure to

□ plot one set of variables

□ enhance the appearance of a plot

□ create multiple plots on separate pages

□ create multiple plots on the same page

□ plot multiple sets of variables on the same pair of axes.

Suppose you want to create a SAS data set containing information about the high and low values of the Dow Jones Industrial Average from 1954 to 1987. You include the following variables in the data set:

YEAR   is the year that the observation describes.

HDATE   is the date on which the Dow Jones reached its highest value during the year.

HIGH   is the value of the Dow Jones on HDATE.

LDATE   is the date on which the Dow Jones reached its lowest value during the year.

LOW   is the value of the Dow Jones on LDATE.

The following program creates the SAS data set STOCKS.HIGHLOW. *
Output 27.1 shows the resulting data set.

```
libname stocks 'your-data-library';

data stocks.highlow;
    infile 'your-input-file';
    input year ∂7 hdate date7. high ∂24 ldate date7. low;
    format hdate ldate date7.;
run;

proc print data=stocks.highlow;
    title 'The SAS Data Set STOCKS.HIGHLOW';
run;
```

Output 27.1
The SAS Data Set
STOCKS.HIGHLOW

```
                        The SAS Data Set STOCKS.HIGHLOW                      1

         OBS    YEAR      HDATE       HIGH       LDATE       LOW

           1    1954    31DEC54     404.39     11JAN54     279.87
           2    1955    30DEC55     488.40     17JAN55     388.20
           3    1956    06APR56     521.05     23JAN56     462.35
           4    1957    12JUL57     520.77     22OCT57     419.79
           5    1958    31DEC58     583.65     25FEB58     436.89
           6    1959    31DEC59     679.36     09FEB59     574.46
           7    1960    05JAN60     685.47     25OCT60     568.05
           8    1961    13DEC61     734.91     03JAN61     610.25
           9    1962    03JAN62     726.01     26JUN62     535.76
          10    1963    18DEC63     767.21     02JAN63     646.79
          11    1964    18NOV64     891.71     02JAN64     768.08
          12    1965    31DEC65     969.26     28JUN65     840.59
          13    1966    09FEB66     995.15     07OCT66     744.32
          14    1967    25SEP67     943.08     03JAN67     786.41
          15    1968    03DEC68     985.21     21MAR68     825.13
          16    1969    14MAY69     968.85     17DEC69     769.93
          17    1970    29DEC70     842.00     06MAY70     631.16
          18    1971    28APR71     950.82     23NOV71     797.97
          19    1972    11DEC72    1036.27     26JAN72     889.15
          20    1973    11JAN73    1051.70     05DEC73     788.31
          21    1974    13MAR74     891.66     06DEC74     577.60
          22    1975    15JUL75     881.81     02JAN75     632.04
          23    1976    21SEP76    1014.79     02JAN76     858.71
          24    1977    03JAN77     999.75     02NOV77     800.85
          25    1978    08SEP78     907.74     28FEB78     742.12
          26    1979    05OCT79     897.61     07NOV79     796.67
          27    1980    20NOV80    1000.17     21APR80     759.13
          28    1981    27APR81    1024.05     25SEP81     824.01
          29    1982    27DEC82    1070.55     12AUG82     776.92
          30    1983    29NOV83    1287.20     03JAN83    1027.04
          31    1984    06JAN84    1286.64     24JUL84    1086.57
          32    1985    16DEC85    1553.10     04JAN85    1184.96
          33    1986    02DEC86    1955.57     22JAN86    1502.29
          34    1987    25AUG87    2722.42     19OCT87    1738.74
```

_____

*   Refer to the Appendix for a complete listing of the input data.

Plotting One Set of Variables

To produce a simple plot of one set of variables, use the following form of the PROC PLOT statement:

> **PROC PLOT** <DATA=*SAS-data-set*>;
>   **PLOT** *vertical*horizontal*;

where

SAS-data-set   is the name of the SAS data set containing the variables you want to plot.

vertical   is the name of the variable to plot on the vertical axis.

horizontal   is the name of the variable to plot on the horizontal axis.

This form of the PLOT procedure automatically selects plotting symbols. It uses the data to determine how to label the axes, how frequently to place tick marks on the axes, and what values to assign to the tick marks. Figure 27.1 shows the axes, values, and tick marks on a plot.

Figure 27.1
Diagram of Axes, Values, and Tick Marks

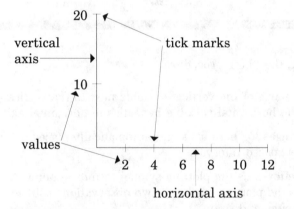

To produce a simple plot showing the trend in high Dow Jones values from 1954 to 1987, use the following program. Output 27.2 shows the plot.

```
options pagesize=40 linesize=76;

proc plot data=stocks.highlow;
   plot high*year;
run;
```

Note: All output in this chapter is created with the page size set to 40 and the line size set to 76 in the OPTIONS statement. Once you set the PAGESIZE= and LINESIZE= options, they remain in effect until you reset them or end the SAS session. Therefore, the OPTIONS statement appears in this example but not in subsequent ones.

Output 27.2
Default Plot for
HIGH versus
YEAR

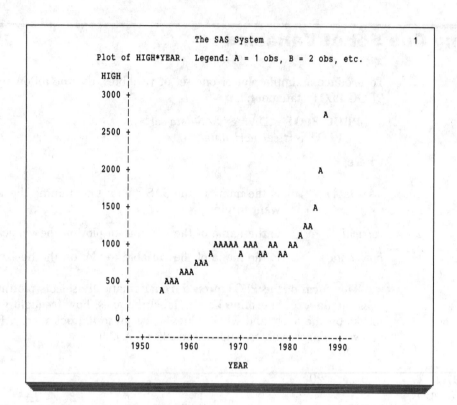

By default, the PLOT procedure

□ prints the name of the vertical variable next to the vertical axis and the name of the horizontal variable beneath the horizontal axis

□ chooses ranges for both axes and automatically places tick marks at reasonably spaced intervals

□ uses the letter A as the plotting symbol to indicate one observation; the letter B as the plotting symbol if two observations coincide; the letter C if three coincide, and so on

□ prints a legend naming the variables in the plot and explaining the plotting symbols.

While this plot conveys the trend in the high Dow Jones value over the years, you can present the information more clearly. The following sections describe how to enhance the plot to increase its effectiveness.

Adding Titles and Labels to a Plot

Add titles and labels to a plot by using TITLE and LABEL statements. The following program adds a title to the output and uses labels for the variables HIGH and YEAR. Output 27.3 shows the plot. Notice that PROC PLOT centers the title across the top of the plot and centers the label for each variable parallel to its axis.

```
        proc plot data=stocks.highlow;
           plot high*year;
           title 'Dow Jones Industrial Average';
           label high='Highest Value'
                 year='Year';
        run;
```

Output 27.3
Adding a Title and
a Label to the
Default Plot

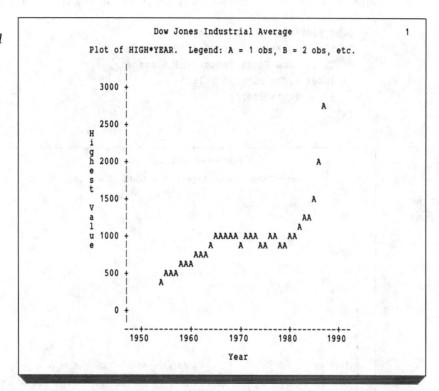

Specifying Values for Tick Marks

In the plots you have seen so far, the range on the horizontal axis is 1950 to 1990. Tick marks and their labels appear every ten years. You can control the selection of the range and the interval on the horizontal axis with the HAXIS= option in the PLOT statement. A corresponding PLOT statement option, VAXIS=, controls tick mark selection on the vertical axis.

The forms of the HAXIS= and VAXIS= options follow. You must precede the first option in a PLOT statement with a slash.

PLOT *vertical*horizontal* / HAXIS=*tick-value-list*;
PLOT *vertical*horizontal* / VAXIS=*tick-value-list*;

where *tick-value-list* is a list of all values to assign to tick marks.

For example, you can specify tick marks every five years from 1950 to 1990 with the following option:

```
haxis=1950 1955 1960 1965 1970 1975 1980 1985 1990
```

Or, you can abbreviate the list of tick marks like this:

```
haxis=1950 to 1990 by 5
```

The following program incorporates the HAXIS= option into the example. Output 27.4 shows the plot. Note that the tick marks on the horizontal axis now appear at five-year intervals, as specified in the HAXIS= option.

```
proc plot data=stocks.highlow;
    plot high*year / haxis=1950 to 1990 by 5;
    title 'Dow Jones Industrial Average';
    label high='Highest Value'
          year='Year';
run;
```

Output 27.4
Controlling the
Range and
Intervals on the
Horizontal Axis

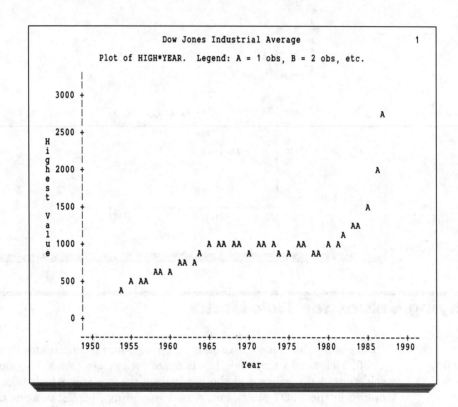

Specifying Plotting Symbols

By default, PROC PLOT uses the letter A as the plotting symbol to indicate one observation, the letter B as the plotting symbol if two observations coincide, the letter C if three coincide, and so on. The letter Z represents 26 or more coinciding observations.

In many instances, particularly if you are plotting two sets of data on the same pair of axes, you use the following form of the PLOT statement to specify your own plotting symbols:

PLOT *vertical* *horizontal='*symbol*';

For example, to specify an asterisk as the plotting symbol for the plot of HIGH versus YEAR, make the following modification to the program. Note that you must enclose the plotting symbol in single or double quotes. Output 27.5 shows the plot.

```
proc plot data=stocks.highlow;
    plot high*year='*' / haxis=1950 to 1990 by 5;
    title 'Dow Jones Industrial Average';
    label high='Highest Value'
          year='Year';
run;
```

Output 27.5
Specifying a
Plotting Symbol

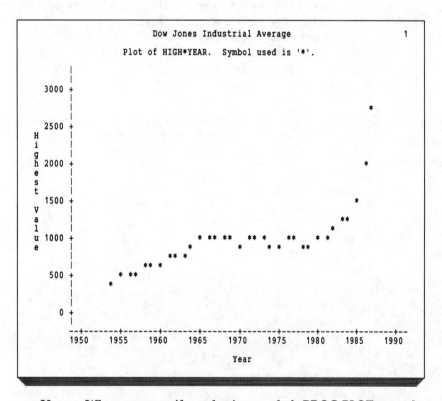

Note: When you specify a plotting symbol, PROC PLOT uses that symbol for all points on the plot regardless of how many observations may coincide. If observations coincide, a message appears at the bottom of the plot telling you how many observations are hidden.

Creating Multiple Plots on Separate Pages

If you want to compare the performance of the low Dow Jones value to the high value, you need two plots. To request more than one plot from the same SAS data set, simply specify additional sets of variables in the following form of the PLOT statement:

PLOT *vertical-1*horizontal-1 vertical-2*horizontal-2*;

All options you list in a PLOT statement apply to all plots the statement produces.

The following program shows how to produce separate plots of the highest and the lowest values of the Dow Jones Industrial Average over the years from 1950 to 1990. Output 27.6 shows the plots.

```
proc plot data=stocks.highlow;
    plot high*year='*' low*year='o' / haxis=1950 to 1990 by 5;
    title 'Dow Jones Industrial Average';
    label high='Highest Value'
          low='Lowest Value'
          year='Year';
run;
```

Output 27.6
Creating Multiple Plots, on Separate Pages

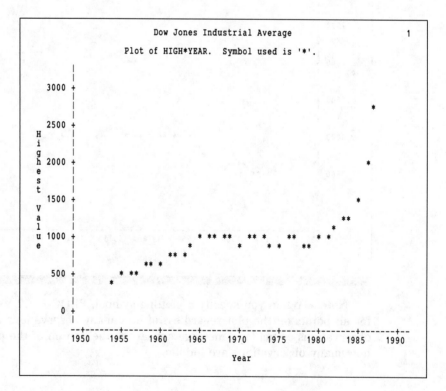

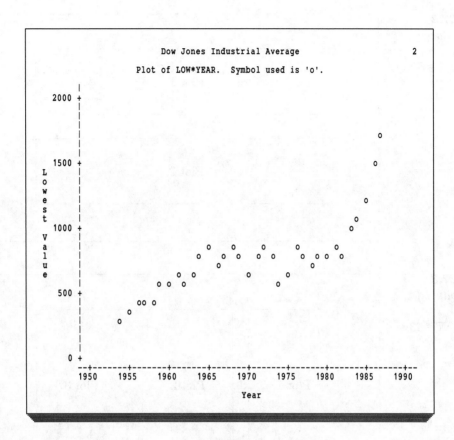

Creating Multiple Plots on the Same Page

You can more easily compare the trends in the high and low Dow Jones values if the two plots appear on the same page. PROC PLOT provides two options that print multiple plots on the same page: the VPERCENT= option and the HPERCENT= option. You can specify these options in the PROC PLOT statement, using one of the following forms:

PROC PLOT <DATA=*SAS-data-set*> VPERCENT=*number*;
PROC PLOT <DATA=*SAS-data-set*> HPERCENT=*number*;

where *number* is the percent of the vertical or horizontal page to give each plot. You can use the aliases VPCT= and HPCT= for these options.

To fit two plots on a page, one beneath the other as in Figure 27.2, use VPERCENT=50; to fit three plots, use VPERCENT=33; and so on. To fit two plots on a page, side by side, use HPERCENT=50; to fit three plots as in Figure 27.3, use HPERCENT=33; and so on. Figure 27.4 illustrates using both of these options in the same PLOT statement. Because the VPERCENT= option and the HPERCENT= option appear in the PROC PLOT statement, they affect all plots created in the PROC PLOT step.

Figure 27.2
Plots Produced
with
VPERCENT=50

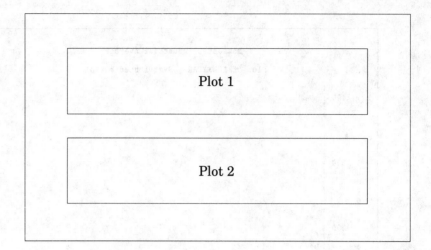

Figure 27.3
Plots Produced
with
HPERCENT=33

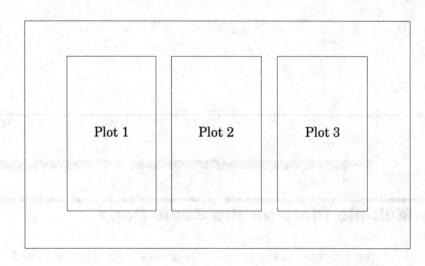

Figure 27.4
Plots Produced
with
VPERCENT=50
and
HPERCENT=33

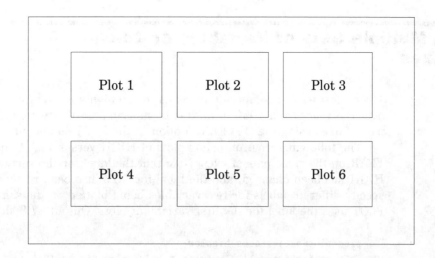

To print both plots in Output 27.6 on the same page, one beneath the other, use the following program. Output 27.7 shows the plot.

```
proc plot data=stocks.highlow vpercent=50 ;
   plot high*year='*' low*year='o' / haxis=1950 to 1990 by 5;
   title 'Dow Jones Industrial Average';
   label high='Highest Value'
         low='Lowest value'
         year='Year';
run;
```

Output 27.7
Creating Multiple
Plots on the Same
Page

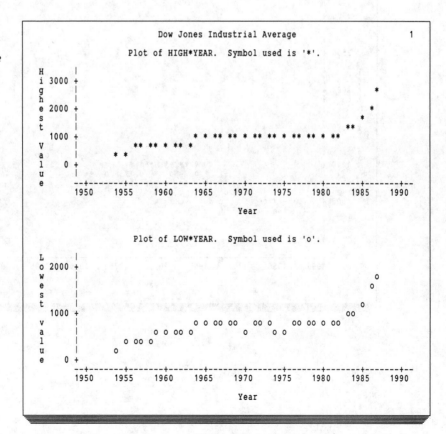

Plotting Multiple Sets of Variables on the Same Axes

The easiest way to compare the trends in the high and low Dow Jones values over the years from 1950 to 1990 is to superimpose the two plots on the same pair of axes using the OVERLAY option in the PLOT statement.

The following program prints plots of HIGH versus YEAR and LOW versus YEAR on the same pair of axes. Note that the label for the vertical variable HIGH has been changed, and the label for LOW has been removed. If you specify different labels for two variables being plotted on the same axis, PROC PLOT uses the label for the first variable it plots. Output 27.8 shows the plot.

```
proc plot data=stocks.highlow;
    plot high*year='*' low*year='o' / haxis=1950 to 1990 by 5
                                       overlay;
    title 'Dow Jones Industrial Average';
    label high='High or Low'
          year='Year';
run;
```

Output 27.8
Overlaying Two
Plots

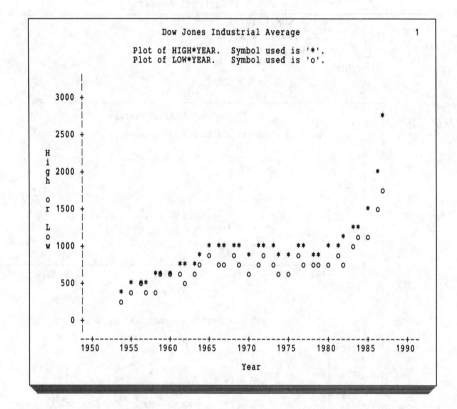

Removing the Legend and Boxing the Output

You can make a few simple changes to the plot in Output 27.8 to improve its appearance. This section shows you how to draw a box around the plot and remove the legend generated by PROC PLOT. The legend is superfluous when the labels clearly identify the variables in the plot and when the association between the plotting symbols and the variables is clear.

To draw a box around the output, use the BOX option in the PLOT statement. To remove the legend, use the NOLEGEND option in the PROC PLOT statement. The following program produces the plot in Output 27.9.

```
proc plot data=stocks.highlow nolegend;
    plot high*year='*' low*year='o' / haxis=1950 to 1990 by 5
                                      overlay box;
    title 'Dow Jones Industrial Average';
    label high='High or Low'
          year='Year';
run;
```

Output 27.9
Removing the
Legend and
Boxing the Output

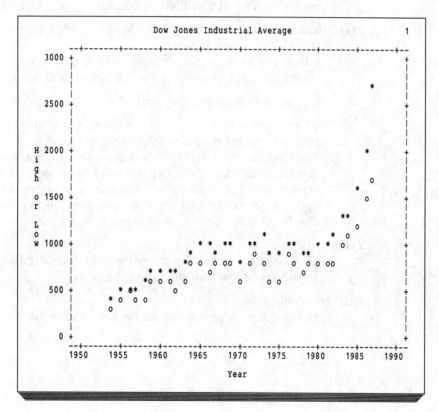

SAS Tools

This chapter discusses the PLOT procedure:

PROC PLOT <DATA=*SAS-data-set*> <VPERCENT=*number*>
        <HPERCENT=*number*> <NOLEGEND>;
  PLOT *request-list* </ <HAXIS=*tick-value-list*> <VAXIS=*tick-value-list*>
      <OVERLAY> <BOX>>;
  TITLE '*title*';
  LABEL *variable*='*label*';

PROC PLOT <DATA=*SAS-data-set*> <VPERCENT=*number*>
        <HPERCENT=*number*> <NOLEGEND>;
        starts the PLOT procedure. The DATA= option specifies the *SAS-data-set*
        containing the variables you want to plot. If you omit the DATA=
        option, the PLOT procedure uses the SAS data set created most recently
        in the current job or session. The VPERCENT= and HPERCENT=
        options determine how many plots appear on a page. The value of
        number is the percentage of the vertical or horizontal space to give to
        each plot. The NOLEGEND option suppresses the default legend.

PLOT *request-list* </ <HAXIS=*tick-value-list*> <VAXIS=*tick-value-list*>
      <OVERLAY> <BOX>>;
        allows you to request individual plots in the *request-list* in the PLOT
        statement. Each element in the list has the following form:

            vertical*horizontal<='*symbol*'>

        where *vertical* and *horizontal* are the names of the variables that appear
        on the axes and *symbol* is the character to use for all points on the plot.
        The HAXIS= and VAXIS= options determine the range of the variables
        and the frequency of the tick marks on each axis. Each *tick-value-list*
        consists of a list of all values to use for tick marks. The OVERLAY
        option superimposes all the plots requested on the same pair of axes.
        The BOX option draws a box around the output.

  TITLE '*title*';
        places a *title* you specify above the default description of the plot and the
        legend that appear on the top of the page.

  LABEL *variable*='*label*';
        replaces the *variable* name on the axes with a *label* you specify.

Learning More

□ Chapter 28, "Charting the Values of a Variable," describes how to make a variety of charts using the CHART procedure. When you are preparing graphics presentations, some data lend themselves to plots, while other data are better suited for charts.

□ The *SAS Procedures Guide, Version 6, Third Edition* describes many more ways to use the PLOT procedure to tailor your output to suit your needs. For example, you can

   □ produce contour plots

   □ draw reference lines on your plots

   □ change the characters used to draw the borders of the plot.

□ The *SAS Procedures Guide* describes using PROC PLOT as an interactive procedure. Once you issue the PROC PLOT statement, you can continue to submit any statements that are valid with the procedure without resubmitting the PROC statement. Therefore, you can easily and quickly experiment with changing labels, values for tick marks, and so on. Any options you submit in the PROC PLOT statement remain in effect until you resubmit the statement.

□ *SAS/GRAPH Software: Reference, Version 6, First Edition* provides complete documentation on using SAS/GRAPH software. If your site has SAS/GRAPH software, you can use the GPLOT, G3D, and GCONTOUR procedures to take advantage of the high-resolution graphics capabilities of output devices to produce plots that include color, different fonts, and text.

414

Chapter **28** Charting the Values of a Variable

Introduction

Charts, like plots, provide a way of presenting data graphically. You can use a chart to show the values of a single variable or several variables.

This chapter shows you how to use the CHART procedure to make

☐ vertical and horizontal bar charts

☐ pie charts

☐ block charts

The charts produced here range in complexity from simple frequency bar charts to more complex charts that group variables and include simple descriptive statistics.

Suppose you are the instructor of an introductory chemistry course. Fifty students are enrolled in the class. All students attend lectures, and each student attends a discussion section one day a week. You have data about each student that you want to put into a SAS data set using the following variables:

NAME   is the student's last name (and first initial if necessary).

SEX   is an F or an M indicating the student's sex.

SECTION   is the day of the week of the student's discussion section (Mon, Wed, or Fri).

GRADE   is the student's grade on the first exam.

Use the following program to create the SAS data set INTRCHEM.GRADES.*
Output 28.1 shows the data set.

```
options pagesize=60;
libname intrchem 'your-data-library';

data intrchem.grades;
   infile 'your-data-source';
   input name $ 1-14 sex $ 15 section $ 17-19 grade;
run;

proc print data=intrchem.grades;
   title 'The SAS Data Set INTRCHEM.GRADES';
run;
```

Note: Most output in this chapter is created with the page size set to 40 and the line size set to 76 in the OPTIONS statement. An OPTIONS statement appears in any example using a different line size or page size. Once you set the PAGESIZE= and LINESIZE= options, they remain in effect until you reset them or end the SAS session.

Output 28.1
The Data Set
INTRCHEM.GRADES

```
                  The SAS Data Set INTRCHEM.GRADES                      1

        OBS     NAME          SEX     SECTION     GRADE

          1     Abdallah       F       Mon          46
          2     Anderson       M       Wed          75
          3     Aziz           F       Wed          67
          4     Bayer          M       Wed          77
          5     Black          M       Fri          79
          6     Blair          F       Fri          70
          7     Blue           F       Mon          63
          8     Brown          M       Wed          58
          9     Bush           F       Mon          63
         10     Chung          M       Wed          85
         11     Davis          F       Fri          89
         12     Drew           F       Mon          49
         13     DuPont         M       Mon          41
         14     Elliott        F       Wed          85
         15     Farmer         F       Wed          58
         16     Franklin       F       Wed          59
         17     Freeman        F       Mon          79
         18     Friedman       M       Mon          58
         19     Gabriel        M       Fri          75
         20     Grant          M       Mon          79
         21     Harding        M       Mon          49
         22     Hazelton       M       Mon          55
         23     Hinton         M       Fri          85
```

---
* Refer to the Appendix for a complete listing of the input data.

```
        24    Hope         F      Fri       98
        25    Jackson      F      Wed       64
        26    Janeway      F      Wed       51
        27    Jones K      F      Mon       39
        28    Jones M      M      Mon       63
        29    Judson       F      Fri       89
        30    Keller       F      Mon       89
        31    LeBlanc      F      Fri       70
        32    Lee          M      Fri       48
        33    Litowski     M      Fri       85
        34    Malloy       M      Wed       79
        35    Meyer        F      Fri       85
        36    Nichols      M      Mon       58
        37    Oliver       F      Mon       41
        38    Parker       F      Mon       77
        39    Patton       M      Wed       73
        40    Randleman    F      Wed       46
        41    Robinson     M      Fri       64
        42    Shien        M      Wed       55
        43    Simonson     M      Wed       62
        44    Smith N      M      Wed       71
        45    Smith R      M      Mon       79
        46    Sullivan     M      Fri       77
        47    Swift        M      Wed       63
        48    Wolfe        F      Fri       79
        49    Wolfson      F      Fri       89
        50    Zabriski     M      Fri       89
```

You want to use this data set to

□ describe the distribution of grades

□ assign a letter grade to each student

□ compare the number of students in each section

□ compare the number of males and females in each section

□ compare the performance of the students in different sections.

The following sections show you how to perform these tasks using PROC CHART.

Using the CHART Procedure

The form of PROC CHART used in this chapter is

PROC CHART <DATA=*SAS-data-set*>;
    chart-type variable-list <*option-list*>;

where

SAS-data-set	is the name of the *SAS-data-set* containing variables you want to chart.
chart-type	specifies the kind of chart and can be VBAR, HBAR, BLOCK, or PIE.
variable-list	is a list of variables to chart (called the *chart variables*).
option-list	is a list of options.

The *chart-type, variable-list,* and *option-list* make up a *chart statement.* You can use any number of chart statements in one PROC CHART step. A list of options pertains to a single chart statement.

Charting Frequencies

By default, PROC CHART creates a frequency chart in which each bar, section, or block in the chart represents a range of values. By default, PROC CHART selects ranges based on the values of the chart variable. At the center of each range is a *midpoint.* A midpoint may or may not correspond to an actual value of the chart variable in an observation. The size of each bar, block, or section represents the number of observations that fall in that range.

PROC CHART makes several different types of charts. The shape of each type emphasizes a certain aspect of the data. The type you choose depends on the nature of your data and the aspect you want to emphasize.

Creating Vertical Bar Charts

A vertical bar chart emphasizes individual ranges. The differences in the heights of the bars clearly indicate which ranges contain many observations and which contain only a few.

Use the VBAR statement in the following program to create a vertical bar frequency chart of the variable GRADE. Output 28.2 shows the frequency chart.

```
libname intrchem 'your-data-library';

proc chart data=intrchem.grades;
   vbar grade;
   title 'Vertical Bar Chart';
run;
```

When you use the VBAR statement without any options, PROC CHART automatically

□ labels the axes

□ selects midpoints and ranges

□ places tick marks on the vertical axis based on the ranges it selects.

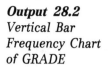

Output 28.2
Vertical Bar
Frequency Chart
of GRADE

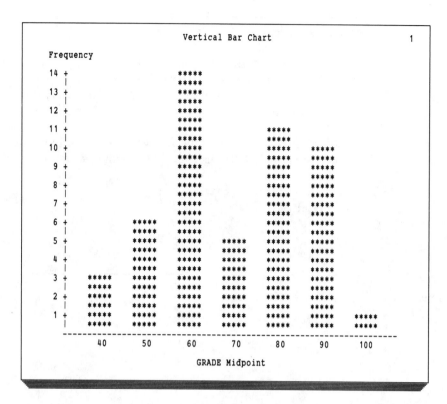

In the preceding example, which charts a numeric variable, PROC CHART selects midpoints ranging from 40 to 100 at intervals of 10. The corresponding ranges are 35 to 44, 45 to 54, 55 to 64, and so on.

Note: Because PROC CHART selects the size of the ranges and the location of their midpoints based on all values of the chart variable, the highest and lowest ranges used in charting a numeric variable often extend beyond the values in the data. For instance, in this example the lowest grade is 39 and the lowest range extends from 35 to 44. Similarly, the highest grade is 98 and the highest range extends from 95 to 104.

If you are charting a character variable, PROC CHART creates a bar for each value of the chart variable.

PROC CHART makes similar decisions for you when you create frequency charts of differing shapes.

Creating Pie Charts

Pie charts emphasize the relationship of each range to the whole. Charting the distribution of grades as a pie chart shows you the size of each range relative to the others just as the vertical bar chart does. However, the pie chart also shows you at a glance how the number of grades in a range compares to the total number of grades.

Use the PIE statement in the following program to create a pie frequency chart of the variable GRADE. Output 28.3 shows the pie chart.

```
proc chart data=intrchem.grades;
   pie grade;
   title 'Pie Chart';
run;
```

Output 28.3
*Pie Frequency
Chart of GRADE*

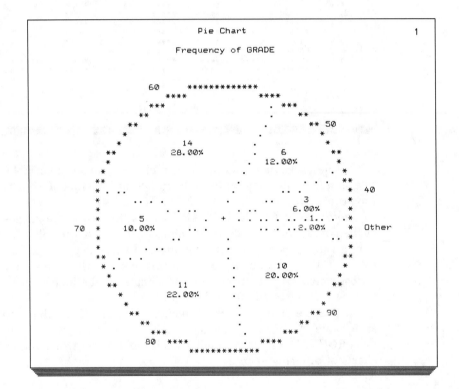

The number of sections in a pie chart corresponds to the number of bars in a vertical bar chart, with one exception. When creating a pie chart, PROC CHART combines all very small sections into one section called "other." In this sample chart the "other" section represents the one grade in the range with a midpoint of 100. The size of a section corresponds to the number of observations that fall in its range.

PROC CHART prints the values of the midpoints around the perimeter of the pie chart. Inside each section of the chart, PROC CHART prints both the number of observations that have values in the range represented by that section and the percent of observations represented by that number.

Creating Block Charts

A block chart is similar to a vertical bar chart in its emphasis on individual ranges; however, a block chart offers a more elegant presentation of the data. On the other hand, a block chart is less precise than a bar chart because the maximum height of a block is ten lines.

Use the BLOCK statement to create a block frequency chart of the variable GRADE. Note that in this case you must also increase the line size to 120. Output 28.4 shows the block chart.

```
options linesize=120;

proc chart data=intrchem.grades;
   block grade;
   title 'Block Chart';
run;
```

Once again, PROC CHART selects the same midpoints. The procedure prints the midpoints beneath the chart and the number of observations represented by each block beneath the block. The height of a block is proportional to this number.

Block charts are also used to create three-dimensional charts (see "Creating a Three-Dimensional Chart" later in this chapter).

Output 28.4   *Block Frequency Chart of GRADE*

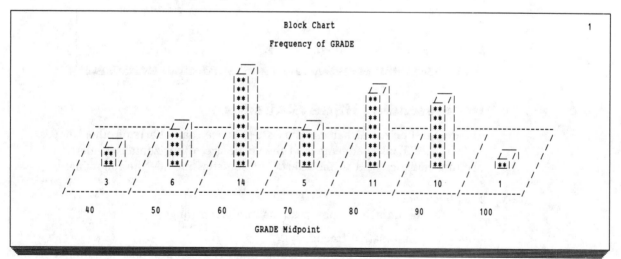

Note: If either the line size or the page size is insufficient for the procedure to create a block chart, PROC CHART creates a horizontal bar chart instead. The procedure sends a message to your SAS log telling you what happened.

Creating a Horizontal Bar Chart

A horizontal bar chart is similar to a vertical bar chart that is turned on its side: that is, the horizontal axis is frequency, and the vertical axis is the chart variable. Like a vertical bar chart, a horizontal bar chart emphasizes individual ranges. However, by default, PROC CHART displays some statistics with a horizontal bar chart that can help you understand the data.

Use the HBAR statement to create a horizontal bar chart of the frequency of the variable GRADE. Output 28.5 shows the horizontal bar chart. The following section explains the statistics.

```
proc chart data=intrchem.grades;
   hbar grade;
   title 'Horizontal Bar Chart';
run;
```

Output 28.5
Horizontal Bar
Frequency Chart
of GRADE

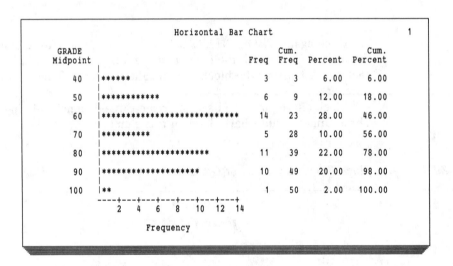

Understanding HBAR Statistics

The default horizontal bar chart uses less space than charts of other shapes. PROC CHART takes advantage of the small size of horizontal bar charts by printing statistics next to the chart. The statistics include the following:

Freq (frequency)
> is the number of observations in a given range.

Cum. Freq (cumulative frequency)
> is the number of observations in all ranges up to and including a given range. The cumulative frequency for the last range is equal to the number of observations in the data set.

Percent
> is the percentage of observations in a given range.

Cum. Percent (cumulative percent)
> is the percentage of observations in all ranges up to and including a given range. The cumulative percentage for the last range is always 100.

In the preceding example, the cumulative percent shows that the median grade for this exam (the grade that 50% of observations lie above and 50% below) lies in the range that has 70 as its midpoint.

Selecting or Removing Statistics

You may want to display only some of the available statistics with your horizontal bar chart, or you may want to remove them altogether. You can use the following options to select the statistics you want: FREQ, CFREQ, PERCENT, and CPERCENT. Each option selects the corresponding statistic. If you use one or more of these options, PROC CHART prints only the statistics you request. The NOSTAT option eliminates all statistics.

The following program produces the same horizontal bar chart as the previous one, but it eliminates all statistics. Output 28.6 shows the chart.

Note: If you use any options in a chart statement, put a slash before the first option.

```
proc chart data=intrchem.grades;
   hbar grade / nostat;
   title 'Removing Statistics from a Horizontal Bar Chart';
run;
```

Output 28.6
Removing
Statistics with the
NOSTAT Option

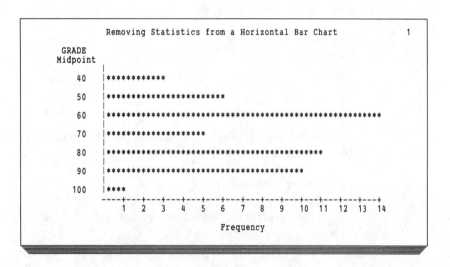

Changing the Number of Ranges

Suppose you want to use the charts of the variable GRADE to assign letter grades. If you look at any of the bar charts of GRADE, you see that the bars don't form the type of curve normally used when assigning grades. You can change the appearance of the charts by

□ using the MIDPOINTS= option to specify midpoints in the middle of the traditional grade ranges, that is, 95 for an A, 85 for a B, and so on

□ using the LEVELS= option to specify the number of bars on the chart (one for each letter grade) and letting PROC CHART select the midpoints.

Note: Most of the remaining examples in this chapter use vertical bar charts. However, unless the text states otherwise, you can use all options shown in the examples with PIE, BLOCK, and HBAR statements.

Specifying Midpoints for a Numeric Variable

To specify midpoints for a numeric variable, use the MIDPOINTS= option in the chart statement. The form of this option is

VBAR *variable* / MIDPOINTS=*midpoints-list*;

where *midpoints-list* is a list of the numbers to use as midpoints.

For example, you can specify the traditional grading ranges with midpoints from 55 to 95, with the following option:

```
midpoints=55 65 75 85 95
```

Or, you can abbreviate this list of midpoints like this:

```
midpoints=55 to 95 by 10
```

The corresponding ranges are

```
50 to 59
60 to 69
70 to 79
80 to 89
90 to 99
```

The following program incorporates the MIDPOINTS= option into the example. Output 28.7 shows the chart.

```
proc chart data=intrchem.grades;
   vbar grade / midpoints=55 to 95 by 10;
   title 'Specifying Your Own Midpoints';
run;
```

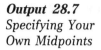

Output 28.7
Specifying Your
Own Midpoints

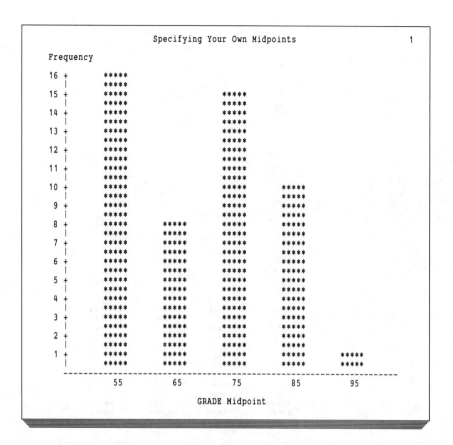

The MIDPOINTS= option forces PROC CHART to center the bars around the traditional midpoints for grades. However, if you assign grades based on these midpoints and the traditional pass/fail boundary of 60, a substantial portion of the class will fail the exam because more observations fall in the bar around the midpoint of 55 than in any other bar.

Specifying the Number of Midpoints in a Chart

Given that you will fail a large number of students if you use the traditional grading ranges, you may prefer to assign the grades a different way. The LEVELS= option allows you to specify the number of midpoints you want in the chart rather than the values of the midpoints. The procedure selects the midpoints.

The form of the option is

VBAR *variable* / LEVELS=*number-of-midpoints*;

where *number-of-midpoints* specifies the number of midpoints.

The following program creates a bar chart with five bars. Output 28.8 shows the bar chart. If you assign grades based on the chart in Output 28.8, only three students will fail.*

```
proc chart data=intrchem.grades;
   vbar grade / levels=5;
   title 'Specifying Five Midpoints';
run;
```

Output 28.8
Specifying Five
Midpoints

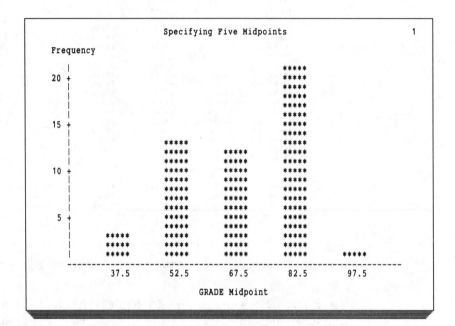

PROC CHART typically produces bars that represent more than one value of the numeric variable. For instance, in Output 28.8 the middle bar represents all grades between 60 and 74. If you want to create a frequency chart that has a bar for every value of the variable GRADE, add the DISCRETE option to the VBAR statement. Output 28.9 shows the chart.

Charting Every Value

```
proc chart data=intrchem.grades;
   vbar grade / discrete;
   title 'Specifying a Bar for Each Value of GRADE';
run;
```

---

*   You may want to normalize your data before creating this chart.

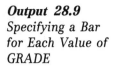

Output 28.9
Specifying a Bar
for Each Value of
GRADE

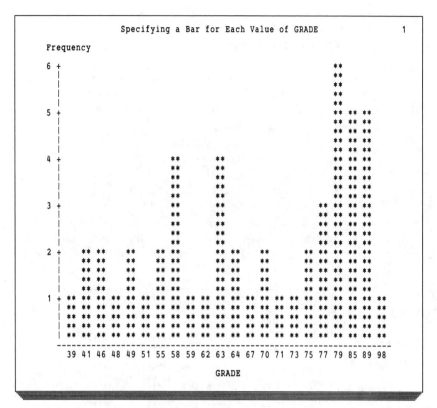

The chart shows that in most cases only one or two students earned a given grade. However, clusters of three or more students earned grades of 58, 63, 77, 79, 85, and 89. The most frequently earned grade was 79.

Charting the Frequency of a Character Variable

So far, all the examples in this chapter have created charts of the numeric variable GRADE. You can also create charts of a character variable. For instance, if you want to compare enrollment among sections, you can create a chart showing the number of students in each section.

The most important difference between charting a numeric variable and charting a character variable is how PROC CHART selects the midpoints. By default, PROC CHART uses each value of a character variable as a midpoint, as if the DISCRETE option were in effect. You can limit the selection of midpoints (see "Specifying Midpoints for a Character Variable" later in this chapter) to a subset of the variable's values, but, unless you define a format for the chart variable, a single bar, block, or section represents a single value of the variable.

Creating the Default Frequency Chart

Creating a frequency chart of a character variable is the same as creating a frequency chart of a numeric variable. To create a vertical bar chart showing the number of students in each section, use the following program. Output 28.10 shows the frequency chart.

```
proc chart data=intrchem.grades;
   vbar section;
   title 'Frequency Chart for SECTION';
run;
```

The chart in Output 28.10 shows that the Monday and Wednesday sections have the same number of students; the Friday section has one fewer student.

Output 28.10
Default Frequency Chart for the Character Variable SECTION

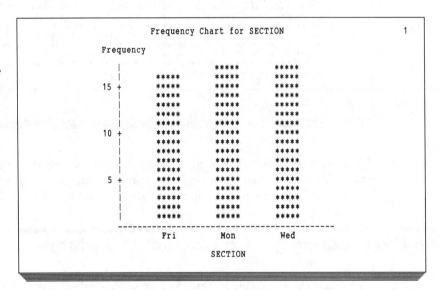

By default, when PROC CHART prints midpoints for character variables, it prints them in alphabetical order. However, you can easily rearrange the order of the midpoints.

Specifying Midpoints for a Character Variable

If you don't want all values of the variable in the chart or if you don't want the values printed in alphabetical order, use the MIDPOINTS= option. When you use the MIDPOINTS= option for character variables, you must enclose the value of each midpoint in single or double quotes, and the values must match values in the data set. Therefore, to alter the chart in Output 28.10 so that the days of the week appear in chronological rather than alphabetical order, add the MIDPOINTS= option to the VBAR statement. Output 28.11 shows the chart.

```
proc chart data=intrchem.grades;
   vbar section / midpoints='Mon' 'Wed' 'Fri';
   title 'Specifying Midpoints for a Character Variable';
run;
```

Output 28.11
Placing Character
Midpoints in
Chronological
Order

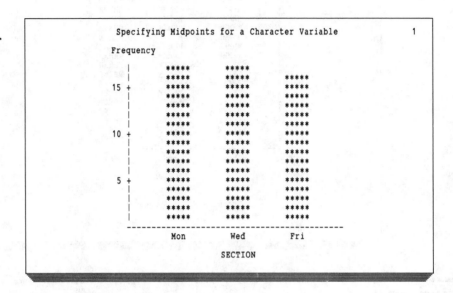

Creating Subgroups within a Range

You can use the SUBGROUP= option to show how a subgroup contributes to each bar or block. For example, you might want to explore patterns in enrollment within the population count. Using the SUBGROUP= option, you can show how many members of each section are male and how many are female.

The SUBGROUP= option defines a variable called the *subgroup variable*. PROC CHART fills each bar or block with characters that show the contribution of each value of the subgroup variable to the total. Each fill character is the first character of one of the values of the subgroup variable. If the variable is formatted, PROC CHART uses the first character of the formatted value. (The PIE statement doesn't support this option.)

The following program defines SEX as the subgroup variable. Output 28.12 shows the chart.

```
proc chart data=intrchem.grades;
   vbar section / midpoints='Mon' 'Wed' 'Fri'
               subgroup=sex;
   title 'Charting with a Subgroup';
run;
```

In Output 28.12 each bar in the chart is filled with the characters representing the value of the variable SEX. The portion of the bar filled with Fs represents the number of observations for which the value of SEX is **F**; the portion filled with Ms represents the number for which the value of SEX is **M**.

Because the value of SEX is a single character (F or M), the symbol used as the fill character is identical to the value of the variable.

Output 28.12
Frequency Chart
of SECTION with
Subgrouping by
SEX

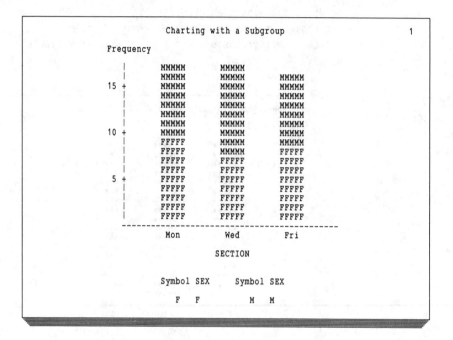

```
                              Charting with a Subgroup                        1

            Frequency
                    |
                    |   MMMMM         MMMMM
                    |   MMMMM         MMMMM
                 15 +   MMMMM         MMMMM         MMMMM
                    |   MMMMM         MMMMM         MMMMM
                    |   MMMMM         MMMMM         MMMMM
                    |   MMMMM         MMMMM         MMMMM
                    |   MMMMM         MMMMM         MMMMM
                 10 +   MMMMM         MMMMM         MMMMM
                    |   FFFFF         MMMMM         MMMMM
                    |   FFFFF         MMMMM         FFFFF
                    |   FFFFF         FFFFF         FFFFF
                    |   FFFFF         FFFFF         FFFFF
                  5 +   FFFFF         FFFFF         FFFFF
                    |   FFFFF         FFFFF         FFFFF
                    |   FFFFF         FFFFF         FFFFF
                    |   FFFFF         FFFFF         FFFFF
                    |   FFFFF         FFFFF         FFFFF
                    ---------------------------------------------
                         Mon           Wed           Fri

                                     SECTION


                          Symbol SEX      Symbol SEX

                            F    F          M    M
```

Grouping Bars

You may find it more effective to create a separate bar for each subgroup. The GROUP= option defines a variable called the *group variable*. PROC CHART creates a set of bars or blocks for each value of this variable. (The PIE statement doesn't support this option.) For example, you can use the GROUP= option to produce

□ a chart showing two groups of SECTION data: one group for males and one group for females. In this case, you group the values of SECTION by their values of SEX.

□ a chart showing three groups of SEX data: one group for the Monday section, one group for the Wednesday section, and one group for the Friday section. In this case, you group the values of SEX by their values of SECTION.

For instance, the first VBAR statement in the following program requests a set of bars for SECTION for each value of the group variable, SEX. The second VBAR statement, which swaps the chart and group variables, requests a set of bars for SEX for each value of SECTION. Output 28.13 shows the charts.

```
proc chart data=intrchem.grades;
    vbar section / midpoints='Mon' 'Wed' 'Fri'
                  group=sex;
    vbar sex     / group=section;
    title 'Comparison of Grouping SECTION by SEX';
    title2 'to grouping SEX by SECTION';
run;
```

Output 28.13
Grouping
Variables in Two
Different Ways;
Using the
GROUP= Option

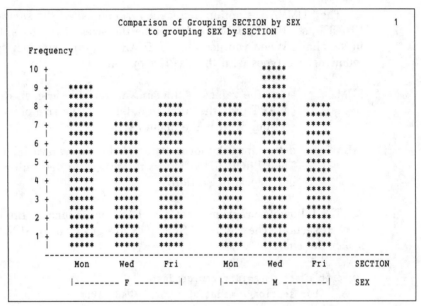

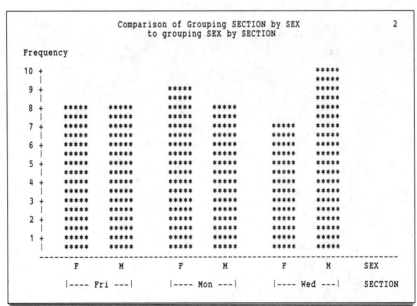

Note: PROC CHART displays groups in alphabetical order. Therefore, the days of the week in Output 28.13 aren't chronological. By creating formats with leading blanks for Monday and Wednesday, you can force the output to be chronological because the sorting order is then ' Mon', ' Wed', 'Fri'.

Charting Sums and Means

Suppose that instead of comparing the number of students in each section you want to compare the grades of the students in each section. In this case, you want the size of a bar, block, or pie section to correspond not to the number of observations in the range, but to the values for the variable GRADE in those observations.

The SUMVAR= option defines a variable called the *sumvar variable*. PROC CHART uses this variable to determine the sizes of the bars, blocks, or sections in the chart. When you use the SUMVAR= option, you can specify one of the following two types with the TYPE= option:

SUM   sums the values of the sumvar variable in each range. Then PROC CHART uses the sums to determine the size of each bar, block, or section. SUM is the default type.

MEAN   determines the mean value of the sumvar variable in each range. Then PROC CHART uses the means to determine the size of each bar, block, or section.

The following program creates a chart that compares the sum of all grades in each section. The values of SECTION are grouped by SEX. Output 28.14 shows the chart.

```
proc chart data=intrchem.grades;
   vbar section / midpoints='Mon' 'Wed' 'Fri'
                  group=sex
                  sumvar=grade type=sum;
   title 'Using the SUMVAR= Option';
run;
```

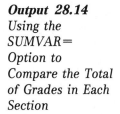

Output 28.14
Using the
SUMVAR=
Option to
Compare the Total
of Grades in Each
Section

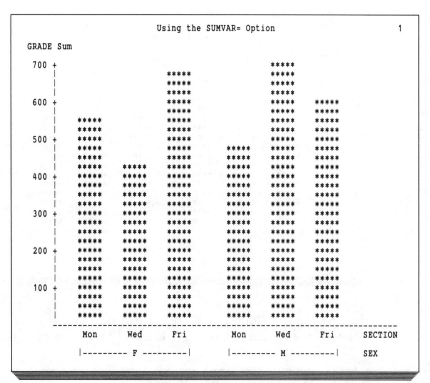

The chart in Output 28.14 shows that, as a group, the males in the Wednesday section achieved the highest grades. However, because the different sections contain different numbers of students, comparing the sum of the grades doesn't accurately reflect the performance of each group. To compare the mean grade for each group, simply change the type of the chart you request from SUM to MEAN. Output 28.15 shows the chart.

```
proc chart data=intrchem.grades;
    vbar section / midpoints='Mon' 'Wed' 'Fri'
                    group=sex
                    sumvar=grade type=mean;
    title 'Using the SUMVAR= option to Compare the Mean GRADE';
    title2 'among Sections';
run;
```

Output 28.15
Using the
SUMVAR=
Option to
Compare the
Mean GRADE
among Sections

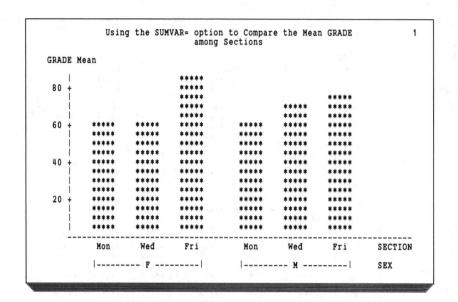

The chart in Output 28.15 shows that the females in the Friday section achieved the highest mean grade, followed by the males in the same section.

Creating a Three-Dimensional Chart

Complicated relationships like the ones charted with the GROUP= option are easier to understand if you present them as block charts because the resulting chart is three-dimensional. To create a three-dimensional chart, change the VBAR statement to a BLOCK statement, and increase the line size. Output 28.16 shows the chart.

```
options linesize=120;

proc chart data=intrchem.grades;
   block section / midpoints='Mon' 'Wed' 'Fri'
                   group=sex
                   sumvar=grade type=mean;
   title 'Comparing the Mean for GRADE among Sections';
run;
```

Output 28.16   *Block Chart Comparing the Mean for GRADE in Each Section, Grouped by SEX*

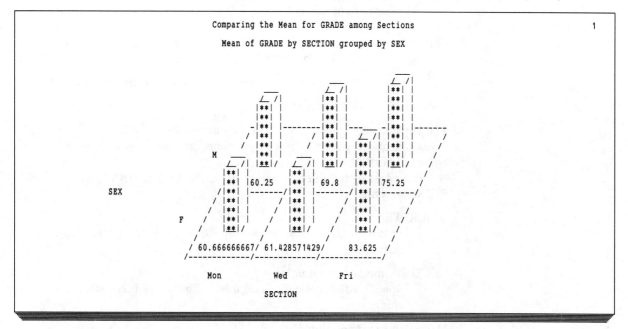

In Output 28.16 the number printed beneath each block is the mean of GRADE for that combination of SECTION and SEX. You can easily see that both females and males in the Friday section earned higher grades than their counterparts in the other sections.

Note: PROC CHART selects the default format when it prints the values of the mean of GRADE beneath each block. To specify the number of decimals you want the procedure to print, use a FORMAT statement like this one:

```
format grade 4.2;
```

SAS Tools

This chapter discusses the CHART procedure:

PROC CHART <DATA=*SAS-data-set*>;
     chart-type variable-list <*option-list*>;

PROC CHART <DATA=*SAS-data-set*>;
          starts the CHART procedure. The DATA= option specifies the
          SAS-data-set containing the variables you want to chart. If you omit the
          DATA= option, the CHART procedure uses the SAS data set created
          most recently in the current job or session.

chart-type variable-list <*option-list*>;
　　is a chart statement where

chart-type　　specifies the kind of chart and may be any of the
　　　　　　　following: VBAR, HBAR, BLOCK, or PIE.

variable-list　is a list of variables to chart (called the *chart variables*).

option-list　　is a list of options.

You can use any number of chart statements in one PROC CHART step.
A list of options pertains to a single chart statement. Not all types of
chart support all options.
　　You can use the following options in the VBAR, HBAR, BLOCK, and
PIE statements:

DISCRETE
　　creates a bar, block, or section for every value of the chart
　　variable.

LEVELS=*number-of-midpoints*
　　specifies the *number-of-midpoints*. The procedure selects the
　　midpoints.

MIDPOINTS=*midpoints-list*
　　specifies the values of the midpoints.

SUMVAR=*variable*
　　specifies the *variable* to use to determine the size of the bars,
　　blocks, or sections.

TYPE=SUM | MEAN
　　specifies the type of chart to create where

　　SUM　　sums the values of the sumvar variable in each
　　　　　　range. Then PROC CHART uses the sums to
　　　　　　determine the size of each bar, block, or section.

　　MEAN　　determines the mean value of the sumvar variable in
　　　　　　each range. Then PROC CHART uses the means to
　　　　　　determine the size of each bar, block, or section.

You can use the following options in the VBAR, HBAR, and BLOCK
statements:

GROUP=*variable*
　　produces a set of bars or blocks for each value of *variable*.

SUBGROUP=*variable*
　　proportionally fills each block or bar with characters
　　representing different values of *variable*.

You can use the following options in the HBAR statement:

NOSTAT
　　suppresses the printing of the statistics that accompany the chart
　　by default.

FREQ
> requests frequency statistics.

CFREQ
> requests cumulative frequency statistics.

PERCENT
> requests percentage statistics.

CPERCENT
> requests cumulative percentage statistics.

Learning More

□ Chapter 27, "Plotting the Relationship between Variables," describes how to use the PLOT procedure. When you are preparing graphics presentations, some data lend themselves to charts, while other data are better suited for plots.

□ The *SAS Procedures Guide, Version 6, Third Edition* provides complete documentation on the CHART procedure. In addition to the features described in this chapter, you can also use PROC CHART to create star charts, to draw a reference line at a particular value on a bar chart, and to change the symbol used to draw charts. In addition, you can create charts based, not only on frequency, sum, and mean, but also on cumulative frequency, percent, and cumulative percent.

□ The *SAS Procedures Guide* presents information on creating your own formats using the FORMAT procedure. See also *SAS Language: Reference, Version 6, First Edition* for information on using formats, both your own and those provided by the SAS System.

□ *SAS/GRAPH Software: Reference, Version 6, First Edition* provides complete documentation on using SAS/GRAPH software. If your site has SAS/GRAPH software, you can use the GCHART procedure to take advantage of the high-resolution graphics capabilities of output devices and produce charts that include color, different fonts, and text.

438

Part 8
Designing Your Own Output

Chapter 29 Writing Output

Introduction

In previous chapters you learned to store data values in a SAS data set and to use SAS procedures to produce a report on the data values. The form of the report was determined by the procedure. The PRINT procedure produced lists with columns, the TABULATE procedure produced tables, and so on. This chapter teaches you how to produce reports using the DATA step instead of a procedure. Using the DATA step allows you to design the output by writing data values and character strings in particular columns and lines of an output file.

This chapter focuses on using the PUT statement in the DATA step to write data. It also discusses the FILE statement, which directs data to a particular destination, and the DATA _NULL_ statement, which prevents the SAS System from creating an additional data set when all you need is the report.

Suppose you want to write a report that deals with morning and evening newspaper circulation in two states, Alabama and Maine. The data are in a disk file that looks like this:

```
Alabama    256.3   480.5   1984
Alabama    291.5   454.3   1985
Alabama    303.6   454.7   1986
Alabama      .     454.5   1987
Maine        .       .     1984
Maine        .      68.0   1985
Maine      222.7    68.6   1986
Maine      224.1    66.7   1987
```

The file contains the name of the state, the morning and evening circulation figures (in thousands), and the year the data represent.

The following sections explain how to use the PUT and DATA _NULL_ statements and how to write the report.

Writing Simple Text

Use a PUT statement to write text in a DATA step. The basic form of the PUT statement is

> **PUT** <*variable* <*format*>> <*'character string'*>;

where *variable* is the variable you want to write, *format* is an optional format, and *character string* is a character string enclosed in quotes. In later sections, you learn how to specify the column and line location of text with the PUT statement.

In many cases, when you use a DATA step to write a report, you don't need to create a new SAS data set at the same time. The special data set name _NULL_ increases program efficiency considerably by causing the SAS System to go through the DATA step as usual but without outputting observations to a data set. A DATA statement using _NULL_ appears below:

```
data _null_;
```

Writing a Character String

In the simplest form, the PUT statement writes the character string you specify to the destination you specify. If you omit the destination, the string goes to the SAS log. Consider the following example:

```
data _null_;
   infile 'your-input-file';
   input state $ morn even year;
   put '***';
run;
```

The SAS System executes the PUT statement once during each iteration of the DATA step. Output 29.1 shows the SAS log that results.

Output 29.1
Writing a
Character String

```
7           data _null_;
8               infile 'your-input-file';
9               input state $ morn even year;
10              put '***';
11          run;

NOTE: The infile 'your-input-file' is:
      Dsname=your-input-file

***
***
***
***
***
***
***
***
NOTE: 8 records were read from the infile 'your-input-file'.
```

In this example you don't give the SAS System any directions about writing a value; you simply tell the SAS System the value to write. By default, the SAS System begins writing on a new line each time it encounters a PUT statement. Writing a character string or variable without giving the SAS System any directions about where to put the value is called *list output*.

Suppose you want to write a message when data lines contain missing values. The following program identifies missing values for MORN and writes a message. Output 29.2 shows the SAS log.

```
data _null_;
   infile 'your-input-file';
   input state $ morn even year;
   if morn=. then put '*** MORN missing';
run;
```

Output 29.2
Writing a
Character String
for an Individual
Observation

```
7           data _null_;
8               infile 'your-input-file';
9               input state $ morn even year;
10              if morn=. then put '*** MORN missing';
11          run;

NOTE: The infile 'your-input-file' is:
      Dsname=your-input-file

*** MORN missing
*** MORN missing
*** MORN missing
NOTE: 8 records were read from the infile 'your-input-file'.
```

Writing Variable Values

Output 29.2 shows that the value for MORN is missing for some of the observations in your data set, but it doesn't show which observations. To find out which observations have the missing MORN values, write the value of one or more variables along with the character string. The following program writes the value of YEAR and STATE, as well as the character string. Output 29.3 shows the SAS log.

```
data _null_;
   infile 'your-input-file';
   input state $ morn even year;
   if morn=. then put '*** MORN missing for ' year state;
run;
```

Output 29.3
Writing a
Character String
and Variable
Values

```
7          data _null_;
8             infile 'your-input-file';
9             input state $ morn even year;
10            if morn=. then put '*** MORN missing for ' year state;
11         run;

NOTE: The infile 'your-input-file' is:
      Dsname=your-input-file

*** MORN missing for 1987 Alabama
*** MORN missing for 1984 Maine
*** MORN missing for 1985 Maine
NOTE: 8 records were read from the infile 'your-input-file'.
```

Notice that in Output 29.3 the last character in the string is a blank. In list output, the SAS System automatically moves one column to the right after writing a variable value, but not after writing a character string. The simplest way to include the required space is to include it in the character string, as shown in Output 29.3.

The SAS System keeps track of its position in the output line with a *pointer*. Another way to describe the action in this PUT statement is to say that in list output the pointer moves one column to the right after writing a variable value but not after writing a character string. In later sections of this chapter, you learn ways to move the pointer to control where the next piece of text is written.

Using More than One PUT Statement

You can use any number of PUT statements in a DATA step. For example, the program below flags missing values for MORN and EVEN in separate statements. Output 29.4 shows the SAS log.

```
data _null_;
   infile 'your-input-file';
   input state $ morn even year;
   if morn=. then put '*** MORN missing for ' year;
   if even=. then put '****** EVEN missing for ' year;
run;
```

Output 29.4
Using More than
One PUT
Statement

```
7          data _null_;
8              infile 'your-input-file';
9              input state $ morn even year;
10             if morn=. then put '*** MORN missing for ' year;
11             if even=. then put '****** EVEN missing for ' year;
12         run;

NOTE: The infile 'your-input-file' is:
      Dsname=your-input-file

*** MORN missing for 1987
*** MORN missing for 1984
****** EVEN missing for 1984
*** MORN missing for 1985
NOTE: 8 records were read from the infile 'your-input-file'.
```

Writing on the Same Line More than Once

As Output 29.4 shows, each PUT statement begins on a new line by default. However, you can write on the same line with more than one PUT statement. To hold a line for use by a later PUT statement, end the current PUT statement with a *trailing @ (at-sign)*. Output 29.5 shows the SAS log.

```
data _null_;
    infile 'your-input-file';
    input state $ morn even year;
    if morn=. then put '*** MORN missing for ' year @;
    if even=. then put '**** EVEN missing for ' year @;
run;
```

Output 29.5
Writing More than
Once on the Same
Line

```
7          data _null_;
8              infile 'your-input-file';
9              input state $ morn even year;
10             if morn=. then put '*** MORN missing for ' year @;
11             if even=. then put '**** EVEN missing for ' year @;
12         run;

NOTE: The infile 'your-input-file' is:
      Dsname=your-input-file

*** MORN missing for 1987 *** MORN missing for 1984 **** EVEN missing for
1984 *** MORN missing for 1985
NOTE: 8 records were read from the infile 'your-input-file'.
```

The trailing @ is a type of *pointer control* called a line-hold specifier. Pointer controls are one way to specify where the SAS System writes text. In this case, using the trailing @ causes the SAS System to write the item in the second PUT statement on the same line rather than on a new line. In this program, execution of either PUT statement holds the output line for further writing. The SAS System continues to write on that line both when a later PUT statement in the same iteration of the DATA step is executed and when a PUT statement in a later iteration is executed.

If the output line were long enough, the SAS System would write all four messages about missing data on a single line. Since the line isn't long enough, the SAS System continues writing on the following line. When it determines that an individual data value or character string doesn't fit on a line, the SAS System brings the entire item down to the following line; it doesn't split a data value or character string.

Releasing a Held Line

You can tell from the output created so far that several values for the variable MORN are missing, and one value for the variable EVEN is missing. You can improve the appearance of your report by writing all the missing variables for each observation on a separate line. Therefore, when both variables MORN and EVEN are missing, two PUT statements write to the same line; when either MORN or EVEN is missing, only one PUT statement writes to that line. To do this, the SAS System has to do two things: first, tell that the line needs to be released and second, release the line. The SAS System determines these two things by the presence of the trailing @ in the PUT statement. Executing a PUT statement with a trailing @ causes the SAS System to hold the current output line for further writing, either in the current iteration of the DATA step or in a future iteration. Executing a PUT statement without a trailing @ releases a held line.

Note: If you don't need to write anything when releasing a line, use a null PUT statement:

PUT;

A null PUT statement works like other PUT statements: by default it begins on a new line, writes what is specified (nothing in this case), and releases the line when finished. If a trailing @ is in effect, the null PUT statement begins on the current line, writes nothing, and releases the line.

The following program shows how to write one or more items to the same line. When MORN is missing, the first PUT statement holds the line in case EVEN is missing for that observation. If the value of EVEN is missing, the next PUT statement writes a message and releases the line. If EVEN isn't missing but a message has been written for MORN (MORN=.), the null PUT statement releases the line. If EVEN isn't missing and MORN isn't missing, the line doesn't need to be released and no PUT statement is executed. Output 29.6 shows the SAS log.

```
data _null_;
   infile 'your-input-file';
   input year $ morn even year;
   if morn=. then put '*** MORN missing for ' year @;
   if even=. then put '***** EVEN missing for ' year;
   else if morn=. then put;
run;
```

Output 29.6
Writing One or
More Times to a
Line and
Releasing the Line

```
7               data _null_;
8                  infile 'your-input-file';
9                  input year $ morn even year;
10                 if morn=. then put '*** MORN missing for ' year @;
11                 if even=. then put '***** EVEN missing for ' year;
12                 else if morn=. then put;
13              run;

NOTE: The infile 'your-input-file' is:
      Dsname=your-input-file

*** MORN missing for 1987
*** MORN missing for 1984 ***** EVEN missing for 1984
*** MORN missing for 1985
NOTE: 8 records were read from the infile 'your-input-file'.
```

Writing a Report

This section explains how to combine the techniques you have already seen to create a report. The discussion begins with choosing a destination and then progresses from the simplest aspects of writing a report (in this case the data values) to the more difficult, until the report is complete. The following sections assume that you are working in the SAS Display Manager System and that the procedure output file is the OUTPUT window. The steps you use to write a report and the way your report looks won't change, regardless of the method you use to run your programs. The report described in the following sections has a page size of 24 lines, which is a typical size for display manager's OUTPUT window.

Choosing a Destination

The PUT statement writes lines of text to the SAS log. However, the SAS log isn't usually a good destination for a formal report because it also contains the source statements for the program and messages from the SAS System.

The simplest destination for a printed report is the SAS procedure output file, the same place the SAS System writes output from procedures. The SAS System automatically defines various characteristics such as page numbers for the procedure output file, and you can take advantage of them instead of defining all the characteristics yourself.

To route lines to the procedure output file, use the following FILE statement before the PUT statement:

```
file print;
```

By default, the procedure output file contains the title "The SAS System." Since this report creates another title, you don't need the default one. To remove the default title, specify

```
file print notitles;
```

The NOTITLES option eliminates the default title line and makes that line available for writing. You can also remove the default title with a null TITLE statement:

```
title;
```

However, in that case the SAS System writes a line containing only the date and page number in place of the default title, and the line isn't available for writing other text.

Designing the Report

After choosing a destination for your report, the next step in producing a report is to decide how you want it to look. You must create the design and determine which lines and columns the text must occupy. Planning how you want your final report to look helps you write the necessary PUT statements to produce the report. The rest of this section assumes you want your final report to resemble Figure 29.1.

Figure 29.1
Design for the
Final Report

```
----+----1----+----2----+----3----+----4----+----5----+----6----+----7--
 1                  Morning and Evening Newspaper Circulation
 2
 3      State           Year                    Thousands of Copies
 4                                               Morning     Evening
 5
 6      Alabama         1984                      256.3       480.5
 7                      1985                      291.5       454.3
 8                      1986                      303.6       454.7
 9                      1987                         .        454.5
10                                              ------      ------
11                      Total for each category  851.4      1844.0
12                            Combined total          2695.4
13
14      Maine           1984                         .           .
15                      1985                         .         68.0
16                      1986                      222.7        68.6
17                      1987                      224.1        66.7
18                                              ------      ------
19                      Total for each category  446.8       203.3
20                            Combined total           650.1
----+----1----+----2----+----3----+----4----+----5----+----6----+----7--
```

Writing Data Values

After determining what you want your final report to look like, you're ready to begin programming. You want the data values of the variables YEAR, MORN, and EVEN to be displayed in specific positions; therefore, you write the following program. Output 29.7 shows the output.

```
options pagesize=24;

data _null_;
   infile 'your-input-file';
   input state $ morn even year;
   file print notitles;
   put @26 year @53 morn @66 even;
run;
```

Output 29.7
Writing Data
Values in
Particular
Locations

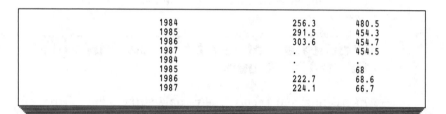

```
                          1984            256.3      480.5
                          1985            291.5      454.3
                          1986            303.6      454.7
                          1987             .         454.5
                          1984             .          .
                          1985             .         68
                          1986            222.7      68.6
                          1987            224.1      66.7
```

The @ followed by a number in the PUT statement is a different kind of pointer control from the trailing @ described earlier. The @*n* symbol is a column-pointer control; it tells the SAS System to move to column *n*. In this example the pointer moves to the location specified, and the PUT statement writes a value at that point using list output. Combining list output with pointer controls is a simple but useful way of writing data values in columns.

Improving the Appearance of Numeric Data Values

In the design for your report, Figure 29.1, all numeric values are aligned on the decimal point. To achieve this result, you have to alter the appearance of the numeric data values. In the input data, all values for MORN and EVEN contain one decimal place; in one case, the decimal value is 0. In list output, the SAS System writes values in the simplest way possible; in this case, it omits the 0s. To show one decimal place for every value and thereby align the values on the decimal, associate a format with a variable in the PUT statement. Output 29.8 shows the formatted values.

```
options pagesize=24;

data _null_;
   infile 'your-input-file';
   input state $ morn even year;
   file print notitles;
   put @26 year @53 morn 5.1 @66 even 5.1;
run;
```

Output 29.8
Using Formats

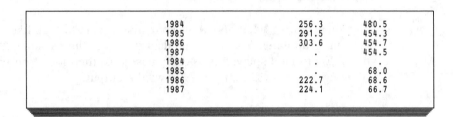

```
                          1984          256.3        480.5
                          1985          291.5        454.3
                          1986          303.6        454.7
                          1987                        454.5
                          1984             .            .
                          1985             .          68.0
                          1986          222.7         68.6
                          1987          224.1         66.7
```

The format used in this program is called the *w.d* format. The *w.d* format specifies the number of columns to be used for writing the entire value, including the decimal point, and the number of columns used for decimal values. In this example the format 5.1 causes the SAS System to use five columns, including one decimal place, for writing each value. Therefore, the SAS System prints the 0s in the decimal place as necessary. The format also aligns the periods for missing values with the decimal points.

Writing a Value at the Beginning of Each BY Group

In creating your report, you're now at the point where you would like to add the name of the state to your output. If you include the name of the state in the PUT statement with other data values, the state will appear on every line. However, remembering what you want your final report to look like, you need to write the name of the state only for the first observation of a given state. Performing a task once for a group of observations requires BY-group processing. Notice the following points about BY-group processing:

□   Make sure observations come from a SAS data set, not an external file.

□   When the data are in BY groups but the groups aren't necessarily in alphabetical order, use the NOTSORTED option in the BY statement, for example,

```
by state notsorted;
```

The following program creates a SAS data set (so the second DATA step can use BY-group processing) and writes the name of the state on the first line of the report for each BY group. Output 29.9 shows the new report.

```
options pagesize=24;
libname save 'your-data-library';

data save.circrep1;
   infile 'your-input-file';
   input state $ morn even year;
run;
```

```
data _null_;
   set save.circrep1;
   by state notsorted;
   file print notitles;
   if first.state then put / @7 state @;
   put @26 year @53 morn 5.1 @66 even 5.1;
run;
```

Output 29.9
Adding BY-Group
Processing

Alabama	1984	256.3	480.5
	1985	291.5	454.3
	1986	303.6	454.7
	1987	.	454.5
Maine	1984	.	.
	1985	.	68.0
	1986	222.7	68.6
	1987	224.1	66.7

During the first observation for a given state, a PUT statement writes the name of the state and holds the line for further writing (that is, the year and circulation figures). The next PUT statement writes the year and circulation figures and releases the held line. In observations after the first, only the second PUT statement is processed; it simply writes the year and circulation figures and releases the line as usual.

The first PUT statement contains a slash (/), a pointer control that moves the pointer to the beginning of the next line. In this example, the PUT statement prepares to write on a new line (the default action). Then the slash moves the pointer to the beginning the next line; as a result, the SAS System skips a line before writing the value of STATE. In Output 29.9, a blank line separates the data for Alabama from the data for Maine; the output for Alabama also begins one line farther down the page than it would have otherwise. (That blank line is used later in the development of the report.)

Calculating Totals

The next step is to calculate the total morning circulation figures, total evening circulation figures, and total overall circulation figures for each state. Sum statements accumulate the totals, and assignment statements start the accumulation at 0 for each state. When the last observation for a given state is being processed, an assignment statement calculates the overall total, and a PUT statement writes the totals and some additional descriptive text. Output 29.10 shows the report at this stage.

```
options pagesize=24;

data _null_;
   set save.circrep1;
   by state notsorted;
   file print notitles;
```

```
          /* Set values of accumulator variables to 0 */
          /* at beginning of each BY group.           */
      if first.state then
        do;
           mtot=0;
           etot=0;
           put / @7 state @;
        end;
      put @26 year @53 morn 5.1 @66 even 5.1;

          /* Accumulate separate totals for morning and */
          /* evening circulations.                      */
      mtot+morn;
      etot+even;

          /* Calculate total circulation at the end of  */
          /* each BY group.                             */
      if last.state then
        do;
           alltot=mtot+etot;
           put @52 '------' @65 '------' /
               @26 'Total for each category'
               @52 mtot 6.1 @65 etot 6.1 /
               @35 'Combined total' @59 alltot 6.1;
        end;
    run;
```

Output 29.10
Calculating and
Writing Totals for
Each BY Group

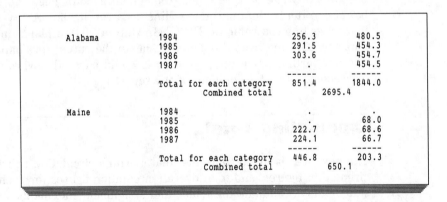

```
        Alabama        1984               256.3        480.5
                       1985               291.5        454.3
                       1986               303.6        454.7
                       1987                 .          454.5
                                          ------       ------
                Total for each category   851.4        1844.0
                        Combined total          2695.4

        Maine          1984                 .            .
                       1985                 .          68.0
                       1986               222.7        68.6
                       1987               224.1        66.7
                                          ------       ------
                Total for each category   446.8        203.3
                        Combined total          650.1
```

Notice that sum statements ignore missing values when they accumulate totals. Also, by default, sum statements assign the accumulator variables (in this case MTOT and ETOT) an initial value of 0. Therefore, although the assignment statements in the DO group are executed for the first observation for both states, you need them only for the second state.

Writing a Simple Heading

The report is complete except for the title lines and column headings. Because this is a simple, one-page report, you can write the heading with a PUT statement executed only during the first iteration of the DATA step. The automatic variable _N_ counts the number of times the DATA step has iterated

or looped; therefore, execute the PUT statement when the value of _N_ is 1.
The complete program follows. Output 29.11 shows the final report.

```
options pagesize=24;

data _null_;
   set save.circrep1;
   by state notsorted;
   file print notitles;
   if _n_=1 then put a16 'Morning and Evening Newspaper Circulation' //
      a7  'State' a26 'Year' a51 'Thousands of Copies' /
      a51 'Morning         Evening';
   if first.state then
      do;
         mtot=0;
         etot=0;
         put / a7 state a;
      end;
   put a26 year a53 morn 5.1 a66 even 5.1;
   mtot+morn;
   etot+even;
   if last.state then
      do;
         alltot=mtot+etot;
         put a52 '------' a65 '------' /
            a26 'Total for each category'
            a52 mtot 6.1 a65 etot 6.1 /
            a35 'Combined total' a59 alltot 6.1;
      end;
run;
```

Output 29.11
Executing a PUT
Statement Only
during the First
Iteration of the
DATA Step

```
                     Morning and Evening Newspaper Circulation
        State            Year                         Thousands of Copies
                                                       Morning     Evening

        Alabama          1984                            256.3       480.5
                         1985                            291.5       454.3
                         1986                            303.6       454.7
                         1987                               .         454.5
                                                        ------      ------
                         Total for each category         851.4      1844.0
                                     Combined total            2695.4

        Maine            1984                               .           .
                         1985                               .          68.0
                         1986                            222.7         68.6
                         1987                            224.1         66.7
                                                        ------      ------
                         Total for each category         446.8        203.3
                                     Combined total             650.1
```

Notice that a blank line appears between the last line of the heading and the
first data for Alabama although the PUT statement for the heading doesn't write
a blank line. The line comes from the slash (/) in the PUT statement that writes
the value of STATE in the first observation of each BY group.

Executing a PUT statement during the first iteration of the DATA step is a simple way to produce headings, especially when a report takes only one page. Chapter 30, "Customizing Output," shows other ways to write headings, including headings that change on each page of a multipage report.

SAS Tools

This chapter discusses the following elements for producing a report:

PUT <*variable* <*format*>> <*'character string'*>;
> writes lines to the destination specified in the FILE statement; if no FILE statement is present, the PUT statement writes to the SAS log. By default, each PUT statement begins on a new line, writes what is specified, and releases the line. A DATA step can contain any number of PUT statements.

> By default, the SAS System writes a *variable* or *'character-string'* at the current position in the line. The SAS System automatically moves the pointer one column to the right after writing a variable value but not after writing a character string; that is, the SAS System places a blank after a variable value but not after a character string. This form of output is called list output. If you place a *format* after a variable name, the SAS System writes the value of the *variable* beginning at its current position in the line and using the *format* you specify. The position of the pointer after a formatted value is the following column; that is, the SAS System doesn't automatically skip a column. Using a format in a PUT statement is called formatted output. You can combine list and formatted output in a single PUT statement.

PUT <*@n*> <*variable* <*format*>> <*'character-string'*> </> <*@*>;
> writes lines to the destination specified in the FILE statement; if no FILE statement is present, the PUT statement writes to the SAS log. The @n pointer control moves the pointer to column *n* in the current line. The / moves the pointer to the beginning of a new line; you can use slashes anywhere in the PUT statement to skip lines. Multiple slashes skip multiple lines. The trailing @, if present, must be the last item in the PUT statement. Executing a PUT statement with a trailing @ holds the current line for use by a later PUT statement either in the same iteration of the DATA step or a later iteration. Executing a PUT statement without a trailing @ releases a held line.

PUT;
> by default begins a new line and releases a previously held line. A PUT statement that doesn't write any text is known as a null PUT statement.

FILE PRINT <NOTITLES>;
> directs output to the SAS procedure output file. Place the FILE statement before the PUT statements that write to that file. The NOTITLES option suppresses any titles currently in effect and makes the line available for writing other text.

TITLE;
> suppresses the default title when you write output to the SAS procedure output file. The lines normally used by the default title aren't available for writing other text.

BY *variable-1* < . . . *variable-n*> <NOTSORTED>;
> indicates that all observations with common values of the BY *variables* are grouped together. The NOTSORTED option indicates that the *variables* are grouped but that the groups aren't necessarily in alphabetical or numeric order.

_N_

> is an automatic variable whose value is the number of times the SAS System has begun executing the DATA step (1, 2, 3, and so on). You can use _N_ in programming statements in the DATA step, but it isn't added to any SAS data sets being created.

Learning More

- □ Part 2, "Getting Your Data into Shape," and Part 3, "Basic Programming," discuss the DATA step programming shown in this chapter. Chapter 24, "Printing Detail Reports," discusses SAS formats for numeric variables. For complete reference information on DATA step programming and on SAS formats, refer to *SAS Language: Reference, Version 6, First Edition*.

- □ Chapter 3, "Starting with Raw Data," discusses using a pointer to read data lines with the INPUT statement.

- □ *SAS Language: Reference* describes additional pointer controls available for use in the PUT statement. A common pointer control is the plus sign (+), which moves the pointer a number of columns relative to its current position. Another common pointer control is the pound sign (#), which moves the pointer to a specific line on the page.

- □ *SAS Language: Reference* provides details on using the N= option in the FILE statement to treat a group of lines as a unit. The examples in this chapter illustrate writing on one line. It's also possible to treat a group of lines or an entire page as a unit and move back and forth between lines (for example, to produce a multicolumn report such as a telephone listing).

456

Chapter **30** Customizing Output

Introduction

This chapter shows you how to customize your reports and other output. Topics include

☐ creating titles and column headings for reports longer than one page

☐ writing different amounts of text on different pages of a report

☐ writing to destinations other than the procedure output file.

This chapter also shows how report-writing techniques can be used to read and write data values in situations other than report production.

The report discussed here builds on the report developed in Chapter 29, "Writing Output"; complete details of the report are included there. As in Chapter 29, the examples assume that you are working in a SAS Display Manager session and are directing the report to the SAS procedure output file (that is, the OUTPUT window); therefore, most examples in this chapter are run with a page size of 24. To print a hardcopy of the report, give the PRINT command on the command line of the OUTPUT window, for example,

```
print
```

The input data for your report deal with morning and evening newspaper circulation figures for several states and look like this:

```
Colorado  738.6 210.2 1984
Colorado  742.2 212.3 1985
Colorado  731.7 209.7 1986
Colorado  789.2 155.9 1987
Alaska     51.0  80.7 1984
Alaska     58.7  78.3 1985
Alaska     59.8  70.9 1986
Alaska     64.3  64.6 1987
Alabama   256.3 480.5 1984
Alabama   291.5 454.3 1985
```

```
Alabama   303.6 454.7 1986
Alabama     .   454.5 1987
Maine       .     .   1984
Maine       .   68.0  1985
Maine     222.7 68.6  1986
Maine     224.1 66.7  1987
```

The data contain the name of the state, the morning and evening circulation figures (in thousands), and the year the data represent.

Figure 30.1 shows the report you want to produce. For reference, column and line rulers appear beside the output.

Figure 30.1
A Multipage
Report

```
----+----1----+----2----+----3----+----4----+----5----+----6----+----7--
1          Morning and Evening Newspaper Circulation          Page 1
2
3   State          Year                    Thousands of Copies
4                                           Morning      Evening
5
6   Colorado       1984                      738.6        210.2
7                  1985                      742.2        212.3
8                  1986                      731.7        209.7
9                  1987                      789.2        155.9
10                                          ------       ------
11                 Total for each category  3001.7        788.1
12                       Combined total          3789.8
13
14  Alaska         1984                       51.0         80.7
15                 1985                       58.7         78.3
16                 1986                       59.8         70.9
17                 1987                       64.3         64.6
18                                          ------       ------
19                 Total for each category   233.8        294.5
20                       Combined total           528.3
----+----1----+----2----+----3----+----4----+----5----+----6----+----7--
```

```
----+----1----+----2----+----3----+----4----+----5----+----6----+----7--
           Morning and Evening Newspaper Circulation          Page 2

    State          Year                    Thousands of Copies
                                            Morning      Evening

    Alabama        1984                      256.3        480.5
                   1985                      291.5        454.3
                   1986                      303.6        454.7
                   1987                        .          454.5
                                            ------       ------
                   Total for each category   851.4       1844.0
                         Combined total          2695.4

    Maine          1984                        .            .
                   1985                        .           68.0
                   1986                      222.7         68.6
                   1987                      224.1         66.7
                                            ------       ------
                   Total for each category   446.8        203.3
                         Combined total           650.1
----+----1----+----2----+----3----+----4----+----5----+----6----+----7--
```

Controlling the Appearance of Pages

You can produce titles and column headings at the beginning of a report by executing a PUT statement when the value of the automatic variable _N_ is 1. Those headings appear only once, at the top of the first page of the report. In this section you learn to produce headings that appear on each page.

Writing Centered Titles and Column Headings

A TITLE statement writes the title you specify at the top of every page:

TITLE<*n*> '*text*';

where *n* can be 1 to 10. If you omit *n*, the SAS System assumes you mean TITLE1. You can use up to 10 TITLE statements. By default, a title is centered.

As shown below, you can modify the final program in Chapter 29 to produce headings with TITLE statements. Output 30.1 shows the report.

```
options pagesize=24;
libname save 'your-data-library';

data save.circrep2;
   infile 'your-input-file';
   input state $ morn even year;
run;

title 'Morning and Evening Newspaper Circulation';
title2;
title3
   'State          Year              Thousands of Copies';
title4
    '                                   Morning     Evening';
```

```
data _null_;
    set save.circrep2;
    by state notsorted;
    file print;
    if first.state then
        do;
            mtot=0;
            etot=0;
            put / @7 state @;
        end;
    put @26 year @53 morn 5.1 @66 even 5.1;
    mtot+morn;
    etot+even;
    if last.state then
        do;
            alltot=mtot+etot;
            put @52 '------' @65 '------' /
                @26 'Total for each category'
                @52 mtot 6.1 @65 etot 6.1 /
                @35 'Combined total' @59 alltot 6.1;
        end;
run;
```

Output 30.1
Headings
Produced with
TITLE Statements

```
                    Morning and Evening Newspaper Circulation                  1

            State        Year                    Thousands of Copies
                                                 Morning      Evening

         Colorado        1984                     738.6        210.2
                         1985                     742.2        212.3
                         1986                     731.7        209.7
                         1987                     789.2        155.9
                                                 ------       ------
                         Total for each category 3001.7        788.1
                                    Combined total       3789.8

         Alaska          1984                      51.0         80.7
                         1985                      58.7         78.3
                         1986                      59.8         70.9
                         1987                      64.3         64.6
                                                 ------       ------
                         Total for each category  233.8        294.5
                                    Combined total       528.3

         Alabama         1984                     256.3        480.5
                         1985                     291.5        454.3
                         1986                     303.6        454.7
```

```
                    Morning and Evening Newspaper Circulation                  2

            State        Year                    Thousands of Copies
                                                 Morning      Evening
                         1987                         .        454.5
                                                 ------       ------
                         Total for each category  851.4       1844.0
                                    Combined total       2695.4

         Maine           1984                         .            .
                         1985                         .         68.0
                         1986                     222.7         68.6
                         1987                     224.1         66.7
                                                 ------       ------
                         Total for each category  446.8        203.3
                                    Combined total       650.1
```

The titles and column headings appear on every page. Producing the centered titles with TITLE statements is simple, but producing column headings isn't so easy. You must insert the correct number of blanks in the TITLE statements so that the entire title, when centered, causes the text to fall in the correct columns.

If you create titles and column headings with TITLE statements, remember three important points:

□ The NOTITLES option in the FILE PRINT statement causes the TITLE statements to be canceled

□ The PUT statement pointer begins on the first line after the last TITLE statement; the SAS System doesn't skip a line before beginning the text as it does with procedure output. In this example, the blank line between the TITLE4 statement and the first line of each state's data is produced by the slash (/) in the PUT statement in the FIRST.STATE group.

□ Unless you specify the NONUMBER system option, the SAS System writes page numbers on title lines by default; therefore, page numbers appear in this report.

Writing Titles and Column Headings in Particular Columns

The easiest way to program headings in specific columns is to use a PUT statement. Instead of calculating the exact number of blanks required to make text fall in particular columns, you simply move the pointer to the appropriate column with pointer controls and write the text.

To write headings with a PUT statement, you must execute the PUT statement at the beginning of each page, regardless of the observation being processed or the iteration of the DATA step. The HEADER= option in the FILE statement identifies statements to be executed at the beginning of each page.

The form of a DATA step containing the HEADER= option is shown below:

```
data _null_;
   more SAS statements
   file print header=your-label;
   more SAS statements
   return;
   your-label:
   SAS statements executed at the beginning of each page
   return;
run;
```

Note the following points:

□ *Your-label*, the value of the HEADER= option, is a *statement label*. A statement label points to a location in the DATA step so that execution can move to that position as necessary, bypassing other statements in the step. Statement labels follow the rules for SAS names: one to eight characters, beginning with a letter or underscore and continuing with letters, numbers, or underscores. A colon (:) must follow the label.

□ When you use the HEADER= option, the group of statements that begins with *your-label* near the end of the DATA step and continues to the RETURN statement at the end of the step is a *header routine*. Each time the SAS System begins a new page, execution moves from its current position to *your-label* and continues until the RETURN statement is encountered. The statements in the header routine are usually PUT statements, but other statements such as sum statements and assignment statements can also appear. When execution reaches the RETURN statement at the end of the header routine, it returns to the statement being executed when the SAS System began a new page.

□ The RETURN statement before the header routine marks the end of the main part of the DATA step; it causes execution to return to the beginning of the step for another iteration. Without this RETURN statement, the statements in the header routine would be executed during each iteration of the DATA step, as well as at the beginning of each page.

The following program adds a header routine to the DATA step. Output 30.2 shows the report.

```
options pagesize=24;

data _null_;
   set save.circrep2;
   by state notsorted;
   file print notitles header=pagetop;
   if first.state then
      do;
         mtot=0;
         etot=0;
         put / @7 state @;
      end;
   put @26 year @53 morn 5.1 @66 even 5.1;
   mtot+morn;
   etot+even;
   if last.state then
      do;
         alltot=mtot+etot;
         put @52 '------' @65 '------' /
            @26 'Total for each category'
            @52 mtot 6.1 @65 etot 6.1 /
            @35 'Combined total' @59 alltot 6.1;
      end;
```

```
        return;
      pagetop:
      put @16 'Morning and Evening Newspaper Circulation' //
          @7 'State' @26 'Year' @51 'Thousands of Copies' /
          @51 'Morning      Evening'  ;
        return;
    run;
```

Output 30.2
Creating Headings
with the
HEADER= Option

```
                  Morning and Evening Newspaper Circulation
          State         Year                    Thousands of Copies
                                                 Morning      Evening

          Colorado      1984                      738.6        210.2
                        1985                      742.2        212.3
                        1986                      731.7        209.7
                        1987                      789.2        155.9
                                                 ------       ------
                        Total for each category  3001.7       788.1
                                 Combined total        3789.8

          Alaska        1984                       51.0         80.7
                        1985                       58.7         78.3
                        1986                       59.8         70.9
                        1987                       64.3         64.6
                                                 ------       ------
                        Total for each category   233.8        294.5
                                 Combined total         528.3

          Alabama       1984                      256.3        480.5
                        1985                      291.5        454.3
                        1986                      303.6        454.7
```

```
                  Morning and Evening Newspaper Circulation
          State         Year                    Thousands of Copies
                                                 Morning      Evening
                        1987                          .        454.5
                                                 ------       ------
                        Total for each category   851.4       1844.0
                                 Combined total        2695.4

          Maine         1984                          .            .
                        1985                          .         68.0
                        1986                      222.7         68.6
                        1987                      224.1         66.7
                                                 ------       ------
                        Total for each category   446.8        203.3
                                 Combined total         650.1
```

In this example, the header routine is named PAGETOP. The PAGETOP routine uses pointer controls in the PUT statement to write the title, skip two lines, and then write column headings in specific locations.

Note the following important points about creating headings with the HEADER= option:

□ The HEADER= option can be used only for print files. (Print files are discussed in the section "Writing Reports to Destinations Other than the Procedure Output File," later in this chapter.) The SAS procedure output file is a print file by default.

□ If you eliminate the title lines with the NOTITLES option in the FILE statement, those lines are available for the PUT statements. Unless you specify the NONUMBER system option, the SAS System writes page numbers on title lines.

Changing a Portion of a Heading

You can use variable values to create headings that change on every page. For example, if you eliminate the default page numbers in the procedure output file, you can create your own page numbers as part of the heading. You can also write the numbers differently from the default method, for example, Page 1 rather than simply 1. Page numbers are an example of a heading that changes with each new page.

The following program creates page numbers using a sum statement and writes the numbers as part of the header routine. Output 30.3 shows the report.

```
options pagesize=24;

data _null_;
   set save.circrep2;
   by state notsorted;
   file print notitles header=pagetop;
   if first.state then
      do;
         mtot=0;
         etot=0;
         put / a7 state a;
      end;
   put a26 year a53 morn 5.1 a66 even 5.1;
   mtot+morn;
   etot+even;
   if last.state then
      do;
         alltot=mtot+etot;
         put a52 '------' a65 '------' /
            a26 'Total for each category'
            a52 mtot 6.1 a65 etot 6.1 /
            a35 'Combined total' a59 alltot 6.1;
      end;
   return;
   pagetop:
   pagenum+1;
   put a16 'Morning and Evening Newspaper Circulation'
      a67 'Page ' pagenum //
      a7 'State' a26 'Year' a51 'Thousands of Copies' /
      a51 'Morning      Evening'  ;
   return;
run;
```

Output 30.3
Customizing Page
Numbers with the
HEADER=
Option

```
              Morning and Evening Newspaper Circulation        Page 1
       State         Year                Thousands of Copies
                                         Morning      Evening
       Colorado      1984                 738.6        210.2
                     1985                 742.2        212.3
                     1986                 731.7        209.7
                     1987                 789.2        155.9
                                         ------       ------
                     Total for each category 3001.7     788.1
                          Combined total        3789.8
       Alaska        1984                  51.0         80.7
                     1985                  58.7         78.3
                     1986                  59.8         70.9
                     1987                  64.3         64.6
                                         ------       ------
                     Total for each category 233.8      294.5
                          Combined total      528.3
       Alabama       1984                 256.3        480.5
                     1985                 291.5        454.3
                     1986                 303.6        454.7
```

```
              Morning and Evening Newspaper Circulation        Page 2
       State         Year                Thousands of Copies
                                         Morning      Evening
                     1987                   .          454.5
                                         ------       ------
                     Total for each category 851.4     1844.0
                          Combined total       2695.4
       Maine         1984                   .            .
                     1985                   .           68.0
                     1986                 222.7         68.6
                     1987                 224.1         66.7
                                         ------       ------
                     Total for each category 446.8      203.3
                          Combined total      650.1
```

Controlling Page Divisions

Creating page divisions is the final step in producing this multipage report. The reports in Output 30.3 and 30.4 automatically split the data for Alabama over two pages. To make attractive page divisions, you need to know that there's enough space on a page to print all the data for a particular state before you print any data for it.

First, you must know how many lines are needed to print a group of data. Then use the LINESLEFT= option in the FILE statement to create a variable whose value is the number of lines remaining on the current page. Before you begin printing a group of data, compare the number of lines needed to the value of that variable. If more lines are needed than are available, use the _PAGE_ pointer control to advance the pointer to the first line of a new page.

In your report, the maximum number of lines needed for any state is eight (four years of circulation data for each state plus four lines for the underline, the totals, and the blank line between states). The following program creates a variable named CKLINES and compares its value to eight at the beginning of each BY group. If the value is less than eight, the SAS System begins a new page before printing that state. Output 30.4 shows the final report.

```
options pagesize=24;

data _null_;
   set save.circrep2;
   by state notsorted;
   file print notitles header=pagetop linesleft=cklines;
   if first.state then
      do;
         mtot=0;
         etot=0;
         if cklines<8 then put _page_;
         put / @7 state @;
      end;
   put @26 year @53 morn 5.1 @66 even 5.1;
   mtot+morn;
   etot+even;
   if last.state then
      do;
         alltot=mtot+etot;
         put @52 '------' @65 '------' /
            @26 'Total for each category'
            @52 mtot 6.1 @65 etot 6.1 /
            @35 'Combined total' @59 alltot 6.1;
      end;
   return;
   pagetop:
   pagenum+1;
   put @16 'Morning and Evening Newspaper Circulation'
      @67 'Page ' pagenum //
      @7  'State' @26 'Year' @51 'Thousands of Copies' /
      @51 'Morning      Evening';
   return;
run;
```

Output 30.4
Checking the
Number of Lines
Left on a Page

```
          Morning and Evening Newspaper Circulation        Page 1
    State            Year                   Thousands of Copies
                                            Morning       Evening

    Colorado         1984                    738.6         210.2
                     1985                    742.2         212.3
                     1986                    731.7         209.7
                     1987                    789.2         155.9
                                            ------        ------
                     Total for each category 3001.7        788.1
                            Combined total          3789.8

    Alaska           1984                     51.0          80.7
                     1985                     58.7          78.3
                     1986                     59.8          70.9
                     1987                     64.3          64.6
                                            ------        ------
                     Total for each category  233.8         294.5
                            Combined total           528.3
```

```
           Morning and Evening Newspaper Circulation        Page 2
   State           Year                       Thousands of Copies
                                              Morning      Evening
   Alabama         1984                         256.3        480.5
                   1985                         291.5        454.3
                   1986                         303.6        454.7
                   1987                             .        454.5
                                               ------       ------
                   Total for each category      851.4       1844.0
                             Combined total          2695.4
   Maine           1984                             .            .
                   1985                             .         68.0
                   1986                         222.7         68.6
                   1987                         224.1         66.7
                                               ------       ------
                   Total for each category      446.8        203.3
                             Combined total           650.1
```

Writing to Destinations Other than the Procedure Output File

In this chapter, the examples direct reports to the SAS procedure output file, which is the simplest destination for a printed report because the SAS System sets up many default characteristics for the report. If you create a report to be printed using another file, you need to specify certain characteristics for the file.

The most important characteristic to specify for the file is *carriage-control characters*. A carriage-control character tells the printer when to begin a new page, when to skip a line, and so on. The SAS System creates carriage-control characters automatically when you use the PRINT option in the DATA step FILE statement, for example,

```
file 'your-output-file' print;
```

The PRINT option identifies *your-output-file* as a file containing carriage-control characters. (Files containing carriage-control characters are known as *print files*.) The PRINT option can apply to any output file. Don't confuse the PRINT option with the PRINT destination, which is shown in other examples in this chapter and you specify like this:

```
file print;
```

The PRINT destination sends lines to the SAS procedure output file.

Customizing Other Kinds of Output

The preceding sections have described how to customize printed reports. You can use the same techniques to create many other kinds of output.

For example, in the circulation data the first field is the name of the state, followed by the morning circulation figures, the evening circulation figures, and the year the data represent; however, suppose you need to create a new file in which the year follows the name of the state. Since you don't need a SAS data set, use a DATA _NULL_ step. First read the fields into SAS variables and then write the variable values in the new order. The following program shows the DATA _NULL_ step:

```
data _null_;
   infile 'your-input-file';
   input state $ morn even year;
   file 'your-output-file';
   put @1 state @10 year @15 morn 5.1 @21 even 5.1;
run;
```

Here's the new external file:

```
Colorado 1984 738.6 210.2
Colorado 1985 742.2 212.3
Colorado 1986 731.7 209.7
more data lines
```

SAS Tools

This chapter discusses the following SAS statements that you can use to customize output:

TITLE<*n*> '*text*';

specifies a title to be printed at the top of each page. You can use up to 10 TITLE statements. The PUT statement pointer begins on the first line after the last title; the SAS System does not automatically skip a line in report writing as it does with procedure output.

FILE PRINT <NOTITLES> <HEADER=*your-label*>
<LINESLEFT=*variable*>;

specifies the SAS procedure output file (destination PRINT). *Your-label* in the HEADER= option identifies a group of statements that are executed each time the SAS System begins a new page. If you use the HEADER= option to create the titles, be sure to specify NOTITLES to suppress the default titles. The value of the LINESLEFT= option is a *variable* whose value is the number of lines remaining on the current page.

FILE *your-output-file* <NOTITLES> <PRINT <HEADER=*your-label*>
<LINESLEFT=*variable*>>;

identifies the file to which lines are to be written. This form is an alternative to the preceding form when you don't route the report to the SAS procedure output file. If the output is to be a printed report, use the PRINT option to produce carriage-control characters in the report. Files containing carriage-control characters are known as print files. If the file is a print file, you can use the HEADER= and LINESLEFT= options as described above.

This chapter discusses the following pointer control for the PUT statement:

PAGE

> causes the pointer to move to the first line of a new page. Then the SAS System executes any remaining actions in the PUT statement. The _PAGE_ pointer control and the HEADER= option in the FILE statement have no effect on each other; the SAS System treats them independently.

This chapter discusses the following command:

PRINT '*your-output-file*'

> is a display manager command that writes the contents of the OUTPUT window to *your-output-file* and adds carriage-control characters to indicate where a new page begins.

Learning More

□ Chapter 25, "Creating Summary Tables," discusses the TITLE statement.

□ *SAS Language: Reference, Version 6, First Edition* provides information on creating two or more reports in the same DATA step. Use a separate FILE statement for each report; follow each FILE statement with the program statements for that report.

□ *SAS Language: Reference* completely documents the PUT statement, the TITLE statement, and statement labels.

□ The *SAS Applications Guide, 1987 Edition* presents other examples of DATA step reports and other applications of FILE and PUT statements.

□ The documentation provided by the vendor for your host system provides information on creating a print file to be used with the PRINT option in the FILE statement; print files differ from one operating system to another.

470

Part 9

Storing and Managing Data in SAS® Files

Chapter **31** SAS® Data Libraries

Introduction

A *SAS data library* is a collection of one or more SAS files. Each file is a *member* of the library. SAS data libraries help you organize your work. If you have an application that uses more than one SAS file, you can keep all the files in the same library. Organizing your files in data libraries makes it easier to locate SAS files and reference these files in your SAS program.

This chapter explains the concept of the SAS data library and tells you how to use data libraries in your SAS programs. Because the handling of data libraries is one of the most operating-system specific parts of the SAS System, this chapter gives only general information. Discussion of the intricacies of each operating system is beyond the scope of this book.

What Is a SAS Data Library?

Under most operating systems, a SAS data library is a logical concept roughly corresponding to the level of organization that the operating system uses to organize files. For instance, under directory-based operating systems, a SAS data library is a group of SAS files in the same directory. The directory may contain other files, but only the SAS files are part of the SAS data library. Under the CMS operating system, a SAS data library is a group of SAS files with the same filetype. Under the MVS and VSE operating systems, a SAS data library is a specially formatted MVS or VSE data set. This kind of data set can contain only SAS files.

Identifying a SAS Data Library

No matter which operating system you use, the way you identify and access a SAS data library is the same. You assign a *library reference (libref)* to each SAS data library you need to access. Then you reference files in a library by using the corresponding libref in your SAS program.

Generally, you assign a libref with a LIBNAME statement. Under some operating systems, you can use either the LIBNAME statement or an operating system command to assign a libref. Under the VSE operating system, you *must* use an operating system command to assign a libref. Refer to the SAS documentation for your host system for information on assigning librefs with operating system commands.

Although the LIBNAME statement has other functions, in this book it's used only to assign a libref to a SAS data library. When you use the LIBNAME statement this way, it associates a SAS name with an existing directory, minidisk, or MVS data set. The appropriate form of the statement is

LIBNAME *libref 'your-data-library'*;

where

libref	is the name to associate with the SAS data library. This name must conform to the rules for SAS names. Under the MVS operating system the libref must also conform to the rules for operating system names.
	Except under the CMS operating system, you can view the libref as the SAS System's abbreviation for the operating system's name for the library. On these systems, because the libref endures only for the duration of the SAS session, you don't have to use the same libref for a particular SAS data library each time you use the SAS System.
	Under the CMS operating system, the libref typically specifies the filetype of all files in the data library. In this case, you must always use the same libref for a given SAS data library because the filetype doesn't change.
your-data-library	is the directory name (under directory-based operating systems), the minidisk (CMS), or the data set name (MVS) of the data library.

Once you establish a libref for a SAS data library, you use the libref throughout your SAS program to read SAS files already in that data library or to create new ones (see the section "Referencing Files in a SAS Data Library" later in this chapter).

When you assign a libref with the LIBNAME statement, the SAS System writes a note to the log confirming the assignment. This note includes the operating system's name for the SAS data library and the name of the engine used to access the files in that library.

Note: Version 6 of the SAS System includes a variety of *engines*. An engine is the SAS System's mechanism for reading from or writing to a file. Each engine allows the SAS System to access files with a particular format. At this point, you don't need to be concerned about engines.

Types of Files in a SAS Data Library

You store all SAS files in a SAS data library. A *SAS file* is a specially structured file that is created, organized, and, optionally, maintained by the SAS System. A file of SAS statements, even one created during a SAS session, is usually *not* a SAS file. The SAS System assigns a member type to each file in a SAS data library. The following sections briefly describe the different types of SAS files.

SAS Data Sets

Every SAS data set consists of two parts: a descriptor portion, which describes the variables in the data set, and a set of observations containing values for the variables. You can think of a SAS data set as a table in which the rows are observations and the columns are variables.

If the descriptor portion and the observations are in the same physical location, the data set is a *SAS data file*. If the descriptor and the observations are stored separately, they form a *SAS data view*. The observations in a SAS data view may be stored in a SAS data set, an external data base, or an external file. The descriptor contains information on where the data are located and which observations and variables to process. You might use a view when you need only a subset of a large amount of data. Rather than actually creating and storing the subset, you can use PROC SQL or SAS/ACCESS software to create a view. You use the view as if it were a SAS data file. In addition to saving storage space, views simplify maintenance because they automatically reflect any changes to the data.

Note: SAS data views usually behave like SAS data files. Other chapters in this book don't distinguish between the two types of files.

SAS data files and the descriptor portion of a SAS data view are stored in SAS data libraries. SAS data files have a file type of DATA; the descriptor portion of a SAS data file has a file type of VIEW.

A SAS data file may have an index associated with it. One purpose of an index is to optimize the performance of the WHERE statement. Basically, an index contains all values of the indexed variable or variables and information on which observations have each value.

Other SAS Files

In addition to SAS data sets, a SAS data library can contain files of the following types:

CATALOG

> The SAS System stores many kinds of information in catalogs. Each catalog can contain multiple *entries*. Each entry has an *entry name* and an *entry type*. Some catalog entries contain system information such as key definitions. Other catalog entries contain application information such as window definitions, help windows, formats, informats, macros, or graphics output.

ACCESS

> Files of type ACCESS are access descriptors. The SAS System uses this information in order to build a SAS data view in which the observations are stored in an external data base. An access descriptor contains information on the layout of an external data base.

PROGRAM

> Files of type PROGRAM contain the compiled form of a SAS DATA step.

> Further discussion of all SAS files except SAS data sets is beyond the scope of this book. For more information, refer to *SAS Language: Reference, Version 6, First Edition.*

Where to Store SAS Files

When you start a SAS session, the SAS System automatically assigns the libref WORK to a special SAS data library. Normally, the files in the WORK library are *temporary files*; that is, usually the SAS System initializes the WORK library when you begin your SAS session and deletes all files in the WORK library when you end the session. Therefore, the WORK library is a useful place for storing SAS files that you don't need to save for use in a subsequent SAS session. The automatic deletion of the WORK library files at the end of the session prevents you from wasting disk space.

Files stored in any SAS data library other than the WORK library are normally *permanent files*; that is, they endure from one SAS session to the next. Store your SAS files in a permanent library if you plan to use them in multiple SAS sessions.

Referencing Files in a SAS Data Library

Every SAS file has a two-level name of the form

`libref.filename`

You can always reference a file with its two-level name. However, you can also use a one-level name (just the filename) to reference a file. A one-level name references a file in the WORK library unless you define the libref USER. This section explains how to use one- and two-level names and how to use the libref USER.

Note: This chapter separates the issues of permanent versus temporary files and one-level versus two-level names. Other chapters in this book assume typical use of the WORK library and refer to files referenced with a one-level name as temporary and to files referenced with a two-level name as permanent.

Using a One-Level Name

When you reference a file by a one-level name, the SAS System

1. looks for the libref USER. If this libref is assigned to a SAS data library, it becomes the default libref for one-level names.

2. uses WORK as the default libref for one-level names if the libref USER hasn't been assigned.

Therefore, if you define the libref USER, you must use a two-level name (for example, WORK.TEST) to access a file in the WORK library.

You assign the libref USER as you do any other libref, for example,

```
libname user 'your-data-library';
```

Therefore, if you define the libref USER, the following program creates a SAS data set named USER.GRADES:

```
data grades;
    infile 'your-data-source';
    input name $ 1-14 sex $ 15 section $ 17-19 grade;
run;
```

If you don't define USER, the same program creates the SAS data set WORK.GRADES. The two data sets are the same, but they are in different SAS data libraries.

Similarly, if you define the libref USER and you want to print the data set WORK.GRADES, you must use a two-level name in the PROC PRINT statement:

```
proc print data=work.grades;
run;
```

To print USER.GRADES when you have defined USER, use the same SAS statements but replace the two-level name WORK.GRADES with the one-level name GRADES.

If you define the libref USER, you need to make only one change in order to use the same program with files of the same name in different SAS data libraries. Instead of specifying two-level names, simply define USER differently in each case. For instance, the following program concatenates five SAS data sets in *your-data-library-1* and puts them in a new SAS data set, WEEK, in the same library:

```
libname user 'your-data-library-1';

data week;
    set mon tues wed thurs fri;
run;
```

By changing just the name of the SAS data library in the LIBNAME statement, you can combine files with the same names in another SAS data library, *your-data library-2*:

```
libname user 'your-data-library-2';

data week;
    set mon tues wed thurs fri;
run;
```

Note: Most SAS documentation assumes that the libref USER isn't defined. Therefore, in other chapters of this book you read that all files referenced by one-level names are in the WORK library. In fact, if the USER libref is defined, files referenced with a one-level name are in the USER library.

At your site, the libref USER may be created for you when you start your SAS session. Your SAS Software Consultant knows whether the libref is defined.

Using a Two-Level Name

You can always reference a SAS file with a two-level name, whether the libref you use is WORK, USER, or some other libref you have assigned. Normally, any two-level name with a libref other than WORK references a permanent SAS file.

Consider the following program:

```
libname intrchem 'your-data-library';

data intrchem.grades;
    infile 'your-data-source';
    input name $ 1-14 sex $ 15 section $ 17-19 grade;
run;
```

The LIBNAME statement establishes a connection between the SAS name INTRCHEM and *your-data-library*, which is an existing minidisk, MVS data set, or directory. The DATA step creates the SAS data set GRADES in the SAS data library INTRCHEM. The SAS System uses the INPUT statement to construct the data set from the raw data in *your-data-source*.

Once you have created the SAS file INTRCHEM.GRADES, you read from it by using its two-level name. The following program reads the file INTRCHEM.GRADES and creates a new SAS data set, INTRCHEM.FRIDAY, which is a subset of the original data set:

```
data intrchem.friday;
   set intrchem.grades;
   if section='Fri';
run;
```

The following program displays the SAS data set INTRCHEM.GRADES:

```
proc print data=intrchem.grades;
run;
```

SAS Tools

This chapter discusses the LIBNAME statement:

LIBNAME *libref 'your-data-library'*;
> allows you to identify a SAS data library to the SAS System on most operating systems. *Libref* is the name to associate with the SAS data library; *your-data-library* is the directory name (all directory-based operating systems), the minidisk (CMS), or the data set name (MVS) of the data library.

> **Note:** Under the VSE operating system you must use an operating system command to assign a libref.
> You can reference any SAS file by a two-level name of the form

> *libref.filename*

By default, if you use a one-level name to identify a SAS file, the SAS System uses the libref USER. If you don't define USER, the SAS System uses the libref WORK.

Learning More

□ Chapter 1, "What Is the SAS System?" and Chapter 2, "Introduction to DATA Step Processing," provide more information on naming and creating SAS data sets.

□ *SAS Language: Reference, Version 6, First Edition* provides more information on all types of SAS files. *SAS Guide to the SQL Procedure: Usage and Reference, Version 6, First Edition* provides detailed information on PROC SQL views.

□ *SAS Language: Reference* discusses the engines that the SAS System supports.

□ *SAS Language: Reference* provides more information on indexes.

□ *SAS Language: Reference* discusses the WORKINIT/NOWORKINIT options and the WORKTERM/NOWORKTERM options, which control when the SAS System initializes the WORK library.

Note: These options are implemented slightly differently on the VMS operating system. For details, refer to the *SAS Companion for the VMS Environment, Version 6, First Edition*.

□ *SAS Language: Reference* provides information on using the WORK configuration option to specify the location of the WORK library or to give the library an alternate libref.

□ *SAS Language: Reference* documents the USER= option, which you can use instead of the LIBNAME statement to define the USER libref. If you define the libref both ways or if you define it more than once with either method, the last definition holds.

□ The SAS documentation for your host system provides information on operating system specifics.

□ The documentation provided by the vendor for your host system presents information on creating temporary and permanent files. From the SAS System's point of view, the files in the WORK library are temporary unless you specify the NOWORKINIT and NOWORKTERM options, and the files in all other SAS data libraries are permanent. However, your operating system's point of view may be entirely different. For example, the operating system may allow you to create a temporary directory, minidisk, or MVS or VSE data set, that is, one that is deleted when you log off. Since all files in a SAS data library are deleted if the underlying operating system structure is deleted, it's the way the operating system views the SAS data library that determines whether the library endures from one session to the next.

Chapter 32 Managing SAS® Data Libraries

Introduction

As your use of SAS software products expands and you accumulate and manipulate increasing numbers of SAS files, you will need some means of managing SAS data libraries. Managing data libraries generally involves using some SAS procedure or operating system command to perform routine tasks such as

□ getting information about the contents of data libraries

□ renaming and deleting files

□ renaming variables

□ copying libraries and files.

The remaining chapters in this part describe how to use the DATASETS procedure to perform these tasks. This chapter tells you what tools are available for managing SAS data libraries and gives an overview of the DATASETS procedure.

Choosing Your Tools

Before Release 6.06 of the SAS System, you couldn't use operating system commands to manage SAS files stored on mainframe operating systems such as MVS or VSE. Beginning with Release 6.06, you can use operating system commands, but their use is restricted to the library level. To delete or copy individual data sets or files, it's still necessary to use SAS utility procedures. For SAS files stored on directory-based minicomputers and microcomputers and CMS, you can use operating system utilities at both the library and file level.

One advantage of learning and using SAS utility procedures is that they work on any operating system at any level. Once you learn SAS procedures, you can handle any file management task for your SAS libraries without knowing the corresponding operating system commands.

There are several SAS System features and utility procedures available for performing all the basic file management activities. You can use these features alone or in combination, depending on what works best for you.

□ The SAS System includes LIBNAME, DIR, VAR, and CATALOG windows that allow you to perform most file management tasks in a windowing environment in the SAS Display Manager System or in full-screen procedures.

□ The COPY procedure provides statements for copying all the members of a library or individual files within the library.

□ The CONTENTS procedure lists the contents of libraries and data sets and provides general information about their size and characteristics.

□ The DATASETS procedure combines all library management functions into one procedure. If your location doesn't have display manager, or if the SAS System executes in a batch or interactive line mode, using this procedure can save you time and resources.

The next three chapters focus on using the DATASETS procedure to manage data libraries whose members are primarily data sets. Once you have mastered the statements in the DATASETS procedure, you can use any file management tools available in the SAS System. However, there are some special features of the DATASETS procedure that you should understand before you start.

Understanding the DATASETS Procedure

The DATASETS procedure is an interactive procedure; that is, it remains active after a RUN statement is executed. Once you start the procedure, you can continue to manipulate files within a library until you have finished all the tasks you planned. This capability can save time and resources when you plan a number of tasks for one session.

The DATASETS procedure behaves in other ways that make it different from many other SAS procedures. The following paragraphs summarize some of the differences that are important to remember.

You specify the input library in the PROC DATASETS statement.

When you start the DATASETS procedure, you can also specify a default input library. If you don't specify an input library, the SAS System uses the temporary library WORK as the source of files. To specify a new default library, you must start the procedure again.

Statements execute in the order they're written.

If you write a program that does several things to the same library, the SAS System completes those tasks in the order they appear in the program. For example, if you want to see the contents of a data set, copy in a data set from another library, and then compare the contents of the second data set with the first, the statements that perform those tasks must be written in that order so they execute correctly.

Groups of statements can execute without a RUN statement.

For the DATASETS procedure *only*, the SAS System recognizes the following statements as implied RUN statements:

- □ APPEND statement

- □ CONTENTS statement

- □ MODIFY statement

- □ COPY statement

- □ PROC DATASETS statement.

The SAS System reads the program statements associated with one task until it reaches one of these statements. It executes all the preceding statements immediately and then continues reading until it reaches another of these statements. To cause the last task to execute, you must still submit a RUN statement.

Note: If you're running in interactive line mode, this feature means you can receive messages that statements have already executed before you submit a RUN statement. You should plan your tasks carefully if you are using this environment for submitting DATASETS statements.

The procedure remains active until you submit statements to stop it.

To stop the DATASETS procedure, you must issue a QUIT statement, a new PROC statement, or a DATA step. Submitting a QUIT statement executes any statements that haven't executed and ends the procedure.

Looking at a PROC DATASETS Session

The following example illustrates how the DATASETS procedure behaves in a typical session. The tasks and the action of the SAS System are listed in the order they occur in the program. The program is arranged in groups to show which statements are executed as one complete task. Each numbered group of code corresponds to a numbered item in the list of tasks.

A common time to manipulate files is at the beginning of a project when you need to create a test library, generally from existing production files. In this example, a file from a library REALDATA is used to create a test file in the library TEST89. You want to copy the file INCOME88 and check its contents to be sure the variables are compatible with an existing file in the test library.

```
proc datasets library=test89;     1

copy in=realdata out=test89;      2
select income88;

contents data=income88;    3
run;

modify income88;     4
rename sales=sales88;

quit;    5
```

1. Start the DATASETS procedure and specify the input library TEST89.

2. Copy INCOME88 from the library REALDATA. The SAS System recognizes these statements as one task. When it reads the CONTENTS statement, it immediately copies INCOME88 into the library TEST89. The CONTENTS statement acts as an implied RUN statement, causing the COPY statement to execute. This action is more noticeable if you are running your SAS session in interactive line mode.

3. Check the contents of the data set to make sure the variables are compatible with an existing SAS data set. When the SAS System receives the RUN statement, it checks the contents of INCOME88. Because the previous task has been executed, it finds the data set in the default library TEST89.

After checking the contents, you find it is necessary to rename the variable SALES before leaving the procedure. Because the DATASETS procedure is still active, you can submit more statements.

4. Rename the variable SALES to SALES88.

5. Stop the DATASETS procedure. The SAS System executes the last two program statements and ends the DATASETS procedure.

Learning More

□ Part 10, "Understanding Your SAS Environment," and *SAS Language: Reference, Version 6, First Edition* present information on managing SAS files through the SAS Display Manager System.

□ The *SAS Procedures Guide, Version 6, Third Edition* provides complete reference information on the DATASETS procedure, as well as the COPY and CONTENTS procedures.

□ The SAS documentation for your host system provides information on using operating system commands to manage SAS files created by Release 6.06 of the SAS System.

Chapter 33 Getting Information about Your Data Sets

Introduction

As you create libraries of SAS data sets, the SAS System generates and maintains information about where the library is stored in your operating system, how and when the data sets were created, and how their contents are defined. The DATASETS procedure allows you to view this information without printing the contents of the data set or referring to additional documentation.

This chapter tells you how to get the following information about your SAS data libraries and data sets:

☐ names and types of SAS files included in a library

☐ names and attributes for variables in SAS data sets

☐ summary information about operating system storage parameters

☐ summary information about the history and structure of SAS data sets.

Requesting a Library Directory

A *directory* is a list of files in a SAS data library. Each file is called a member, and each member has a *member type* that was assigned to it by the SAS System. When processing statements, the SAS System not only looks for the specified file, it verifies that the file has a member type that can be processed by the statement.

The directory listing contains two parts: a heading and a list of library members and their member types. The following sections tell you how to obtain a directory for a library of SAS data sets that contain facts about the climate of the United States. The library also contains two catalogs.

Listing All Files in a Library

To obtain a directory of all members in the library, you need only the PROC
DATASETS statement and its LIBRARY= option. The library containing climate
information has the libref USCLIM.* When you use the following program, the
SAS System sends the directory to the SAS log in Output 33.1.

```
libname usclim 'your-data-library';

proc datasets library=usclim;
```

Output 33.1
Directory for
Library USCLIM

```
NOTE: Libref USCLIM was successfully assigned as follows:
      Engine:        V606
      Physical Name: 'your-data-library'
61        libname usclim 'your-data-library';

62        proc datasets library=usclim;
                    -----Directory-----  1

               Libref:           USCLIM
               Engine:           V606
               Physical Name:    'your-data-library'

               #  Name 2     Memtype 3   Indexes 4
               ----------------------------------
               1  BASETEMP   CATALOG
               2  HIGHTEMP   DATA
               3  HURICANE   DATA
               4  LOWTEMP    DATA
               5  REPORT     CATALOG
               6  TEMPCHNG   DATA
```

The directory contains these items. (The numbers in the following list
correspond to the numbers in the SAS log in Output 33.1)

1. Heading
     This part of the directory gives the physical name as well as the libref
     for the library. Note that some operating systems provide additional
     information. The information shown here is common to all operating
     systems.

2. Name
     This column contains the second-level SAS name you assigned to the file
     when you created it. You can have two files of the same name in one
     library if the files are different member types.

3. Memtype
     The memtype, or member type, column indicates the type of SAS file.
     The most common member types are DATA and CATALOG. The library
     USCLIM contains two catalogs and four data sets.

---

* The DATA steps that created the data sets in the SAS data library USCLIM are shown in the
Appendix.

4. Indexes

> The last column indicates whether a data set is indexed. If the field contains a YES value, one or more variables in the data set are indexed. If the data set is not indexed, the field is blank.

Listing Files of the Same Member Type

Suppose you're interested only in the data sets stored in the library USCLIM. You can use the MEMTYPE= option in the DATASETS statement to show only certain types of SAS files in the directory listing. The following program gives a listing for USCLIM containing only data set information. Output 33.2 shows the SAS log, which lists only the data sets in USCLIM. You can list catalogs by specifying CATALOG after the MEMTYPE option. The examples in this book focus on using PROC DATASETS to manage only data sets.

```
proc datasets library=usclim memtype=data;
```

Output 33.2
Directory of Data
Sets Only in
USCLIM

```
7          proc datasets library=usclim memtype=data;
                      -----Directory-----

          Libref:           USCLIM
          Engine:           V606
          Physical Name:    'your-data-library'

          #  Name      Memtype  Indexes
          ------------------------------
          1  HIGHTEMP  DATA
          2  HURICANE  DATA
          3  LOWTEMP   DATA
          4  TEMPCHNG  DATA
```

Requesting Contents Information for SAS Data Sets

You can use the DATASETS procedure to look at the contents of a SAS data set without printing the data. The CONTENTS statement and its options provide descriptive information about data sets and a list of variables and their attributes.

Listing the Contents of One Data Set

The library USCLIM contains four data sets. Suppose you want to find the data set that contains extreme changes in temperature. You might begin by looking at the variables in the data set TEMPCHNG. Use the DATA= option in the following program to specify the name of the data set. Output 33.3 shows a contents listing for the data set TEMPCHNG. The results from the CONTENTS statement are sent to the SAS output file rather than to the SAS log.

```
contents data=tempchng;
run;
```

Output 33.3
Contents Listing
for the Data Set
TEMPCHNG

```
                              The SAS System                            1

                           DATASETS PROCEDURE          1

Data Set Name: USCLIM.TEMPCHNG          Observations:           5
Member Type:   DATA                     Variables:              6
Engine:        V606                     Indexes:                0
Created:       09AUG89:15:53:20         Observation Length:     53
Last Modified: 09AUG89:15:53:20         Deleted Observations:   0
Data Set Type:                          Compressed:             NO
Label:

        -----Alphabetic List of Variables and Attributes-----    2

      #    Variable   Type   Len   Pos   Format    Informat
      --------------------------------------------------------
      2    DATE       Num     8    13    DATE7.    DATE7.
      6    DIFF       Num     8    45
      4    END_F      Num     8    29
      5    MINUTES    Num     8    37
      3    START_F    Num     8    21
      1    STATE      Char   13     0              $CHAR13.
```

The output from the CONTENTS statement varies for different operating
systems. The following list describes the information you might find in a
contents listing. (The numbers in the following list correspond to the numbers in
the contents listing in the Output 33.3.)

1. Heading

    The heading contains field names. The fields are left empty if the field
    doesn't apply to the data set. The field names are listed below:

    Data Set Name

       is the two-level name assigned to the data set.

    Member Type

       is the type of member of the SAS data library.

    Engine

       is the access method the SAS System uses to read from or write
       to the data set.

    Created

       is the date the data set was created.

    Last Modified

       is the last date the data set was modified.

    Data Set Type

       applies only to files with the member type DATA. Information in
       this field indicates that the data set contains special observations
       and variables for use with SAS statistical procedures.

    Label

       is the descriptive information you supply in a LABEL= data set
       option to identify the data set.

    Observations

       is the total number of observations currently in the data set.

    Variables

       is the number of variables in the data set.

Indexes
>is the number of indexes on the data set.

Observation Length
>is the length of each observation in bytes.

Deleted Observations
>is the number of observations marked for deletion, if applicable.

Compressed
>indicates whether the data are in fixed-length or variable-length records. If the data set is compressed, an additional field indicates whether new observations are added to the end of the data set or written to unused space within the data set.

2. Alphabetic List of Variables and Attributes
This table lists all the variable names in the data set in alphabetical order and describes the attributes assigned to the variable when it was defined. The attributes are described below:

\#
>is the relative position of the variable in the observation.

Variable
>is the name of the variable.

Type
>indicates whether the variable is character or numeric.

Len
>is the length of the variable in bytes.

Pos
>is the physical position in the observation buffer of the first byte of the variable's associated value.

Format
>is the format of the variable.

Informat
>is the informat of the variable.

Label
>is the label for the variable.

In addition, the output you produce may provide information about how the data set is stored within your operating system. The field names vary according to the engine used to access the data set and the operating system. If the variables are part of a SAS index, the output also displays a table describing the indexes.

Listing the Contents of All Data Sets in a Library

You can list the contents of all the data sets in the library USCLIM by substituting the SAS keyword _ALL_ for the file in the DATA= option. The statement below produces a directory listing for the library in the SAS output file and then prints a contents listing for each data set listed in the directory:

```
contents data=_all_;
```

If you want to send only a directory listing to the output file, add the NODS option after the DATA=_ALL_ statement. This statement prints the directory and then suppresses printing of the contents for individual data sets. Use this form if you want the directory for the default library:

```
contents data=_all_ nods;
```

Include the libref if you want the directory for another library, for example, the library STORM:

```
contents data=storm._all_ nods;
```

Requesting Contents Information in Different Formats

If you want a variation of the contents listing, you can use the POSITION or SHORT options to modify the CONTENTS statement.

To obtain the list of variables in the data set TEMPCHNG in order of their relative position within an observation, write the CONTENTS statement as shown in the following program. Output 33.4 shows that the contents are listed in both alphabetical and position order.

```
contents data=tempchng position;
run;
```

Output 33.4
Listing Contents of
Data Set
TEMPCHNG in
Position Order

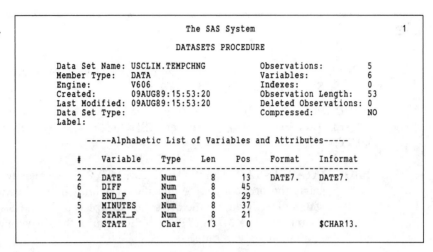

```
                               The SAS System                                  1

                            DATASETS PROCEDURE

     Data Set Name: USCLIM.TEMPCHNG          Observations:          5
     Member Type:   DATA                     Variables:             6
     Engine:        V606                     Indexes:               0
     Created:       09AUG89:15:53:20         Observation Length:    53
     Last Modified: 09AUG89:15:53:20         Deleted Observations:  0
     Data Set Type:                          Compressed:            NO
     Label:

          -----Alphabetic List of Variables and Attributes-----

          #    Variable   Type   Len   Pos   Format    Informat
          -------------------------------------------------------
          2    DATE       Num     8    13    DATE7.    DATE7.
          6    DIFF       Num     8    45
          4    END_F      Num     8    29
          5    MINUTES    Num     8    37
          3    START_F    Num     8    21
          1    STATE      Char   13     0              $CHAR13.
```

```
                               The SAS System                                  2

                            DATASETS PROCEDURE

             -----Variables Ordered by Position-----

          #    Variable   Type   Len   Pos   Format    Informat
          -------------------------------------------------------
          1    STATE      Char   13     0              $CHAR13.
          2    DATE       Num     8    13    DATE7.    DATE7.
          3    START_F    Num     8    21
          4    END_F      Num     8    29
          5    MINUTES    Num     8    37
          6    DIFF       Num     8    45
```

If you don't need all the information in the contents listing, request an abbreviated version by using the SHORT option in the CONTENTS statement. To end the DATASETS procedure, issue the QUIT statement, a new PROC statement, or a DATA step as shown in the following program. Output 33.5 lists the variable names.

```
contents data=tempchng short;
run;
quit;
```

Output 33.5
Listing Variable
Names Only for
Data Set
TEMPCHNG

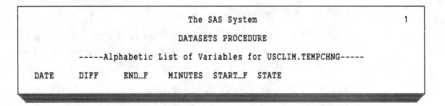

```
                               The SAS System                                  1

                            DATASETS PROCEDURE

          -----Alphabetic List of Variables for USCLIM.TEMPCHNG-----

     DATE     DIFF     END_F    MINUTES  START_F  STATE
```

SAS Tools

This chapter discusses using the DATASETS procedure to get information about your SAS data libraries and data sets:

PROC DATASETS LIBRARY=*libref* <MEMTYPE=*member-type*>;
   CONTENTS DATA=*SAS-data-set* <SHORT> <POSITION> <NODS>;
QUIT;

PROC DATASETS LIBRARY=*libref* <MEMTYPE=*member-type*>;
   starts the procedure and specifies a default input library for subsequent statements. It automatically sends a directory to the SAS log when it is submitted. The MEMTYPE= option limits the directory listing to files of one member type only.

CONTENTS DATA=*SAS-data-set* <SHORT> <POSITION> <NODS>;
   generates a list of variable names and attributes for the *SAS-data-set* you specify in the DATA= option. The SHORT option produces an alphabetical list of variable names only. The POSITION option prints the contents listing in order of relative position of the variable in the *SAS-data-set*. You can use the NODS option with the keyword _ALL_ in the DATA= option to produce a directory of the library in a SAS output file.

QUIT;
   executes any preceding statements that haven't already run and stops the procedure.

Learning More

□ Chapter 39, "Mastering Your Environment with Selected Windows," presents details on using the DIR, VAR, LIBNAME, and CATALOG windows in the SAS Display Manager System to combine the functions of the CONTENTS statement with the convenience of windows. This feature is available if you're using the SAS System in a full-screen environment.

□ *SAS Language: Reference, Version 6, First Edition* discusses indexes and compressed data sets.

□ The *SAS Procedures Guide, Version 6, Third Edition* provides complete reference information on the DATASETS procedure. You can use the DATASETS procedure to manage SAS files of all member types.

□ The *SAS Procedures Guide* documents the CONTENTS procedure, which provides all the functions of the CONTENTS statement in the DATASETS procedure.

□ The *SAS Procedures Guide* documents the CATALOG procedure, which you can use to obtain contents information about catalogs.

Chapter 34 Modifying Data Set Names and Attributes

Introduction

The SAS System allows you to modify data set names and attributes without creating new data sets. This chapter describes statements in the DATASETS procedure you can use to

- ☐ rename data sets

- ☐ rename variables

- ☐ change, add, or delete variable formats

- ☐ change, add, or delete variable labels.

Note that you can't use the DATASETS procedure to change the values of observations, create or delete variables, or change the type or length of variables. These manipulations are performed through the statements and functions of the DATA step.

Although this chapter focuses on using the DATASETS procedure to modify data sets, you can use some of the statements and options illustrated to modify other SAS files.

Renaming Data Sets

Renaming data sets is often required for effective data library management. You might rename data sets as you archive them or as you add new data values. If you're copying data sets from one library to another, you can rename data sets that have the same name but different data to prevent the output data set from being overwritten. Use the CHANGE statement of the DATASETS procedure to rename data sets. The form of the CHANGE statement is

CHANGE *old-name=new-name*;

where

old-name   is the current *name* of the data set.

new-name   is the *name* you want to give the data set.

Suppose you have a SAS data library, USCLIM, that contains information about the climate of the United States. You want to rename two data sets in USCLIM. The following program starts the DATASETS procedure and changes the name of the data set HIGHTEMP to USHIGH and the name of the data set LOWTEMP to USLOW.* As it processes these statements, the SAS System sends messages to the SAS log, as shown in Output 34.1. These messages verify that the data sets have been renamed.

```
libname usclim 'your-data-library';

proc datasets library=usclim;
   change hightemp=ushigh lowtemp=uslow;
run;
```

Output 34.1
Renaming Data
Sets in Library
USCLIM

```
NOTE: Libref USCLIM was successfully assigned as follows:
      Engine:        V606
      Physical Name: 'your-data-library'
5          libname usclim 'your-data-library';
6
7          proc datasets library=usclim;
                    -----Directory-----

                    Libref:         USCLIM
                    Engine:         V606
                    Physical Name:  'your-data-library'

               #  Name      Memtype  Indexes
               ----------------------------
               1  BASETEMP  CATALOG
               2  HIGHTEMP  DATA
               3  HURICANE  DATA
               4  LOWTEMP   DATA
               5  REPORT    CATALOG
               6  TEMPCHNG  DATA
8          change hightemp=ushigh lowtemp=uslow;
9      run;

NOTE: Changing the name USCLIM.HIGHTEMP to USCLIM.USHIGH (memtype=DATA).
NOTE: Changing the name USCLIM.LOWTEMP to USCLIM.USLOW (memtype=DATA).
```

---

*   The DATA steps that created the data sets in the SAS data library USCLIM are shown in the Appendix in "Data Sets for Chapter 33."

Renaming Variables

One circumstance under which you might want to rename variables is when you are combining data sets with one or more identical variable names. You can rename one or more variables by using the MODIFY statement in the DATASETS procedure and its associated RENAME statement. The form of these statements is

> **MODIFY** *SAS-data-set*;
> **RENAME** *old-name*=*new-name*;

where

SAS-data-set	is the name of the *SAS-data-set* containing the variable you want to rename.
old-name	is the current *name* of the variable.
new-name	is the *name* you want to give the variable.

Suppose you want to rename two variables in the data set HURICANE, which is in your library USCLIM. The following program changes the variable name STATE to PLACE and the variable name DEATHS to USDEATHS. Remember that you already started the DATASETS procedure. The SAS log messages verifying that the variables are renamed to PLACE and USDEATHS appear in Output 34.2. All other attributes assigned to these variables remain unchanged.

```
modify huricane;
rename state=place deaths=usdeaths;
run;
```

Output 34.2
Renaming
Variables in the
Data Set
HURICANE

```
8          modify huricane;
9          rename state=place deaths=usdeaths;
NOTE: Renaming variable STATE to PLACE.
NOTE: Renaming variable DEATHS to USDEATHS.
10         run;
```

Modifying Variable Attributes

The SAS System allows you to assign and store descriptive labels and formats that are used by many SAS procedures during printing. The MODIFY statement and its associated FORMAT and LABEL statements enable you to change, add, or delete these attributes. Note that you can't use the MODIFY statement to change fixed attributes such as type or length of the variable.

Adding, Changing, or Deleting Formats

Adding, changing, or deleting a format changes the way the data values are printed or displayed after processing. You can change the format to a SAS format or to a format that you have defined and stored using the FORMAT procedure.

To assign a new format or delete a format, use the MODIFY statement and the FORMAT statement. The form of these statements is

> **MODIFY** *SAS-data-set*;
> **FORMAT** *variable format*;

where

SAS-data-set	is the name of the *SAS-data-set* containing the variable whose format you want to modify.
variable	is the name of the *variable* whose format you want to change, add, or delete.
format	is the *format* you want to give the variable.

Follow these rules when adding or changing a format:

□ List the variable names before the format.

□ List multiple variable names or use abbreviated variable lists if you want to assign the format to more than one variable.

□ Don't use any punctuation to separate items in the list.

The following example illustrates ways to include many variables and formats in the same FORMAT statement:

```
format date1-date5 mmddyy6. cost1 cost2 dollar4.2 place $char25.;
```

The variables DATE1 through DATE5 are written in abbreviated list form, and the format MMDDYY6. is assigned to all five variables. The variables COST1 and COST2 are listed individually before their format. The format $CHAR25. is assigned to the variable PLACE.

You must follow two more rules when you are deleting formats from variables:

□ List the variable names only.

□ Place the variable names last in the list if you're using the same FORMAT statement to add or change formats.

Suppose in your data set HURICANE you want to change the format for the variable DATE from a full spelling of the month, date, and year to an abbreviation of the month and year. You also want to delete the format for the variable MILLIONS. Because the FORMAT statement doesn't send any messages to the SAS log, you must use the CONTENTS statement if you want to make sure the changes were made. The following program changes the format for the variable DATE, deletes the format for MILLIONS, and displays the contents of the data set HURICANE before and after these changes. Output 34.3 shows the output from the CONTENTS statements. You can see that the format for the variable DATE was changed from WORDDATE18. to MONYY5. and that the format for the variable MILLIONS was deleted.

```
contents data=huricane;
   modify huricane;
   format date monyy5. millions;
contents data=huricane;
run;
```

Output 34.3
Modifying
Variable Formats
in the Data Set
HURICANE

```
                        The SAS System                            1
                      DATASETS PROCEDURE

   Data Set Name: USCLIM.HURICANE      Observations:        5
   Member Type:   DATA                 Variables:           5
   Engine:        V606                 Indexes:             0
   Created:       18AUG89:12:01:07     Observation Length:  43
   Last Modified: 18AUG89:12:05:45     Deleted Observations: 0
   Data Set Type:                      Compressed:          NO
   Label:

          -----Alphabetic List of Variables and Attributes-----

   #   Variable   Type   Len   Pos   Format       Informat   Label
   -----------------------------------------------------------------
   2   DATE       Num    8     11    WORDDATE18.  DATE7.
   4   MILLIONS   Num    8     27    DOLLAR6.                 Damage
   5   NAME       Char   8     35
   1   PLACE      Char   11    0                  $CHAR11.
   3   USDEATHS   Num    8     19
```

```
                        The SAS System                            2
                      DATASETS PROCEDURE

   Data Set Name: USCLIM.HURICANE      Observations:        5
   Member Type:   DATA                 Variables:           5
   Engine:        V606                 Indexes:             0
   Created:       18AUG89:12:01:07     Observation Length:  43
   Last Modified: 18AUG89:12:06:30     Deleted Observations: 0
   Data Set Type:                      Compressed:          NO
   Label:

          -----Alphabetic List of Variables and Attributes-----

   #   Variable   Type   Len   Pos   Format    Informat   Label
   -----------------------------------------------------------------
   2   DATE       Num    8     11    MONYY5.   DATE7.
   4   MILLIONS   Num    8     27                          Damage
   5   NAME       Char   8     35
   1   PLACE      Char   11    0               $CHAR11.
   3   USDEATHS   Num    8     19
```

Adding, Changing, or Deleting Labels

A label is the descriptive information that identifies variables in tables, plots, and graphs. You generally assign labels when you create the variable. If you don't assign a label, the SAS System prints the variable name. You can use the MODIFY statement and its associated LABEL statement to add, replace, or remove labels for variables. The form of these statements is

> **MODIFY** *SAS-data-set*;
> **LABEL** *variable*='*new-label*';

where

SAS-data-set	is the name of the *SAS-data-set* containing the variable whose label you want to modify.
variable	is the name of the *variable* whose label you want to add, delete, or change.
new-label	is the *label* you want to give the variable.

When writing the LABEL statement, follow these rules:

□ Enclose the text of the label in single or double quotes.

□ Limit the label to no more than 40 characters, including blanks.

□ Use a blank as the text of the label to remove a label. The format is *variable*=' '.

The following program changes the label for the variable MILLIONS and adds a label for the variable PLACE in the data set HURICANE. Use the CONTENTS statement to verify that the changes were made because the LABEL statement doesn't send any messages to the SAS log. To stop working with the DATASETS procedure, issue the QUIT statement, another PROC statement, or a DATA statement. Output 34.4 shows the results from the CONTENTS statements. You can see that the label for the variable MILLIONS is replaced and that a label is included in the description of the variable PLACE.

```
contents data=huricane;
  modify huricane;
  label millions='Damage in Millions' place='State Hardest Hit';
contents data=huricane;
run;
quit;
```

Output 34.4
Modifying
Variable Labels in
the Data Set
HURICANE

```
                          The SAS System                              1
                        DATASETS PROCEDURE

   Data Set Name: USCLIM.HURICANE      Observations:          5
   Member Type:   DATA                 Variables:             5
   Engine:        V606                 Indexes:               0
   Created:       18AUG89:12:01:07     Observation Length:   43
   Last Modified: 18AUG89:12:06:30     Deleted Observations:  0
   Data Set Type:                      Compressed:           NO
   Label:

           -----Alphabetic List of Variables and Attributes-----

   #    Variable   Type   Len   Pos   Format     Informat   Label
   -----------------------------------------------------------------
   2    DATE       Num     8    11    MONYY5.    DATE7.
   4    MILLIONS   Num     8    27                          Damage
   5    NAME       Char    8    35
   1    PLACE      Char   11     0               $CHAR11.
   3    USDEATHS   Num     8    19
```

```
                          The SAS System                              2
                        DATASETS PROCEDURE

   Data Set Name: USCLIM.HURICANE      Observations:          5
   Member Type:   DATA                 Variables:             5
   Engine:        V606                 Indexes:               0
   Created:       18AUG89:12:01:07     Observation Length:   43
   Last Modified: 18AUG89:12:07:01     Deleted Observations:  0
   Data Set Type:                      Compressed:           NO
   Label:

           -----Alphabetic List of Variables and Attributes-----

   #    Variable   Type   Len   Pos   Format    Informat   Label
   ----------------------------------------------------------------
   2    DATE       Num     8    11    MONYY5.   DATE7.
   4    MILLIONS   Num     8    27                         Damage in Millions
   5    NAME       Char    8    35
   1    PLACE      Char   11     0              $CHAR11.   State Hardest Hit
   3    USDEATHS   Num     8    19
```

SAS Tools

This chapter discusses using the DATASETS procedure for renaming SAS data sets and variables and for modifying variable attributes such as labels and formats:

PROC DATASETS LIBRARY=*libref*;
  CHANGE *old-name=new-name*;
  MODIFY *SAS-data-set*;
    RENAME *old-name=new-name*;
    FORMAT *variable format*;
    LABEL *variable='new-label'*;
QUIT;

PROC DATASETS LIBRARY=*libref*;
      starts the procedure and specifies a default input library for subsequent statements.

CHANGE *old-name=new-name*;
> renames the data set you specify with *old-name* to the name you specify
> with *new-name*. You can rename more than one data set in the same
> library using one CHANGE statement. All new names must be valid SAS
> names.

MODIFY *SAS-data-set*;
> identifies the *SAS-data-set* that you want to change.
>> You can use the following statements with the MODIFY statement:

> **RENAME** *old-name=new-name*;
>> changes the name of the variable you specify with *old-name* to
>> the name you specify with *new-name*. You can rename more than
>> one variable in the same data set using one RENAME statement.
>> All the names must be valid SAS names.

> **FORMAT** *variable format*;
>> adds, replaces, or removes the format assigned to the variable
>> you specify with *variable* using the format you specify with
>> *format*. You can give more than one variable the same format by
>> listing more than one variable before the format. Leave the
>> *format* off if you want to delete a format.

> **LABEL** *variable='new-label'*;
>> adds, replaces, or removes the label assigned to the variable you
>> specify with *variable*. To remove a label, place a blank space
>> inside the quotes.

QUIT;
> executes any preceding statements that have not already run and stops
> the procedure.

Learning More

□ Chapter 4, "Starting with SAS Data Sets," discusses creating and deleting
variables in the DATA step.

□ *SAS Language: Reference, Version 6, First Edition* provides additional
information on the LABEL statement and writing and using variable labels.

□ *SAS Language: Reference* provides information on using the RENAME= data
set option or the RENAME statement in the DATA step to rename the
variables of SAS data sets. You can also rename variables as you create new
data sets.

□ *SAS Language: Reference* discusses the many standard informats and formats
available for reading and printing data values.

□ The *SAS Procedures Guide, Version 6, Third Edition* describes additional
statements available with the MODIFY statement for changing informats and
creating and deleting indexes for variables.

Chapter **35** Copying, Moving, and Deleting
SAS® Data Sets

Introduction

Copying, moving, and deleting data sets are the library management tasks you do
most frequently. You perform these tasks to create test files, make backups,
archive files, and remove unused files. The DATASETS procedure allows you to
work with all the files in a SAS data library or with parts of the library. This
chapter provides information on how to use the DATASETS procedure to

□ copy all files in a library at one time

□ copy data sets

□ move data sets

□ delete data sets

□ delete all files in a library at one time.

This chapter focuses on using the DATASETS procedure to copy, move, or delete data sets, but you can also use the statements and options illustrated to copy, move, or delete other SAS files.

▶ *Caution* .... *When used incorrectly, the procedures and statements illustrated in this chapter can damage or permanently remove files. The SAS System does not notify you of duplicate file names or variable names before copying, and it does not ask you to verify delete operations.* ▲

Copying Data Libraries

You can use the COPY statement in the DATASETS procedure to copy all SAS data sets from one library to another. When copying data sets, the SAS System duplicates the contents of each file, including the descriptor information, and updates information in the directory for each library.

Suppose you have five SAS data libraries that contain sample data sets used to collect and store weather statistics for the United States and other countries. The data libraries have the librefs PRECIP, USCLIM, CLIMATE, WEATHER, and STORM. This example sets up all the libnames used in the chapter: *

```
libname precip 'your-data-library';
libname usclim 'your-data-library';
libname climate 'your-data-library';
libname weather 'your-data-library';
libname storm 'your-data-library';
```

As you make changes to libraries, it's helpful to obtain directories of the input and output libraries before copying files. This step is important because the libraries might contain data sets with the same name but different data.

▶ *Caution* .... *During processing, the SAS System automatically writes the data from the input library into the output data set of the same name. You do not receive a warning message that there are duplicate data set names before copying starts.* ▲

The next two sections explain how to copy all the files in a library. They also show you how to use the IN= and OUT= options in the COPY statement so that you can copy files regardless of the library you specify as the default input library in the PROC DATASETS statement.

---

* The DATA steps that created the data sets in the SAS data libraries CLIMATE, PRECIP, and STORM are shown in the Appendix. The data steps that created the data sets in the SAS data library USCLIM are also shown in the Appendix in "Data Sets for Chapter 33."

Copying from the Default Library

To copy files from the default library you specify in the PROC DATASETS statement, use the COPY statement. The form of this statement is

COPY OUT=*libref*;

where *libref* is the libref of the library to which you want to copy the files. Note that you must specify an output library in the OUT= option. If you don't specify a library to copy to, the files aren't copied.

The library PRECIP contains international records for snowfall and rainfall amounts. Another library, CLIMATE, contains records on temperature. After compiling these statistics, you might find it easier to work with the data sets if they were in one library.

To copy all the files in PRECIP into the library CLIMATE, first issue the PROC DATASETS statement to start the procedure and to specify the name of the default library. Then use the CONTENTS statement to obtain a directory of each library and make sure that none of the data sets in the two libraries has the same name. Output 35.1 shows the contents listings.

```
proc datasets library=precip;
   contents data=_all_ nods;
   contents data=climate._all_ nods;
run;
```

Output 35.1
Checking Directories of PRECIP and CLIMATE before Copying

```
                       The SAS System                     1

                    DATASETS PROCEDURE

                    -----Directory-----

           Libref:         PRECIP
           Engine:         V606
           Physical Name:  'your-data-library'

             #  Name  Memtype  Indexes
             -----------------------------
             1  RAIN  DATA
             2  SNOW  DATA
```

```
                       The SAS System                     2

                    DATASETS PROCEDURE

                    -----Directory-----

           Libref:         CLIMATE
           Engine:         V606
           Physical Name:  'your-data-library'

             #  Name      Memtype  Indexes
             -----------------------------
             1  HIGHTEMP  DATA
             2  LOWTEMP   DATA
```

There are no duplicate names in the directories so you can issue the following COPY statement. The SAS log in Output 35.2 shows the messages you receive as the data sets in the library PRECIP are copied to the library CLIMATE. There are now two copies of the data sets RAIN and SNOW.

```
copy out=climate;
run;
```

Output 35.2
Messages Sent to
the SAS Log
during Copying

```
9          copy out=climate;
10
11         run;

NOTE: Copying PRECIP.RAIN to CLIMATE.RAIN (MEMTYPE=DATA).
NOTE: The data set CLIMATE.RAIN has 5 observations and 4 variables.
NOTE: Copying PRECIP.SNOW to CLIMATE.SNOW (MEMTYPE=DATA).
NOTE: The data set CLIMATE.SNOW has 3 observations and 4 variables.
```

Copying from Other Libraries

You can copy from a library other than the default library without issuing another PROC DATASETS statement. Use the IN= option in the COPY statement to override the default library. The form of this option is

COPY OUT=*libref-1* IN=*libref-2*;

where *libref-1* is the libref of the library you want to copy to and *libref-2* is the libref of the library you want to copy from.

The IN= option is a useful feature when you want to copy more than one library into the output library. You can use one COPY statement for each input library without repeating the PROC DATASETS statement. Remember that in the last example you specified PRECIP as the default library. Use the following program to copy the libraries PRECIP, STORM, CLIMATE, and USCLIM to the library WEATHER. The SAS log in Output 35.3 shows that the data sets from these libraries have been consolidated in the library WEATHER.

```
copy out=weather;
copy in=storm out=weather;
copy in=climate out=weather;
copy in=usclim out=weather;
run;
```

Output 35.3
Copying Four
Libraries into
Library WEATHER

```
12          copy out=weather;
NOTE: Copying PRECIP.RAIN to WEATHER.RAIN (MEMTYPE=DATA).
NOTE: The data set WEATHER.RAIN has 5 observations and 4 variables.
NOTE: Copying PRECIP.SNOW to WEATHER.SNOW (MEMTYPE=DATA).
NOTE: The data set WEATHER.SNOW has 3 observations and 4 variables.
13          copy in=storm out=weather;
NOTE: Copying STORM.TORNADO to WEATHER.TORNADO (MEMTYPE=DATA).
NOTE: The data set WEATHER.TORNADO has 5 observations and 4 variables.
14          copy in=climate out=weather;
NOTE: Copying CLIMATE.HIGHTEMP to WEATHER.HIGHTEMP (MEMTYPE=DATA).
NOTE: The data set WEATHER.HIGHTEMP has 5 observations and 4 variables.
NOTE: Copying CLIMATE.LOWTEMP to WEATHER.LOWTEMP (MEMTYPE=DATA).
NOTE: The data set WEATHER.LOWTEMP has 5 observations and 4 variables.
NOTE: Copying CLIMATE.RAIN to WEATHER.RAIN (MEMTYPE=DATA).
NOTE: The data set WEATHER.RAIN has 5 observations and 4 variables.
NOTE: Copying CLIMATE.SNOW to WEATHER.SNOW (MEMTYPE=DATA).
NOTE: The data set WEATHER.SNOW has 3 observations and 4 variables.
15          copy in=usclim out=weather;
16
17          run;

NOTE: Copying USCLIM.BASETEMP to WEATHER.BASETEMP (MEMTYPE=CATALOG).
NOTE: Copying USCLIM.HURICANE to WEATHER.HURICANE (MEMTYPE=DATA).
NOTE: The data set WEATHER.HURICANE has 5 observations and 5 variables.
NOTE: Copying USCLIM.REPORT to WEATHER.REPORT (MEMTYPE=CATALOG).
NOTE: Copying USCLIM.TEMPCHNG to WEATHER.TEMPCHNG (MEMTYPE=DATA).
NOTE: The data set WEATHER.TEMPCHNG has 5 observations and 6 variables.
NOTE: Copying USCLIM.USHIGH to WEATHER.USHIGH (MEMTYPE=DATA).
NOTE: The data set WEATHER.USHIGH has 6 observations and 5 variables.
NOTE: Copying USCLIM.USLOW to WEATHER.USLOW (MEMTYPE=DATA).
NOTE: The data set WEATHER.USLOW has 7 observations and 5 variables.
```

Copying Data Sets

The SAS System also provides statements for copying only part of a library. You can use one of two methods to limit how much of the library you copy: the SELECT statement or the EXCLUDE statement. The method you choose is generally a matter of convenience or efficiency.

Selecting Data Sets to Copy

Use the SELECT statement with the COPY statement if you want to copy only a few data sets from a large data library. List the data set names after the SELECT statement with no punctuation between them.

The following program copies the data set HURICANE from the library USCLIM to the library STORM. The default library is still PRECIP so the program includes the IN= option to specify another input library. The SAS log in Output 35.4 shows that only the data set HURICANE was copied into the library STORM.

```
copy in=usclim out=storm;
select huricane;
run;
```

Output 35.4
Copying Data Set
HURICANE to
Library STORM

```
10          copy in=usclim out=storm;
11          select huricane;
12
13          run;

NOTE: Copying USCLIM.HURICANE to STORM.HURICANE (MEMTYPE=DATA).
NOTE: The data set STORM.HURICANE has 5 observations and 5 variables.
```

Excluding Data Sets from Copying

Use the EXCLUDE statement with the COPY statement if you want to copy an entire library except for a few data sets. The following program copies the library PRECIP to USCLIM except for the data set SNOW. The SAS log in Output 35.5 shows that only the data set RAIN was copied to USCLIM. The data set SNOW remains in the library PRECIP.

```
copy out=usclim;
exclude snow;
run;
```

If you want to exclude more than one data set from the copy, list the names after the EXCLUDE statement with no punctuation between them.

Output 35.5
Excluding Data
Set SNOW from
Copying to Library
USCLIM

```
9           copy out=usclim;
10
11          exclude snow;
12          run;

NOTE: Copying PRECIP.RAIN to USCLIM.RAIN (MEMTYPE=DATA).
NOTE: The data set USCLIM.RAIN has 5 observations and 4 variables.
```

Moving Libraries and Data Sets

When data sets are moved, they're copied and deleted. The SAS System first copies data sets to the library named in the OUT= option and then deletes them from the input library.

▶ *Caution* . . . . *The MOVE option deletes all or some of the files in the input library immediately after copying them.* ▲

Moving Libraries

To move data sets from one SAS library to another, use the MOVE option in the COPY statement. Use the following program to move the data sets in the library PRECIP to the library CLIMATE. The SAS log in Output 35.6 shows that the data sets in PRECIP were copied into CLIMATE. No messages are sent to the SAS log telling you that all data sets were deleted from PRECIP.

```
copy out=climate move;
run;
```

Output 35.6
Moving Library PRECIP to Library CLIMATE

```
9          copy out=climate move;
10
11         run;
NOTE: Moving PRECIP.RAIN to CLIMATE.RAIN (MEMTYPE=DATA).
NOTE: The data set CLIMATE.RAIN has 5 observations and 4 variables.
NOTE: Moving PRECIP.SNOW to CLIMATE.SNOW (MEMTYPE=DATA).
NOTE: The data set CLIMATE.SNOW has 3 observations and 4 variables.
```

As the following program illustrates, if you ask for a directory listing for PRECIP after copying files with the MOVE option, the SAS output from the CONTENTS statement tells you there are no members in the library. The library CLIMATE contains the only copy of the data sets RAIN and SNOW. Output 35.7 shows the directory for PRECIP.

```
contents data=_all_ nods;
run;
```

Output 35.7
Directory of the Library PRECIP Showing That Data Sets Are Deleted during the Move Operation

```
                        The SAS System                          1

                      DATASETS PROCEDURE

                     -----Directory-----

             Libref:          PRECIP
             Engine:          V606
             Physical Name:   'your-data-library'
ERROR: No matching members in directory.
```

Note: The data sets are removed from the SAS directory for PRECIP, but the SAS libref is still assigned for this session. The name assigned to the library on your operating system isn't removed when you move all files from one SAS library to another.

Moving Data Sets

You can use the SELECT and EXCLUDE statements to move one or more data sets. The data sets you move are deleted from the input library. Use the following program to move the data set HURICANE from the library USCLIM:

```
copy in=usclim out=storm move;
select hurricane;
```

Similarly, you can also use the EXCLUDE statement to move all files except the data set SNOW in the library PRECIP.

```
copy out=usclim move;
exclude snow;
```

Deleting Data Sets

Before using any of the options or statements discussed in this section, check carefully to ensure you're specifying the correct library and data set.

▶ *Caution* . . . . *The SAS System immediately deletes the files in a SAS data library when the program statements are submitted. You are not asked to verify the delete operation before it begins.* ▲

There are two statements for deleting individual data sets or groups of data sets: the DELETE statement and the SAVE statement. The one you choose is a matter of convenience and desired results.

Specifying Data Sets to Delete

Use the DELETE statement to delete one or more data sets from a library. If you want to delete more than one data set, list the names after the DELETE statement with no punctuation between them, or use abbreviated member lists if applicable. The following program deletes the data set HURICANE from the library USCLIM. To specify a new default input library, issue the PROC DATASETS statement. Output 35.8 shows that the SAS System sends messages to the SAS log when processing the DELETE statement.

```
proc datasets library=usclim;
    delete huricane;
run;
```

Output 35.8
Deleting the Data
Set HURICANE
from the Library
USCLIM

```
7          proc datasets library=usclim;
                     -----Directory-----
              Libref:           USCLIM
              Engine:           V606
              Physical Name:    'your-data-library'

                # Name      Memtype  Indexes
               -----------------------------
                1 BASETEMP  CATALOG
                2 HURICANE  DATA
                3 RAIN      DATA
                4 REPORT    CATALOG
                5 TEMPCHNG  DATA
                6 USHIGH    DATA
                7 USLOW     DATA
8          delete huricane;
9       run;

NOTE: Deleting USCLIM.HURICANE (memtype=DATA).
```

Specifying Data Sets to Save

If you want to delete all data sets but a few, you can use the SAVE statement to list the names of the data sets you want to keep. List the data set names with no punctuation between them, or use abbreviated member lists (such as YRDATA1-YRDATA5) if applicable. The following program deletes all data sets from the library USCLIM except the data set TEMPCHNG. Output 35.9 shows the SAS log created during this delete operation. The SAS System sends messages to the SAS log verifying that it has kept the data sets you specified in the SAVE statement and deleted all other members of the library.

```
save tempchng;
run;
quit;
```

Output 35.9
Deleting All
Members of the
Library USCLIM
except the Data
Set TEMPCHNG

```
8          save tempchng;
9       run;
NOTE: Saving USCLIM.TEMPCHNG (memtype=DATA).
NOTE: Deleting USCLIM.BASETEMP (memtype=CATALOG).
NOTE: Deleting USCLIM.RAIN (memtype=DATA).
NOTE: Deleting USCLIM.REPORT (memtype=CATALOG).
NOTE: Deleting USCLIM.USHIGH (memtype=DATA).
NOTE: Deleting USCLIM.USLOW (memtype=DATA).
10         quit;
```

Deleting All Files in a Library

To delete all files in a SAS library at one time, use the KILL option in the PROC DATASETS statement.

► *Caution* . . . . *The KILL option deletes all members of the library immediately after the statement is submitted.* ▲

The following program deletes all data sets in the library WEATHER. Issue the QUIT statement to leave the DATASETS procedure. Output 35.10 shows the SAS log.

```
proc datasets library=weather kill;
run;
quit;
```

Output 35.10
Deleting All
Members of the
Library WEATHER

```
7              proc datasets library=weather kill;
                           -----Directory-----

                   Libref:        WEATHER
                   Engine:        V606
                   Physical Name: 'your-data-library'

                     # Name       Memtype  Indexes
                   -------------------------------
                     1 BASETEMP   CATALOG
                     2 HIGHTEMP   DATA
                     3 HURICANE   DATA
                     4 LOWTEMP    DATA
                     5 RAIN       DATA
                     6 REPORT     CATALOG
                     7 SNOW       DATA
                     8 TEMPCHNG   DATA
                     9 TORNADO    DATA
                    10 USHIGH     DATA
                    11 USLOW      DATA
NOTE: Deleting WEATHER.BASETEMP (memtype=CATALOG).
NOTE: Deleting WEATHER.HIGHTEMP (memtype=DATA).
NOTE: Deleting WEATHER.HURICANE (memtype=DATA).
NOTE: Deleting WEATHER.LOWTEMP (memtype=DATA).
NOTE: Deleting WEATHER.RAIN (memtype=DATA).
NOTE: Deleting WEATHER.REPORT (memtype=CATALOG).
NOTE: Deleting WEATHER.SNOW (memtype=DATA).
```

```
2                       The SAS System

NOTE: Deleting WEATHER.TEMPCHNG (memtype=DATA).
NOTE: Deleting WEATHER.TORNADO (memtype=DATA).
NOTE: Deleting WEATHER.USHIGH (memtype=DATA).
NOTE: Deleting WEATHER.USLOW (memtype=DATA).
8          run;

9          quit;
```

Note: All data sets and catalogs are removed from the SAS directory, but the libref is still assigned for this session. The name assigned to the library in your operating system isn't removed when you delete the files included in a SAS library.

SAS Tools

This chapter discusses using the DATASETS procedure for copying, moving, and deleting SAS data sets:

PROC DATASETS LIBRARY=*libref* <KILL>;
  COPY OUT=*libref* <IN=*libref*> <MOVE>;
    SELECT *SAS-data-set*;
    EXCLUDE *SAS-data-set*;
  DELETE *SAS-data-set*;
  SAVE *SAS-data-set*;
QUIT;

PROC DATASETS LIBRARY=*libref* <KILL>;
       starts the procedure and specifies a default input library for subsequent statements. The KILL option deletes all members and member types from the library you specify in the LIBRARY= option.

COPY OUT=*libref* <IN=*libref*> <MOVE>;
       copies files from the default input library you specify in the PROC DATASETS statement to the output library you specify in the OUT= option. The IN= option specifies an input library other than the default library. The MOVE option deletes files from the input library after copying them to the output library.
       You can use the following statements with the COPY statement:

  SELECT *SAS-data-set*;
           is used with the COPY statement to specify a *SAS-data-set* that you want copied to the output library.

  EXCLUDE *SAS-data-set*;
           is used with the COPY statement to specify a *SAS-data-set* that you want excluded from the copying. Files you don't list in this statement are copied to the output library.

DELETE *SAS-data-set*;
       deletes only the *SAS-data-set* you specify in this statement.

SAVE *SAS-data-set*;
       deletes all members of the library except those you specify in this statement.

QUIT;
       executes any preceding statements that haven't already run and stops the procedure.

Learning More

□ The *SAS Procedures Guide, Version 6, Third Edition* describes the CATALOG procedure in detail. You can use PROC CATALOG to copy, move, or delete entries in SAS catalogs.

□ The *SAS Procedures Guide* provides information on using the DATASETS procedure to copy, move, or delete other member types.

□ The *SAS Procedures Guide* documents the MEMTYPE= option, which you can use with many of the statements described in this chapter to limit the member type of the files to be processed. The *SAS Procedures Guide* gives the default member type for each statement and option.

Part 10

Understanding Your SAS® Environment

Chapter 36 Starting, Running, and Exiting the SAS® System

Introduction

This chapter explains how to start, run, and exit the SAS System. It describes the differences between foreground and background processing and the advantages of each. It explains the following processing methods and gives instructions for each concerning how to start and end a session:

☐ interactive processing with the SAS Display Manager System

☐ interactive processing in line mode

☐ batch processing

☐ noninteractive processing.

This chapter also tells you how to customize a session, including how to

□ set system options automatically

□ execute SAS statements automatically.

Starting a SAS Session

The first step in starting a SAS session is to invoke the SAS System. At the operating system prompt, execute the SAS command, which in most cases will be the following:*

```
sas
```

Your SAS session has begun.

You can customize your SAS session as you start it by specifying SAS system options, which then remain in effect throughout a session. For example, you can use the LINESIZE= system option to specify a line size other than the default for the SAS log and print file. System options include options that you can specify at initialization only and options that you can specify during a SAS session. For details, see the section "Customizing a SAS Session or Program" later in this chapter.

Choosing Your Environment

You can choose one of four ways to run a SAS program:

□ interactive processing with the SAS Display Manager System

□ interactive processing in line mode

□ batch processing

□ noninteractive processing.

These methods of running the SAS System fall into one of two categories:

□ foreground processing

□ background processing.

Discovering Your Options

Figure 36.1 shows the relationship among the four methods of running the SAS System. Since all are considered to be either *background processing* or *foreground processing*, it is important that you understand these concepts.

---

* The SAS command may vary from site to site. Consult your SAS Software Representative if you need information.

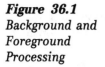

Figure 36.1
Background and
Foreground
Processing

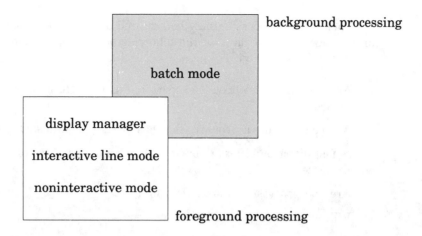

Understanding Foreground Processing

Foreground processing encompasses all the methods except batch. Processing begins immediately, but as your program runs, your current terminal session is occupied, so you can't use it to do anything else.* With foreground processing, you can route your output to the terminal display, to a file, to a printer, or to tape.

If you answer yes to one or more of the following questions, you may want to consider foreground processing:

□ Are you learning SAS programming?

□ Are you testing a program to see if it works?

□ Do you need fast turnaround?

□ Are you processing a fairly small data file?

□ Are you using an interactive application?

Understanding Background Processing

Background processing includes batch processing. Your operating system coordinates all the work, so you can use your terminal session to do other work at the same time your program runs. However, because the operating system also schedules your program for execution and assigns it a priority, it may have to wait in the *input queue* (the operating system's waiting list of jobs to be run) before it is executed. Once your program runs to completion, you can browse, delete, or send your output to a printer.

---

* In a workstation environment, you can switch to another window and continue working.

Background processing may be required at your site. In addition, if you answer yes to one or more of the following questions, you may want to consider background processing:

□   Are you an experienced SAS user, not as likely to make as many errors as a novice?

□   Are you running a program that has already been tested and refined?

□   Is fast turnaround less important than minimizing use of computer resources?

□   Are you processing a large data file?

□   Will your program run for a long time?

□   Are you using a tape?

Processing Interactively in the SAS Display Manager System

When you process in *interactive display manager mode*, you use the SAS Display Manager System to execute SAS programs. Display manager is a full-screen facility that contains windows for, among other things, editing and executing programs, viewing output, and viewing messages about your program.

Because it is an interactive full-screen facility, you can use one session to prepare and submit a program and, if necessary, modify and resubmit it after browsing the output and messages. You can move from window to window and even interrupt and return to a session at the same point you left it.

Invoking the SAS System

To invoke display manager, execute the SAS command followed by any system options that you want to put into effect. The DMS system option activates a display manager session. Display manager is the default method of operation when the SAS System is shipped, but it may not be the default mode at your site. In that case, you can either specify the DMS option in the SAS command or include it in the configuration file, which contains settings for system options. (For more information on this special file, see the section "Customizing a SAS Session or Program" later in this chapter.) You specify options in the SAS command as you do any other command options on your system. For example, specify the DMS option under the VMS and AOS/VS operating systems as shown below:

```
sas/dms
```

Under the MVS operating system, use the OPTIONS operand to specify an option as shown below:

```
sas options ('dms')
```

Under the CMS operating system, specify the DMS option as follows:

```
sas (dms
```

For details on how to specify command options on other systems, refer to the SAS documentation for your host system.

Ending a Session

You can end your display manager session with the BYE or ENDSAS command. Specify either of the following commands and execute it by pressing ENTER or RETURN, depending on which operating system you're using:

```
bye
```

or

```
endsas
```

You can also end your session with the ENDSAS statement in the PROGRAM EDITOR window. Type the following statement on a data line and submit it for execution:

```
endsas;
```

Interrupting a Session

You may occasionally find it necessary to return to your operating system from a SAS session. If you don't want to end your SAS session, you can escape to the host system by using the X command. Simply execute the following command:

```
x
```

From your operating system, you can then return to the same SAS session, as you left it, by executing the host command appropriate for your operating system.*

Use this form of the X command to execute a single operating system command:

X *operating-system-command*

or, if the command contains embedded blanks,

X *'operating-system-command '*

For example, on many systems, you can display the current time by specifying

```
x time
```

When you use this form of the X command, the command executes; then take the appropriate action to return to your SAS session.

For information pertinent to other operating systems, refer to the SAS documentation for your host system.

---

* For example, under the MVS operating system, the host command is RETURN or END; under the VMS operating system, the host command is LOGOFF.

Processing Interactively in Line Mode

You can also process interactively in *line mode*. In line mode, you enter programming statements one line at a time; DATA and PROC steps are executed after you enter a RUN statement or after another step boundary. Program messages and output appear on the terminal display.

You can modify program statements only as you first enter them, before you press ENTER or RETURN, which means that you must type your entries carefully.

Invoking the SAS System

To invoke the SAS System in line mode, execute the SAS command followed by any system options that you want to put into effect. The NODMS system option activates an interactive line mode session. If NODMS isn't the default at your site, you can either specify the option in the SAS command or include the NODMS specification in the configuration file, the file that contains settings for system options that are put into effect at invocation. For example, to specify the NODMS system option in the SAS command under the VMS and AOS/VS operating systems, specify

```
sas/nodms
```

Under the MVS operating system, specify

```
sas options ('nodms')
```

Under the CMS operating system, specify

```
sas (nodms
```

Using the RUN Statement to Execute a Program

In line mode, steps are executed only after you enter a RUN statement or a semicolon ending CARDS data. Output 36.1 shows an example of a line mode session using a RUN statement after each DATA and PROC step.

Output 36.1
Executing a
Program in Line
Mode with the
RUN Statement

```
NOTE: Copyright(c) 1985,1986,1987,1988 SAS Institute Inc., Cary, NC USA.
NOTE: SAS (r) Proprietary Software Release 6.xx.
      Licensed to SAS Institute Inc., Site xxxxxxxx
      For use on IBM Model 3084 Serial Number 000000.

 1? data a;
 2? input c;
 3? cards;
 4> 0
 5> 1
 6> 1
 7> 4
 8> 0
 9> 0
10> 5
11> 3
12> 6
13> ;
NOTE: The data set WORK.A has 9 observations and 1 variables.

14? run;
15? proc chart;
16? vbar c;
17? title 'Executing the CHART Procedure in Line Mode';
18? run;
                    Executing the CHART Procedure in Line Mode                1

        Frequency

    3 +        *****
      |        *****
      |        *****
      |        *****
      |        *****
      |        *****
      |        *****
      |        *****
      |        *****
      |        *****
    2 +        *****        *****        *****        *****
      |        *****        *****        *****        *****
      |        *****        *****        *****        *****
      |        *****        *****        *****        *****
      |        *****        *****        *****        *****
      |        *****        *****        *****        *****
      |        *****        *****        *****        *****
      |        *****        *****        *****        *****
      |        *****        *****        *****        *****
      |        *****        *****        *****        *****
    1 +        *****        *****        *****        *****
      |        *****        *****        *****        *****
      |        *****        *****        *****        *****
      |        *****        *****        *****        *****
      |        *****        *****        *****        *****
      |        *****        *****        *****        *****
      |        *****        *****        *****        *****
      |        *****        *****        *****        *****
      ----------------------------------------------------------
               0           2           4           6

                              C Midpoint

19? endsas;
NOTE: SAS Institute Inc., SAS Circle, PO Box 8000, Cary, NC 27512-8000
```

At the beginning of each line, the SAS System prompts you with a number and a question mark to enter more statements. If you use a CARDS statement, a greater-than symbol (>) replaces the question mark, indicating that data lines are expected.

Note that system and program messages are intermingled with programming statements and raw data. The DATA step ends before the PROC step and immediately triggers the display of the log, or program messages, before the PROC step begins. Similarly, the second RUN statement executes the PROC step and triggers the display of the procedure output. If the PROC step were followed by another PROC or DATA step, the first PROC step would run without a RUN statement, but the output would be intermingled with the next step. Therefore, you should use RUN statements to end each step of a SAS program when you execute in line mode.

Ending a Session

To end your session, type the following statement at the SAS prompt and press ENTER or RETURN:

    endsas;

Your session ends, and you're returned to your operating system environment.

Interrupting a Session

In line mode, you can escape to the operating system by executing the following statement:

    x;

You can return to your SAS session by executing the host command appropriate for your operating system. Use this form of X statement to execute a single operating system command:

> **X** *operating-system-command*;

or, if the command contains embedded blanks,

> **X** '*operating-system-command*';

For example, on many systems you can display the current time by specifying

    x time;

When you use this form of the X command, the command executes, and you're returned to your SAS session.

Processing in Batch Mode

The first step in executing a program in batch mode is to prepare files that include

□ any operating system control language statements required by the operating system you're using to manage the program

□ the SAS statements necessary to execute the program.

Then you submit your file to the operating system, and your terminal session is free for other work while the operating system executes the program. This is called *background processing* because you can't view or change the program in any way until *after* it executes. The log and output are routed to the destination that you specify in the operating system control language; without a specification, they are routed to the default. For examples of batch processing, refer to the SAS documentation for your host system.

Processing Noninteractively

Noninteractive processing has some characteristics of interactive processing and some of batch processing. When you process noninteractively, you execute SAS program statements stored in an external file. You use a SAS command to submit the program statements to your operating system.* As in interactive processing, processing begins immediately, and your current terminal session is occupied. However, as with batch processing, you can't interact with your program.** You don't see the log or procedure output until after the program has run. And to correct or modify your program, you must use an editor to make necessary changes and then resubmit your program.

Executing a Program

When you run a program in noninteractive mode, you don't enter a SAS session as you do in interactive mode; instead of starting a SAS session, you're executing a SAS program. The first step is to enter the SAS statements in a file, just as you would for a batch job. Then, at the system prompt, you specify the SAS command followed by the complete name of the file and any system options you want to specify.

The following example executes the SAS statements in the partitioned data set *your-userid*.UGWRITE.TEXT on the MVS operating system in the member TEMP:

```
sas input(ugwrite.text(temp))
```

Note that the INPUT operand points to the file that contains the SAS statements for a noninteractive session.

The next example executes the SAS statements stored in the subdirectory [USERID.UGWRITE.TEXT] on the VMS operating system in the file TEMP.SAS:

```
$ sas [userid.ugwrite.text]temp
```

Note that the SAS System looks for the file on the current disk.

The following example executes the SAS statements in the CMS file TEMP SAS A:

```
sas temp
```

Note that the SAS System looks for filetype SAS on the A-disk.

For details on how to use noninteractive mode on other operating systems, refer to the SAS documentation for your host system. Consult your SAS Software Consultant for information specific to your site.

Browsing the Log and Output

Depending on your operating system, the log and output go either to files or to your terminal display, where you can browse them.

---

* The SAS command is implemented differently under each operating system. For example, under MVS it is a CLIST, and under CMS it is an EXEC.

** There are some exceptions to this, but they're beyond the scope of this book.

Customizing a SAS Session or Program

The SAS System allows you to customize your SAS session or program by

□ setting options automatically

□ executing SAS statements automatically.

Setting Options Automatically

As mentioned earlier, you can put options into effect for the duration of a SAS session or program. These options, called *system options*, fall into one of two categories:

□ options that you must specify when you invoke the system

□ options that you can specify at any time.

Setting Invocation-Only Options

You can specify some options only when you invoke the SAS System. These options affect

□ the way the SAS System interacts with your operating system

□ the hardware you're using

□ the way in which your session or program is configured.

Usually, the defaults are set when the SAS System is installed at your site.
    You can specify these options on the command line each time you invoke the SAS System. However, for options that you specify every time you run the SAS System, it's more convenient to set the options in a configuration file. Each time you invoke the SAS System, the SAS System looks for that file and uses the customized settings it contains. Be sure to examine the default version before creating your own.
    Note: If you specify an option in the SAS command that also appears in the configuration file, the setting from the SAS command overrides the setting in the file.
    To display the current settings for all options listed in the configuration file as you invoke the system, use the VERBOSE system option in the SAS command.
    A typical list of options in a configuration file under the MVS operating system might include the following:

WORK=MYWORK
SASUSER=SASUSER2
NEWS=*host-filename*
SASMSG=*host-filename*

Setting Other SAS System Options

Other SAS system options determine how

- □ your SAS output appears
- □ files are handled by the SAS System
- □ observations from SAS data sets are processed
- □ system variables are used.

You can change default settings for system options in the SAS command each time you invoke the SAS System. You can also change most options in an OPTIONS statement and in the OPTIONS window of display manager. When you change your system options determines when the change is actually implemented and at what point output is affected. The settings remain in effect until your session ends, unless you change them.

Within a full-screen environment, you can invoke the OPTIONS window to browse a list of current settings for SAS system options that work across all operating systems. Otherwise, you can check the settings of all options with the OPTIONS procedure. To obtain a complete list, submit the following statements:

```
proc options;
run;
```

Executing SAS Statements Automatically

Just as you can set SAS system options automatically when you invoke the SAS System, you can also execute statements automatically when you invoke the SAS System by creating a special autoexec file. Each time you invoke the SAS System, it looks for this special file and executes any of the statements it contains.

You can save time by using this file to execute statements that you use routinely. For example, you might add

- □ OPTIONS statements including system options that you use regularly
- □ FILENAME and LIBNAME statements to define filerefs and librefs you use regularly.

SAS Tools

This chapter discusses the OPTIONS procedure:

PROC OPTIONS *options*;
> lists the current values of all SAS system options.

This chapter discusses the following system options:

LINESIZE=*n*
> specifies the line width for SAS output.

DMS | NODMS
> at invocation, specifies whether the SAS Display Manager System is to be active in a SAS session. A full-screen terminal must be used to invoke display manager.

VERBOSE
> at invocation, displays a listing of all options in the configuration file.

This chapter discusses the following statements:

ENDSAS;
> causes a SAS job or session to terminate at the end of the current DATA or PROC step.

CARDS;
> signals to the SAS System that the data follow immediately.

RUN;
> causes the previously entered SAS step to be executed.

X <*'operating-system-command'*>;
> is used to issue an operating system command from within a SAS session. *Operating-system-command* specifies the command. Omitting the command puts you into the operating system's submode.

OPTIONS *option*;
> changes one or more system options from the default value set at a site.

This chapter discusses the following display manager command-line commands:

BYE
> ends a SAS session.

ENDSAS
> ends a SAS session.

X <*'operating-system-command'*>
> executes the operating system command requested and then prompts you to take the appropriate action to return to the SAS System. Omitting the command puts you into the operating system's submode.

Learning More

- □ Other chapters in Part 10 contain more information on processing interactively in the SAS Display Manager System. *SAS Language: Reference, Version 6, First Edition* provides complete reference information on display manager.

- □ Chapter 1, "What is the SAS System?" and *SAS Language: Reference* discuss processing methods.

- □ *SAS Language: Reference* discusses running the SAS System.

- □ *SAS Language: Reference* contains complete reference information on SAS system options.

- □ *SAS Language: Reference* provides more information on using the QUIT statement. For some procedures, you can continue to enter procedure statements after you enter a RUN statement. To end these procedures, you enter a QUIT statement.

- □ *SAS Language: Reference* discusses the autoexec and configuration files.

- □ The SAS documentation for your host system provides host-specific information concerning

  - □ batch processing
  - □ interrupting a SAS session
  - □ interacting with SAS programs run in interactive mode
  - □ specifying command options.

Chapter 37 Using the SAS® Display Manager System: the Basics

Introduction

This chapter describes in detail the SAS Display Manager System. It tells you how to use display manager to

☐ submit a program for execution

☐ manipulate your output

☐ understand the results of your program.

You can perform all these tasks using display manager's four primary windows:

- □ the PROGRAM EDITOR window
- □ the LOG window
- □ the OUTPUT window
- □ the OUTPUT MANAGER window.

Understanding Display Manager

The SAS Display Manager System is an interactive, full-screen environment. You view the full-screen display through a series of windows, each of which has particular capabilities. For example, when you first invoke display manager, you see two windows: the PROGRAM EDITOR (PGM) window and the LOG window, as shown in Display 37.1. These are two of the four primary windows; you will learn more about them in this chapter.

Display 37.1
The PROGRAM
EDITOR and LOG
Windows

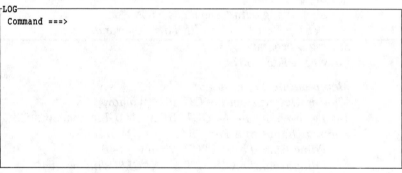

Your keyboard contains function keys, typewriter keys, cursor control keys, and possibly a numeric keypad, which you use to interact with your display manager environment. You can execute commands to alter and move through your environment, and you can enter and submit SAS statements to create and analyze a data set by using various parts of your keyboard within the appropriate windows. Unlike noninteractive processing, interactive processing allows you to make changes as you enter commands and statements. And unlike batch processing, you don't have to wait; processing begins immediately.

Using the Windows

The SAS Display Manager System is a windowing environment. It appears to you through a series of windows, each having one or more functions and many capabilities. The primary windows are

□ the PROGRAM EDITOR window, where you enter, edit, and submit SAS statements and save SAS source files

□ the LOG window, where you browse and scroll the SAS log

□ the OUTPUT window, where you browse and scroll procedure output

□ the OUTPUT MANAGER window, where you browse and manipulate an index of your output.

Display manager includes additional windows with which you can obtain online help, view and change some SAS system options, view and change function key settings, and create and store notepads of information. You can also manage SAS catalogs and data sets and obtain information about variables, filerefs, and librefs. These are just some of the tasks you can accomplish within display manager windows.

Commands: Learning the Ground Rules

Now you recognize display manager as a full-screen interactive environment. But in order to begin to realize the power and flexibility of display manager, you need to understand how to use commands. Display manager offers many different commands with which you can display a window, alter its configuration, or move within it. You can change its color, cut and paste and then store text, and globally search for and alter selected words or phrases. Depending on your particular site, by default, you execute commands on the command line or through the PMENU facility. Whether the command line or the PMENU facility is the default, you can execute line commands in the numbered part of the display. In each case, you can use function keys as an alternative way of executing commands.

Using the Command Line

If the command line is the default at your site, each window in display manager contains a special line, called a *command line*, at the top of the display. It is indicated by the following notation:

```
Command===>
```

To execute a command, type the command keyword on the command line and press the ENTER or RETURN key, depending on which operating system you're using. You can specify a simple one-word command; multiple commands, separated by semicolons; or a command followed by an option. For example, suppose you want to move from the PROGRAM EDITOR window to the LOG window and increase it to occupy the entire display. On the command line of the PROGRAM EDITOR window, specify

```
log; zoom
```

Then press ENTER or RETURN to execute both commands.

When the command line is the default, you can also use the PMENU facility as an alternate way of executing commands. Execute the PMENU command on the command line of a window. An action bar replaces the command line, and then you can use the PMENU facility to execute commands.

Using the PMENU Facility

If the PMENU facility is the default at your site, each window contains an *action bar* instead of a command line. This action bar is made up of several *items*. Select an item by moving the cursor to it and pressing ENTER or RETURN or by using a mouse to point and click. Depending on the item you select, one of three things happens:

1. a command is executed

2. a *pull-down menu* is displayed

3. a *dialog box* is displayed.

From any pull-down menu, you can select a *menu item* to carry out an action. A dialog box appears in response to an action and prompts you for information. You can either supply the information requested or execute the CANCEL command to exit it.

Using Line Commands

In text editing windows, you can execute *line commands* by typing them in the numbered part of your display, in the left-most portion of a window. Line commands are one or more letters that copy, move, delete, and otherwise edit text. Note that although line commands are usually executed in the numbered part of the display or with function keys, they can also be executed from the command line if preceded by a colon.

Using Function Keys

Your keyboard includes function keys to which default values have already been assigned. You can browse or alter those values in the KEYS window. To open the KEYS window, simply execute the following command:

```
keys
```

Then the KEYS window appears. Using the FORWARD command, scroll forward to view all the settings. To change the setting of a key, type the new value over the old value. The new setting takes effect immediately and is permanently saved when you execute the END command to close the window.

Function keys allow you to execute commands with one keystroke, allowing you to work more efficiently, and you can tailor your key settings to meet the needs you have in a given session.

For example, suppose you're submitting a number of programs and constantly moving from the PROGRAM EDITOR window to the OUTPUT window and back again; each time you finish viewing your output, you must type the PGM and ZOOM commands on the command line and press ENTER or RETURN. As a shortcut, define one of your function keys to do that by typing the following commands over an unwanted value or where none existed before:

```
pgm; zoom
```

Then every time you press that function key, the commands are executed, saving you time. You can also use function keys to execute line commands. Simply precede the command with a colon as you would from the command line.

Submitting a Program for Execution

Understanding the PROGRAM EDITOR Window

When you first invoke display manager, you immediately see the PROGRAM EDITOR window (in Display 37.1). One of display manager's four primary windows, it is the window where you

□ enter and submit program statements

□ edit text

□ store your program in a file

□ copy the contents from an already-created file

□ copy the contents into a file.

The PROGRAM EDITOR window is the window you may use most often. It has many capabilities and, as the first window you encounter, it can be used as a starting point to access other windows. In addition, almost all display manager commands are valid in the PROGRAM EDITOR window.

Entering and Submitting SAS Statements

Entering your SAS statements is simple. You need to know the basics of typing, and you need to be familiar with the keyboard at your site, as well as the ground rules for SAS programming (a forgotten semicolon produces an error message here as it does in any other mode).

Once you have typed the text of your program, simply type the following command on the command line and press ENTER or RETURN:

```
submit
```

You can also use a function key or the PMENU facility to execute the SUBMIT command.

Editing Text

The PROGRAM EDITOR window is where you enter and edit text, whether it is SAS programming statements or other text. You can make the editing process most efficient if you use the commands display manager makes available.

Simplifying with Commands

You may find it useful to move, or *scroll*, back and forth through your text as you edit it, especially if it's lengthy. Scrolling commands are easy to remember because they do what their names suggest. When you execute the TOP command, you scroll to the beginning of the PROGRAM EDITOR window; the BOTTOM command scrolls you to the last line of text. With the BACKWARD command, you move backward toward the beginning of text; with the FORWARD command, forward toward the end of text. With the LEFT command, you move left; with the RIGHT command, you move right. You can also move to a particular line by specifying only its number.

Some other commands that you may find especially useful as you enter and submit SAS statements and edit text are listed here.

ZOOM

increases the size of the window to occupy the entire display. Execute the ZOOM command again to return the window to its previous size.

UNDO

cancels the effects of the most recently submitted text editing command. Continuing to execute the UNDO command undoes previous commands, starting with the most recent and moving backwards.

RECALL

brings back to the PROGRAM EDITOR window the most recently submitted block of statements in your current display manager session. Continuing to execute the RECALL command recalls previous statements, starting with the most recent and moving backwards.

CLEAR

clears a window as specified. You can clear the PROGRAM EDITOR, LOG, and OUTPUT windows from another window by executing the CLEAR command with the appropriate option as shown in the examples below:

```
clear pgm

clear log

clear output
```

CAPS

converts everything you type to uppercase.

FIND

searches for a specified string of characters. Enclose the string in quotes if it contains embedded blanks or special characters.

CHANGE

changes a specified string of characters to another. Follow the command keyword with the first string, a space, and then the second string. The rules for embedded blanks and special characters apply. For example, suppose you specify

```
change 'operating system' platform
```

This CHANGE command replaces the first occurrence of operating system with the word platform. Note that the first string must be enclosed in quotes because it contains an embedded blank.

Getting Fast Results with Line Commands

The left-most portion of the PROGRAM EDITOR window includes a numbered field. That is where you enter *line commands,* editing commands denoted by one or more letters that, among other things, move, copy, delete, justify lines of text, or insert blank lines.

To move a line of text, type the letter M (move) in the numbered field next to the text you want to move. To copy a line of text, use the letter C (copy). In both cases, specify a destination by typing the letter B (before) on the line you want the moved text to precede or the letter A (after) on the line you want the moved text to follow. For example, to make the following list alphabetical, place line 1 after what is currently line 5. The first sample of code shows the text after you have typed the line commands but before you have pressed ENTER or RETURN:

```
m 001 Lincoln f Wake Ligon    135   1090
00002 Andrews f Wake Martin   140    998
00003 Black   f Wake Martin   149   1210
00004 Gatlin  m Wake Martin   142   1100
a 005 Jones   m Wake Daniels  137    987
```

The second sample shows the results, after you have pressed ENTER or RETURN:

```
00001 Andrews f Wake Martin   140    998
00002 Black   f Wake Martin   149   1210
00003 Gatlin  m Wake Martin   142   1100
00004 Jones   m Wake Daniels  137    987
00005 Lincoln f Wake Ligon    135   1090
```

Other line commands are equally simple. To delete a line of text, use the letter D (delete). To insert a blank line, use the letter I (insert); one new line is inserted immediately after the line on which you have typed the command. You can use the letter A or B to specify a destination on the line before or after you want the blank line inserted.

Storing a Program

After you have entered, edited, and executed a program, you may want to store it in an external file so you can use it again. You can do this with the FILE command. On the command line, specify the FILE command followed by a fileref or the actual filename. Enclose the actual filename in single or double quotes, as shown in Display 37.2.

Display 37.2
Storing Text with the FILE Command

```
┌LOG─────────────────────────────────────────────────────────────────┐
│ Command ===>                                                        │
│                                                                     │
│                                                                     │
│                                                                     │
│                                                                     │
│                                                                     │
│                                                                     │
│                                                                     │
└─────────────────────────────────────────────────────────────────────┘
┌PROGRAM EDITOR───────────────────────────────────────────────────────┐
│ Command ===> file 'your-output-file'                                │
│                                                                     │
│ 00001 data sats;                                                    │
│ 00002    input test $ 1-8 sex $ 10 year 13-16 score 19-21;          │
│ 00003 cards;                                                        │
│ 00004 verbal m  1967  461                                           │
│ 00005 verbal f  1967  463                                           │
│ 00006 math   f  1967  520                                           │
└─────────────────────────────────────────────────────────────────────┘
```

The FILE command allows you to save all the text in your window, regardless of whether it is visible on your display. Because the FILE command doesn't remove the contents of the window, you can store one copy of your text and continue to modify another copy.

Suppose you inadvertently specify an already-existing file by omitting a fileref or filename or by specifying one that already exists. Then the SAS System displays a *requestor window*, a special type of window used to obtain information before performing an action. This requestor window offers you three courses of action:

□ overwriting the contents of the existing file with the new file

□ appending the new file to the existing file

□ canceling the command.

This check prevents you from accidentally replacing, or writing over, an existing file. Display 37.3 is an example of a requestor window.

Display 37.3
Protecting Files
with a Requestor
Window

```
┌LOG─────────────────────────────────────────────────────────────────────
  Command ===>


        ------------------------------------------------------------------
        |                                                                |
        | WARNING: The file already exists. Enter R to replace it,       |
        | enter A to append to it or enter C to cancel FILE command.     |
        |                                                                |
        ------------------------------------------------------------------




└─────────────────────────────────────────────────────────────────────────

┌PROGRAM EDITOR──────────────────────────────────────────────────────────
  Command ===>

  00001 Andrews  f Wake     Martin   140  998
  00002 Black    m Wake     Martin   149 1210
  00003 Gatlin   m Wake     Martin   142 1100
  00004 Lincoln  f Wake     Ligon    135 1090
  00005
  00006
└─────────────────────────────────────────────────────────────────────────
```

Often you may want to replace a file with an updated version. To suppress the requestor window, add the REPLACE option to the FILE command after the fileref or complete filename. Your file is replaced with no questions asked. To add the text in the PROGRAM EDITOR window to the end of an existing file, specify the APPEND option with the FILE command after the fileref or complete filename.

Copying a File

Storing text in a file for future use may be only part of a two-step process. If you are to reuse the stored text, you must be able to copy it back into the PROGRAM EDITOR window. You can do it easily with the INCLUDE command. Understanding the INCLUDE command is as simple as understanding the FILE command since many of the rules are identical for both.

To copy a file into the PROGRAM EDITOR window, specify the INCLUDE command on the command line followed by an assigned fileref or an actual filename; remember to enclose an actual filename in single or double quotes. The lines of that file are appended to the end of the text already entered in the window or wherever you specify with an A or B line command. It is a copy that the PROGRAM EDITOR window receives; the original remains stored in your file for future use.

If you want to replace the text already in your window, specify the REPLACE option with the INCLUDE command after the fileref or filename. As it is copied into the window, the retrieved text replaces the window's contents.

Manipulating Your Output

Viewing Output from the OUTPUT Window

The previous section explains how to successfully submit a SAS program for execution. The results of submitting a program, if it contains a PROC step that produces output, are usually displayed in the OUTPUT window. One of the four primary windows, the OUTPUT window allows you to browse and scroll procedure output from your current SAS session.

Suppose you finish entering the SAS statements in your SAS program. You check to see that you haven't made any mistakes. Everything is spelled correctly, no semicolons are missing or misplaced, and all statements within the DATA and PROC steps are in proper order. You execute the SUBMIT command and the results appear in the OUTPUT window, as shown in Display 37.4. The OUTPUT window now contains the testing results, which you can browse and scroll.

Display 37.4
Displaying
Procedure Output

```
┌OUTPUT─────────────────────────────────────────────────┐
│ Command ===>                                           │
│                                                        │
│                      Original Data                   1 │
│                                                        │
│          OBS   TEST    SEX   YEAR   SCORE              │
│                                                        │
│           1    verbal   m    1967    463               │
│           2    verbal   f    1967    468               │
│           3    verbal   m    1970    459               │
│           4    verbal   f    1970    461               │
│           5    verbal   m    1975    437               │
│           6    verbal   f    1975    431               │
│           7    verbal   m    1977    431               │
│           8    verbal   f    1977    427               │
│           9    verbal   m    1980    428               │
│          10    verbal   f    1980    420               │
│          11    verbal   m    1981    430               │
│          12    verbal   f    1981    418               │
│          13    verbal   m    1982    431               │
│          14    verbal   f    1982    421               │
│          15    verbal   m    1983    430               │
│          16    verbal   f    1983    420               │
└────────────────────────────────────────────────────────┘
```

Most of the command-line commands described earlier for the PROGRAM EDITOR window can be used in the OUTPUT window. You can move backward and forward or left and right with the scrolling commands. If you have shrunk the OUTPUT window, you can enlarge it with the ZOOM command. You can search for character strings with the FIND command.

The CLEAR command is particularly useful in the OUTPUT window since all output is appended to the previous output within a SAS session. If you don't want to accumulate output, be sure to execute the CLEAR command before you submit your next program. From any other window, you can clear the OUTPUT window by specifying

```
clear output
```

Taking Inventory in the OUTPUT MANAGER Window

Depending on how much output is in the OUTPUT window, you may find it helpful to browse a listing of its contents. The OUTPUT MANAGER window acts as an index for your OUTPUT window, showing the following details for each separate piece of output:

□ the name of the procedure that created it

□ the order in which it falls, compared to other output

□ the beginning page number

□ its length in pages

□ a description, based on the first 40 characters of the title.

Execute the following command to invoke the OUTPUT MANAGER window, shown in Display 37.5.

```
manager
```

Display 37.5
Invoking the
OUTPUT
MANAGER
Window

```
┌OUTPUT MANAGER──────────────────────────────────────────────────┐
│ Command ===>                                                    │
│                                                                 │
│    Procedure  Page#   Pages      Description                    │
│  _ PRINT        1       1         The SAS System                │
│  _ PLOT         2       1         Sales Shown by Region          │
│                                                                 │
│                                                                 │
│                                                                 │
│                                                                 │
│                                                                 │
│                                                                 │
│                                                                 │
│                                                                 │
│                                                                 │
│                                                                 │
│                                                       ─ZOOM─R─  │
└─────────────────────────────────────────────────────────────────┘
```

In addition to browsing an index of the output, you can use the OUTPUT MANAGER window to delete, file, and print output. You can cancel or verify a DELETE command or rename the output's description. You can also edit the output and save the changes in the OUTPUT window.

Routing Output to a File

Filing from the OUTPUT Window

Just as you may choose to file SAS statements and other text, you may also find it necessary to store output for future use. As you did in the PROGRAM EDITOR window, on the command line of the OUTPUT window simply specify the FILE command followed by a fileref or the actual filename. If you haven't specified a file in your current session, the SAS System issues an error message telling you that no default file exists.

The FILE command stores a copy of the entire contents of the OUTPUT window without removing what is on the display. If you specify an existing file, a requestor window appears asking you whether you want the file to overwrite the contents of the existing file or to be appended to the contents of the existing file or whether you want to cancel the FILE command.

Filing from the OUTPUT MANAGER Window

To file output from the OUTPUT MANAGER window, type F in the selection field next to the output you choose; press ENTER or RETURN. A requestor window appears and prompts you to enter the name of the file. Type the filename and press ENTER or RETURN or END. To cancel the command, move your cursor to the field marked CANCEL and press ENTER or RETURN.

Printing Output

You can print output in one of two ways. From the OUTPUT window, simply execute the PRINT command. All the output currently in the window is sent to the default printer at your site. From the OUTPUT MANAGER window, type P in the selection field adjacent to the output you want printed; press ENTER or RETURN. A requestor window again appears with the following prompt:

```
Enter filename ( Default is PRINTER )
```

Press ENTER or RETURN or END to print the output. To cancel the command, move your cursor to the field marked CANCEL and press ENTER or RETURN.

Understanding the Results of Your Program

Using the LOG Window

In order to program successfully, you must

□ recognize when you have made errors

□ understand what is necessary to correct those errors

□ receive feedback on the steps you take to correct them.

The SAS log provides you with all this information. In display manager, this information is contained in the LOG window, another one of the four primary windows. The LOG window shows the SAS statements you have submitted as well as messages from the SAS System concerning your program. Under most operating systems, it tells you

□ when the program was executed

□ the release of the SAS System under which the program was run

□ details about the computer installation and its site number

□ the number of observations and variables for a given output data set

□ the computer resources each step used.

(Note that because of the system options used, some of this information is suppressed in the SAS logs shown in this chapter.)

In the LOG window, you can use the command-line commands described earlier for the OUTPUT window. Be sure to follow the same guidelines already described for these commands.

Storing Your Session

If you're having problems with your program, it's a good idea to save the log for debugging. To route the contents of the LOG window to an external file, execute the FILE command followed by a fileref or an actual filename; enclose an actual file name in quotes. The FILE command stores a copy of the LOG window without removing what is displayed. As in the PROGRAM EDITOR and OUTPUT windows, if you specify an existing file, a requestor window appears and offers you three courses of action: overwriting the contents of the existing file with the new file, appending the new file to the existing file, or canceling the command.

Browsing a SAS Session

Suppose you execute the PRINT procedure to obtain a simple printout. A record of your session appears in the LOG window, as shown in Display 37.6. The messages in the LOG window tell you how many observations and variables your data set contains. Because the program contained no errors, no error messages appear in the LOG window.

Display 37.6
Recording the
Session in the
LOG Window

```
┌LOG─────────────────────────────────────────────────────────────┐
│ Command ===>                                                    │
│                                                                 │
│ 109  data sales;                                                │
│ 110     input salesrep $ 1-8 sales 10-15 region $ 19-23         │
│ 111        machine $ 29-39;                                     │
│ 112     cards;                                                  │
│                                                                 │
│ NOTE: The data set WORK.SALES has 15 observations and 4 variables. │
│                                                                 │
│ 128  ;                                                          │
│ 129  run;                                                       │
│ 130  proc print;                                                │
│ 131  run;                                                       │
│                                                                 │
│                                                                 │
│                                                                 │
│                                                                 │
│                                                                 │
│                                                           ─ZOOM─│
└─────────────────────────────────────────────────────────────────┘
```

However, suppose your program contains errors. For example, the CARDS statement is missing a semicolon, and the PROC PRINT statement is misspelled. Display 37.7 shows the results.

Display 37.7
Viewing Error
Messages

```
┌LOG─────────────────────────────────────────────────────────────┐
│ Command ===>                                                    │
│                                                                 │
│ 155  data sales;                                                │
│ 156     input salesrep $ 1-8 sales 10-15 region $ 19-23         │
│ 157        machine $ 29-39;                                     │
│ 158     cards                                                   │
│ 159  Wilson   10498    west     SC                              │
│      ------                                                     │
│      76                                                         │
│ 160  Lambert   9876    west     O                               │
│ 161  Parker    8967    east     O                               │
│ 162  Davis    12335    north    SC                              │
│ 163  Mohar    14567    south    O                               │
│ 164  McVeigh  14066    west     O                               │
│ 165  Early    11446    east     O                               │
│ 166  Dillon    9565    south    SC                              │
│ 167  Lingle   10775    south    SC                              │
│ 168  Lea      12600    north    O                               │
│ 169  Carter   13450    east     O                               │
│ 170  Shelby   10982    west     SC                              │
│ NOTE: The SAS System stopped processing this step because of errors. │
│ NOTE: The data set WORK.SALES has 0 observations and 4 variables. │
│                                                           ─ZOOM─│
└─────────────────────────────────────────────────────────────────┘
```

```
┌─LOG─────────────────────────────────────────────────────────────────────┐
│ Command ===>                                                             │
│                                                                          │
│ WARNING: File SALES was not saved because this step was aborted.         │
│ 171   Evan     9400    north    0                                        │
│ 172   Lucas    12075   south    SC                                       │
│ 173   Black    11150   west     SC                                       │
│ 174   ;                                                                  │
│ 175   run;                                                               │
│       ---                                                                │
│       180                                                                │
│                                                                          │
│ ERROR 76-322: Syntax error, statement will be ignored.                   │
│                                                                          │
│ ERROR 180-322: Statement is not valid or it is used out of proper order. │
│                                                                          │
│                                                                          │
│ 176   proc paint;                                                        │
│ 177   run;                                                               │
│                                                                          │
│ ERROR: Procedure PAINT not found.                                        │
│                                                                          │
│                                                                          │
│                                                                 ─ZOOM─   │
└──────────────────────────────────────────────────────────────────────────┘
```

Three error messages reveal that the SAS System has detected a syntax error and that the PAINT procedure can't be found. Two other notes and one warning appear as a result of these errors.

SAS Tools

This chapter discusses using the SAS Display Manager System. All the windows available in display manager can be invoked by specifying the name of the window (or an alias) on the command line. The window-call commands introduced in this chapter are PROGRAM (PGM), OUTPUT (LISTING), MANAGER, and LOG.

The following commands are also discussed in this chapter:

ZOOM

increases the size of the window to occupy the entire display or returns the window to the default size.

PMENU

activates or deactivates the PMENU facility for all windows.

SUBMIT

submits the statements in the PROGRAM EDITOR window to the SAS System for processing.

CANCEL

cancels changes in a window and removes it from the display.

END

closes a window and removes it from the display.

UNDO

cancels the effects of the previous text editing command.

RECALL
> brings back to the PROGRAM EDITOR window the most recently submitted block of statements.

CLEAR
> clears a window as specified.

CAPS
> converts everything that you type to uppercase.

FIND
> searches for a specified string of characters.

CHANGE
> changes one string of characters to another.

FILE
> stores text in an external file.

INCLUDE
> copies stored text into a window.

The following options are used with the FILE and INCLUDE commands and are discussed in this chapter:

REPLACE
> suppresses the requestor window and replaces a file.

APPEND
> adds text to the end of the existing file.

Learning More

- ☐ Chapter 20, "Understanding and Enhancing Your Output," contains more information on procedure output.

- ☐ Chapter 21, "Analyzing Your SAS Session with the SAS Log," discusses the SAS log.

- ☐ Chapter 23, "Diagnosing and Avoiding Errors," presents more information on error messages. Display 37.7 is just one example of a log containing error messages.

- ☐ Chapter 36, "Starting, Running, and Exiting the SAS System," discusses other methods of running the SAS System.

- ☐ Chapter 38, "Using Commands to Manipulate Your Full-Screen Environment," and Chapter 39, "Mastering Your Environment with Selected Windows," contain more information on the SAS Display Manager System. Chapter 38 also discusses line commands and command-line commands. Chapter 39 contains information on function keys.

- ☐ *SAS Language: Reference, Version 6, First Edition* contains complete reference information on display manager.

- ☐ *SAS Language: Reference* provides complete reference information on the text editor.

□   *SAS Language: Reference* presents more information on the PMENU facility.
See also the *SAS Procedures Guide, Version 6, Third Edition.*

Chapter 38 Using Commands to Manipulate Your Full-Screen Environment

Introduction

This chapter discusses both display manager and text editing commands. Although some display manager commands are window specific, many are valid in all or most windows. Text editing commands are part of the SAS text editor, a full-screen editing facility available not only in base SAS software but in SAS/FSP and SAS/AF software. This chapter concentrates on the commands you may use most often.

In Chapter 37, "Using the SAS Display Manager System: the Basics," you learned the ground rules for using commands. Remember that you can execute *command-line commands* by typing keywords on the command line and pressing the ENTER or RETURN key, by using function keys, or by using the PMENU facility. You usually execute *line commands* by typing them in the numbered part of the display or by using function keys, although they can be executed from the command line.

Using Display Manager Commands

Of the commands already discussed, several are valid in most or all windows. It might be easiest for you to remember these commands grouped by the kinds of tasks they allow you to perform.

Calling Windows and Making Them Active

The SAS Display Manager System has numerous windows, in addition to the four primary windows, through which you can move and accomplish tasks. Use a *window-call command* to open a window and make it active; as you do, the cursor immediately moves to that window.* The window-call commands correspond to the name or nickname for each window, as shown in the following list of window-call commands:

- □ AF C=*library.catalog.entry.type*
- □ APPOINTMENT
- □ CALCULATOR
- □ CATALOG
- □ DIR
- □ FILENAME
- □ FOOTNOTES
- □ FSFORMS *form-name*
- □ HELP
- □ KEYS
- □ LIBNAME
- □ LOG
- □ MANAGER | MGR
- □ NOTEPAD
- □ OPTIONS
- □ OUTPUT | LISTING
- □ PROGRAM | PGM
- □ SETINIT
- □ SITEINFO
- □ TITLES
- □ VAR

Because you can use the window-call commands anywhere, you can use them to move from any one display manager window to another. You may find it efficient to use multiple commands when you use window-call commands.

---

* Note that PROGRAM, or PGM, is the window-call command for the PROGRAM EDITOR window; MANAGER, or MGR, is the window-call command for the OUTPUT MANAGER. FSFORMS *form-name* is the window-call command for the FORM window.

For example, suppose you want to correct an error in a lengthy set of SAS statements in the PROGRAM EDITOR window. From the LOG window, specify

```
pgm; zoom; change paint print
```

Display 38.1 shows that the cursor immediately moves to the PROGRAM EDITOR window, which now occupies the entire display. The word *paint* has been changed to *print*, and the cursor rests after the last character of that text string. With one execution, you have accomplished three tasks.

Display 38.1
Executing a
Window-Call
Command in a
Series

```
┌PROGRAM EDITOR───────────────────────────────────────────────┐
  Command ===>

  00041 math      point    m 1983 493
  00042 math      point    f 1983 445
  00043 math      point    m 1984 495
  00044 math      point    f 1984 449
  00045 math      point    m 1985 499
  00046 math      point    f 1985 452
  00047 math      point    m 1986 501
  00048 math      point    f 1986 451
  00049 ;
  00050 run;
  00051 proc sort;
  00052    by test sex;
  00053 run;
  00054 proc means noprint;
  00055    by test sex;
  00056    var score;
  00057    output out=summary mean=avescore;
  00058 proc print data=summary; _
  00059    title 'Using the MEANS Procedure';
  00060 run;
                                                        ─ZOOM─
```

Managing Windows

The NEXT and PREVWIND commands also allow you to move from one window to another. They are examples of *window management commands*, commands that help you manage windows and thereby use them efficiently. The PREVWIND command moves the cursor to the previous open window and makes it active; the NEXT command moves the cursor to the next open window and makes it active.*

---

* Both the NEXT and PREVWIND commands access windows only if you have already opened them with a window-call command. Otherwise, they access only three of the four primary windows: the PROGRAM EDITOR, LOG, and OUTPUT windows.

The following list includes the commands you may use most often to manage your windows:

□ BYE

□ CLEAR

□ END

□ NEXT

□ PREVWIND

□ RECALL

□ ZOOM

You should already be familiar with the ZOOM command. Execute it once to increase a window to occupy the entire display. Execute it again to return the window to its previous size. The BYE command ends a SAS session, and the END command closes a window, removing it from the display. In the PROGRAM EDITOR window, the END command acts like the SUBMIT command.

Clearing a Window

The CLEAR command removes all text from the active window. You can also clear the PROGRAM EDITOR, LOG, and OUTPUT windows from any display manager window. Suppose you want to clear the LOG window from the PROGRAM EDITOR window, before you submit your SAS statements. Simply specify

```
clear log
```

Then you can submit your SAS statements, and the LOG window contains only your new log messages.

Scrolling Windows

Scrolling commands allow you to maneuver within text, and they're easy to remember because they do what their names suggest. The following are scrolling commands:

□ BACKWARD

□ FORWARD

□ LEFT

□ RIGHT

□ TOP

□ BOTTOM

□ HSCROLL

□ VSCROLL

You can move the contents of a window backward and forward with the BACKWARD and FORWARD commands or left and right with the LEFT and RIGHT commands. With the TOP command, you can move the cursor to the first character of the first line in a window. With the BOTTOM command, you can display the last line of text. Using the TOP and BOTTOM commands allows you to move quickly to the beginning or end of a lengthy program. Display 38.2 shows the results of using the BOTTOM command.

Display 38.2
Fast Forwarding with the BOTTOM Command

```
┌PROGRAM EDITOR─────────────────────────────────────────────────────────┐
│ Command ===>                                                           │
│                                                                        │
│ 00055    by test sex;                                                  │
│ 00056    var score;                                                    │
│ 00057    output out=summary mean=avescore;                            │
│ 00058 proc print data=summary;                                         │
│ 00059    title 'Using the MEANS Procedure';                           │
│ 00060 run;                                                             │
│ 00061                                                                  │
│ 00062                                                                  │
│ 00063                                                                  │
│ 00064                                                                  │
│ 00065                                                                  │
│ 00066                                                                  │
│ 00067                                                                  │
│ 00068                                                                  │
│ 00069                                                                  │
│ 00070                                                                  │
│ 00071                                                                  │
│ 00072                                                                  │
│ 00073                                                                  │
│ 00074                                                                  │
└────────────────────────────────────────────────────────────────ZOOM──┘
```

The amount you move to the left or the right is determined by the HSCROLL command; the amount you move forward or backward is determined by the VSCROLL command. With both the HSCROLL and VSCROLL commands, you can choose from the following options to set the amount you scroll automatically. If you don't specify any of these options, the SAS System assigns HALF as the default.

PAGE   is the entire amount showing in the window.

HALF   is half the amount showing in the window.

MAX   is the maximum portion to the left or right or to the top or bottom showing in the window.

n is n lines or columns, where n is the number you specify.

CURSOR   is the left or right of the display, depending on whether the LEFT or RIGHT command is subsequently executed.*

---

* You can use the CURSOR option only in windows that allow editing.

For example, if you want to make the automatic horizontal scrolling amount five columns, specify

```
hscroll 5
```

Now, when you execute the LEFT or RIGHT command, you move five columns in whichever direction you specify. If you want to make the automatic vertical scrolling amount half a page, specify

```
vscroll half
```

Then, when you execute the FORWARD command, half of the previous page remains on the display and half of a new page is scrolled into view.

Occasionally, you need to scroll a specific number of lines forward or backward to position the text so you can see portions of your program in the window at one time. Instead of changing the VSCROLL amount to the number of lines you want to scroll, simply use the scroll amount on the FORWARD command to temporarily override the default scrolling amount. You can specify any of the scrolling amounts with the BACKWARD and FORWARD commands and the LEFT and RIGHT commands.

Changing Color and Highlighting in Windows

With the COLOR command, the SAS System offers you a simple way to customize your environment if your display terminal supports color. Display manager windows are assigned colors, which you can change with the COLOR command. Simply specify the COLOR command followed by the *field*, or part of the window, you want changed and the desired color. You may also be able to change highlighting attributes, such as blinking and reverse video.

For example, to change the text to red, specify

```
color text red
```

Text you subsequently enter appears in red. In the PROGRAM EDITOR window, existing text also changes to red.

Other available colors are blue, green, cyan, pink, yellow, white, black, magenta, gray, brown, and orange. If the color you specify isn't available, the SAS System attempts to match a color to its closest counterpart.

Finding and Changing Text

You may often want to search for a character string and change it. You can locate the character string by specifying first the FIND command and then the character string. Then the cursor moves to the first occurrence of the string you want to locate. Remember to enclose a string in quotes if CAPS ON is in effect. You can change a string by specifying first the CHANGE command, then a space and the current character string, and then a space and the new character string. Remember to enclose in quotes any string that contains an embedded blank or special characters. For both the FIND and CHANGE commands, the character string can be any length.

With both the FIND and CHANGE commands, you can specify the following options to locate or change a particular occurrence of a string:

□ ALL

□ FIRST

□ LAST

□ NEXT

□ PREFIX

□ PREV

□ SUFFIX

□ WORD

For details on which options you can use together, see *SAS Language: Reference, Version 6, First Edition.* Note that the option ALL finds or changes all occurrences of the specified string. In the following example, all occurrences of host are changed to operating system:

```
change host 'operating system' all
```

To resume the search for a string previously specified with the FIND command, specify the RFIND command. To continue changing a string previously specified with the CHANGE command, specify the RCHANGE command. To find the previous occurrence of a string, specify the BFIND or FIND PREV command; you can use the PREFIX, SUFFIX, and WORD options with the BFIND command.

Cutting, Pasting, and Storing Text

With the cut and paste facility, you can

□ identify the text you want to manipulate

□ store a copy of the text in a temporary storage place called a *paste buffer*

□ insert text

□ list the names of all current paste buffers or delete them.

You can manipulate and store text using the following commands:

MARK   identifies the text that you want to cut or paste.

CUT   removes the marked text from the display and stores it in the paste buffer.

STORE   copies the marked text and stores it in the paste buffer.

PASTE   inserts the text that you have stored in the paste buffer at the cursor location.

Managing Files

In Chapter 37, you learned how to use the FILE command to store the contents of the PROGRAM EDITOR, LOG, and OUTPUT windows in an external file. You also learned how to use the INCLUDE command to copy text from an external file into the PROGRAM EDITOR window.

Using the SAS Text Editor

Discovering the Possibilities

The SAS text editor is a full-screen editing facility available in the PROGRAM EDITOR and NOTEPAD windows of base SAS software and in SAS/FSP and SAS/AF software. You can edit text with various command-line and line commands. The SAS text editor also uses most of the display manager commands that aren't window specific.

Editing Text

To edit text, you can use command-line commands, line commands, function keys, or the PMENU facility. Several of these commands are explained briefly in Chapter 37. This section provides you with more details about those commands and new information about others.

Moving and Rearranging Text

In Chapter 37 you learned the basics of moving, deleting, inserting, and copying single lines of text. The ground rules are similar for working with a block of text. Simply use double letters on the beginning and ending lines you want to edit.

For example, alphabetizing the following list requires that you move a block of text. Note the MM (move) block command on lines 5 and 6 and the B line command on line 1 of the example.

```
b 001    c signifies the line command copy
  00002  d signifies the line command delete
  00003  i signifies the line command insert
  00004  m signifies the line command move
mm 05    a signifies the line command after
mm 06    b signifies the line command before
  00007  r signifies the line command repeat
```

The operation is complete after you press the ENTER or RETURN key. Here are the results:

```
00001   a signifies the line command after
00002   b signifies the line command before
00003   c signifies the line command copy
00004   d signifies the line command delete
00005   i signifies the line command insert
00006   m signifies the line command move
00007   r signifies the line command repeat
```

Mastering just a few more commands greatly increases the complexity of what you can do within the text editor. Several commands allow you to justify text. Specify the JL (justify left) command to left justify, the JR (justify right) command to right justify, and the JC (justify center) command to center text. To justify blocks of text, use the JJL, JJR, and JJC commands. For example, suppose you want to center the following text:

```
00001 Study of Gifted Seventh Graders
00002 Burns County Schools, North Carolina
00003 Conducted by Educomp, Inc.
```

Simply add the JJC block command on the first and last lines and press ENTER or RETURN.

You can also shift text right or left the number of spaces you choose by executing the following set of line commands:

>[n]   shifts text to the right the number of spaces you specify; the default is one space.

<[n]   shifts text to the left the number of spaces you specify; the default is one space.

To shift a block of text left, specify the following command on the beginning and ending line numbers of the block:

<<[n]

Specify the following to shift a block of text right:

>>[n]

Displaying Column and Line Numbers

To display column numbers in the text editor, specify the COLS line command. This command is especially useful if you are writing an INPUT statement in column mode, as shown in Display 38.3.

Display 38.3
Executing the
COLS Command

```
┌PROGRAM EDITOR─────────────────────────────────────────────────────────────┐
│ Command ===>                                                                │
│                                                                             │
│ 00001 data sales;                                                           │
│ 00002    input salesrep $ 1-8 sales 10-15 region $ 19-23                    │
│ 00003        machine $ 29-30;                                               │
│ 00004    cards;                                                             │
│ *COLS ----|----10---|----20---|----30---|----40---|----50---|----60---|----7│
│ 00006 Wilson   10498    west     SC                                         │
│ 00007 Lambert   9876    west     O                                          │
│ 00008 Parker    8967    east     O                                          │
│ 00009 Davis    12335    north    SC                                         │
│ 00010 Mohar    14567    south    O                                          │
│ 00011 McVeigh  14066    west     O                                          │
│ 00012 Early    11446    east     O                                          │
│ 00013 Dillon    9565    south    SC                                         │
│ 00014 Lingle   10775    south    SC                                         │
│ 00015 Lea      12600    north    O                                          │
│ 00016 Carter   13450    east     O                                          │
│ 00017 Shelby   10982    west     SC                                         │
│ 00018 Evan      9400    north    O                                          │
│ 00019 Lucas    12075    south    SC                                         │
│ 00020 Black    11150    west     SC                                         │
└────────────────────────────────────────────────────────────────────ZOOM───┘
```

To remove the COLS line command or any other pending line command, execute the RESET command on the command line. You can also execute the D (delete) line command on the line where you have specified the COLS command to achieve the same results.

The NUMBERS command numbers the data lines in the PROGRAM EDITOR and NOTEPAD windows. Specify the following command to add numbers to the data lines:

    numbers on

To remove the numbers, specify

    numbers off

You can also use the NUMBERS command without an argument like an on or off switch, executing the command once to turn it on and again to turn it off.

Uppercasing and Lowercasing Text

Uppercasing and lowercasing text involves two sets of commands to accomplish two kinds of tasks:

□   the CAPS command, which changes the default

□   the CU and CL line commands, which change the case of existing text.

Changing the Default with the CAPS Command

After you execute the CAPS command, the text that you enter is uppercased as soon as you press ENTER or RETURN. Under some operating systems, with CAPS ON, characters entered or modified are translated into uppercase when you move the cursor from the line. Character strings that you specify with a

FIND, RFIND, or BFIND command are interpreted as having been entered in uppercase unless you enclose the character strings in quotes.

For example, suppose you want to find the word *value* in the LOG window. On the command line, specify

```
find value
```

If the CAPS command has already been specified, the SAS System searches for the word *VALUE* instead of *value*. You receive a message indicating that no occurrence of *VALUE* has been found, as shown in Display 38.4.

Display 38.4
The Results of the FIND Command with CAPS ON

```
┌LOG───────────────────────────────────────────────────────────────────┐
│ Command ===>                                                           │
│ WARNING: No occurrences of "VALUE" found.                              │
│ 178   data sales;                                                      │
│ 179      input salesrep $ 1-8 sales 10-15 region $ 19-23               │
│ 180          machine $ 29-39;                                          │
│ 181      cards;                                                        │
│                                                                        │
│ NOTE: The data set WORK.SALES has 15 observations and 4 variables.     │
│                                                                        │
│ 197   ;                                                                │
│ 198   run;                                                             │
│ 199   proc print;                                                      │
│ 200   run;                                                             │
│                                                                        │
│                                                                        │
│                                                                        │
│                                                                        │
│                                                               ─ZOOM─   │
└────────────────────────────────────────────────────────────────────┘
```

However, specify the following command and the SAS System searches for the word *value*, and finds it:

```
find 'value'
```

The CAPS command remains in effect until the end of your session or until you turn it off. You can execute the CAPS command by specifying

```
caps on
```

To discontinue it, specify

```
caps off
```

You can also use the CAPS command like an on or off switch, executing it once to turn it on and again to turn it off.

Changing the Case of Existing Text

To uppercase or lowercase text that has already been entered, use the line commands CU and CL. Execute the CU (case upper) command to uppercase a line of text and the CL (case lower) command to lowercase a line of text. For a block of text, you have two choices. First, you can execute the CCU block command to uppercase a block of text and the CCL block command to lowercase a block of text. Be sure to position the block command on both the first and last lines of text you want converted. Second, you can designate a number of lines to be uppercased or lowercased by specifying a numeric *argument*, as shown below.

```
cu3 1 Study of Gifted Seventh Graders
00002 Burns County Schools, North Carolina
00003 Conducted by Educomp, Inc.
```

Press ENTER or RETURN to execute the command. The three lines of text are converted to uppercase, as shown below:

```
00001 STUDY OF GIFTED SEVENTH GRADERS
00002 BURNS COUNTY SCHOOLS, NORTH CAROLINA
00003 CONDUCTED BY EDUCOMP, INC.
```

Combining and Separating Text

A number of line commands allow you to combine and separate pieces of text. With the TC (text connect) command, you can connect two lines of text. For example, suppose you want to join the following lines. Type the TC line command as shown below. Note that the second line is deliberately started in column 2 to create a space between the last word of the first line and the first word of the second line.

```
tc001 This study was conducted by
00002  Educomp, Inc., of Annapolis, Md.
```

Press ENTER or RETURN to execute the command, and the lines flow as shown below.

```
00001 This study was conducted by Educomp, Inc., of Annapolis, Md.
```

Conversely, the TS (text split) command shifts text after the cursor's current position to the beginning of a new line.

Remember that you can also use a function key to execute the TC line command, the TS line command, or any other line command as long as you precede it with a colon.

SAS Tools

Many of the commands discussed in this chapter were introduced in Chapter 37. The commands discussed in more detail in this chapter are summarized below. This chapter discusses the following command-line commands:

NEXT
> moves the cursor to the next window and makes it active.

PREVWIND
> moves the cursor to the previous window and makes it active.

CLEAR
> clears a window as specified.

COLOR
> changes the color of a part of the window.

FIND
> searches for a specified character string.

CHANGE
> finds and changes one character string to another.

MARK
> identifies the text that you want to cut or paste.

CUT
> removes marked text from the display and stores it in the paste buffer.

STORE
> copies marked text in display to the paste buffer. The text isn't removed from the display.

PASTE
> inserts the text that is stored in the paste buffer at the cursor location.

NUMBERS
> adds or removes line numbers.

CAPS
> changes the default case of text.

This chapter discusses the following line commands:

mm
> moves a block of text.

JL or JJL
> left justifies text.

JR or JJR
> right justifies text.

JC or JJC
> centers text.

>[*n*] or >>[*n*]
>> shifts text *n* spaces to the right.

<[*n*] or <<[*n*]
>> shifts text *n* spaces to the left.

COLS
>> displays a line ruler that marks horizontal columns.

CU or CCU
>> uppercases text.

CL or CCL
>> lowercases text.

TC

>> connects two lines of text.

TS

>> splits a line of text.

This chapter discusses the following scrolling commands:

BACKWARD
>> moves the contents of a window backward.

FORWARD
>> moves the contents of a window forward.

LEFT
>> moves the contents of a window to the left.

RIGHT
>> moves the contents of a window to the right.

TOP
>> moves the cursor to the first character of the first line in a window.

BOTTOM
>> moves to the last line of text.

HSCROLL
>> controls the amount you scroll from left to right.

VSCROLL
>> controls the amount you scroll from top to bottom.

You can use the following options with the HSCROLL and VSCROLL commands to set the amount you scroll:

PAGE
>> is the entire amount showing in the window.

HALF
>> is half the amount showing in the window.

MAX
>> is the maximum portion to the left or right or to the top or bottom showing in the window.

n
   is *n* lines or columns, where *n* is the number you specify.

CURSOR
   is the left or right of the display, depending on whether the LEFT or
   RIGHT command is subsequently executed.

Learning More

□ Chapter 37, "Using the SAS Display Manager System: the Basics," and
 Chapter 39, "Mastering Your Environment with Selected Windows," provide
 more information on the SAS Display Manager System.

□ *SAS Language: Reference, Version 6, First Edition* contains complete
 reference information on display manager.

□ *SAS Language: Reference* presents complete reference information on the SAS
 text editor.

□ The SAS documentation for your host system presents host-specific details
 concerning the CAPS command.

Chapter **39** Mastering Your Environment with Selected Windows

Introduction

This chapter acquaints you with some of the windows that allow you to control your environment. With these windows you can

- find help when you need it

- simplify your work

- monitor files

- customize your environment.

Finding Help

As you use the SAS Display Manager System, you may find occasionally that you need help. Perhaps you're familiar with a command or a window but don't fully understand what it accomplishes. Or perhaps you know what you want to do but don't know which command or window to use. In either case, you can obtain the information you need *online*, from the HELP window.

Calling Help Online

You can access the HELP window from any other window. It is an online facility that provides you with information about display manager and the entire SAS System. To access the HELP window, simply specify

```
help
```

Choosing from a Menu

When accessed from one of the four primary windows (PROGRAM EDITOR, LOG, OUTPUT, and OUTPUT MANAGER windows), the HELP window appears as shown in Display 39.1.

Display 39.1
Viewing the HELP
Window

```
┌HELP: SAS System Help──────────────────────────────────────────┐
│ Command ===>                                                   │
│                                                                │
│    SAS SYSTEM HELP: Main Menu                                  │
│                                                                │
│                                                                │
│                                                                │
│    DATA MANAGEMENT        REPORT WRITING        GRAPHICS        │
│                                                                │
│                                                                │
│    DATA ANALYSIS          PLANNING TOOLS        UTILITIES       │
│                                                                │
│                                                                │
│    SAS LANGUAGE           SAS TEXT EDITOR       SAS WINDOWS     │
│                                                                │
│                                                                │
│                           HOST UTILITIES                       │
│                                                                │
│                                INDEX                           │
│                                                                │
│                                                                │
└────────────────────────────────────────────────────────────────┘
```

As Display 39.1 shows, SAS System Help appears to you first through a primary menu. From that primary menu, you can request help information for base SAS software procedures, windows, other components of base SAS software, and other SAS software products. Simply move the cursor to the category you want and press ENTER or RETURN or use a mouse to point and click. The primary window also includes an index for your convenience. If you execute the HELP command within SAS System Help, information is displayed concerning how to use SAS System Help.

For example, if you want more information on the data management procedures, select that category by moving the cursor to DATA MANAGEMENT and pressing ENTER or RETURN. A window is displayed listing all those procedures. Then suppose you want information concerning the DATASETS procedure. You select the DATASETS procedure by moving the cursor to DATASETS and pressing ENTER or RETURN. A *help window* is displayed containing the index entry for the DATASETS procedure. A brief definition is provided. Selecting Introduction displays another help window with additional information about PROC DATASETS, including some of its statements. Selecting Syntax displays a help window with complete syntax for the DATASETS procedure.

Suppose you want information about the DATASETS procedure but don't know which category to select. From the primary menu, select INDEX by moving the cursor to INDEX and pressing ENTER or RETURN. The DATASETS procedure is listed, along with the other base SAS software procedures and other parts of the SAS System. Select the DATASETS procedure. A help window is displayed containing the index entry for the DATASETS procedure. From there, you can either select Introduction or Syntax for more information about PROC DATASETS or close the window.

From any help window, executing the END command closes the current help window and removes it from the display, returning to the previous window. Executing the =X command causes you to exit SAS System Help completely, returning you to the previous display manager window.

Taking Shortcuts

As you become more familiar with the help windows, you can take shortcuts to obtain the information you want. From any of the primary windows in display manager, you can move directly to a help window for the part of the SAS System you choose. For example, to access a help window for the APPEND procedure, specify

```
help append
```

The primary menu is bypassed, and a help window is displayed containing the index entry for the APPEND procedure. From there, you can obtain more information about the APPEND procedure by selecting Introduction or Syntax. If you execute the END command instead, you return to the previous display manager window.

Getting Help from Selected Windows

From any window other than one of the four primary windows, you can directly access information for that window. The primary menu is bypassed. For example, from the command line of the NOTEPAD window, specify

```
help
```

A help window for the NOTEPAD window appears immediately, occupying the entire display, as shown in Display 39.2.

Display 39.2
Getting Help from the NOTEPAD Window

```
┌HELP: Display Manager Windows──────────────────────────────────────
│ Command ===>
│
│    SAS DISPLAY MANAGER WINDOW: NOTEPAD
│
│    The Notepad window displays an area where you can enter and
│    edit any kind of information you wish, using the SAS Text Editor
│    to use within a session, or to save from session to session.
│
│    SAS Display Manager Global Commands can be used in the NOTEPAD window.
│
│
│
│
│
│
│
│
│
│
│
│
│
│
│
│
│
│
└──────────────────────────────────────────────────────────────────
```

Execute the END or =X command to return directly to the previous window.

Simplifying Your Work with the KEYS Window

While the HELP window provides you with information you need, the KEYS window simplifies your work by

□ showing you what commands are assigned to keys

□ letting you set up your own key definitions.

Browsing the KEYS Window

To access the KEYS window, specify

```
keys
```

By now, you should be aware of, and may have used, the function keys at your terminal. With them, you can use one keystroke to execute any command defined by a function key. Depending on the type of terminal you're using, the SAS System assigns default definitions to your terminal's function keys. A sample of typical key settings is displayed in the KEYS window in Display 39.3.

Display 39.3
Viewing Sample
Key Settings

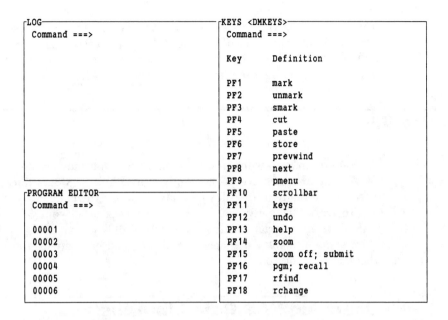

```
┌LOG──────────────────────────┐   ┌KEYS <DMKEYS>─────────────────────┐
│ Command ===>                 │   │ Command ===>                      │
│                              │   │                                   │
│                              │   │ Key       Definition              │
│                              │   │                                   │
│                              │   │ PF1       mark                    │
│                              │   │ PF2       unmark                  │
│                              │   │ PF3       smark                   │
│                              │   │ PF4       cut                     │
│                              │   │ PF5       paste                   │
│                              │   │ PF6       store                   │
│                              │   │ PF7       prevwind                │
│                              │   │ PF8       next                    │
│                              │   │ PF9       pmenu                   │
├PROGRAM EDITOR────────────────┤   │ PF10      scrollbar               │
│ Command ===>                 │   │ PF11      keys                    │
│                              │   │ PF12      undo                    │
│ 00001                        │   │ PF13      help                    │
│ 00002                        │   │ PF14      zoom                    │
│ 00003                        │   │ PF15      zoom off; submit         │
│ 00004                        │   │ PF16      pgm; recall             │
│ 00005                        │   │ PF17      rfind                   │
│ 00006                        │   │ PF18      rchange                 │
└──────────────────────────────┘   └───────────────────────────────────┘
```

Scroll forward to view all of the default settings; execute the END command to exit the window. You can also use most of the other display manager commands already discussed in this chapter and others.

Changing Key Settings

Changing and Adding Commands

To change the definition of any setting, simply type the new definition over an old one. Once defined, a setting takes effect immediately, whether or not you exit the KEYS window.

If you have changed your settings but want to cancel the change before exiting the KEYS window, on the command line specify

    cancel

Your previous settings are restored.

Inserting Text

Aside from changing or adding commands within the KEYS window, you can also define a key to insert text. Simply precede the text string with a tilde (~) in the first column of the field. For example, suppose you are circulating a report and want to indicate to reviewers that more information is needed in certain places. You can define one of your function keys to insert a text string, as shown here:

    ~/*More information needed; please supply.*/

Then every time you press that function key, the text string is inserted at the location of the cursor (without the tilde symbol). Depending on the operating system you're using, the inserted text may or may not overlay text following the cursor. Customizing function keys like this can save you time.

Monitoring Files

As you continue to work in display manager, you may create numerous SAS files, some of which are permanently stored in a SAS data library. You may also need to use many of the files you have stored externally.

To work efficiently, you need to keep track of all your SAS data libraries, SAS files, their variables, and the external files you're using in display manager. With some of display manager's windows, you can rely on the SAS System to do that tracking for you.

Checking SAS Data Libraries and SAS Files

Using the LIBNAME Window

A SAS data library is a collection of SAS files with the same *libref*, or first-level name. All currently assigned librefs are displayed in the LIBNAME window. To display the LIBNAME window, specify

    libname

Display 39.4 shows the LIBNAME window.

Display 39.4
Viewing the
LIBNAME Window

```
┌LOG─────────────    ┌LIBNAME────────────────────────────────────────────
│ Command ===>       │ Command ===>
│                    │
│                    │
│                    │      Libref     Engine    Host Path Name
│                    │
│                    │    - S          V606      YOUR-DATA-LIBRARY1
│                    │    _ SASHELP    V606      YOUR-DATA-LIBRARY2
│                    │    _ SASUSER    V606      YOUR-DATA-LIBRARY3
│                    │    _ WORK       V606      YOUR-DATA-LIBRARY4
│                    │
│                    │
│                    │
│                    │
│                    │
│                    │
┌PROGRAM EDITOR──────│
│ Command ===>       │
│                    │
│ 00001              │
│ 00002              │
│ 00003              │
│ 00004              │
│ 00005              │
│ 00006              │
```

The libref, the name of the engine used to access the library, and the name of the corresponding SAS data library are displayed. To list the SAS files contained in one of the SAS data libraries, move the cursor to the selection field to the left of the libref you choose, type X, and press ENTER or RETURN. Then the DIR window appears as shown in Display 39.5, listing all the SAS files in that SAS data library.

Display 39.5
Reaching the DIR
Window through
the LIBNAME
Window

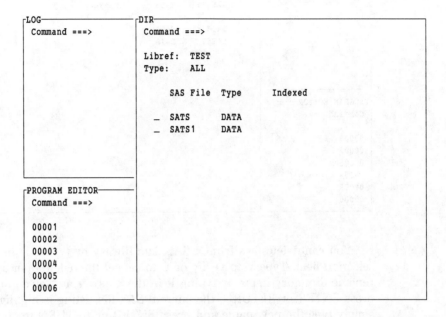

The relationship between the LIBNAME and DIR windows occurs because they are *interactive*; that is, the selections you make in one window trigger information in another window to be displayed. If call for a list of SAS files from the LIBNAME window, the DIR window appears.

Note: The CATALOG window and the VAR window are also interactive. If you call for a list of variables for a given data set, the VAR window appears. If you request a list of entries for a given catalog, the CATALOG window appears.

Using the DIR Window

You can also access the DIR window by executing its window-call command from any display manager window:

```
dir
```

By default, the libref WORK and the type ALL appear at the top of the window. Enter the name of the libref and the type of SAS file in the appropriate selection fields and press ENTER or RETURN to display the listing you want.

Suppose you want to list all the files in the library referenced by the libref OUT. Type OUT over WORK (don't change the type) and press ENTER or RETURN. A list of those SAS files then appears, as shown in Display 39.6.

Display 39.6
Listing SAS Files
in the DIR
Window

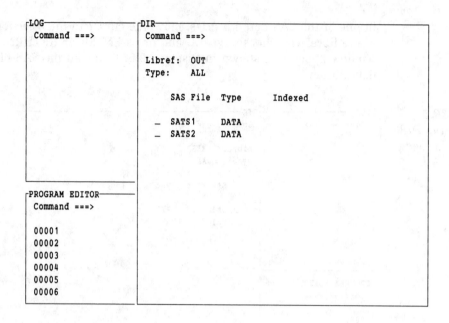

```
┌LOG─────────────────────    ┌DIR──────────────────────────────────
│ Command ===>               │ Command ===>
│                            │
│                            │ Libref:  OUT
│                            │ Type:    ALL
│                            │
│                            │    SAS File  Type      Indexed
│                            │
│                            │ _  SATS1     DATA
│                            │ _  SATS2     DATA
│                            │
│                            │
│                            │
│                            │
│                            │
┌PROGRAM EDITOR───────────   │
│ Command ===>               │
│                            │
│ 00001                      │
│ 00002                      │
│ 00003                      │
│ 00004                      │
│ 00005                      │
│ 00006                      │
```

You can delete files from a SAS data library by typing D in the appropriate selection field. Type V to verify or C to cancel the delete operation. You can rename directory items by typing R in the appropriate selection field. When you press ENTER or RETURN, the current SAS file listing is highlighted and you simply type the new name and press ENTER or RETURN to complete the process.

Use the END command to exit the LIBNAME and DIR windows. In both windows, you can use most of the commands discussed in this chapter and in Chapter 37, "Using the SAS Display Manager System: the Basics," and Chapter 38, "Using Commands to Manipulate Your Full-Screen Environment."

Checking External Files

Although you may store much of your data in SAS files, you may also store your data in external files. You can use a FILENAME statement to associate a *fileref*, or file reference name, with an external file. Then, as you write SAS programs and submit SAS statements in display manager, you can use the fileref as a shorthand way to reference the external file. Assigned filerefs are listed in the FILENAME window, which you can display with the following window-call command:

    filename

The fileref appears in the left-hand column, and the file's complete name appears in the right-hand column, as shown in Display 39.7.

Display 39.7
Viewing the
FILENAME
Window

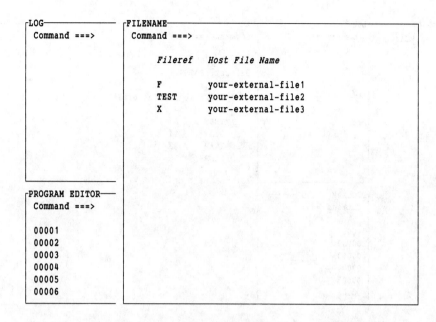

```
┌─LOG─────────        ┌─FILENAME─────────────────────────────────────────┐
│  Command ===>       │  Command ===>                                     │
│                     │                                                   │
│                     │      Fileref    Host File Name                    │
│                     │                                                   │
│                     │      F          your-external-file1               │
│                     │      TEST       your-external-file2               │
│                     │      X          your-external-file3               │
│                     │                                                   │
│                     │                                                   │
│                     │                                                   │
│                     │                                                   │
│                     │                                                   │
├─PROGRAM EDITOR──────│                                                   │
│  Command ===>       │                                                   │
│                     │                                                   │
│  00001              │                                                   │
│  00002              │                                                   │
│  00003              │                                                   │
│  00004              │                                                   │
│  00005              │                                                   │
│  00006              └───────────────────────────────────────────────────┘
```

As with the DIR and LIBNAME windows, you can exit the FILENAME window by executing the END command. You can also use most of the display manager commands already discussed in this chapter.

Checking Variables in SAS Data Sets

The VAR window allows you an easy way to browse a list of variables for a SAS data set, as well as the following for each variable:

□ type and length

□ format

□ informat

□ key indicator

□ label, if assigned.

To display the VAR window, specify

```
var
```

Fill in the selection fields for the libref and the data set to display the information for the data set you choose.

For example, for information about the data set OUT.SATS1, fill in the blanks for libref and data set and press ENTER or RETURN. The data set has three character variables and one numeric variable, as shown in Display 39.8.

Display 39.8
Browsing the VAR
Window

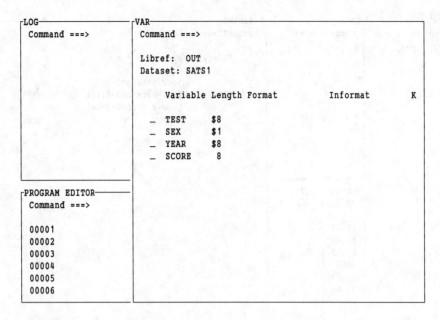

```
┌LOG─────────────         ┌VAR────────────────────────────────────────────────┐
│ Command ===>            │ Command ===>                                       │
│                         │                                                    │
│                         │ Libref:  OUT                                       │
│                         │ Dataset: SATS1                                     │
│                         │                                                    │
│                         │         Variable Length Format      Informat     K │
│                         │                                                    │
│                         │     _   TEST     $8                                │
│                         │     _   SEX      $1                                │
│                         │     _   YEAR     $8                                │
│                         │     _   SCORE     8                                │
│                         │                                                    │
┌PROGRAM EDITOR──         │                                                    │
│ Command ===>            │                                                    │
│                         │                                                    │
│ 00001                   │                                                    │
│ 00002                   │                                                    │
│ 00003                   │                                                    │
│ 00004                   │                                                    │
│ 00005                   │                                                    │
│ 00006                   └────────────────────────────────────────────────────┘
```

Remember that because the VAR window is interactive, you can also reach it through the DIR window. From the DIR window, type the name of a libref in the selection field for the libref and DATA in the selection field for the type; press ENTER or RETURN to list the SAS files. Type X next to the data set for which you want information about variables and press ENTER or RETURN. Then the VAR window appears.

You can use most of the display manager commands in the VAR window that have already been discussed. Execute the END command to exit the window.

Knowing Your Options

Much of this book is dedicated to showing you how to change the appearance of SAS output, handle files, use SAS System variables, and process observations in SAS data sets. For example, Chapter 21, "Analyzing your SAS Session with the SAS Log," tells you how to suppress page numbering, system messages, and SAS statements on your output. You can make these changes and others by using SAS system options.

Browsing the OPTIONS Window

An alphabetical listing of SAS system options that work across all operating systems is contained in the OPTIONS window, which you can invoke from any other window with the following window-call command:

```
options
```

Host options aren't displayed. Display 39.9 shows the OPTIONS window.

Display 39.9
Viewing Current
Options and Their
Values

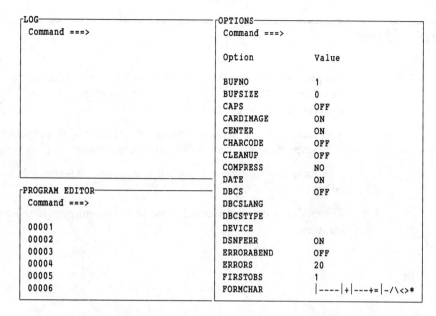

In the OPTIONS window, the left-hand column lists the options; the right-hand column, which can be changed, shows the corresponding value for each. (Note that equal signs aren't shown for options whose arguments are character or numeric strings; the values ON and OFF correspond to the *option*/NO*option* form used for options in the OPTIONS statement.) Scroll forward to continue browsing the list. Use the END command to return to the previous window.

Changing SAS System Options

In addition to listing all the options, the OPTIONS window allows you to alter settings. You can do this by typing over the current value shown in the column labeled Value that corresponds to a given option. The changes take effect immediately and, unless changed again, remain in effect throughout your session. For example, suppose you want to substitute the letter X for the default missing value (.). Simply locate the option MISSING in the left-hand column. Over the default value in the right-hand column, type

```
X
```

Execute the CANCEL command to return to the previous setting without saving your changes; execute the END command to save changes and exit the window.

SAS Tools

You can invoke all the windows available in the SAS Display Manager System by specifying the name of the window (or alias) on the command line. The window-call commands discussed in this chapter are HELP, KEYS, LIBNAME, DIR, FILENAME, VAR, and OPTIONS.

Learning More

- □ Chapter 37, "Using the SAS Display Manager System: the Basics," and Chapter 38, "Using Commands to Manipulate Your Full-Screen Environment," provide more information on display manager.

- □ *SAS Language: Reference, Version 6, First Edition* presents complete reference information on display manager and display manager windows.

- □ *SAS Language: Reference* contains complete reference information on the text editor.

- □ The SAS documentation for your host system provides information on host options.

Part 11
Appendix

Appendix   **Additional Data Sets**

| Appendix | # Additional Data Sets |

Introduction

In general, this book shows within each chapter how to create the data sets used in the chapter. However, when the input data are lengthy or the actual contents of the data set are not crucial to the chapter, the DATA steps or raw data to create data sets are listed in this appendix instead of within the chapter.

This appendix is organized by chapter number; only the raw data or DATA steps not illustrated in detail in the chapter are included here.

Data Sets for Chapter 4

DATA Step to Create IN.NASA

```
libname in 'your-data-library';
data in.nasa;
   input YEAR 4. @7 TOTAL comma6.
         @15 PTOTAL comma6. @20 PFLIGHT comma6.
         @28 PSCIENCE comma6. @37 PAIRTRAN comma6.
         @43 FTOTAL comma6. @49 FFLIGHT comma6.
         @58 FSCIENCE comma6. @64 FAIRTRAN comma6.;
   label    total='Total Outlays'
           ptotal='Performance: Total'
          pflight='Performance: Space Flight'
         pscience='Performance: Space Science Applications'
         pairtran='Performance: Air Transport and Other'
           ftotal='Facilities: Total'
          fflight='Facilities: Space Flight'
         fscience='Facilities: Space Science Applications'
         fairtran='Facilities: Air Transport and Other' ;
   cards;
1966  5,933  5,361 3,819   1,120    422    572    391    63    118
1967  5,426  5,137 3,477   1,160    500    289    172    47     70
1968  4,726  4,599 3,028   1,061    510    127     69    29     29
1969  4,252  4,187 2,754     893    540     65     27    21     17
1970  3,753  3,699 2,195     963    541     54     14    21     19
1971  3,382  3,338 1,877     926    535     44      8     6     30
1972  3,423  3,373 1,727   1,111    535     50     13     7     30
1973  3,316  3,271 1,532   1,220    519     45      5    11     29
1974  3,256  3,181 1,448   1,156    577     75     25    12     38
1975  3,266  3,181 1,500   1,076    606     85     35     9     42
1976  3,670  3,549 1,934     969    646    121     66    11     43
1977  3,945  3,840 2,195   1,002    643    105     56     4     45
1978  3,984  3,860 2,204     964    692    124     56     8     60
1979  4,187  4,054 2,175   1,144    735    133     41     9     83
1980  4,850  4,710 2,556   1,341    813    140     38     5     97
1981  5,241  5,274 3,026   1,380    868    147     26     4    117
1982  6,035  5,926 3,526   1,454    946    109     17     3     89
1983  6,664  6,556 4,027   1,486  1,043    108     26     .     82
1984  7,048  6,856 4,037   1,667  1,152    192     44    20    128
1985  7,251  7,004 3,852   1,834  1,318    247     70    23    154
1986  7,404  7,105 3,787   2,101  1,317    299    107    26    166
;
```

Data Sets for Chapter 20

DATA Step to Create OUT.SATS1

```
libname out 'your-data-library';
data out.sats1;
   input test $ @18 sex $1. year score;
   cards;
verbal           m 1967 463
verbal           f 1967 468
verbal           m 1970 459
verbal           f 1970 461
verbal           m 1975 437
verbal           f 1975 431
verbal           m 1977 431
verbal           f 1977 427
verbal           m 1980 428
verbal           f 1980 420
verbal           m 1981 430
verbal           f 1981 418
verbal           m 1982 431
verbal           f 1982 421
verbal           m 1983 430
verbal           f 1983 420
verbal           m 1984 433
verbal           f 1984 420
verbal           m 1985 437
verbal           f 1985 425
verbal           m 1986 437
verbal           f 1986 426
math             m 1967 514
math             f 1967 467
math             m 1970 509
math             f 1970 465
math             m 1975 495
math             f 1975 449
math             m 1977 497
math             f 1977 445
math             m 1980 491
math             f 1980 443
math             m 1981 492
math             f 1981 443
math             m 1982 493
math             f 1982 443
math             m 1983 493
math             f 1983 445
math             m 1984 495
math             f 1984 449
```

```
math          m 1985 499
math          f 1985 452
math          m 1986 501
math          f 1986 451
;
```

Data Sets for Chapter 21

Raw Data for OUT.SATS3, OUT.SATS4, OUT.SATS5

```
----+----1----+----2----+----3----+----4----+----5----+----6----+----7--
verbal        m 1967 463
verbal        f 1967 468
verbal        m 1970 459
verbal        f 1970 461
verbal        m 1975 437
verbal        f 1975 431
verbal        m 1977 431
verbal        f 1977 427
verbal        m 1980 428
verbal        f 1980 420
verbal        m 1981 430
verbal        f 1981 418
verbal        m 1982 431
verbal        f 1982 421
verbal        m 1983 430
verbal        f 1983 420
verbal        m 1984 433
verbal        f 1984 420
verbal        m 1985 437
verbal        f 1985 425
verbal        m 1986 437
verbal        f 1986 426
math          m 1967 514
math          f 1967 467
math          m 1970 509
math          f 1970 465
math          m 1975 495
math          f 1975 449
math          m 1977 497
math          f 1977 445
math          m 1980 491
math          f 1980 443
math          m 1981 492
math          f 1981 443
math          m 1982 493
math          f 1982 443
math          m 1983 493
math          f 1983 445
----+----1----+----2----+----3----+----4----+----5----+----6----+----7--
```

```
----+----1----+----2----+----3----+----4----+----5----+----6----+----7--
math          m 1984 495
math          f 1984 449
math          m 1985 499
math          f 1985 452
math          m 1986 501
math          f 1986 451
```

Data Sets for Chapter 23

Raw Data for OUT.ERROR1, OUT.ERROR2, OUT.ERROR3

```
----+----1----+----2----+----3----+----4----+----5----+----6----+----7--
verbal        m 1967 463
verbal        f 1967 468
verbal        m 1970 459
verbal        f 1970 461
verbal        m 1975 437
verbal        f 1975 431
verbal        m 1977 431
verbal        f 1977 427
verbal        m 1980 428
verbal        f 1980 420
verbal        m 1981 430
verbal        f 1981 418
verbal        m 1982 431
verbal        f 1982 421
verbal        m 1983 430
verbal        f 1983 420
verbal        m 1984 433
verbal        f 1984 420
verbal        m 1985 437
verbal        f 1985 425
verbal        m 1986 437
verbal        f 1986 426
math          m 1967 514
math          f 1967 467
math          m 1970 509
math          f 1970 465
math          m 1975 495
math          f 1975 449
math          m 1977 497
math          f 1977 445
math          m 1980 491
math          f 1980 443
math          m 1981 492
math          f 1981 443
math          m 1982 493
math          f 1982 443
----+----1----+----2----+----3----+----4----+----5----+----6----+----7--
```

(continued on next page)

(continued from previous page)

```
----+----1----+----2----+----3----+----4----+----5----+----6----+----7--
math          m 1983 493
math          f 1983 445
math          m 1984 495
math          f 1984 449
math          m 1985 499
math          f 1985 452
math          m 1986 501
math          f 1986 451
```

Data Sets for Chapter 24

Raw Data for SALES.ALLYEAR

```
----+----1----+----2----+----3----+----4----+----5----+----6----+----7--
01 1 Hollingsworth Deluxe    260 29.50
01 1 Smith         Standard   41 19.95
01 1 Hollingsworth Standard  330 19.95
01 1 Jones         Standard  110 19.95
01 1 Smith         Deluxe    715 29.50
01 1 Jones         Standard  675 19.95
02 1 Smith         Standard 2045 19.95
02 1 Smith         Deluxe     10 29.50
02 1 Smith         Standard   40 19.95
02 1 Hollingsworth Standard 1030 19.95
02 1 Jones         Standard  153 19.95
02 1 Smith         Standard   98 19.95
03 1 Hollingsworth Standard  125 19.95
03 1 Jones         Standard  154 19.95
03 1 Smith         Standard  118 19.95
03 1 Hollingsworth Standard   25 19.95
03 1 Jones         Standard  525 19.95
03 1 Smith         Standard  310 19.95
04 2 Smith         Standard  150 19.95
04 2 Hollingsworth Standard  260 19.95
04 2 Hollingsworth Standard  530 19.95
04 2 Jones         Standard 1110 19.95
04 2 Smith         Standard 1715 19.95
04 2 Jones         Standard  675 19.95
05 2 Jones         Standard   45 19.95
05 2 Hollingsworth Standard 1120 19.95
05 2 Smith         Standard   40 19.95
05 2 Hollingsworth Standard 1030 19.95
05 2 Jones         Standard  153 19.95
05 2 Smith         Standard   98 19.95
06 2 Jones         Standard  154 19.95
06 2 Hollingsworth Deluxe     25 29.50
06 2 Jones         Standard  276 19.95
06 2 Hollingsworth Standard  125 19.95
----+----1----+----2----+----3----+----4----+----5----+----6----+----7--
```

```
----+----1----+----2----+----3----+----4----+----5----+----6----+----7--
06 2 Smith         Standard  512 19.95
06 2 Smith         Standard 1000 19.95
07 3 Smith         Standard  250 19.95
07 3 Hollingsworth Deluxe     60 29.50
07 3 Smith         Standard   90 19.95
07 3 Hollingsworth Deluxe     30 29.50
07 3 Jones         Standard  110 19.95
07 3 Smith         Standard   90 19.95
07 3 Hollingsworth Standard  130 19.95
07 3 Jones         Standard  110 19.95
07 3 Smith         Standard  265 19.95
07 3 Jones         Standard  275 19.95
07 3 Smith         Standard 1250 19.95
07 3 Hollingsworth Deluxe     60 29.50
07 3 Smith         Standard   90 19.95
07 3 Jones         Standard  110 19.95
07 3 Smith         Standard   90 19.95
07 3 Hollingsworth Standard  330 19.95
07 3 Jones         Standard  110 19.95
07 3 Smith         Standard  465 19.95
07 3 Jones         Standard  675 19.95
08 3 Jones         Standard  145 19.95
08 3 Smith         Deluxe    110 29.50
08 3 Hollingsworth Standard  120 19.95
08 3 Hollingsworth Standard  230 19.95
08 3 Jones         Standard  453 19.95
08 3 Smith         Standard  240 19.95
08 3 Hollingsworth Standard  230 29.50
08 3 Jones         Standard  453 19.95
08 3 Smith         Standard  198 19.95
08 3 Hollingsworth Standard  290 19.95
08 3 Smith         Standard 1198 19.95
08 3 Jones         Deluxe     45 29.50
08 3 Jones         Standard  145 19.95
08 3 Smith         Deluxe    110 29.50
08 3 Hollingsworth Standard  330 19.95
08 3 Smith         Standard  240 19.95
08 3 Hollingsworth Deluxe     50 29.50
08 3 Jones         Standard  453 19.95
08 3 Smith         Standard  198 19.95
08 3 Jones         Deluxe    225 29.50
09 3 Hollingsworth Standard  125 19.95
09 3 Jones         Standard  254 19.95
09 3 Smith         Standard  118 19.95
09 3 Hollingsworth Standard 1000 19.95
09 3 Jones         Standard  284 19.95
09 3 Smith         Standard  412 19.95
09 3 Jones         Deluxe    275 29.50
09 3 Smith         Standard  100 19.95
09 3 Jones         Standard  876 19.95
09 3 Hollingsworth Standard  125 19.95
----+----1----+----2----+----3----+----4----+----5----+----6----+----7--
```

(continued on next page)

(continued from previous page)

```
----+----1----+----2----+----3----+----4----+----5----+----6----+----7--
09 3 Jones       Standard  254 19.95
09 3 Smith       Standard 1118 19.95
09 3 Hollingsworth Standard  175 19.95
09 3 Jones       Standard  284 19.95
09 3 Smith       Standard  412 19.95
09 3 Jones       Deluxe    275 29.50
09 3 Smith       Standard  100 19.95
09 3 Jones       Standard  876 19.95
10 4 Smith       Standard  250 19.95
10 4 Hollingsworth Standard  530 19.95
10 4 Jones       Standard  975 19.95
10 4 Hollingsworth Standard  265 19.95
10 4 Jones       Standard   55 19.95
10 4 Smith       Standard  365 19.95
11 4 Hollingsworth Standard 1230 19.95
11 4 Jones       Standard  453 19.95
11 4 Smith       Standard  198 19.95
11 4 Jones       Standard   70 19.95
11 4 Smith       Standard  120 19.95
11 4 Hollingsworth Deluxe    150 29.50
12 4 Smith       Standard 1000 19.95
12 4 Jones       Standard  876 19.95
12 4 Hollingsworth Deluxe    125 29.50
12 4 Jones       Standard 1254 19.95
12 4 Hollingsworth Standard  175 19.95
----+----1----+----2----+----3----+----4----+----5----+----6----+----7--
```

Data Sets for Chapter 25

Raw Data for SALES.YEAR

```
----+----1----+----2----+----3----+----4----+----5----+----6----+----7--
01 1 Hollingsworth Deluxe    260 29.50
01 1 Smith       Standard   41 19.95
01 1 Hollingsworth Standard  330 19.95
01 1 Jones       Standard  110 19.95
01 1 Smith       Deluxe    715 29.50
01 1 Jones       Standard  675 19.95
02 1 Smith       Standard 2045 19.95
02 1 Smith       Deluxe     10 29.50
02 1 Smith       Standard   40 19.95
02 1 Hollingsworth Standard 1030 19.95
02 1 Jones       Standard  153 19.95
02 1 Smith       Standard   98 19.95
03 1 Hollingsworth Standard  125 19.95
03 1 Jones       Standard  154 19.95
03 1 Smith       Standard  118 19.95
03 1 Hollingsworth Standard   25 19.95
----+----1----+----2----+----3----+----4----+----5----+----6----+----7--
```

```
----+----1----+----2----+----3----+----4----+----5----+----6----+----7--
03 1 Jones       Standard  525 19.95
03 1 Smith       Standard  310 19.95
04 2 Smith       Standard  150 19.95
04 2 Hollingsworth Standard  260 19.95
04 2 Hollingsworth Standard  530 19.95
04 2 Jones       Standard 1110 19.95
04 2 Smith       Standard 1715 19.95
04 2 Jones       Standard  675 19.95
05 2 Jones       Standard   45 19.95
05 2 Hollingsworth Standard 1120 19.95
05 2 Smith       Standard   40 19.95
05 2 Hollingsworth Standard 1030 19.95
05 2 Jones       Standard  153 19.95
05 2 Smith       Standard   98 19.95
06 2 Jones       Standard  154 19.95
06 2 Hollingsworth Deluxe     25 29.50
06 2 Jones       Standard  276 19.95
06 2 Hollingsworth Standard  125 19.95
06 2 Smith       Standard  512 19.95
06 2 Smith       Standard 1000 19.95
07 3 Smith       Standard  250 19.95
07 3 Hollingsworth Deluxe     60 29.50
07 3 Smith       Standard   90 19.95
07 3 Hollingsworth Deluxe     30 29.50
07 3 Jones       Standard  110 19.95
07 3 Smith       Standard   90 19.95
07 3 Hollingsworth Standard  130 19.95
07 3 Jones       Standard  110 19.95
07 3 Smith       Standard  265 19.95
07 3 Jones       Standard  275 19.95
07 3 Smith       Standard 1250 19.95
07 3 Hollingsworth Deluxe     60 29.50
07 3 Smith       Standard   90 19.95
07 3 Jones       Standard  110 19.95
07 3 Smith       Standard   90 19.95
07 3 Hollingsworth Standard  330 19.95
07 3 Jones       Standard  110 19.95
07 3 Smith       Standard  465 19.95
07 3 Jones       Standard  675 19.95
08 3 Jones       Standard  145 19.95
08 3 Smith       Deluxe    110 29.50
08 3 Hollingsworth Standard  120 19.95
08 3 Hollingsworth Standard  230 19.95
08 3 Jones       Standard  453 19.95
08 3 Smith       Standard  240 19.95
08 3 Hollingsworth Standard  230 29.50
08 3 Jones       Standard  453 19.95
08 3 Smith       Standard  198 19.95
08 3 Hollingsworth Standard  290 19.95
08 3 Smith       Standard 1198 19.95
08 3 Jones       Deluxe     45 29.50
----+----1----+----2----+----3----+----4----+----5----+----6----+----7--
```

(continued on next page)

(continued from previous page)

```
----+----1----+----2----+----3----+----4----+----5----+----6----+----7--
08 3 Jones        Standard  145 19.95
08 3 Smith        Deluxe    110 29.50
08 3 Hollingsworth Standard  330 19.95
08 3 Smith        Standard  240 19.95
08 3 Hollingsworth Deluxe     50 29.50
08 3 Jones        Standard  453 19.95
08 3 Smith        Standard  198 19.95
08 3 Jones        Deluxe    225 29.50
09 3 Hollingsworth Standard  125 19.95
09 3 Jones        Standard  254 19.95
09 3 Smith        Standard  118 19.95
09 3 Hollingsworth Standard 1000 19.95
09 3 Jones        Standard  284 19.95
09 3 Smith        Standard  412 19.95
09 3 Jones        Deluxe    275 29.50
09 3 Smith        Standard  100 19.95
09 3 Jones        Standard  876 19.95
09 3 Hollingsworth Standard  125 19.95
09 3 Jones        Standard  254 19.95
09 3 Smith        Standard 1118 19.95
09 3 Hollingsworth Standard  175 19.95
09 3 Jones        Standard  284 19.95
09 3 Smith        Standard  412 19.95
09 3 Jones        Deluxe    275 29.50
09 3 Smith        Standard  100 19.95
09 3 Jones        Standard  876 19.95
10 4 Smith        Standard  250 19.95
10 4 Hollingsworth Standard  530 19.95
10 4 Jones        Standard  975 19.95
10 4 Hollingsworth Standard  265 19.95
10 4 Jones        Standard   55 19.95
10 4 Smith        Standard  365 19.95
11 4 Hollingsworth Standard 1230 19.95
11 4 Jones        Standard  453 19.95
11 4 Smith        Standard  198 19.95
11 4 Jones        Standard   70 19.95
11 4 Smith        Standard  120 19.95
11 4 Hollingsworth Deluxe    150 29.50
12 4 Smith        Standard 1000 19.95
12 4 Jones        Standard  876 19.95
12 4 Hollingsworth Deluxe    125 29.50
12 4 Jones        Standard 1254 19.95
12 4 Hollingsworth Standard  175 19.95
----+----1----+----2----+----3----+----4----+----5----+----6----+----7--
```

Data Sets for Chapter 27

Raw Data for STOCKS.HIGHLOW

```
----+----1----+----2----+----3----+----4----+----5----+----6----+----7--
1954   31DEC54   404.39   11JAN54   279.87
1955   30DEC55   488.40   17JAN55   388.20
1956   06APR56   521.05   23JAN56   462.35
1957   12JUL57   520.77   22OCT57   419.79
1958   31DEC58   583.65   25FEB58   436.89
1959   31DEC59   679.36   09FEB59   574.46
1960   05JAN60   685.47   25OCT60   568.05
1961   13DEC61   734.91   03JAN61   610.25
1962   03JAN62   726.01   26JUN62   535.76
1963   18DEC63   767.21   02JAN63   646.79
1964   18NOV64   891.71   02JAN64   768.08
1965   31DEC65   969.26   28JUN65   840.59
1966   09FEB66   995.15   07OCT66   744.32
1967   25SEP67   943.08   03JAN67   786.41
1968   03DEC68   985.21   21MAR68   825.13
1969   14MAY69   968.85   17DEC69   769.93
1970   29DEC70   842.00   06MAY70   631.16
1971   28APR71   950.82   23NOV71   797.97
1972   11DEC72  1036.27   26JAN72   889.15
1973   11JAN73  1051.70   05DEC73   788.31
1974   13MAR74   891.66   06DEC74   577.60
1975   15JUL75   881.81   02JAN75   632.04
1976   21SEP76  1014.79   02JAN76   858.71
1977   03JAN77   999.75   02NOV77   800.85
1978   08SEP78   907.74   28FEB78   742.12
1979   05OCT79   897.61   07NOV79   796.67
1980   20NOV80  1000.17   21APR80   759.13
1981   27APR81  1024.05   25SEP81   824.01
1982   27DEC82  1070.55   12AUG82   776.92
1983   29NOV83  1287.20   03JAN83  1027.04
1984   06JAN84  1286.64   24JUL84  1086.57
1985   16DEC85  1553.10   04JAN85  1184.96
1986   02DEC86  1955.57   22JAN86  1502.29
1987   25AUG87  2722.42   19OCT87  1738.74
----+----1----+----2----+----3----+----4----+----5----+----6----+----7--
```

Data Sets for Chapter 28

Raw Data for INTRCHEM.GRADES

```
----+----1----+----2----+----3----+----4----+----5----+----6----+----7--
Abdallah    F Mon  46
Anderson    M Wed  75
Aziz        F Wed  67
Bayer       M Wed  77
Black       M Fri  79
Blair       F Fri  70
Blue        F Mon  63
Brown       M Wed  58
Bush        F Mon  63
Chung       M Wed  85
Davis       F Fri  89
Drew        F Mon  49
DuPont      M Mon  41
Elliott     F Wed  85
Farmer      F Wed  58
Franklin    F Wed  59
Freeman     F Mon  79
Friedman    M Mon  58
Gabriel     M Fri  75
Grant       M Mon  79
Harding     M Mon  49
Hazelton    M Mon  55
Hinton      M Fri  85
Hope        F Fri  98
Jackson     F Wed  64
Janeway     F Wed  51
Jones K     F Mon  39
Jones M     M Mon  63
Judson      F Fri  89
Keller      F Mon  89
LeBlanc     F Fri  70
Lee         M Fri  48
Litowski    M Fri  85
Malloy      M Wed  79
Meyer       F Fri  85
Nichols     M Mon  58
Oliver      F Mon  41
Parker      F Mon  77
Patton      M Wed  73
Randleman   F Wed  46
Robinson    M Fri  64
Shien       M Wed  55
Simonson    M Wed  62
Smith N     M Wed  71
Smith R     M Mon  79
Sullivan    M Fri  77
----+----1----+----2----+----3----+----4----+----5----+----6----+----7--
```

```
----+----1----+----2----+----3----+----4----+----5----+----6----+----7--
Swift        M Wed  63
Wolfe        F Fri  79
Wolfson      F Fri  89
Zabriski     M Fri  89
```

Data Sets for Chapter 33

DATA Step to Create
USCLIM.HIGHTEMP

```
libname usclim 'your-data-library';
data usclim.hightemp;
   input state $char14. city $char14. temp_f date $ elev;
   cards;
Arizona      Parker        127 07jul05 345
Kansas       Alton         121 25jul36 1651
Nevada       Overton       122 23jun54 1240
North Dakota Steele        121 06jul36 1857
Oklahoma     Tishomingo    120 26jul43 6709
Texas        Seymour       120 12aug36 1291
;
```

DATA Step to Create
USCLIM.HURICANE

```
libname usclim 'your-data-library';
data usclim.huricane;
   input @1 state $char11. @13 date date7. deaths millions name $;
   format date worddate18. millions dollar6.;
   informat state $char11. date date7.;
   label millions='Damage';
   cards;
Mississippi 14aug69 256 1420 Camille
Florida     14jun72 117 2100 Agnes
Alabama     29aug79 5   2300 Frederick
Texas       15aug83 21  2000 Alicia
Texas       03aug80 28  300  Allen
;
```

DATA Step to Create USCLIM.LOWTEMP

```
libname usclim 'your-data-library';
data usclim.lowtemp;
   input state $char14. city $char14. temp_f date $ elev;
   cards;
Alaska         Prospect Creek -80 23jan71 1100
Colorado       Maybell        -60 01jan79 5920
Idaho          Island Prk Dam -60 18jan43 6285
Minnesota      Pokegama Dam   -59 16feb03 1280
North Dakota   Parshall       -60 15feb36 1929
South Dakota   McIntosh       -58 17feb36 2277
Wyoming        Moran          -63 09feb33 6770
;
```

DATA Step to Create USCLIM.TEMPCHNG

```
libname usclim 'your-data-library';
data usclim.tempchng;
   input @1 state $char13. @15 date date7. start_f end_f minutes;
   diff=end_f-start_f;
   informat state $char13. date date7.;
   format date date7.;
   cards;
North Dakota  21feb18 -33 50   720
South Dakota  22jan43 -4  45   2
South Dakota  12jan11 49  -13  120
South Dakota  22jan43 54  -4   27
South Dakota  10jan11 55  8    15
;
```

Note on the Catalogs, USCLIM.BASETEMP and USCLIM.REPORT

The catalogs USCLIM.BASETEMP and USCLIM.REPORT are used to illustrate how the DATASETS procedure processes both SAS data sets and catalogs. The contents of these catalogs aren't important in the context of this book. In most cases, you use SAS/AF, SAS/FSP, or other SAS software products to create catalog entries. You can test the examples in this chapter without having these catalogs.

Data Sets for Chapter 35

DATA Step to Create CLIMATE.HIGHTEMP

```
libname climate 'your-data-library';
data climate.hightemp;
   input place $ 1-13 date $ deg_f deg_c;
   cards;
Libya         13sep22 136 58
California    10jul13 134 57
Israel        21jun42 129 54
Argentina     11dec05 120 49
Saskatchewan  05jul37 113 45
;
```

DATA Step to Create CLIMATE.LOWTEMP

```
libname climate 'your-data-library';
data climate.lowtemp;
   input place $ 1-13 date $ deg_f deg_c;
   cards;
Antarctica    21jul83 -129 -89
Siberia       06feb33 -90  -68
Greenland     09jan54 -87  -66
Yukon         03feb47 -81  -63
Alaska        23jan71 -80  -67
;
```

DATA Step to Create PRECIP.RAIN

```
libname precip 'your-data-library';
data precip.rain;
   input place $ 1-12 @13 date date7. inches cms;
   format date date7.;
   cards;
La Reunion  15mar52 74 188
Taiwan      10sep63 49 125
Australia   04jan79 44 114
Texas       25jul79 43 109
Canada      06oct64 19 49
;
```

DATA Step to Create PRECIP.SNOW

```
libname precip 'your-data-library';
data precip.snow;
   input place $ 1-12 @13 date date7. inches cms;
   format date date7.;
   cards;
Colorado    14apr21 76 193
Alaska      29dec55 62 158
France      05apr69 68 173
;
```

DATA Step to Create STORM.TORNADO

```
libname storm 'your-data-library';
data storm.tornado;
   input state $ 1-12 @13 date date7. deaths millions;
   format date date7. millions dollar6.;
   label millions='Damage in Millions';
   cards;
Iowa        11apr65 257 200
Texas       11may70 26  135
Nebraska    06may75 3   400
Connecticut 03oct79 3   200
Georgia     31mar73 9   115
;
```

Glossary

action bar

a list of selections that appears when the PMENU command is executed. The action bar is used by placing your cursor on the selection that you want and pressing ENTER or, if you are using a mouse, by pointing and clicking on the item you want. This either executes a command or displays a pull-down menu.

alignment form unit

a group of Xs printed in a rectangular block by the FORMS procedure. Alignment form units are the same size as the form units they represent and are used to test whether the output from the FORMS procedure will line up correctly on the continuous feed-form paper. See also the entry for form unit.

analysis variable

in some SAS procedures, such as the TABULATE procedure, a numeric variable identified in the VAR statement. It often contains quantitative or continuous values, but this is not a requirement. You can request a variety of descriptive statistics for analysis variables.

argument

(1) the data values within parentheses on which a SAS function or CALL routine performs the indicated operation. (2) in syntax descriptions, any keyword in a SAS statement other than the statement name.

arithmetic operator

an infix operator used to perform arithmetic calculations, such as addition, subtraction, multiplication, division, and exponentiation.

array

(1) a method of grouping variables of the same type for processing under a single name. (2) a method of defining an area of memory as a unit of information.

array name

a name selected to identify a group of variables or temporary data elements. It must be a valid SAS name that is not the name of a variable in the same DATA step.

array reference

a description of the element to be processed in an array.

ASCII collating sequence

an ordering of characters that follows the order of the characters in the American Standard Code for Information Interchange (ASCII) character set. The following operating systems supported by the SAS System use the ASCII collating sequence: AOS/VS, MS-DOS, OS/2, PC DOS, PRIMOS, UNIX and its derivatives, and VMS.

AUTOEXEC file

a file containing SAS statements that are executed automatically when the SAS System is invoked. The AUTOEXEC file is usually used to specify SAS system options and librefs and filerefs that are commonly used.

automatic variable

a variable that is created automatically by the DATA step. Every DATA step creates the _N_ and _ERROR_ variables. Some DATA step statements create additional automatic variables. The SAS macro facility also creates automatic macro variables.

base SAS software

software that includes a programming language that manages your data, procedures that are software tools for data analysis and reporting, a macro facility, help menus, and a windowing environment for text editing and file management.

batch mode

on mainframes and minicomputers, a method of running SAS programs in which you prepare a file containing SAS statements and any necessary operating system control statements and submit the file to the operating system. Execution is completely separate from other operations at your terminal and is sometimes referred to as running in background. This method of running SAS programs is not available in PC and workstation environments.

Boolean operator (logical operator)

See the entry for logical operator (Boolean operator).

buffer

a temporary storage area reserved for holding data after they are read or before they are written.

BY group

all observations with the same values for all BY variables.

BY-group processing

the process of using the BY statement to process observations that are ordered, grouped, or indexed according to the values of one or more variables. Many SAS procedures and the DATA step support BY-group processing. For example, you can use BY-group processing with the PRINT procedure to print separate reports for different groups of observations in a single SAS data set.

BY value

the value of a BY variable.

BY variable

a variable named in a BY statement.

CALL routine

(1) a program that can be called in the DATA step of a SAS program by issuing a CALL statement. (2) an alternate form of one of the SAS random number functions that allows more control over the seed stream and random number stream.

carriage-control character

a specific symbol that tells the printer how many lines to advance the paper, when to begin a new page, when to skip a line, and when to hold the current line for overprint.

catalog

See the entry for SAS catalog.

catalog entry

See the entry for entry type.

cell

a single unit of a table produced by a SAS procedure, such as the TABULATE procedure. The value contained in the cell is a summary statistic for the input data set. The contents of the cell are described by the page, row, and column that contain the cell.

character comparison

a process in which character operands are compared character by character from left to right, yielding a numeric result. If the character operands are equal, the result is the value 1; if they are not equal, the result is the value 0.

character constant

characters enclosed in quotes in a SAS statement (sometimes called a character literal). The maximum number of characters allowed is 200.

character format

instructions to the SAS System to write character data values using a specific pattern.

character function

a function that enables you to perform character string manipulations.

character informat

instructions to the SAS System to read character data values into character variables using a specific pattern.

character literal

See the entry for character constant.

character string

See the entry for character constant.

character value

a value that can contain alphabetic characters, numeric characters 0 through 9, and other special characters. Character values are stored in character variables.

character variable

a variable whose values can contain alphabetic and special characters as well as numeric characters.

class variable

in some SAS procedures, such as the TABULATE procedure, a variable identified in the CLASS statement. Class variables can have character, integer, or even continuous values, but they typically have a few discrete values that define the classifications of the variable.

collating sequence

an order assigned to characters and symbols in a character set (for example, ASCII or EBCDIC).

column input

a style that gives column specifications in the INPUT statement for reading data in fixed columns.

column output

a style that gives column specifications in the PUT statement for writing data in fixed columns.

comment

descriptive text to explain or document a program. A comment is denoted by the symbols /* beginning the comment and the symbols */ ending the comment or by an asterisk (*) beginning the comment and a semicolon (;) ending the comment.

comparison operator

an infix operator that tests a relationship between two values. If the comparison (or relationship) is true, the result of carrying out the operation is the value 1; if the comparison is false, the result is the value 0.

compilation

the automatic translation of SAS statements into code.

compound expression

an expression using more than one operator.

concatenating

(1) a process in which the SAS System combines two or more SAS data sets, one after the other, into a single data set. (2) a process in which the SAS System combines two or more character values, one after the other, into a single character value. (3) in the TABULATE procedure, the operation that instructs the procedure to join information for two or more table elements by placing the output for the second element immediately after the output for the first element.

condition

one or more numeric or character expressions whose value some decision depends upon.

configuration file

an external file containing SAS system options. The options in the file are put into effect when the SAS System is invoked.

configuration option
a SAS option that can be specified on the command line or during invocation in a configuration file. Configuration options affect how the SAS System interfaces with the computer hardware and operating system.

constant
a number or a character string in quotes that indicates a fixed value.

crossing
the operation that instructs some SAS procedures, such as the TABULATE procedure, to combine the effects of two or more elements.

data error
a type of execution error that occurs when the data being analyzed by a SAS program contain invalid values. For example, a data error occurs if you specify numeric variables in the INPUT statement for character data. Data errors do not cause a program to stop, but instead they produce notes.

data set label
a user-defined field in a SAS data set that can consist of up to 40 characters. It can be used for purposes of documenting the SAS data set.

data set option
an option that appears in parentheses after a SAS data set name. Data set options specify actions that are applicable only to the processing of that SAS data set.

DATA step
a group of statements in a SAS program that begin with a DATA statement and end with a RUN statement, another DATA statement, a PROC statement, the end of the job, or the line after in-stream input data that contains one or four semicolon(s). The DATA step enables you to read raw data or other SAS data sets and use programming logic to create a SAS data set, write a report, or write to an external file.

data value
(1) a unit of information. (2) the intersection of a row (observation) and a column (variable) in the rectangular form of a SAS data set.

date and time format
instructions that tell the SAS System how to write data values that represent dates, times, and datetimes.

date and time informat
instructions that tell the SAS System how to read data values that represent dates, times, and datetimes.

date value
See the entry for SAS date value.

declarative statement
a statement that supplies information to the SAS System and that takes effect when the system compiles program statements.

delimiter

a character that serves as a boundary; it separates elements of a character string, programming statement, or data line.

descriptor portion

the descriptive information the SAS System creates and maintains about each SAS data set. It includes such information as the names of all the data set variables, the attributes of all the variables, the number of observations in the data set, and the time and date when the data set was created.

detail report

a report with output that lists all the data that are processed.

dialog box

a feature of the PMENU facility that appears in response to an action, usually selecting a menu item. The purpose of dialog boxes is to obtain information, which you supply by filling in a field or choosing a selection from a group of fields. You can execute the CANCEL command to exit the dialog box.

dimension expression

in the TABULATE procedure, the portion of the TABLE statement that defines what variables and statistics make up a single dimension of the table. The format of a dimension expression is the same for any of the three dimensions: page, row, and column.

directory

(1) a list of the members and associated information in a SAS data library. (2) a list of entries and associated information in a SAS catalog.

    Note: Directory has a different meaning outside of the SAS System under some operating systems.

display manager

See the entry for SAS Display Manager System.

display manager mode

an interactive windowing method of running SAS programs in which you edit a group of statements, submit the statements, and then review the results of the statements in various windows.

DO group

a sequence of statements headed by a DO statement and ended by a corresponding END statement. DO groups can be executed repeatedly in a DO loop, or they can simply be a collection of statements that are executed only when certain conditions are met.

DO loop

the repetitive execution of the same statement or statements by use of an iterative DO, DO WHILE, or DO UNTIL statement.

double trailing at sign (@ @)

a special symbol used to hold a line in the input buffer across iterations of the DATA step.

duration

an integer representing the difference, in elapsed time or days, between any two time or date values.

EBCDIC collating sequence

an ordering of characters in the Extended Binary Coded Decimal Interchange Code (EBCDIC) 8-bit character coding scheme. The following operating systems supported by the SAS System use the EBCDIC collating sequence: CMS, MVS, and VSE.

engine

a part of the SAS System that reads from or writes to a file. Each engine allows the SAS System to access files with a particular format.

entry

a unit of information stored in a SAS catalog.

entry type

a part of the name for an entry in a SAS catalog that is assigned by the SAS System to identify what type of information is stored in the entry. For example, HELP is the entry type for an entry containing help information for applications developed with the BUILD procedure in SAS/AF software.

executable statement

a SAS statement not completed after compilation and one that can be executed on an individual observation. Only executable statements can occur in a THEN or ELSE clause and can have a statement label applied to them.

execution

(1) the process in which the SAS System carries out the statements in the DATA step for each observation or record in the step. (2) the process in which the SAS System processes items other than statements in the DATA step, such as SAS macros, procedures, and global statements.

execution mode

See the entry for methods of running the SAS System.

explicit array

an array that consists of an array name, an optional reference to the number of variables or temporary data elements, and an optional list of the array elements. In an explicit array, you must explicitly specify the subscript in the reference when referring to an element. See also the entry for implicit array.

explicit array reference

a description of the element to be processed in an explicit array.

expression

a sequence of operators and operands that form a set of instructions used to produce a value.

external file
a file created and maintained on the host operating system from which you can read data or stored SAS programming statements or to which you can write procedure output or output created by PUT statements in a DATA step.

field
the smallest logical unit of data in an external file.

***field-type* of a window**
as part of the COLOR command, the area of a window or type of text where color is changed. Field types include background, banner, data, notes, and source.

file reference
another name for fileref.

fileref
the name used to identify an external file to the SAS System. You assign a fileref with a FILENAME statement or with operating system control language.

first-level name
See the entry for libref.

FIRST.*variable*
a temporary variable that the SAS System creates to identify the first observation of each BY group. It is not added to the SAS data set.

format
the instructions the SAS System uses to write each value of a variable. There are two types of formats: formats supplied by SAS software and user-written formats created using the FORMAT procedure.

format, variable
See the entry for format.

format modifier
(1) a special symbol used in the INPUT and PUT statements that enables you to control the way the SAS System reads input data and writes output data. (2) in the TABULATE procedure, an element of the form F=*format* that can be crossed in a dimension expression to indicate how the values in cells should be formatted.

formatted input
a style that uses special instructions called informats for reading data in the INPUT statement.

formatted output
a style that uses special instructions called formats for writing data in the PUT statement.

form layout
the number and arrangements of form units, such as mailing labels, on a page of continuous-feed paper (a form page).

form page

a sheet of continuous-feed paper on which form units, such as mailing labels, are printed. A form page has a line size and page size associated with it.

form unit

the data printed in a rectangular block by the FORMS procedure. For example, a mailing label is a form unit. See also the entry for alignment form unit.

full-screen facility

a form of screen presentation in which the contents of an entire terminal display can be displayed at once.

function

a built-in expression that returns a value resulting from zero or more arguments.

global option

See the entry for system option.

header routine

a group of DATA step statements identified by the HEADER= option in the FILE statement that is used to produce a page header. The group begins with a statement label and continues to a RETURN statement.

heading

the text located near the beginning of each page of output. This includes lines produced by HEADER= options in FILE statements, lines written with TITLE statements, and default information such as date and page numbers.

host

the operating system that provides facilities, computer services, and the environment for software applications.

implicit array

an array that consists of an array name, an optional index variable, and a list of array elements. In an implicit array, you do not have to explicitly specify the subscript in the reference when referring to an element. See also the entry for explicit array.

index

a feature of a SAS data set that enables the SAS System to access observations in the SAS data set quickly and efficiently. The purpose of SAS indexes is to optimize WHERE-clause processing and facilitate BY-group processing.

informat

the instructions that specify how the SAS System reads raw data values to create variable values. There are two types of informats: informats supplied by SAS software and user-written informats created using the FORMAT procedure.

informat, variable

See the entry for informat.

input buffer
the temporary area of memory into which each record of data is read when the INPUT statement executes.

interactive facility
a system that alternately accepts and responds to input. An interactive facility is conversational; that is, a continuous dialog exists between user and system. The SAS Display Manager System is interactive.

interactive line-mode
a method of running SAS programs without using the SAS Display Manager System. You enter one line of a SAS program at a time. The SAS System processes each line immediately after you enter it.

interleaving
a process in which the SAS System combines two or more sorted SAS data sets into one sorted SAS data set based on the values of the BY variables.

item
one of the choices displayed in a pull-down menu or an action bar of the PMENU facility. Selecting an item either executes a command, displays a pull-down menu, or displays a dialog box.

label
See the entries for data set label, statement label, and label, variable.

label, variable
a descriptive label of up to 40 characters that can be printed by certain procedures instead of, or in addition to, the variable name.

LAST.*variable*
a temporary variable that the SAS System creates to identify the last observation of each BY group. It is not added to the SAS data set.

length, variable
the number of bytes used to store each of a variable's values in a SAS data set.

length variable
(1) a numeric variable created by the LENGTH= option in the INFILE statement to store the length of the current input record. (2) a numeric variable used with the $VARYING informat or format to specify the actual length of a character variable whose length varies.

library reference
another name for libref.

libref (first-level name)
the name temporarily associated with a SAS data library. You assign a libref with a LIBNAME statement or with operating system control language. The libref is the first-level name of a two-level name. For example, A is the libref in the two-level name A.B. The default libref is WORK unless the USER libref is defined. See also the entry for USER library.

line-hold specifier
a special symbol used in INPUT statements (trailing @ or double trailing @ signs) and in PUT statements (trailing @ sign) that enables you to hold a record in the input or output buffer for further processing.

line mode
See the entry for interactive line-mode.

list input, modified
a style that uses special instructions called informats and format modifiers in the INPUT statement to scan input records for data values that are separated by at least one blank or other delimiter, and in some cases, by two blanks.

list input, simple
a style that gives only variable names and dollar signs ($) in the INPUT statement to scan input records for data values that are separated by at least one blank or other delimiter.

list output
a style in which a character string or variable is specified in a PUT statement without explicit directions that specify where the SAS System should place the string or value.

literal
(1) a SAS constant. See also the entry for constant. (2) in syntax descriptions, a part of the SAS language that you must specify using the exact set of characters that the language expects. For example, in the statement

BY *variables*;

BY is a literal because in order for the SAS System to understand the term you must spell it with the two characters B and Y. The term *variable* is not a literal because you can supply any list of valid variable names.

logical operator (Boolean operator)
an operator used in expressions to link sequences of comparisons. The logical operators are AND, OR, and NOT.

macro facility
a tool that allows you to extend and customize features of the SAS System.

macro variable
a variable belonging to the macro language whose value is a string that remains constant until you change it.

master data set
in an update operation, the data set containing the information you want to update.

match-merging
a process in which the SAS System joins observations from two or more SAS data sets according to the values of the BY variables.

member

(1) a file in a SAS data library. (2) a single element of a partitioned data set under the MVS operating system.

member name

(1) the name of a file in a SAS data library. When you reference a file with a two-level name, such as A.B, the member name is the second part of the name (the libref is the first part). (2) the name of a single element of a partitioned data set under the MVS operating system.

member type

the classification of a file in a SAS data library that is assigned by the SAS System to identify what type of information is stored in the file. For example, CATALOG is the member type for catalogs.

merging

the process of combining observations from two or more SAS data sets into a single observation in a new SAS data set.

methods of running the SAS System

one of the following modes used to run SAS programs: display manager mode, interactive line mode, noninteractive mode, batch mode.

missing value

incomplete SAS data. In input, use a period or a blank as a placeholder for missing values of character variables, and use a period, a blank, or a special missing character (assigned with the MISSING= system option) as a placeholder for numeric variables. The SAS System displays a blank to represent a missing value for a character variable and a period or a special character to represent a missing value for a numeric variable.

mnemonic operator

a letter abbreviation of mathematical or Boolean (logical) symbols that is used to request a comparison, logical operation, or arithmetic calculation (for example, EQ, OR, and AND).

mode of execution

See the entry for methods of running the SAS system.

name, variable

the identifying attribute of a variable. A variable name must conform to SAS naming rules.

noninteractive mode

a method of running SAS programs in which you prepare a file of SAS statements and submit the program to the computer system. The program runs immediately and occupies your current terminal session.

numeric constant

a number that appears in a SAS statement.

numeric format

instructions to the SAS System to write numeric variable values using a specific pattern.

numeric informat

instructions to the SAS System to read numeric data values using a specific pattern to create numeric variable values.

numeric value

a value that usually contains only numbers, including numbers in E-notation and hexadecimal notation, and sometimes a decimal point, plus sign, or minus sign. Numeric values are stored in numeric variables.

numeric variable

a variable that can contain only numeric values. In the SAS System, all numeric variables are stored in floating-point representation.

observation

a row in a SAS data set that contains the specific data values for an individual entity.

one-to-one merging

the process of using the MERGE statement (without a BY statement) to combine observations from two or more data sets based on the observations' positions in the data sets. See also the entry for match-merging.

operator

a symbol that requests a comparison, logical operation, or arithmetic calculation. The SAS System uses two major kinds of operators: prefix operators and infix operators.

output buffer

in the DATA step, the area of memory to which a PUT statement writes before writing to a designated file or output device.

padding a value with blanks

a process in which the SAS System adds blanks to the end of a character value that is shorter than the length of the variable.

page size

(1) the size of the page of printed output. (2) the number of bytes of data that the SAS System moves between external storage and memory in one input/output operation.

period

the default character used for a missing value for a numeric variable.

permanent SAS data library

a library that is not deleted when the SAS session terminates; it is available for subsequent SAS sessions. Unless the USER libref is defined, you use a two-level name to access a file in a permanent library. The first-level name is the libref, and the second-level name is the member name.

permanent SAS file
a SAS file in a library that is not deleted when the SAS session or job terminates.

physical filename
the name the operating system uses to identify a file.

PMENU facility
a menuing system that is used instead of the command line as a way to execute commands.

pointer
in the DATA step, a programming tool the SAS System uses to keep track of its position in the input or output buffer.

pointer control
the process of instructing the SAS System to move the pointer before reading or writing data.

print file
an external file containing carriage-control (printer-control) information.

PROC step
a group of SAS statements that call and execute a procedure, usually with a SAS data set as input.

procedures
(1) often called SAS procedures, a collection of built-in SAS programs that are used to produce reports, manage files, and analyze data. They enable you to accept default output or to tailor your output by overriding defaults. (2) usually called user-written procedures, a self-contained user-written program, written in a language other than the SAS language, that interfaces with the SAS System and is accessed with a PROC statement.

program data vector
the temporary area of memory, or storage area, where the SAS System builds a SAS data set, one observation at a time.

programming error
an execution-time logic error that causes a SAS program to fail or to produce incorrect results.

propagation of missing values
a method of treating missing values in which using a missing value in an arithmetic expression causes the SAS System to set the result of the expression to missing. Using that result in another expression causes the next result to be missing.

pull-down menu
the list of choices that appears when you choose an item from an action bar or from another pull-down menu in the PMENU facility. The choices in the list are called items.

raw data

(1) data stored in an external file that have not been read into a SAS data set.
(2) in statistical analysis, data (including SAS data sets) that have not had a particular operation, such as standardization, performed on them.

record

a unit of data in an external file that contains the specific data values for all fields of an individual entry.

requestor window

a window that the SAS System displays so that you can confirm, cancel, or modify an action.

SAS catalog

a SAS file that stores many different kinds of information in smaller units called entries. Some catalog entries contain system information such as key definitions. Other catalog entries contain application information such as window definitions, help windows, formats, informats, macros, or graphics output.

SAS command

a command that invokes the SAS System. This command may vary depending on operating system and site.

SAS data file

a SAS data set that stores descriptor information and observations in the same location.

SAS data library

a collection of one or more SAS files that are recognized by the SAS System. Each file is a member of the library.

SAS data set

descriptor information and its related data values organized as a table of observations and variables that can be processed by the SAS System. A SAS data set can be either a SAS data file or a SAS data view.

SAS data set option

See the entry for data set option.

SAS data view

a SAS data set in which the descriptor portion and the observations are stored in separate locations. SAS data views store the information required to retrieve data values that are stored in other files.

SAS date constant

a date in the form *ddMMMyy* in quotes followed by the character d (for example, '06JUL89'd).

SAS date value

the number of days between January 1, 1960, and another date.

SAS datetime constant
a datetime in the form *ddMMMyy:hh:mm:ss* in quotes followed by the characters dt (for example, '06JUL89:09:53:22'dt).

SAS datetime value
the number of seconds between midnight, January 1, 1960, and another date and time.

SAS Display Manager System
an interactive windowing environment in which actions are performed with a series of commands or function keys. Within one session, multiple tasks can be accomplished. It can be used to prepare and submit programs, view and print the results, and debug and resubmit the programs.

SAS file
a specially structured file that is created, organized, and, optionally, maintained by the SAS System. A SAS file can be a SAS data set, a catalog, a stored program, or an access descriptor.

SAS invocation
the process of initializing a SAS session.

SAS keyword
a literal that is a primary part of the SAS language. Keywords are the words DATA and PROC, statement names, function names, macro names, and macro function names.

SAS language
(1) the statements that direct the execution of the SAS System. (2) as a grouping in SAS documentation, all parts of base SAS software except procedures.

SAS log
a file that can contain the SAS statements you enter and messages about the execution of your program.

SAS name
a name that can appear in a SAS statement, including items such as names of variables and SAS data sets. SAS names can be up to eight characters long. The first character must be a letter or an underscore. Subsequent characters can be letters, numbers, or underscores. Blanks and special characters (except the underscore) are not allowed.

SAS operator
See the entry for operator.

SAS procedure output file
an external file that contains the result of the analysis or the report produced. Procedures write output to the procedure output file by default. DATA step reports that contain the FILE statement with the PRINT destination also go to this file.

SAS procedures
See the entry for procedures.

SAS program

a sequence of related SAS statements.

SAS statement

a string of SAS keywords, SAS names, and special characters and operators ending in a semicolon that instructs the SAS System to perform an operation or gives information to the SAS System.

SAS system option

See the entry for system option.

SAS text editor

a full-screen editing facility available in some windows of the SAS Display Manager System, as well as in windows of SAS/AF, SAS/FSP, and SAS/GRAPH software.

SAS time constant

a time in the form *hh:mm:ss* in quotes followed by the character t (for example, '09:53:22't).

SAS time value

the number of seconds between midnight of the current day and another time value.

SAS windowing environment

See the entry for SAS Display Manager System.

second-level name

See the entry for member name.

selection field

the portion of a display manager window (shown on the display as an underscore) where you can enter a short command to perform an action, such as B for Browse.

selection field command

a command that enables you to perform actions from a display manager window. For example, entering the letter D in the DIRECTORY window's selection command field beside the name of a SAS data set enables you to delete that SAS data set.

simple expression

an expression that uses only one operator.

site number

the number used by SAS Institute to identify the site to which the SAS System is licensed. The site number appears near the top of the log in every SAS session.

statement label

a word that prefixes a statement in the DATA step so that execution can move to that position as necessary, bypassing other statements in the step. Statement labels follow the rules for SAS names.

statement option

an option specified in a given SAS statement that affects only that statement.

summary table

output that provides a concise overview of the relationships that exist among variables in a data set.

syntax checking

a process in which the SAS System checks each statement to be sure it is used properly, that all keywords are spelled correctly, that all names meet the requirements for SAS names, and so forth.

syntax error

an error in the spelling or grammar of SAS statements. The SAS System finds syntax errors as it compiles each SAS step before execution.

system option

an option that affects the appearance of SAS output, the handling of some of the files used by the SAS System, the use of system variables, the processing of observations in SAS data sets, the features of SAS System initialization, the SAS System's interface with your computer hardware, and the SAS System's interface with the operating system.

temporary file

a SAS file in a SAS data library (usually the WORK library) that is deleted at the end of the SAS session or job.

temporary SAS data library

a library that exists only for the current SAS session or job. The most common temporary library is the WORK library.

text editing command

a command specific to the text editor.

title

a heading printed at the top of each page of SAS output or log.

toggle

the on/off switch process where you can go back and forth (switch) between two different actions.

trailing at sign (@)

a special symbol used to hold a line for use by a later INPUT or PUT statement.

transaction data set

in an update operation, the data set containing the information with which to update the master data set.

type, variable

See the entry for variable type.

updating

a process in which the SAS System replaces the values of variables in the master data set with values from observations in the transaction data set.

USER library

a SAS data library defined with the libref USER. When the libref USER is defined, the SAS System uses it as the default libref for one-level names.

user-written format

See the entry for format.

user-written informat

See the entry for informat.

variable

the set of data values in the program data vector or in a SAS data set that describe a given characteristic. See also the entry for macro variable.

variable attributes

the name, label, format, informat, type, and length associated with a particular variable.

variable list

a list of variables. You can use abbreviated variable lists in many SAS statements instead of listing all the variable names.

variable type

one of two divisions, numeric or character, into which the SAS System classifies variables.

window

a resizable, movable object on the display.

window field type

See the entry for *field-type* of a window.

windowing environment

See the entry for SAS Display Manager System.

WORK library

the temporary library automatically defined by the SAS System at the beginning of each SAS session or job to store temporary files. When the libref USER is not defined, the SAS System uses WORK as the default library for one-level names.

Index

Your Turn

If you have comments or suggestions about *SAS Language and Procedures: Usage, Version 6, First Edition*, please send them to us on a photocopy of this page or send us electronic mail.

For comments about this book, please return the photocopy to

> SAS Institute Inc.
> Publications Division
> SAS Campus Drive
> Cary, NC 27513
> **e-mail:** yourturn@unx.sas.com

For suggestions about the software, please return the photocopy to

> SAS Institute Inc.
> Technical Support Division
> SAS Campus Drive
> Cary, NC 27513
> **e-mail:** suggest@unx.sas.com